# REASONING

## VERBAL, NONVERBAL & ANALYTICAL

F-2/16, Ansari Road, Daryaganj, New Delhi-110002
*E-mail:* info@unicornbooks.in • Website: www.unicornbooks.in
☎ 011-23275434, 23262683, 23250704

**Branch** : Mumbai
23-25, Zaoba Wadi, Thakurdwar, Mumbai-400002
☎ 022-22010941, 022-22053387
*E-mail:* rapidex@bom5.vsnl.net.in



ISBN: 978-81-7806-397-3

**Edition:** 2017



***Printed at :*** *Param Offsetters, Okhla, New Delhi-110020*

# Preface

Reasoning forms the most important section in any competitive examination today as it tests the thinking power and mind applicability skills of the candidates; and those who believe in and depend on rote learning may not be able to crack these exams.

Non-verbal reasoning assesses a child's ability to see patterns and relationships, independent of language, using shapes, pictures and patterns.

The questions on reasoning asked in various competitive examinations are not easy and can only be solved if one has had enough practice.

*Trailblazer's* book of Reasoning – Verbal, Non-Verbal and Analytical, has been developed keeping in mind the increasing significance of reasoning as a major subject of study for various examinations, and dearth of useful materials on this subject in the market. It has been divided into 2 sections - Verbal Reasoning and Non-Verbal Reasoning. The verbal reasoning section includes chapters on analytical reasoning as well. Each section consists of a number of chapters with different types of questions of multiple patterns asked in various exams.

The Verbal part contains 26 chapters whereas the Non-Verbal part contains 14 chapters.

The Verbal Reasoning section covers Analogy, Clocks, Calendar, Puzzles, Coding-Decoding, Classification, Number Series, Letter Series, Blood Relations, etc. whereas, the Analytical Reasoning section covers Statement & Arguments, Statement & Assumptions, Course of Action, Cause & Effects, Syllogism, etc.

The Non-Verbal Reasoning section covers Analogy, Classification, Completion of Figures, Cubes, Paper Folding, Mirror Image, Water Image, Figure Matrix, etc. Previous year's questions of different competitive examinations including MAT and other MBA entrances, Bank PO, Clerk, SSC, LIC, RBI, RRB, B.Ed. etc along with their authentic and detailed solutions have been covered in the exercises.

The ample number of questions will help the candidates get an insight into the trends and types of questions and master the tricks of the trade, as this book covers all the three types of reasoning comprehensively, and offers in-depth practice at every level.

Lastly, we request all the readers to let us know of the errors and deficiencies which, in-spite of our best efforts might have crept in; and also to send us their suggestions so that we can improve upon the contents of this book further.

Good luck to all aspirants who want to crack CAT, MAT, XAT, ATMA, JMET, GMAT, FMS, Hotel Management courses, SSC, Bank, Railway, IAS/PCS, B.Ed., etc. and Campus Interviews!

**Publishers**

# Contents

## Part-1
## Reasoning : Verbal

## Part-2
## Reasoning : Nonverbal

## Other Books on Competitive Examinations

| | | |
|---|---|---|
| ISBN: 9788178063492 | A Comprehensive Guide for CLAT *(Common Law Admission Test) & LL.B Entrance Examinations* (SET, AILET, LSAT) | ₹495/- |
| ISBN: 9788178063805 | OBJECTIVE ENGLISH *for Competitive Examinations* | ₹450/- |
| ISBN: 9788178063737 | QUANTITATIVE APTITUDE *for Competitive Examinations* | ₹350/- |
| ISBN: 9788178062013 | Indian & Western Educational Philosophy *for M.Ed. & B.Ed. Students and Aspirants to the Civil Services* | ₹195/- |
| ISBN: 9788178063775 | सामान्य ज्ञान | ₹375/- |
| ISBN: 9788178063614 | भारत का इतिहास | ₹325/- |
| ISBN: 9788178063881 | भारतीय संविधान | ₹275/- |
| ISBN: 9788178061764 | सामान्य हिन्दी एवं संक्षिप्त व्याकरण | ₹150/- |
| ISBN: 9788178062983 | वस्तुनिष्ठ सामान्य हिन्दी | ₹150/- |

# REASONING

## VERBAL

# 1

# Analogy

## INTRODUCTION

Analogy means 'similarity' or 'similar relationship' or 'correspondence'.

Analogy literally means "resemblance of one object to another in certain respects between things which are otherwise different".

The candidates are required to establish the relationship between the given set of variables. It is the process of reasoning from parallel cases.

## KINDS OF ANALOGY

Analogy may be broadly divided into the following:

(1) Word Analogy (2) Alphabet Analogy (3) Number Analogy

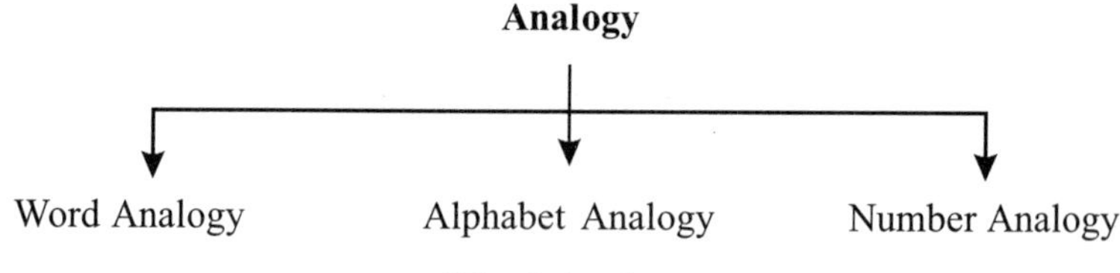


**Word Analogy**

The aim of the word analogy is to test the candidate's ability to discover the relationship between the question pair and then to find the required pair of words that is most similar to that relationship.

### Important Points

(*i*) Read the initial pair of words, substituting words for the colons.

(*ii*) The first colon (:) means "is to".

(*iii*) The two colons (: :) means "as".

(*iv*) Then define the logical relationship between the pair of words.

These type of questions cover every type of relationships that one can think of. There are many ways of establishing a relationship like quantity and unit, worker and wages, cause and effect, word-synonym, word-antonym, country and capital, state and capital, country and currency, animal and the young ones (kid), male and female, animals and their resting places, games and places of playing, occupation and their working, place and their work.

Here, some relationships are given, which are useful for solving questions based on analogy

| Country | Capital | Currency |
|---|---|---|
| Bangladesh | Dhaka | Taka |
| Iraq | Baghdad | Dinar |
| China | Beijing | Yuan |
| India | Delhi | Rupee |
| UK | London | Pound |
| Japan | Tokyo | Yen |
| USA | Washington DC | Dollar |
| Russia | Moscow | Rouble |
| Greece | Athens | Euro |
| **Occupation** | **Working Place** | **Working** |
| Lawyer | Court | Legal Practice |
| Servant | House | Service |
| Beautician | Parlour | Make up |
| Mechanic | Garage | Repairing |
| Waiter | Restaurant | Serving |
| Teacher | School | Teaching |
| Chef | Kitchen | Cooking |
| Sailor | Ship | Sailing |

| States of India | Capital |
|---|---|
| Sikkim | Gangtok |
| West Bengal | Kolkata |
| Goa | Panaji |
| Tamil Nadu | Chennai |
| Odisha | Bhubaneshwar |
| Bihar | Patna |

| Male | Female |
|---|---|
| Dog | Bitch |
| Horse | Mare |
| Bull | Cow |
| Cock | Hen |
| Son | Daughter |
| Brother | Sister |

| Individual | Class |
|---|---|
| Frog | Amphibian |
| Rat | Rodent |
| Cup | Crockery |
| Snake | Reptile |
| Man | Mammal |
| Ostrich | Bird |
| Whale | Mammal |
| Pen | Stationery |

| Animal | Sound |
|---|---|
| Cock | Crow |
| Duck | Quack |
| Cat | Meow |
| Frog | Croak |
| Snake | Hiss |
| Owl | Hoot |
| Jackal | Howl |
| Donkey | Bray |

| Quantity | Unit |
|---|---|
| Power | Watt |
| Pressure | Pascal |
| Current | Ampere |
| Area | Hectare |
| Time | Second |
| Mass | Kilogram |
| Work | Joule |
| Volume | Litre |
| Force | Newton |

| Word | Synonym |
|---|---|
| Assign | Allot |
| Substitute | Replace |
| Abduct | Kidnap |
| Haughty | Proud |
| Dissipate | Squander |
| Brim | Edge |
| Dearth | Scarcity |

| Word | Antonym |
|---|---|
| Robust | Weak |
| Deep | Shallow |
| Chaos | Peace |
| Cruel | Kind |
| Gentle | Harsh |
| Kind | Cruel |
| Lethargy | Alertness |
| Mourn | Rejoice |

| Individual | Dwelling (Place) |
|---|---|
| Lion | Den |
| Spider | Web |
| Horse | Stable |
| Bird | Nest |
| King | Palace |
| Eskimo | Igloo |

| Instrument | Measurement |
|---|---|
| Sphygmomanometer | Blood pressure |
| Seismograph | Earthquake |
| Barometer | Pressure |
| Ammeter | Current |
| Odometer | Speed |

| Game | Place of Playing |
|---|---|
| Tennis | Court |
| Wrestling | Arena |
| Boxing | Ring |
| Race | Track |
| Badminton | Court |

| Occupation | Product |
|---|---|
| Farmer | Crop |
| Architect | Designs |
| Producer | Films |
| Teacher | Education |
| Tailor | Clothes |

| Animal | Young One |
|---|---|
| Dog | Puppy |
| Hen | Chick |
| Cat | Kitten |
| Cow | Calf |
| Bear | Cub |

## SOLVED EXAMPLE

### TYPES OF QUESTIONS

Different types of questions, based on analogy that are asked in various competitive exams have been given below.

### Type 1 Direct/Simple Analogy

In this type of analogy, we deal with questions which have three components. Two have some relationship and you have to choose from the alternatives which has the same relationship with the third component.

**1.** College is related to student in the same way as Hospital is related to ...
(*a*) Doctor (*b*) Nurse (*c*) Medicine (*d*) Patient

**Sol. (*d*)** In the College, education is given to students, in the same way treatment given to Patient in Hospital.

**2.** Major is related to Lieutenant in the same way as Squadron Leader is related to ...
(*a*) Group Captain (*b*) Flying Attendant
(*c*) Flying Officer (*d*) Pilot Officer

**Sol. (*c*)** Major and Squadron Leader are equivalent ranks in the Army and the Air Force, respectively. Same as Lieutenant and Flying Officer are equivalent ranks in the Army and the Air force.

### Type 2 Completing the Analogous Pair

In this type of questions, two words are given. These words are related to each other in some way. Another word is also given. The candidate is required to find out the relationship between the first two words and choose the word from the given alternatives, which have the same relationship to the third word, as their is between the first two.

**3.** Boat : Oar : : Bicycle : ?
(*a*) Pedal (*b*) Seat (*c*) Road (*d*) Wheel

**Sol. (*a*)** Denotes that part of the first, on which the effort is applied to move it.

**4.** Traveller : Journey : : Sailor : ?
(*a*) Water (*b*) Ship (*c*) Voyage (*d*) Crew

**Sol. (*c*)** Second is the name given to the process of travel of the first.

### Type 3 Choosing the Analogous Pair

In this type of questions, a pair of words is given, followed by four pairs of alternatives. You are required to choose the pair in which the words bear the same relationship as borne by words given in the question.

**5.** Apostate : Religion
(*a*) Teacher : Education (*b*) Traitor : Country
(*c*) Potentate : Kingdom (*d*) Jailor : Law

**Sol. (*b*)** Apostate is one who renounces Religion. Similarly, Traitor is one who betrays his Country.

**6.** Gland : Enzyme
(*a*) Muscle : Spasm (*b*) Generator : Current
(*c*) Organ : Kidney (*d*) Brain : Cortex

**Sol. (*b*)** As, Gland produces Enzyme. Similary, Genrator produces the Current.

### Type 4 Choosing a Similar Word

In this type of questions, a group of three words is given, followed by four other words as alternatives. The candidate is required to choose the alternative, which is similar to the given group of words.

**7.** Kolkata, Mumbai, Mangalore
(*a*) Delhi (*b*) Lucknow (*c*) Cochin (*d*) Hyderabad

**Sol. (*c*)** All are port cities of India.

**8.** Bhilai, Durgapur, Bokaro
(*a*) Baroda (*b*) Chennai (*c*) Chandigarh (*d*) Rourkela

**Sol. (*d*)** All cities are famous for steel plants.

## NUMBER ANALOGY

In this type of analogy, questions have two numbers/group of numbers bearing a relationship. There is also a third number/group of number which have the same relationship from the alternative. You are required to find that alternative.

**9.** 2 : 8 : : 3 : ?
(*a*) 20 (*b*) 21 (*c*) 24 (*d*) 27

**Sol. (*d*)** Second number is the cube of first number in the same way 27 is the cube of 3.

i.e., $2^3 = 8$; $3^3 = 27$.

**10.** 5 : 35 : : ?

(*a*) 7 : 77 (*b*) 9 : 45 (*c*) 11 : 45 (*d*) 3 : 28

**Sol. (*a*)** The first number is multiplied by the next prime number to obtain the second number.

i.e., $7 \times 11 = 77$

7 and 11 are prime numbers.

So, the missing pair is 7 : 77.

## ALPHABET ANALOGY

In this type of analogy, first two group of letters are related to each other in some way, you are required to find out this relationship and then choose another group which is related in the same way, as first two letters / group of letters.

**11.** MUMBAI : LTLAZH : : DELHI : ?

(*a*) CDKGG (*b*) IHLED (*c*) CDKGH (*d*) BCKGH

**Sol. (*c*)** Each letter of the first group is moved one step backward to obtain the corresponding letter of the second group.

So DELHI → CDKGH.

**12.** NEWS : 14,5,23,19 : : PAPER : ?

(*a*) 16,5,16,1,18 (*b*) 18,5,16,1,16 (*c*) 16,1,16,5,18 (*d*) 32,2,32,10,36

**Sol. (*c*)** Each letter of english alphabet is assigned a serial number based on its position from left.

So, PAPER → 16,1,16,5,18.

**13.** FILM : 10 : : HOTEL : ?

(*a*) 12 (*b*) 15 (*c*) 18 (*d*) 30

**Sol. (*a*)** As, F I L M

↓ ↓ ↓ ↓

$6 + 9 + 12 + 13 = 40$

$40 \div 4 = 10$

Similarly, H O T E L

↓ ↓ ↓ ↓ ↓

$8 + 15 + 20 + 5 + 12 = 60$

$60 \div 5 = 12$

## EXERCISE

### WORD ANALOGY

**Directions (Qs. 1-19):** *In each of the following questions two words are paired which have a certain relation. Select the correct option to subtitute question-mark so as to make a similar relational pair with the word given after double colon (: :).*

**1.** Safe : Secure : : Protect : ?
(*a*) Conserve (*b*) Sure (*c*) Guard (*d*) Lock

**2.** Foresight : Anticipation : : Insomnia : ?
(*a*) Treatment (*b*) Unrest (*c*) Disease (*d*) Sleeplessness

**3.** Venerate : Worship : Extol : ?
(*a*) Glorify (*b*) Homage (*c*) Compliment (*d*) Recommend

**4.** Denigrate : Devalue : : Upgrade : ?
(*a*) Revalue (*b*) Praise (*c*) Demote (*d*) Promote

**5.** Novice : Learner : : Harbinger : ?
(*a*) Robber (*b*) Messenger (*c*) Pick Pocket (*d*) Thief

**6.** Inteligentsia : Elitist
(*a*) Outer shell : Sea Shell (*b*) Gentry : Public
(*c*) Commonality : Common class (*d*) Rabble : Plebeian

**7.** Vehicle : Cart
(*a*) Music : Jazz (*b*) Man : Child
(*c*) Country : State (*d*) Ocean : Sea

**8.** Abomination : Abhorrence
(*a*) Wail : Weep (*b*) Write : Read (*c*) Ripe : Eat (*d*) Dance : Jump

**9.** Pusillanimous : Coward
(*a*) Optimistic : Pessimist (*b*) Magnanimous : Misanthrope
(*c*) Plebeian : Entrepreneur (*d*) Impecunious : Mendicant

**10.** Racism : Apartheid
(*a*) Nationalism : Identity (*b*) Sexism : Chauvinism
(*c*) Communalism : Religion (*d*) Parochialism : Linguism

**11.** Reproof : Scold
(*a*) Chastise : Erring (*b*) Romantic : Strong
(*c*) Respite : Spite (*d*) Salient : Prominent

**12.** Cliche : Commonplace
(*a*) Annoy : Destroy (*b*) Maxim : Terse
(*c*) Serious : Play (*d*) Bitter : Pill

**13.** Giant : Dwarf : : Genius : ?
(*a*) Gentle (*b*) Idiot (*c*) Tiny (*d*) Wicked

**14.** Import : Export : : Expenditure : ?
(*a*) Sharp (*b*) Saving (*c*) Interest (*d*) Shrewd

**15.** Savage : Civilized
(*a*) Illiterate : Book (*b*) Dark : Lighted
(*c*) Wild : Animal (*d*) Brutal : Heroic

**16.** Intimidate : Wheedle
(*a*) Resolute : Impetuous (*b*) Coordinate : Dissent
(*c*) Defile : Rebuke (*d*) Extol : Disparage

**17.** Dubious : Certain
(*a*) Hot : Angry (*b*) Cold : Warm
(*c*) Long : Elongated (*d*) Short : Dwarf

**18.** Dunce ; Clever
(*a*) Flower : Petals (*b*) Worry : Poor
(*c*) Beautiful : Attractive (*d*) Fearful : Courageous

**19.** Mellifluous: Cacophony
(*a*) Dulcet : Euphony (*b*) Florid : Embellishment
(*c*) Thrifty : Parsimony (*d*) Fragrant : Noisome

**Directions (Qs. 20-29):** *In each of the following questions, the first word has a definite relationship. Choose one word of the given four alternatives which will fill in the blank space and show the same relationship with the third word as between the first two.*

**20.** *Leer* is to *Lust* as *Scowl* is to ........ ?
(*a*) Glower (*b*) Glance (*c*) Embarassment (*d*) Anger

**21.** *Loiter* is related to *Dwandle* in the same way as *Impugn* is related to ...?
(*a*) Revenge (*b*) Challenge (*c*) Gamble (*d*) Confiscate

**22.** *Guild* is related to *Association* in the same way as *Fleet* is related to ...?
(*a*) Vessel (*b*) Water (*c*) Ship (*d*) Armada

**23.** *Abduction* is related to *Kidnapping* in the same way as *Larceny* is related to .... ?
(*a*) Sin (*b*) Crime (*c*) Blackmail (*d*) Theft

**24.** *Forfeit* is related to *Surrender* in the same way as *Remit* is related to ... ?
(*a*) Exempt (*b*) Confiscate (*c*) Perceive (*d*) Cancel

**25.** *Pull* is related to *Push* in the same way as *Low* is related to ......... ?
(*a*) Long (*b*) More (*c*) Medium (*d*) High

**26.** *Town* is related to *village* in the same way as *Urban* is related to ......... ?
(*a*) Semi-Urban (*b*) Metropolis (*c*) City (*d*) Rural

**27.** *Young* is related to *Old* in the same way as *Wide* is related to ......... ?
(*a*) Long (*b*) Insufficient (*c*) Big (*d*) Narrow

**28.** *Sympathy* is related to *Virtue* in the same way as *Cruelty* is related to ......?
(*a*) Animosity (*b*) Kindness (*c*) Emotion (*d*) Vice

**29.** *Dream* is related to *reality* in the same as *Falsehood* is related to ......... ?
(*a*) Correctness (*b*) Fairness (*c*) Truth (*d*) Untruth

## ALPHABET ANALOGY

**Directions (Qs. 30-40):** *Each of the following questions consists of a pair of letter groups that have a certain relationship to each other, followed by four other pairs of letter-group given as alternatives. Select the pair in which the letter-groups are similarly related as in the given pair.*

**30.** AHOP : CKSU : : BJMR : ?
(*a*) EZUQ (*b*) DMQW (*c*) DQKM (*d*) CJWN

**31.** OT : PS
(*a*) TV : SW (*b*) IL : HK (*c*) PN : PM (*d*) BE : FC

**32.** ABCD : NPRT : : FGHI : ?
(*a*) KLMN (*b*) OQRT (*c*) RTUW (*d*) SUWY

**33.** EJOT : VQLG : : BGLQ : ?
(*a*) AEIM (*b*) AFKP (*c*) YTOJ (*d*) ZUPK

**34.** BLOCKED : YLOXPVW : : ? : OZFMXS
(*a*) LAUNCH (*b*) DEBATE (*c*) LABOUR (*d*) RESULT

**35.** BUCKET : ACTVBDJLDFSU : : BONUS : ?
(*a*) ACMNMOTVRT (*b*) SUNOB
(*c*) ACNPMOTVRT (*d*) ACMNMOTURT

**36.** computer : fqprxvht : : language : ?
(*a*) oxpixdig (*b*) ocqicying (*c*) ocqixcjg (*d*) ocqixcig

**37.** BEGK is related to ADFJ in the same way as PSVY is related to ..........?
(*a*) LOQT (*b*) ROUX (*c*) OTUZ (*d*) ORUX

**38.** In English alphabet, ‘BDG’ is to ‘CFJ’ in the same way as ‘EGJ’ is to?
(*a*) FIL (*b*) FJM (*c*) FIM (*d*) FIM

**39.** AFHO : GBDJ : : CHFM : ?
(*a*) GBIM (*b*) GBLD (*c*) GPLD (*d*) IDBH

**40.** GREAT : 25 : : NUMBER : ?
(*a*) 36 (*b*) 38 (*c*) 27 (*d*) 24

## NUMBER ANALOGY

**Directions (Qs. 41-49):** *In each of the following questions, there is a certain relationship between two given numbers one on side of : : and one number is given another side of : : while another number is to be found from the given alternatives, having the same relationship with this number as the numbers of the given pair bear. Choose the best alternative.*

**41.** 11 : 101 : : 91 : ?
(*a*) 225 (*b*) 810 (*c*) 205 (*d*) 901

**42.** 26 : 5 : : 65 : ?
(*a*) 6 (*b*) 7 (*c*) 8 (*d*) 9

**43.** 16 : 56 : : 32 : ?
(*a*) 96 (*b*) 112 (*c*) 118 (*d*) 128

**44.** 5 : 124 : : 7 : ?
(*a*) 125 (*b*) 248 (*c*) 342 (*d*) 343

**45.** 7584 : 5362 : : 4673 : ?
(*a*) 2367 (*b*) 2451 (*c*) 2531 (*d*) None of these

**46.** 5 : 100, 4 : 64 : : 4 : 80, 3 : ?
(*a*) 26 (*b*) 48 (*c*) 54 (*d*) 60

**47.** 11 : 1210 : : ?
(*a*) 6 : 216 (*b*) 7 : 1029 (*c*) 8 : 448 (*d*) 9 : 729

**48.** 6 : 222 : : 7 : ?
(*a*) 210 (*b*) 336 (*c*) 343 (*d*) 350

**49.** 14 : 9 : : 26 : ?
(*a*) 12 (*b*) 13 (*c*) 15 (*d*) 31

**Directions (Qs. 50-54):** *In each of the following questions, choose similar number/numbers to the numbers in the given set.*

**50.** Given Set: (6, 36, 63)
(*a*) (7, 49, 98) (*b*) (8, 64, 46) (*c*) (9, 84, 45) (*d*) (11, 111, 84)

**51.** Given Set: (63, 49, 35)
(*a*) (72, 40, 24) (*b*) (72, 48, 24) (*c*) (64, 40, 28) (*d*) (81, 63, 45)

**52.** Given Set : (32, 24, 8)
(*a*) (26, 32, 42) (*b*) (34, 24, 14) (*c*) (24, 16, 0) (*d*) (42, 34, 16)

**53.** Given Set: (6, 15, 28)
(*a*) (46, 56, 66) (*b*) (50, 59, 71) (*c*) (60, 69, 72) (*d*) (60, 69, 82)

**54.** Given Set : (2, 14, 16)
(*a*) (2, 7, 8) (*b*) (2, 9, 16) (*c*) (3, 21, 24) (*d*) (4, 16, 18)

## ANSWERS

| 1 | 2 | 3 | 4 | 5 | 6 | 7 | 8 | 9 | 10 |
|---|---|---|---|---|---|---|---|---|---|
| (*c*) | (*d*) | (*a*) | (*d*) | (*b*) | (*d*) | (*a*) | (*a*) | (*d*) | (*b*) |
| **11** | **12** | **13** | **14** | **15** | **16** | **17** | **18** | **19** | **20** |
| (*d*) | (*b*) | (*b*) | (*b*) | (*b*) | (*d*) | (*b*) | (*d*) | (*d*) | (*d*) |
| **21** | **22** | **23** | **24** | **25** | **26** | **27** | **28** | **29** | **30** |
| (*b*) | (*d*) | (*d*) | (*d*) | (*d*) | (*d*) | (*d*) | (*d*) | (*c*) | (*b*) |
| **31** | **32** | **33** | **34** | **35** | **36** | **37** | **38** | **39** | **40** |
| (*a*) | (*d*) | (*c*) | (*a*) | (*c*) | (*c*) | (*d*) | (*c*) | (*d*) | (*a*) |
| **41** | **42** | **43** | **44** | **45** | **46** | **47** | **48** | **49** | **50** |
| (*d*) | (*c*) | (*b*) | (*c*) | (*b*) | (*b*) | (*c*) | (*d*) | (*c*) | (*b*) |
| **51** | **52** | **53** | **54** | | | | | | |
| (*d*) | (*c*) | (*d*) | (*c*) | | | | | | |

## SOME SELECTED EXPLANATORY ANSWERS

**1.** 'Safe is synonym of 'Secure'.
Similarly, 'Protect' is synonym of 'Guard'.

**2.** 'Foresight' is synonym of 'Anticipation'.
Similarly, 'Insomnia' is synonym of 'Sleeplessness'.

**3.** 'Venerate' is synonym of 'Worship'.
Similarly, 'Extol' is synonym of 'Glorify'.

**4.** 'Denigrate' is synony of 'Devalue'.
Similarly, 'Upgrade' is synonym of 'Promote'.

**5.** 'Novice' is synonym of 'Learner'.
Similarly, 'Harbinger' is synonym of 'Messenger'.

**6.** 'Intelligentsia' is synonym of 'Elitist'.
Similarly, 'Rabble' is synonym of 'Plebeian'.

**7.** 'Vehicle' is synonym of 'cart'.
Similarly, 'Music' is synonym of 'Jazz'.

**8.** 'Abomination' is synonym of 'Abhorrence'.
Similarly, 'Wail' is synonym of 'Weep'.

**9.** 'Pusillanimous' is synonym of 'Coward'.
Similarly, 'Impecunious' is synonym of 'Mendicant'.

**10.** 'Racism' is synonym of 'Apartheid'.
Similarly, 'Sexism' is synonym of 'Chauvinism'.

**11.** 'Reproof' is synonym of 'Scold'.
Similarly, 'Salient' is synonym of 'Prominent'.

**12.** 'Cliche' is synonym of 'Common place'.
Similarly, 'Maxim' is synonym of 'Terse'.

**13.** 'Giant', is antonym of 'Dwarf'.
Similarly, 'Genius' is antonym of 'Idiot'.

**14.** 'Import' is antonym of 'Export'.
Similarly, 'Expenditure' is antonym of 'Saving'.

**15.** 'Savage' is antonym of 'Civilized'.
Similarly, 'Dark' is antonym of 'Lighted'.

**16.** 'Intimidate' is antonym of 'wheedle'.
Similarly, 'Extol' is antonym of 'Disparage'.

**17.** 'Dubious' is antonym of 'Certain'.
Similarly, 'Cold' is antonym of 'Warm'.

**18.** 'Dunce' is antonym of 'Clever'.
Similarly, 'Fearful' is antonym of 'Courageous'.

**19.** 'Mellifluous' is antonym of 'Cacophony'.
Similarly, 'Fragrant' is antonym of 'Noisome'.

**20.** 'Leer' is synonym of 'Lust'
Similarly, 'Scowl' is synonym of 'Anger'.

**21.** 'Loiter' is synonym of 'Dwandle'.
Similarly, 'Impugn' is synonym of 'Challenge'.

**22.** 'Guild' is synonym of 'Association'.
Similarly, 'Fleet' is synonym of 'Armada'.

**23.** 'Abduction' is synonym of 'Kidnapping'.
Similarly, 'Larceny' is synonym of 'Theft'.

**24.** 'Forfeit' is synonym of 'Surrender'.
Similarly, 'Remit' is synonym of 'Cancel'.

**26.** 'Town' is antonym of 'Village'.
Similarly, 'Urban' is antonym of 'Rural'.

**27.** 'Young' is antonym of 'Old'.
Similarly, 'Wide' is antonym of 'Narrow'.

**28.** 'Cruelty' is antonym of 'Sympathy'.
Similarly, 'Vice' is the antonym of 'Virtue'.

**29.** Dream is antonym of 'Reality'
Similary Falsehood is antonym of 'Truth'

**30.**
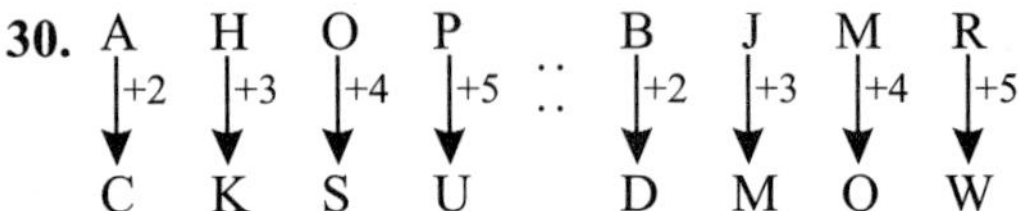


**31.** The pattern is as follows:

O T : P S
15 + 20 : 16 + 19
⇒ 35 : 35

Similarly, T V : S W
20 + 22 : 19 + 23
⇒ 42 : 42

**32.** The pattern is as follows:

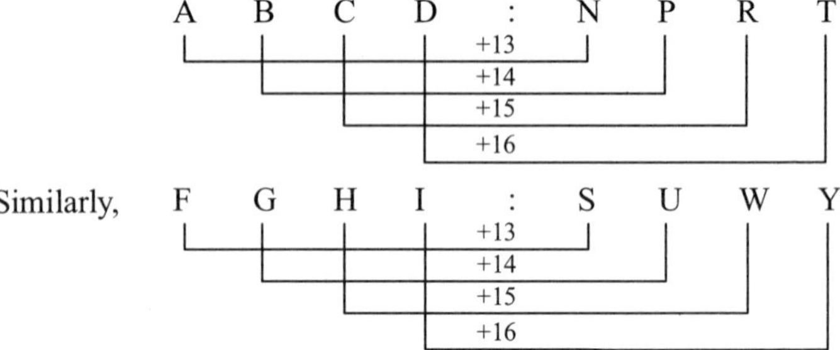


**33.** The pattern is as follows:

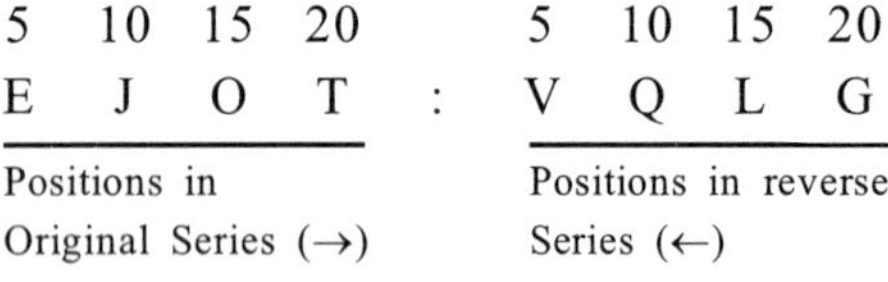


Similarly, 2 7 12 17 : 2 7 12 17
B G L Q : Y T O J
Positions in Original Series (→) Positions in reverse Series (←)

**34.** The pattern is as follows:

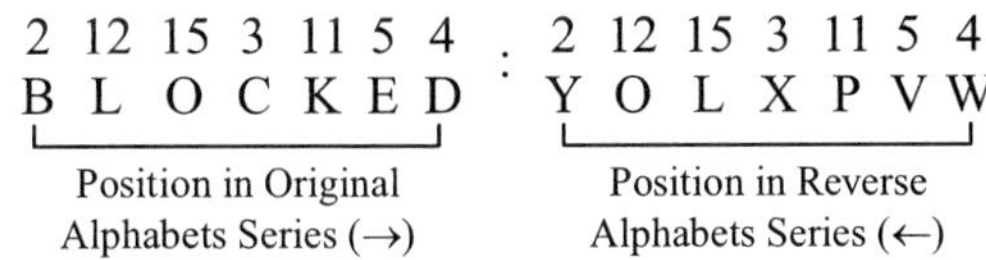


Similarly,

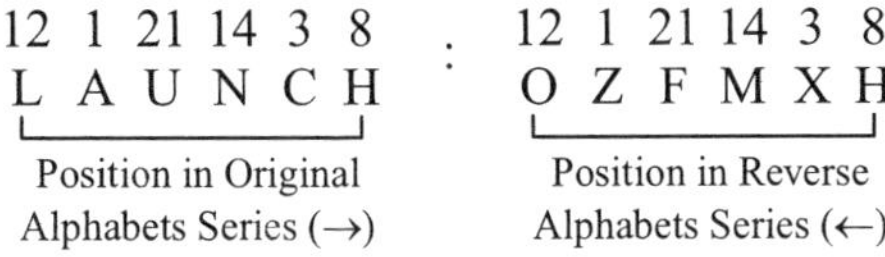


**35.** The pattern is as follows:

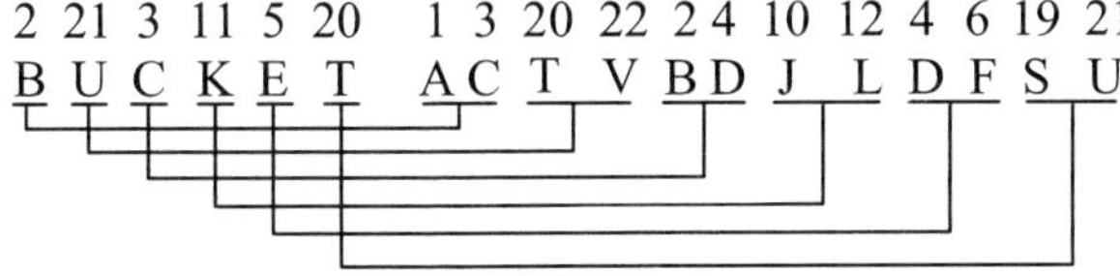


1 2 3 20 21 22 2 3 4 10 11 12 4 5 6 19 20 21
i.e., A B C : T U V : B C D : J K L : D E F : S T U

Similarly,

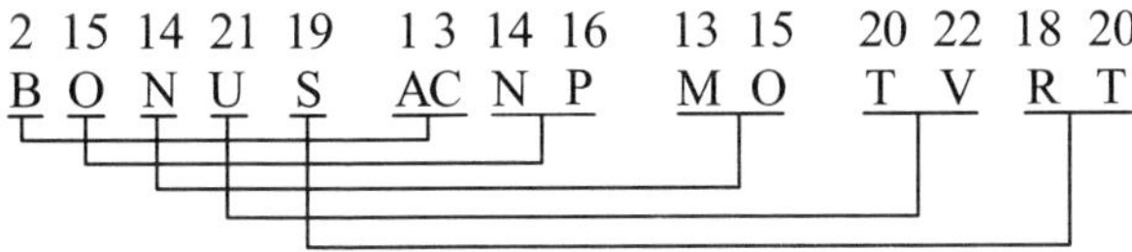


**36.** The pattern is as follows:

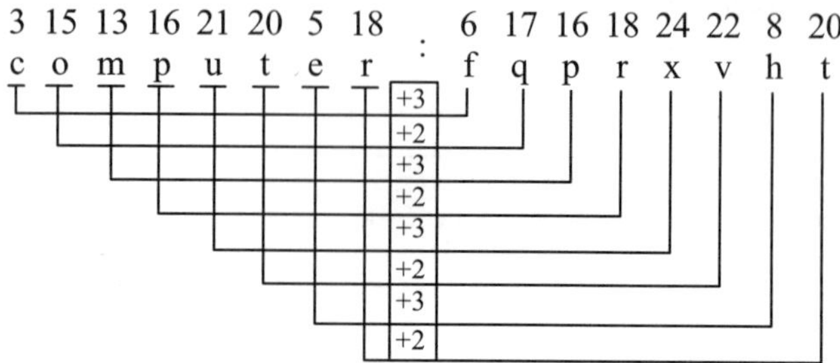


Similarly,

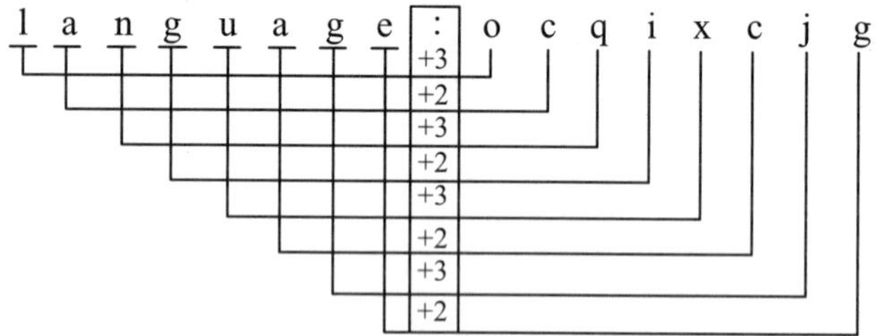


**37.** The pattern is as follows:

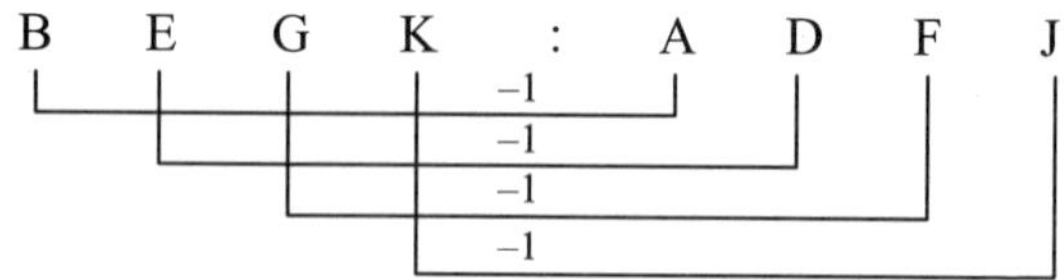


Similarly,

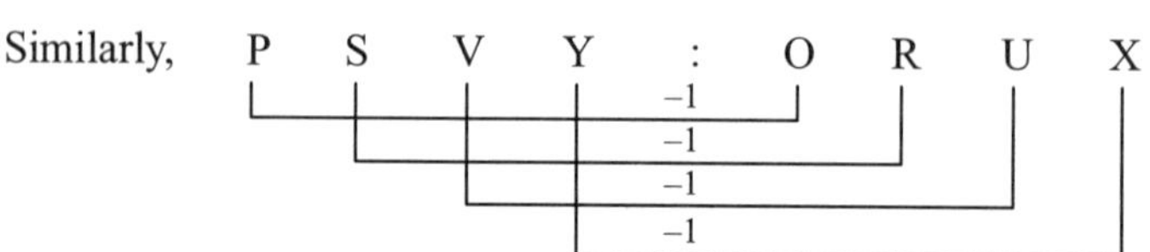


**38.**

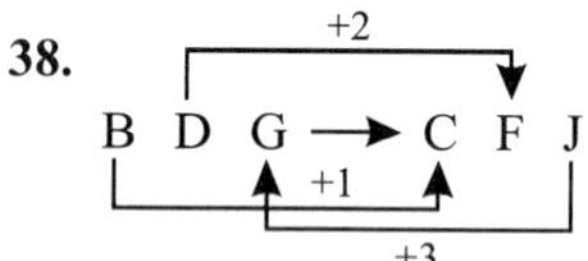


Similarly, code for EGJ is given as

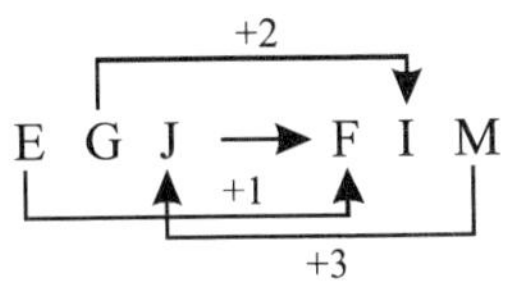


**39.** As, A F H O

$\downarrow$ +2, +2, –2, –2

C H F M

Similarly,

G B D J

$\downarrow$ +2, +2, –2, –2

I D B H

**40.** In word GREAT, the number of alphabets = 5

$\therefore$ GREAT = $(5)^2 = 25$

In the same way, in word NUMBER, the number of alphabets = 6

$\therefore$ NUMBER = $(6)^2 = 36$

**41.** The pattern is as follows:

Zero is inserted in between the digits of the first number to obtain the second number.

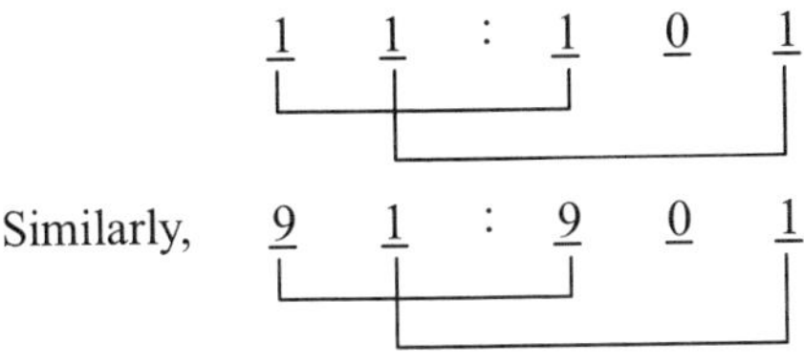


**42.** The pattern is as follows:

$(X^2 + 1) : X$

i.e. 26 : 5 ($5^2 + 1$)

Similarly, 65 : 8 ($8^2 + 1$)

**43.** The pattern is as follows : $X : \frac{7X}{2}$

i.e., 16 : 56

$7 \times \frac{16}{2}$

Similarly, 32 : 112

$7 \times \frac{32}{2}$

**44.** The pattern is X : ($X^3$ – 1)

5 : 124 ($5^3 - 1$)  7 : 342 ($7^3 - 1$)

**45.** The pattern is as follows:

X : (X – 2222)

i.e. 7584 : 5362 (7584 – 2222)

Similarly, 4673 : 2451 (4673 – 2222)

**46.** The pattern is as follows:

X : 20X; X : 16X; X : 20X; X : 16X

5 : 100 : 4 : 64 : 4 : 80 : 3 : 48

X20  X16  X20  X16

**47.** The pattern is X : $X^3 - X^2$

11 : 1210 : 8 : 448

$11^3 - 11^2$  $8^3 - 8^2$

**48.** The pattern is as follows:

X : ($X^3$ + X)

i.e. 6 : 222 ($6^3 + 6$)

Similarly, 7 : 350 ($7^3 + 7$)

**49.** The pattern is as follows : (2X – 4) : X

i.e. 14 : 9 (2 × 9 – 4)

Similarly, 26 : 15 (2 × 15 – 4)

**50.** The pattern is as follows:
Second number = (first number)$^2$
Third number = Interchange digits of Second number.

**51.** The pattern is as follows:

X × 9; X × 7, X × 5 where X = 7 and 9

63 = 7 × 9; 49 = 7 × 7; 35 = 7 × 5

Similarly, 81 = 9 × 9; 63 = 9 × 7; 45 = 9 × 5

Therefore, the required triplet = (81, 63, 45)

**52.** The pattern is as follows:

2nd number = 1st number – 8

3rd number = 2nd number – 16

i.e., 24 = 32 – 8 and 8 = 24 – 16

Therefore, the required triplet = (24, 16, 0).

**53.** The pattern is as follows:

Difference between the 2nd and 1st number = 15 – 6 = 9

Difference between the 3rd and 2nd number = 28 – 15 = 13

Therefore, the required triplet = (60, 69, 82)

**54.** The pattern is as follows:

2nd number = 1st number × 7 and

3rd number = 1st number × 8

i.e. 14 = 2 × 7 and 16 = 2 × 8

Therefore, the required triplet = (3, 21, 24).

2

# Coding-Decoding

## INTRODUCTION

*Coding'* is used for conveying secret messages from one place to another, especially in defence services. The codes are based on various patterns/principles such that the message can be easily deciphered or decoded at the other end. In coding, a particular code or pattern is used to express a word in English language to express it as a different word or in a different form.

Decoding is the process of arriving at the equivalent english word from the given code word. The candidates are required to encode and decode words and sentences after observing the patterns and principles involved.

In questions on coding-decoding, a word (basic word) is coded in a particular way and the candidates are asked to code other words in the same way. The coding and decoding tests are set up to judge the candidate's ability to decipher the rule that has been followed to code a particular word/message.

Some methods/techniques are given below to remember the positions of English alphabets in forward or backward order.

**Order of the English Alphabet**

| Forward order position | 1 | 2 | 3 | 4 | 5 | 6 | 7 | 8 | 9 | 10 | 11 | 12 | 13 | 14 | 15 | 16 | 17 | 18 | 19 | 20 | 21 | 22 | 23 | 24 | 25 | 26 |
|---|---|---|---|---|---|---|---|---|---|---|---|---|---|---|---|---|---|---|---|---|---|---|---|---|---|---|
| Alphabetes | A | B | C | D | E | F | G | H | I | J | K | L | M | N | O | P | Q | R | S | T | U | V | W | X | Y | Z |
| Backward order position | 26 | 25 | 24 | 23 | 22 | 21 | 20 | 19 | 18 | 17 | 16 | 15 | 14 | 13 | 12 | 11 | 10 | 9 | 8 | 7 | 6 | 5 | 4 | 3 | 2 | 1 |

## SOLVED EXAMPLE

**1.** In a certain code, LAKE is written as OZPV. How will BACK be in that same code?

(*a*) ZYXP (*b*) ZYPX (*c*) YZXP (*d*) YZPX

**Sol.** (*c*) As,

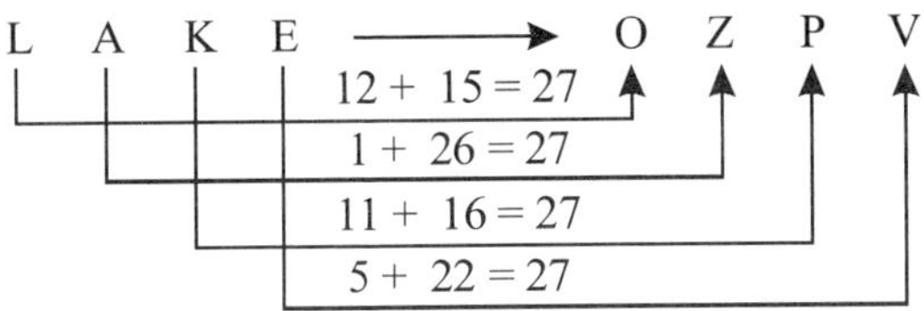


Similarly,

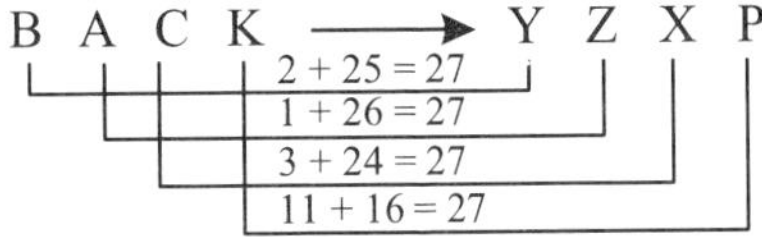


**2.** In a certain code language, 'GIVE' is written as 'VIEG' and 'OVER' is written as 'EVRO'. How will 'DISK' be written in that same code?
(*a*) SIDK (*b*) KISD (*c*) KDSI (*d*) SIKD

**Sol.** (*d*) Here,

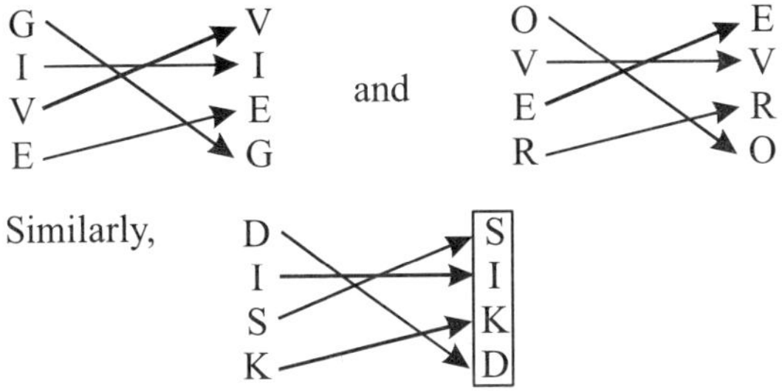


**3.** In a certain coding system, 'SHEEP' is written as 'GAXXR' and 'BLEAT' as 'HPXTN'. How can 'SLATE' be written in that same coding system?
(*a*) GPTNX (*b*) GPTXN (*c*) GPXNT (*d*) PTGXN

**Sol.** (*a*) In both the words 'SHEEP' and 'BLEAT', the letter E is common and code for E is substituted X. Hence, using direct letter coding method, we have

S ⟶ G and B ⟶ H
H ⟶ A L ⟶ P
E ⟶ X E ⟶ X
E ⟶ X A ⟶ T
P ⟶ R T ⟶ N

Similarly, using the direct codes

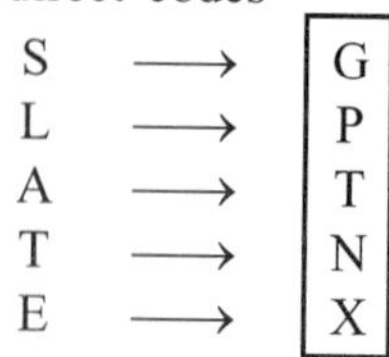


**4.** In a certain code language, 'it pit sit' means 'I am boy', 'it nit sit' means 'I am girl', which of the following means 'girl'?

(*a*) it (*b*) pit (*c*) sit (*d*) nit

**Sol. (*d*)** We have,

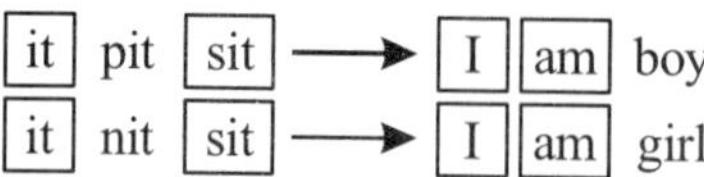


Here, 'it' and 'sit' is common in both the messages and 'I' and 'am' is common in both codes. Hence, code for girl will be 'nit'.

**5.** In a certain code language, '786' means 'study very hard', '958' means 'hard work pays' and '645' means 'study and work'. Which of the following is the code for 'very'?

(*a*) 8 (*b*) 6

(*c*) 7 (*d*) Cannot be determined

**Sol. (*c*)** Given,

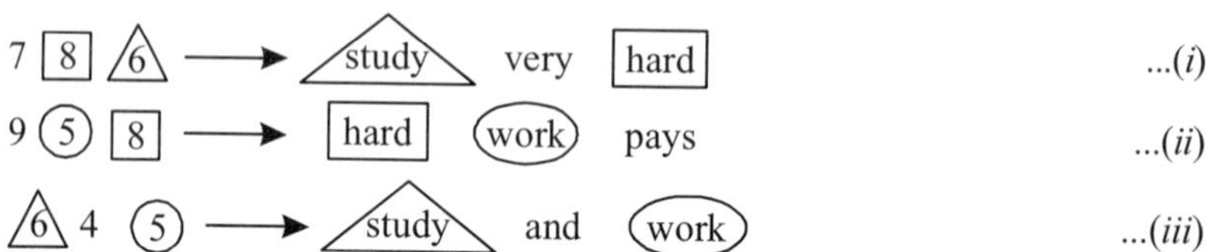


In the first and second statements, the common code digit is '8' and the common word is 'hard'. So, '8' means 'hard'. In the first and third statements, the common code digit is '6' and the common word is 'study'. So, '6' means 'study'.

From Eqs. (*i*) and (*ii*), 8 ⟶ hard

From Eqs. (*i*) and (*iii*), 6 ⟶ study

Hence, very ⟶ 7

**6.** If 'Parrot' is known as 'Peacock', 'Peacock' is known an 'Swallow', 'Swallow' is known as 'Pigeon' and 'Pigeon' is known as 'Sparrow', then what would be the name of Indian National Bird?

(*a*) Parrot (*b*) Swallow (*c*) Peacock (*d*) Pigeon

**Sol. (*b*)** We know that, Peacock is the Indian National Bird but here Peacock is known as Swallow. So, the answer is Swallow.

## EXERCISE

**1.** In a certain code DESIRABLE is written as JTFEQFMCB. How will DIMENSION be written in that code?
(*a*) FNJEMTJPO (*b*) FNJEOOPJT (*c*) FNJEMOPJT (*d*) EJNFMOPJT

**2.** In a certain code CLIMATE is written as BUFLJMD. How will ORDERLY be written in that code?
(*a*) SMZDESP (*b*) ZMSDPSE (*c*) ZMSDESP (*d*) ZMSFESP

**3.** If in a certain code CORPORATIONS is written as PROCTAROSNOL, then how will JUDICIAL be written in that code?
(*a*) IDUJLAIC (*b*) UJIDLAIC (*c*) UJIDICLA (*d*) IDUJICLA

**4.** If in a certain code, CERTAIN is coded as XVIGZRM, SEQUENCE is coded as HVJFVMXV, then how would MUNDANE be coded?
(*a*) NFMWZMX (*b*) NFMWZMV (*c*) NFMXZMV (*d*) None of these

**5.** In a certain code language, BEAT is written as YVZG, then what will be the code of MILD?
(*a*) ONRW (*b*) NOWR (*c*) ONWR (*d*) NROW

**6.** If the word 'TABLECLOTH' is coded as 'XEMRANRIST', how will 'HOTEL' be written?
(*a*) RIXAT (*b*) TIXAR (*c*) TAXIR (*d*) RAXIT

**7.** If 'CARING' is coded as 'EDVGCK', and SHARES is coded as 'UKEPBO'. How will CASKET be coded as in the same code?
(*a*) EDXIBP (*b*) EDWIAP (*c*) EDWPAI (*d*) EDWIBP

**8.** If DEMOCRATIC is written as EDMORCATCI, how CONTINUOUS will be written in the same code?
(*a*) OCTNNIOUSU (*b*) OTCNINUOUS
(*c*) OCNTNIUOSU (*d*) OTNCINUOSU

**9.** If in a certain code, 'DAUGHTER' is written as 'TERDAUGH', how will 'APTITUDE' be written in that code?
(*a*) DEUAPTIT (*b*) UDEAPTIT (*c*) DUEAPTIT (*d*) DAUEPTIT

**10.** If 'DELHI' is coded as '73541' and 'CALCUTTA' as '82589662', how will 'CALICUT' be coded?
(*a*) 5279431 (*b*) 5978213 (*c*) 8251896 (*d*) 8543691

**11.** In a certain code, FAVOUR is written as EBUPTS. How will DANGER be written in that code?
(*a*) CBFFDS (*b*) CBMHDS (*c*) EBFHDS (*d*) EBHHFS

**12.** In a certain code GOAL is written as AGLO and BEAR is written as ABRE. How will SEND be written in that code?
(*a*) SNED (*b*) NOES (*c*) DENS (*d*) NSDE

**13.** If ROAST is coded as PQYUR in a certain language, then how will SLOPPY be coded in that language?
(*a*) MRNAQN (*b*) NRMNQA (*c*) QNMRNA (*d*) RANNMQ

**14.** If HEALTH is written as GSKZDG, then how will NORTH be written in that code?
(*a*) OPSUI (*b*) GSQNM (*c*) FRPML (*d*) IUSPO

**15.** If in a code, MIND becomes KGLB and ARGUE becomes YPESC, then what will DIAGRAM be in that code?
(*a*) BGYEPYK (*b*) BGYPYEK (*c*) GLPEYKB (*d*) LKBGYPK

**16.** In a certain code PHYSICAL is written as MQBIDZJT. How will BREAKING be written in that code?
(*a*) HCOQJFLB (*b*) HCOSJFLB (*c*) HCOSLJKB (*d*) HCOTJFLB

**17.** If BE QUICK is coded as ZC OSGAI, then the code of the last letter of the third word in the sentence I LOVE MY COUNTRY is:
(*a*) A (*b*) T (*c*) U (*d*) W

**18.** In a certain code language RUSTICATE is written as QTTUIDBSD, how would STATISTIC be written in that code?
(*a*) RSBUJTUHB (*b*) RSBUITUHB (*c*) RSBUIRSJD (*d*) TUBUITUMB

**19.** In a certain code TEACHER is written is as VGCEJGT. How will CHILDREN be written in that code?
(*a*) EJKNEGTP (*b*) EGKNFITP (*c*) EJKNFGTO (*d*) EJKNFTGP

**20.** In a certain code BREAKTHROUGH is written as EAOUHRBRGHKT. How will DISTRIBUTION be written in that code?
(*a*) RISTTIBUDION (*b*) TISTBUONDRII
(*c*) STTIBUONRIDI (*d*) STTIBUDIONRI

**21.** If a certain code, FIRE is written as QHOE and MOVE as ZMWE. Following the same rule of coding, what should be the code for the word OVER?
(*a*) MWED (*b*) MWEO (*c*) MWOE (*d*) MWZO

**22.** In a coding system PEN is written as NZO and BARK as CTSL. How can we write PRANK in that coding system?
(*a*) CSTZN (*b*) NSTOL (*c*) NTSLO (*d*) NZTOL

**23.** If the word PORTER can be coded as MBNZQN, how can REPORT be written?
(*a*) NQMNBZ (*b*) NQMBNZ (*c*) NBQMNZ (*d*) NQBMNZ

**24.** If the word EARTH be written as QPMZS in coded form how would HEART be written following the same coding?
(*a*) SQPZM (*b*) SQMPZ (*c*) SPQZM (*d*) SQPMZ

**25.** In a certain code, STOVE is written as FNBLK, then how will VOTES be written in the same code?
(*a*) FLKBN (*b*) LBNKF (*c*) LKNBF (*d*) LNBKF

**Directions (Qs. 26–30):** *In each of these questions a group of digits is given followed by four combinations of letter / symbol codes numbered (a), (b), (c) & (d). The group of digits is to be coded as per the folio wing scheme and conditions. The serial number of the combination that represent the group of digits is your answer. If none of the combinations is correct, your answer is (e), i.e., 'None of these'.*

| Digit | 5 | 1 | 4 | 8 | 9 | 3 | 6 | 2 | 7 | 0 |
|---|---|---|---|---|---|---|---|---|---|---|
| Letter / Symbol Code | Q | T | % | # | E | F | $ | L | W | @ |

**Conditions:**

(*i*) If the first digit is odd and the last digit is even, their codes are to be swapped.

(*ii*) If the first as well as the last digit is even both are to be coded by the code of the first digit.

(*iii*) If the first digit is even and the last digit is odd, both are to be coded by the code for odd digit.

**26.** 584632
(*a*) Q#%$FL (*b*) L#$%FQ (*c*) L#%$QF
(*d*) L#%$FQ (*e*) None of these

**27.** 431068
(*a*) %FT@$# (*b*) %FT$@# (*c*) %FT@$%
(*d*) #FT@$# (*e*) None of these

**28.** 384695
(*a*) F#%$EF (*b*) F#%$EQ (*c*) Q#%$EQ
(*d*) Q#%$EF (*e*) None of these

**29.** 803279
(*a*) E@FLWE (*b*) #@FLWE (*c*) #@FLW#
(*d*) E@FLW# (*e*) None of these

**30.** 765984
(*a*) W$QE#% (*b*) W$QE#W (*c*) %$QE#%
(*d*) %$QE#L (*e*) None of these

**31.** In a certain code, DECEMBER is written as ERMBCEDE. Which word will be written as ERMBVENO in that code?
(*a*) AUGUST (*b*) SEPTEMBER (*c*) OCTOBER (*d*) NOVEMBER

**32.** If NARGRUED is the code for GRANDEUR, which word is coded as SERPEVRE?
(*a*) PERSEVER (*b*) PRESEVER (*c*) PERSERVE (*d*) PRESERVE

**33.** In acertain code, REFRIGERATOR is coded as ROTAREGIRFER. Which word would be coded as NOITINUMMA?
(*a*) ANMOMIUTNI (*b*) AMNTOMUIIN
(*c*) AMMUNITION (*d*) NMMUNITIOA

**34.** In a certain language, POPULAR is coded as QPQVMBS, which word would be coded as GBNPVT?
(*a*) FARMER (*b*) FAMOUS (*c*) FARMES (*d*) FAMOTH

**35.** In a certain code BAKE is written as 5796 and FIRE is written as 3146. How would FEAR be written in that code?
(*a*) 3564 (*b*) 3674 (*c*) 3574 (*d*) 3654

**36.** In a certain code MODERN is written as 5% 38# @ and WIN is written as 6©@. How is RIDE written in that code?
(*a*) #©38 (*b*) #@38 (*c*) #©83 (*d*) ©@38

**37.** In a certain code RAID is written as % # © * $, RIPE is written as % * @©. How is DEAR written up in that code?
(*a*) @©#% (*b*) $@#% (*c*) @$#% (*d*) $©#%

**38.** In a certain code ROPE is written as % 57 $, DOUBT is written as 35#8* and LIVE is written as @ 24$. How is TROUBLE written in that code?
(*a*) * % 5#8 @$ (*b*) *%#58@$ (*c*) *%5#8@4 (*d*) *%#58$@

**39.** If MACHINE is coded as 19–7–9–14–15–20–11, how will you code DANGER?
(*a*) 11–7–20–16–11–24 (*b*) 13–7–20–9–11–25
(*c*) 10–7–20–13–11–24 (*d*) 13–7–20–10–11–25

**40.** If E = 5, PEN = 35, then PAGE = ?
(*a*) 27 (*b*) 28 (*c*) 29 (*d*) 36

**41.** In a certain code language 'ja na da' means 'what you want', 'na pa ka' means 'they want food', and 'ka ho ni' means 'food and water'. What does 'da' mean in that code language?
(*a*) what (*b*) you
(*c*) what or you (*d*) Data inadequate

**42.** In a certain code language 'nee muk pic' means 'grave and concern', 'ill die so' means 'every body else' and 'tur muk so' means 'body and soul'. Which of the following would means 'every concern'?

(*a*) die pic (*b*) ill nee
(*c*) pic nee (*d*) can not be determined

**43.** In a certain code language 'food is good' is written as 'ho na ta', 'eat food regularly' is written as 'sa ta da' and 'keep good health' is written as 'la na ja'. How is 'eat' written in that code language?

(*a*) la (*b*) sa or da
(*c*) sa (*d*) Data Inadequate

**44.** In a certain code 'nik ma de' means 'he has come', 'de lit pa' means 'comehere fast' and 'ma la se' means 'she has gone'. What is the code for 'he'?

(*a*) nik (*b*) ma
(*c*) de (*d*) Can not be determined

**Directions (Qs. 45–47):** *According to a certain code language:*

'min fin bin gin' means 'Trains are always late'
'gin din cin hin' means 'Drivers were always punished'
'bin cin vin rin' means 'Drivers stopped all trains'
'din lin fin vin' means 'All passengers were late'

**45.** Which word is represented by 'vin'?

(*a*) Trains (*b*) Drivers (*c*) Late (*d*) All

**46.** 'Drivers were late' would be written as:

(*a*) fin cin din (*b*) min cin din (*c*) fin din gin (*d*) gin hin min

**47.** 'hin min lin' would mean:

(*a*) Always late train (*b*) All passenger trains
(*c*) Passenger are late (*d*) Passenger are punished

**Directions (Qs. 48–50):** *In a certain code language meanings of some words are as follows:*

(*a*) 'pit na sa' means 'you are welcome'
(*b*) 'na ho pa la' means 'they are very good'
(*c*) 'ka da la' means 'who is good'
(*d*) 'ho od pit la' means 'they welcome good people'

**48.** Which of the following means 'people' in that code language?

(*a*) ho (*b*) pit (*c*) la (*d*) od

**49.** Which of the following means 'very' in that code language?

(*a*) na (*b*) da
(*c*) pa (*d*) Data inadequate

**50.** Which of the following statements is redundant to answer the above two questions?
(*a*) None (*b*) (*i*) and (*iii*) (*c*) (*ii*) and (*iv*) (*d*) None of these

**51.** If 'Lily is called 'Lotus', 'Lotus' is called 'Rose', 'Rose' is called 'Sunflower' and 'Sunflower' is called 'Marigold', then which will be the national flower of India?
(*a*) Lily (*b*) Lotus (*c*) Rose (*d*) Marigold

**52.** In another place, the local terminology for 'earth', 'water', 'light', 'air' and 'sky' are 'sky', 'light', 'air', 'water' and 'earth', respectively. If someone is thirsty there, what would he drink?
(*a*) Light (*b*) Air (*c*) Sky (*d*) Water

**53.** If the animals which can walk are called 'swimmers', animals who crawl are called 'flying', those living in water are called 'snakes' and those which fly in the sky are called 'hunters', then what will a lizard be called?
(*a*) Swimmers (*b*) Snakes (*c*) Flying (*d*) Hunters

**54.** If 'orange' is called 'butter', 'butter' is called 'soap', 'soap' is called 'ink', 'ink' is called 'honey' and 'honey' is called 'orange', then which of the following will be used for washing clothes?
(*a*) Honey (*b*) Butter (*c*) Orange (*d*) Ink

**55.** If 'bucket' is known as 'tub', 'tub' is known as 'glass', 'glass' is known as 'saucer', 'saucer' is known as 'spoon', then which utensil will be used for drinking water?
(*a*) Tub (*b*) Saucer (*c*) Glass (*d*) Spoon

**Directions (Qs. 56–59):** *A code language has been used to write the words in English in column I and Greek letters in column II. Greek letters in column II do not appear in the same order as letters in column I. Decode the language and choose the correct code for the word given in each question, from amongst the alternatives provided.*

| Column I | Column II |
|---|---|
| CLEAR | γβωπθ |
| VIEW | νεγδ |
| TURN | ηρπσ |
| BUTTER | σρασπγ |
| OILY | δλθμ |
| WRITE | γπσνδ |
| VOWEL | νλεγθ |

**56.** CYCLE
(*a*) βθγμβ (*b*) βμβνπ (*c*) πρπεω (*d*) πλβνπ

**57.** TROUBLE
(*a*) ναβδγηλ (*b*) νσωδγθε (*c*) δγηλωεν (*d*) σλρπαγθ

**58.** LIVER
(*a*) θδεγπ (*b*) δγθπε (*c*) ρσωεν (*d*) αβδγη

**59.** BROWN
(*a*) ωενλω (*b*) ωδπρν (*c*) πανλη (*d*) πρβνε

## ANSWERS

| 1 | 2 | 3 | 4 | 5 | 6 | 7 | 8 | 9 | 10 |
|---|---|---|---|---|---|---|---|---|---|
| (*c*) | (*a*) | (*a*) | (*b*) | (*d*) | (*b*) | (*d*) | (*c*) | (*b*) | (*c*) |
| **11** | **12** | **13** | **14** | **15** | **16** | **17** | **18** | **19** | **20** |
| (*b*) | (*d*) | (*c*) | (*b*) | (*a*) | (*b*) | (*d*) | (*b*) | (*d*) | (*d*) |
| **21** | **22** | **23** | **24** | **25** | **26** | **27** | **28** | **29** | **30** |
| (*b*) | (*b*) | (*b*) | (*d*) | (*b*) | (*d*) | (*c*) | (*b*) | (*a*) | (*e*) |
| **31** | **32** | **33** | **34** | **35** | **36** | **37** | **38** | **39** | **40** |
| (*d*) | (*d*) | (*c*) | (*b*) | (*b*) | (*a*) | (*d*) | (*a*) | (*c*) | (*c*) |
| **41** | **42** | **43** | **44** | **45** | **46** | **47** | **48** | **49** | **50** |
| (*c*) | (*d*) | (*b*) | (*a*) | (*d*) | (*a*) | (*d*) | (*d*) | (*c*) | (*d*) |
| **51** | **52** | **53** | **54** | **55** | **56** | **57** | **58** | **59** | |
| (*c*) | (*a*) | (*c*) | (*d*) | (*b*) | (*a*) | (*d*) | (*a*) | (*c*) | |

## SOME SELECTED EXPLANATORY ANSWERS

**1.** The pattern is as follows:

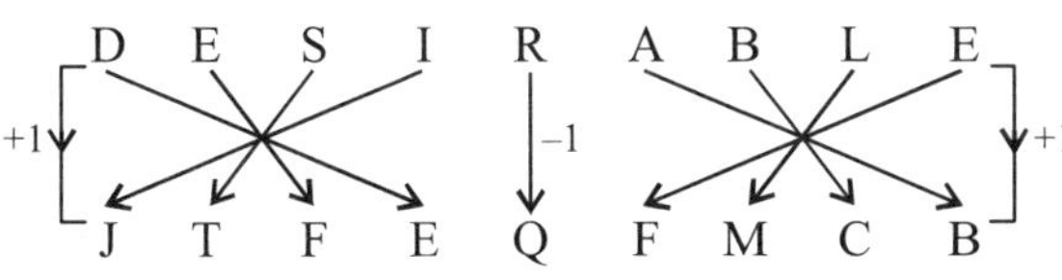


Similarly,

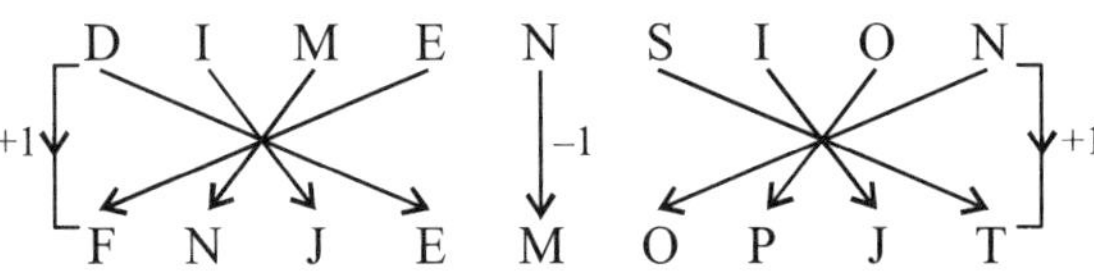


Therefore, the required code is 'FNJEMOPJT'

**2.** The pattern is as follows:

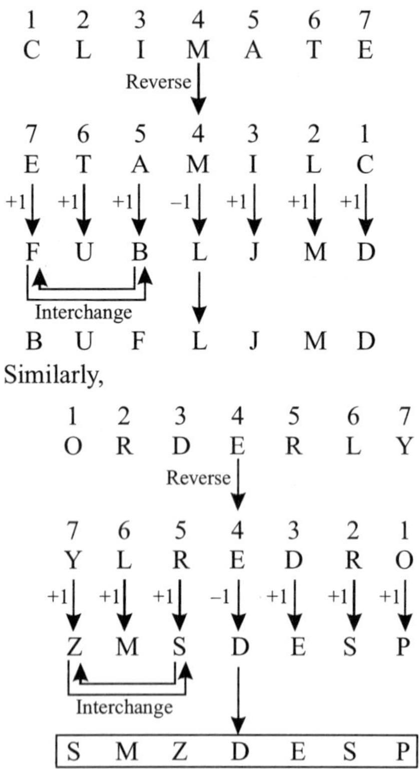


**3.** The pattern is as follows:

The word is divided into equal parts and the letters of each part are written in reverse order.

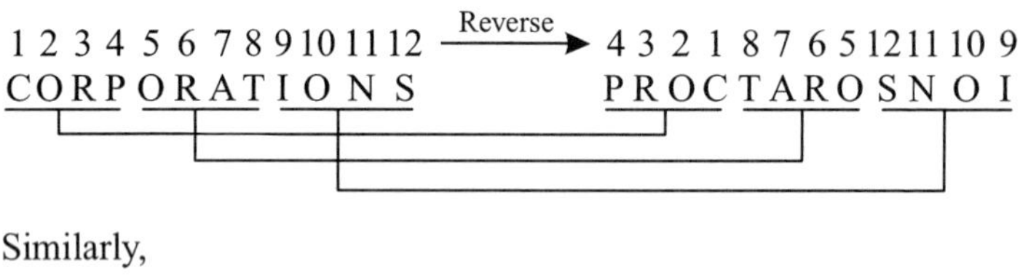


Similarly,

1 2 3 4 5 6 7 8 Reverse → 4 3 2 1 8 7 6 5

JUDI CIAL → IDUJ LAIC

**4.** The pattern of coding is as follows:

| | | | | | | | |
|---|---|---|---|---|---|---|---|
| Letters in Original series (→) | C | E | R | T | A | I | N |
| | ↓ | ↓ | ↓ | ↓ | ↓ | ↓ | ↓ |
| Letters in Reverse series (←) [code] | X | V | I | G | A | R | M |
| Position of letters | 3rd | 5th | 18th | 20th | 1st | 9th | 14th |

Similarly, S E Q U E N C E ⇒ H V J F V M X V

Similarly,

| | | | | | | | |
|---|---|---|---|---|---|---|---|
| Letters in Original series (→) | M | U | N | D | A | N | E |
| | ↓ | ↓ | ↓ | ↓ | ↓ | ↓ | ↓ |
| Letters in Reverse series (←) [code] | N | F | M | W | Z | M | V |
| | ↓ | ↓ | ↓ | ↓ | ↓ | ↓ | ↓ |
| Position of letters | 13rd | 21st | 14th | 4th | 1st | 14th | 5th |

**5.** The pattern of coding is as follows:

| | | | | |
|---|---|---|---|---|
| Letters in Original series (→) | B | E | A | T |
| | ↓ | ↓ | ↓ | ↓ |
| Letters in Reverse series (←) | Y | V | Z | G |
| | ↓ | ↓ | ↓ | ↓ |
| Position of letters | 2nd | 5th | 1st | 20th |

Smilarly,

| | | | | |
|---|---|---|---|---|
| Letters in Original series | M | I | L | D |
| | ↓ | ↓ | ↓ | ↓ |
| Letters in Reverse series | N | R | O | W |
| | ↓ | ↓ | ↓ | ↓ |
| Position of letters | 13th | 9th | 12th | 4th |

**6.** As,

| | | | | | | | | | |
|---|---|---|---|---|---|---|---|---|---|
| T | A | B | L | E | C | L | O | T | H |
| ↓ | ↓ | ↓ | ↓ | ↓ | ↓ | ↓ | ↓ | ↓ | ↓ |
| X | E | M | R | A | N | R | I | X | T |

Similarly,

| | | | | |
|---|---|---|---|---|
| H | O | T | E | L |
| ↓ | ↓ | ↓ | ↓ | ↓ |
| T | I | X | A | R |

**7.** As,

| | | | | | |
|---|---|---|---|---|---|
| C | A | R | I | N | G |
| ↓ +2 | ↓ +3 | ↓ +4 | ↓ –2 | ↓ –3 | ↓ –4 |
| E | D | V | G | K | C |

and S H A R E S
↓+2 ↓+3 ↓+4 ↓–2 ↓–3 ↓–4
U K E P B O

Similarly,

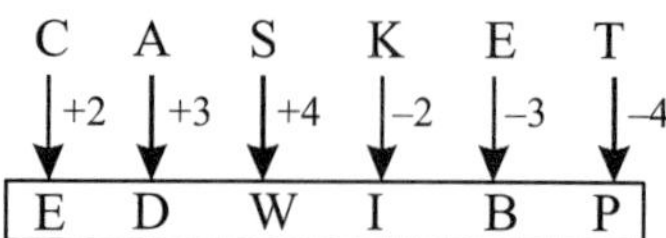


**8.** As,

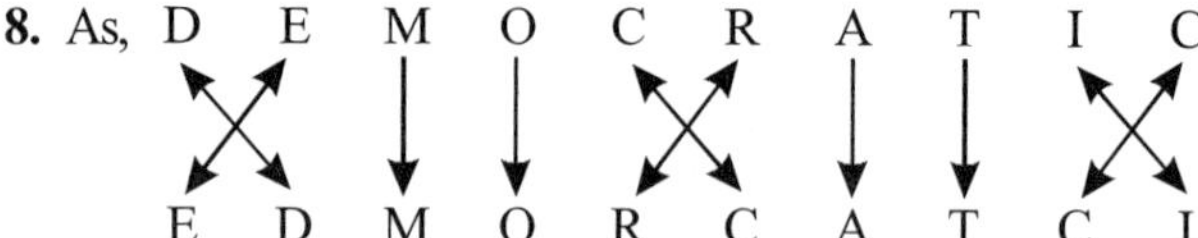


Similarly,

**9.** As, 1 2 3 4 5 6 7 8 → 6 7 8 1 2 3 4 5
D A U G H T E R → T E R D A U G H

Similarly, 1 2 3 4 5 6 7 8 → 6 7 8 1 2 3 4 5
A P T I T U D E → U D E A P T I T

**10.** If

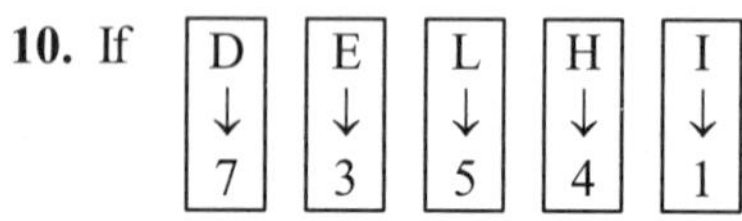


and

| C | A | L | C | U | T | T | A |
|---|---|---|---|---|---|---|---|
| ↓ | ↓ | ↓ | ↓ | ↓ | ↓ | ↓ | ↓ |
| 8 | 2 | 5 | 8 | 9 | 6 | 6 | 2 |

Then,

| C | A | L | I | C | U | T |
|---|---|---|---|---|---|---|
| ↓ | ↓ | ↓ | ↓ | ↓ | ↓ | ↓ |
| 8 | 2 | 5 | 1 | 8 | 9 | 6 |

**11.** The pattern is as follows:

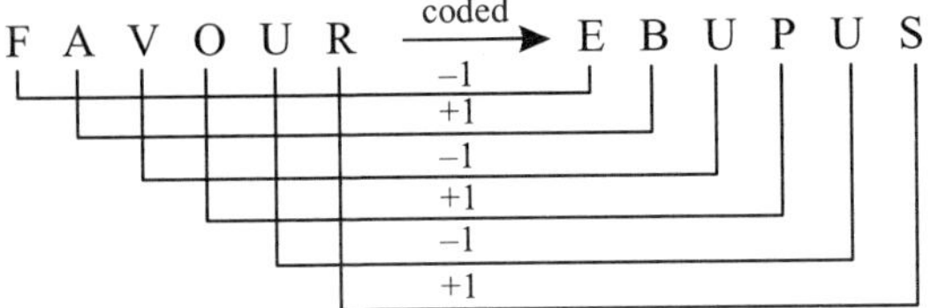


Similarly,

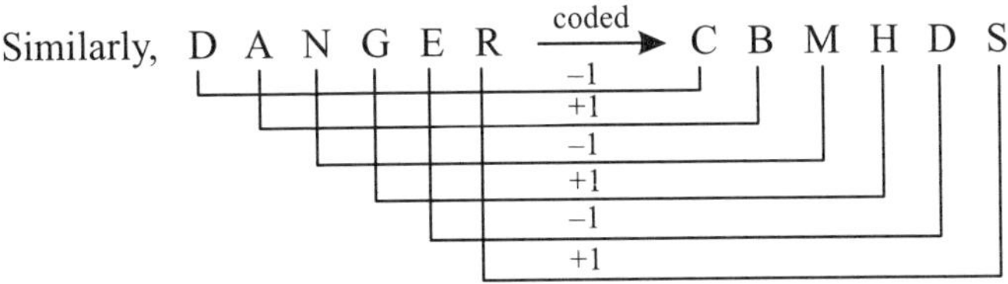


**12.** The pattern is as follows:

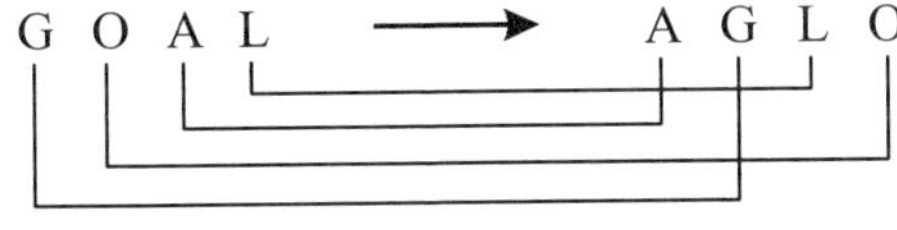


and,

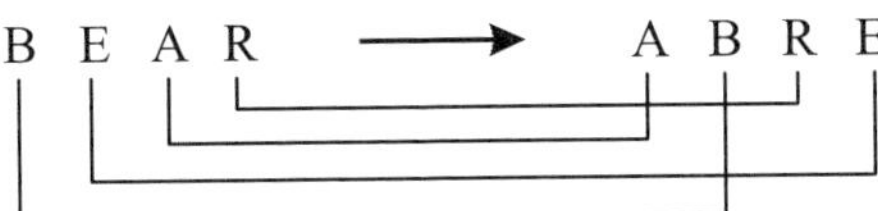


Therefore,

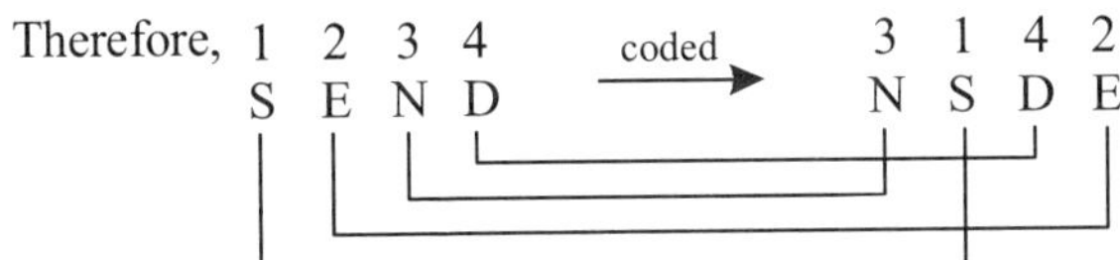


**13.** The pattern is as follows:

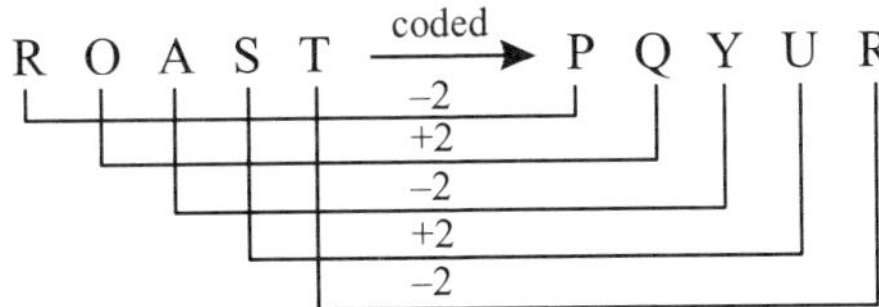

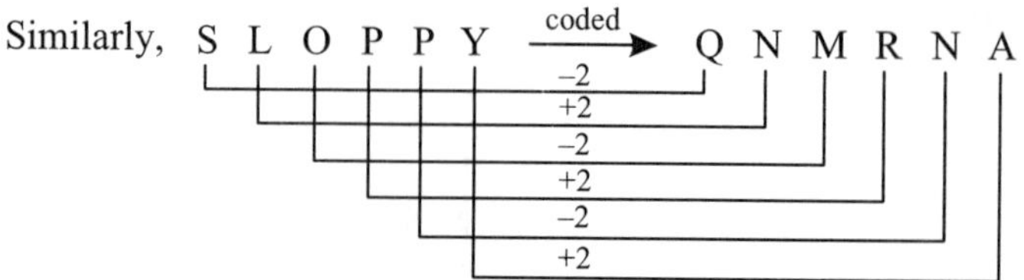


**14.** The pattern is as follows:

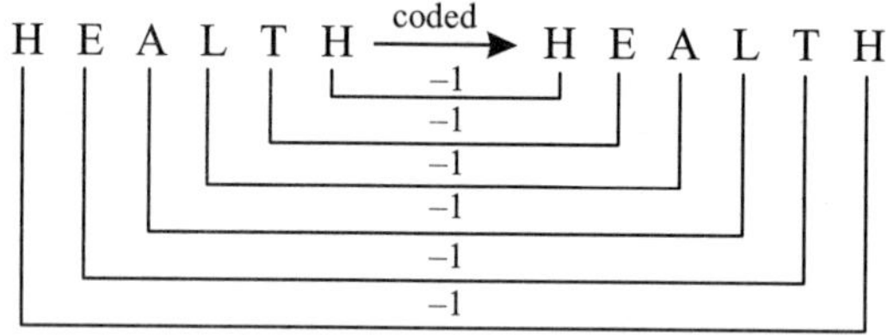


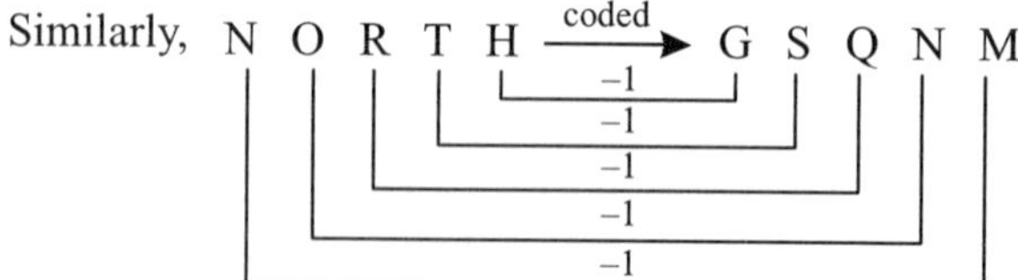


**15.** The pattern is as follows:

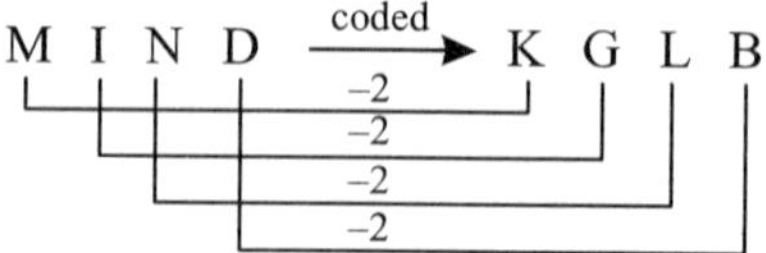


Similarly,

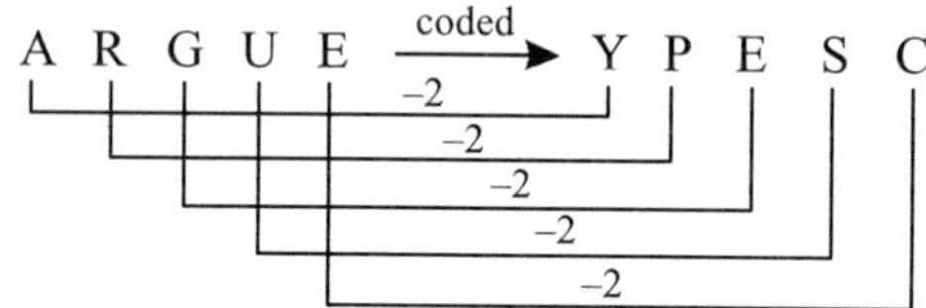


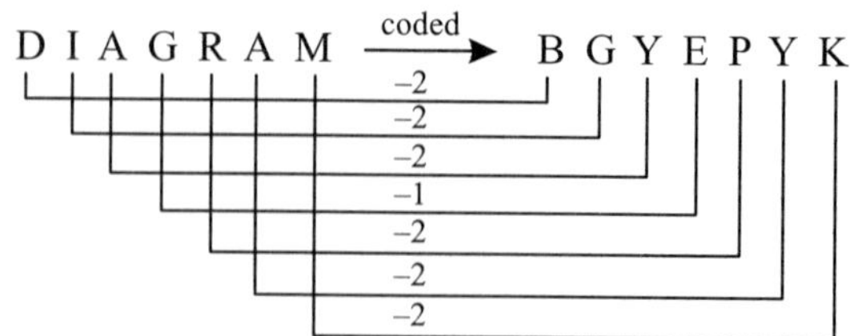

**16.** The pattern is as follows:

| | | | | | | | | | |
|---|---|---|---|---|---|---|---|---|---|
| 1 2 3 4 5 6 7 8 | coded → | 8 | 1 | 7 | 2 | 6 | 3 | 5 | 4 |
| P H Y S I C A L | | L | P | A | H | C | Y | I | S |
| | | +1 ↓ | +1 ↓ | +1 ↓ | +1 ↓ | +1 ↓ | +1 ↓ | +1 ↓ | +1 ↓ |
| | | M | Q | B | I | D | Z | J | T |

Similarly,

| | | | | | | | | | |
|---|---|---|---|---|---|---|---|---|---|
| 1 2 3 4 5 6 7 8 | coded → | 8 | 1 | 7 | 2 | 6 | 3 | 5 | 4 |
| B R E A K I N G | | G | B | N | R | I | E | K | A |
| | | +1 ↓ | +1 ↓ | +1 ↓ | +1 ↓ | +1 ↓ | +1 ↓ | +1 ↓ | +1 ↓ |
| | | H | C | O | S | J | F | L | B |

**17.** The pattern is as follows:

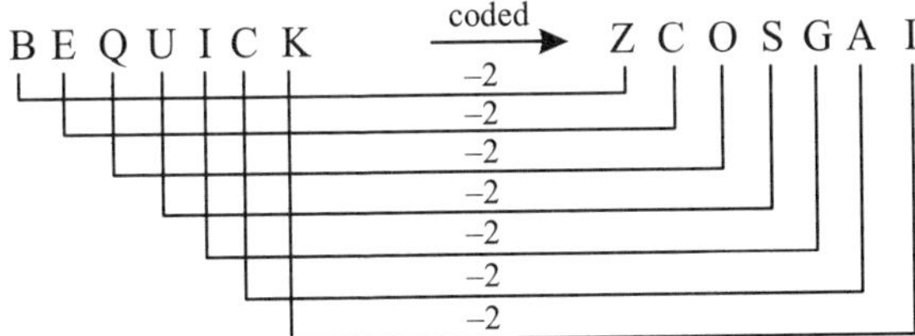


Similarly,

| I | L | O | V | E | M | Y | C | O | U | N | T | R | Y |
|---|---|---|---|---|---|---|---|---|---|---|---|---|---|
| –2 ↓ | –2 ↓ | –2 ↓ | –2 ↓ | –2 ↓ | –2 ↓ | –2 ↓ | –2 ↓ | –2 ↓ | –2 ↓ | –2 ↓ | –2 ↓ | –2 ↓ | –2 ↓ |
| G | J | M | T | C | K | W | A | M | S | L | R | P | W |

Therefore, the code of the last letter of the third word in this sentence = W.

**18.** The pattern is as follows:

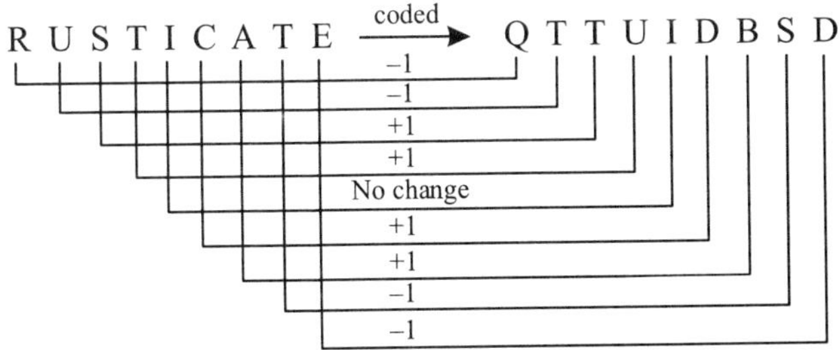

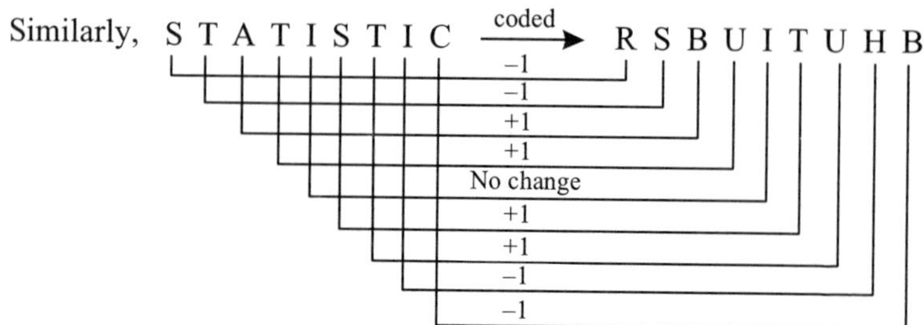


**19.** The pattern is as follows:

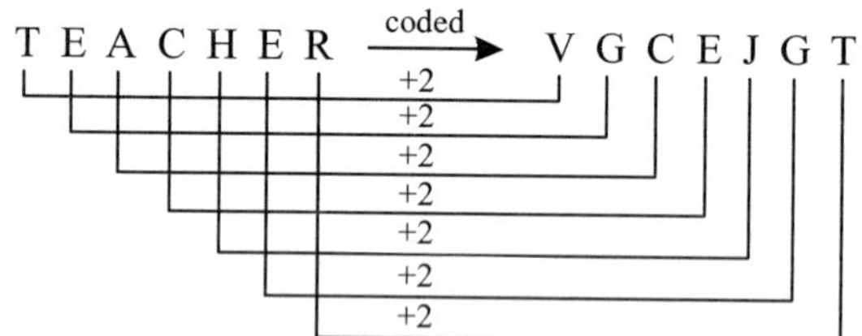


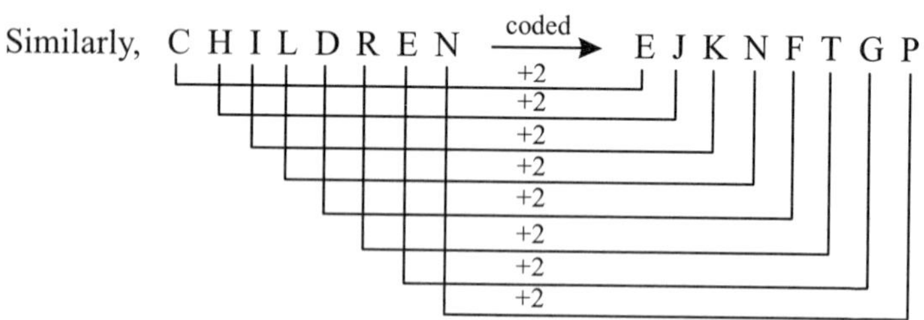


**20.** The pattern is as follows:

1 2 3 4 5 6 — 2 5 4 1 6 3

BR EA KT HR OU GH $\xrightarrow{\text{coded}}$ EA OU HR BR GH KT

Similarly,

1 2 3 4 5 6 — 2 5 4 1 6 3

DI ST RI BU TI ON $\xrightarrow{\text{coded}}$ ST TI BU DI ON RI

**21.** According to the question:

| Letter | F | I | R | M | O | V | E |
|---|---|---|---|---|---|---|---|
| Code | Q | H | O | Z | M | W | E |

Therefore Word : O V E R

↓ ↓ ↓ ↓

Code : M W E O

**22.** According to the question:

| Letter | P | E | N | B | A | R | K |
|---|---|---|---|---|---|---|---|
| Code | N | Z | O | C | T | S | L |

Therefore Word : P R A N K
↓ ↓ ↓ ↓ ↓
Code : N S T O L

**23.** According to the question:

| Letter | P | O | R | T | E | R |
|---|---|---|---|---|---|---|
| Code | M | B | N | Z | Q | N |

Therefore Word : R E P O R T
↓ ↓ ↓ ↓ ↓ ↓
Code : N Q M B N Z

**24.** According to the question:

| Letter | E | A | R | T | H |
|---|---|---|---|---|---|
| Code | Q | P | M | Z | S |

Therefore Word : H E A R T
↓ ↓ ↓ ↓ ↓
Code : S Q P M Z

**25.** According to the question:

| Letter | S | T | O | V | E |
|---|---|---|---|---|---|
| Code | F | N | B | L | K |

Therefore Word : V O T E S
↓ ↓ ↓ ↓ ↓
Code : L B N K F

**26.** Condition (*i*) follows i.e. 5 → L, 2 → Q (interchanged)

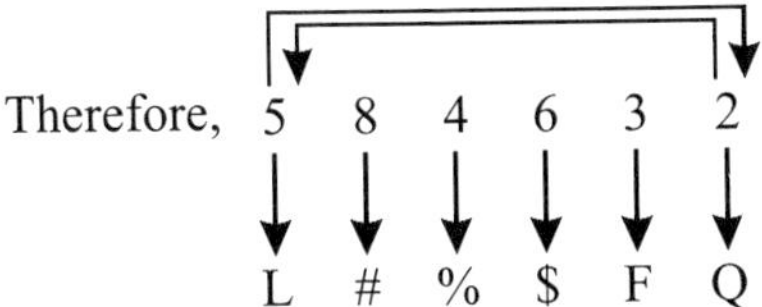

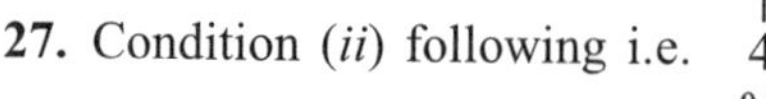

**27.** Condition (*ii*) following i.e. 4   8

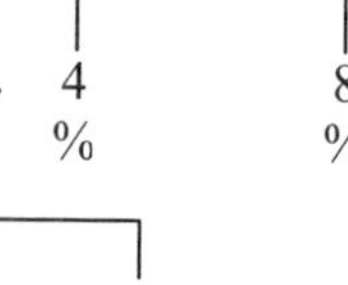

%   %

Therefore, 4 3 1 0 6 8

↓ ↓ ↓ ↓ ↓ ↓

% F T @ $ %

**28.** No Condition follows

Therefore, 3 8 4 6 9 5

↓ ↓ ↓ ↓ ↓ ↓

F # % $ E Q

**29.** Condition (*iii*) follows i.e. 8   9

E   E

Therefore, 8 0 3 2 7 9

↓ ↓ ↓ ↓ ↓ ↓

E @ F L W E

**30.** Condition (*i*) follows i.e. 7   4

%   W

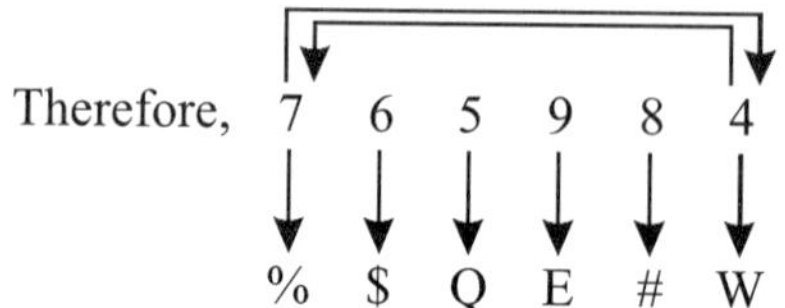

Therefore, 7 6 5 9 8 4

↓ ↓ ↓ ↓ ↓ ↓

% $ Q E # W

**31.** The pattern is as follows:

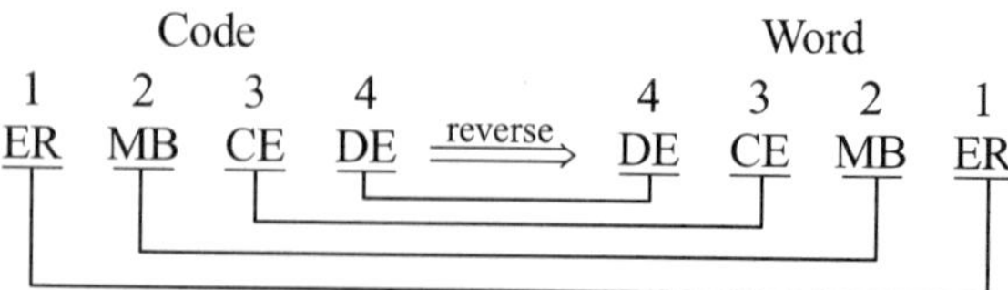

Similarly,

| Code | | | | | Word | | | |
|---|---|---|---|---|---|---|---|---|
| 1 | 2 | 3 | 4 | | 4 | 3 | 2 | 1 |
| ER | MB | VE | NO | $\xrightarrow{\text{reverse}}$ | NO | VE | MB | ER |

So the required word is 'NOVEMBER'.

**32.** The pattern is as follows:

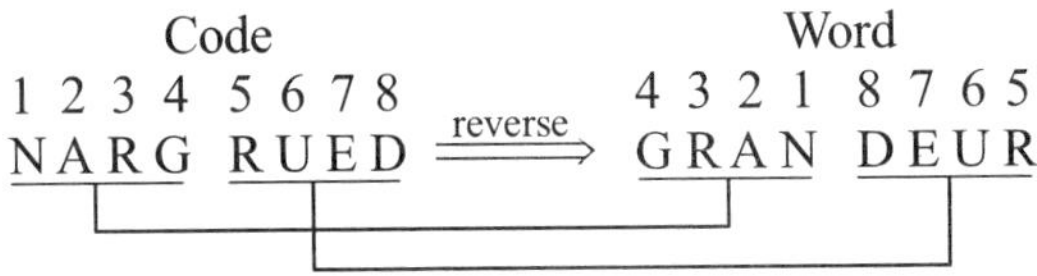


Similarly,

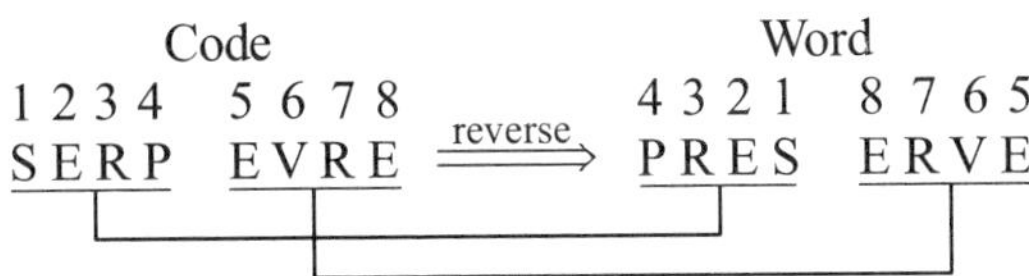


So, the required word is 'PRESERVE'

**33.** The pattern is as follows:

| Code | | Word |
|---|---|---|
| 1 2 3 4 5 6 7 8 9 10 11 12 | $\xrightarrow{\text{reverse}}$ | 12 11 10 9 8 7 6 5 4 3 2 1 |
| R O T A R E G I R F E R | | R E F R I G E R A T O R |

Similarly,

| | | |
|---|---|---|
| 1 2 3 4 5 6 7 8 9 10 | $\xrightarrow{\text{reverse}}$ | 10 9 8 7 6 5 4 3 2 1 |
| N O I T I N U M M A | | A M M U N I T I O N |

So, the required word is 'AMMUNITION'

**34.** The pattern is as follows:

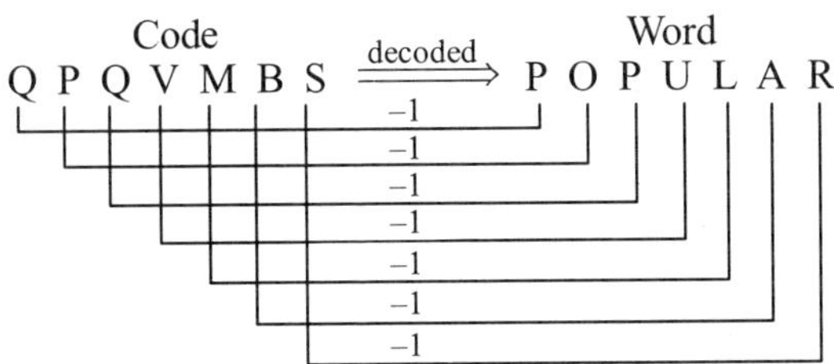

Similarly,

| Code | | Word |
|---|---|---|
| G B N P V T | $\xrightarrow{\text{decoded}}$ | F A M O U S |

G → −1 → F
B → −1 → A
N → −1 → M
P → −1 → O
V → −1 → U
T → −1 → S

So, the required word is 'FAMOIS'.

**35.** According to the question:

| Letters | B | A | K | E | F | I | R | E |
|---|---|---|---|---|---|---|---|---|
| Digit / Code | 5 | 7 | 9 | 6 | 3 | 1 | 4 | 6 |

Therefore, F E A R
↓ ↓ ↓ ↓
3 6 7 4

**36.** According to the question:

| Letters | M | O | D | E | R | N | W | I | N |
|---|---|---|---|---|---|---|---|---|---|
| Digit/Symbol Code | 5 | % | 3 | 8 | # | @ | 6 | © | @ |

Therefore, R I D E
↓ ↓ ↓ ↓
# © 3 8

**37.** According to the question:

| Letters | R | A | I | D | R | I | P | E |
|---|---|---|---|---|---|---|---|---|
| Symbol Code | % | # | * | $ | % | * | @ | © |

Therefore, D E A R
↓ ↓ ↓ ↓
$ © # %

**38.** According to the question:

| Letters | R | O | P | E | D | O | U | B | T | L | I | V | E |
|---|---|---|---|---|---|---|---|---|---|---|---|---|---|
| Symbol Code | % | 5 | 7 | $ | 3 | 5 | # | 8 | * | @ | 2 | 4 | $ |

Therefore, T R O U B L E
↓ ↓ ↓ ↓ ↓ ↓ ↓
* % 5 # 8 @ $

**39.** According to the English alphabet

| 13 | 1 | 3 | 8 | 9 | 14 | 5 |
|---|---|---|---|---|---|---|
| M | A | C | H | I | N | E |
| +6↓ | +6↓ | +6↓ | +6↓ | +6↓ | +6↓ | +6↓ |
| 19 | 7 | 9 | 14 | 15 | 20 | 11 |

Therefore,

| 4 | 1 | 14 | 7 | 5 | 18 |
|---|---|---|---|---|---|
| D | A | N | G | E | E |
| +6↓ | +6↓ | +6↓ | +6↓ | +6↓ | +6↓ |
| 10 | 7 | 20 | 13 | 11 | 24 |

**40.** According to the English alphabet

16 5 14

P E N = 16 + 5 + 14 = 35.

E = 5. (Given)

Therefore,

16 1 7 5

P A G E = 16 + 1 + 7 + 5 = 29.

**41.** The pattern of coding is as follows:

| **Code** | | **Word** | |
|---|---|---|---|
| ja (na) da | ⇒ | What you (want) | ...(*i*) |
| (na) pa △ka | ⇒ | they (want) △food | ...(*ii*) |
| △ka ho ni | ⇒ | △food and water | ....(*iii*) |

From (*i*) & (*ii*)

Common word = 'want'

Common code = 'na'

So, 'Want' $\xrightarrow{\text{Code}}$ 'na' ...(*iv*)

Using (*iv*) in (*i*), we get

'What' $\xrightarrow{\text{Code}}$ either 'ja' or 'da' ...(*v*)

So, word for code 'da' = either 'What' or 'you'. [From (*v*)]

**42.** The pattern of coding is as follows:

| **Code** | | **Word** | |
|---|---|---|---|
| nee muk pic | ⇒ | grave and concern | ...(*i*) |
| ill die so | ⇒ | every body else | ...(*ii*) |
| tur muk so | ⇒ | body and soul | ....(*iii*) |

From (*ii*) & (*iii*)

Common word = 'body'

Common code = 'so'.

So, 'body' $\xrightarrow{\text{Code}}$ 'So' ...(*iv*)

From (*i*) and (*iii*)

'and' $\xrightarrow{\text{Code}}$ 'muk' ...(*v*)

From (*iv*) & (*v*), it is clear that

'every' $\xrightarrow{\text{Code}}$ either 'ill' or 'dic'. ...(*vi*)

and 'concern' $\xrightarrow{\text{Code}}$ either 'nee' or 'pic'. ...(*vii*)

So, it cannot be determined exactly.

**43.** The pattern is as follows:

| **Code** | | **Word** | |
|---|---|---|---|
| food is good | ⇒ | ho na ta | ...(*i*) |
| eat food regularly | ⇒ | sa ta da | ...(*ii*) |
| keep good health | ⇒ | la na ja | ....(*iii*) |

From (*i*) & (*ii*)

Common-word = 'food'

Common-Code = 'ta'

So, 'food' $\xrightarrow{\text{Code}}$ 'ta' ...(*iv*)

From (*i*), (*ii*) & (*iv*), we get

'eat' ⇒ either 'sa' or 'da'.

**44.** According to the question

| **Code** | | **Word** | |
|---|---|---|---|
| nik ma de | ⇒ | he has come | ...(*i*) |
| de lit pa | ⇒ | come here fast | ...(*ii*) |
| ma la se | ⇒ | she has gone | ....(*iii*) |

From (*i*) & (*iii*)
Common word = 'has'
Common code = 'ma'

So, 'has' $\xrightarrow{\text{Code}}$ 'ma' ...(*iv*)

From (*i*) & (*ii*)
Common word = 'come'
Common code = 'de'

So, 'come' $\xrightarrow{\text{Code}}$ 'de' ...(*v*)

From (*i*), (*iv*) & (*v*), it is clear that

'he' $\xrightarrow{\text{Code}}$ 'nik'.

**45-47.**

| **Code** | | **Word** | |
|---|---|---|---|
| min fin bin gin | ⟹ | Trains are always late | ...(*i*) |
| gin din cin hin | ⟹ | Drivers were always punished | ...(*ii*) |
| bin cin vin rin | ⟹ | Drivers stopped all trains | ...(*iii*) |
| din lin fin vin | ⟹ | All passengers were late | ...(*iv*) |

Hence, din = were, gin = always, cin = drivers, bin = trains, fin = late, and vin = all

**48-50.**

| **Code** | | **Word** | |
|---|---|---|---|
| pit na sa | ⟹ | you are welcome | ...(*i*) |
| ho na pa la | ⟹ | they are very good | ...(*ii*) |
| ka da la | ⟹ | who is good | ...(*iii*) |
| ho od pit la | ⟹ | they welcome good people | ...(*iv*) |

**51.** We know that, national flower of India is Lotus and here Lotus is called Rose.

**52.** Water quenches thirst and here water is called as light.

**53.** Lizard will be called flying.

**54.** Soap is used for washing clothes and here soap is called ink.

**55.** Glass is used for drinking water and here glass is called as saucer.

**Hints (56-59):** *The pattern of coding is as following:*

| | WORD | | CODE | |
|---|---|---|---|---|
| (*i*) | C L E A R | ⇒ | γ β ω π θ | ... (*i*) |
| (*ii*) | V I E W | ⇒ | ν ε γ δ | ... (*ii*) |
| (*iii*) | T U R N | ⇒ | η ρ π σ | ... (*iii*) |
| (*iv*) | B U T T E R | ⇒ | σ ρ α σ π γ | ... (*iv*) |
| (*v*) | O I L Y | ⇒ | δ λ θ μ | ... (*v*) |
| (*vi*) | W R I T E | ⇒ | γ π σ ν δ | ... (*vi*) |
| (*vii*) | V O W E L | ⇒ | ν λ ε γ θ | ... (*vii*) |

From (*i*) to (*vii*)

| Letters | E | I | R | L | O | Y | W | T | V | U | N | B | C | A |
|---|---|---|---|---|---|---|---|---|---|---|---|---|---|---|
| Code in Greek letter | γ | δ | π | θ | λ | μ | ν | σ | ε | ρ | η | α | β or ω | β or ω |

**56.** C Y C L E $\xrightarrow{\text{coded}}$ β μ β θ γ or, β θ γ μ β

**57.** T R O U B L E $\xrightarrow{\text{coded}}$ σ π λ ρ α θ γ or, σ λ ρ π α γ θ

**58.** L I V E R $\xrightarrow{\text{coded}}$ θ δ ε γ π

**59.** B R O W N $\xrightarrow{\text{coded}}$ α π λ ν η or, π α ν λ η

3

# Sequences and Series

## INTRODUCTION

Sequences and series consist of questions where you are supposed to understand the logic behind a given sequence or series of numbers/alphabets. Based on this understanding you are supposed to determine either:

(*a*) A continuation to the series

(*b*) The immediate next term of the series or

(*c*) A missing term/terms within the series.

While preparing yourself to solve such questions, you should improve your ability to spot a particular relationship between terms within the series. The common logical premises used for questions are given here.

## SERIES BASED ON NUMBERS

1. Arithmetic series : 1, 2, 3, 4, 5, ...
2. Geometric series : 2, 4, 8, 16, ...
3. Harmonic series : $1, \frac{1}{2}, \frac{1}{3}, \frac{1}{4} \ldots$
4. Squares, Squares + something or squares – something e.g. next term in the series 24, 35, 48, 63, 80... will be 99 since the series is $(5^2 - 1), (6^2 - 1)$, etc.
5. Cubes, cubes + something, cubes – something
6. Series of constantly changing additions or multiplications, e.g.,
   (*i*) 2, 6, 24, 120, ... (The terms are got by × 3, × 4, × 5, and so on.)
   (*ii*) 11, 16, 22, 29, 37, ... (The series follows a logic of +5, +6, +7, +8, and so on.)
7. Intermingled series— *e.g.*, 2, 5, 6, 10, 18, 15, 54 ...
   In this series alternate terms starting with the first term form a Geometric Progression ($a, ar, ar^2, ar^3, ar^4$, etc.) with common ratio $r = 3$, while the 2nd, 4th, 6th terms form an Arithmetic Progression ($a, a + d, a + 2d, a + 3d$, etc.) with a common difference $d = 5$.

## SERIES BASED ON ALPHABETS

In such series, the most crucial aspect is to know the position of each alphabet in the alphabet series A to Z both from start to end.

Thus, the following reference numbers for each alphabet become important:

| Going Forward | 1 | 2 | 3 | 4 | 5 | 6 | 7 | 8 | 9 | 10 | 11 | 12 | 13 |
|---|---|---|---|---|---|---|---|---|---|---|---|---|---|
| Alphabet | A | B | C | D | E | F | G | H | I | J | K | L | M |
| Going Back from Z | 26 | 25 | 24 | 23 | 22 | 21 | 20 | 19 | 18 | 17 | 16 | 15 | 14 |

| Going Forward | 14 | 15 | 16 | 17 | 18 | 19 | 20 | 21 | 22 | 23 | 24 | 25 | 26 |
|---|---|---|---|---|---|---|---|---|---|---|---|---|---|
| Alphabet | N | O | P | Q | R | S | T | U | V | W | X | Y | Z |
| Going back from Z | 13 | 12 | 11 | 10 | 9 | 8 | 7 | 6 | 5 | 4 | 3 | 2 | 1 |

Notice that M and N are the two middle points of this series.

Let us now look at a few solved examples before we go into the practice exercise.

### SOLVED EXAMPLE

**1.** Which of the numbers given below would come next in the series of numbers?

1, 9, 25, ....

(*a*) 36 (*b*) 49 (*c*) 64 (*d*) 81

**Sol.** The first number is 1, second is 9 and third is 25. We can easily observe that the numbers in the series are squares of consecutive odd numbers. Hence, the next number would be the square of 7 which would be 49. Thus Option (*b*) is correct.

**2.** Which of the following letters would come next in the series of letters?

Z, W, R, K, ....

(*a*) A (*b*) C (*c*) B (*d*) D

**Sol.** In the given series from the end of the alphabet series, Z is the 1st alphabet, W is the 4th alphabet, R is the 9th alphabet and K is the 16th alphabet.

Thus the next letter in the series will be the 25th alphabet from the end or the second from the start. Hence, the next alphabet must be B. Thus (*c*) is the correct option.

**3.** What would come next in the following series of numbers?

1, 2, 10, 37, ....., 226

(*a*) 62 (*b*) 101 (*c*) 125 (*d*) 175

**Sol.** The series is following the +1, +8, +27 routine. Hence, the next number must be at an interval of +64 and should be 101. Thus Option (*b*) is the correct answer.

**4.** What would come next in the following series?

$A_{10}$, $D_{15}$, $G_{20}$, $J_{25}$ ....

(*a*) $N_{18}$ (*b*) $O_{20}$ (*c*) $M_{16}$ (*d*) $M_{30}$

**Sol.** In the series of letters represented above there is a gap of 2 letters between every two consecutive terms and hence, the next letter will be M (after skipping K and L). Thus, the correct answer should be $M_{30}$. Thus Option (*d*) is correct.

**5.** What should come next in the series below?

122343456 ..................

(*a*) 45678 (*b*) 6789 (*c*) 34567 (*d*) None of these

**Sol.** We can see that the series is a group of joined series as 12, 234, 3456 and hence the next terms should be 45678. Thus Option (*a*) is correct.

## EXERCISE

### NUMBER SERIES

**Directions:** *In each of the following questions, a number series is given with one term missing. Choose the correct alternative that will continue the same pattern and replace the question mark in the given series.*

**1.** 0, 2, 8, 14, ?, 34

(*a*) 25 (*b*) 23 (*c*) 20 (*d*) 24

**2.** 325, 259, 204, 160, 127, 105, ?

(*a*) 96 (*b*) 98 (*c*) 100 (*d*) 94

**3.** 28, 33, 31, 36, ?, 39

(*a*) 32 (*b*) 34 (*c*) 38 (*d*) 40

**4.** 10000, 11000, 9900, 10890, 9801, ?

(*a*) 10929 (*b*) 10241 (*c*) 10423.3 (*d*) 10781.1

**5.** 96 107 129 162 206 ?
(*a*) 260 (*b*) 261 (*c*) 258 (*d*) 256

**6.** 60.5 72 84.5 98 112.5 ?
(*a*) 127 (*b*) 125 (*c*) 126 (*d*) 128

**7.** 12 14 17 13 8 14 21 13 4 ?
(*a*) 15 (*b*) 2 (*c*) 13 (*d*) 14

**8.** 289 303 324 352 387 429 ?
(*a*) 473 (*b*) 487 (*c*) 558 (*d*) 478

**9.** 4, 8, 28, 80, 244, ?
(*a*) 628 (*b*) 728 (*c*) 278 (*d*) 428

**10.** 3 20 87 392 ?
(*a*) 1963 (*b*) 2025 (*c*) 1612 (*d*) None of these

**11.** 114 115 107 134 70 ?
(*a*) 140 (*b*) 195 (*c*) 150 (*d*) None of these

**12.** 4, 6, 9, $13\frac{1}{2}$, ?
(*a*) 19 (*b*) $22\frac{3}{4}$ (*c*) $17\frac{1}{2}$ (*d*) $20\frac{1}{4}$

**13.** 3, 7, 15, ? 63, 127
(*a*) 52 (*b*) 30 (*c*) 47 (*d*) 31

**14.** 30 46 78 126 190 270 ?
(*a*) 398 (*b*) 382 (*c*) 356 (*d*) 366

**15.** 0.4 2.4 ? 27.4 114.6 579
(*a*) 6.4 (*b*) 4.2 (*c*) 8.3 (*d*) 7.8

**16.** 3 10 32 100 ?
(*a*) 460 (*b*) 308 (*c*) 345 (*d*) None of these

**17.** 12 22 69 272 1365 ?
(*a*) 6830 (*b*) 8195 (*c*) 8196 (*d*) 8184

**18.** 4 6 9 13.5 20.25 30.375 ?
(*a*) 48.5625 (*b*) 42.7525 (*c*) 40.25 (*d*) 45.5625

**19.** 19, 2, 38, 3, 114, 4, ?
(*a*) 352 (*b*) 256 (*c*) 228 (*d*) 456

**20.** 2, 9, 28, ? 126, 217, 344
(*a*) 82 (*b*) 65 (*c*) 50 (*d*) 70

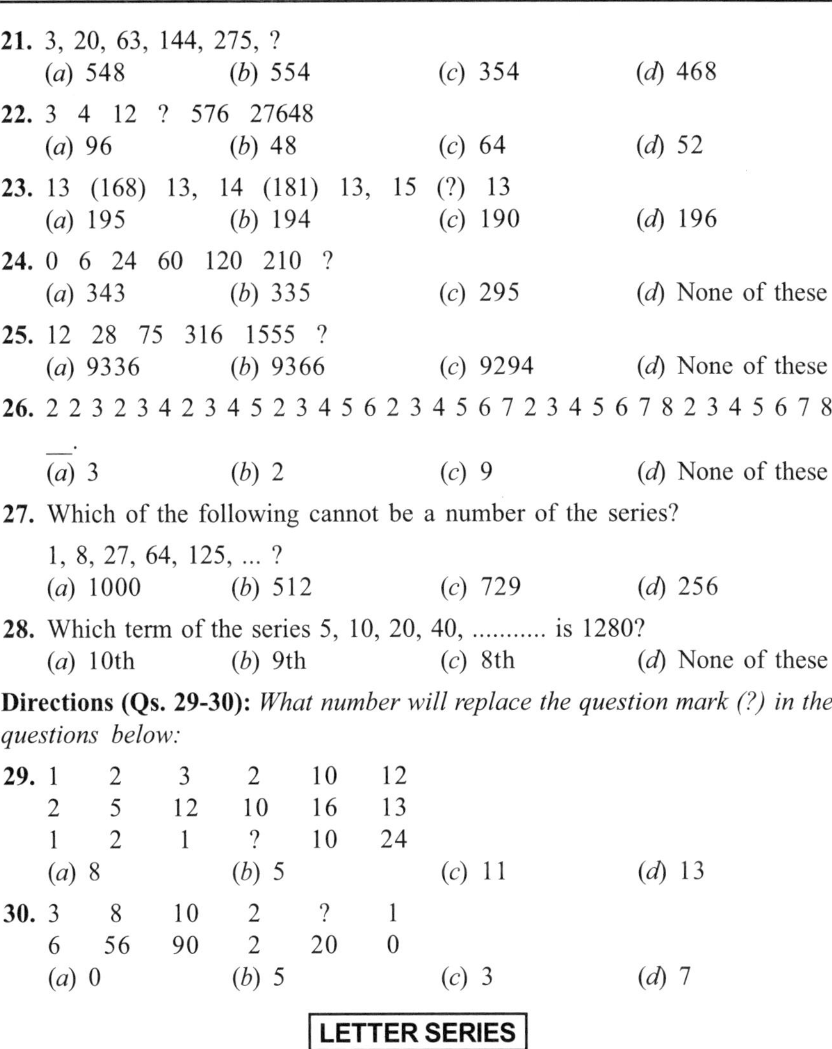

**21.** 3, 20, 63, 144, 275, ?
(*a*) 548 (*b*) 554 (*c*) 354 (*d*) 468

**22.** 3 4 12 ? 576 27648
(*a*) 96 (*b*) 48 (*c*) 64 (*d*) 52

**23.** 13 (168) 13, 14 (181) 13, 15 (?) 13
(*a*) 195 (*b*) 194 (*c*) 190 (*d*) 196

**24.** 0 6 24 60 120 210 ?
(*a*) 343 (*b*) 335 (*c*) 295 (*d*) None of these

**25.** 12 28 75 316 1555 ?
(*a*) 9336 (*b*) 9366 (*c*) 9294 (*d*) None of these

**26.** 2 2 3 2 3 4 2 3 4 5 2 3 4 5 6 2 3 4 5 6 7 2 3 4 5 6 7 8 2 3 4 5 6 7 8 __.
(*a*) 3 (*b*) 2 (*c*) 9 (*d*) None of these

**27.** Which of the following cannot be a number of the series?
1, 8, 27, 64, 125, ... ?
(*a*) 1000 (*b*) 512 (*c*) 729 (*d*) 256

**28.** Which term of the series 5, 10, 20, 40, ........... is 1280?
(*a*) 10th (*b*) 9th (*c*) 8th (*d*) None of these

**Directions (Qs. 29-30):** *What number will replace the question mark (?) in the questions below:*

**29.**

| | | | | | |
|---|---|---|---|---|---|
| 1 | 2 | 3 | 2 | 10 | 12 |
| 2 | 5 | 12 | 10 | 16 | 13 |
| 1 | 2 | 1 | ? | 10 | 24 |

(*a*) 8 (*b*) 5 (*c*) 11 (*d*) 13

**30.**

| | | | | | |
|---|---|---|---|---|---|
| 3 | 8 | 10 | 2 | ? | 1 |
| 6 | 56 | 90 | 2 | 20 | 0 |

(*a*) 0 (*b*) 5 (*c*) 3 (*d*) 7

## LETTER SERIES

**Directions (Qs. 31-71):** *In each of the following questions, various terms of an alphabet series are given with one or more terms missing as shown by (?). Choose the missing terms out of the given alternatives.*

**31.** A, C, F, J, ?
(*a*) K (*b*) O (*c*) M (*d*) N

**32.** A, Z, D, Y, G, X, ?, ?
(*a*) W, J (*b*) J, W (*c*) W, K (*d*) K, W

**33.** B, I, P, ?, D
(*a*) U (*b*) W (*c*) S
(*d*) R (*e*) None of these

**34.** E, J, ?, T, Y, D
(*a*) B (*b*) O (*c*) F
(*d*) J (*e*) None of these

**35.** A, C, F, J, ?, ?
(*a*) L, P (*b*) M, O (*c*) O, U (*d*) R, V

**36.** A,D, E, H, I, L, ?, ?
(*a*) M, P (*b*) M, N (*c*) M, O (*d*) M, Q

**37.** C, F, I, L, O, ?
(*a*) R (*b*) S (*c*) T
(*d*) U (*e*) None of these

**38.** D, H, L, P, T, ?
(*a*) Z (*b*) A (*c*) B
(*d*) X (*e*) None of these

**39.** A, I, B, J, C, K, ?, ?
(*a*) E, M (*b*) E, L (*c*) D, L (*d*) D, M

**40.** W, T, P, M, I, F, B, ?, ?
(*a*) Z, V (*b*) X, U (*c*) Y, U (*d*) Y, V

**41.** X, Q, K, F, ?
(*a*) E (*b*) B (*c*) C (*d*) D

**42.** W, T, Q, N
(*a*) J (*b*) K (*c*) L (*d*) M

**43.** A, Z, B, Y, C, X, ?, ?
(*a*) E, V (*b*) W, D (*c*) D, W (*d*) Y, V

**44.** A, P, C, Q, E, R, G, ?, ?
(*a*) S, I, (*b*) H, I (*c*) I, S (*d*) T, J

**45.** NZ, OY, PX, QW, RV, ?
(*a*) FS (*b*) SU (*c*) UF (*d*) TU

**46.** AC, FH, K ..., PR, UW
(*a*) L (*b*) J (*c*) M (*d*) N

**47.** AZ, BY, CX, ?
(*a*) EW (*b*) EU (*c*) GH (*d*) DW

**48.** DF, GI, KM, NQ, RT, ?
(*a*) UW (*b*) YZ (*c*) XZ (*d*) UX

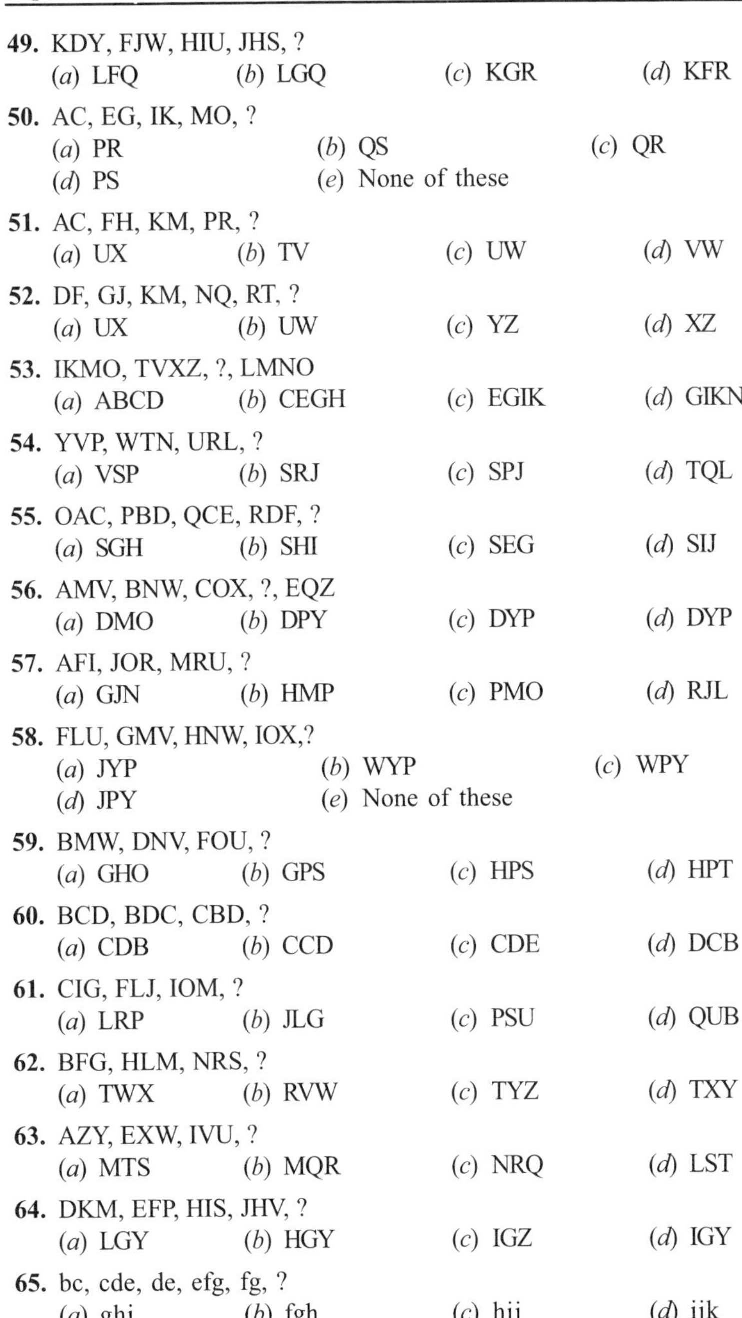

**49.** KDY, FJW, HIU, JHS, ?
(*a*) LFQ (*b*) LGQ (*c*) KGR (*d*) KFR

**50.** AC, EG, IK, MO, ?
(*a*) PR (*b*) QS (*c*) QR
(*d*) PS (*e*) None of these

**51.** AC, FH, KM, PR, ?
(*a*) UX (*b*) TV (*c*) UW (*d*) VW

**52.** DF, GJ, KM, NQ, RT, ?
(*a*) UX (*b*) UW (*c*) YZ (*d*) XZ

**53.** IKMO, TVXZ, ?, LMNO
(*a*) ABCD (*b*) CEGH (*c*) EGIK (*d*) GIKN

**54.** YVP, WTN, URL, ?
(*a*) VSP (*b*) SRJ (*c*) SPJ (*d*) TQL

**55.** OAC, PBD, QCE, RDF, ?
(*a*) SGH (*b*) SHI (*c*) SEG (*d*) SIJ

**56.** AMV, BNW, COX, ?, EQZ
(*a*) DMO (*b*) DPY (*c*) DYP (*d*) DYP

**57.** AFI, JOR, MRU, ?
(*a*) GJN (*b*) HMP (*c*) PMO (*d*) RJL

**58.** FLU, GMV, HNW, IOX,?
(*a*) JYP (*b*) WYP (*c*) WPY
(*d*) JPY (*e*) None of these

**59.** BMW, DNV, FOU, ?
(*a*) GHO (*b*) GPS (*c*) HPS (*d*) HPT

**60.** BCD, BDC, CBD, ?
(*a*) CDB (*b*) CCD (*c*) CDE (*d*) DCB

**61.** CIG, FLJ, IOM, ?
(*a*) LRP (*b*) JLG (*c*) PSU (*d*) QUB

**62.** BFG, HLM, NRS, ?
(*a*) TWX (*b*) RVW (*c*) TYZ (*d*) TXY

**63.** AZY, EXW, IVU, ?
(*a*) MTS (*b*) MQR (*c*) NRQ (*d*) LST

**64.** DKM, EFP, HIS, JHV, ?
(*a*) LGY (*b*) HGY (*c*) IGZ (*d*) IGY

**65.** bc, cde, de, efg, fg, ?
(*a*) ghi (*b*) fgh (*c*) hij (*d*) ijk

**66.** OTE, PUF, QVG, RWH, ?
(*a*) SYJ (*b*) TXI (*c*) SXJ (*d*) SXI

**67.** CEG, IKM, OQS, ?
(*a*) VXZ (*b*) TVX (*c*) TUV (*d*) UWY

**68.** CFL, EIK, GLJ, IOI, ?
(*a*) KRH (*b*) KRJ (*c*) JRU (*d*) KOV

**69.** BXF, DVI, FTL, HRO, ?
(*a*) IOL (*b*) KPM (*c*) KPL (*d*) JPR

**70.** BEAG, DGCI, FIKE, ?
(*a*) HMIE (*b*) HKGM (*c*) HGKJ (*d*) HKLJ

**71.** ABCD, BCDA, CDAB, ? ABCD
(*a*) DADC (*b*) DABC (*c*) DBAC (*d*) DACB

**72.** What should come next in the following letter series?

A B C D P Q R S A B C D E P Q R S T A B C D E F P Q R S T
(*a*) A (*b*) V (*c*) U
(*d*) W (*e*) None of these

**73.** What should come next in the following letter series?

P Q P Q R P Q R S P Q R S T P Q R S T U P Q R S T U V P Q R S T
(*a*) S (*b*) U (*c*) Q
(*d*) R (*e*) None of these

**74.** What should come next in the following letter series?

A B C D E F Z Y X W V U A B C D E Z Y X W V U A B C D Z Y X W V
(*a*) U (*b*) A (*c*) B
(*d*) Z (*e*) None of these

**Directions (Qs. 75-84):** *These questions are based on the letter series. In each of these series, some letters are missing. Select the correct alternative.*

**75.** ab_d_ _b_dm_ _x_ _
(*a*) xmaxabda (*b*) xmaxabdam (*c*) mxaxabdm (*d*) mxaxbadm

**76.** mc_m_a_ca_ca_c_mc
(*a*) acmmma (*b*) camcam (*c*) aacmm (*d*) acmmc

**77.** b_ab_b_aab_b
(*a*) abbb (*b*) abba (*c*) baaa (*d*) aaba

**78.** _bcab_cabc_abca_b
(*a*) abca (*b*) aabc (*c*) bbca (*d*) abac

**79.** _ _r_ttp_ _s_ _tp_ _ _s_ _ _
(*a*) pqrssqtpqrtp (*b*) pqstrsqptrst (*c*) pqsqrsqrrtpq (*d*) pqrsqtpqsrtp

**80.** pqr _ _ rs _ rs _ _ s _ q _
(*a*) spqpprr (*b*) pqrrppq (*c*) sqppqpr (*d*) sqprrqr

**81.** bc _ bca _ cab _ ab _ a _ ca
(*a*) abcab (*b*) cabac (*c*) abccb (*d*) cabca

**82.** _ bb _ c _ bg _ b _ g
(*a*) cbgbc (*b*) cgbcb (*c*) cgbcc (*d*) gbcbb

**83.** a _ c _ ba _ ca _ cb
(*a*) abcc (*b*) acba (*c*) bcaa (*d*) bcba

**84.** _OPQ, N_PQ, NO_Q, NOP_
(*a*) ONQP (*b*) NOQP (*c*) NOPQ (*d*) PQNO

**Directions (Qs. 85-94):** *In each of the following questions, a letter series is given. Some of the letters of the series are missing. These missing letters are given in the same order as one of the four alternatives below the series. Find out the correct alternative.*

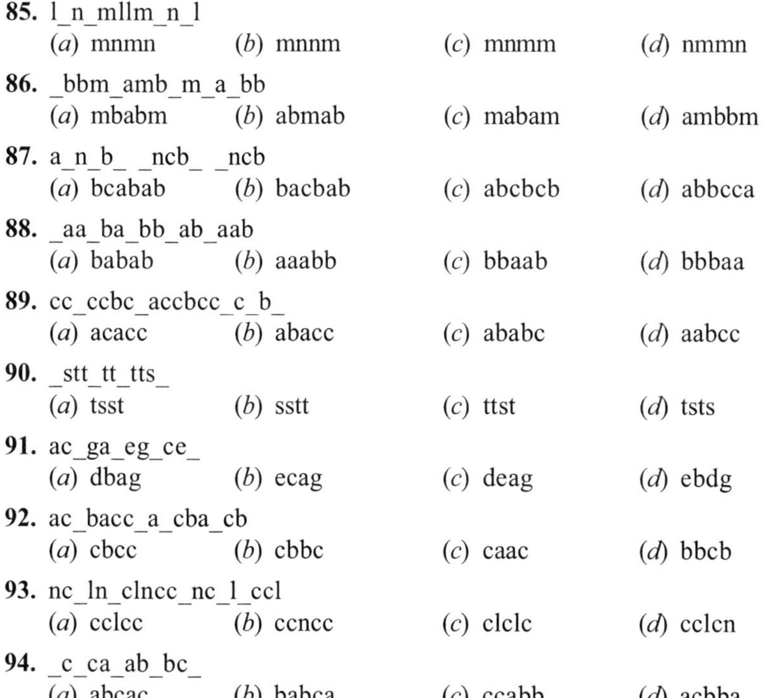

**85.** l_n_mllm_n_l
(*a*) mnmn (*b*) mnnm (*c*) mnmm (*d*) nmmn

**86.** _bbm_amb_m_a_bb
(*a*) mbabm (*b*) abmab (*c*) mabam (*d*) ambbm

**87.** a_n_b_ _ncb_ _ncb
(*a*) bcabab (*b*) bacbab (*c*) abcbcb (*d*) abbcca

**88.** _aa_ba_bb_ab_aab
(*a*) babab (*b*) aaabb (*c*) bbaab (*d*) bbbaa

**89.** cc_ccbc_accbcc_c_b_
(*a*) acacc (*b*) abacc (*c*) ababc (*d*) aabcc

**90.** _stt_tt_tts_
(*a*) tsst (*b*) sstt (*c*) ttst (*d*) tsts

**91.** ac_ga_eg_ce_
(*a*) dbag (*b*) ecag (*c*) deag (*d*) ebdg

**92.** ac_bacc_a_cba_cb
(*a*) cbcc (*b*) cbbc (*c*) caac (*d*) bbcb

**93.** nc_ln_clncc_nc_l_ccl
(*a*) cclcc (*b*) ccncc (*c*) clclc (*d*) cclcn

**94.** _c_ca_ab_bc_
(*a*) abcac (*b*) babca (*c*) ccabb (*d*) acbba

**Directions (Qs No. 95-104):** *In each of the following letter series, some of the letters are missing, which are given in the same order as one of the alternatives below it. Choose the correct alternative.*

**95.** _cb_ca_bacb_ca_bac_d
(*a*) addddb (*b*) addbbb (*c*) bddddb (*d*) bbbddd

**96.** c_bba_cab_ac_ab_ac
(*a*) bcacb (*b*) babcc (*c*) abcbc (*d*) acbcb

**97.** a_bc_a_bcda_ccd_bcd_
(*a*) abddbd (*b*) acbdbb (*c*) adbbad (*d*) adbcad

**98.** _c_bd_cbcda_a_db_a
(*a*) bdbcba (*b*) daabbc (*c*) cdbbca (*d*) adabcd

**99.** a_bc_c_abb_bca_
(*a*) abbba (*b*) accba (*c*) cccbc (*d*) cbbac

**100.** _A′B_B′AA′_BB′_A
(*a*) A′BAB′ (*b*) A′B′AB (*c*) ABAB (*d*) AB′A′B

**101.** _zy_zxy_yxzx_zyx_xy
(*a*) yxyzz (*b*) zxyzy (*c*) yzxyx (*d*) xyzzy

**102.** a_ba_c_aad_aa_ea
(*a*) babbb (*b*) babbd (*c*) babbc (*d*) bacde

**103.** aa_aabb_b_aa_aabb_bb
(*a*) bbbaa (*b*) bbbba (*c*) aabbb (*d*) babba

**104.** ab_y abc_xw abcdev_
(*a*) z, d, u (*b*) d, x, u (*c*) c, d, u
(*d*) z, y, w (*e*) None of these

**Directions (Qs. 105-109):** *In each of the following questions, a letter series is given. Some of the letters of the series are missing. These missing letters are given in the same order as one of the four alternatives below the series. Find out the correct alternative.*

**105.** H_JH_IJHHI_HH_JH
(*a*) IHJI (*b*) HIHI (*c*) IHIJ (*d*) HJHJ

**106.** ZYX_W_YZZ_XWWXY_
(*a*) WXYZ (*b*) WYXZ (*c*) WXZY (*d*) XYZW

**107.** ZX_TR_NLJ_FD_
(*a*) VPHB (*b*) VRHB (*c*) UPJB (*d*) VPJB

**108.** ac_cab_baca_aaa_aba
(*a*) aabc (*b*) aacb (*c*) babb (*d*) bcbb

**109.** _b_baaabb_a_ _bb_a_
(*a*) abbaaba (*b*) ababbaa (*c*) babaaba (*d*) baabaab

## MIXED SERIES

**Directions (Qs. 110-117):** *In each of the following series, one or more terms are missing as shown by (?). Choose the missing terms out of the given alternatives.*

**110.** J2Z, K4X, I7V, ?, H16R, M22P
(*a*) L 12 T (*b*) I 11 T (*c*) L 11 S (*d*) L 11 T

**111.** 4A, 12D, 28G, 60J, 124M, ?
(*a*) 246 S (*b*) 256 T (*c*) 248 Q (*d*) 252 P

**112.** D – 4, F – 6, H – 8, J – 10, ?, ?
(*a*) K – 12, M – 14 (*b*) K – 12, M – 13
(*c*) L –12, M – 14 (*d*) L – 12, N – 14

**113.** 2 Z 5, 7 Y 7, 14 X 9, 23 W 11, 34 V 13, ?
(*a*) 14 V 14 (*b*) 27 U 24 (*c*) 45 U 15 (*d*) 47 U 15

**114.** Q 1 F, S 2 E, U 6 D, W 21 C, ?
(*a*) Z 88 B (*b*) Y 44 B (*c*) Y 66 B (*d*) Y 88 B

**115.** B 0 R, G 3 U, E 3 P, J 7 S, H 9 N
(*a*) G 3 U (*b*) E 3 P (*c*) H 9 N (*d*) J 7 S

**116.** G 4 T, J 10 R, M 20 P, P 43 N, S 90 L
(*a*) G 4 T (*b*) M 20 P (*c*) S 90 L (*d*) J 10 R

**117.** 2, A, 9, B, 6, C, 13, D ?
(*a*) 19 (*b*) 9 (*c*) 12 (*d*) 10

**Directions (Qs. 118-122):** *In each of the following question, a series of letters and numbes are given, which follow certain definite pattern in groups. Choose the correct alternatives.*

**118.** 2 3 B _, 6 _ F G, _ 5 D _, 8 _ H I
(*a*) C, 7, 4, E, 9 (*b*) D, 8, 6, C, 7
(*c*) E, 8, 7, D, 9 (*d*) W, 8, 7, I, 6

**119.** Z _ 2 5 Y B 2 3 X C _ W _ 19 _ E 17
(*a*) A, 21, D, V (*b*) A, 27, C, V
(*c*) X, 21, C, W (*d*) X, 27, F, W

**120.** D _ 6 E G P _ H J _ 1 2 K M B 1 5 _
(*a*) E, 7, J, L, (*b*) F, 8, M, K (*c*) G, 9, I, M (*d*) J, 9, V, N

**121.** F _ U 6 _ 9 I _ T 7 _ 20 _ 4 D 23
(*a*) 11, G, 16, K, U (*b*) 13, H, 15, L, M
(*c*) 17, J, 19, R, S (*d*) 21, R, 18, G, W

**122.** X W C _ T S 20 _ P 12 _ L 1 5 K _ P _ G S 7

(*a*) 17, F I, S, T (*b*) 19, E, R, L, H

(*c*) 21, G, L, N, F (*d*) 23, H, K, O, H

**123.**

| | | | |
|---|---|---|---|
| KP | 42 | 0 | JX |
| GS | 9 | 30 | MY |
| TB | ? | ? | OL |

(*a*) 23, 52 (*b*) 0, 0 (*c*) 73, 48 (*d*) 40, 180

## ANSWERS

| 1 | 2 | 3 | 4 | 5 | 6 | 7 | 8 | 9 | 10 |
|---|---|---|---|---|---|---|---|---|---|
| (*d*) | (*d*) | (*b*) | (*d*) | (*b*) | (*d*) | (*d*) | (*d*) | (*b*) | (*d*) |
| **11** | **12** | **13** | **14** | **15** | **16** | **17** | **18** | **19** | **20** |
| (*b*) | (*d*) | (*d*) | (*d*) | (*d*) | (*b*) | (*d*) | (*d*) | (*d*) | (*b*) |
| **21** | **22** | **23** | **24** | **25** | **26** | **27** | **28** | **29** | **30** |
| (*d*) | (*b*) | (*b*) | (*d*) | (*b*) | (*c*) | (*d*) | (*b*) | (*d*) | (*b*) |
| **31** | **32** | **33** | **34** | **35** | **36** | **37** | **38** | **39** | **40** |
| (*b*) | (*b*) | (*b*) | (*b*) | (*c*) | (*a*) | (*a*) | (*d*) | (*c*) | (*c*) |
| **41** | **42** | **43** | **44** | **45** | **46** | **47** | **48** | **49** | **50** |
| (*b*) | (*b*) | (*c*) | (*a*) | (*b*) | (*c*) | (*d*) | (*d*) | (*b*) | (*b*) |
| **51** | **52** | **53** | **54** | **55** | **56** | **57** | **58** | **59** | **60** |
| (*c*) | (*a*) | (*a*) | (*c*) | (*c*) | (*b*) | (*b*) | (*d*) | (*d*) | (*a*) |
| **61** | **62** | **63** | **64** | **65** | **66** | **67** | **68** | **69** | **70** |
| (*a*) | (*d*) | (*a*) | (*a*) | (*a*) | (*d*) | (*d*) | (*a*) | (*d*) | (*b*) |
| **71** | **72** | **73** | **74** | **75** | **76** | **77** | **78** | **79** | **80** |
| (*b*) | (*c*) | (*b*) | (*a*) | (*b*) | (*a*) | (*d*) | (*a*) | (*c*) | (*c*) |
| **81** | **82** | **83** | **84** | **85** | **86** | **87** | **88** | **89** | **90** |
| (*c*) | (*b*) | (*d*) | (*c*) | (*b*) | (*c*) | (*a*) | (*c*) | (*a*) | (*a*) |
| **91** | **92** | **93** | **94** | **95** | **96** | **97** | **98** | **99** | **100** |
| (*b*) | (*a*) | (*d*) | (*b*) | (*a*) | (*d*) | (*c*) | (*d*) | (*b*) | (*c*) |
| **101** | **102** | **103** | **104** | **105** | **106** | **107** | **108** | **109** | **110** |
| (*a*) | (*d*) | (*c*) | (*a*) | (*a*) | (*a*) | (*a*) | (*a*) | (*a*) | (*d*) |
| **111** | **112** | **113** | **114** | **115** | **116** | **117** | **118** | **119** | **120** |
| (*d*) | (*d*) | (*d*) | (*d*) | (*d*) | (*d*) | (*d*) | (*a*) | (*a*) | (*d*) |
| **121** | **122** | **123** | | | | | | | |
| (*d*) | (*d*) | (*b*) | | | | | | | |

## SOME SELECTED EXPLANATORY ANSWERS

**1.** The given sequence follows the pattern:
+2, +6, +6, +10, +10, ... .

i.e. 0 → 2 → 8 → 14 → [24] → 34
(+2, +6, +6, +10, +10)

Therefore, Missing term = 14 + 10 = 24.

**2.** The given sequence follows the pattern:

–66, –55, –44, –33, –22, –11.

i.e. –11 × 6 = –66; –11 × 5 = –55; –11 × 4 = –44;
–11 × 3 = –33; –11 × 2 = –22; –11 × 1 = –11.

325 → 259 → 204 → 160 → 127 → 105 → [94]
(–66, –55, –44, –33, –22, –11)

Therefore, Missing term = 105 – 11 = 94.

**3.** The given sequence follows the pattern:

28 → 33 → 31 → 36 → [34] → 39
(+5, –2, +5, –2, +5)

Therefore, Missing term = 36 – 2 = 34.

**4.** The given sequence follows the pattern:

X + (10% of X); X – (10% of X) and so on.

10000 → 11000 → 9900 → 10890 → 9801 → [10781.1]
(+(10% of 10000), –(10% of 11000), +(10% of 9900), –(10% of 10890), +(10% of 9801))

Therefore, Missing term = 9801 + (10% of 9801)

$$= 9804 + \frac{10}{100} \times 9801$$

$$= 9801 + 980.1 = 10781.1.$$

**5.** The given sequence of number follows the pattern:
+11 × 1 = +11; +11 × 2 = +22; +11 × 3 = + 33;
= 11 × 4 = +44; +11 × 5 = +55;

96 → 107 → 129 → 162 → 206 → [261]
(+11, +22, +33, +44, +55)

Therefore, Missing number = 206 + 55 = 261.

**6.** The given sequence of number follows the pattern:

11.5; 11.5 + 1.0 = 12.5; 12.5 + 1.0 = 13.5; 13.5 + 1.0 = 14.5; 14.5 + 1.0 = + 15.5.

60.5 72 84.5 98 112.5 [128]

+11.5 +12.5 +13.5 +14.5 +15.5

Therefore, Missing number = 112.5 + 15.5 = 128.

**7.** The given sequence of number follows the pattern:
+2; +3; –5; +6; +7; –8; –9; +10.

12 14 17 13 8 14 21 13 4 [14]

+2 +3 –4 –5 +6 +7 –8 –9 +10

Therefore, Missing number = 4+ 10 = 14.

**8.** The given sequence of number follows the pattern:

14; 14 + 7 = 21; 21 + 7 = 28; 28 + 7 = 35; 35 + 7 = 42; 42 + 7 = 49.

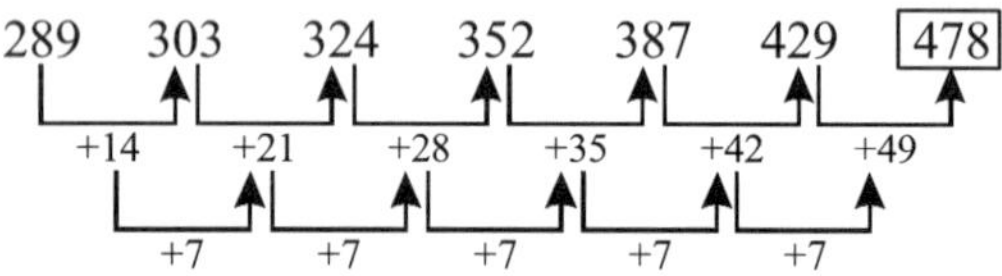


Therefore, Missing number = 428 + 49 = 478.

**9.** The given sequence of number follows the pattern:

$3^1 + 1, 3^2 - 1, 3^3 + 1, 3^4 - 1, 3^5 + 1, 3^6 - 1$

| 4 | 8 | 28 | 80 | 244 | 728 |
|---|---|---|---|---|---|
| ↓ | ↓ | ↓ | ↓ | ↓ | ↓ |
| $3^1 + 1$ | $3^2 - 1$ | $3^3 + 1$ | $3^4 - 1$ | $3^5 + 1$ | $3^6 - 1$ |

Therefore, Missing term = $3^6 - 1 = 728$.

**10.** The given sequence of number follows the pattern:

3 20 87 392 [1003]

$+1^2 + 16$ $+(9)^2 - 14$ $+(17)^2 + 16$ $+(25)^2 - 14$

Therefore, Missing number = $392 + (25)^2 - 14 = 1003$.

**11.** The given sequence of number follows the pattern:

114 115 107 134 70 [195]

$+1^3$ $-2^3$ $+3^3$ $-4^3$ $+5^3$

Therefore, Missing number = $70 + 5^3 = 195$.

**12.** The given sequence of number follows the pattern

$4 \xrightarrow{\times \frac{3}{2}} 6 \xrightarrow{\times \frac{3}{2}} 9 \xrightarrow{\times \frac{3}{2}} 13\frac{1}{2} \xrightarrow{\times \frac{3}{2}} \boxed{20\frac{1}{4}}$

Therefore, Missing number $= \frac{27}{2} \times \frac{3}{2} = \frac{81}{4} = 20\frac{1}{4}$

**13.** The given sequence of number follows the pattern:

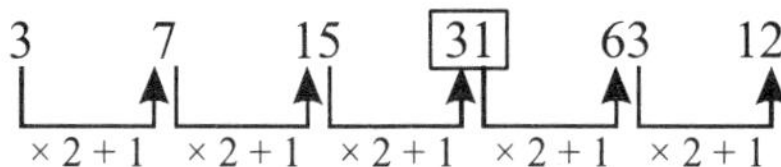


Therefore, Missing number = (15 × 2) + 1 = 31.

**14.** The given sequence of number follows the pattern:

$30 \xrightarrow{+16\times 1} 46 \xrightarrow{+16\times 2} 78 \xrightarrow{+16\times 3} 126 \xrightarrow{+16\times 4} 190 \xrightarrow{+16\times 5} 270 \xrightarrow{+16\times 6} \boxed{366}$

Therefore, Missing number = 270 + 16 × 6 = 366.

**15.** The given sequence of number follows the pattern:

$0.4 \xrightarrow{\times 1+2} 2.4 \xrightarrow{\times 2+3} \boxed{7.8} \xrightarrow{\times 3+4} 27.4 \xrightarrow{\times 4+5} 114.6 \xrightarrow{\times 5+6} 579$

Therefore, Missing number = 2.4 × 2 + 3 = 7.8.

**16.** The given sequence of number follows the pattern:

$3 \xrightarrow{\times 3+1} 10 \xrightarrow{\times 3+2} 32 \xrightarrow{\times 3+4} 100 \xrightarrow{\times 3+8} \boxed{308}$

Therefore, Missing number = 100 × 3 + 8 = 308.

**17.** The given sequence of number follows the pattern:

$12 \xrightarrow{\times 2-2} 22 \xrightarrow{\times 3+3} 69 \xrightarrow{\times 4-4} 272 \xrightarrow{\times 5+5} \boxed{1365} \xrightarrow{\times 6-6} 8184$

Therefore, Missing number = 1365 × 6 – 6 = 8184.

**18.** The given sequence of number follows the pattern:

×1.5

$4 \xrightarrow{\times 1.5} 6 \xrightarrow{\times 1.5} 9 \xrightarrow{\times 1.5} 13.5 \xrightarrow{\times 1.5} 20.25 \xrightarrow{\times 1.5} 30.375 \xrightarrow{\times 1.5} \boxed{45.5625}$

Therefore, Missing number = 30.375 × 1.5 = 45.5625.

**19.** The given series of number follows the pattern:

Series I : 19 38 114 [456]
×2 ×3 ×4

Series II : 2 3 4
+1 +1

Therefore, Missing number = 114 × 4 = 456.

**20.** The given series of number follows the pattern:

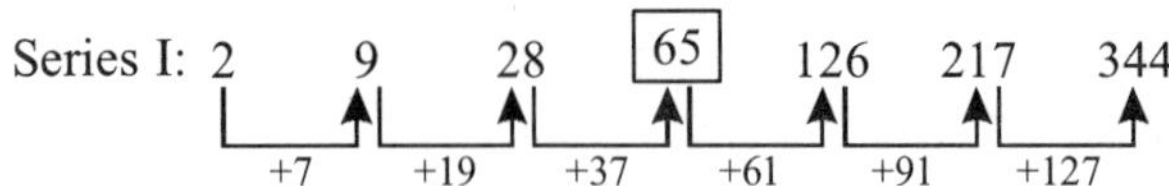


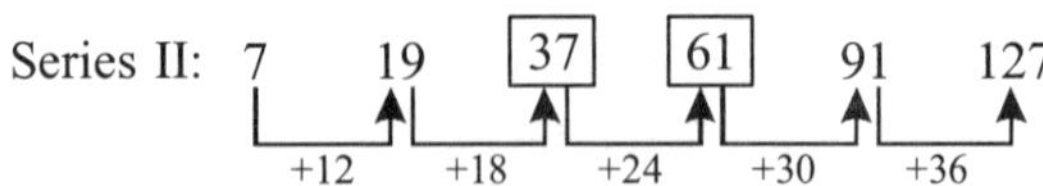


Series III: 12 [18] [24] [30] 36
+6 +6 +6 +6

So, Missing terms in Series III = 18 24 30
+6 +6

Missing terms in series II = 37 and 61.
i.e. 19 + <u>18</u>, and 37 + <u>24</u>
Therefore, Missing number in series I = 28 + <u>37</u> = 65.

**21.** The given series of number follows the pattern:

Series I: 3 20 63 144 275 [468]
+17 +43 +81 +131 +193

Series II: 17 43 81 131 [193]
+26 +38 +50 +62

Series III: 26 38 50 [62]
+12 +12 +12

So, Missing term in Series III = 50 + 12 = 62.
Missing term in Series II = 131 + 62 = 193
Therefore, Missing term in Series I = 275 + 193 = 468.

**22.** The given sequence of number follows the pattern:

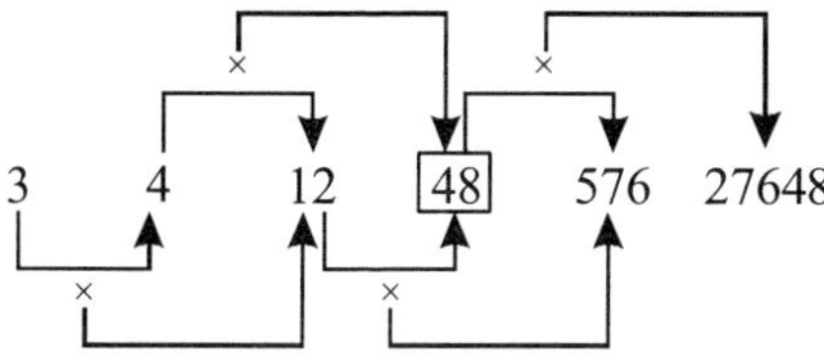


i.e. $3 \times 4 = 12$; $4 \times 12 = \boxed{48}$

$12 \times 48 = 576$; $48 \times 576 = 27648$

Therefore, Missing number = 48.

**23.** The given series of number follows the pattern,

Number within the bracket = Multiply of numbers on its adjacent sides – 1

i.e. $(13 \times 13) - 1 = 168$; $(14 \times 13) - 1 = 181$

Therefore, Missing number = $(15 \times 13) - 1 = 194$.

**24.** The given sequence of number follows the pattern:

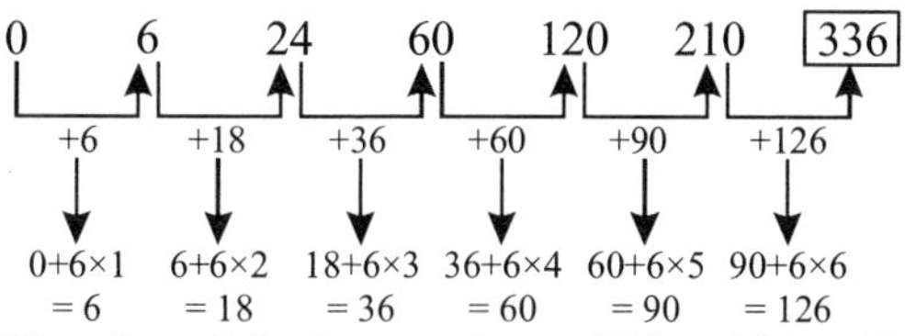


Therefore, Missing number = 210 + 126 = 336.

**25.** The given sequence of number follows the pattern:

12 28 75 316 1555 $\boxed{9366}$

$\times 2 + 2^2$ $\times 3 - 3^2$ $\times 4 + 4^2$ $\times 5 - 5^2$ $\times 6 + 6^2$

Therefore, Missing number = $1555 \times 6 + 6^2 = 9366$.

**26.** The given sequence of number follows the pattern:

<u>2</u> <u>23</u> <u>234</u> <u>2345</u> <u>23456</u> <u>234567</u> <u>2345678</u> <u>2345678</u>.

Therefore, Next number = $\boxed{9}$

**27.** The given sequence of number follows the pattern Cubes of natural numbers

| 1 | 8 | 27 | 64 | 125 | $\boxed{512}$ | $\boxed{729}$ | $\boxed{1000}$ |
|---|---|---|---|---|---|---|---|
| ↓ | ↓ | ↓ | ↓ | ↓ | ↓ | ↓ | ↓ |
| $1^3$ | $2^3$ | $3^3$ | $4^3$ | $5^3$ | $8^3$ | $9^3$ | $10^3$ |

But '256' is not a cube of any number

Therefore, '256' cannot be a number of the series.

**28.** The given series is a G.P. with first term $a = 5$ and common ratio $= r$

$$= \frac{10}{5} = 2$$

Let 1280 be the $n$th term

$\because$ $\quad n\text{th term} = ar^{n-1}$

or, $\quad 1280 = ar^{n-1}$

Put $\quad a = 5;\ r = 2$

$\quad 1280 = 5.(2)^{n-1}$

or, $\quad 256 = (2)^{n-1}$

or, $\quad 2^8 = (2)^{n-1}$

or, $\quad 8 = n - 1$

or, $\quad n = \boxed{9}$

Therefore, required term = 9th.

**30.** The given sequence follow the pattern:

Upper number in each column divides the lower number completely

| 3 | 8 | 10 | 2 | [5] | 1 |
|---|---|---|---|---|---|
| 6 | 56 | 90 | 2 | 20 | 0 |

$\therefore$ Only 5 divides 20 completely.

Therefore, Missing number = 5.

**31.**

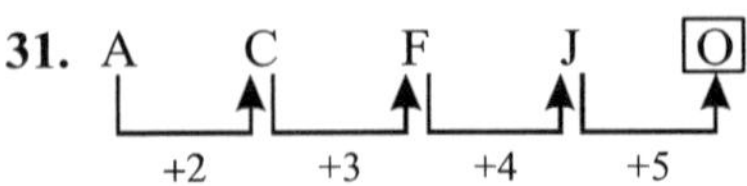


**32.**

−1 −1 −1

A Z D Y G X [J] [W]

+3 +3 +3

**33.** B I P [W] D

+7 +7 +7 +7

**34.** E J [O] T Y D

+5 +5 +5 +5 +5

**35.** A C F J [O] [U]

+2 +3 +4 +5 +6

**36.** 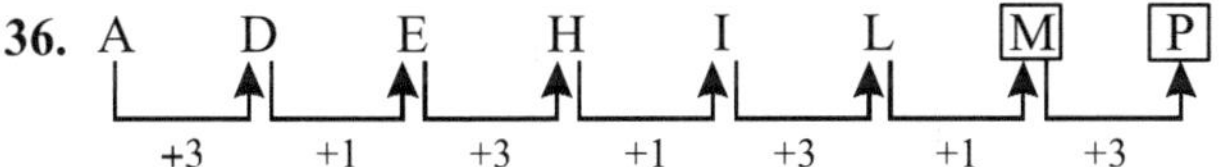


**37.** C F I L O R
+3 +3 +3 +3 +3

**38.** D H L P T X
+4 +4 +4 +4 +4

**39.** 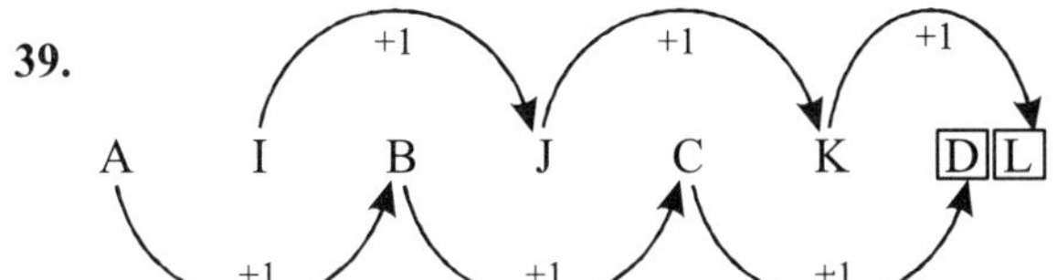


**40.** W T P M I F B Y U
–3 –4 –3 –4 –3 –4 –3 –4

**41.** X Q K F B
–7 –6 –5 –4

**42.** W T Q N K
–3 –3 –3 –3

**43.**
–1 –1 –1
A Z B Y C X D W
+1 +1 +1

**44.**
+1 +1 +1
A P C Q E R G S I
+2 +2 +2 +2

**45.**
–1 –1 –1 –1 –1
NZ OY PX QW RV SU
+2 +2 +2 +2 +2

**46.** 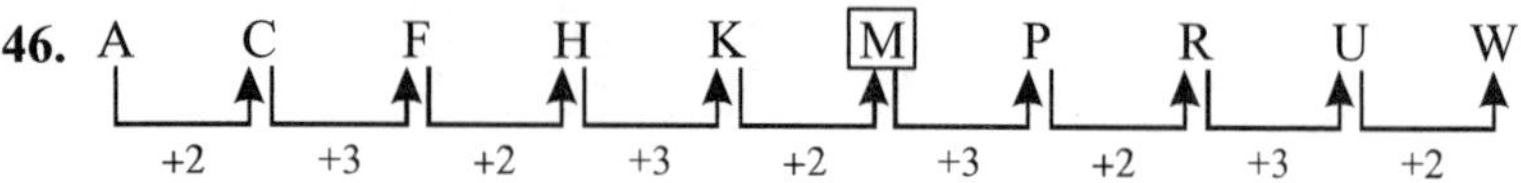


**47.** 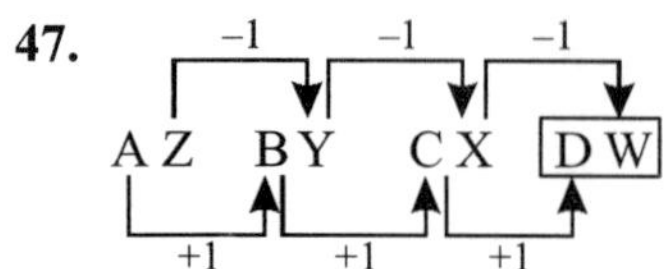


**48.** 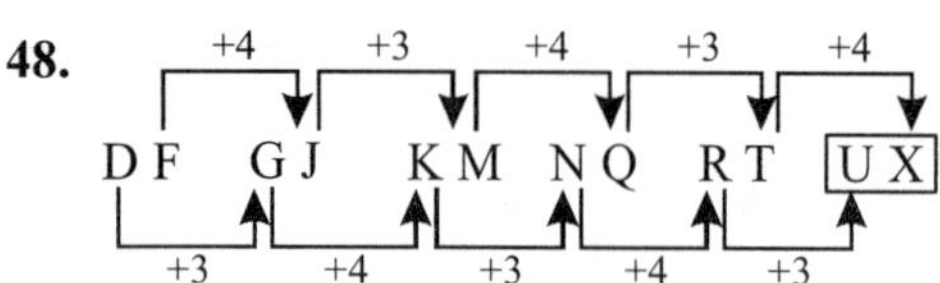


**50.** A $\xrightarrow{+4}$ E $\xrightarrow{+4}$ I $\xrightarrow{+4}$ M $\xrightarrow{+4}$ Q

C $\xrightarrow{+4}$ G $\xrightarrow{+4}$ K $\xrightarrow{+4}$ O $\xrightarrow{+4}$ S

**51.** A C F H K M P R U W

+2 +3 +2 +3 +2 +3 +2 +3 +2

**52.**

+3 +4 +3 +4 +3

DF GJ KM NQ RT UX

+4 +3 +4 +3 +4

**53.** 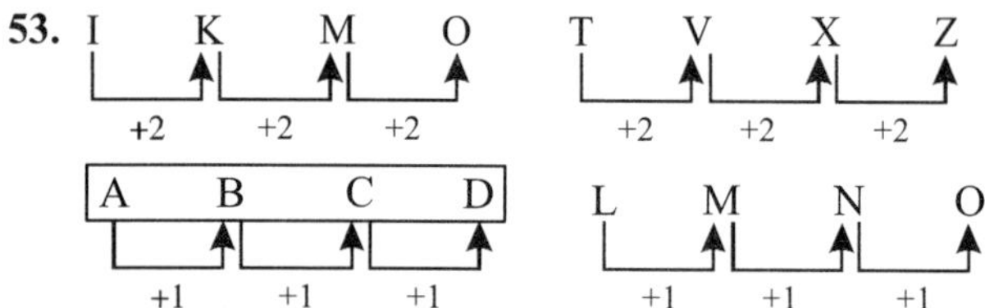


**54.** 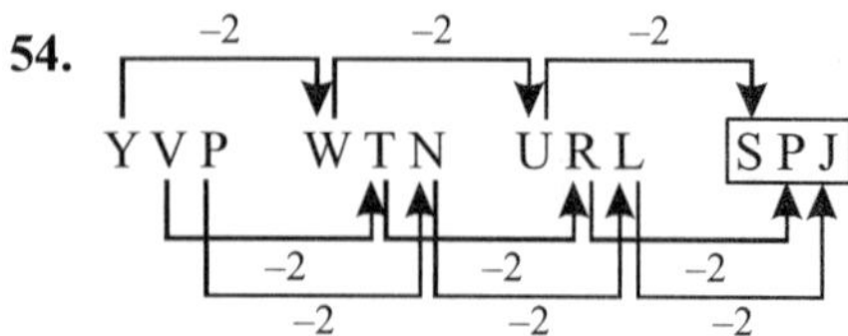

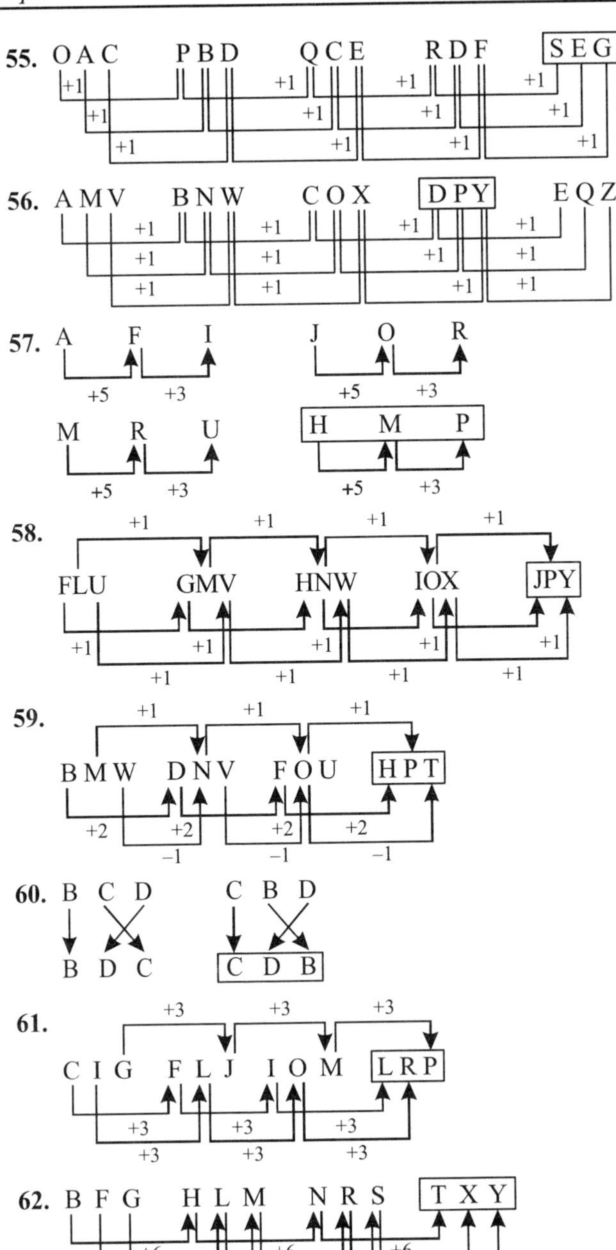
55. O A C P B D Q C E R D F S E G
+1 +1 +1 +1 +1 +1 +1 +1 +1 +1 +1 +1
56. A M V B N W C O X D P Y E Q Z
+1 +1 +1 +1 +1 +1 +1 +1 +1 +1 +1 +1
57. A F I J O R
+5 +3 +5 +3
M R U H M P
+5 +3 +5 +3
58. FLU GMV HNW IOX JPY
+1 +1 +1 +1
59. BMW DNV FOU HPT
+1 +1 +1 +2 +2 +2 +2 −1 −1 −1
60. B C D C B D
B D C C D B
61. C I G F L J I O M L R P
+3 +3 +3
62. B F G H L M N R S T X Y
+6 +6 +6

**63.**

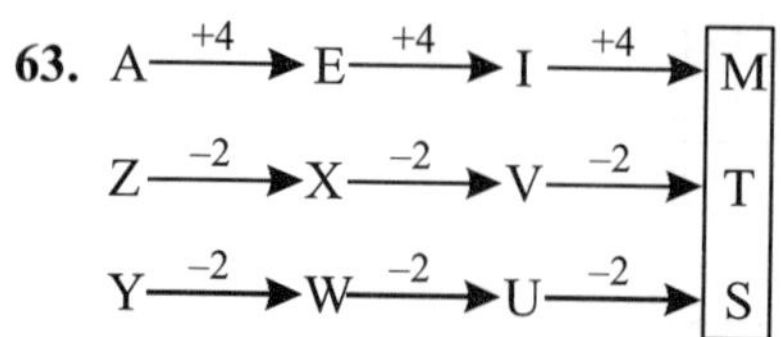


**64.**

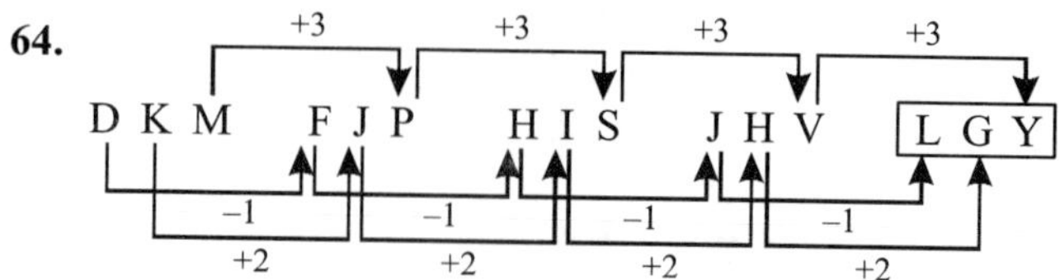


**65.** bc, cde, de, efg, fg, ghi

In this series, last letter of a term starts a new term and next two letters are included in the term.

**66.**

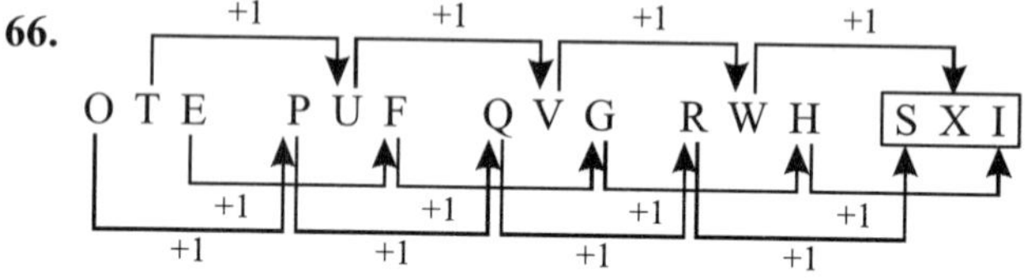


**67.**

| | | |
|---|---|---|
| C + 2 = E | | O + 2 = Q |
| E + 2 = G | | Q + 2 = S |
| G + 2 = I | | S + 2 = U |
| I + 2 = K | | U + 2 = W |
| K + 2 = M | | W + 2 = Y |
| M + 2 = O | | |

**68.**

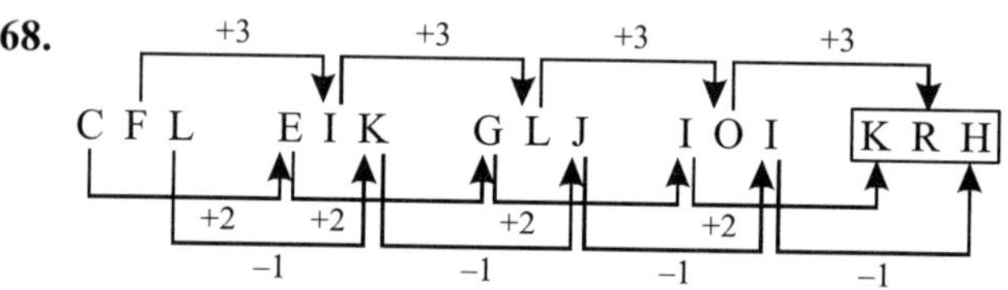


**69.**

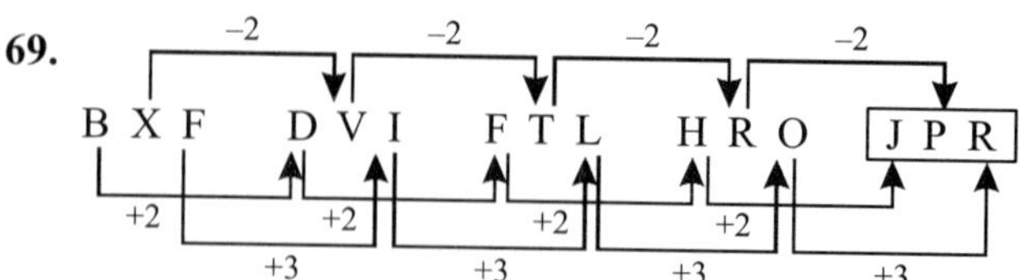

**70.** 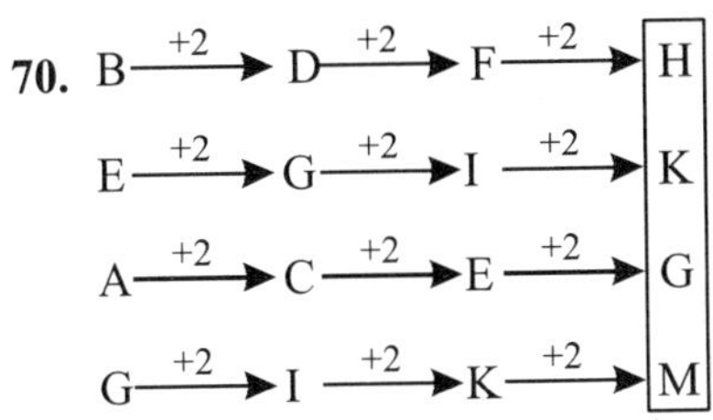


**71.** ABCD/BCDA/CDAB/DABC/ABCD

**72.** ABCD/PQRS/ABCDE/PQRST/ABCDEF/PQRST U

**73.** PQ/PQR/PQRS/PQRST/PQRSTU/PQRSTUV/PQRST U

**74.** ABCDEF/ZYXWVU/ABCDE/ABCDE/ZYXWVU/ABCD/ZYXWV U

**75.** Here, repeated block is 'abxdm'.
Now, abxdmabxdmabxdm

**76.** m c a/ m c a/ m c a/ m c a/m c a/ mc

**77.** ba/ab/ab/ba/ab/ab

**78.** abc/abb/cab/cca/bca/ab

**79.** The last letter of each previous block is moved to the beginning of the successive block.
Now, pqrst/tpqrs/stpqr/rstpq

**80.** Set 'sqppqpr' completes the given letter series.
pqrs/qrsp/rspq/spqr

**81.** In the series, the pattern abc is repeated. Hence, the series is
bc/abc/abc/abc/abc/abc/a = abccb

**82.** cbbg/cbbg/cbbg ⇒ cgbcb

**83.** By option (*d*).
abc/cba/bca/acb ⇒ bcba

**84.** N O P Q, N O P Q, N O P Q, N O P Q ⇒ NOPQ

**85.** lmn/nml/lmn/nml ⇒ mnnm
The sequence is repeat of alternative two blocks lmn and nml.

**86.** mbb/maa/mbb/maa/mbb ⇒ mabam
The sequence is repeat of alternative two blocks mbb and maa.

**87.** abncb/abncb/abncb ⇒ bcabab
The pattern is abncb.

**88.** The pattern is baab.
Now, baab/baab/baab/baab ⇒ bbaab

**89.** cca/ccb/cca/ccb/cca/ccb/c ⇒ acacc
The sequence is made of two blocks cca and ccb alternately.

**90.** tst/tst/tst/tst ⇒ tsst
The sequence is made of repetition of block tst.

**91.** aceg/aceg/aceg ⇒ ecag
The series is made of repetition of block aceg.

**92.** accb/accb/accb/accb ⇒ cbcc
The series is made of repetition of block accb.

**93.** nccl/nccl/nccl/nccl/nccl ⇒ cclcn
The series is made of repetition of block nccl.

**94.** bca/cab/abc/bca ⇒ babca

**95.** acbd/cadb/acbd/cadb/acbd ⇒ addddb
The sequence is made of repetition of two blocks acbd, cadb alternatively.

**96.** cab/bac/cab/bac/cab/bac ⇒ acbcb
The sequence is made of repetition of two blocks cab and bac alternatively.

**97.** aabcd/abbcd/abccd/abcdd ⇒ adbbad

**98.** acdb/dacb/cdab/acdb/da ⇒ adabcd

**99.** aabcc/ccabb/bbcaa ⇒ accba

**100.** AAB/BB′A/A′AB/B′BA ⇒ ABAB

**101.** From option (*a*)
yzy/xzx/yzy/xzx/yzy/xzx/y ⇒ yxzyz

**102.** abba/acca/adda/aeea
Hence, set bacde will come in gap, respectively.

**103.** aaaaa/bbabb/aabaa/bbbbb
Hence, set aabbb will come in gap respectively.

**104.** abzy/abcdxw/abcdevu ⇒ zdu

**105.** HIJH/HIJH/HIJH/HIJH ⇒ IHJI
The sequence is made of repetition of block HIJH.

**106.** ZYXWWXYZ/ZYXWWXYZ ⇒ WXYZ

**107.** ZXVTRPNLJHFDB ⇒ VPHB
The sequence is made of (–2) letters, respectively.

**108.** aca/cab/aba/cab/aaa/cab/a ⇒ aabc

**109.** abb/baa/abb/baa/abb/baa ⇒ abbaaba

**110.** The given sequence of group of letter number follows the pattern:

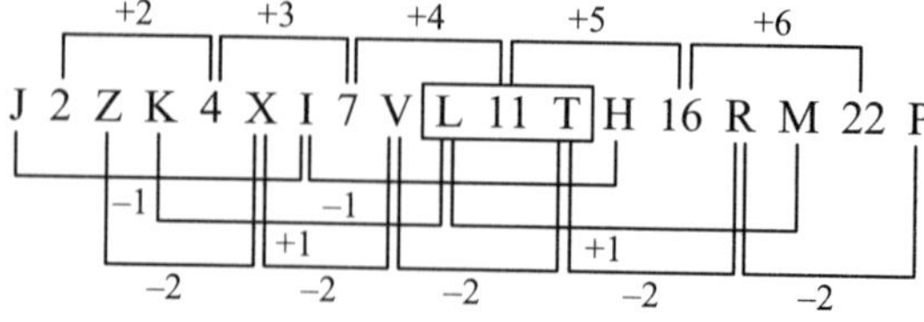

Therefore, missing letter number group = L 11 T.

**111.** The given sequence of group of letter number follows the pattern:

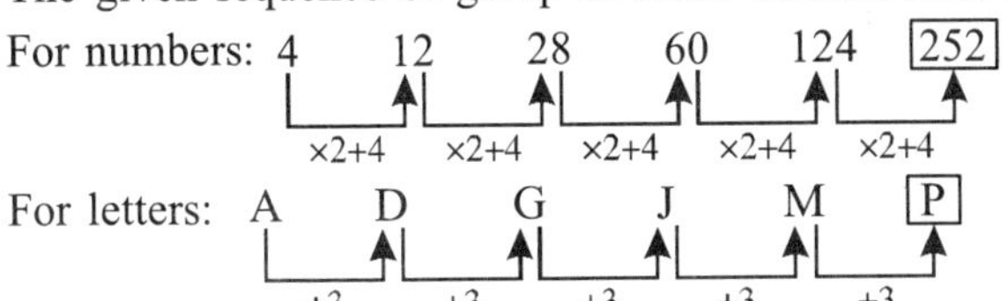


Therefor, missing group of letter and number are P and 252 respectively

**112.** The given sequence of group of letter number follows the pattern:

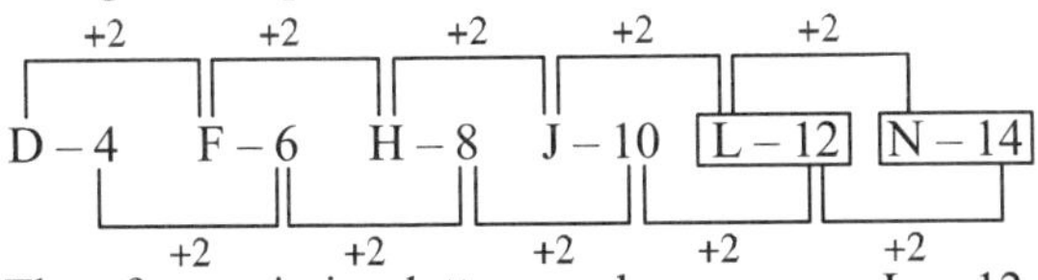


Therefore, missing letter number group = L – 12 and N – 14.

**113.** The given sequence of group of letter number follows the pattern:

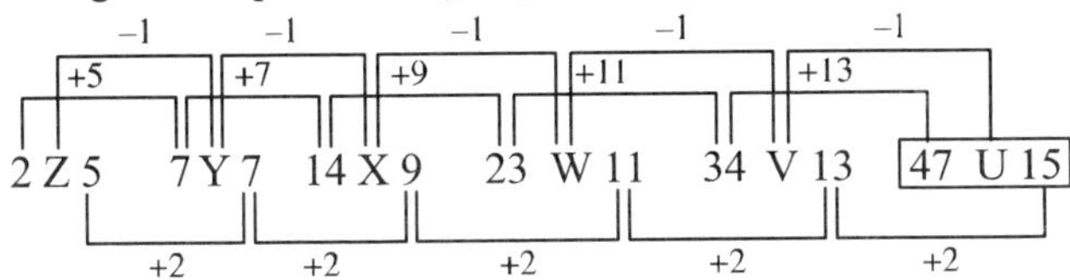


**114.** The given sequence of group of letter number follows the pattern:

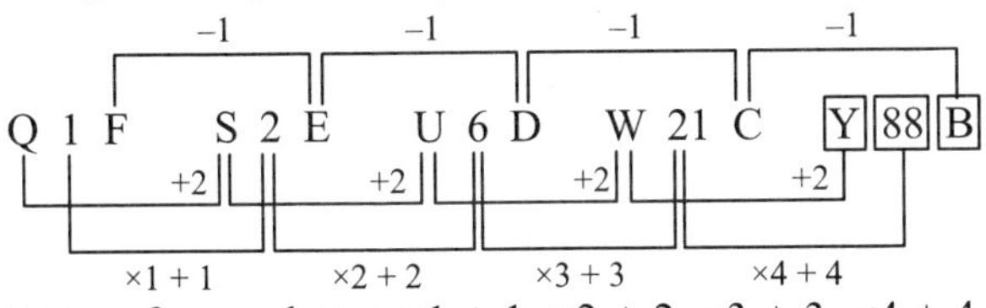


Pattern for numbers : ×1 + 1, ×2 + 2, ×3 + 3, ×4 + 4

Therefore, missing letter number group = Y 88 B

**115.** The given sequence of group of letter number follows the pattern:

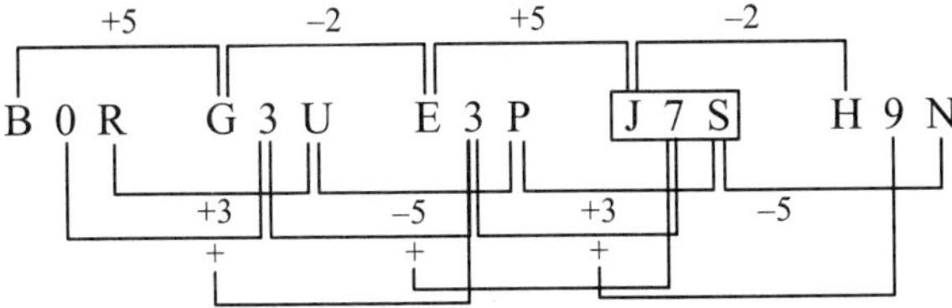


Numbers = Sum of two preceding numbers i.e.

0 + 3 = 3, 3 + 3 = <u>6</u>, <u>6</u> + 3 = 9 ∴ 3 + 3 = <u>6</u>

The correct group = ‘J 6 S’

Therefore, the letter number group 'J7S' does not fit into the series.

**116.** The given sequence of group of letter number follows the pattern:

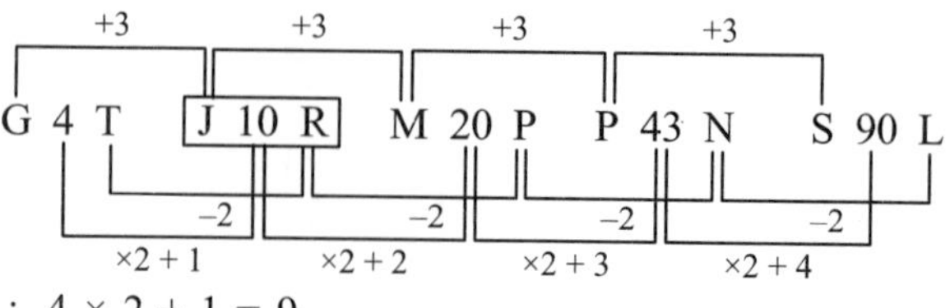


$\therefore\ 4 \times 2 + 1 = 9$

The correct group = 'J 9 R'

Therefore, the letter-number group 'J 10 R' does not fit into the series.

**117.** The given sequence of letter number is a combination of series and follows the pattern:

+7, –3, +7, –3 in series I and +1 in series II respectively.

Series I: 2 9 6 13 10

+7 –3 +7 –3

Series II: A B C D

+1 +1 +1

Therefore, missing term in letter number series = 10.

**118.** The given letter-number series based upon the respective positions follows the pattern:

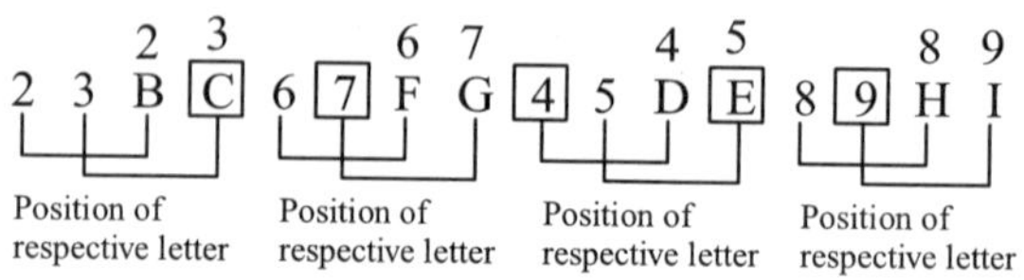


**119.** The given letter-number series follows the pattern: Number = Difference of position of respective letters

i.e. Z – A = 26 – 1 = 25

Y – B = 25 – 2 = 23

X – C = 24 – 3 = 21

W – D = 23 – 4 = 19

V – E = 22 – 5 = 17

26 1   25 2   24 3   23 4   22 5

Z A 25 Y B 23 X C 21 W D 19 V E 17

26 – 1   25 – 2   24 – 3   23 – 4   22 – 5

**121.** The given letter number series follows the pattern:

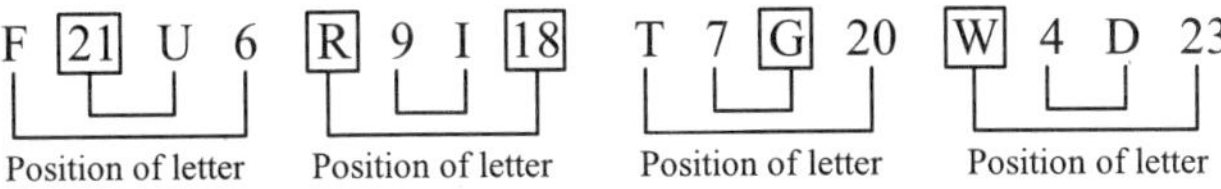


**122.** The given letter number series follows the pattern:

First two letter or number : –1, –1, –4, –4, –1

Any two letter in each group : Same position from beginning and end

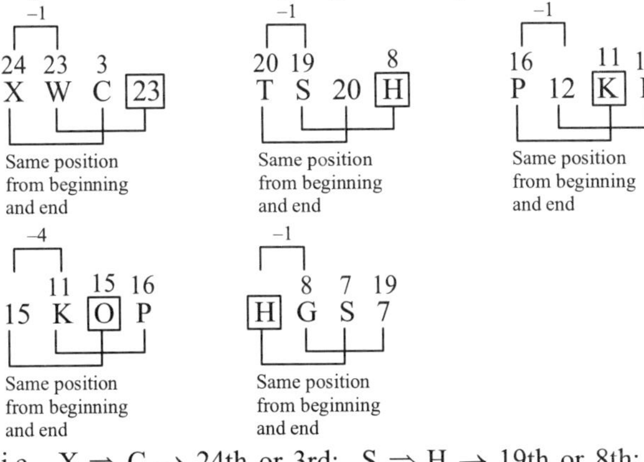


i.e. $X \Rightarrow C \rightarrow$ 24th or 3rd; $S \Rightarrow H \rightarrow$ 19th or 8th;
$P \Rightarrow K \rightarrow$ 16th or 11th; $K \Rightarrow P \rightarrow$ 11th or 16th;
$H \Rightarrow S \rightarrow$ 8th or 19th respectively.

**123.** The given sequence of letter number follows the pattern:

$K^{11} \times P^{16} = 11 \times 16 = 176 \Rightarrow 1 \times 7 \times 6 \Rightarrow 42$

$J^{10} \times X^{24} = 10 \times 24 = 240 \Rightarrow 2 \times 4 \times 0 \Rightarrow 0$

$G^{7} \times S^{19} = 7 \times 19 = 133 \Rightarrow 1 \times 3 \times 3 \Rightarrow 9$

$M^{13} \times Y^{25} = 13 \times 25 = 325 \Rightarrow 3 \times 2 \times 5 \Rightarrow 30$

$T^{20} \times B^{2} = 20 \times 2 = 40 \Rightarrow 4 \times 0 \Rightarrow 0$

$O^{15} \times L^{12} = 15 \times 12 = 180 \Rightarrow 1 \times 8 \times 0 \Rightarrow 0$

Therefore, missing numbers = 0 and 0

# 4

# Classification

## INTRODUCTION

Classification means 'to assort the items' of a given group on the basis of a certain common quality they possess and then spot the stranger or 'odd one out'.

These questions are based on words, letters and numerals. In these types of problems, we consider the defining quality of particular things. In these questions, four or five elements are given, out of which one does not belong to the group. You are required to find the 'odd one'.

**Note:** *There may be possibility of more than one logic to be applicable but we need to apply optimum and best logic of all possibilities.*

There are several types of questions that can be asked on classification in different catagories. Some of the types are discussed below.

## SOLVED EXAMPLE

### Type 1 Choosing the Odd Word

In these type of problems, some words are given which belong to real world. They have some common features except the odd one. You are required to find the 'odd one out'.

**Directions (Qs 1-3):** *In each of the following questions, four words have been given out of which three are alike in some manner while the fourth one is different. Choose the odd one.*

**1.** (*a*) Pear (*b*) Apple (*c*) Litchi (*d*) Orange

**Sol. (*d*)** Out of given fruits orange is citrus fruit. So, it is different from others.

**2.** (*a*) Deck (*b*) Quay (*c*) Stern (*d*) Bow

**Sol. (*b*)** All except quay are parts of a ship.

**3.** (*a*) Tomato (*b*) Gourd (*c*) Brinjal (*d*) Potato

**Sol. (*d*)** All the vegetables except potato grow above the ground level.

### Type 2 Choosing the Odd Pair of Words

In this type of classification, different pairs are classified on the basis of some common features/properties like names, places, usage, situations, origin, etc.

**Directions (Qs. 4-5):** *In each of the following questions, four/five pairs of words are given out of which words in three/four pairs bear a certain common relationship. Choose the pair in which the words are differently related.*

**4.** (*a*) Gold : Ornaments (*b*) Cloth : Garments
(*c*) Wood : Furniture (*d*) Earthen pots : Clay

**Sol. (*d*)** Except pair (*d*), in all other pairs, the first is the raw material used to make the second.

**5.** (*a*) Broad : Wide (*b*) Light : Heavy
(*c*) Tiny : Small (*d*) Big : Large

**Sol. (*b*)** Light is antonym of heavy. But in other pairs words are synonyms.

### Type 3 Choosing the Odd Letter Group

In this type of problems, some groups of letters are given. One of them is different and this is the relevent answer.

**Directions (Qs. 6-7):** *Choose the group of letters which is different from others.*

**6.** (*a*) GE (*b*) MK (*c*) WU (*d*) QN

**Sol. (*d*)** Here,

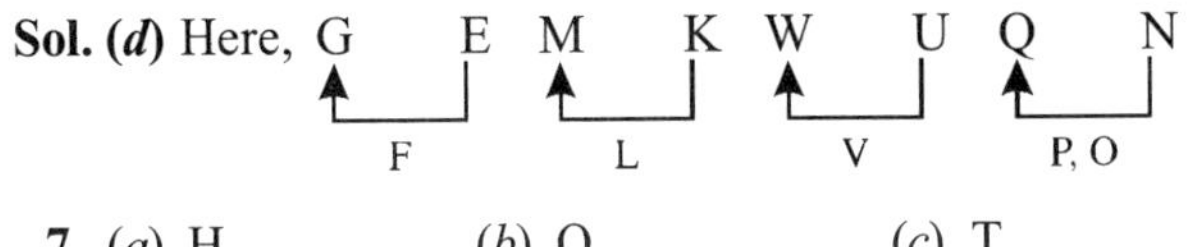


**7.** (*a*) H (*b*) Q (*c*) T (*d*) Z

**Sol. (*b*)** All other letters except (*b*), occupy the even-numbered positions in the English alphabets.

### Type 4 Choosing the Odd Number/Pair of Numbers

In this type of classification, certain numbers/pair of numbers are given, out of which except one, all have some common characteristics and hence are alike. The 'different one' is to be choosen as the answer.

**Directions (Qs. 8-9):** *In each of the following questions, four/five numbers are given. Out of these, three/four are alike in a certain way. Choose the one which is different from the rest.*

**8.** (*a*) 57 (*b*) 87 (*c*) 131 (*d*) 133

**Sol. (*c*)** Except 131, all other numbers are non-prime (composite) numbers.

9. (*a*) 2 (*b*) 32 (*c*) 56 (*d*) 128

**Sol. (c)** Each of the numbers except 56, can be expressed in terms of powers of 2.

## EXERCISE

**Directions (Qs. 1-12):** *In each of the following questions, three of the given four are alike in a certain way and form a group. Which is the one that does not belong to that group in the following questions?*

1. (*a*) 4566 (*b*) 5686 (*c*) 2346 (*d*) 1236
2. (*a*) 246 (*b*) 356 (*c*) 527 (*d*) 639
3. (*a*) 728 (*b*) 455 (*c*) 546 (*d*) 284
4. (*a*) 53 (*b*) 125 (*c*) 147 (*d*) 85
5. (*a*) 156 (*b*) 110 (*c*) 72 (*d*) 152
6. (*a*) 6958 (*b*) 7948 (*c*) 6895 (*d*) 9783
7. (*a*) 2 (*b*) 65 (*c*) 215 (*d*) 126
8. (*a*) 216 (*b*) 729 (*c*) 129 (*d*) 648
9. (*a*) 125 (*b*) 64 (*c*) 27 (*d*) 144
10. (*a*) 257 (*b*) 143 (*c*) 195 (*d*) 224
11. (*a*) 145 (*b*) 35 (*c*) 197 (*d*) 65
12. (*a*) 15 (*b*) 57 (*c*) 7 (*d*) 31

**Directions (Qs. 13-15):** *In each of the following questions, four numbers are given. Out of these three are alike in a certain way but one is different. Choose the one which is different from the rest.*

13. (*a*) 14, 17, 23 (*b*) 19, 22, 28 (*c*) 17, 20, 26 (*d*) 21, 23, 30
14. (*a*) 9, 49 (*b*) 13, 121 (*c*) 10, 61 (*d*) 7, 25
15. (*a*) 0-3-8 (*b*) 9-12-16 (*c*) 17-20-24 (*d*) 51-54-58
16. Find out the set among the four sets which is like the given set.

(23 : 30 : 37)

(*a*) (6 : 13 : 20) (*b*) (7 : 15 : 22)
(*c*) (21 : 28 : 34) (*d*) (12 : 19 : 25)

17. Find out the set among the four sets which is like the given set.

Given set is (6 : 12 : 18)

(*a*) (4 : 8 : 14) (*b*) (10 : 20 : 26)
(*c*) (12 : 24 : 36) (*d*) (30 : 36 : 42)

**18.** Find out the set among the four sets which is like the given set.

(13 : 20 : 27)

(*a*) (3 : 11 : 18)
(*b*) (18 : 25 : 32)
(*c*) (18 : 27 : 72)
(*d*) (7 : 14 : 28)

**Directions (Qs. 19-25):** *Find the odd one out.*

| | | | |
|---|---|---|---|
| **19.** (*a*) 5-21 | (*b*) 29-45 | (*c*) 48-68 | (*d*) 71-87 |
| **20.** (*a*) 12-24 | (*b*) 14-28 | (*c*) 23-46 | (*d*) 36-70 |
| **21.** (*a*) 547-563 | (*b*) 71-55 | (*c*) 517-523 | (*d*) 248-231 |
| **22.** (*a*) 8-15 | (*b*) 25-36 | (*c*) 49-64 | (*d*) 81-100 |
| **23.** (*a*) 42-4 | (*b*) 36-6 | (*c*) 32-2 | (*d*) 15-5 |
| **24.** (*a*) 8-11 | (*b*) 1-4 | (*c*) 7-10 | (*d*) 3-5 |
| **25.** (*a*) 80-9 | (*b*) 64-8 | (*c*) 36-6 | (*d*) 49-7 |

**Directions (Qs. 26-40):** *In each of the following questions, four words have been given out of which three are alike in some manner, which the fourth one is different. Choose the odd one out.*

| | | | |
|---|---|---|---|
| **26.** (*a*) Goggles | (*b*) Accessories | (*c*) Bangles | (*d*) Ring |
| **27.** (*a*) Van | (*b*) Truck | (*c*) Cargo | (*d*) Trolley |
| **28.** (*a*) Guava | (*b*) Orange | (*c*) Apple | (*d*) Lichi |
| **29.** (*a*) Brass | (*b*) Iron | (*c*) Aluminium | (*d*) Zinc |
| **30.** (*a*) Gourd | (*b*) Cucumber | (*c*) Brinjal | (*d*) Papaya |
| **31.** (*a*) Raddish | (*b*) Carrot | (*c*) Garlic | (*d*) Gourd |
| **32.** (*a*) Coal | (*b*) Aluminium | (*c*) Plastic | (*d*) Iron |
| **33.** (*a*) Green | (*b*) Yellow | (*c*) Grey | (*d*) Red |
| **34.** (*a*) Cabbage | (*b*) Brinjal | (*c*) Sweet Gourd | (*d*) Pumpkin |
| **35.** (*a*) August | (*b*) December | (*c*) July | (*d*) May |
| **36.** (*a*) Kerosene | (*b*) Water | (*c*) Petrol | (*d*) LPG |
| **37.** (*a*) Stone | (*b*) Sand | (*c*) Cement | (*d*) Rock |
| **38.** (*a*) Cumin | (*b*) Groundnut | (*c*) Cinnamon | (*d*) Pepper |
| **39.** (*a*) Dog | (*b*) Horse | (*c*) Goat | (*d*) Fox |
| **40.** (*a*) Tomato | (*b*) Carrot | (*c*) Ginger | (*d*) Potato |

**Directions (Qs. 41-55):** *In each of the following questions, some letters or groups of letters are given, all of which except one, share a common similarity while one is different. Choose the odd one out.*

41. (*a*) 1P6 (*b*) 2X4 (*c*) 1K1 (*d*) 2N0
42. (*a*) 20K9 (*b*) 14D10 (*c*) 9G2 (*d*) 18P16
43. (*a*) D12B (*b*) O43B (*c*) K62T (*d*) Y60E
44. (*a*) DH6 (*b*) UO18 (*c*) XP20 (*d*) NB10
45. (*a*) ACDF (*b*) FGKL (*c*) HIVW (*d*) TUOP
46. (*a*) DECB (*b*) GDFE (*c*) HKIJ (*d*) JFHG
47. (*a*) SUWY (*b*) MOQS (*c*) CEGI (*d*) HJMO
48. (*a*) TPLH (*b*) SOKG (*c*) ZVRN (*d*) UQMJ
49. (*a*) CXGT (*b*) EVBY (*c*) DXEY (*d*) AZDW
50. (*a*) BFCGD (*b*) LPMQN (*c*) NROSP (*d*) YCDZA
51. (*a*) DBa : dbA (*b*) biD : dIB (*c*) sUd : sUd (*d*) eMR : Emr
52. (*a*) WITH : TIHW (*b*) JUST : SUTJ (*c*) DONE : NOED (*d*) HAVE : AVEH
53. (*a*) LOCATE : OCLTAE (*b*) EXAMIN : XAEIMN (*c*) PLENTY : LEPTYN (*d*) COWARD : OWCRAD
54. (*a*) SUNDAY : NSVYDB (*b*) MOTHER : TMPRHD (*c*) PARENT : RPBTEO (*d*) MOSTLY : SMPYTM
55. (*a*) DiZuBeS (*b*) SuAPaTJ (*c*) KBoXaRuS (*d*) dPrULmD

## ANSWERS

| 1 | 2 | 3 | 4 | 5 | 6 | 7 | 8 | 9 | 10 |
|---|---|---|---|---|---|---|---|---|---|
| (*b*) | (*b*) | (*d*) | (*c*) | (*d*) | (*d*) | (*c*) | (*d*) | (*d*) | (*a*) |
| **11** | **12** | **13** | **14** | **15** | **16** | **17** | **18** | **19** | **20** |
| (*b*) | (*b*) | (*d*) | (*c*) | (*a*) | (*a*) | (*c*) | (*b*) | (*c*) | (*d*) |
| **21** | **22** | **23** | **24** | **25** | **26** | **27** | **28** | **29** | **30** |
| (*d*) | (*a*) | (*a*) | (*d*) | (*a*) | (*b*) | (*c*) | (*d*) | (*a*) | (*d*) |
| **31** | **32** | **33** | **34** | **35** | **36** | **37** | **38** | **39** | **40** |
| (*d*) | (*c*) | (*c*) | (*a*) | (*d*) | (*b*) | (*c*) | (*b*) | (*d*) | (*a*) |
| **41** | **42** | **43** | **44** | **45** | **46** | **47** | **48** | **49** | **50** |
| (*d*) | (*d*) | (*b*) | (*d*) | (*a*) | (*d*) | (*d*) | (*d*) | (*c*) | (*d*) |
| **51** | **52** | **53** | **54** | **55** | | | | | |
| (*b*) | (*d*) | (*c*) | (*b*) | (*d*) | | | | | |

## SOME SELECTED EXPLANATORY ANSWERS

1. In all other numbers, First three digits = Consecutive Numerals of the number.
2. Sum of the first two digits = Third digit
   i.e. $246 \Rightarrow 2 + 4 = 6$
   $527 \Rightarrow 5 + 2 = 7$
   $639 \Rightarrow 6 + 3 = 9$
   But $356 \Rightarrow 3 + 5 = 8 \neq 6$.
3. First two digits ÷ Third digit = 9
   i.e. $728 \Rightarrow \frac{72}{8} = 9$ $455 \Rightarrow \frac{45}{5} = 9$
   $546 \Rightarrow \frac{54}{6} = 9$
   But $284 \Rightarrow \frac{28}{4} = 7$
4. Except 147, all others are in $X^2 + 4$ pattern
   i.e. $53 = 7^2 + 4$; $125 = 11^2 + 4$; $85 = 9^2 + 4$;
   But $147 = 12^2 + 3$.
5. Except 152, all others are in $X^2 - X$ pattern
   i.e. $156 = 13^2 - 13$; $110 = 11^2 - 11$; $72 = 9^2 - 9$;
   But $152 = 12^2 + 8$.
6. Sum of the digits of the number = 28
   i.e. $6958 \Rightarrow 6 + 9 + 5 + 8 = 28$
   $7948 \Rightarrow 7 + 9 + 4 + 8 = 28$
   $6895 \Rightarrow 6 + 8 + 9 + 5 = 28$
   But $9783 \Rightarrow 9 + 7 + 8 + 3 = 27$
7. Except 215, all others are in $X^3 + 1$ pattern
   i.e. $1^3 + 1 = 2$; $4^3 + 1 = 65$; $5^3 + 1 = 126$;
   But $6^3 - 1 = 215$.
8. Except 648, all others are perfect cube.
9. Except 144, all others are perfect cube.
   i.e. $125 = 5^3$; $64 = 4^3$; $27 = 3^3$.

**10.** Except 257, all others are in $X^2 - 1$ pattern
i.e. $143 = 12^2 - 1$; $195 = 14^2 - 1$; $224 = 15^2 - 1$;
But $257 = 16^2 + 1$.

**11.** Except 35, all others are in $X^2 + 1$ pattern
i.e. $145 = 12^2 - 1$; $197 = 14^2 - 1$; $65 = 8^2 + 1$;
But $35 = 6^2 - 1$.

**12.** Except 57, all others are in $2^x - 1$ pattern
i.e. $15 = 2^4 - 1$; $7 = 2^3 - 1$; $31 = 2^5 - 1$
But $57 = 2^6 - 7$.

**13.** In every pair first two number has same diference and diference between second and third number is also same but option (d) has not follow this pattern.

**14.** In all the pairs except option (c), the first number is an odd number and second number is (1st number $-2)^2$.

**15.**

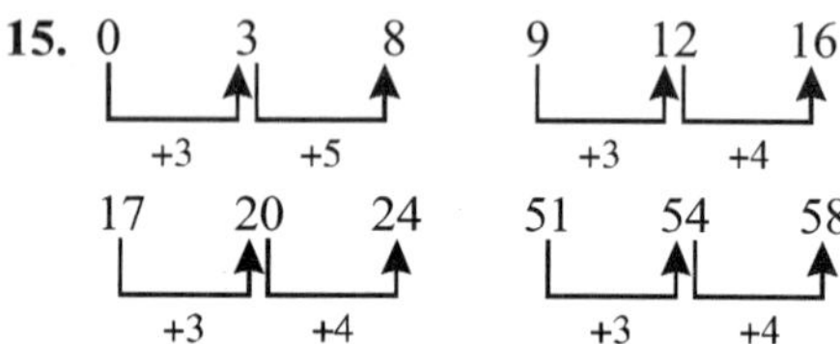


Hence, 0-3-8 is different from other three.

**16.** 23 : 30 : 37 = 23 $\xrightarrow{+7}$ 30 $\xrightarrow{+7}$ 37

Similarly, 6 : 13 : 20 = 6 $\xrightarrow{+7}$ 13 $\xrightarrow{+7}$ 20

**17.** As, 6 $\xrightarrow{+6}$ 12 $\xrightarrow{+6}$ 18

Similarly, 12 $\xrightarrow{+12}$ 24 $\xrightarrow{+12}$ 36

**18.** As, $13 + 7 = 20 \rightarrow 20 + 7 = 27$
Similarly, $18 + 7 = 25 \rightarrow 25 + 7 = 32$

**19.** $5 \xrightarrow{+16} 21$, $29 \xrightarrow{+16} 45$
$71 \xrightarrow{+16} 87$, $48 \xrightarrow{+20} 68$
So, '48-68' is different from other three.

**20.** Except 'option (*d*) second number is twice of first number.

**21.** Except option (*d*) difference of all other numbers are divisible by 2.

**22.** Except '8-15', in all the options, both the numbers are squares of a natural number.

**23.** Except option '(*a*)', in all options first number is divisible by the second number.

**24.** $8 + 3 = 11$ $\quad 1 + 3 = 4$
$7 + 3 = 10$ $\quad 3 + 3 = 6 \neq 5$

**25.** Except '80-9', in all options first number is square of second number.

**26.** All the others are items of accessories.

**27.** Except Cargo, all others are carriers of load. 'Cargo' means load.

**28.** Except Lichi, all others have many Seeds. 'Lichi' has only one seed.

**29.** Except Brass, all others are metals. 'Brass' is an alloy.

**30.** Except Papaya, all others are Vegetables. 'Papaya' is a fruit.

**31.** Except Gourd, all others grow beneath the ground.

**32.** Except plastic, all others are natural resources. 'Plastic' is prepared by human beings.

**33.** Except Grey, all others are colours. 'Grey' is a shade.

**34.** Except Cabbage, all others are fruits. 'Cabbage' is a Vegetable.

**35.** Except May, all others are either followed or preceded by a month of 31 days.

**36.** Except Water, all others are petroleum products used as fuel.

**37.** Except Cement, all others are found in Nature. 'Cement' is prepared by human beings.

**41.** The digits in each group denotes the position of the given letter in the English alphabet series:

i.e. 1P6 $\Rightarrow$ 16 = P
2X4 $\Rightarrow$ 24 = X
1K1 $\Rightarrow$ 11 = K
2N0 $\Rightarrow$ 20 = T but N = 14

Therefore 2N0 is the odd one.

**42.** The difference of the numbers in each group denotes the position of the letter in the English alphabet.

i.e. 20K9 $\Rightarrow$ 20 – 9 = 11 = K

14D10 $\Rightarrow$ 14 – 10 = 4 = D

9G2 $\Rightarrow$ 9 – 2 = 7 = G

But 18P16 $\Rightarrow$ 18 – 16 = 2 = B $\neq$ P

Therefore 18P16 is the odd one.

**43.** In all other groups,

Middle number = 2 × (Sum of positions of first and last letters)

i.e. 12 $\Rightarrow$ 2 × (D + B) $\Rightarrow$ 2 × (4 + 2)

62 $\Rightarrow$ 2 × (K + T) $\Rightarrow$ 2 × (11 + 20)

60 $\Rightarrow$ 2 × (Y + E) $\Rightarrow$ 2 × (25 + 5)

But, 2 × (O + B) $\Rightarrow$ 2 × (15 + 2) = 34 $\neq$ 43

Therefore, O43B is the odd one.

**44.** In all other groups,

Number at the end = $\frac{1}{2}$ × (Sum of positions of first and last letters)

i.e. $\frac{1}{2}(D + H) \Rightarrow \frac{1}{2}(4 + 8) = 6$

$\frac{1}{2}(U + O) \Rightarrow \frac{1}{2}(21 + 15) = 18$

$\frac{1}{2}(X + P) \Rightarrow \frac{1}{2}(24 + 16) = 20$

But, $\frac{1}{2}(N + B) \Rightarrow \frac{1}{2}(14 + 2) = 8 \neq 10$

Therefore, NB10 is the odd one.

**45.** Except ACDF, in all other groups, the first and second letters; the third and fourth letters are consecutive.

**46.** Except JFHG, in all other groups, they are consecutive letters but not in order.

**47.** Except HJMO, in all other groups, they are alternate letters.

**48.** Except UQMJ, in all other groups, each of the first three letters is four steps forward to the next letter.

**49.** Except DXEY, in all other groups, first and second letters as well as third and fourth letters are equidistant from the beginning and end respectively in the alphabetical series.

**50.** Except YCDZA, in all other groups, the first, third and fifth as well as the second and fourth letters are consecutive letters. Also, the second letter is two steps forward of the fifth letter.

**51.** Except biD : dIB, all other pairs, only vowel is in small letter in the first group and in second group only the consonant is in small letter.

**52.** Except HAVE : AVEH, all other pair of groups follow the pattern.

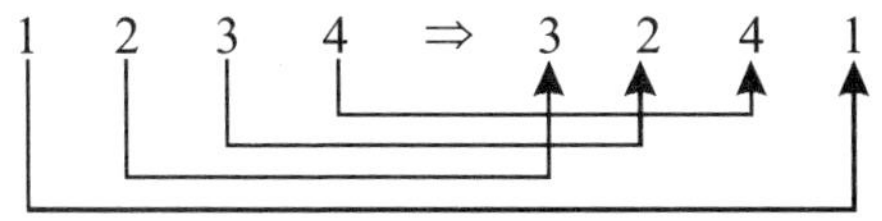


e.g. D O N E : N O E D
1 2 3 4 3 2 4 1

**53.** Except PLENTY : LEPTYN, all other pair of groups follow the pattern.

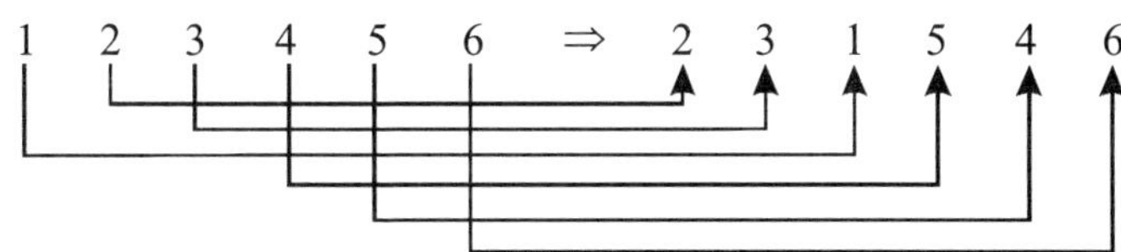


**54.** Except MOTHER : TMPRHD, all other pair of groups follows the pattern.

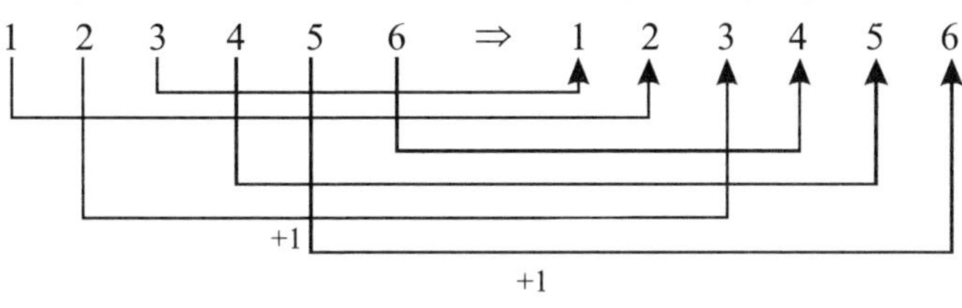


3 1 2 6 4 5
e.g. S U N D A Y : N S V Y D B
1 2 3 4 5 6 1 2 3 4 5 6

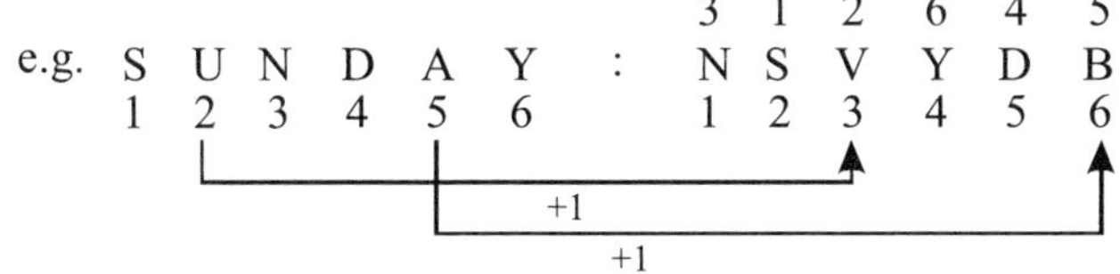


**55.** Except dPrULmD, in all other groups, the small letters are vowels.

# Blood Relation & Coded Relation

## INTRODUCTION

Blood Relation Test involves analysis of information showing blood relationship among the members of a family.

In the exams, the success of a candidate in the questions on blood relations depends upon his knowledge about various blood relations.

Some of which are summarised below to help solve these tests.

## CHART OF USEFUL RELATIONS

The following chart would prove immensely beneficial to you for solving such questions:

Mother's or Father's son: **Brother**

Mother's or Father's daughter: **Sister**

Mother's or Father's brother: **Uncle**

Mother's or Father's sister: **Aunt**

Mother's or Father's mother: **Grandmother**

Mother's or Father's father: **Grandfather**

Son's wife: **Daughter-in-law**

Daughter's husband: **Son-in-law**

Husband's or wife's sister: **Sister-in-law**

Husband's or wife's Brother: **Brother-in-law**

Brother's son: **Nephew**

Brother's daughter: **Niece**

Uncle or aunt's son or daughter: **Cousin**

Sister's husband: **Brother-in-law**

Brother's wife: **Sister-in-law**

Grandfather's only son: **Father**

Grandmother's only son: **Father**

Grandfather's son: **Father or uncle**

Grandmother's son: **Father or uncle**

Grandfather's only daughter-in-law: **Mother**

Grandmother's only daughter-in-law: **Mother**

## SOLVED EXAMPLE

**1.** Pointing to a man in a photograph, a woman said, 'His brother's father is the only son of my grandfather.' How is the woman related to the man in the photographs?

(*a*) Mother (*b*) Aunt (*c*) Sister
(*d*) Daughter (*e*) Grandmother

**2.** Sanjeev said to Rohit, 'That boy playing with football is the younger of the two brothers of the daughter of my father's wife'. How is the boy playing football related to Sanjeev?

(*a*) Mother (*b*) Aunt (*c*) Sister
(*d*) Daughter (*e*) Grandmother

**3.** Read the following information carefully and answer the questions given below:

**Directions:** *All the six members of a family A, B, C, D, E and F are travelling together, B is the son of C but C is not the mother of B. A and C are a married couple. E is the brother of C. D is the daughter of A. F is the brother of B.*

**I.** How many male members are there in the family?

(*a*) 1 (*b*) 3 (*c*) 2
(*d*) 4 (*e*) 5

**II.** Who is the mother of B?

(*a*) D (*b*) F (*c*) E
(*d*) A (*e*) None of these

**III.** How many children does A have?

(*a*) One (*b*) Two (*c*) Three
(*d*) Four (*e*) None of these

**IV.** Who is the wife of E?

(*a*) A (*b*) F (*c*) B
(*d*) Can't be determined (*e*) None of these

**V.** Which of the following is a pair of females?

(*a*) AE (*b*) BD (*c*) DF
(*d*) AD (*e*) None of these

**VI.** How is E related to D?

(*a*) Father (*b*) Brother (*c*) Uncle
(*d*) Can't be determined (*e*) None of these

**Backtracking:** For questions like Ex 1 and Ex 2, it is best to use 'backtrack', *i.e.*, start with the last information and proceed backwards. For example, if it is given that he is the son of the mother of my grandfather's daughter, then we proceed with the last information: 'grandfather's daughter'. Grandfather's daughter means aunt (sister of father). Now 'mother of my grandfather's daughter' becomes 'mother of my aunt'. Mother, of my aunt is my grandmother. Hence, he is the son of the mother of my grandfather's daughter becomes 'son of my grandmother' which is father or uncle.

**Sol. 1:** His brother's father is *only son of my grandfather* ⇒ His brother's father is my father (Since only son of my grandfather = my father)

Now, brother's father is my father

⇒ His brother is my brother

⇒ He is my brother.

**Answer:** (c)

**Sol. 2:** Younger of the two brothers of the daughter of *my father's wife* (Since my father's wife = my mother)

⇒ Younger of the two brothers of the *daughter of my mother.*

(Since daughter of my mother = my sister)

⇒ Younger of the two brothers of my sister

⇒ my younger brother.

**3.** In questions of this type one is required to establish the relationships within the whole family and not between only two persons. For this, *one should have the ability to draw a family-tree* which is essential in order to easily solve such problems. Here we suggest a convenient method of drawing family-trees.

## Drawing a Family Tree

(*a*) Vertical or diagonal lines should be used to represent parent-child relationships.

(*b*) A double horizontal line (like ⇔) should be used to represent marriages.

(*c*) a dashed line should be used to represent brother or sister relationships.

[**Note:** Apart from dashed lines, brother or sister relationships are also easily established if two persons have the same root (*i.e.* parents depicted by vertical or diagonal lines).]

(*d*) Put a + sign before someone who is a male and a - sign before someone who is, a female.

(*e*) Whenever something is not known put a ? mark or some such symbol (*x*, *y*, *z* etc., for example) before it.

For example, consider the following diagram:

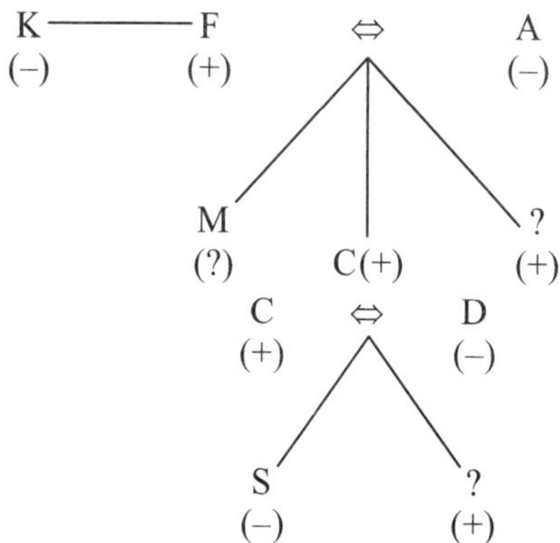


The above diagram tells us that:

(*i*) F and A are a couple; F is the husband while A is the wife.

(*ii*) F has a sister K.

(*iii*) The couple, F and A, has three children: M, C and another son, whose name is not known. C is also a son while the sex of M is not known.

(*iv*) M and the other unknown son are unmarried while C is married to D.

(*v*) The couple, C and D, has a daughter S and a son whose name is not known.

(II) Now that you have learnt the methods of drawing the family tree, let us see the actual method of solving problems such as Ex 3.

### To solve such problems

(*i*) Read the data quickly. This would give you a 'feel' of the problem.

(*ii*) Separate the actual information from the negative information.

(*iii*) Each of the actual information would give you some information that can be used to draw a part of the family tree. **It is advisable to begin with a sentence that gives information about parent-child relationship. Grandfather-grandson relationships and brother-sister relationships should be touched later. (Very Imp)**

(*iv*) Go on reading the actual information, one by one, and make diagrams for each of these informations. These diagrams would be like parts or components of the final family tree. Simultaneously, try your best that you do not draw a new diagram for every new information that you read. Instead, try to 'add' to the existing diagram on reading a new information. The USI and the negative information would be of immense use in this regard.

(*v*) Finally, with the help of all the given information etc. combine all these components into a family tree and answer the questions.

Hence, we can interpret the relationships mentiond in **question 3** as follows and then answer the questions.

**Sol. 3:**

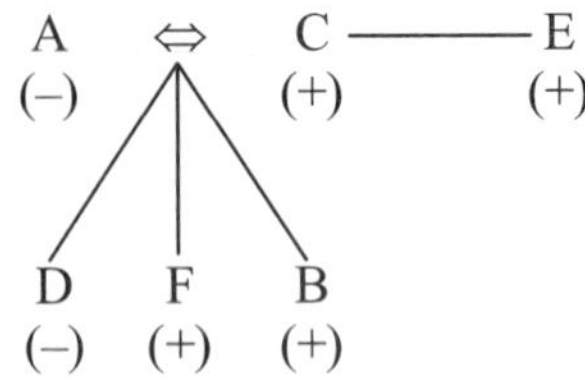


Now, read the questions and check your answers.

| | | |
|---|---|---|
| **I.** (*d*) | **II.** (*d*) | **III.** (*c*) |
| **IV.** (*d*) | **V.** (*d*) | **VI.** (*c*) |

## Problems on blood relations and professions

These problems are very much similar to the problems on blood relations. Only, in these questions another dimension is added. The professions of various family members are also incorporated into the data. Some sample questions are provided below:

**4. Directions:** *Read the following information carefully and answer the questions given below it:*

(1) There is a group of six persons A, B, C, D, E.and F in a family. They are Psychologist, Manager, Lawyer, Jeweller, Doctor and Engineer.

(2) The doctor is the grandfather of F who is a Psychologist.

(3) The Manager D is married to A.

(4) C, the Jeweller, is married to the Lawyer.

(5) B is the mother of F and E.

(6) There are two married couples in the family.

**I.** What is the profession of E?

(*a*) Doctor (*b*) Jeweller (*c*) Manager
(*d*) Psychologist (*e*) None of these

**II.** How is A related to E?

(*a*) Brother (*b*) Uncle (*c*) Father
(*d*) Grandfather (*e*) None of these

**III.** How many male members are there in the family?

(*a*) One (*b*) Three (*c*) Four
(*d*) Two (*e*) Can't be determined

**IV.** What is the profession of A?

(*a*) Doctor (*b*) Lawyer (*c*) Jeweller
(*d*) Manager (*e*) None of these

**V.** Which of the following is one of the pairs of couples in the family?

(*a*) AB (*b*) AC (*c*) AD
(*e*) Cannot be determined (*e*) None of these

**Sol.** The 1st sentence and the 6th sentence are general. Let us begin with the 5th sentence because it has a parent-child relationship. The diagram is:

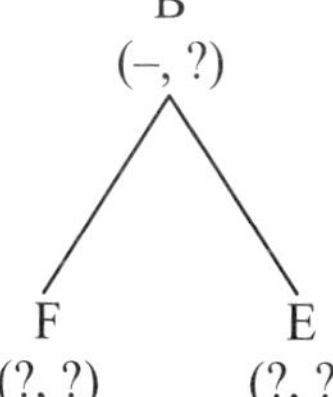


[B is the mother of F and E]

Now, we should look for another sentence that involves B or F or E. We see that the only such sentence is the 2nd which gives some information about F. Please note that if the doctor is the grandfather of F and if B is the mother of F, then B must be the daughter-in-law of the doctor. The diagram becomes:

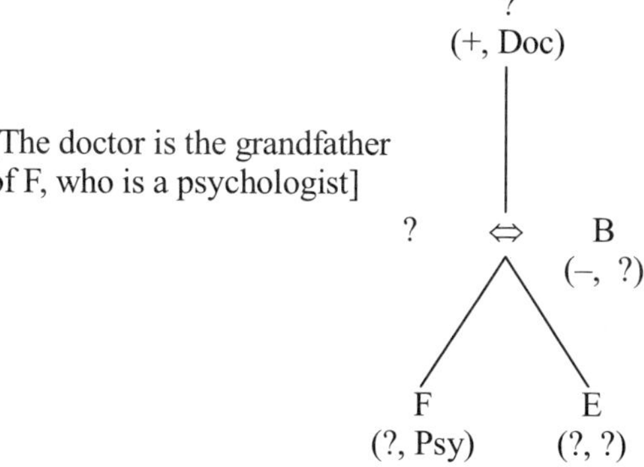


Now the only two sentences remaining are 3rd and 4th. Their diagrams are:

| | | | |
|---|---|---|---|
| D | ⇔ | A | [The manager D is |
| (?, Man) | | (?, ?) | married to A] |
| C | ⇔ | ? | [C, the Jeweller, is married |
| (?, Jew) | | (?, Law) | to the lawyer] |

We see that we have made three components or three different diagrams. How do we combine these informations into one? Since all the actual informations are exhausted, we turn to the only information remaining. It is the last sentence that says that there are two married couples in the family. It means (look at the first diagram) that the doctor's wife is alive. She must be the manager D and the doctor must be A because the professions of the other couple are jeweller and lawyer and not doctor. Now, C, the only one remaining, must be the husband of B, and hence B must be the lawyer. Hence, we have:

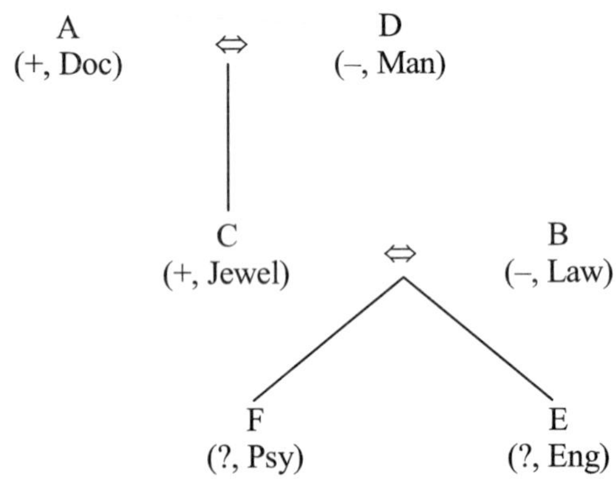


Note that the sex of F and E can't be determined. But the profession of E must be Engineer. Now read the questions and check your answers:

**I.** (*e*) **II.** (*d*) **III.** (*e*)
**IV.** (*a*) **V.** (*c*)

## Coded Relationship

In this type of problems the candidate is required to analyse some given codes and decode each and every relation between a set of persons or to represent a given relationship in the coded form.

The relationship are represented *by* certain specific symbols or codes.

Such codes or Symbols: +, –, ×, ÷, ( ), of, =, $, *, @, £, #, %, ?, □, 0, α, β, γ, Δ, © etc.

## Important tricks to solve coded relationship

**I. Check Sex :**

Check the sex of the required person i.e a male or a female. Example:

(*i*) X is the aunt of Y.
Here 'X' must be female.

(*ii*) A is the grandson of B.
Here 'A' must be 'male'.

So, the answer choices start with informations contrary to the question can be easily eliminated.

According to the statement (*i*), 'X' must be a 'female'.

So, the answer choices start with informations that 'X' is a 'male' (father, brother, son etc.) can be easily eliminated.

**II. Draw a relationship chart or a family tree diagram.**

Draw a relationship chart or a family tree diagram to solve the coded relationships easily and quickly.

**Our Conventions:**

(*i*) ⇌ ⇒ Married couples

(*ii*) | or ∧ ⇒ parent - child relationship

(*iii*) —— ⇒ brother or sister relationship

(*iv*) '+' sign ⇒ male.

(*v*) '–' sign ⇒ female.

(*vi*) '?' sign ⇒ unknown sex

**5.** If 'A $ B' means 'A is father of B', 'A # B' means 'A is daughter of B', 'A @ B' means 'A is sister of B', then how is K related to M in H @ K $ L # M ?

(*a*) Husband (*b*) Uncle (*c*) Father
(*d*) Cannot be determined (*e*) None of these

**Sol.** H @ K ⇒ H is sister of K.

K $ L ⇒ K is father of L.

L # M ⇒ L is daughter of M.

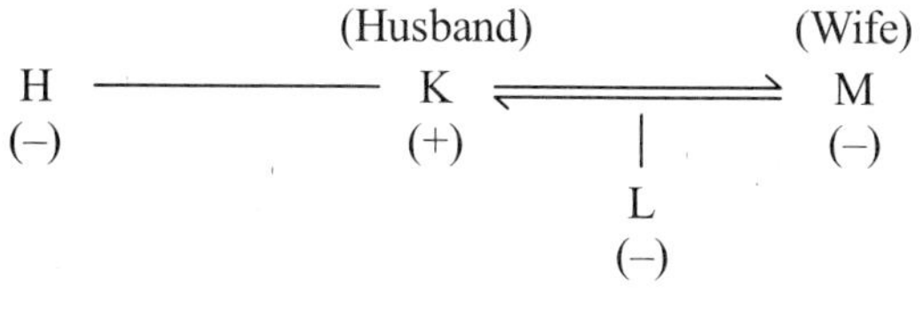

```
                       (Husband)              (Wife)
H ———————————————————— K  ⇌—————————————————  M
(–)                    (+)          |          (–)
                                    L
                                   (–)
```

Therefore, 'K' is the *husband* of 'M' **Ans (*a*)**

## EXERCISE

**1.** Introducing a lady a man said, her mother's husband's sister is my aunt. How is the lady related to the man?
(*a*) Mother (*b*) Sister (*c*) Aunt
(*d*) Daughter (*e*) Granddaughter

**2.** Pointing to Rekha, Rahul said, "She is the daughter of my grandfather's son." How is Rekha related to Rahul?
(*a*) Aunt (*b*) Sister (*c*) Niece
(*d*) Mother (*e*) Sister-in-law

**3.** Pointing to a photograph, Ranjit said, "She is the daughter of the son of my grandfather's only brother." How is the lady related to Ranjit?
(*a*) Sister (*b*) Niece (*c*) Cousin
(*d*) Can't say (*e*) None of these

**4.** Introducing to a lady in the photograph, Sanjeev said, "This woman is my sister's father's son-in-law's wife". How is Sanjeev related to the woman?
(*a*) Mother (*b*) Sister (*c*) Can't be determined
(*d*) Wife (*e*) None of these

**5.** Monica introduces to a photograph as "He is the brother of the son of my grandfather's only daughter. "How is the man related to Monica.
(*a*) Brother (*b*) Cousin (*c*) Nephew
(*d*) Can't say (*e*) None of these

**6.** Pointing to a joker, Madhu says, "He is the son of my father's brother's only sister-in-law." How is the joker related to Madhu?
(*a*) Son (*b*) Brother (*c*) Cousin
(*d*) Uncle (*e*) None of these

**7.** Introducing to a photograph Arun said, "She is the mother of my brother's son's wife's daughter". How is Arun related to the lady?
(*a*) cousin (*b*) aunt (*c*) daughter-in-law
(*d*) uncle (*e*) None of these

**8.** Introducing to a gentleman, Panas says, 'He is the son of the daughter of the father of my father'. How is the person related to Panas?
(*a*) cousin (*b*) nephew (*c*) uncle
(*d*) brother (*e*) brother-in-law

**9.** Pointing to a man, Yugnirmal recalled, 'He is the son of the mother of the father of my daughter.' How is Yugnirmal related to the man?
(*a*) cousin (*b*) brother (*c*) nephew
(*d*) uncle (*e*) son

**10.** Rohit said about a Person that 'He is the younger of the two brothers of the daughter of my father's wife'. How is the person related to Rohit?
(*a*) nephew (*b*) son (*c*) uncle
(*d*) brother (*e*) father

**11.** Pointing to a woman, Anil said, 'She is the daughter of my grandfather's only son's wife.' How is Anil related to that girl?
(*a*) Brother (*b*) cousin (*c*) Father
(*d*) Uncle (*e*) Husband

**12.** Pointing to a boy in a photograph, Akhil said, "He is the son of my mother's only son." How is Akhil related to that boy?
(*a*) Uncle (*b*) Brother (*c*) Father
(*d*) Cousin (*e*) None of these

**13.** Meena says about a boy, "He is the son of my grandfather's only son." How is the boy's mother related to Meena?
(*a*) Mother (*b*) Aunt (*c*) Sister
(*d*) Data inadequate (*e*) None of these

**14.** Introducing Sarita, Meena said, "She is the only daughter of my father's only daughter." How is Meena related to Sarita?
(*a*) Niece (*b*) Cousin (*c*) Aunt
(*d*) Data inadequate (*e*) None of these

**Directions (Qs. 15-16):** *Study the information given below and answer the questions following it:*

Mohan is son of Arun's father's sister. Prakash is son of Reva, who is mother of Vikash and grandmother of Arun. Pranab is father of Neela and grandfather of Mohan. Reva is wife of Pranab.

**15.** How is Mohan related to Reva?
(*a*) Grandson (*b*) Son (*c*) Nephew
(*d*) Data inadequate (*e*) None of these

**16.** How is Vikash's wife related to Neela?
(*a*) Sister (*b*) Niece (*c*) Sister-in-law
(*d*) Data inadequate (*e*) None of these

**17.** Introducing Kedar, Veena-said, 'His mother's brother is the father of my son Nitin.' How is Kedar related to Veena?
(*a*) Niece (*b*) Aunt (*c*) Nephew
(*d*) Sister-in-law (*e*) None of these

**18.** Pointing to a boy, Namrata says, "He is the son of my grandfather's only child." How is the boy related to Namrata?
(*a*) Brother (*b*) Cousin (*c*) Uncle
(*d*) Data inadequate (*e*) None of these

**19.** Kalyani is mother-in-law of Veena who is Sister-in-law of Ashok. Dheeraj is father of Sudeep, the only brother of Ashok. How is Kalyani related to Ashok?
(*a*) Mother-in-law (*b*) Aunt (*c*) Wife
(*d*) Cousin (*e*) None of these

**20.** Pointing to a girl, Abhishek said, "She is daughter of the only child of my father." How is Abhishek's Wife related to that girl?
(*a*) Daughter (*b*) Mother (*c*) Aunt
(*d*) Sister (*e*) None of these

**21.** If P $ Q means P is father of Q, P # Q means P is mother of Q, P * Q means P is sister of Q, then how is Q related to N in N # L $ P * Q?
(*a*) Grandson (*b*) Granddaughter (*c*) Nephew
(*d*) Data inadequate (*e*) None of these

**22.** A $ B means B is father of A; A # B means B is mother of A; A * B means B is sister of A; and A @ B means B is husband of A; then which of the following indicates the relationship 'N is grandmother of P'?
(*a*) P*Q#M$N (*b*) P@Q$M#N (*c*) P#Q$N*M
(*d*) P$Q#M@N (*e*) None of these

**23.** If 'A + B' means 'A is brother of B', 'A – B' means 'A is sister of B', 'A × B' means 'A is wife of B', and 'A ÷ B' means 'A is father of B', then which of the following indicates 'S is son of P'?
(*a*) P × Q ÷ R + S – T (*b*) P × Q ÷ S – R + T (*c*) P × Q ÷ R – T + S
(*d*) P × Q ÷ R – S + T (*e*) None of these

**Directions (Qs. 24-25):** *Study the following information carefully and answer the given questions based on it:*
(A) 'P × Q' means 'Q is mother of P'.
(B) 'P + Q' means 'P is father of Q'.
(C) 'P – Q' means 'Pis brother of Q'.
(D) 'P ÷ Q' means 'Q is sister of P'.

**24.** Which of the following means 'M is niece of T'?
(*a*) M ÷ D + T × R (*b*) T – D + R ÷ M (*c*) T × D + R ÷ M
(*d*) Cannot be determined (*e*) None of these

**25.** Which of the following statements is redundant to answer the above question.

(*a*) A only (*b*) B only (*c*) Either A or B only
(*d*) Either C or D only (*e*) All are required

**Directions (Qs. 26-27):** *Study the following information carefully and answer the given questions following it.*

(*i*) 'P × Q' means 'P is brother of Q'
(*ii*) 'P + Q' means 'Q is mother of P'
(*iii*) 'P – Q' means 'Q is sister of P'
(*iv*) 'P ÷ Q' means 'P is father of Q'

**26.** Which of the following means T is nephew of R?

1. R × J ÷ T 2. R – M + T – J 3. R × J ÷ T × K

(*a*) 1 only (*b*) 2 only (*c*) 3 only
(*d*) Either 2 or 3 (*e*) None of these

**27.** Which of the following is superfluous to answer the above question?

(*a*) (*i*) only (*b*) (*ii*) only (*c*) Either (*ii*) or (*iii*)
(*d*) (*iii*) only (*e*) All are required

**Directions (Qs. 28-29):** *Study the following information and answer the questions given below.*

(*i*) 'P ÷ Q' means 'Q is father of P'.
(*ii*) 'P × Q' means 'P is sister of Q'.
(*iii*) 'P + Q' means 'P is brother of Q'.
(*iv*) 'P – Q' means 'Q is mother of P'.

**28.** Which of the following means R is nephew of T?

(*a*) R + N – Q × T (*b*) R – Q × N × T (*c*) R – N × T
(*d*) T + M ÷ R (*e*) T – Q ÷ R

**29.** Which of the following is/are redundant to answer the above question?

(*a*) (*ii*) only (*b*) (*i*) only (*c*) (*i*) and (*iv*) only
(*d*) Either (*i*) and (*iii*) or (*ii*) and (*iv*)
(*e*) Either (*i*) and (*ii*) or (*iii*) and (*iv*)

**30.** P – Q' means 'Q' is son of 'P' and 'P × Q' means 'P' is brother of 'Q', 'P ÷ Q' means 'Q' is sister of 'P', and 'P + Q' means 'P' is mother of 'Q'. Which of the following is definitely TRUE about 'N × K – M ÷ L'?

(*a*) 'K' is father of L and M.
(*b*) 'L' is the daughter of 'K' and is the niece of her uncle 'N'.

(*c*) 'K' is the father of 'M' and 'L' - his son and daughter respectively.
(*d*) 'M' is the uncle of K's brother N.
(*e*) None of these

**31.** A + B means B is brother of A; A × B means B is husband of A; A – B means A is mother of B; and A ÷ B means A is father of B. Then which of the following expressions indicates 'P' is grandmother of 'T'?
(*a*) Q – P + R ÷ T (*b*) P × Q ÷ R – T (*c*) P × Q ÷ R + T
(*d*) P + Q ÷ R – T (*e*) None of these

**32.** If A + B means "A is the sister of B", A × B means "A is the wife of B", A ÷ B means "A is the father of B" and A – B means "A is the brother of B", then which of following expresses the relationship that "T is the daughter of P"?
(*a*) P × Q ÷ R + S – T (*b*) P × Q ÷ R – T + S (*c*) P × Q ÷ R + T – S
(*d*) P × Q ÷ R + S + T (*e*) None of these

**33.** If 'A $ B' means 'A is brother of B', 'A @ B' means 'A is wife of B', 'A # B' means 'A is daughter of B' and 'A * B' means 'A is father of B', then which of the following expressions indicates the relationship 'U is father-in-law of P?
(*a*) P@Q$T#U*W (*b*) P@W$Q*T#U (*c*) P@Q$W*T#U
(*d*) P@Q$T#W*U (*e*) None of these

**34.** If 'M × N' means 'M is the daughter of N', 'M + N' means 'M is the father of N', 'M ÷ N' means 'M is the mother of N', and 'M – N' means 'M is the brother of N' then in the expression 'P ÷ Q + R – T × K', how 'P is related to K'?
(*a*) Daughter-in-law (*b*) Sister-in-law (*c*) Aunt
(*d*) Mother (*e*) None of these

**Directions (Qs. 35-39):** *If A + B means A is daughter of B,*
*A – B* means *A* is husband of *B*,
*A* × *B* means *A* is brother of *B*.

**35.** What does the relation $p \times q - r$ show?
(*a*) *p* is son-in-law of *r* (*b*) *p* is brother of *r* (*c*) *r* is wife of *p*
(*d*) *p* is father of *r* (*e*) None of these

**36.** If $h + i \times j + k \times l + m \times n$, then what is the present generation of *h*. Assume that the oldest generation in this group is the first generation?
(*a*) 2nd (*b*) 3rd (*c*) 4th
(*d*) 5th (*e*) None of these

**37.** Which of the following statements does not apply?

(*a*) $A + B \times C$ (*b*) $A - B \times C$ (*c*) $A + B + C$
(*d*) $A + B - C$ (*e*) None of these

**38.** From the statement $A \times B \times C \times D$, which of the following statement is not necessarily true?

(*a*) *B* is the brother of *A* (*b*) *C* is the brother of *A*
(*c*) *D* is brother of *C* (*d*) *A, B, C* are male
(*e*) None of these

**39.** From the statement $p - q + r \times s$, how is *q* related to *s*?

(*a*) Niece (*b*) Sister (*c*) Mother
(*d*) Sister-in-law (*e*) None of these

**Directions (Qs. 40-42):** *A * B means A is brother of B*
*A @ B means A is the daughter of B*
*A $ B means A is the sister of B*

**40.** Which of the following shows the relationship *p* is the paternal uncle of *n*?

(*a*) *n$o@p* (*b*) *n@o$p* (*c*) *n@o*p*
(*d*) *n*o@p* (*e*) None of these

**41.** From the following statement, what is the relationship between *n* and *s*?
*n$o@p*q$r*s*

(*a*) Grandmother (*b*) Grandfather (*c*) Aunt
(*d*) Mother (*e*) Can't be determined

**42.** If *a$b$c@d@e*f*g*, then how many males and females are there respectively?

(*a*) 4, 3 (*b*) 3, 4 (*c*) 5, 2
(*d*) 2, 3 (*e*) Can't be determined

**Directions (Qs. 43-44):** *Study the following information carefully and answer the questions given below.*

P, Q, R, S, T, U and V are seven members of a family belonging to three generations. There are two married couples—one each of first and second generation respectively. They travel in three different cars—Bentley, Lamborghini and Ferrari so that no car has more than three members and there is at least one female in each car. R, who is granddaughter, does not travel with her grandfather and grandmother. Q travels with his father T in Lamborghini.

U travels with her granddaughter S in Bentley. P travels with her daughter in Ferrari.

**43.** How many female members are there in the family?
(*a*) Three (*b*) Four (*c*) Five
(*d*) Six (*e*) None of these

**44.** Which of the following is one of the married couples?
(*a*) Q & S (*b*) Q & R (*c*) T & U
(*d*) U & V (*e*) None of these

**Direction (Qs 45):** *Read the information given carefully and answer the question.*

In a family of six persons—Pranay, Qayamat, Ravi, Shashi, Tanveer, Umed, there are three males and three females. There are two married couples and two persons are unmarried. Each one of them reads different magazines, which are Cosmopolitan, Vogue, India Today, Economist, Stardust and Femina.

The following facts about the family members are also known:

Tanveer, who reads Cosmopolitan, is mother-in-law of Pranay, who is wife of Ravi. Shashi is the father of Umed and he does not read Vogue or Femina. Qayamat reads Stardust and is the sister of Umed, who reads India Today. Ravi does not read Femina.

**45.** Who among the following reads *Vogue* and what is the relation between the person who reads *Vogue* and *Qayamat*?
(*a*) Ravi, Sister (*b*) Ravi, Father (*c*) Umed, sister
(*d*) Shashi, Father (*e*) None of these

## ANSWERS

| 1 | 2 | 3 | 4 | 5 | 6 | 7 | 8 | 9 | 10 |
|---|---|---|---|---|---|---|---|---|---|
| (*b*) | (*b*) | (*c*) | (*b*) | (*d*) | (*b*) | (*e*) | (*a*) | (*b*) | (*d*) |
| **11** | **12** | **13** | **14** | **15** | **16** | **17** | **18** | **19** | **20** |
| (*a*) | (*c*) | (*a*) | (*e*) | (*a*) | (*c*) | (*c*) | (*a*) | (*e*) | (*b*) |
| **21** | **22** | **23** | **24** | **25** | **26** | **27** | **28** | **29** | **30** |
| (*d*) | (*e*) | (*d*) | (*b*) | (*a*) | (*c*) | (*e*) | (*a*) | (*b*) | (*b*) |
| **31** | **32** | **33** | **34** | **35** | **36** | **37** | **38** | **39** | **40** |
| (*b*) | (*b*) | (*a*) | (*e*) | (*e*) | (*c*) | (*b*) | (*c*) | (*a*) | (*c*) |
| **41** | **42** | **43** | **44** | **45** | | | | | |
| (*e*) | (*e*) | (*c*) | (*c*) | (*a*) | | | | | |

## SOME SELECTED EXPLANATORY ANSWERS

1. As is given, lady's aunt is man's aunt, therefore, lady is man's sister.
2. Rahul grandfathers only son = Rahul father
   Now, Rahul father's daughter = Rahul sister = Rekha.
3. Grandfather's → brother

   Ranjit → Daughter
   Hence cousin.
4. Sister's father means father
   Father's son-in-law's wife means sister
   Hence Sanjeev's sister.
5. Her grandfather's only daughter may be her mother or aunt.
6. Brother's only sister-in-law = Wife
   Father's wife = Mother
   Son of mother = Brother
7. The lady in question is Arun's brother's daughter-in-law. Thus Arun is father-in-law's brother of the lady.
8. 

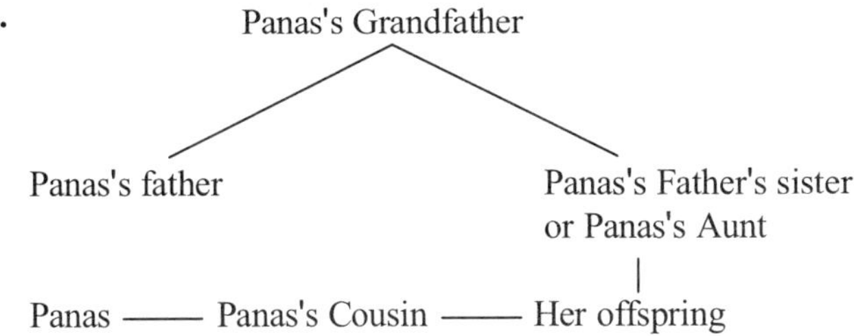


9. Yugnirmal's daughter's father → Yugnirmal.
   Mother of Yugnirmal's daughter's father → Yugnirmal's mother.
   Son other than Yugnirmal of Yugnirmal's mother → Yugnirmal's brother.
10. My father's wife ⇒ my mother
    Daughter of my mother ⇒ my sister.
    Brother of my sister ⇒ myself or my brother.
11. Anil's grandfather's only son's wife = Anil's mother, Anil's mother's daughter

is his sister. Therefore Anil is the girl's brother.

**12.** Photograph is of the son of Akhil's mother's only son.
or, Photograph is the son of Akhil.
and, Akhil is the father of the boy.

**13.** One's grandfather's only son ⇒ one's father. And the son of one's father ⇒ One's brother or oneself. Hence, the mother of the boy is Meena's mother.

**14.** Daughter of my father means Meena's daughter, hence Meena is the mother of that girl.

**15-16.** Pranab ⇔ Reva
(+) (–)
|
* or Neela Prakash Vikash
(–) (–) (+)
| |
Mohan Arun
(+)

Hence, Mohan is grand son of Reva and Vikash's wife is sister-in-law of Neela.

**17.** ** * Veena
(–) — (+) ⇔ (–)
| |
Kedar (+) Nitin

Hence, Kedar is Veena's nephew.

**18.** Son of Namrata's grandfather's only child is Namrata's brother

**19.** Kalyani (–) ⟷ Dheeraj (+)

(+) Ashok Sudeep (+) ⟷ Veena (–)

Clearly, Kalyani is mother of Ashok.

**20.** Girl is daughter of the only child of Abhishek's father or, Girl is daughter of Abhishek

Hence girl is daughter of Abhishek's wife.

**21.** N is mother of L and L is father of both P and Q. So N is the grandmother of P and Q. But we dont know sex of Q. Therefore we can't say wether Q is grandson or granddaughter of N.

**22.** The family-chain should be: N (–)

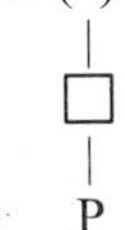


**23.** As 'S' is a female in option (*a*) and (*b*), they can be rejected directly. The sex of 'S' in option (*c*) is not known, hence it can also be eliminated. Now, check option (*d*).

(–) P ↔ Q (+)
|
R (–) —S(+) — T

[Clearly, S is son of P.]

**24.** T(+) — D(+) = T is brother of D
D + R = D is father of R
R ÷ M = M is sister of R
⇒ D is father of M
Hence, Ans. is (*b*)

**26.** (*a*) $R_{(+)}$ — $J_{(+)}$
|
T

But we do not know whether T is a male or female. (Rejected)

(*b*) $T_{(-)}$ — $J_{(-)}$
|
R — $M_{(-)}$

Here T is a female. (Rejected)

(*c*) $R_{(+)}$ — $J_{(+)}$
|
$T_{(+)}$ — K

Here, T is the nephew of R.

**27.** To check the equations [(*a*), (*b*) and (*c*)] we need all the statements (*i*), (*ii*), (*iii*) and (*iv*).

**28.** If R is nephew of T then the required equation must depict R as a male. Reject (*b*) and (*c*) because in these equations the symbol '–' denotes the sex of Q and N respectively. The sex of R remains unknown. Reject (*d*) and (*e*) because these equations depict R older then T. Now, check (*a*).

$Q_{(-)}$ — T
|
$R_{(+)}$ — N

Obviously, R is the nephew of T.

**29.** R + N – Q × T "the required equation to answer the previous question. Here the used symbols are '+', '–' and '×'. Therefore, redundant part of the symbols given in the direction is statement (*i*).

**30.**
```
N — K
(+)   |
      M — L
      (+)  (–)
```
(*a*) and (*c*) are definitely not true because we don't know the sex of K. So, K may be the mother.

**31.** Option (*c*) is ruled out because we need two generation-change signs (– and ÷) between P and T. Same is the case with (*a*). Again, (*d*) is ruled out because P + Q does not give the sex of P. Now, check (*b*)

```
P(–) ↔ Q(+)
         |
        R(–)
         |
         T
```

**32.** Options (*a*) and (*d*) can be rejected at first sight because the sex of T is not known here. In option (*c*), T is male, so can be rejected as well. Now, check option (*b*)

```
  P(–) ↔ Q(+)
          |
    (+)R — T(–) —S.
```

Clearly, T is the daughter of 'P'.

**33.** The sex of 'U' is not known in options (*b*), (*c*) and (*d*). And hence can be rejected directly. Now, check option (*a*):

```
                  U(+)
                   |
(–)P ⇔ Q(+) — T(–) — W
```

(Clearly, 'U' is father-in-law of 'P'.)

**34.**
```
P(–)
 |
Q(+) ⇔ K(–)
 |
(+)R — T(–)
```
(Clearly, 'P' is mother-in-law of 'K'.)

**35.** $p \times q - r$ can be read as $p$ is the brother of $q$ and $q$ is the husband of $r$. Thus $p$ must be the brother-in-law of $r$. Hence, option (*d*) is correct.

**36.** $h + i \times j + k \times l + m \times n$ means $h$ is the daughter of $i$, $i$ is the brother of $j$, $j$ is the daughter of $k$, $k$ is the brother of $l$, $l$ is the daughter of $m$ and $m$ is the brother of $n$. Thus, if $m$ and $n$ are the first generation, $k$ and $l$ are the second, $i$ and $j$ are the third generation, $h$ is the fourth generation. To solve this question in short, you only need to realise that the use of the + sign signifies a generation change. Since the + sign is used thrice, $h$ must be the fourth generation. Hence, option (*c*) is the answer.

**37.** Option (*b*) says: $A - B \times C$, this does not hold since $A$ must be the husband of $B$ (who is a female) and $B$ is the brother of $C$ (which cannot happen). Hence, option (*b*) is the answer.

**38.** $A \times B \times C \times D$ means $A$ is the brother of $B$, $B$ is the brother of $C$ and $C$ is the brother of $D$. This makes options (*a*), (*b*) and (*d*) as correct. Only option (*c*) is not necessarily true since $D$ could be $B$'s sister too. Hence, (*c*) is the answer.

**39.** $p - q + r \times s$ reads as $p$ is the husband of $q$, $q$ is the daughter of $r$ and $r$ is the brother of $s$. Thus, $q$ must be $s$'s niece. Hence, option (*a*) is the correct answer.

**40.** $n@o*p$ reads, $n$ is the daughter of $o$ and $o$ is the brother of $p$. Hence, $p$ becomes $n$'s paternal uncle. So, option (*c*) is correct.

**41.** It is clear that $s$'s sex cannot be determined. Hence, the relationship between $n$ and $s$ cannot be determined. Option (*d*) is the answer.

**42.** Again here, $g$'s sex is indeterminable. Hence, the answer cannot be determined. Option (*e*) is the answer.

**Solutions to 43 and 44**

On the basis of the given clues we get the following information:

| Car | Persons travelling in car |
|---|---|
| Bentley | U(F), S(F) |
| Lamborghini | Q(M), T(M) |
| Ferrari | P(F), ?(F) |

Besides this we came to know that R is a female but we still do not know the gender of V. But it is given that there is at least one female in each car. The above table shows that Lamborghini has a vacant seat for a female passenger. Hence, the seventh person must be a female to fulfill the condition. Hence, V is a female. But we still do not know in which car R and V are travelling knowing that both are not in the same car. Now we need to construct a family tree:

$$[T(M) \leftrightarrow U(F)] \longrightarrow [Q(M) \leftrightarrow P(F)] \longrightarrow [R(F) + S(F)]$$

FIRST SECOND THIRD

Since R does not travel with her grandfather and grandmother, R is not in Bentley, hence R is in Lamborghini. We are still not aware of V's position in the family tree.

**43.** Option (*c*)

**44.** Option (*c*)

**45.** From the given information of the readership, we can build a table as follows:

| | **Payal** | **Qayamat** | **Ravi** | **Shashi** | **Tanveer** | **Umed** |
|---|---|---|---|---|---|---|
| *Cosmopolitan* | × | × | × | × | ✓ | × |
| *Vogue* | × | × | ✓ | × | × | × |
| *India Today* | × | × | × | × | × | ✓ |
| *Economist* | × | × | × | ✓ | × | × |
| *Stardust* | × | ✓ | × | × | × | × |
| *Femina* | ✓ | × | × | × | × | × |

(*a*) Tanveer and Shashi are a couple.
(*b*) Pranay and Ravi are a couple.
(*c*) Ravi, Umed and Qayamat are brothers and sisters.

Hence, Option (*a*) is the correct answer.

# 6

# Direction Sense

Direction is a measurement of position of one thing with respect to another thing and displacement is the measurement of distance between the starting and the final point.

Direction Sense Test checks *'the sense of direction'* of the candidate.

## BASIC CONCEPTS

To solve these type of questions, the candidate should be aware of the directions. The following diagram shows the four main directions:

(*i*) North (N) (*ii*) South (S)

(*iii*) East (E) (*iv*) West (W)

**Four cardinal directions:**

(*i*) North East (NE) (*ii*) North West (NW)

(*iii*) South East (SE) (*iv*) South West (SW)

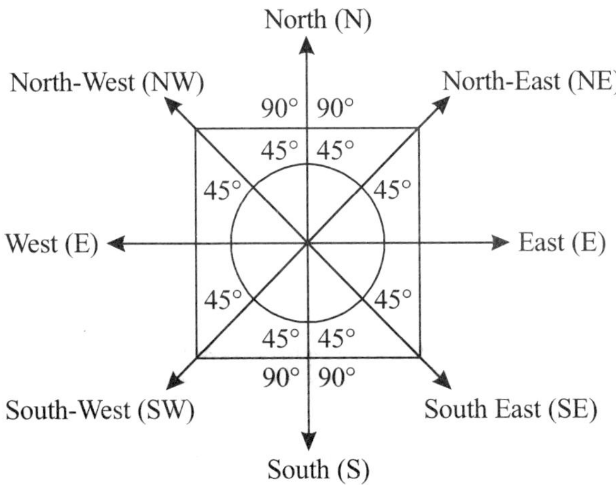


**Fig.:** *Basic Direction Diagram*

If your face is towards NORTH, your left hand is towards WEST and your right hand is towards EAST. Similarly the positions of the directions of the hands can be fixed when you move in any of the other three directions as given below in table. Commonly, North-South direction is referred to as "vertical" direction and the East-West direction is referred to as the "horizontal" direction as shown in the diagram.

## DIRECTION TABLE

Take care of the change in direction when a person or vehicle takes a right or left turn.

| Direction before taking the turn | Direction in-which the person or Vehicle taking the turn will be moving after | |
|---|---|---|
| | **Right** | **Left** |
| (*i*) North | East | West |
| (*ii*) South | West | East |
| (*iii*) East | South | North |
| (*iv*) West | North | South |
| (*v*) North-West | North-East | South-West |
| (*vi*) South-West | North-West | South-East |
| (*vii*) South-East | South-West | North-East |
| (*viii*) North-East | South-East | North-West |

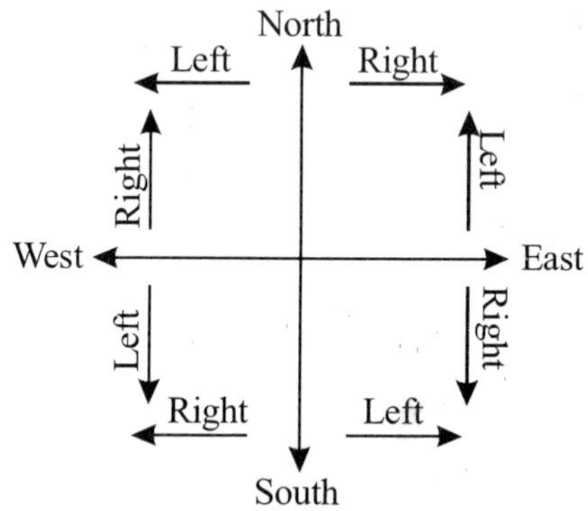


**Fig.:** *Direction after taking turn (Right or Left)*

If the movement is on right side of the four directoins: Clockwise direction.

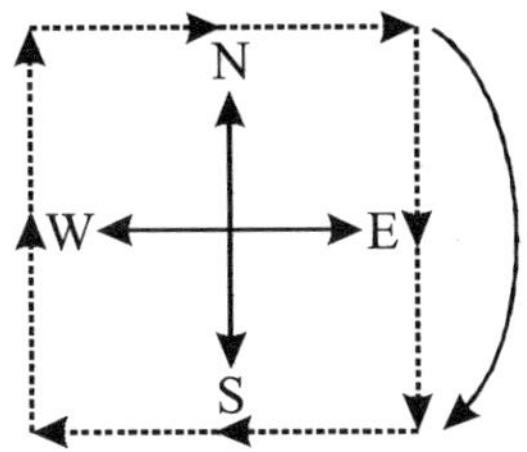


**Fig.:** *Clockwise direction Diagram*

If the movement is on left side of the four directions: Anti Clockwise direction.

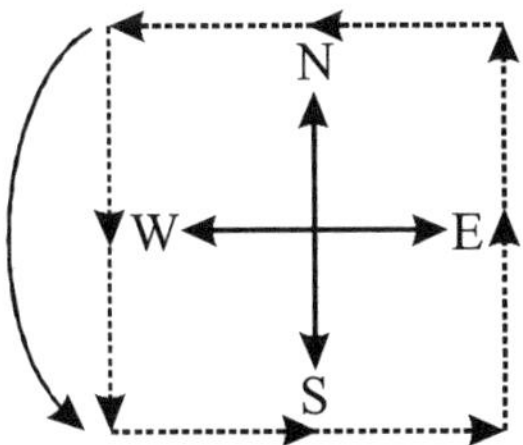


**Fig.:** *Anti clockwise direction diagram*

## SOLVED EXAMPLE

**1.** After walking 5 km Panas turned right and covered a distance of 2 km, then turned left and covered a distance of 6 km. In the end, he was moving towards the north. From which direction did he start the journey?

(*a*) North (*b*) South (*c*) East
(*d*) West (*e*) None of these

**Sol.** (*b*) From the Fig., It is clear that Panas started the journey from South and moved northwards.

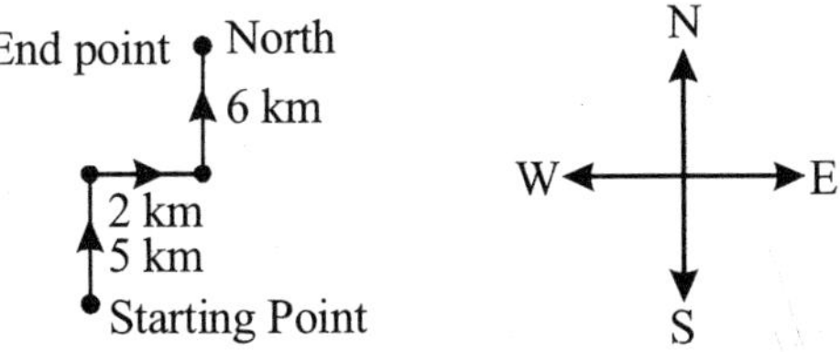


Therefore, Panas started the journey from South.

**2.** Jyoti is facing towards west and turns through 45° clockwise, again 180° clockwise and then turns through 270° anticlockwise. In which direction is she facing now?

(*a*) West (*b*) North-west (*c*) South
(*d*) South-west (*e*) None of these

**Sol.** (*d*) From the Fig. it is clear that Jyoti initially faces the direction OP. Then on moving 45° clockwise, Jyoti faces in the direction OQ. On further moving 180° clockwise, She faces in the direction OR.

Then, She finally faces in the direction OS after moving 270° anticlockwise.

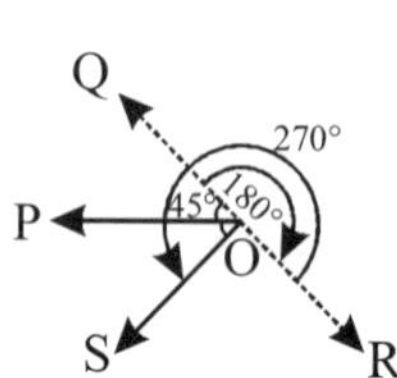

Final movement Second movement

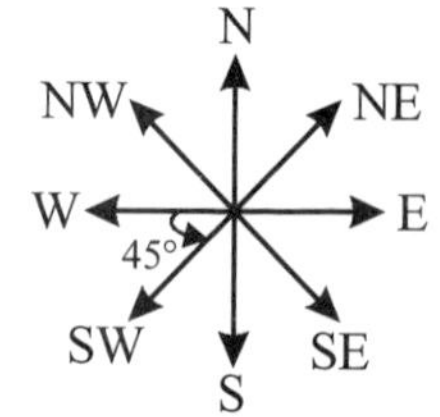

Basic Direction Diagram

From the basic direction diagram, it is clear that direction OS is South-west.

Therefore, Jyoti is now facing South-west.

**Shortcut method:**

Clockwise directions: 45° + 180° = 225°

Anticlockwise direction : 270°

The required direction = Clockwise direction + Anticlockwise direction

= 225° + (–270°) = 225° – 270° = –45°

*i.e.*, 45° anticlockwise from initial position.

Therefore, the required direction is south-west.

**3.** Prakash walked 5 metres facing towards East, then took a right turn and walked a distance of 9 metres. The then took a left turn and walked a distance of 7 metres. How far is he from the starting point?

(*a*) 15 metres (*b*) 21 metres (*c*) 18 metres
(*d*) cannot be determined (*e*) None of these

**Sol.** (*a*) The journey of Prakash is as shown in Fig.

A = Starting point; D = End point

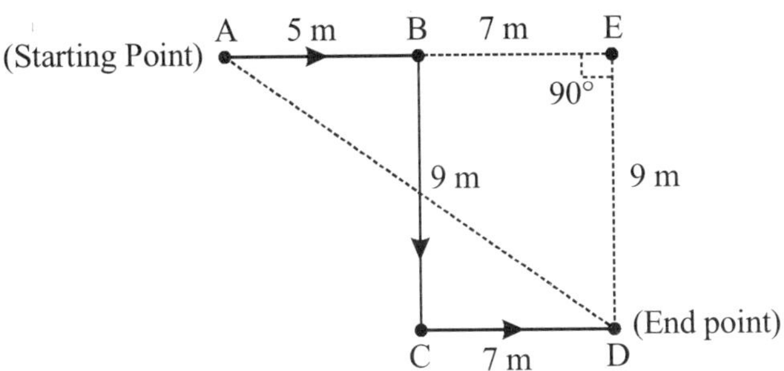


$\therefore \quad AD = \sqrt{AE^2 + ED^2}$

$= \sqrt{12^2 + 9^2} = \sqrt{144 + 81} = \sqrt{225} = 15m$

$\therefore$ Praksh's distance from starting point A = AD = 15 m.

**4.** Satyam walks 10 metres towards the South. Turning to the left, he walks 20 metres and then moves to his right. After moving a distance of 20 metres, he turns to the right and walks 20 metres. Finally, he turns to the right and moves a distance of 10 metres. How far and in which direction is he from the starting point?

(*a*) 10 metres North (*b*) 20 metres South (*c*) 20 metres North
(*d*) 10 metres South (*e*) None of these

**Sol.** (*b*) The journey of Satyam from A to F is as shown in Fig.

A = Starting point; F = End point

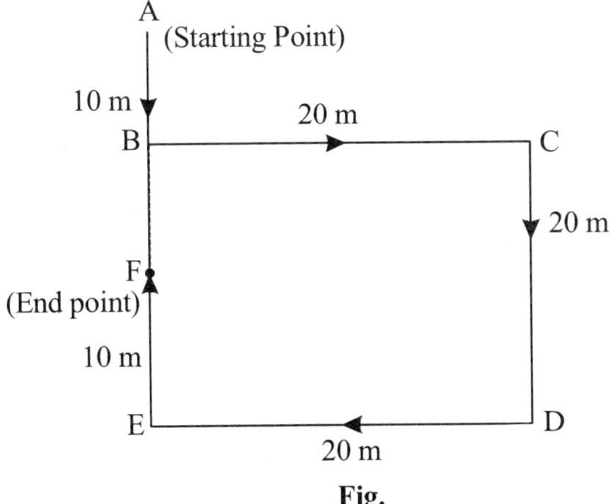


**Fig.**

Satyam's distance from starting point A = AF = (AB + BF)

= AB + (BE – EF)

= AB + (CD – EF)

= [10 + (20 – 10)] m = (10 + 10) m = 20 m

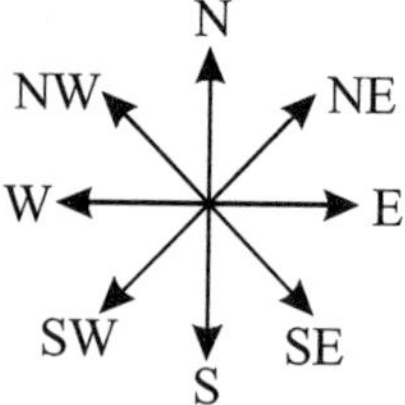


**Fig.:** *Basic direction diagram*

Also, according to the Basic direction diagram, it is clear that F lies to the South of A.

Therefore, Satyam is 20 metres to the South of his starting point.

**5.** A clock is so placed that at 12 noon its minute hand points towards north-east. In which direction does its hour hand point at 1:30 p.m.?

(*a*) North (*b*) South (*c*) East
(*d*) West (*e*) None of these

**Sol.** (*c*) The positions of the minute and hour hands at 12 noon and 1:30 p.m. are shown in Fig. I and Fig. II respectively.

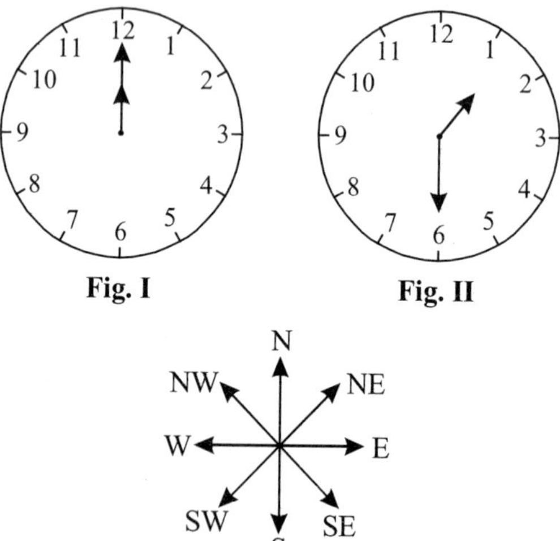


**Fig. I** **Fig. II**

**Fig. III:** *Basic direction diagram*

According to the question, at 12 noon minute hand points towards North-East.

So, the changed direction is shown in Fig. IV

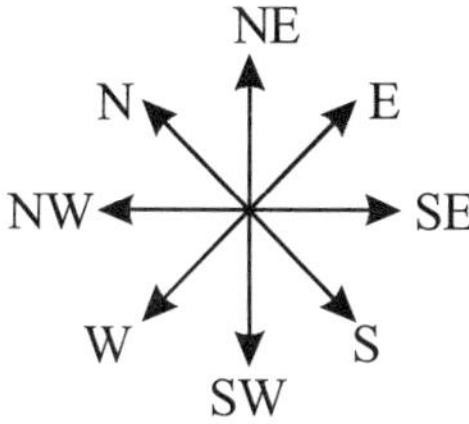


**Fig. IV:** *(According to the question)*

Therefore, clearly the hour hand at 1:30 p.m. points towards the East as shown in Fig. I. and Fig. II

## EXERCISE

**1.** A rat runs 20' towards East and turns to right, runs 10' and turns to right, runs 9' and again turns to left, runs 5' and then turns to left, runs 12' and finally turns to left and runs 6'. Now which-direction is the rat facing?

(*a*) East (*b*) West (*c*) North
(*d*) South (*e*) None of these

**2.** A policeman goes 20 km east and then turning to the south he goes 30 km and then again turns to his left and goes 10 km. How far is he from his starting point?

(*a*) 30 km (*b*) 20 km (*c*) 10 km
(*d*) 40 km (*e*) None of these

**3.** If Southeast becomes east and Northwest becomes west and all the other directions are changed in the same direction. Then what will be the direction for north?

(*a*) Northwest (*b*) Southeast (*c*) Southwest
(*d*) Northeast (*e*) None of these

**4.** If Northwest becomes south and southwest becomes east and all the other directions change in the similar manner, then what will be the direction for north?

(*a*) Southeast (*b*) Northeast (*c*) West
(*d*) North (*e*) None of these

**5.** Karan's house is south facing. From the front door of his house Karan started walking and after walking 20 metres straight he turned to his left and walked 50 metres. After this he turned to his right and walked

80 metres. Find the distance between the point from where he finished his walk and the door of his house.

(*a*) $50\sqrt{5}$ metres (*b*) $5\sqrt{50}$ metres (*c*) 100 metres
(*d*) 120 metres (*e*) None of these

**6.** A man started walking towards north, he walks 10 metres and then turns to his right, walks 5 metres and turns to his right again and walks 10 metres and turns to his left, walks 7 metres and then turns to his right. At this point in which direction is he facing?

(*a*) East (*b*) South (*c*) Southeast
(*d*) Southwest (*e*) None of these

**7.** A man walks 5 metres straight and then 10 metres to the right. After this he continuously turns left and every time walks 10, 5 and 10 meters respectively. How far is he now from his starting point?

(*a*) $5\sqrt{3}$ metres (*b*) $3\sqrt{5}$ metres (*c*) $5\sqrt{2}$ metres
(*d*) 10 metres (*e*) None of these

**8.** I walk 1 km to my east then turn to the south and walk for 5 km. Next, I turn east and walk 2 km. After this I turn to the north and walk for 9 km. How far am I from my starting point?

(*a*) 5 km (*b*) 4 km (*c*) 6 km
(*d*) Can't be determined (*e*) None of these

**9.** 'A' is east of 'B' and west of 'C', 'H' is south-west of 'C' and 'B' is south-east of 'X'. Who is the farthest west?

(*a*) C (*b*) A (*c*) B
(*d*) B (*e*) H

**10.** Vishnu walked 30 metres towards East, took a right turn and walked 40 metres. Then he took a left turn and walked 30 metres. In which direction is he now from the starting point?

(*a*) North-East (*b*) East (*c*) South-East
(*d*) South (*e*) None of these

**11.** Kittu walks 10 metres in front and 10 metres to the right. Then every time turning to her left, she walks 5, 15 and 15 metres respectively. How far is she now from her starting point?

(*a*) 10 metres (*b*) 15 metres (*c*) 20 metres
(*d*) 5 metres (*e*) 23 metres

**12.** The post office is to the east of my school while my house is to the south of the school. The market is to the north of the post office. If the distance of the market from the post office is equal to the distance of my house from the school, in which direction is the market with respect to my school?

(*a*) North (*b*) East (*c*) South
(*d*) South-West (*e*) North-East

**13.** Sajid walks a distance of 3 km towards north, then turns to his left and walks for 2 km. He again turns left and walks for 3 km. At this point he again turns to his left and walks for 3 km. How many kilometers is he from the starting point?
(*a*) 1 km (*b*) 2 m (*c*) 3 km
(*d*) 5 km (*e*) None of these

**14.** Of the five villages P, Q, R, S and T situated close to each other, P is to the west of Q, R is to the south of P, and T is to north of Q and S is to the east of T. Then R is in which direction with respect to S?
(*a*) North-west (*b*) South-east (*c*) South-west
(*d*) Data inadequate (*e*) None of these

**15.** One morning after sunrise, Rinku and Sweety were talking to each other face to face at Tilak Square. If Sweety's shadow was exactly to the right of Rinku, in which direction Sweety was facing?
(*a*) North (*b*) South (*c*) East
(*d*) Data inadequate (*e*) None of these

**16.** I am facing South. I turn right and walk 20 m. I turn right again and walk 10 m. I turn left and walk 10 m and then turning right walk 20 m. I turn right again and walk 60 m. In which direction am I from the starting point?
(*a*) North (*b*) North-west (*c*) East
(*d*) North-east (*e*) South

**17.** A postman was returning to the post office which was in front of him to the north. When the post office was 100 metres away from him, he turned to the left and moved 50 metres to deliver the last letter at Shantivilas. He then moved in the same direction for 40 metres, turned to his right and moved 100 metres. How many metres was he away from the post office?
(*a*) 0 (*b*) 90 (*c*) 150
(*d*) 100 (*e*) None of these

**18.** If you are facing north-east and move 10 m forwards, turn left and move 7.5 m, then you are
(*a*) North to your initial position (*b*) South to your initial position
(*c*) East to your initial position (*d*) 12 m from your initial position
(*d*) Both (*c*) and (*d*)

**19.** Ramesh wants to go to the university. He starts from his home which is in east and comes to a crossing. The road to the left ends in a theatre, straight ahead is the hospital. In which direction is the university?

(*a*) North (*b*) South (*c*) East
(*d*) West (*e*) None of these

**20.** A villager went to meet his uncle in another village situated 5 km away in the North-east direction of his own village. From there he came to meet his father-in-law living in a village situated 4 km in the south of his uncle's village. How far away and in what direction is he now?
(*a*) 3 km in the North (*b*) 3 km in the East (*c*) 4 km in the East
(*d*) 4 km in the West (*e*) None of these

**21.** Shakti starts from a point A and travels 3 km eastwards to B and then turns left and travels thrice that distance to reach C. He again turns left and travels five times the distance he covered between A and B and reaches his destination D. The shortest distance between the starting point and the destination is
(*a*) 12 km (*b*) 15 km (*c*) 16 km
(*d*) 18 km (*e*) 21 km

**22.** Sanjay and Mithlesh start walking in opposite direction. Sanjay walked 3 km and Mithlesh walked 4 km. Then Sanjay turned right and walked 4 km and Mithlesh turned left and walked 3 km. How far is each from the starting point?
(*a*) 4.5 km (*b*) 6 km (*c*) 8 km
(*d*) 5 km (*e*) 9 km

**23.** Dipak walks 1 km towards East and then he turns to South and walks 5 km. Again he turns to east and walks 2 km, after this he turns to North and walks 9 km. Now, how far is he from his starting point?
(*a*) 3 km (*b*) 4 km (*c*) 5 km
(*d*) 7 km (*e*) None of these

**24.** Shahid left for his office in his car. He drove 15 km towards north and then 10 km towards west. He then turned to the south and covered 5 km. Further, he turned to the east and moved 8 km. Finally, he turned right and drove 10 km. How far and in which direction is he from his starting point?
(*a*) 2 km West (*b*) 5 km East (*c*) 6 km South
(*d*) 6 km North (*e*) None of these

**Directions (Qs. 25 to 27):** *Read the situation given below to answer these questions.*

*j, k, 1, m, n, o, p, q* and *r* are nine huts. *l* is 2 km east of *k*. *j* is 1 km north of *k* and *q* is 2 km south of *j*. *p* is 1 km west of *q* while *m* is 3 km east of *p* and *o* is 2 km north of *p*. *r* is situated just in middle of *k* and 1 while *n* is just in middle of *q* and *m*.

**25.** Distance between *k* and *l* is:
(*a*) 2 km (*b*) 1 km (*c*) 5 km
(*d*) 1.2 km (*e*) 4 km

**26.** Distance between *k* and *r* is:
(*a*) 1.41 km (*b*) 3 km (*c*) 3.5 km
(*d*) 1 km (*e*) 2 km

**27.** Distance between *p* and *q* is:
(*a*) 4 km (*b*) 2 km (*c*) 1 km
(*d*) 3 km (*e*) 2.5 km

**Directions (Qs. 28 to 32):** *Study the following information carefully to answer the questions. All the streets of a city are either perpendicular or parallel to one another. The streets are all straight. Streets N, O, P, Q and R are parallel to one another. Streets S, T, U, V, W, X and Y are parallel to one another.*

(*i*) Street N is 1 km east of Street O.
(*ii*) Street O is 1/2 km west of Street P.
(*iii*) Street Q is 1 km west of Street R.
(*iv*) Street S is 1/2 km south of Street T.
(*v*) Street U is 1 km north of Street V.
(*vi*) Street W is 1/2 km north of Street X.
(*vii*) Street W is 1 km south of Street Y.

**28.** If street R is between O and P, then distance between N and Q is:
(*a*) 1/2 km (*b*) 1 km (*c*) 1.5 km
(*d*) 1.5 – 2 km (*e*) None of these

**29.** If W is parallel to U and W is 1/2 km south of V and 1 km north of T, then which two streets would be 1 & 1/2 km apart?
(*a*) U and W (*b*) V and S (*c*) V and T
(*d*) W and V (*e*) None of these

**30.** Which of the following is necessarily true (given the basic clues)?
(*a*) R and O intersect
(*b*) W is 1 km North of X
(*c*) V is 1.5 km South of T
(*d*) Distance between U and T is maximum
(*e*) Y is 1.5 km North of X.

**31.** If R is between O and P, then which of the following is false?
(*a*) Q is 1.75 km west of N (*b*) P is less than 1 km from Q
(*c*) R is less than 1 km from N (*d*) Q is less than 1 km from O
(*e*) None of these

**32.** Which of the following possibilities would make two streets coincide?
(*a*) X is 1/2 km north of U (*b*) P is 1 km west of Q
(*c*) Q is 1/2 km east of N (*d*) R is 1/2km east of O
(*e*) None of these

**33.** I start from my home and go 2 km straight. Then, I turn towards my right and go 1 km. I turn again towards my right and go 1 km again. If I am north-west from my house, then in which direction did I go in the beginning?
(*a*) North (*b*) South (*c*) East
(*d*) West (*e*) None of these

**34.** A river flows west to east and on the way turns left and goes in a semi-circle round a hillock, and then turns left at right angles. In which direction is the river finally flowing?
(*a*) West (*b*) East (*c*) North
(*d*) South (*e*) None of these

**Directions (Qs. 35 and 36 ):** *Study the information given below carefully and answer the questions that follow:*

On a playing ground, Pankaj, Vinod, Uday, Raja and Prashant are standing as described below facing the North.

(*i*) Vinod (V) is 40 metres to the right of Raja (R)
(*ii*) Pankaj (PJ) is 60 metres to the south of Vinod (V)
(*iii*) Uday (U) 25 metres to the west Raja (R)
(*iv*) Prashant (P) is 90 metres to the north of Pankaj (PJ).

**35.** Who is to the north-east of the person who is to the left of Vinod (V)?
(*a*) Pankaj (PJ)
(*b*) Uday (U)
(*c*) Either Uday (U) and Pankaj (PJ)
(*d*) Prashant (P)
(*e*) None of these

**36.** If a boy walks from Uday (U), meets Raja (R), followed by Vinod (V), Pankaj (PJ) and then Prashant (P), how many metres has he walked if he has travelled the straight distance all through?
(*a*) 155 metres (*b*) 185 metres (*c*) 215 metres
(*d*) 235 metres (*e*) 245 metres

**Directions (Qs. 37 to 41):** *The following questions are based on the diagram given below showing four persons stationed at the four corners of a square piece of plot as shown.*

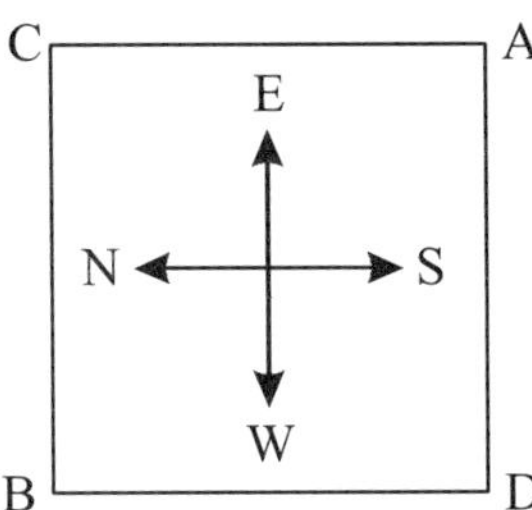


**37.** From the positions in the given figure, C and A move diagonally to opposite corners and then one side each clockwise and anti-clockwise respectively. B and D move two sides each clockwise and anticlockwise respectively. Where is A now?

(*a*) At the North-west corner
(*b*) At the North-east corner
(*c*) At the South-east corner
(*d*) At the South-west corner
(*e*) Midway between original positions of B and D

**38.** After the movements given in above question, who is at the north-west corner?

(*a*) A (*b*) B (*c*) C
(*d*) D (*e*) None of these

**39.** From the original position B and D move one and a half length of sides clockwise and anti-clockwise respectively. Which one of the following statements is true?

(*a*) B and D are both at the midpoint between A and C
(*b*) D is at the midpoint between A and C, and B at the corner originally occupied by C
(*c*) B is at the midpoint between A and C, and D at the midpoint between original positions of B and C
(*d*) B and D are both at the midpoint between A and D
(*e*) None of these

**40.** From the original position given in the above figure, A starts crossing the field diagonally. After walking half the distance, he turns right, walks some distance and turns left. Which direction is A facing now?

(*a*) North-east (*b*) North-west (*c*) North
(*d*) South-east (*e*) South-west

**41.** From the original position given in the above figure A and B move one arm length clockwise and then cross over to the corner diagonally opposite; C and D move one arm length anti-clockwise and cross over the corner diagonally opposite. The original configuration ADBC has now changed to

(*a*) CBDA (*b*) BDAC (*c*) DACB
(*d*) ACBD (*e*) BCAD

**Directions (Qs. 42 and 43):** *Daya, Kamini and Shilpa are standing at the corners of an equilateral triangle piece of plot as shown below in Fig.*

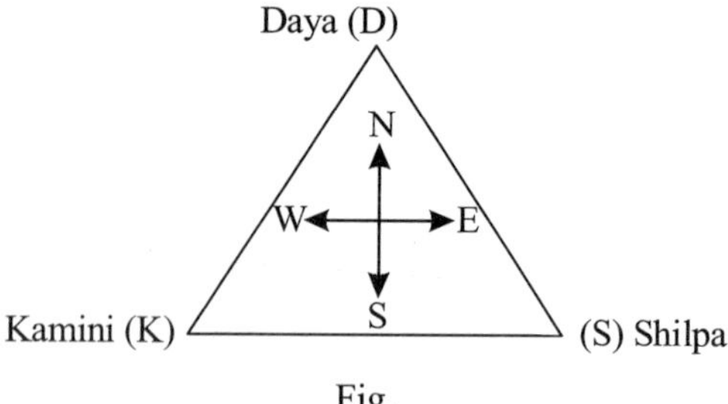


Fig.

The following questions are based on the diagram given above.

**42.** Daya, Kamini and Shilpa run along the sides in clockwise direction from the original position and stop after covering (One and a half) $1\frac{1}{2}$ of sides. Which one of the following statements is true?

(*a*) Kamini is to the North-west of Daya
(*b*) Daya is to the South-west of Shilpa
(*c*) Daya is to the South-east of Kamini
(*d*) Daya is to the South-west of Kamini
(*e*) Daya is to the West of Shilpa

**43.** From the positions mentioned in Q. 42 above, if all of them run in the anticlock wise direction covering two side and then stop. Which one of the following statement is true?

(*a*) Daya is to the South of Shilpa
(*b*) Kamini is to the South-west of Shilpa
(*c*) Daya is to the south of Kamini
(*d*) Daya is to the East of Shilpa
(*e*) Daya is to the South-east of Shilpa

**44.** A square field ABCD of side 90 m is so located that its diagonal AC is from north to south and the corner B is to the west of D. Rohan and Rahul start walking along the sides from B and C respectively in the clockwise and anticlockwise directions with speeds of 8 km/hr and 10 km/hr. Where shall they cross each other the second time?

(*a*) On AD at a distance of 30 m from A
(*b*) On BC at a distance of 10 m from B

(*c*) On AD at a distance of 30 m from D
(*d*) On BC at a distance of 10 m from C
(*e*) None of these

**45.** Sheela starts at point T, walks straight to point U which is 4 ft away. She turns left at 90° and walks to W which is 4 ft away, turns 90° right and goes 3 ft to P, turns 90° right and walks 1 ft to Q, turns left at 90° and goes to V, which is 1 ft away and once again turns 90° right and goes to R, 3 ft away. What is the distance between T and R.

(*a*) 4 ft (*b*) 5 ft (*c*) 6 ft
(*d*) 7 ft (*e*) 8 ft

## ANSWERS

| 1 | 2 | 3 | 4 | 5 | 6 | 7 | 8 | 9 | 10 |
|---|---|---|---|---|---|---|---|---|---|
| (*c*) | (*e*) | (*a*) | (*e*) | (*a*) | (*b*) | (*c*) | (*a*) | (*d*) | (*c*) |
| **11** | **12** | **13** | **14** | **15** | **16** | **17** | **18** | **19** | **20** |
| (*d*) | (*e*) | (*a*) | (*c*) | (*a*) | (*d*) | (*b*) | (*a*) | (*a*) | (*b*) |
| **21** | **22** | **23** | **24** | **25** | **26** | **27** | **28** | **29** | **30** |
| (*b*) | (*d*) | (*c*) | (*a*) | (*a*) | (*d*) | (*c*) | (*d*) | (*a*) | (*e*) |
| **31** | **32** | **33** | **34** | **35** | **36** | **37** | **38** | **39** | **40** |
| (*b*) | (*d*) | (*d*) | (*b*) | (*d*) | (*c*) | (*d*) | (*c*) | (*a*) | (*b*) |
| **41** | **42** | **43** | **44** | **45** | | | | | |
| (*a*) | (*d*) | (*b*) | (*d*) | (*e*) | | | | | |

## SOME SELECTED EXPLANATORY ANSWERS

**1.** In the fig. we see that that the movement is from A to G.

The journey of the rat is from A to B, B to C, C to D, D to E, E to F and F to G.

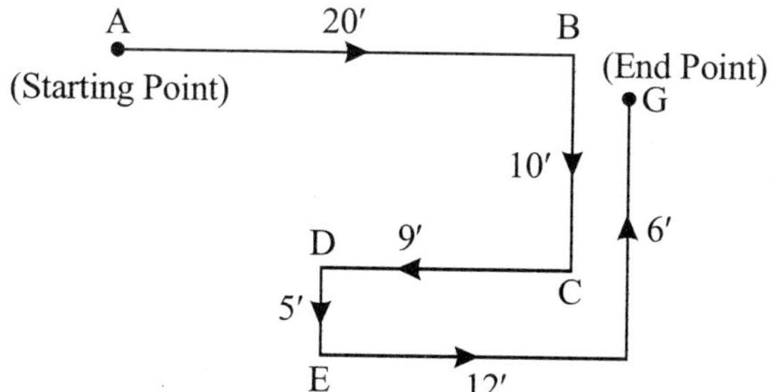


Therefore, the final movement is in the direction FG *i.e.*, North.

2.

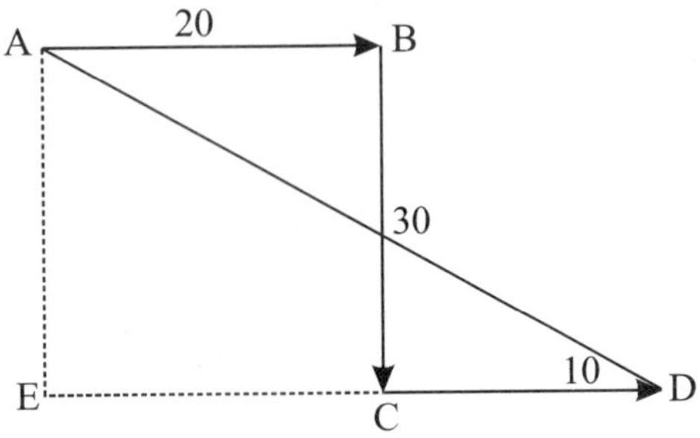


Distance AD = $\sqrt{1800} = 30\sqrt{2}$

Hence, Option (*e*) is the correct answer.

5.

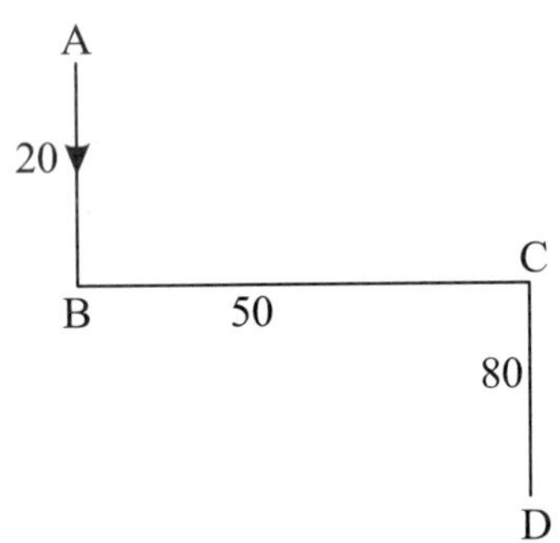


$$AD = \sqrt{50^2 + 100^2}$$

$$\sqrt{12500} = 50\sqrt{5} \text{ metres}$$

Hence, Option (*a*) is the correct answer.

7.

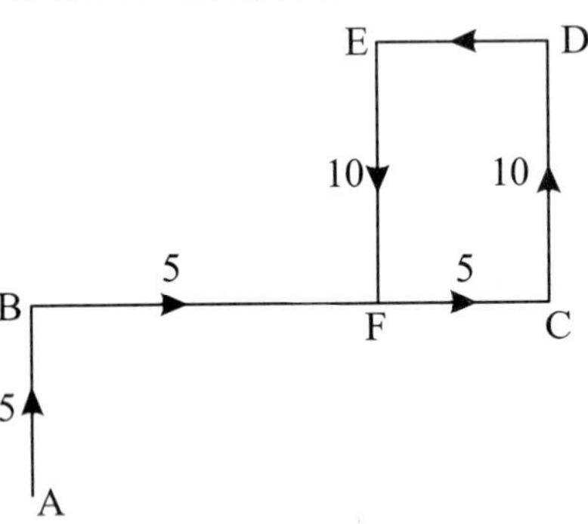


If A is the starting point:

The required distance is seen on AF = $\sqrt{50} = 5\sqrt{2}$.

Hence, Option (*c*) is the correct answer.

**8.**

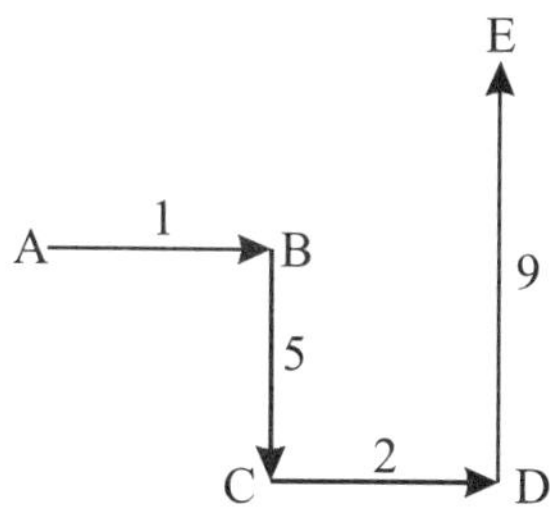


AE = $\sqrt{3^2 + 4^2}$ = 5 km

Hence, Option (*a*) is the correct answer.

**9.** From the Fig. it is clear the B is the farthest west.

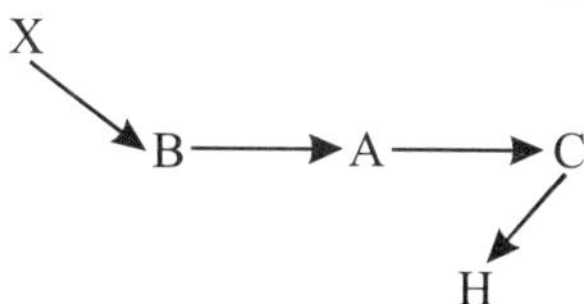


**10.** The movements of Vishnu are as like this:

A to B, B to C and C to D.

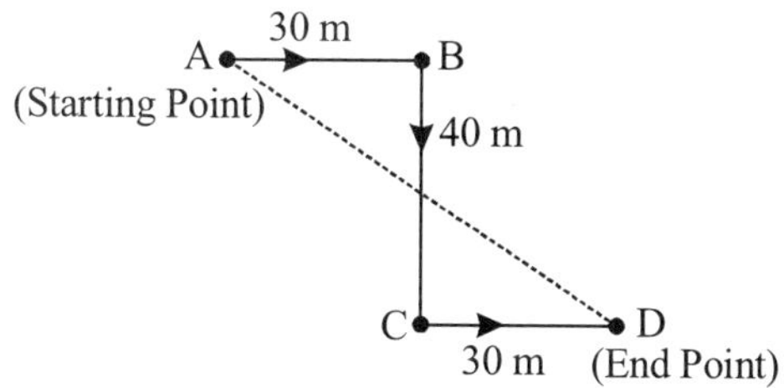


∴ Therefore, his final position is D which is to the South-east of the starting point A.

**11.** The movements of Kittu are as like this:

A to B, B to C, C to D, D to E and E to F.

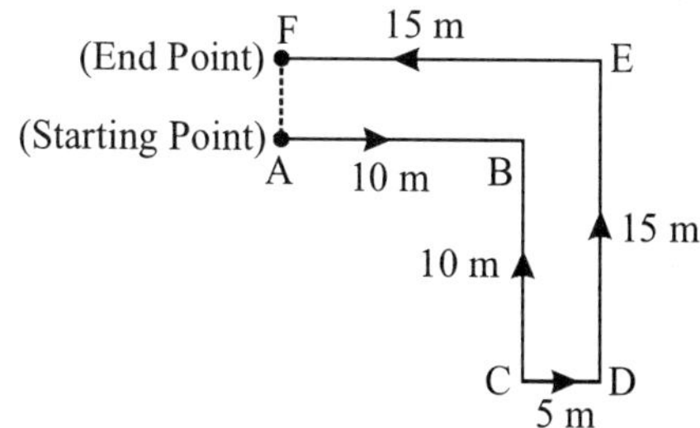

Clearly, FE = AB + CD

So, F is in line with A.

Therefore, Kittu's distance from the starting point

A = AF = (DE – BC)

= (15 – 10)m = 5m.

**12.** From question,

The positions of various places are as shown in Fig.

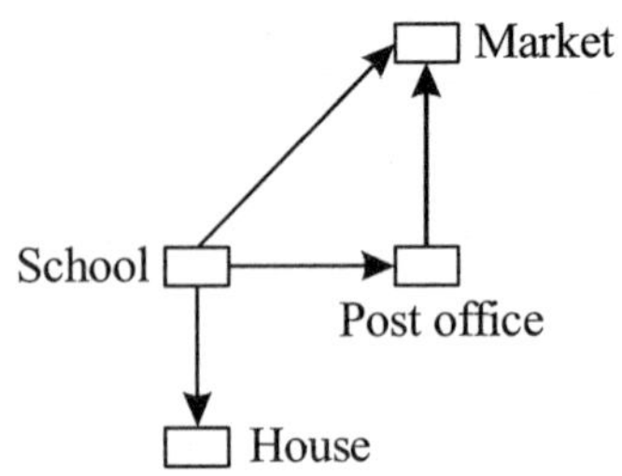


Therefore, the market is to the North-east of school.

**13.** The movements of Sajid are as like this:

A to B, B to C, C to D and D to E.

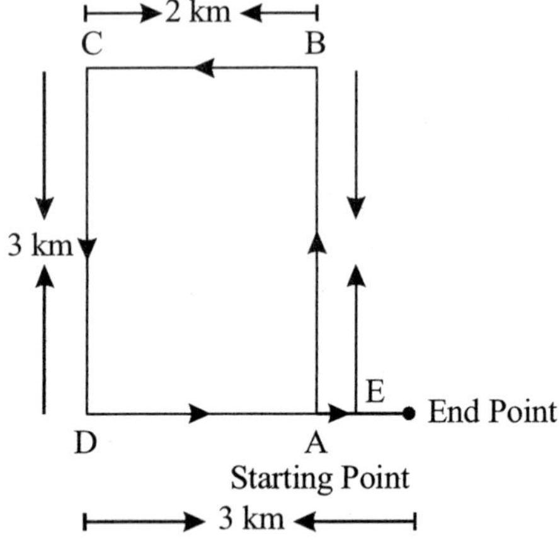


∴ AD = BC = 2 km

Therefore, the required distance = AE

= (DE – AD)

= (3 – 2) = 1 km

**14.** From question, the location of village is as shown in the fig.

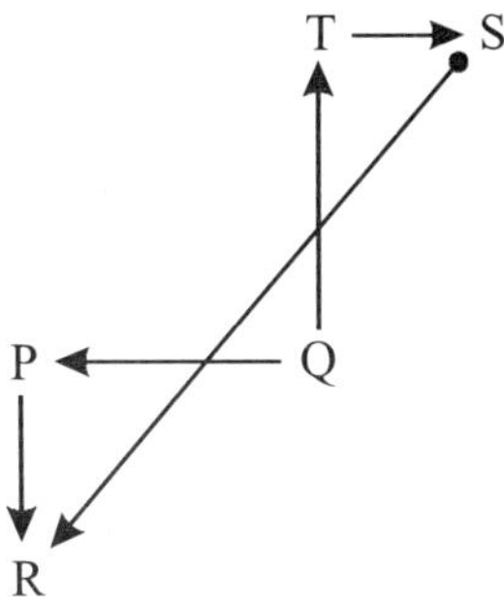


Therefore, R lies to the South-west of S.

**15.** We know that sun rises in the east.

So, the shadow falls towards the west.

Now, Sweety's shadow falls to the right of Rinku as shown in Fig. (*i*) & (*ii*)

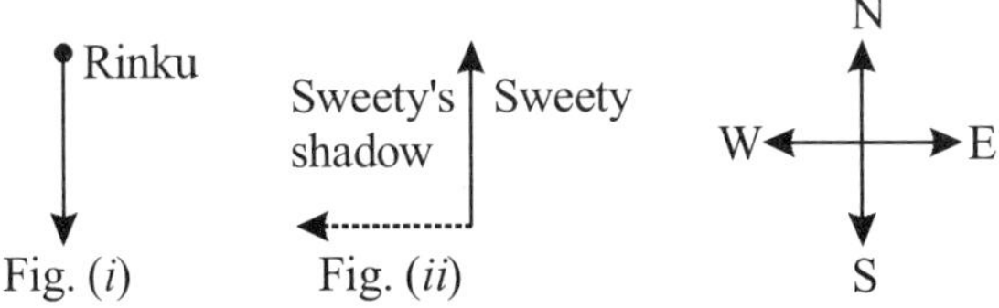


Fig. (*i*) Fig. (*ii*)

Therefore, Rinku is facing south and Sweety is facing North.

**16.** The movements are as shown in Fig. *i.e.*, P to Q, Q to R, R to S, S to T and T to U.

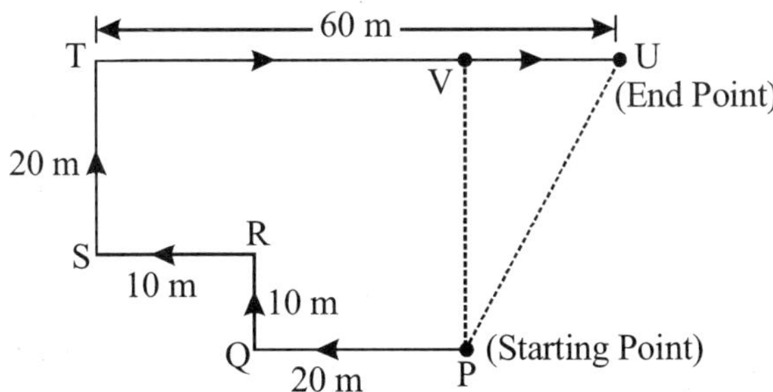


Therefore, the final position is U which is to the North-East of the starting point P.

**17.** The journey of the postman is as shown in Fig. *i.e.*, P to Q, Q to R, R to

S, and S to T.

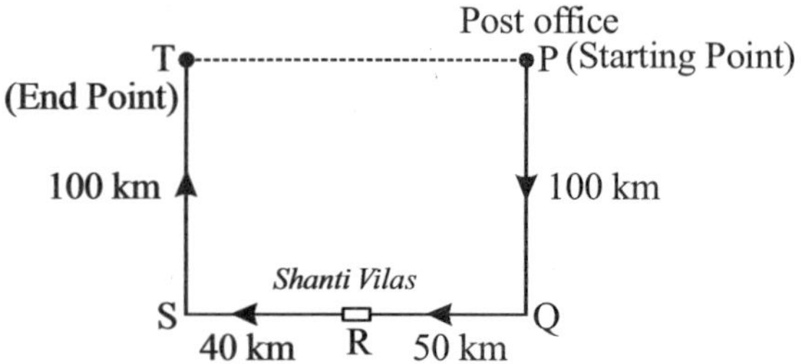


Therefore, at the end point, the distance of Postman from post office TP = QS = (QR + RS) = (50 + 40) m = 90 m

**18.** You starts from P, moves towards North-east a distance of 10 m upto Q, turns left (90° anticlockwise) and moves 7.5 m upto R.

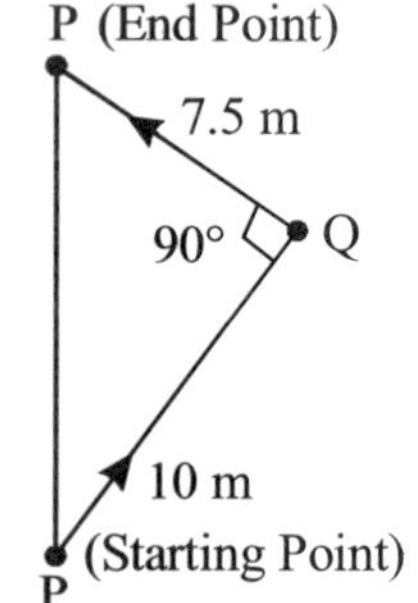


So, R lies to the north of P.

Clearly, ΔPQR is right angled at Q.

So, $PR^2 = PQ^2 + QR^2$

$= (10)^2 + (7.5)^2 = 100 + 56.25$

$= 156.25$

$\Rightarrow \quad PR = \sqrt{156.25}\text{ m} = 12.5\text{ m}$

Therefore, you are 12.5 m to the North of your initial position.

**19.** From question Ramesh moves westwards, after starting from his house in the East. Then, the theatre, which is to the left, will be in the South. Then, the hospital, which is straight ahead, will be to the West.

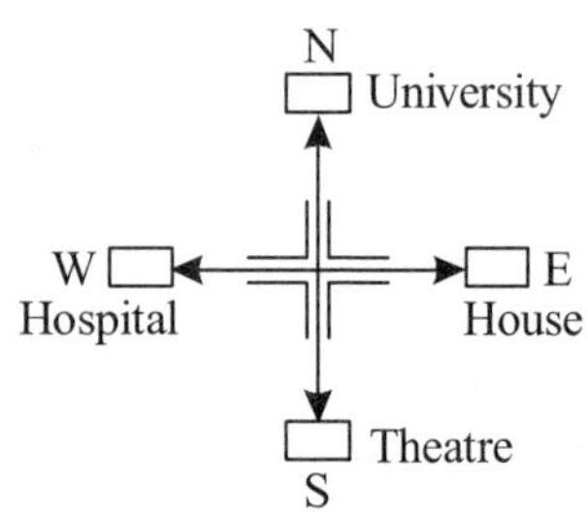

Therefore, the university will be to the North as shown in above Fig.

**20.** From question The movements of the villager are:
*i.e.*, P to Q and Q to R.

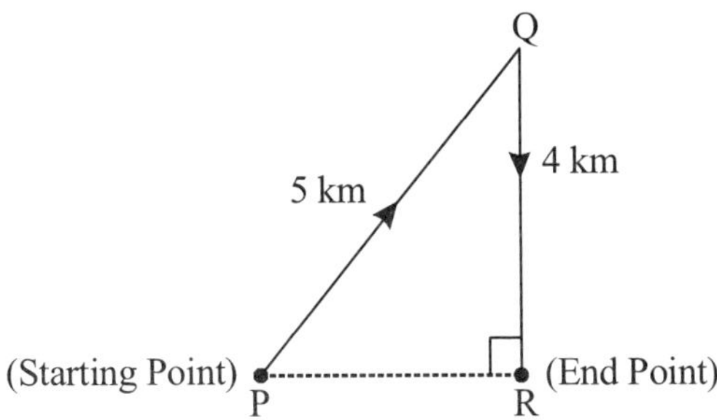


Clearly, ΔPRQ is right and angled at R.

So, $PQ^2 = PR^2 + QR^2$

$\Rightarrow \quad PR^2 = PQ^2 - QR^2$

$\Rightarrow \quad PR = \sqrt{25 - 16}$ km $= \sqrt{9}$ km $= 3$ km

Therefore, R is 3 km to the east of his initial position P.

**21.** The movements of the Shakti is shown below *i.e.*, A to B, B to C and C to D.

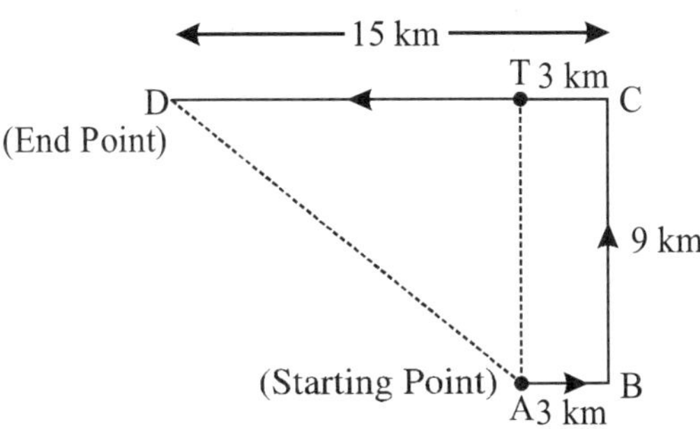


AB = 3 km;

BC = (3 × 3) km = 9 km;

CD = (5 × 3) km = 15 km

Shortest distance AD = $\sqrt{9^2 + 12^2}$ km = $\sqrt{225}$ km = 15 km

Therefore, the required distance AD = 15 km.

22.

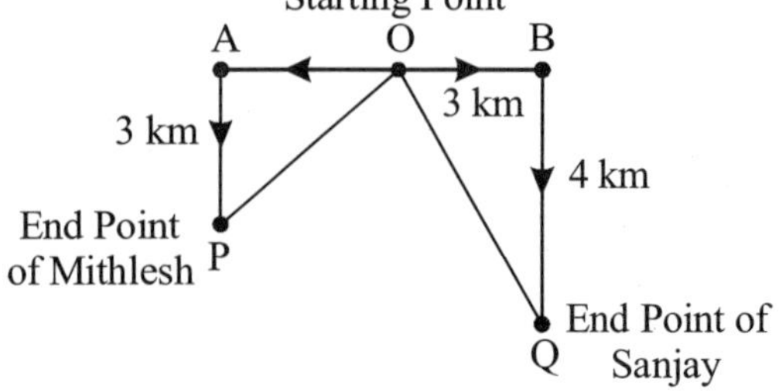


The movements of Mithlesh and Sanjay are as shown in Fig. *i.e.,* O to A & A to P and O to B & B to Q respectively.

Therefore, the required distance from the starting point.

$$O = OP = OQ = \sqrt{4^2 + 3^2} = \sqrt{25} = 5\text{km}$$

**23.** The movements of Dipak is as shown in fig. *i.e.*, P to Q, Q to R, R to S and S to T.

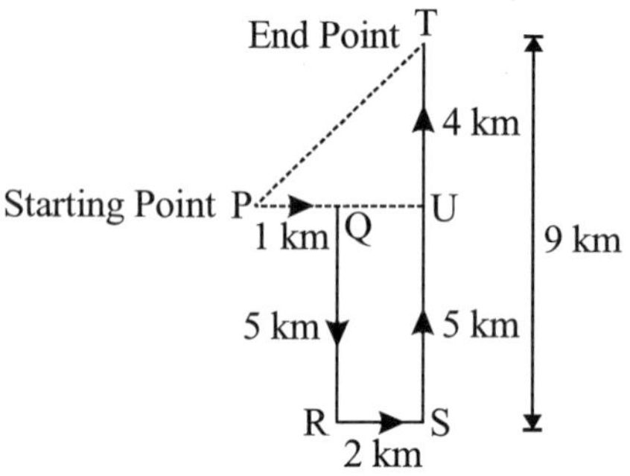


SU = QR = 5 km

TU = (ST – SU) = (9 – 5) km = 4 km

QU = RS = 2 km

PU = PQ + QU = PQ + RS = (1 + 2) km = 3 km

Therefore, Dipak's distance from starting point

$$P = PT = \sqrt{PU^2 + TU^2}$$

$$= \sqrt{3^2 + 4^2} = \sqrt{25} = 5 \text{ km.}$$

**24.** The movements of Shahid is like this: P to Q, Q to R, R to S, S to T and T to U.

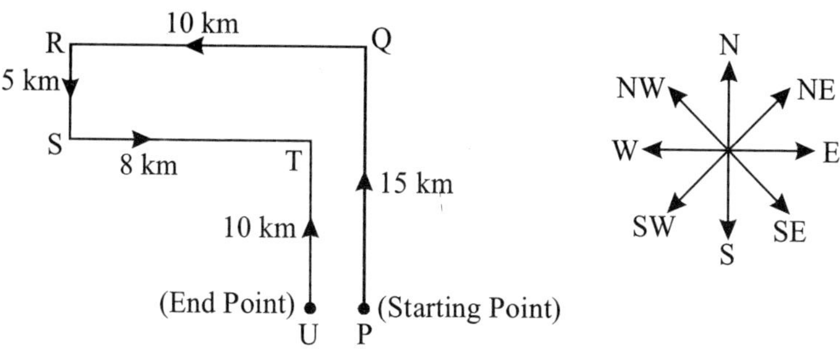


Clearly, P and U lie in the same straight line and U lies to the west of P. Therefore, distance from the starting point

$$P = PU = (QR - ST)$$
$$= (10 - 8) \text{ m} = 2 \text{ km}.$$

**28 to 32.**

The vertical North South streets are N, O, P, Q, R. From the basic information we have two relative positions are available-one between O, P and N and the other between Q and R.

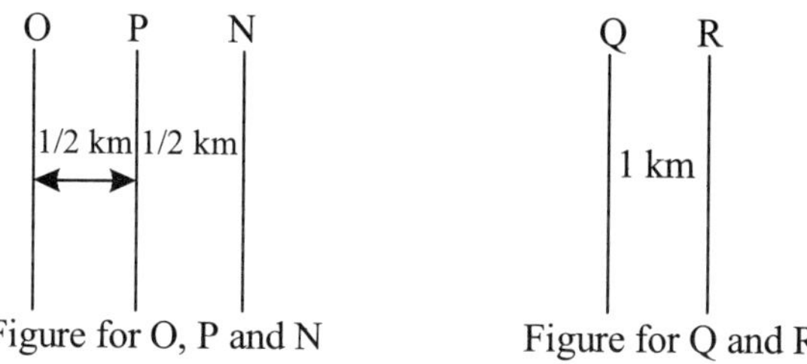


Figure for O, P and N Figure for Q and R

The horizontal eastwest streets are: S, T, U, V, W, X, Y.

Of these seven streets the relative positioning is given in 3 distinct parts as shown here.

T
1/2 km
S

U
1 km
V

Y
1 km
W
1/2 km
X

**28.** If R is placed between O and P, Q to N would be a minimum of 1.5 and a maximum of 2 kms. Option (*d*) is correct.

**29.** The solution is visible from the figure below. Option (*a*) is correct.

| | |
|---|---|
| | U |
| 1/2 km | |
| | Y |
| 1/2 km | |
| | V |
| 1/2 km | |
| | W |
| 1/2 km | |
| | X |
| 1/2 km | |
| | T |
| 1/2 km | |
| | S |

**30.** Y is 1.5 km north of X is correct in all cases as the figure between X, W and Y shows. Option (*e*) is correct.

**31.** If R is between O and P, then Q being 1 km to the west of R, would be more than 1 km to the west of P. Option (*b*) is correct.

**32.** If R 1/2 km east of O, then R and P would coincide. Option (*d*) makes two streets coincide.

**33.** From question The journey of the person is like this: P to Q, Q to R and R to S.

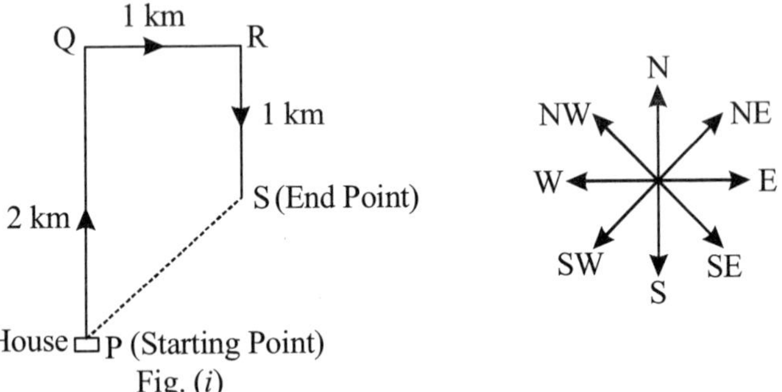


Fig. (*i*)

Also, it is given that the person is finally to the north-west of his house. So, we have to rotate Fig. (*i*) 90° anticlockwise to satisfy the specified conditions.

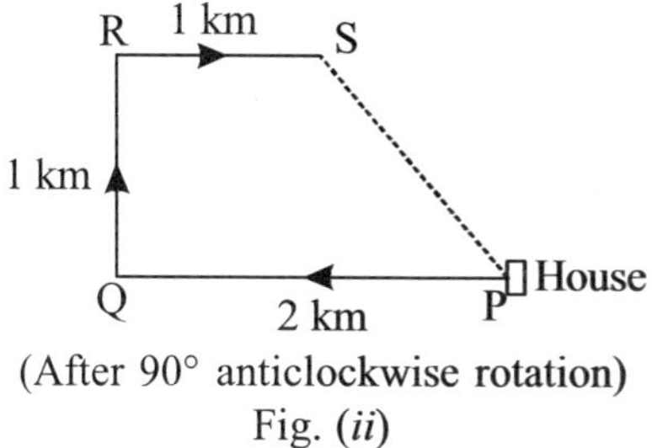

(After 90° anticlockwise rotation)
Fig. (*ii*)

Therefore, from Fig. (*ii*) itis clear that the direction of walking in the beginning was West.

**34.** From the question it is clear that the river flows eastwards from P towards Q. Then turns left and follows a semi-circular path to reach R where it again turns left and finally flows towards S *i.e.*, eastwards.

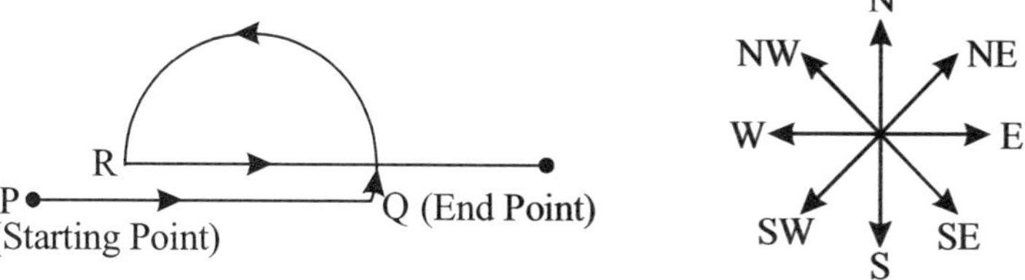


Therefore, River is finally flowing in East direction.

**36.** According to the given arrangement

The required distance

$$= UR + RV + V(PJ) + (PJ)P$$
$$= (25 + 40 + 60 + 90)\text{ m} = 215\text{ m}$$

**37.** Based on question New positions of A, B, C and D are shown in the fig. within the circles.

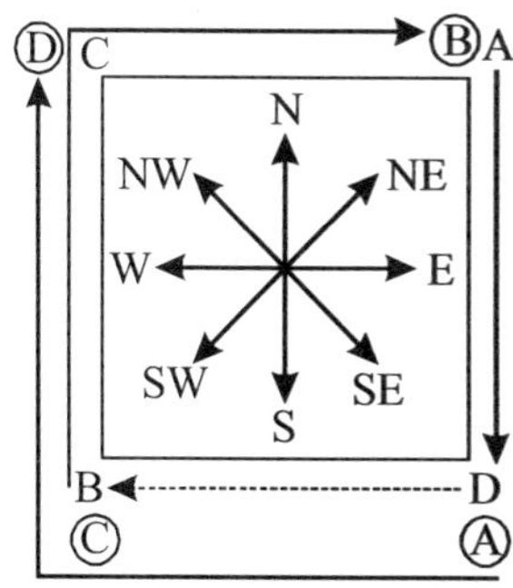


Therefore, 'A' is in the South-west corner.

**38.** From the above Fig. it is clear that 'C' is at the North-west corner.

**39.** The movements of B and D are shown in Fig.

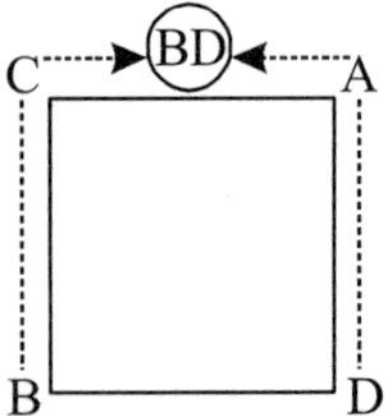


Therefore, B and D are both at the midpoint between A and C.

**40.** The route of 'A' is like this:

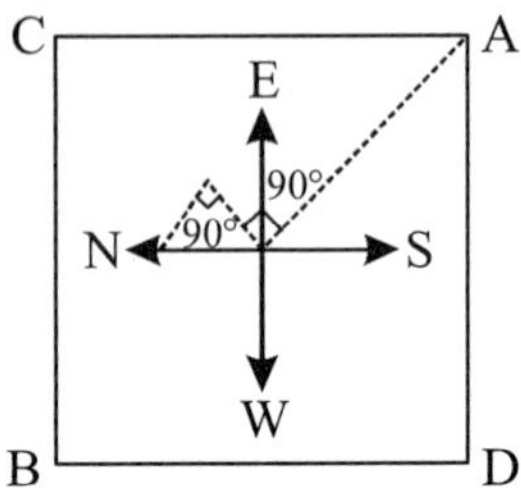


From the Fig., it is clear that A is facing North-west.

**41.** In Fig., $A_1$, $B_1$, $C_1$ and $D_1$ are original positions of A, B, C, & D. $A_2$, $B_2$, $C_2$ and $D_2$ are positions after 1[st] movement of A, B, C and D. $A_3$, $B_3$, $C_3$ and $D_3$ are final positions.

Therefore, the final configuration of ADBC has now CBDA.

$C_1B_2A_3$ $A_1D_2C_3$

$B_2$ $D_2$

$C_2$ $A_2$

$B_1C_2D_3$ $D_1A_2B_3$

**42.**

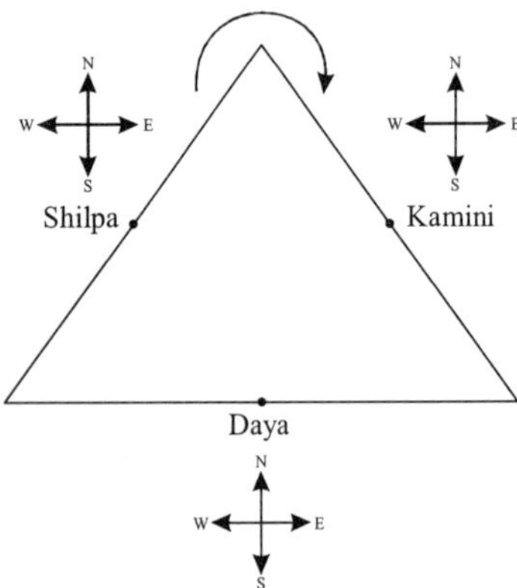


From the given Fig., it is clear that Daya is to the South-west of Kamini.

**43.**

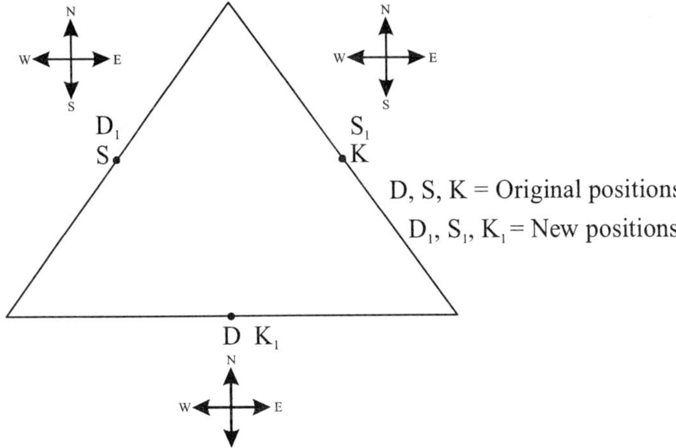


From the given Fig., it is clear that Kamini is to the South-west of Shilpa.

**44.** Based on the question the arrangement of two is as shown in the Fig.

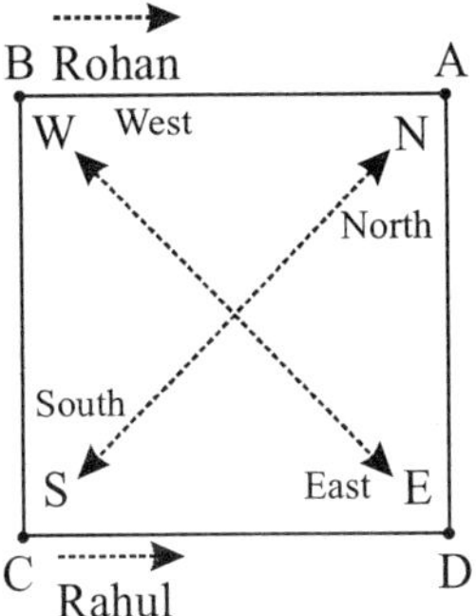


Rohan takes the route BADCB at 8 km/hr

$$\frac{8000}{60 \times 60} = \frac{20}{9} \text{ m/sec.}$$

Rahul takes the route CDABC at 10 km/hr

$$\frac{10000}{60 \times 60} = \frac{25}{9} \text{ m/sec.}$$

Let's assume they meet first time at time t. Therefore, distance covered by Rohan = $\frac{20}{9}$t and distance covered by Rahul = $\frac{25}{9}$t.

When they meet first time, they have together covered total of 3 sides i.e., $90 \times 3 = 270$ m. So $\frac{20}{9}t + \frac{25}{9}t = 270$

This gives t = 54 sec. So distance (Rahul) = $\frac{25}{9} \times 54 = 150$ m and

distance (Rohan) = $\frac{20}{9} \times 54 = 120$ m. This meeting point is between A and D at distance of 30 m from A.

When they meet the second time, they have travelled the entire perimeter of the square together. Again assuming that they meet after time T; so now the equation becomes

$$\frac{20}{9}T + \frac{25}{9}T = 90 \times 4 \Rightarrow T = 72 \text{ sec.}$$

So distance (Rahul) = $\frac{25}{9} \times 72 = 200$ m and

distance (Rohan) = $\frac{20}{9} \times 72 = 160$ m.

Therefore, on BC at a distance of 10 m from C they cross each other the second time.

**45.** It is clear from the question that T to U, U to W, W to P, P to Q, Q to V and V to R are the movements of Sheela.

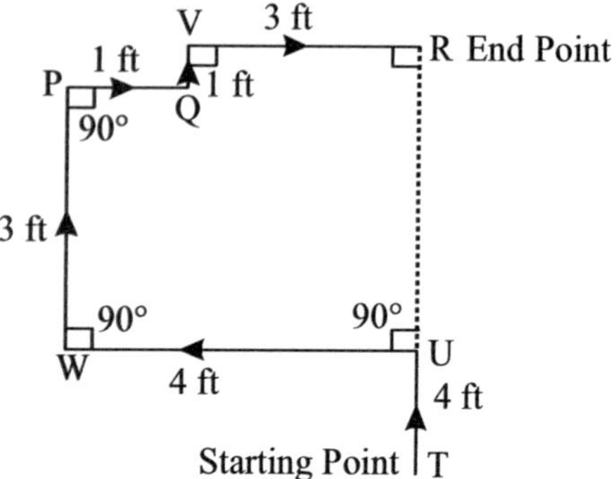


∴ Therefore, distance between T and R

$$= TR = TU + UR$$
$$= TU + PW + QV$$
$$= (4 + 3 + 1) \text{ ft} = 8 \text{ ft.}$$

# Row & Rank

## INTRODUCTION

Row and Ranking is based on arrangement of characters/persons/objects in a particular order based on some specific characteristics.

In these type of questions, the candidate has to find out the number of objects in a row, queue or lane; or to find a person's rank both from the top and from the bottom in a class of certain number of persons; or to find the total number of persons in a given row.

## SOLVED EXAMPLE

**1.** How many even numbers are there in the following series of numbers, each of which is preceded by an odd number, but not followed by an even number?

5 3 4 8 9 7 1 6 5 3 2 9 8 7 3 5

(*a*) Nil (*b*) 1 (*c*) 2 (*d*) 3

**Sol.** (*d*) 5 3 4 8 9 7 1 6 5 3 2 9 8 7 3 5

There are three such even numbers 6, 2 and 8 each of which is preceded by an odd number and not followed by an even number.

**2.** In a class of 42 students, Pana's rank is 16th from the bottom. What is his rank from the top?

(*a*) 25th (*b*) 26th (*c*) 24th (*d*) 27th

**Sol.** (*d*) Number of students ahead of Pana's = 42 – 16 = 26

Now Pana's rank from top = 26 + 1 = 27

So, Pana's rank is 27th from the top.

This question can be solved by formula also.

Rank of a person from upper or left end = (Total number of persons in the row) – (Rank of that person from lower or right end) + 1

∴ Panas rank from the top = 42 – 16 + 1 = 27.

**3.** If every second Saturdays and all Sundays are holidays in a 30 days month beginning on Saturday, then how many working days are there in that month?

(*a*) 20 (*b*) 21 (*c*) 22 (*d*) 23

**Sol.** (*d*) As the month begins on Saturday. So, 2nd, 9th, 16th, 23rd, 30th days are Sundays, while 8th and 22nd are second Saturdays. Thus, there are 7 holidays in all.

∴ Number of working days = 30 – 7 = 23.

## EXERCISE

**1.** Dipak ranks eighteenth in a class of 48 students. What is his rank from the last?
(*a*) 31 (*b*) 32 (*c*) 19 (*d*) 18

**2.** In a class of 45 students, Yogesh is ranked 20th. When two boys joined, his rank dropped by one. What is his new rank from the end?
(*a*) 25th (*b*) 26th (*c*) 27th (*d*) 28th

**3.** In a row of girls, there are 16 girls between deepa and Nada. Deepa is thirty-second from the left end of the row. If Deepa is nearer than Nada to the right end of the row, then how far away is Nada from the left end of the row?
(*a*) 16th (*b*) 15th
(*c*) Data Inadequate (*d*) None of these

**4.** Tinku ranks seventh from the top and twenty-sixth from the bottom in a class. How many students are there in the class?
(*a*) 31 (*b*) 32 (*c*) 33 (*d*) 34

**5.** In a class of 35 students, Ganesh is placed 7th from the bottom whereas Abhishek is placed 9th from the top. Seema is placed exactly in between Ganesh and Abhishek. What is Ganesh's position from Seema?
(*a*) 9th (*b*) 11th (*c*) 13th (*d*) 10th

**6.** There are 25 boys in a horizontal row. Satyam was shifted by three places towards his right side and he occupies the middle position in the row. What was his origianl position from the left end of the row?
(*a*) 15th (*b*) 16th (*c*) 12th (*d*) 10th

**7.** In a row of children, Parul is fifteenth from the left end of the row. If she is shifted towards the right end of the row by four places, she becomes eighth from the right end. How many children are there in the row?
(*a*) 24 (*b*) 28 (*c*) 26 (*d*) None of these

**8.** Manas is fourteenth from the right end in a row of 40 girls. What is his position from the left end?
(*a*) 26th (*b*) 28th (*c*) 25th (*d*) 27th

**9.** The positions of how many digits in the number '5314687' will remain unchanged after the digits are rearranged in ascending order?
(*a*) None (*b*) One (*c*) Two (*d*) Three

**10.** How many '8s' are followed by an even number and also preceded by an odd number?

184381483287848568784186

(*a*) 3 (*b*) 4 (*c*) 9 (*d*) 5

**11.** Three person Ahmed, Vishwas and Rajat are standing in a queue. There are five persons between Ahmed and Vishwas and eight persons between Vishwas and Rajat. If there are three persons ahead of Rajat and 21 behind Ahmed then what could be the minimum number of persons in the queue?

(*a*) 26 (*b*) 27 (*c*) 29 (*d*) 28

**12.** Raja walks slower than Raghu and Raghu walks as fast as Guru and Krishna walks faster than Guru. Who walks the fastest?

(*a*) Raghu (*b*) Raja

(*c*) Krishna (*d*) Both Raghu and Guru

**13.** If the 5th date of a month is Tuesday, what date will be 3 days after the 3rd Friday in the month?

(*a*) 19 (*b*) 18 (*c*) 17 (*d*) 22

**14.** In a row of boys facing the north, Sunil is sixteenth from the left end and Ajay is sixteenth from the right end. Dinesh, who is fourth to the right of Sunil, is fifth to the left of Ajay in the row. How many boys are there in the row?

(*a*) 38 (*b*) 42 (*c*) 43 (*d*) 40

**15.** The positions of how many digits in the number 837912 will remain unchanged after the digits within the number are rearranged in descending order (from left to right)?

(*a*) None (*b*) One (*c*) Two (*d*) Three

**16.** Consider five people A, B, C, D and E, each having different age. A is younger only to B. C is elder than D. D is not the youngest. Who amongst the following are elder than C?

(*a*) A and B (*b*) E, B and A (*c*) A and E (*d*) E and B

**17.** In a queue of children, Lovely is fifth from the left and Riya is sixth from the right. When they interchange their places among themselves, Lovely becomes thirteenth from the left. Then, what will be Riya's position from the right?

(*a*) 15th (*b*) 14th (*c*) 9th (*d*) 8th

**18.** In a queue I am the last person while my friend is Seventh from the front. If the person exactly between me and my friend is on the 23rd position from the front, what is my position in the queue?

(*a*) 37 (*b*) 36 (*c*) 38 (*d*) 39

**19.** In a queue, Mr. X is fourteenth from the front and Mr. Y is seventeenth from the end, while Mr. Z is exactly in between Mr. X and Mr. Y. If Mr. X is ahead of Mr. Y and there are 48 persons in the queue, how many persons are there between Mr. X and Mr. Z?

(*a*) 6 (*b*) 7 (*c*) 8 (*d*) 9

**20.** Praveen correctly remembers that his father's birthday is after 21st May but before 27th May whereas his sister correctly remembers that their father's birthday is after 24th May but before 30th May. On which day in May was definitely their father's birthday?

(*a*) 25th (*b*) 24th (*c*) 26th (*d*) 25th or 26th

**21.** If in a clock, 12 is replaced by 1, 11 by 2, 10 by 3 and so on, and the clock is running anticlockwise then what will be the time in that clock corresponding to 'twenty minutes past three in the usual Clock'?

(*a*) Twenty minutes past eleven (*b*) Forty minutes past ten
(*c*) Forty minutes past nine (*d*) Twenty minutes past ten

**22.** There are 30 plants of Chiku, Guava, Sitafal and Mango in a row. There is one pair of Mango plants after Chiku and Guava which are followed by one Chiku and one Sitafal plant and so on. If the row begins with a plant of Chiku, then which of the following will be the last in the row?

(*a*) Guava (*b*) Mango (*c*) Chiku (*d*) Sitafal

**23.** In a group of five districts, Lakhisarai is smaller than Barh, Biharsharif is bigger than Sheikhpura and Patna is bigger than Barh but not as big as Sheikhpura. Which district is the biggest?

(*a*) Lakhisaria (*b*) Barh (*c*) Biharsharif (*d*) Sheikhpura

**24.** Five birds Crow, Pigeon, Little pigeon, Big crow and Eagle fly one after other from a tree branch. Big crow flew after Crow but is ahead of Eagle. Pigeon is between Crow and Big crow. Little pigeon is before Crow. Which bird is in the last?

(*a*) Pigeon (*b*) Big crow (*c*) Eagle (*d*) None of these

**25.** In a shop, the items were arranged in a shelf consisting of six rows. Biscuits were arranged above the tins of chocolates but below the rows of packets of chips. Cakes were at the bottom and the bottles of peppermints were below the chocolates the topmost row had the display of jam bottles. Where exactly were the bottles of peppermints? (Mention the place from the top.)

(*a*) 2nd (*b*) 3rd (*c*) 4th (*d*) 5th

**26.** In a class, Neha's rank is 21st from the top and 30th from the bottom. What is the total number of students in that class?

(*a*) 48 (*b*) 49 (*c*) 50 (*d*) 51

**27.** Fifteen students are standing in a horizontal row from left to right. If all the odd numbered students in the row are shifted to successive odd-numbered positions, what will be the position of Sonam who was 7th from the left end in the row initially?

(*a*) 8th from the left end (*b*) 7th from the right end
(*c*) 8th from the right end (*d*) 7th from the left end

**28.** Sneha correctly remembers that her father's birthday is before 16th June but after 11th June whereas, her younger brother correctly remembers that their father's birthday is after 13th June but before 18th June and her elder brother birthday is on an even date. On what date, in June, is definitely their father's birthday?
(*a*) 15th (*b*) 13th (*c*) 14th (*d*) None of these

**Directions (Qs. 29-30):** *Study the following arrangement of numbers carefully and answer the questions that follow.*

5 7 9 4 8 2 4 2 5 7 8 4 2
9 2 4 8 7 5 2 1 2 5 4 9 7

**29.** How many such digits are there in the above arrangement each of which is followed by a digit which has a greater value than the previous digit?
(*a*) Eleven (*b*) Seven (*c*) Eight (*d*) None of these

**30.** How many such even digits are there in the above arrangement which is immediately preceded and also immediately followed by an odd number?
(*a*) Three (*b*) Four (*c*) Five (*d*) Six

**Directions (Qs. 31-35):** *Study the sets of numbers given below and answer the questions.*

972 682 189 298 751

**31.** If one is added to the lowest number and two is added to the highest number, what will be the difference between the second digit of the smallest number and third digit of the highest number?
(*a*) 5 (*b*) 7 (*c*) 9 (*d*) 8

**32.** If in each number, first and the last digit are interchanged, which one of the following will be the third highest number?
(*a*) 972 (*b*) 682 (*c*) 189 (*d*) 298

**33.** If in each number, all the three digits are arranged in descending order, which of the following will be the third highest number?
(*a*) 972 (*b*) 682 (*c*) 189 (*d*) 298

**34.** If in each number, second and third digit are interchanged, what will be the sum of first digit of the smallest number and last digit of highest number?
(*a*) 7 (*b*) 6 (*c*) 9 (*d*) 8

**35.** If one is added to the smallest odd number and one is subtracted from the highest odd number, which of the following will be obtained, if the second digit of that higher odd number is subtracted from the second digit of that lower odd number thus formed?
(*a*) 6 (*b*) 5 (*c*) 4 (*d*) 3

## ANSWERS

| 1 | 2 | 3 | 4 | 5 | 6 | 7 | 8 | 9 | 10 |
|---|---|---|---|---|---|---|---|---|---|
| (*a*) | (*c*) | (*b*) | (*b*) | (*d*) | (*d*) | (*c*) | (*d*) | (*c*) | (*b*) |
| **11** | **12** | **13** | **14** | **15** | **16** | **17** | **18** | **19** | **20** |
| (*d*) | (*c*) | (*b*) | (*d*) | (*b*) | (*a*) | (*b*) | (*d*) | (*c*) | (*d*) |
| **21** | **22** | **23** | **24** | **25** | **26** | **27** | **28** | **29** | **30** |
| (*c*) | (*d*) | (*c*) | (*c*) | (*d*) | (*c*) | (*b*) | (*c*) | (*d*) | (*a*) |
| **31** | **32** | **33** | **34** | **35** | | | | | |
| (*a*) | (*b*) | (*a*) | (*d*) | (*c*) | | | | | |

## SOME SELECTED EXPLANATORY ANSWERS

**1.** Dipak's rank from the start or front = 18th.
So, Dipak's rank from the last

$$= (48 - 18) + 1 = 30 + 1 = 31.$$

**Trick:** Ranking of a student from the last or bottom = (total no. of students – Ranking of a student from the top) + 1.

**2.** When two boys joined, the rank of the boy dropped by one i.e., it became 21st from 20th among 47 students.

Then his rank from behind = 47- 21 + 1 = 27th.

**3.** Deepa's rank from the left end = 32nd
∵ Deepa is nearer than Nada to the right end.
Therefore, Nada's rank from the left end

$$= [32 - (16 + 1)]$$
$$= 15\text{th or, } (32 - 18) + 1 = 14 + 1 = 15\text{th}$$

**4.** Total student in the class = 7 + 26 – 1 = 33 – 1 = 32.

**5.** Ganesh's rank from the bottom = 7th
Abhishek's rank from the top = 9th
So, Ganesh's rank from the top = (35 – 7) + 1 = 29th

Seema's rank from the top = $\dfrac{9 + 29}{2}$ = 19th

So, Ganesh's rank or position from Seema = (29 – 19) = 10th.

**6.** When Satyam was shifted by three places towards his right side, then he occupies the middle position, *i.e.*, 13th position.

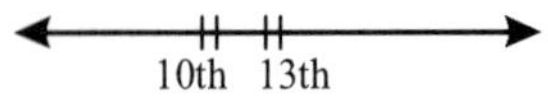


Thus, his original position from the left end of the row = 13 – 3 = 10th

**7.** Parul's rank from the left end = 15th

Parul's rank from the left end after shifting 4 places = (15 + 4) = 19th.

Parul's rank from the right end after shifting = 8th.

So, total number of children in the row = (19 + 8) – 1 = 27 – 1 = 26.

**8.** Manas's rank from the right end = 14th.

Manas's rank from the left end = (40 – 14) + 1 = 26 + 1 = 27th.

[**Trick:** *Requred rank from the left end = (total no. of girls – rank from the right end) + 1.*]

**9.**

| 5 | 3 | 1 | 4 | 6 | 8 | 7 |
|---|---|---|---|---|---|---|
| 1 | 3 | 4 | 5 | 6 | 7 | 8 |

Hence, two digits 3 and 6 will remain unchanged.

**10.** 184381 4832878485 68784186

There are four such pairs which are followed by even number and preceded by odd number.

**11.** Rajat's rank from the top = 4th

Ahmed's rank from the top = 7th (3 people + 4th Rajat + 2 people)

Ahmed's rank from the bottom = 22nd

To find minimum number of persons in the queue, assume Vishwas is behind Ahmed.

So, the minimum number of persons in the queue = (7 + 22) – 1 = 28.

**12.** Based on the question the arrangement of four in increasing order

Raja < Raghu < Guru < Krishna

Hence, Krishna is the fastest from all of them.

**13.** If the 5th day of the month is Tuesday. Then, first day of the month will be Friday. The third Friday will fall on 15th of the month. So, the date 3 days after 3rd Friday will be 18th.

**14.** Sunil's rank from the left end = 16th

Ajay's rank from the right end = 16th

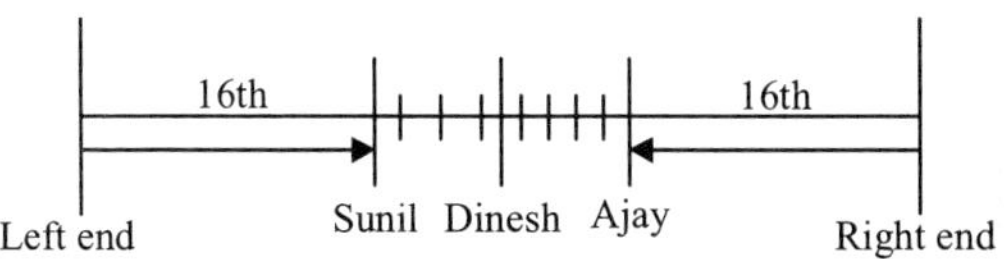


So, total no. of boys in the row = 40.

**15.** Given number — 8 3 7 9 1 2

Descending order — 9 8 7 3 2 1

Hence, only one number 7's position will remain unchanged.

**16.** Arrange the people according to their age,

$$B > A > C > D > E \quad ...(i)$$

From Eq. (*i*), we can say that A and B are older than C.

**17.** **Before Interchanging:**

Lovely's rank from the left end = 5th

Riya's rank from the right end = 6th

**After Interchanging:**

Lovely's rank from the left end = 13th

So, total number of children = (13 + 6) – 1 = 18.

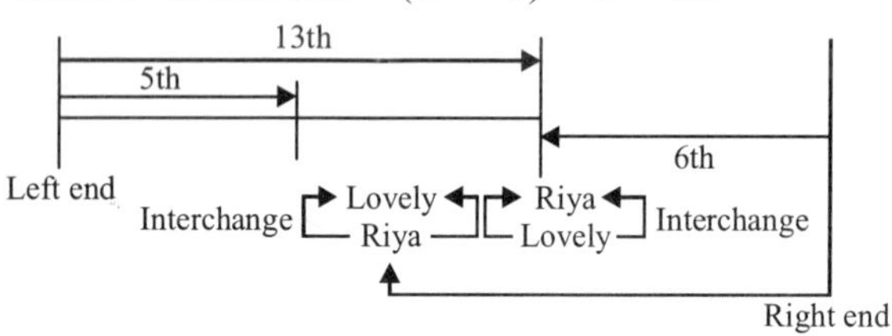


So, Riya's position or rank from the right end

= (18 – 5) + 1 = 14th.

**18.** Friend's rank from the front i.e. left end = 7th

Persons's rank from the front i.e. Left end = 23rd

Therefore people in between my friend and person = 15. So 15 more people stand between myself and the person as well.

∴ My position from left = (23 + 15) + 1 = 39th.

**19.** The arrangement can be drawn as

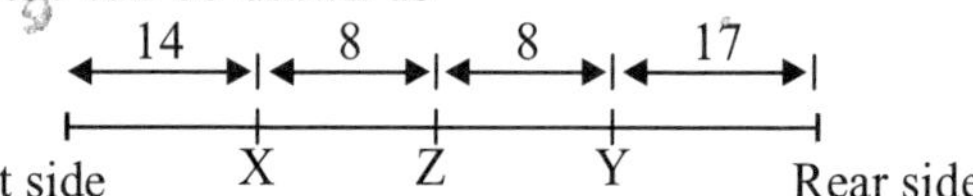


Position of Z will be after (14 + 8) = 22th place.

Hence, Number of Person between X and Z is 8.

**20.** According to Praveen — 22, 23, 24, (25), (26)

According to his sister — (25), (26), 27, 28, 29

So, Common date is 25 or 26.

**21.** 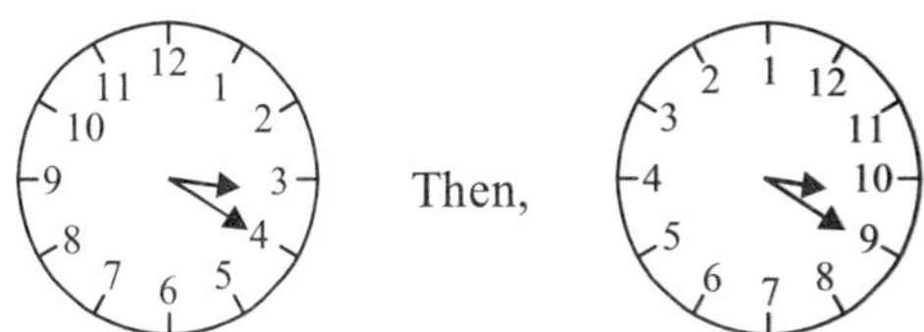


Normal clock Number change clock

So, the time will be 'Forty minute past nine'. (Clock rotates anticlockwise)

**22.** The order of given plants is as follows:

| | | Pair | | | | |
|---|---|---|---|---|---|---|
| Chiku | Guava | Mango | Mango | Chiku | Sitafal | ......... |
| 1 | 2 | 3 | 4 | 5 | 6 | 7 |

Therefore, the required 30th plant = Sitafal.

**23.** Based on question, the arrangement of five districts from smallest to largest is like this:

Lakhisarai < Barh < Patna < Sheikhpura < Biharsharif.

Hence, biggest district is Biharsharif.

**24.** Arranging all birds in descending order according to distance,

Little pigeon > Crow > Pigeon > Big crow > Eagle.

Hence, Eagle is in the last.

**25.** 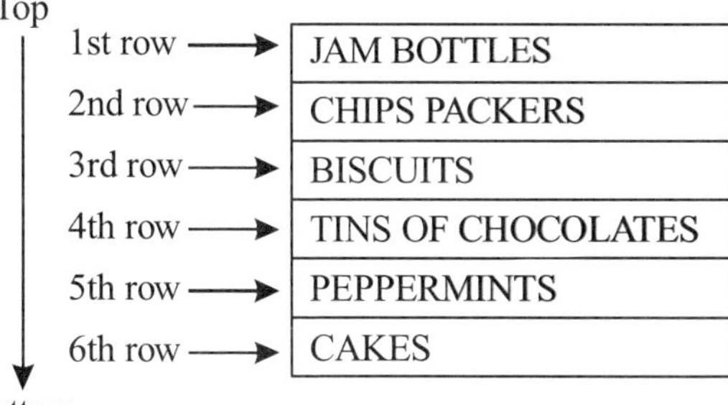


Bottom

Therefore, Peppermints from the top = 5th.

**26.** Total number of students = Total of both side rank – 1

= 21 + 30 – 1 = 50

**27.** Initially, Sonam's rank from the left end = 7th

So, Sonam's rank after shifting to successive odd-numbered

= 7th from the right end.

**28.** According to — Birth Date

| According to | Birth Date |
|---|---|
| Sneha | 12, 13, (14), 15 |
| Younger Brother | (14), 15, 16, 17 |
| Elder Brother | ..., (14), 16, ... |

Hence, confirmed date is fourteenth.

**29.** 5 $\underline{7}$ $\underline{9}$ 4 $\underline{8}$ 2 $\underline{4}$ 2 $\underline{5}$ $\underline{7}$ $\underline{8}$ 4 2 $\underline{9}$ 2 $\underline{4}$ $\underline{8}$ 7 5 2 1 $\underline{2}$ $\underline{5}$ 4 $\underline{9}$ 7

⇒ Thirteen.

**30.** 5 7 9 4 8 2 5 7 8 4 2 9 2 4 8 7 5 $\underline{2}$ 1 $\underline{2}$ 5 $\underline{4}$ 9 7 ⇒ Three

**31.** Given, 972, 682, 189, 298, 751

Make Changes +2 +1

Changed Series 974, 682, 190, 298, 751

∴ Difference = 9 – 4 = 5.

**32.** Changed Series →

| 279, | 286, | 981, | 892, | 157 |
|---|---|---|---|---|
| $\boxed{4}$ | $\boxed{3}$ | $\boxed{1}$ | $\boxed{2}$ | $\boxed{5}$ |

**33.** Series in desending order

| 972, | 862, | 981, | 982, | 751 |
|---|---|---|---|---|
| $\boxed{3}$ | $\boxed{4}$ | $\boxed{2}$ | $\boxed{1}$ | $\boxed{5}$ |

**34.** After interchanging

927, 628, 198, 289, 715

Sum

8

**35.** Series 972, 682, 189, 298, 751

+1 –1

972, 682, 190, 298, 750

Series changed difference = 9 – 5 = 4.

✧✧✧✧

# 8

# Puzzle Test

## INTRODUCTION

Reasoning puzzles are a favourite question type in all aptitude examinations.

As the name suggests, questions on puzzles challenge you to match multiple factors (like name, colour of shirt, place of living, car model driven, etc.). The key skills involved in solving questions on puzzles include knowledge but are not limited to it. These also include:

(*i*) The ability to make a relevant tabular structure for using the clues seamlessly: For example, suppose you have 5 people A, B, C, D, E wearing 5 colour of shirts red, yellow, green, blue and white and drinking 5 kinds of soft drinks Coke, Pepsi, Mirinda, Thums Up and Seven Up. The solution table structure would look like as given on the next page.

(*ii*) The ability to order the clues in the correct order of usage (as explained in the theory of logical reasoning): This includes the ability to perceive the direct clues and use them first to set up the 'framework' of problem solving.

(*iii*) The ability to perceive what indirect clues are given and how to use them;

(*iv*) The ability to convert clues written in language form into visual clues so that you do not need to read the text again and again. Also, converting the language clues to visual clues is critical for the purpose of being able to 'see' all the clues at one go.

Illustrated below are the solutions to a few typical questions on puzzles. We would advise you to first have a look at the questions and try to solve the same on your own before looking at the step-by-step process of solving the same.

| Red | Yellow | Green | Blue | White | Coke | Pepsi | Mirinda | Thums Up | Seven Up |
|---|---|---|---|---|---|---|---|---|---|
| A | | | | | | | | | |
| B | | | | | | | | | |
| C | | | | | | | | | |
| D | | | | | | | | | |
| E | | | | | | | | | |
| Coke | | | | | | | | | |
| Pepsi | | | | | | | | | |
| Mirinda | | | | | | | | | |
| Thums UP | | | | | | | | | |
| Seven Up | | | | | | | | | |

## SOLVED EXAMPLE

At a fancy dress party people were asked to dress as an object that represented their professions.

Mr. Abhijit, Mrs. Banerjee, Mrs. Chatterjee, Mr. Dipanjan De and Mr. Elangovan were among the guests. The costumes included a leaf, a pen, a fork, a camera reel, and a stethoscope. The professions included a photographer, a gardener, a compounder, a teacher, and a cook.

Mr. Abhijit is a teacher.

Neither Mrs. Banerjee nor Mrs. Chatterjee was dressed as a fork.

None of the men is a compounder.

Mr. Dipanjan De is dressed as a camera reel.

Mrs. Chatterjee is a gardener.

**1.** Which person is dressed as a stethoscope?
(*a*) Abhijit (*b*) Banerjee (*c*) Chatterjee (*d*) Dipanjan

**2.** What is Elangovan's profession?
(*a*) Cook (*b*) Gardener (*c*) Compounder (*d*) Teacher

**Sol.** Putting the direct Clues 1 and 4 in the we get:

| Male | Female | Female | Male | Male |
|---|---|---|---|---|
| Abhijit<br>Pen<br>Teacher<br>From Clue 1 | Banerjee | Chatterjee | Dipanjan De<br>Camera reel<br>Photographer<br>From Clue 4 | Elangovan |

At this point if we use Clue 2, it is evident that it must be Elangovan who is dressed as a fork. Also using clue 5 (Mrs. Chatterjee is a gardener) completes the solution.

| **Male** | **Female** | **Female** | **Male** | **Male** |
|---|---|---|---|---|
| Abhijit<br>Pen<br>Teacher | Banerjee | Chatterjee<br>Leaf<br>Gardener<br><br>From<br>Clue 5 | Dipanjan De<br>Camera reel<br>Photographer | Elangovan<br>Cook<br>Fork<br><br>From Clue 2<br>once we know<br>the details of<br>Dipanjan and<br>Abhijit. |

Obviously, Mrs. Banerjee would be the compounder.

The solutions are: 1. Banerjee Option (*b*)

2. Elangovan is the cook. Option (*a*) is correct.

**Directions:** *Read the following information given below to answer these questions that follows.*

(*i*) Aarti is elder than Sanya.

(*ii*) Muskan is elder than Aarti but younger than Kashish.

(*iii*) Kashish is elder than Sanya.

(*iv*) Sanya is younger than Muskan.

(*v*) Gargi is the eldest.

**1.** Agewise, who is in the middle?

(*a*) Kashish (*b*) Aarti (*c*) Muskan (*d*) Sanya

**Sol.** According to the statements,

(*i*) Aarti > Sanya

(*ii*) Kashish > Muskan > Aarti

(*iii*) Kashish > Sanya

(*iv*) Sanya < Muskan

Clearly, Kashish > Muskan > Aarti > Sanya, but Gargi is the eldest of all.

Hence, Gargi > Kashish > Muskan > Aarti > Sanya.

(*c*) Agewise, Muskan is in the middle.

## EXERCISE

**Directions (Qs 1-3):** *Read the following informations and answer the questions given below:*

(*i*) A finance company's office has 3 windows W1, W2 and W3 for handling various transactions.

(*ii*) W1 is open between 10 a.m. and 2 p.m. on Monday, Wednesday and Thursday and between 2.30 p.m. and 4.30 p.m. on Tuesday, Friday and Saturday.

(*iii*) W2 is open between 9 a.m. and 12 noon on Tuesday, Thursday and Friday and between 1 p.m. and 3 p.m. on Monday, Wednesday and Saturday.

(*iv*) W3 is open between 8 a.m. and 11 a.m. on Monday, Tuesday and Thursday and 12 noon and 2 p.m. on Wednesday, Friday and Saturday.

**1.** On which day before noon, all the three windows are simultaneously open at least for some time?
(*a*) Saturday (*b*) Thursday (*c*) Wednesday (*d*) Monday

**2.** On which day, more than one windows are not open simultaneously at any given time?
(*a*) Thursday (*b*) Wednesday (*c*) Friday (*d*) Saturday

**3.** On which day's afternoon, only Wl and W2 are open simultaneously for some time?
(*a*) Saturday (*b*) Thursday (*c*) Monday (*d*) Tuesday

**Directions (Qs 4-7):** *Read the following information and answer the given questions:*

(*i*) Six friends Ramesh, Dinesh, Lokesh, Nilesh, Shailesh and Hitesh work in different companies, namely 'P', 'Q', 'R' 'S', 'T' and 'U', and each one wears company-sponsored different coloured tie, i.e. Blue, Green, Pink, Yellow, Purple and Red, though not necessarily in the same order.

(*ii*) The one wearing Blue tie works in company 'S' and the one wearing Green tie works in company 'P'.

(*iii*) Hitesh does not work in company 'R' or 'T'.

(*iv*) Ramesh wears Pink tie and works in company 'Q'.

(*v*) Nilesh does not work in company 'T' and purple colour tie is not sponsored by company 'R'.

(*vi*) Shailesh works in company 'U' and neither Nilesh nor Dinesh works in company 'S'.

(*vii*) Company 'T' does not sponsor Purple or Yellow coloured tie and Lokesh works in company 'P'.

**4.** Which coloured tie is sponsored by Company 'R'?
(*a*) It can not be ascertained (*b*) Blue
(*c*) Green (*d*) Yellow

**5.** Which of the following "colour of tie-company-person" combinations is correct?
(*a*) Green-R-Nilesh (*b*) Blue-S-Lokesh
(*c*) Red-T-Dinesh (*d*) Yellow R-Shailesh

**6.** Which of the following is true?
(*a*) Company 'U' sponsors Green tie
(*b*) Shailesh wears Red tie
(*c*) Nilesh works in Company 'T'
(*d*) Red colour is sponsored by company 'T'

**7.** Which of the following sequence of companies represents Ramesh, Dinesh, Lokesh, Nilesh, Shailesh and Hitesh in the same order?
(*a*) Q, P, T, R, U, S (*b*) Q, T, P, R, U, S
(*c*) Q, P, T, S, U, R (*d*) Q, T, S, U, R, P

**Directions (Qs. 8-10):** *Read the following information carefully and answer the questions given below.*

(*i*) Five friends Amar, Kapil, Sarvesh, Rohan and Nagesh wear shirts of different colours, viz. red, yellow, blue, white and green (not necessarily in the same order) while going for a party.

(*ii*) Each one of them has different tastes viz. reading, playing, travelling, singing and writing.

(*iii*) Kapil, who likes singing, does not wear a yellow shirt. Sarvesh wears red shirt and does not like reading or writing. Nagesh likes to play and does not wear a blue or yellow shirt. Amar likes writing and Rohan does not wear a yellow or green shirt.

**8.** What is the colour of Kapil's shirt?
(*a*) White (*b*) Green
(*c*) Blue (*d*) Data inadequate

**9.** Who likes reading?
(*a*) Rohan (*b*) Amar
(*c*) Kapil (*d*) Data inadequate

**10.** Which of the following combinations of 'person-colour-liking' is correct?
(*a*) Rohan-Blue-Reading (*b*) Negesh-White-Playing
(*c*) Amar-Yellow-Writing (*d*) Nagesh-Green-Playing

**Directions (Qs. 11-13):** *Read the following information carefully and answer the questions given below.*

Six persons A, B, C, D, E and F took up a job with a firm in a week from Monday to Saturday. Each of them joined for different posts on different days. The posts were of— Clerk, Officer, Technician, Manager, Superviser and Sales Executive, though not respectively.

F joined as a Manager on the first day. B joined as a Supervisor but neither on Wednesday nor Friday. D joined as a Technician on Thursday. Officer joined the firm on Wednesday. E joined as a Clerk on Tuesday. A joined as a Sales Executive.

**11.** Who joined the firm on Wednesday?
(*a*) B (*b*) C (*c*) B or C (*d*) Data inadequate

**12.** Who was the last person to join the firm?
(*a*) E (*b*) F (*c*) A (*d*) B

**13.** On which of the following days did the Sales Executive join?
(*a*) Tuesday (*b*) Thursday (*c*) Saturday (*d*) None of these

**Directions (Qs. 14-18):** *Read the following information carefully and answer the questions given below:*

(*i*) P, Q, R, S, T and U are six teachers in a school teaching different subjects-Mathematics, Physics, Sociology, Biology, Geography and History, not necessarily in the same order. There are only four female teachers.

(*ii*) Q teaches History. No female teaches Biology or Mathematics. S, who teaches Sociology, is the eldest. P is elder than R and teaches Physics. The youngest teaches Biology and U is not the youngest. T teaches Mathematics and is elder than P but younger than Q and U.

**14.** Which of the following is the group of females?
(*a*) RPSU (*b*) RSTQ (*c*) PQTU (*d*) PQSU

**15.** Which subject does U teach?
(*a*) Geography (*b*) Sociology
(*c*) Geography or Sociology (*d*) Data inadequate

**16.** Who teaches Biology?
(*a*) P (*b*) S (*c*) R (*d*) Data inadequate

**17.** If all the teachers are arranged in descending order of their ages, what will be the position of the two male teachers respectively?
(*a*) II and VI (*b*) IV and VI (*c*) III and VI (*d*) Data inadequate

**18.** Who is the youngest in the group?
(*a*) Q (*b*) T (*c*) P (*d*) None of these

**Directions (Qs. 19-23):** *Study the following information carefully and answer the questions given below:*

(*i*) Six students P, Q, R, S, T and U are in different branches of Engineering, viz. civil, mechanical, chemical, electrical, metallurgy and electronics but not necessarily in the same order.

(*ii*) Each of them is a resident of a different city viz. Mumbai, Kolkata, Chennai, Delhi, Hyderabad and Bengaluru. R is the resident of Delhi but he is not in chemical or electrical, T, who is in mechanical, is not the resident of Mumbai or Hyderabad. Q is from Calcutta and he is in electrical. The student from Chennai is in electronics and S is from Mumbai. P is in metallurgy.

**19.** Which of the following is not the correct combination of student and subject?
(*a*) P-metallurgy (*b*) Q-electrical (*c*) U-electronics (*d*) S-civil

**20.** Which student is from Chennai?
(*a*) R (*b*) U (*c*) S (*d*) T

**21.** P is from which city?
(*a*) Chennai (*b*) Kolkatta (*c*) Hyderabad (*d*) Data inadequate

**22.** Which student is from Bengaluru?
(*a*) T (*b*) Q (*c*) S (*d*) None of these

**23.** R is studying which subject?
(*a*) Electronics (*b*) Mechanical (*c*) Metallurgy (*d*) Data inadequate

**Directions (Qs. 24-28):** *Study the following information carefully and answer the questions given below:*

(*i*) M, N, P, Q, S and T are six members of a group in which three are female members. Females work in three departments — Accounts, Administration and Personnel — and sit on three different floors — 1st, IInd and IIIrd. Persons working in the same department are not on the same floor. On each floor two persons work.

(*ii*) No two females work in the same department or on the same floor. N and S work in the same department but not in Personnel. Q works in administration. S and M are on the 1st and IIIrd floors respectively and work in the same department. Q, a female, does not work on IInd floor. P, a male, works on 1st floor.

**24.** Which of the following groups of persons are females?
(*a*) SQT (*b*) QMT (*c*) QPT (*d*) Data inadequate

**25.** Which of the following pairs of persons work in Administration?
(*a*) QP (*b*) QN (*c*) SP (*d*) Data inadequate

**26.** 'T' works in which department?
(*a*) Accounts (*b*) Administration
(*c*) Personnel (*d*) Accounts or Personnel

**27.** Which of the following pair works on IInd floor?
(*a*) PT (*b*) SM (*c*) QN (*d*) None of these

**28.** If T is transferred to Accounts and S is transferred to Administration, who is to be transferred to Personnel to maintain the original distribution of females on each floor?
(*a*) P (*b*) N (*c*) Q or N (*d*) Data inadequate

**Directions (Qs. 29-33):** *Study the following information carefully and answer the questions given below:*

There are seven students — P, Q, R, S, T, V and W — in a class. Each of them has a different-favourite subject, viz Science, Chemistry, Biology, French, English, Mathematics and Hindi. Each of the students secured different marks in their favourite subject. R has scored second highest marks and neither Science nor French is her favourite subject T scored the least marks and neither Mathematics nor Chemistry is his favourite subject. The favourite subject of S is Biology and he scored more marks than Q and W but less than the marks of P. The favourite subject of Q is English and his marks is more than the marks of T but less than the marks of W.

The favourite subject of P is Hindi and he has not secured the highest marks. The student whose favourite subject is French, got the highest marks. The favourite subject of R is not Chemistry.

**29.** Which is the favourite subject of T?
(*a*) Chemistry (*b*) Science (*c*) English (*d*) Data inadequate

**30.** What is the favourite subject of W?
(*a*) Chemistry (*b*) Mathematics
(*c*) Either Chemistry of Mathematics
(*d*) Data inadequate

**31.** Who got the second lowest marks?
(*a*) W (*b*) S (*c*) R (*d*) None of these

**32.** French is the favourite subject of
(*a*) R (*b*) P (*c*) W (*d*) V

**33.** When all the seven students are arranged according to their marks in their favourite subjects in descending order, what is the position of P from the top?
(*a*) Second (*b*) Fourth (*c*) Third (*d*) Data inadequate

**Directions (Qs 34-38):** *Study the following information carefully and answer the question given below:*

A, B, C, D, E, F and G are seven members of a family belonging to three generations. There are two married couples one each of first and second generations respectively. They travel in three different cars P, Q and R so that no car has more than three members and there is at least one female in each car. C, who is the granddaughter, does not travel with her Grandfather and Grandmother. B travels with his father E in car Q. F travels with her granddaughter D in car P. A travels with her daughter in car R.

**34.** How many female members are there in the family?
(*a*) Three (*b*) Four (*c*) Five (*d*) Data inadequate

**35.** Which of the following is one of the married couples?
(*a*) DB (*b*) BC (*c*) EF (*d*) Data inadequate

**36.** In which car are three members travelling?
(*a*) P (*b*) Q (*c*) Either P or Q (*d*) R

**37.** How is D related to E?
(*a*) Daughter (*b*) Niece (*c*) Granddaughter (*d*) Data inadequate

**38.** How is G related to A?
(*a*) Daughter (*b*) Sister (*c*) Mother-in-law (*d*) Data inadequate

**Directions (Qs. 39-43):** *Study the following information carefully and answer the questions given below:*

P, Q, R, S, T, V and W are seven members in a family, out of which there are three females and four males. There are two managers, two lawyers, one teacher, one engineer and one doctor. No female is either teacher or engineer. R is a lawyer and is married to P, who is a teacher. V, the engineer, is married to S, who is neither lawyer nor doctor. No two ladies have the same profession. Q is the sister of W, who is a manager.

**39.** What is T's profession?
(*a*) Manager (*b*) Lawyer
(*c*) Manager or Lawyer (*d*) Data inadequate

**40.** Which of the following is the group of males?
(*a*) PQVW (*b*) TVSW (*c*) PRTV (*d*) PTVW

**41.** What is Q's profession?
(*a*) Doctor (*b*) Manager (*c*) Lawyer (*d*) Data inadequate

**42.** Who among them has the same profession as that of W?
(*a*) R (*b*) T (*c*) S (*d*) Data inadequate

**43.** Which of the following pairs have the same profession?
(*a*) PS (*b*) RS (*c*) TP (*d*) None of these

**Directions (Qs. 44-48):** *Study the following information carefully and answer the questions given below:*

P, Q, R, S, T, V and W are seven friends who left for seven different destinations — Delhi, Chennai, Hyderabad, Bangalore, Kolkata, Chandigarh and Jaipur — each one on a different day of the week. R left for Jaipur on Monday. On the last day of the week (saturday) the person left for Bangalore. T left the next day of P, who left for Chandigarh and on the previous day of W. S left for Kolkata on Friday. Q did not leave for either Hyderabad or Bangalore and W left for Delhi.

**44.** On which day of the week did Q leave?
(*a*) Sunday (*b*) Saturday (*c*) Wednesday (*d*) Data inadequate

**45.** Who left for Bangalore?
(*a*) T (*b*) P (*c*) V (*d*) Data inadequate

**46.** On which day of the week did T leave?
(*a*) Tuesday (*b*) Thursday (*c*) Sunday (*d*) Wednesday

**47.** Which of the following combinations of person-place is not correct?
(*a*) R—Jaipur (*b*) P—Chandigarh
(*c*) T—Hyderabad (*d*) All are correct

**48.** Who left on Tuesday?
(*a*) P (*b*) W (*c*) Q (*d*) V

**Directions (Qs. 49-53):** *Study the following information carefully and answer the questions given below.*

(*i*) Seven persons A, B, C, D, E, F and G teach seven subjects History, Geography, Physics, Chemistry, Maths, Biology and English from Monday to Friday. Each person teaches a different subject and not more than two subjects are taught on any particular day.

(*ii*) Chemistry is taught by B on Tuesday.

(*iii*) D teaches on Friday but neither Geography nor Physics.

(*iv*) F teaches History but neither on Thursday nor on Friday.

(*v*) A teaches English on the day oh which History is taught.

(*vi*) C teaches Maths on Monday.

(*vii*) Geography and Chemistry are taught on the same day.

(*viii*) G teaches on Thursday.

**49.** English is taught on which day?
(*a*) Wednesday (*b*) Monday (*c*) Tuesday (*d*) Data inadequate

**50.** Which of the following subjects is taught by 'G'?
(*a*) Biology (*b*) Geography (*c*) Physics (*d*) Chemistry

**51.** Geography is taught on which day?
(*a*) Monday (*b*) Tuesday (*c*) Wednesday (*d*) Thursday

**52.** Which subject is taught on Friday?
(*a*) Physics (*b*) History (*c*) Geography (*d*) Biology

**53.** Which of the following pairs of persons teaches on Tuesday?
(*a*) B and D (*b*) A and B (*c*) B and F (*d*) None of these

**Directions (Qs. 54-57):** *Read the following information and answer the questions given below.*

(*i*) Rajiv, a medical representative (M. R.), has to meet 7 doctors M, N, O, P, Q, R and S on a particular day between 9 am to 4 pm.

(*ii*) He takes 30 minutes with each doctor and keeps a gap of 25 minutes between two appointments for travel and preparation except after 5th visit, when he takes 50 minutes' break for lunch, travel and preparation

(*iii*) He has to meet doctor M immediately before Q but immediately after R, who is the third doctor to be met.

(*iv*) 'S' does not give time for M.R. before 9.30 am and after 10.30 am. 'P' and 'N' meet MR between 2 pm and 3.30 pm only.

**54.** Who among the followings was likely to be the first doctor of that day?
(*a*) S (*b*) O (*c*) R (*d*) Q

**55.** Who will be the last doctor to be visited by him on that day?
(*a*) N (*b*) P (*c*) Either N or P (*d*) Data inadequate

**56.** At what time is he likely to meet doctor 'S'?
(*a*) 9.55 am (*b*) 9.30 am (*c*) 9 am (*d*) Data inadequate

**57.** If doctor 'R' asks him to visit again 25 minutes after his scheduled seventh visit is over, then at what time can he meet doctor 'R'?
(*a*) 3.55 pm (*b*) 3.40 pm (*c*) 3.25 pm (*d*) None of these

**Directions (Qs. 58-62):** *Study the following information carefully and answer the questions given below:*

P, Q, R, S, T, V and W are travelling in three different vehicles. There are at least two passengers in each Vehicle — I, II & III, and of the two only one of them is a male. There are two engineers, Two doctors and three teachers among them.

(*i*) R is a lady doctor and she does not travel with the pair of sisters, P and V.

(*ii*) Q, a male engineer, travels with only 'W', a teacher in vehicle I.

(*iii*) S is a male doctor.

(*iv*) Two persons belonging to the same profession do not travel in the same vehicle.

(*v*) P is not an engineer and travels in vehicle II.

**58.** What is V's profession?
(*a*) Engineer (*b*) Teacher (*c*) Doctor (*d*) Data inadequate

**59.** In which vehicle does R travel?
(*a*) I (*b*) II (*c*) III (*d*) II or III

**60.** Which of the following represents the three teachers?
(*a*) WTV (*b*) WTP (*c*) WTV or WTP (*d*) Data inadequate

**61.** Which of the following is not correct?
(*a*) T-Male-Teacher (*b*) Q-Male-Engineer
(*c*) P-Female-Teacher (*d*) V-Female-Teacher

**62.** How many lady members are there among them?
(*a*) Three (*b*) Four (*c*) Three or Four (*d*) Data inadequate

**Directions (Qs. 63-67):** *Read the given information carefully and answer the questions given below:*

Eight persons L, M, N, P, Q, R, S and T are sitting in a round table conference facing the centre.

(*i*) R sits between L and S.

(*ii*) S, who is the neighbour of Q, sits 3 places to the right of T.

(*iii*) Q sits 2 places to the right of T.

(*iv*) M sits 3 places to the left of R.

**63.** Who sits opposite to M?
(*a*) P (*b*) L (*c*) Q (*d*) T

**64.** Between which two persons is S sitting?
(*a*) L – Q (*b*) M – Q (*c*) R – Q (*d*) L – M

**65.** Who sits opposite to S?
(*a*) N (*b*) P (*c*) T (*d*) Either N or P

**66.** Who among the following is Q's neighbour?
(*a*) P (*b*) R (*c*) L (*d*) S

**67.** Who is L's neighbour on his left?
(*a*) R (*b*) S (*c*) Q (*d*) T

**Directions (Qs. 68-72):** *Read the given information carefully and answer the questions given below:*

Five books A, B, C, D and E have to be proofread in 6 hours where one hour needs to be spent per book.

(*i*) A break of one hour has to be taken in the third or the fourth hour.

(*ii*) The proofreading cannot start with A and has to end with C.

(*iii*) D has to immediately follow B with no break in-between.

(*iv*) A cannot be done imediately after D.

(*v*) A has to immediately precede E with no break in-between.

**68.** In which hour is the break taken?
(*a*) Sixth (*b*) Fourth (*c*) Fifth (*d*) Third

**69.** Which is the first book to be proofread?
(*a*) D (*b*) A (*c*) B (*d*) C

**70.** Which book is to be proofread immediately after the break?
(*a*) E (*b*) D (*c*) B (*d*) A

**71.** Which book is to be proofread immediately after D?
(*a*) B (*b*) E (*c*) C (*d*) None of these

**72.** Which book is to be proofread immediately after E?
(*a*) A (*b*) D (*c*) C (*d*) B

## ANSWERS

| **1** | **2** | **3** | **4** | **5** | **6** | **7** | **8** | **9** | **10** |
|---|---|---|---|---|---|---|---|---|---|
| (*b*) | (*c*) | (*c*) | (*d*) | (*c*) | (*d*) | (*b*) | (*d*) | (*a*) | (*c*) |
| **11** | **12** | **13** | **14** | **15** | **16** | **17** | **18** | **19** | **20** |
| (*b*) | (*d*) | (*d*) | (*d*) | (*a*) | (*c*) | (*b*) | (*d*) | (*d*) | (*b*) |
| **21** | **22** | **23** | **24** | **25** | **26** | **27** | **28** | **29** | **30** |
| (*c*) | (*a*) | (*d*) | (*a*) | (*d*) | (*c*) | (*d*) | (*b*) | (*b*) | (*a*) |
| **31** | **32** | **33** | **34** | **35** | **36** | **37** | **38** | **39** | **40** |
| (*d*) | (*d*) | (*c*) | (*c*) | (*c*) | (*b*) | (*c*) | (*d*) | (*b*) | (*d*) |
| **41** | **42** | **43** | **44** | **45** | **46** | **47** | **48** | **49** | **50** |
| (*a*) | (*c*) | (*d*) | (*a*) | (*c*) | (*d*) | (*d*) | (*a*) | (*a*) | (*c*) |
| **51** | **52** | **53** | **54** | **55** | **56** | **57** | **58** | **59** | **60** |
| (*b*) | (*d*) | (*d*) | (*b*) | (*c*) | (*a*) | (*d*) | (*a*) | (*c*) | (*b*) |
| **61** | **62** | **63** | **64** | **65** | **66** | **67** | **68** | **69** | **70** |
| (*d*) | (*b*) | (*b*) | (*c*) | (*d*) | (*d*) | (*a*) | (*d*) | (*c*) | (*d*) |
| **71** | **72** | | | | | | | | |
| (*d*) | (*c*) | | | | | | | | |

## SOME SELECTED EXPLANATORY ANSWERS

**1-3.**

| | **Mon** | **Tue** | **Wed** | **Thu** | **Fir** | **Sat** |
|---|---|---|---|---|---|---|
| $W_1$ | 10 pm-2 pm | 2.30 pm-4.30 pm | 10 am-2 pm | 10 am-2 pm | 2.30 pm-4.30 pm | 2.30 pm-4.30 pm |
| $W_2$ | 1 pm-3 pm | 9 pm-12 noon | 1 am-3 pm | 9 am-12 noon | 9 am-12 noon | 1 pm-3 pm |
| $W_3$ | 8 am-11 am | 8 pm-11 am | 12 noon-2 pm | 8 am-11 am | 12 noon-2 pm | 12 noon-2 pm |

**4-7.**

| **Tie** | **Company** | **Name** |
|---|---|---|
| Blue | S | Hitesh |
| Green | P | Lokesh |
| Pink | Q | Rakesh |
| Purple | U | Shailesh |
| Yellow | R | Nilesh |
| Red | T | Dinesh |

**8-10.**

| **Friend** | **Shirt** | **Liking** |
|---|---|---|
| Amar | yellow | writing |
| Kapil | White/blue/green | singing |
| Sarvesh | red | travelling |
| Rohan | blue/white | reading |
| Nagesh | green/white | playing |

**11-13.**

| **Person** | **Post** | **Day** |
|---|---|---|
| F | Manager | Monday |
| B | Supervisor | Saturday |
| D | Technician | Thursday |
| C | Officer | Wednesday |
| E | Clerk | Tuesday |
| A | Sales executive | Friday |

**14-18.**

| Teacher | Sex | Subject | Relative age |
|---|---|---|---|
| Q | F | History | 4/5 |
| R | M | Biology | 1 |
| T | M | Mathematics | 3 |
| S | F | Sociology | 6 |
| P | F | Physics | 2 |
| U | F | Geography | 5/4 |

**19-23.**

| Student | State | Branch |
|---|---|---|
| R | Delhi | Chem, Electrical (×) |
| T | Mumbai, Hyder (×) | Mech |
| Q | Calcutta | Electrical |
| | Chennai | Electronics |
| S | Mumbai | |
| P | | Metallurgy |

The empty boxes can be filled easily with the given information.

| | | |
|---|---|---|
| R | Delhi | Civil |
| T | Bangalore | Mechanical |
| Q | Calcutta | Electrical |
| U | Chennai | Electronics |
| S | Mumbai | Chemical |
| P | Hyderabad | Metallurgy |

**24-28.**

| Person | Sex | Floor | Department |
|---|---|---|---|
| P | Male | I | Personnel/Administration |
| S | Female | I | Accounts |
| N | Male | II | Accounts |
| T | Female | II | Personnel |
| Q | Female | III | Administration |
| M | Male | III | Accounts |

**29-33.**

| Student's Name | Favourite Subject | | | | | | | Rank in Descending order of Performance |
|---|---|---|---|---|---|---|---|---|
| | S | C | B | F | E | M | H | |
| P | | | | | | | ✓ | 3 |
| Q | | | | | ✓ | | | 6 |
| R | | | | | | ✓ | | 2 |
| S | | | ✓ | | | | | 4 |
| T | ✓ | | | | | | | 7 |
| V | | | | ✓ | | | | 1 |
| W | | ✓ | | | | | | 5 |

S-Science, C-Chemistry, B-Biology, F-French, E-English, M-Mathematics, H-Hindi.

**34-38.**

On the basis of the given clues we get the following information:

| **Car** | **Persons travelling in car** |
|---|---|
| P | F(–), D(–) |
| Q | B(+), E(+), G |
| R | A(–), C(–) |

$\left(\begin{matrix} + \Rightarrow \text{male} \\ - \Rightarrow \text{female} \end{matrix}\right)$

Besides this, we also came to know C is a female but still we do not know about the sex of G. But it is given that there is atleast one female in each car. The above table shows that the car Q needs a female to fulfil the condition described above. Hence, seventh person is a female, *i.e.* G is a female. Let us proceed to draw a family tree.

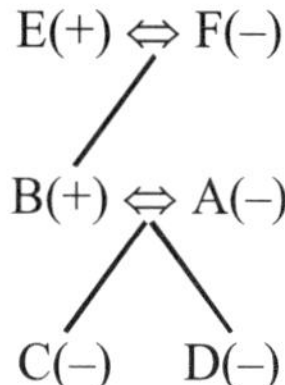

Since C does not travel with her grandfather and grandmother, C is not in the car P and in Q. Hence, C is in the car R and G is in the car Q. Still we are not aware of G's position in the family tree.

**39-43.** Based on given information, we get

| **Person** | **Profession** | **Sex** |
|---|---|---|
| P | Teacher | Male |
| Q | Doctor | Female |
| R | Lawyer | Female |
| S | Manager | Female |
| T | Lawyer | Male |
| V | Engineer | Male |
| W | Manager | Male |

**44-48.** The given information can be summarised as follow:

| **No.** | **Person** | **Desination** | **Day** |
|---|---|---|---|
| 1. | R | Jaipur | Monday |
| 2. | V | Bangalore | Saturday |
| 3. | P | Chandigarh | Tuesday |
| 4. | S | Kolkata | Friday |
| 5. | W | Delhi | Thursday |
| 6. | T | Hyderabad | Wednesday |
| 7. | Q | Chennai | Sunday |

**49-53.** The obtained information can be summarised as follow:

| No. | Person | Subject | Day |
|---|---|---|---|
| 1. | E | Geography | Tuesday |
| 2. | B | Chemistry | Tuesday |
| 3. | C | Maths | Monday |
| 4. | G | Physics | Thursday |
| 5. | D | Biology | Friday |
| 6. | F | History | Wednesday |
| 7. | A | English | Wednesday |

**54-57.** Following table represents the time duration in which Rajiv met the doctors:

| Order | Doctor | Duration of meeting | Gap (in min) |
|---|---|---|---|
| 1. | O | 9 am – 9.30 am | 25 |
| 2. | S | 9.55 am – 10.25 am | 25 |
| 3. | R | 10.50 am – 11.20 pm | 25 |
| 4. | M | 11.45 am – 12.15 pm | 25 |
| 5. | Q | 12.40 pm – 1.10 pm | 50 |
| 6. | P/N | 2 pm – 2.30 pm | 25 |
| 7. | N/P | 2.55 pm – 3.25 pm | — |

**58-62.**

| **Vehicle** | **Person** |
|---|---|
| I. | Q, W |
| II. | P, S, V |
| III. | T, R |

The obtained information can be summarised as below:

| Person | Profession | Vehicle | Sex |
|---|---|---|---|
| Q | Engineer | I | Male |
| W | Teacher | I | Female |
| P | Teacher | II | Female |
| S | Doctor | II | Male |
| V | Engineer | II | Female |
| T | Teacher | III | Male |
| R | Doctor | III | Female |

**63-67**

S sits 3 places to the right of T and Q sits two places to the right of T. Let's fix up these positions first.

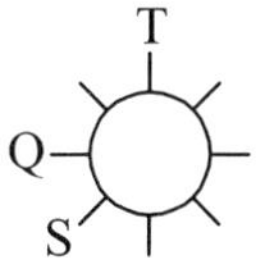

Now, if R has to sit between L and S, it has to be to the right of S else Q will clash with R. We can also get the positions of M relative to R. However, the positions of N and P cannot be determined for sure.

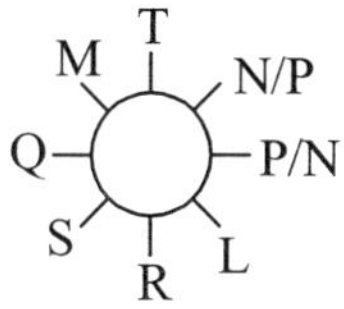

**63.** L sits opposite M.

**64.** S is sitting between R and Q.

**65.** Either N or P sits opposite S.

**66.** S is Q's neighbour.

**67.** R is to the left of L.

**68-72**

C is the last book. The combination B-D and A-E in that order have to compulsorily exist. Now, the order will have to start with B-D, since A cannot be started with (from (*ii*)).

| 1 | 2 | 3 | 4 | 5 | 6 |
|---|---|---|---|---|---|
| B | D | | | | C |

If the fourth hour is the break, then the combination A-E cannot be fitted without a break in-between.

| 1 | 2 | 3 | 4 | 5 | 6 |
|---|---|---|---|---|---|
| B | D | | X | | C |

Hence, the break has to be in the third hour and the arrangement is as follows:

| 1 | 2 | 3 | 4 | 5 | 6 |
|---|---|---|---|---|---|
| B | D | X | A | E | C |

**68.** 3rd hour is the break.

**69.** B is the first book to be proofread.

**70.** A is to be proofread immediately after the break.

**71.** None of these.

**72.** C is to be proofread immediately after E.

# 9

# Mathematical Operations

## INTRODUCTION

Questions on Mathematical operations will first start with either defining a new meaning to the existing symbols or define a new symbol and its mathematical meaning.

You are then required to evaluate the value of an expression by assuming the meaning of the symbols as defined in the question. The following examples will make these question types clear to you.

## SOLVED EXAMPLE

**1.** If '+' means '–', '–' means '×', '×' means '÷' and '÷' means '+' then which of the following will be the value of the given expression?

$32 + 8 \times 2 - 3 \div 4$

(*a*) 12 (*b*) 20 (*c*) 0 (*d*) 24

**Sol.** Putting the changed signs, the expression can be rewritten as

$32 - 8 \div 2 \times 3 + 4$

Using BODMAS rule,

$$= 32 - 4 \times 3 + 4 = 32 - 12 + 4 = 24$$

Hence, the correct option is (*d*).

**2.** If A implies '+', B implies '–', C implies '×', D implies '÷', then calculate the value of the expression 2A3B4C5D1.

(*a*) 15 (*b*) 0 (*c*) –15 (*d*) –12

**Sol.** Using the proper signs, the above expression can be written as

$$2 + 3 - 4 \times 5 \div 1 = 5 - 20 = -15$$

Hence, option (*c*) is correct.

**3.** Which of the following changes would make the given expression correct?

$4 + 4 \times 4 - 4 \div 4 = 4$

(*a*) '+' and '×' (*b*) '–' and '÷' (*c*) '+' and '÷' (*d*) both '*b*' and '*c*'

**Sol.** By making inter-changes given in 'a' we get the expression as:
$4 \times 4 + 4 - 4 \div 4 = 4$ which is false.
By making interchanges given in '*b*', we get expression as
$4 + 4 \times 4 \div 4 - 4 = 4$ which is true.
By making interchanges given in option '*c*', we get the expression as
$4 \div 4 \times 4 - 4 + 4 = 4$ which is also true.
Hence, option (*d*) is correct.

**4.** If A"B means add B to A, A'B implies subtract B from A, A@ B implies divide A by B, A*B means multiply A with B.

If a train travels with a speed of $S_1$ from point A to B and returns with a speed of $S_2$. The average speed will be represented using the above explained notations as?

(*a*) $(2*S_1"S_2)/(S_1"S_2)$ (*b*) $(2*S_1*S_2)/(S_1"S_2)$
(*c*) $(2*S_1"S_2)/(S_1'S_2)$ (*d*) $(2*S_1@S_2)/(S_1'S_2)$

**Sol.** We know that the formula for average speed is given by
$2S_1S_2/(S_1 + S_2)$
Hence the correct option is (*b*).

**5.** If (*l*, *m*, *n*) is represented as $\sqrt{[(l + 1)\ (m + 1)/(n + 1)]}$:
What is the value of (48, 63, 80)?

(*a*) 56/9 (*b*) 55/9 (*c*) 6 (*d*) 7

**Sol.** Putting the value in the above equation we get
$\sqrt{[(48 + 1)(63 + 1)/(80 + 1)]}$
$= \sqrt{(49 \times 64/81)} = (7 \times 8)/9 = 56/9$
Hence, the correct option is (*a*).

## EXERCISE

**Directions (Qs. 1 to 4):** *In each of the following questions if the given interchanges are made in signs and numbers, which one of the four equations would be correct?*

**1.** Given interchanges, signs '–' and '÷' and numbers 4 and 8

(*a*) $4 - 8 \div 12 = -23/4$ (*b*) $4 \div 8 - 2 = 8$
(*c*) $8 \div 2 - 4 = -15/4$ (*d*) None of these

**2.** Given interchanges: 3 and 2, ÷ and –

(*a*) $1 + 3 \times 4 - 2 \div 1 = 5$ (*b*) $1 + 2 - 3 \times 8 \div 4 = 9$
(*c*) $3 - 1 \times 4 + 2 \div 1 = 11$ (*d*) None of these

**3.** Given interchanges, × and +, 10, and 1.

(*a*) $5 \times 1 + 10 - 2 = 5$ (*b*) $8 + 8 - 10 \times 1 = 75$
(*c*) $4 - 6 \times 10 + 1 = 6$ (*d*) $3 + 4 - 12 \times 1 \div 10 = 10$

**4.** Given interchanges: 0.4 and 0.04,
(*a*) $1 + 2 - 0.04 \times 0.4 = 1$ (*b*) $0.4 + 0.04 - 2 \times 2 = 1.76$
(*c*) $0.04 \times 0.4 - 1 = 0.18$ (*d*) None of these

**5.** If '+' implies '–', '_' implies '×', '×' implies '÷' and '÷' implies '+', then insert the proper signs between the figures in the given equation

12__8__4__2__1 = 15
(*a*) ÷, ×, –, + (*b*) ÷, –, +, × (*c*) +, –, ×, ÷ (*d*) –, +, ÷, ×

**6.** Insert proper arithmetical signs between the figures in the following equation

12_4_2_1 = 24
(*a*) –, ÷, × (*b*) ×, ÷, × (*c*) +, ×, ÷ (*d*) None of these

**7.** Find out the two signs to be interchanged for making the following equation to be correct:
$5 + 3 - 5 \times 5 \div 1 = 15$
(*a*) × and – (*b*) × and + (*c*) ÷ and – (*d*) + and –

**8.** If '*a*' implies '+', '*b*' implies '–', '*c*' implies '×' and '*d*' implies '÷', insert proper letters between the figures in the following equation:

40_ 20_ 30_6 = 55
(*a*) *a*, *b*, *c* (*b*) *b*, *c*, *d* (*c*) *a*, *b*, *d* (*d*) *d*, *b*, *a*

**9.** Which of the following two signs need to be inter-changed to make the given equation correct?
$4 + 2 - 5 \times 7 \div 12 = -21$
(*a*) ÷ and – (*b*) ÷ and + (*c*) × and + (*d*) × and –

**Directions (Qs. 10 to 12):** *If 'a' means +, 'b' means –, 'c' means × and 'd' means ÷*

**10.** Calculate (8*c*7)*c*(7*a*5)*b*(6*d*3)*d*(3*b*2)
(*a*) 650 (*b*) 375 (*c*) 670 (*d*) None of these

**11.** Calculate the value of 6*a*7*b*8*c*8*d*2
(*a*) –17 (*b*) 12 (*c*) –19 (*d*) None of these

**12.** What is the value of 9*a*10*b*11*c*15*d*0
(*a*) 1 (*b*) 2 (*c*) 3 (*d*) undefined

**13.** If $\alpha = +$, $\beta = -$, $\gamma = \times$, $\delta = \div$
Insert the correct notations between the numbers in the given sum
10__8__6__4__2 = 6
(*a*) β, α δ, γ (*b*) α, β, γ, δ (*c*) β, δ, γ, α (*d*) None of these

**Directions (Qs 14 to 18):** *If a + b implies a – b*
*a* – *b* implies *a* × *b*

$a \times b$ implies $a \div b$
$a \div b$ implies $a + b$

**14.** Which of the following is true?
(*a*) $6 + 2 - 3 \times 1 \div 4 = 12$
(*b*) $10 + 4 - 3 \times 1 \div 2 = 5$
(*c*) $6 + 4 - 2 \times 2 \div 1 = 3$
(*d*) None of these

**15.** What will come at the question mark (?)?
$(1 + 2 - 3 \times 1 \div 4)/(4 + 5 - 4 \times 2 \div 1) = ?$
(*a*) –1/5 (*b*) 1/5 (*c*) 1 (*d*) None of these

**16.** With which statement can you find the value of 8?
(*a*) $1 + 2 - 6 \times 3 \div 8$
(*b*) $1 - 2 + 6 \times 3 \div 8$
(*c*) $1 - 2 \times 6 + 3 \times 8$
(*d*) None of these

**17.** Calculate $5 + 8 - 25 \times 5 \div 40$
(*a*) 5 (*b*) –5 (*c*) 0 (*d*) 10

**18.** Find the value of
$(4 + 3 - 5 \times 1 \div 4) \times (5 + 2 - 3 \times 1 \div 4)$
(*a*) –7/3 (*b*) –8/3 (*c*) 1 (*d*) None of these

**Directions (Qs. 19 to 21):** *If*

A implies +
M implies –
P implies ×
Q implies ÷

**19.** Calculate 5A6M3P4Q8
(*a*) 10 (*b*) 9 (*c*) 9.5 (*d*) 10.5

**20.** Calculate (2A3M4P5)P(5M6P8Q4)
(*a*) –105 (*b*) –120 (*c*) 120 (*d*) None of these

**21.** Which of the following equations is correct?
(*a*) 30Q10A4P2M2 = 15
(*b*) 5P2A4Q2P2 = 14
(*c*) 2Q3B5P6A7 = –5
(*d*) None of these

**Directions (Qs. 22 and 23):** *If '*' indicates either '+' or '×', then solve the following questions.*

**22.** What is the minimum value of
1*2*3*4
(*a*) 10 (*b*) 9 (*c*) 11 (*d*) 14

**23.** What is the maximum value of
1*2*3*4*5*6*7
(*a*) 5040 (*b*) 5041 (*c*) 7112 (*d*) None of these

**Directions (Qs.24 to 26):** *If*

$12 + 2 = 6$
$27 + 9 = 3$
and $15 + 5 = 3$ are true, then solve the following.

**24.** Calculate $(10 + (6 + (3 + (2 + 1))))$
(*a*) 4 (*b*) 5 (*c*) 8 (*d*) None of these

**25.** Calculate the value of $182 + 13$
(*a*) 14 (*b*) 1.4 (*c*) 0.14 (*d*) None of these

**26.** Calculate the value of $50 + [50 + 10]$
(*a*) 10 (*b*) 100 (*c*) 110 (*d*) 5

**Directions (Qs. 27 to 31):** *If*

AXB implies $A^2 + B^2$
AYB implies $A^2 - B^2$
AZB implies $(A + B)^2$
AMB implies $(A - B)^2$

**27.** Calculate (3Z4) – (5M5)
(*a*) 49 (*b*) 25 (*c*) 64 (*d*) None of these

**28.** Calculate the value of (2Z2)M(4Y4)
(*a*) 16 (*b*) 256 (*c*) 25 (*d*) None of these

**29.** Calculate the value of (373M413)
(*a*) 1600 (*b*) 900 (*c*) 400 (*d*) 2500

**30.** Calculate the value of (4X5)Y(6X7)
(*a*) 5544 (*b*) –5544 (*c*) 500 (*d*) None of these

**31.** If (AMB) = (AZB) then which of the following is true.
(*a*) $A - B = O$ (*b*) $A^2 = B^2$ (*c*) $A.B = 0$ (*d*) $A = 0$

**Directions (Qs. 32 to 35):** *If*

$3 \times 4 = 5$
$5 \times 12 = 13$

Then solve the following question.

**32.** Calculate the value of $8 \times 9$
(*a*) 145 (*b*) $\sqrt{145}$ (*c*) 12 (*d*) 12.5

**33.** $9 \times ? = 41$
(*a*) 35 (*b*) 30 (*c*) 40 (*d*) None of these

**34.** Obtain $\{3 \times (5 \times 6)\} = ?$
(*a*) 5 (*b*) $\sqrt{70}$ (*c*) $5\sqrt{3}$ (*d*) None of these

**35.** Calculate the value of 7 × 24
(*a*) 12 (*b*) 48 (*c*) 10 (*d*) None of these

**Directions (Qs. 36 to 40):** *If*
M means greater than
N means equal to
O means not less than
P means less than
Q means not equal to
and R means not greater than

**36.** If aP0 and b + 2Pa, then which of the following is true?
(*a*) bM –2 (*b*) bN – 2 (*c*) bP – 2 (*d*) None of these

**37.** 10aM6b and 12bM20c, then which of the following is true?
(*a*) 5aMc (*b*) aM5c (*c*) aNc (*d*) None of these

**38.** If yPz and zNa, then which of the following is true?
(*a*) yMa (*b*) yPa (*c*) yOa (*d*) None of these

**39.** If $|t - u|$ M0, then which of the following is/are true
(*a*) uMt (*b*) tMu
(*c*) uNt (*d*) (*a*) or (*b*) could be true

**40.** If sOt, tRu and tRv then which of the following could be true about *s* and *u*/*v* or *u* and *v*?
(*a*) sMu (*b*) sPv
(*c*) uNv (*d*) can't be determined

**Directions (Qs. 41 to 43):** *If*
A indicates >
B indicates <
C indicates =
D indicates ≠
E indicates +
F indicates –
G indicates *
H indicates ÷

**41.** Calculate (32H(2H(6H3)))
(*a*) 16 (*b*) 32 (*c*) 8 (*d*) None of these

**42.** Calculate 5E3F4G6H2
(*a*) 1.5 (*b*) 1 (*c*) –4 (*d*) None of these

**43.** Which of the following is false?
(*a*) (5E7)A(4E3)A(1E2) (*b*) (5E6)A(6E12)A(13E6)
(*c*) (12H3)C(40H10)C(60H15) (*d*) All of these are fals

**Directions (Qs. 44 to 46):**

A"B implies A + B
A'b implies A – B
A@B implies A ÷ B
A*B implies A × B

**44.** Jadugar has a jadoo box whose length, breadth and height can be represented by '*x*', '*a*', '*c*' respectively. What is the formula for its total surface area?

(*a*) 2[(*x*'*a*)*(*a*"*c*)*(*x*"*c*)] (*b*) 2[(*x**a*)"(*a**c*)"(*x**c*)]
(*c*) 2[(*x*'*a*)*(*a**c*)*(*x**c*)] (*d*) None of these

**45.** A man travels with a speed of f from A to B and returns from B to A with speed *h*. What is the average speed of the man over the entire journey?

(*a*) 2f'h/f'h (*b*) 2f@h/f'h (*c*) 2f*h/f@h (*d*) None of these

**46.** At the Wave cinemas in Sector 18 in Noida, charges for parking are as follows

1. For cycles ₹ 2
2. For scooters ₹ 5
3. For cars ₹ 20

On a particular day there were '25' cycles, '40' scooters and '100' cars parked at the stand, what was the amount collected in that particular day?

(*a*) (25"2)*(40"5)*(100"20) (*b*) (25'2)@(40'5)@(100'20)
(*c*) (25*2)"(40*5)"(100*20) (*d*) None of these

## ANSWERS

| 1 | 2 | 3 | 4 | 5 | 6 | 7 | 8 | 9 | 10 |
|---|---|---|---|---|---|---|---|---|---|
| (*d*) | (*b*) | (*d*) | (*d*) | (*a*) | (*b*) | (*a*) | (*c*) | (*b*) | (*c*) |
| **11** | **12** | **13** | **14** | **15** | **16** | **17** | **18** | **19** | **20** |
| (*c*) | (*d*) | (*b*) | (*c*) | (*b*) | (*b*) | (*a*) | (*a*) | (*c*) | (*d*) |
| **21** | **22** | **23** | **24** | **25** | **26** | **27** | **28** | **29** | **30** |
| (*b*) | (*b*) | (*b*) | (*d*) | (*a*) | (*a*) | (*a*) | (*b*) | (*a*) | (*b*) |
| **31** | **32** | **33** | **34** | **35** | **36** | **37** | **38** | **39** | **40** |
| (*c*) | (*b*) | (*c*) | (*b*) | (*d*) | (*c*) | (*a*) | (*b*) | (*d*) | (*d*) |
| **41** | **42** | **43** | **44** | **45** | **46** | | | | |
| (*b*) | (*c*) | (*b*) | (*b*) | (*d*) | (*c*) | | | | |

## SOME SELECTED EXPLANATORY ANSWERS

**2.** The given expression will become $1 + 3 \div 2 \times 8 - 4 = 9$. Option (*b*) is the answer.

**4.** Checking each of the four options we will get none of these the answer. Hence, option (*d*) is the answer.

**5.** $12 \div 8 \times 4 - 2 + 1$ would mean $12 + 8 \div 4 \times 2 - 1 = 12 + 4 - 1 = 15$. Hence, the order given in option (*a*) is correct.

**6.** Insertion of $\times$, $\div$, $\times$ in that order will make $12 \times 4 \div 2 \times 1 = 24$. Hence, option (*b*) is correct.

**7.** If the signs are changed according to the first option the equation is satisfied. Hence, option (*a*) is correct.

**8.** $40 + 20 - 30 \div 6 = 60 - 5 = 55$. Hence, *a*, *b*, *d*. Option (*c*) is correct.

**9.** If the signs are changed according to the second option the equation is satisfied. Hence, option (*b*) is correct.

**10.** $(8c7)c(7a5)b(6d3)d(3b2)$ becomes $56 \times 12 - 2 \div 1 = 670$. Option (*c*) is the answer.

**11.** $6a7b8c8d2 = 6 + 7 - 8 \times 8 \div 2 = -19$. Hence, (*c*) is the answer.

**12.** The expression contains a division by 0, hence is undefined. Option (*d*) is the answer.

**14.** Option (*c*) gives us $6 - 4 \times 2 \div 2 + 1 = 3$. Hence, this is correct.

**15.** $(1 + 2 - 3 \times 1 \div 4)/(4 + 5 - 4 \times 2 \div 1)$
$= (1 - 2 \times 3 \div 1 + 4)/(4 - 5 \times 4 \div 2 + 1)$
$= -1/-5 = 1/5$. Hence, (*b*) is the answer.

**16.** Looking at option (*b*), we get, $1 - 2 + 6 \times 3 \div 8$ becomes
$1 \times 2 - 6 \div 3 + 8 = 8$. Hence, option (*b*) is the correct answer.

**17.** The expression will become $5 - 8 \times 25 \div 5 + 40$.
Using the BODMAS rule we will get:
$5 - 40 + 40 = 5$. Hence, option (*a*) is correct.

**18.** $(4 + 3 - 5 \times 1 \div 4) \times (5 + 2 - 3 \times 1 \div 4)$
$= (4 - 3 \times 5 \div 1 + 4) \div (5 - 2 \times 3 \div 1 + 4)$
$= -7/3$. Hence, option (*a*) is the answer.

**22.** The minimum value we will get if we use multiplication between 1 and 2 and addition between 2, 3, and 4. The value will be $1 \times 2 + 3 + 4 = 9$. Hence, option (*b*) is the answer.

**23.** The maximum value will be obtained when we use multiplication between 2 to 7 and addition between 1 and 2. Hence, option (*b*) is the answer.

**30.** $41^2 - 85^2 = 1681 - 7225 = -5544$. Hence, option (*b*) is a correct answer.

**31.** The given expression tells us that $(A - B)^2 = (A + B)^2$. This can only occur when $2AB = -2AB = 0$. Hence, option (*c*) is correct.

**Solutions 32 to 35**

The relationship that is defined through $a \times b = \sqrt{(a^2 + b^2)}$

Thus, $3 \times 4 = \sqrt{25} = 5$ and $5 \times 12 = \sqrt{(25 + 144)} = 13$.

**32.** $8 \times 9 = \sqrt{(64 + 81)} = \sqrt{145}$. Hence, option (*b*) is the answer.

**33.** The required value will be got by the square root of the difference between $41^2$ and $9^2 \rightarrow 1681 - 81 = 1600$. Hence, the required answer is 40. Correct answer is option (*c*).

**34.** The required value would be square root of $61 + 9 = \sqrt{70}$. Hence, option (*b*) is the answer.

**35.** $7 \times 24 = \sqrt{625} = 25$. Hence, option (*d*) is the answer.

**36.** *a* is negative and $b + 2$ is less than *a* implies that *b* must be below –2. Hence, option (*c*) is correct.

**37.** 10*a* is greater than 6*b* and 12*b* is greater than 20*c*. This implies that 20*a* is greater than 20*c*. Thus, *a* is greater than *c*. So 5*a* is obviously greater than *c*. Option (*a*) is correct.

**38.** yPz means that y is less than *z* and zNa means $z = a$. Thus, *y* is less than a → yPa. Option (*b*) is correct.

**39.** The modulus value can give 2 results: either $(t - u) > 0$ or $-(t - u) > 0$.This means that either $t > u$ or $u > t$. Hence, option (*d*) is correct.

**40.** Nothing can be said about the relationships between *s*, *u* or *v* or for that matter about *u* and *v*. Hence, the relationship cannot be determined. The correct answer is option (*d*).

**43.** It can be seen that options 1 and 3 are correct, but option (*b*) is wrong. Hence, option (*b*) is the correct answer.

**44.** The surface area of a cuboid box is equal to twice the areas of 3 different sides. Hence, option (*b*) is correct.

**45.** It can be seen that none of these is correct. Hence, (*d*) is the answer.

✦✦✦✦

# 10

# Symbolic Conclusion

## INTRODUCTION

In this type of questions, certain relationship between different sets of elements is given (in terms of less than', 'greater than', or 'equal to'), using either the real symbols or substituted symbols. The candidate is required to read the given statements and then choose which one of the conclusions is definitely true.

## SOLVED EXAMPLE

**Directions (Qs. 1-3):** *In the following questions, the symbols δ, @, ©, % and are used with the meaning as indicated below.*

'P © Q' means 'P is not smaller than Q'.

'P % Q' means 'P is neither smaller than nor equal to Q'.

'P  Q' means 'P is neither greater than nor equal to Q'.

'P δ Q' means 'P is not greater than Q'.

'P @ Q' means 'P is neither greater than nor smaller than Q'.

Now, in each of the following questions assuming the given statements to be true, find which one of the four conclusions I, II, III and IV, given below them, is/are definitely true, give your answer accordingly.

**1. Statements:** D δ T, T @ R, R © M, M % K

**Conclusions:** I. R @ D  II. R % D  III. K  T  IV. M δ T

(*a*) Only either I or II is true
(*b*) III and IV are true
(*c*) Either I or II and III are true
(*d*) Either I or II and IV are true
(*e*) Either I or II and III and IV are true

**2. Statements:** J @ F, F δ N, N % H, H © G

**Conclusions:** I. G  N  II. N © J  III. F  J  IV. J δ G

(*a*) I and II are true
(*b*) I, II and III are true
(*c*) I, III and IV are true
(*d*) All I, II, III and IV are true
(*e*) None of the above

**3. Statements:** R  K, K % D, D @ V, V δ M

**Conclusions:** I. R  D  II. V  R  III. D @ M  IV. M % D

(*a*) None is true
(*b*) Only III is true
(*c*) Only IV is true
(*d*) Either III or IV is true
(*e*) Either III or IV and II are true

**Sol. (Qs. 1-3):** Finally, © ⇒ ≥

% ⇒ >

 ⇒ <

δ ⇒ ≤

@ ⇒ =

**1.** (*e*) Here, D δ T ⇒ $D \le T$

T @ R ⇒ $T = R$

R © M ⇒ $R \ge M$

M % K ⇒ $M > K$

So, $D \le T \Rightarrow R \ge M > K$

Now, R @ D ⇒ $R = D$ (may be)

R % D ⇒ $R > D$ (may be)

K  T ⇒ $K < T$ (true)

M δ T ⇒ $M \le T$ (true)

From first two statements only one can be true. Hence, either I or II and III and IV are true.

**2.** (*a*) Here, J @ F ⇒ $J = F$

F δ N ⇒ $F \le N$

N % H ⇒ $N > H$

H © G ⇒ $H \ge G$

So, $J = F \le N > H \ge G$

Now, G  N ⇒ $G < N$ (true)

N © J ⇒ $N \ge J$ (true)

F  J ⇒ $F < J$ (false)

J δ G ⇒ $J \le G$ (false)

Hence, I and II are true.

**3.** (*d*) Here, R  K ⇒ $R < K$

K % D ⇒ $K > D$

D @ V ⇒ $D = V$

V δ M ⇒ $V \le M$

So, $R < K > D = V \le M$

Now, R  D ⇒ R < D (false)
V  R ⇒ V < R (false)
D @ M ⇒ D = M (may be)
M % D ⇒ M > D (may be)

Hence, either III or IV is true.

## EXERCISE

**Directions (Qs. 1-5):** In the following questions, the symbols @, @̲, =, © and ©̲ are used with the following meaning:

P @ Q means P is greater than Q.

P @̲ Q means P is either greater than or equal to Q.

P = Q means P is equal to Q.

P © Q means P is smaller than Q.

P ©̲ Q means P is either smaller than or equal to Q.

Now in each of the following questions assuming the given statements to be true, find which of the two conclusions I and II given below them is/are definitely true? Give answer

(*a*) if only conclusion I is true, (*b*) if only conclusion II is true,
(*c*) if either I or II is true, (*d*) if neither I nor II is true, and
(*e*) if both I and II are true.

1. **Statements:** B@V, K © C, C ©̲ B
**Conclusions:** I. V @ C II. B @ K

2. **Statements:** K @ T, S = K, T ©̲ R
**Conclusions:** I. S @ R II. T = R

3. **Statements:** U = M, P @̲ U, M @̲ B
**Conclusions:** I. P = B II. P @ B

4. **Statements:** L @̲ N, J ©̲ P, P @̲ L
**Conclusions:** I. J = L II. P = N

5. **Statements:** H @̲ G, D @ E, H = E
**Conclusions:** I. D @ H II. G © D

**Directions (Qs. 6-10):** *In the following questions, the symbol $, @, *, ** and # are used with the following meaning:*

A $ B means A is greater than B
A @ B means A is either greater than or equal to B
A * B means A is equal to B
A ** B means A is smaller than B
A # B means A is either smaller than or equal to B

Now in each of the following questions assuming the given statements to be true, find which one of the two conclusions I and II given below them is/are definitely True? Give answer

(*a*) if only conclusion I is true. (*b*) if only conclusion II is true.
(*c*) if either I or II is true. (*d*) if neither I nor II is true.
(*e*) if both I and II are true.

**6. Statements:** P @ Q, Q * M # N, N ** Q
**Conclusions:** I. P $ M II. N # P

**7. Statements:** D ** X, F @ Y, D $ F
**Conclusions:** I. X @ Y II. Y # D

**8. Statements:** M ** P, S $ T, M @ T
**Conclusions:** I. S * M II. T ** P

**9. Statements:** U * V, X $ W, U ** W
**Conclusions:** I. W $ V II. U ** X

**10. Statements:** G $ H, J # K, H * K
**Conclusions:** I. H $ J II. J * H

**Directions (Qs. 11-15):** *In the questions given below, certain symbols are used with the following meanings:*

A @ B means A is greater than B.
A * B means A is either greater than or equal to B.
A # B means A is equal to B.
A $ B means A is either smaller than or equal to B.
A + B means A is smaller than B.

Now in each of the following questions, assuming the given statements to be true, find which one of the two conclusions I and II given below them is/are definitely true? Give answer

(*a*) if only conclusion I is true.
(*b*) if only conclusion II is true.
(*c*) if either conclusion I or II is true.
(*d*) if neither conclusion I nor II is true.
(*e*) if both conclusions I and II are true.

**11. Statements:** B+D, E$T, T*P, P@B
**Conclusions:** I. P $ D II. P @ D

**12. Statements:** E*F, G$H, H#E, G@K
**Conclusions:** I. H@K II. H*F

**13. Statements:** P$Q, N#M, M@R, R*P
**Conclusions:** I. P+N II. Q$M

**14. Statements:** D+T, E$V, F*T, E@D
**Conclusions:** I. D$V II. D+F

**15. Statements:** T*U, U$W, V@L, W+V
**Conclusions:** I. V@T II. L#W

**Directions (Qs. 16-20):** *In the following questions, the symbols +, ×, =, ÷ and – are used with the following meaning:*

P + Q means P is greater than Q.
P × Q means P is either greater than or equal to Q.
P = Q means P is equal to Q.
P ÷ Q means P is smaller than Q.
P – Q means P is either smaller than or equal to Q.

Now in each of the following questions assuming the given statements to be true, find which one of the two conclusions I and II given below them is/are definitely true. Give answer

(*a*) if only conclusion I is true. (*b*) if only conclusion II is true.
(*c*) if either I or II is true. (*d*) if neither I nor II is true.
(*e*) if both I and II are true.

**16. Statements:** U+V, W–Y, Y×U
**Conclusions:** I. W+U II. W÷V

**17. Statements:** B÷A, D×E, E+A
**Conclusions:** I. D+A II. B÷E

**18. Statements:** S×Q, R+T, R-S
**Conclusions:** I. S+T II. Q =T

**19. Statements:** M÷N, P×Q, P+N
**Conclusions:** I. N+Q II. N-Q

**20. Statements:** G-H, K×L, L-G
**Conclusions:** I. G÷K II. L-H

**Directions (Qs. 21-25):** *In the following questions, the symbols @, c, £, ? and $ are used with the following meanings:*

A @ B means A is neither equal to nor smaller than B.
A c B means A is neither greater nor smaller than B.
A £ B means A is not equal to B.
A ? B means A is neither greater than nor equal to B.
A $ B means A is either greater or equal to B.

Now, in each of the following questions, assuming the given statements to be true, find which one of the two conclusions I and II given below them is/are definitely true. Give answer

(*a*) if only conclusion I is true. (*b*) if only conclusion II is true.
(*c*) if either I or II is true. (*d*) if neither I nor II is true.
(*e*) if both I and II are true.

**21. Statements:** N?S, S@P, P£M
**Conclusions:** I. S@M II. PcN

**22. Statements:** JcP, P$N, J£H
**Conclusions:** I. JcN II. H@P

**23. Statements:** Z@D, FcD, F$G
**Conclusions:** I. DcG II. Z@G

**24. Statements:** L@T, P?T, K$L
**Conclusions:** I. L@P II. K@T

**25. Statements:** RcU, U?Q, W$R
**Conclusions:** I. WcU II. W@U

**Directions (Qs. 26-30):** *In the following questions, the symbols @, &, *, $ and ? are used with the following meanings:*

P ? Q means P is either equal to or smaller than Q.
P $ Q means P is neither greater than nor smaller than Q.
P * Q means P is neither greater than nor equal to Q.
P @ Q means P is either greater than or equal to Q.
P & Q means P is not equal to Q.

Now in each of the following questions, assuming the given statements to be true, find which one of the two conclusions I and II given below them is/are definitely true. Give answer

(*a*) if only conclusion I is true. (*b*) if only conclusion II is true.
(*c*) if either I or II is true. (*d*) if neither I nor II is true; and
(*e*) if both I and II are true.

**26. Statements:** K$M, N&M, J@K
**Conclusions:** I. J?M II. K$N

**27. Statements:** K@R, L&B, B?K
**Conclusions:** I. B?R II. R*L

**28. Statements:** J*M, W$E, J@W
**Conclusions:** I. M?W II. J?E

**29. Statements:** R@S, S?U, T$R
**Conclusions:** I. T$S II. T?U

**30. Statements:** A*B, B?C, C@D
**Conclusions:** I. A$D II. B?D

**Directions (Qs. 31-35):** *In the following questions the symbols +, ×, ?, @ and $ are used with the following meanings:*

P + Q means P is neither smaller nor greater than Q.
P × Q means P is neither equal to nor smaller than Q.
P ? Q means P is neither greater than nor equal to Q.
P @ Q means P is either greater than or equal to Q.
P $ Q means P is not equal to Q.

Now in each of the following questions assuming the given statements to be true, find which of the two conclusions I and II given below them is/are, definitely true. Give answer

(*a*) if only conclusion I is true. (*b*) if only conclusion II is true.
(*c*) if either I or II is true. (*d*) if neither I nor II is true; and
(*e*) if both I and II are true.

**31. Statements:** P $ Q, Q × R, P + R
**Conclusions:** I. Q × P II. P ? Q

**32. Statements:** A + B, B $ C, C ? A
**Conclusions:** I. C $ A II. B + C

**33. Statements:** Y @ Z, Z × Q, Q $ P
**Conclusions:** I. Y ? Q II. Y ? P

**34. Statements:** E × F, F @ L, L + N
**Conclusions:** I. N + F II. E × L

**35. Statements:** H @ J, J ? K, K × M
**Conclusions:** I. H @ M II. M × J

**Directions (Qs. 36-40):** *In the following questions, the symbols #, @, $, © and % are used with the following meaning as illustrated below:*

'P # Q' means 'P is neither greater than nor equal to Q'.
'P @ Q' means 'P is neither greater than nor smaller than Q'.
'P $ Q' means 'P is not smaller than Q'.
'P © Q' means 'P is neither smaller than nor equal to Q'.
'P % Q' means 'P is not greater than Q'.

Now in each of the following questions, assuming the given statements to be true, find which one of the two conclusions 1 and II given below them is/are definitely true? Give answer

(*a*) if only Conclusion I is true.
(*b*) if only Conclusion II is true.
(*c*) if either Conclusion I or II is true.
(*d*) if neither Conclusion I nor II is true.

(*e*) if both Conclusions I and II are true.

**36. Statements:** M©R, R%T, T@N
**Conclusions:** I. N©R II. N@R

**37. Statements:** D@K, K$F, H#F
**Conclusions:** I. H#D II. D©F

**38. Statements:** J%V, V#T, T©R
**Conclusions:** I. R@J II. R#J

**39. Statements:** K@ W, B%W, N#B
**Conclusions:** I. K@N II. N#K

**40. Statements:** R©E, D@E, M$D
**Conclusions:** I. D#R II. E@R

## ANSWERS

| 1 | 2 | 3 | 4 | 5 | 6 | 7 | 8 | 9 | 10 |
|---|---|---|---|---|---|---|---|---|---|
| (*b*) | (*d*) | (*c*) | (*d*) | (*e*) | (*a*) | (*d*) | (*b*) | (*e*) | (*c*) |
| **11** | **12** | **13** | **14** | **15** | **16** | **17** | **18** | **19** | **20** |
| (*c*) | (*e*) | (*a*) | (*b*) | (*d*) | (*d*) | (*e*) | (*a*) | (*c*) | (*b*) |
| **21** | **22** | **23** | **24** | **25** | **26** | **27** | **28** | **29** | **30** |
| (*d*) | (*d*) | (*b*) | (*e*) | (*c*) | (*d*) | (*d*) | (*d*) | (*d*) | (*d*) |
| **31** | **32** | **33** | **34** | **35** | **36** | **37** | **38** | **39** | **40** |
| (*e*) | (*a*) | (*d*) | (*b*) | (*d*) | (*c*) | (*a*) | (*d*) | (*b*) | (*a*) |

## SOME SELECTED EXPLANATORY ANSWERS

**1.** $B > V$ ... (*i*); $K < C$ ... (*ii*); $C \leq B$ ... (*iii*)
No relationship can be found out between V and C.
Hence, I does not follow.
From (*ii*) and (*iii*), $B > K$. Hence II follows.

**2.** $K > T$ ... (*i*); $S = K$ ... (*ii*); $T \leq R$ .... (*iii*)
Neither relationship can be established.

**3.** $U = M$ ... (*i*); $P \geq U$ ... (*ii*); $M \geq B$.... (*iii*)
Combining, we get $P \geq U = M \geq B \Rightarrow P \geq B$
$\Rightarrow P = B$ or $P > B$.

**4.** $L \geq N$ .... (*i*); $J \leq P$ ... (*ii*); $P \geq 1$ ... (*iii*)
Neither relationship can be established.

**5.** H ≥ G ... (*i*); D > E ... (*ii*); H = E ... (*iii*)
Combining, we get D > E = H ≥ G ⇒ D > H and G < D.

**6.** P ≥ Q ... (*i*), M ≤ N ... (*ii*), N < Q ... (*iii*)
Combining all these, we get
P ≥ Q > N ≥ M ⇒ P > M. Hence, I follows
From (*i*) and (*iii*), P ≥ Q > N ⇒ P > N. Hence, II is false.

**7.** D < X ... (*i*), F ≥ Y ... (*ii*), D > F ... (*iii*)
From (*ii*) and (*iii*), D > F ≥ Y ... (*iv*) ⇒ D > Y. Hence, II may be correct but not necessarily so.
From (*i*) and (*iv*), X > D > F ≥ Y ⇒ X > Y. Hence, I may be correct but not necessarily so.

**11.** B < D ...(*i*), E ≤ T ... (*ii*), T ≥ P ... (*iii*), P > B ... (*iv*)
From (*i*) and (*iv*), we get, P > B < D ⇒ no conclusion. But the exhaustive possibilities are P > D, P = D and P < D. Hence, either I or II is true.

**12.** E ≥ F ... (*i*), G ≤ H ... (*ii*), H = E ... (*iii*), G > K ... (*iv*)
From (*ii*) and (*iv*), we get, H ≥ G > K ⇒ H > K. Hence, I is true.
From (*i*) and (*iii*), we get, H = E ≥ F ⇒ H ≥ F. Hence, II is true.

**13.** P ≤ Q ... (*i*), N = M ... (*ii*), M > R ... (*iii*), R ≥ P ... (*iv*)
From (*ii*), (*iii*) and (*iv*), we get, N = M > R ≥ P
⇒ N > R For P < N. Hence, I is true.
From (*iii*), (*iv*) and (*i*), we get, M > R ≥ P ≤ Q ⇒ No conclusion about the relationship between M and Q can be established.

**16.** U > V ... (*i*), W ≤ Y ... (*ii*), Y ≥ U ... (*iii*)
From (*ii*) and (*iii*), W ≤ Y ≥ U ⇒ No relationship between W and U can be determined, Hence, I is not true. Now, using (*i*), again no relationship between W and V can be determined.

**17.** B < A ... (*i*), D ≥ E ... (*ii*), E > A ... (*iii*)
From (*ii*) and (*iii*), we get D ≥ E > A ⇒ D > A. Hence, I is true.
From (*i*) and (*iii*), we get B < A < E ⇒ B < E. Hence, II is true.

**18.** S ≥ Q ... (*i*), R > T ... (*ii*), R ≤ S ... (*iii*)
Combining all, we get, Q ≤ S ≥ R > T ⇒ No relationship between Q and T can be determined. Hence II is not true. But S > T. Hence, I is true.

**19.** M < N ... (*i*), P ≥ Q ... (*ii*), P > N ... (*iii*)
From (*ii*) and (*iii*), we get N < P ≥ Q ⇒ No relationship between N and Q can be established. But I and II together are exhaustive. Hence, either I or II is true.

**20.** $G \leq H$ ... (*i*), $K \geq L$ ... (*ii*), $L \leq G$ ... (*iii*)
From (*ii*) and (*iii*), we get, $K \geq L \leq G \Rightarrow$ I can't be established.
From (*i*) and (*iii*), we get, $L \leq G \leq H \Rightarrow L \leq H$. Hence, II is true.

**21–25.** In these questions the negative meaning of these symbols is given to establish the relation between A and B, which can be easily converted to its simple and positive meaning. Expressing them mathematically, we get @ $\rightarrow >$ (greater than), c $\rightarrow =$ (equal to), £ $\rightarrow \neq$ (means either greater than or smaller than, but no definite conclusion), ? $\rightarrow <$ (smaller than), and \$ $\rightarrow \geq$.

**21.** $N < S$ ... (*i*), $S > P$ ... (*ii*), $P \neq M$ ... (*iii*)
From (*ii*) and (*iii*), no definite relationship between S and M can be established. Hence, I is not true.
From (*i*) and (*ii*), we get, $N < S > P \Rightarrow$ no conclusion. Hence, II is not true.

**22.** $J = P$ ... (*i*), $P \geq N$ ... (*ii*), $J \neq H$ ... (*iii*)
From (*i*) and (*ii*), we get, $J = P \geq N \Rightarrow J \geq N$
$\Rightarrow$ I may be true but not necessarily so.
From (*i*) and (*iii*), $P = J \neq H \Rightarrow P \neq H$. Hence, again II may be true but $H < P$ may be other possibility. Hence II is not true.

**27.** $K \geq R$ ... (*i*), $L \neq B$ ...(*ii*), $B \leq K$ ... (*iii*)
From (*iii*) and (*i*), we get $B \leq K \geq R \Rightarrow$ no conclusion.
Hence, I does not follow. No relationship between R and L can be determined. Hence, II does not follow.

**28.** $J < M$ ... (*i*), $W = E$ ... (*ii*), $J \geq W$ ... (*iii*)
From (*i*) and (*iii*), we get $M > J \geq W \Rightarrow M > W$. Hence, I is not true.
From (*ii*) and (*iii*), we get $J \geq W = E \Rightarrow J \geq E$. Hence, II is not true.

**31.** $P \neq Q$ ... (*i*), $Q > R$ ... (*ii*), $P = R$ ... (*iii*)
From (*ii*) and (*iii*), we get $Q > R = P \Rightarrow Q > P$. Hence, both I and II are true.

**32.** $A = B$ ... (*i*), $B \neq C$ ... (*ii*), $C < A$ ... (*iii*)
From (*iii*), conclusion I is true, II contradicts statement (*ii*), hence, it is not true.

**33.** $Y \geq Z$ ... (*i*), $Z > Q$ ... (*ii*), $Q \neq P$ ... (*iii*)
From (*i*) and (*ii*), we get $Y \geq Z > Q \Rightarrow Y > Q$ ... (A)
Hence I is not true. From (*iii*), two possible relationships between P and Q are;
**Case I:** When $P > Q$
Now, using (A), we get $Y > Q < P \Rightarrow$ no conclusion.

**Case II:** When Q > P

using (A), we get V > Q > P ⇒ Y > P. Hence, II is not true.

**34.** E > F ... (*i*), F ≥ L ... (*ii*), L = N ... (*iii*)

From (*ii*) and (*iii*), we get F ≥ L = N ⇒ F ≥ N or N ≤ F.

Hence, I may be true but not necessarily so.

From (*i*) and (*ii*), we get E > F ≥ L ⇒ E > L

Hence, II is true.

**35.** H ≥ J ... (*i*), J < K ... (*ii*), K > M ... (*iii*)

From (*ii*) and (*iii*), we get J < K > M ⇒ no relationship between J and M can be established. Hence II can't be established. Again, combining all we can't conclude the relationship between H and M. Hence, I is not true.

**36.** M > R ... (*i*); R ≤ T...(*ii*); T = N ... (*iii*)

Combining (*ii*) and (*iii*), we get

T = N ≥ R ⇒ N > R (conclusion I) or N = R (conclusion II)

**37.** D = K ... (*i*); K ≥ F ... (*ii*); H < F ... (*iii*)

Combining all, we get

D = K ≥ F > H ⇒ D > H and D ≥ F.

Hence, conclusion I (H < D) is true but conclusion II (D > F) is not necessarily true.

**38.** J ≤ V ... (*i*); V < T ... (*ii*); T > R ... (*iii*)

Combining (*i*) and (*ii*), we get T > V ≥ J ... (*iv*)

From (*iii*) and (*iv*) we do not get any specific relation between R and J. Hence, neither conclusion I nor conclusion II is necessarily true.

**39.** K = W ... (*i*); B ≤ W ... (*ii*); N < B ... (*iii*)

Combining all, we get

K = W ≥ B > N ⇒ K > N ⇒ N < K (conclusion II)

Hence, conclusion I is not true but conclusion II is true.

**40.** R > E ... (*i*); D = E... (*ii*); M ≥ D ... (*iii*)

Combining (*i*) and (*ii*), we get

R > E = D ⇒ R > D and R > E

⇒ D < R (Conclusion I) and E < R.

Hence, conclusion I is true but conclusion II is not true.

# 11

# Inserting missing Number/Characters in the Figure

## INTRODUCTION

Inserting the missing character is based on diagrammatic arrangement of letters/ numbers in which a missing term needs to be calculated.

In these types of question, a figure, a set of figures, a matrix or an arrangement is given.

Each characters, be it letters, numbers or a combination/group of numbers/ letters, follow a particular rule/pattern for their placement at different places in relation to the figure.

The candidates are required to decipher this rule/pattern and accordingly find the missing character in the figure.

## SOLVED EXAMPLE

**1.**

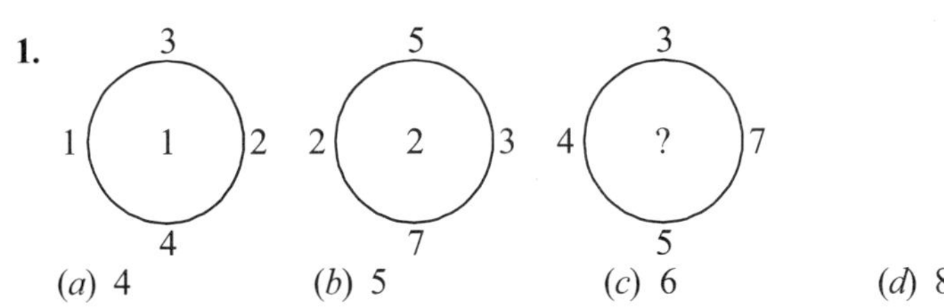


(*a*) 4 (*b*) 5 (*c*) 6 (*d*) 8

**Sol.** (*c*) Clearly, pattern associated with given question is

c

a e b

d

$e = (b - a) \times (d - c)$

= Difference between left and right numbers ×

Difference between bottom and top numbers

So, missing number = (5 – 3) × (7 – 4) = 2 × 3 = 6.

**2.** 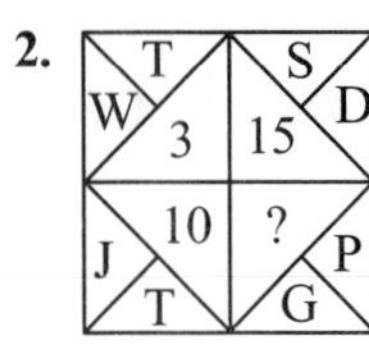


(*a*) 11 (*b*) 13 (*c*) 5 (*d*) 9

**Sol.** (*d*) Put A = 1, B = 2, C = 3 ..... X = 24, Y = 25, Z = 26

Then the pattern is as follow (Moving clockwise):

W – T = 23 – 20 = 3; S – D = 19 – 4 = 15 T – J = 20 – 10 = 10;

Therefore, missing number = P – G = 16 – 7 = 9.

**3.** 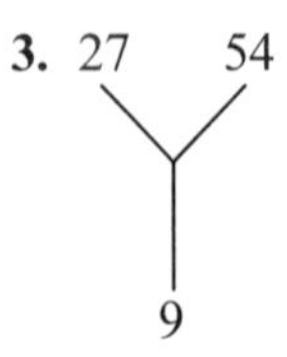


(*a*) 24 (*b*) 21 (*c*) 35 (*d*) 12

**Sol.** (*b*) The pattern is as follows:

$$\frac{27 + 54}{9} = 9; \ \frac{42 + 84}{14} = 9$$

Let the missing number be $x$

Then, $\frac{x + 42}{7} = 9$ or, $x = 21$

Therefore, missing number = 21.

**4.** 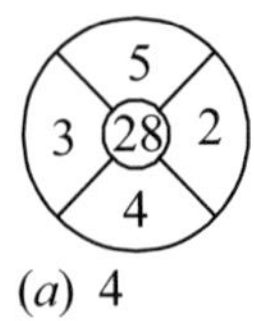


(*a*) 4 (*b*) 2 (*c*) 3 (*d*) 5

**Sol.** (*b*) The pattern is as follows: $\{(5)^2 + (4)^2\} - \{(3)^2 + (2)^2\} = 28$

Let the missing number be $x$

Then $\{(8)^2 + (4)^2\} - \{(8)^2 + (x)^2\} = 12$

or, $x^2 = 4$ or, $x = 2$

Therefore, missing number = 2.

## EXERCISE

**Directions (Qs. 1-45):** *In each question given below which one number/character can be placed at the sign of interrogation?*

**1.**

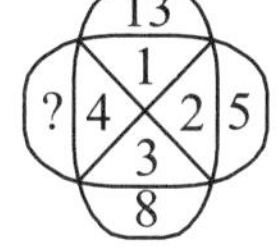


(*a*) 10 (*b*) 11 (*c*) 12 (*d*) 13

**2.**

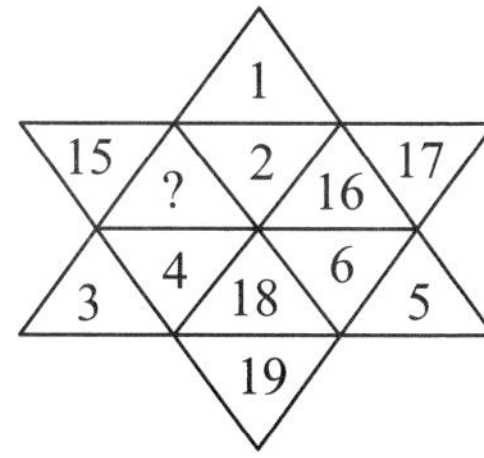


(*a*) 13 (*b*) 14 (*c*) 20 (*d*) 21

**3.**

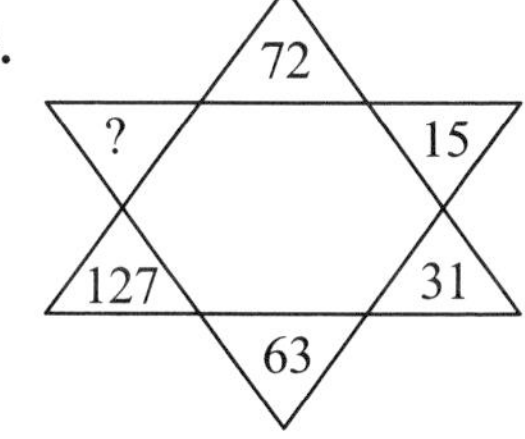


(*a*) 190 (*b*) 221 (*c*) 236 (*d*) 255

**4.** If 213 = 419; 322 = 924; 415 = 16125, then 215 = ?

(*a*) 625 (*b*) 4125 (*c*) 2541 (*d*) 1625

**5.**

28, 2, 3 — 50, 4, 5 — ?, 3, 5

(*a*) 35 (*b*) 40 (*c*) 49 (*d*) 53

**6.**

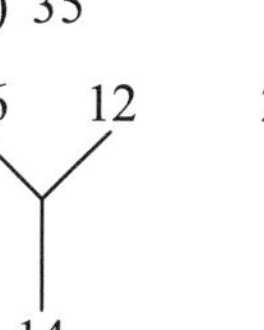


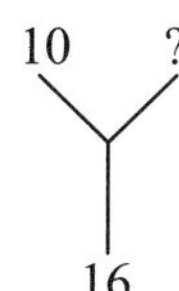


10 ? 16

(*a*) –21 (*b*) 12 (*c*) 32 (*d*) 22

**7.** 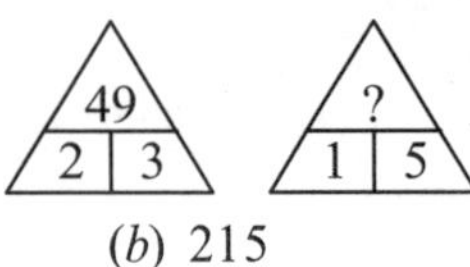


? / 1 5

(*a*) 125 (*b*) 215 (*c*) 251 (*d*) 512

**8.** 13 19 → 4; 71 9 → 10; 128 32 → ?

(*a*) 25 (*b*) 15 (*c*) 10 (*d*) 20

**9.** 36, 25, 27, 23, 30, 21, 33, ?

(*a*) 19 (*b*) 22 (*c*) 32 (*d*) 35

**10.** 12 18 30 → 6; 16 32 40 → 8; 36 18 27 → ?

(*a*) 6 (*b*) 9 (*c*) 12 (*d*) 18

**11.**

| DL | 10 | 14 | ER |
|---|---|---|---|
| RX | 23 | 18 | SM |
| KM | ? | ? | PV |

(*a*) 18, 34 (*b*) 14, 21 (*c*) 56, 84 (*d*) 12, 18

**12.** A, 9, D, 5, G, 4, J, 7; 35

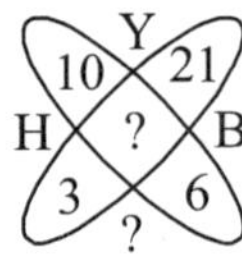


(*a*) F and 75 (*b*) E and 65 (*c*) D and 60 (*d*) C and 58

**13.**

| 7 | A | 5 |
|---|---|---|
| G | 49 | C |
| 4 | E | 3 |

| 8 | I | 4 |
|---|---|---|
| O | 40 | K |
| 6 | M | 2 |

| 5 | Q | 1 |
|---|---|---|
| W | ? | ? |
| 4 | U | 2 |

(*a*) V and 9 (*b*) T and 3 (*c*) S and 6 (*d*) Y and 5

**14.**

| 3 | 5 | 8 | 7 |
|---|---|---|---|
| 4 | 6 | 4 | 6 |
| 5 | 2 | 2 | 3 |
| 58 | 58 | 62 | ? |

(*a*) 126 (*b*) 122 (*c*) 128 (*d*) 124

**15.**

| 63 | 7 | 9 |
|---|---|---|
| 30 | 5 | 6 |
| 20 | 4 | ? |

(*a*) 8 (*b*) 3 (*c*) 5 (*d*) 2

**16.**

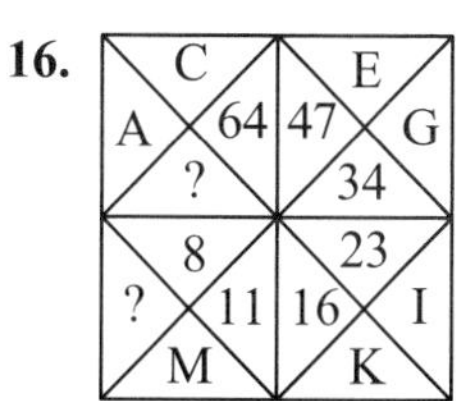


(*a*) J and 80 (*b*) O and 83 (*c*) N and 74 (*d*) P and 85

**17.**

| 1 | 3 | 7 |
|---|---|---|
| 2 | 4 | 4 |
| 4 | 5 | 9 |
| 3 | 2 | 3 |
| 50 | 70 | ? |

(*a*) 23 (*b*) 115 (*c*) 118 (*d*) 220

**18.**

| D | M | V |
|---|---|---|
| F | P | Z |
| H | S | ? |

(*a*) D (*b*) C (*c*) I (*d*) G

**19.**

| 92 | 70 | 48 |
|---|---|---|
| 64 | 53 | 42 |
| 52 | 45 | ? |

(*a*) 36 (*b*) 40 (*c*) 38 (*d*) 42

**20.**

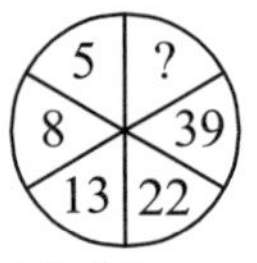


(*a*) 66 (*b*) 72 (*c*) 61 (*d*) 78

**21.** Consider the following matrix:

| 3 | 370 | 7 |
|---|---|---|
| 2 | 224 | 6 |
| 1 | 730 | X |

What is the number at 'X' in the above matrix?

(*a*) 5 (*b*) 8 (*c*) 9 (*d*) 11

**22.**

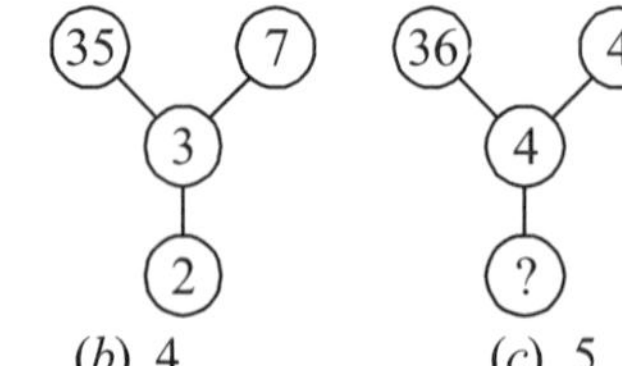


(*a*) 3 (*b*) 4 (*c*) 5 (*d*) 6

**23.**

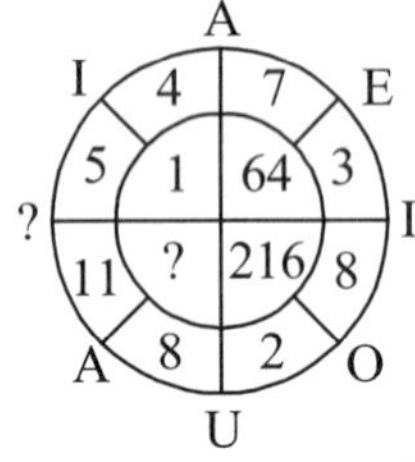


(*a*) U and 28 (*b*) I and 26 (*c*) E and 27 (*d*) A and 25

**24.**

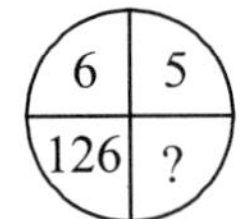


(*a*) 127 (*b*) 31 (*c*) 217 (*d*) 238

**25.**

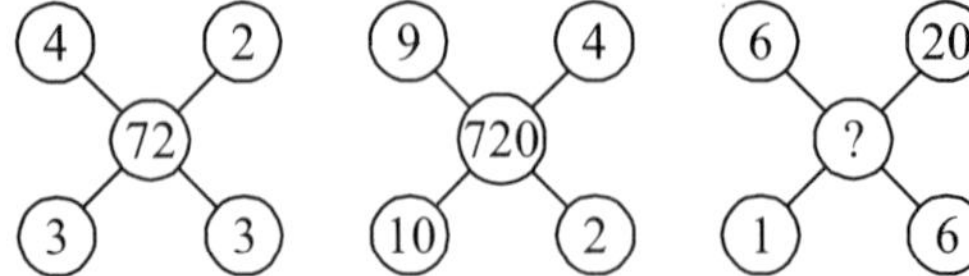


(*a*) 72 (*b*) 720 (*c*) 7200 (*d*) 38

**26.**

| | 3 | | | 4 | | | 7 | |
|---|---|---|---|---|---|---|---|---|
| 3 | (63) | 4 | 6 | (66) | 5 | 6 | (?) | 3 |
| | 6 | | | 2 | | | 5 | |

(*a*) 57 (*b*) 53 (*c*) 39 (*d*) 108

**27.**

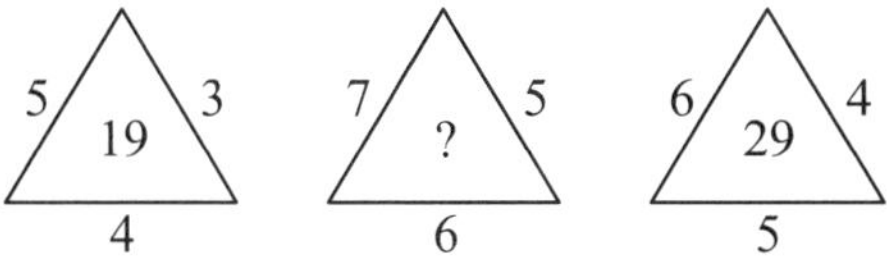

Triangle 1: sides 5, 3, 4; centre 19
Triangle 2: sides 7, 5, 6; centre ?
Triangle 3: sides 6, 4, 5; centre 29

(*a*) 25 (*b*) 37 (*c*) 41 (*d*) 45

**28.**

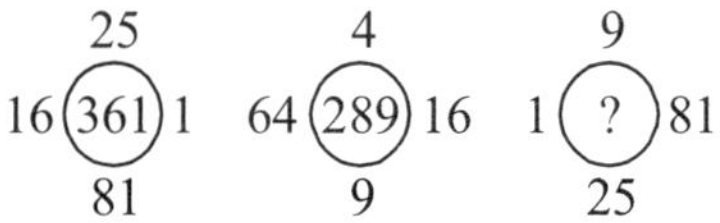

| | 25 | | | 4 | | | 9 | |
|---|---|---|---|---|---|---|---|---|
| 16 | (361) | 1 | 64 | (289) | 16 | 1 | (?) | 81 |
| | 81 | | | 9 | | | 25 | |

(*a*) 429 (*b*) 260 (*c*) 269 (*d*) 324

**29.**

| | 1 | | | 3 | | | 1 | |
|---|---|---|---|---|---|---|---|---|
| 3 | (510) | 5 | 2 | (650) | 4 | 0 | (?) | 2 |
| | 4 | | | 6 | | | 8 | |

(*a*) 610 (*b*) 660 (*c*) 670 (*d*) 690

**30.**

| A2 | C4 | E6 |
|---|---|---|
| G3 | I5 | ? |
| M5 | O9 | Q14 |

(*a*) J15 (*b*) K8 (*c*) K15 (*d*) L10

**31.**

| 2 | 5 | 10 |
|---|---|---|
| 17 | ? | 37 |
| 50 | 65 | 82 |

(*a*) 20 (*b*) 26 (*c*) 27 (*d*) 32

**32.**

| 1 | 4 | 9 | ? |
|---|---|---|---|
| 1 | 2 | 3 | 4 |
| 2 | 4 | 6 | ? |

(*a*) 16, 8 (*b*) 25, 5 (*c*) 36, 4 (*d*) 48, 7

**33.**

? 3
22 5
13 8

(*a*) 26 (*b*) 1 (*c*) 50 (*d*) 39

**34.**

| AZ | BY | CX |
|---|---|---|
| DW | ? | FU |
| GT | HS | IR |

(*a*) DB (*b*) DU (*c*) FH (*d*) EV

**35.**

| $AC_4$ | $BD_6$ | $EG_{12}$ |
|---|---|---|
| $HJ_{18}$ | $KM_{29}$ | ? |
| $QS_{36}$ | $TV_{38}$ | $WY_{76}$ |

(*a*) $PQ_{68}$ (*b*) $NP_{34}$ (*c*) $OQ_{49}$ (*d*) $NP_{49}$

**36.**

| 1 | 2 | 3 |
|---|---|---|
| 4 | 5 | 6 |
| 7 | 8 | 9 |
| 27 | 38 | ? |

(*a*) 52 (*b*) 51 (*c*) 50 (*d*) 49

**37.**

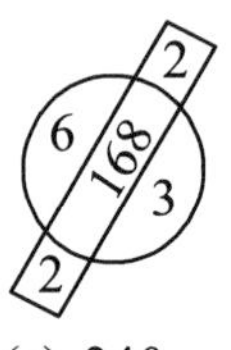

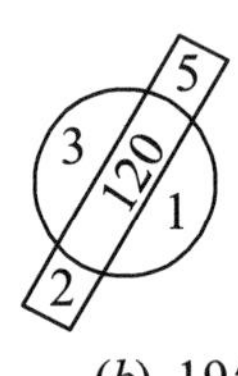

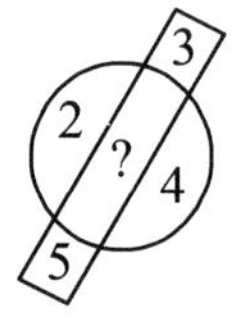


(*a*) 240 (*b*) 195 (*c*) 84 (*d*) None of these

**38.**

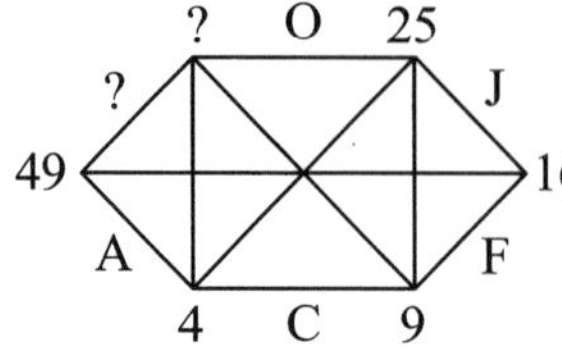


(*a*) Y and 40 (*b*) U and 36 (*c*) W and 64 (*d*) X and 81

**39.** The number of students in Art class is increasing month after month as follows:

| **Month** | Jan | Feb | Mar | Apr | May | June |
|---|---|---|---|---|---|---|
| **Number of students** | 1 | 2 | 4 | 7 | 11 | ? |

Find the number of students in June:
(*a*) 13 (*b*) 14 (*c*) 15 (*d*) 16

**40.** Examine the following three figures in which the numbers follow a specific pattern:

| 84 | | | 81 | | | 88 | |
|---|---|---|---|---|---|---|---|
| 14 | 12 | | 18 | 9 | | ? | 11 |

The missing number (?) in the third figure above is
(*a*) 7 (*b*) 16 (*c*) 21 (*d*) 28

**Directions (Qs. 41-44):** *Numbers in all the four figures given below follow a similar pattern. Find out the missing numbers:*

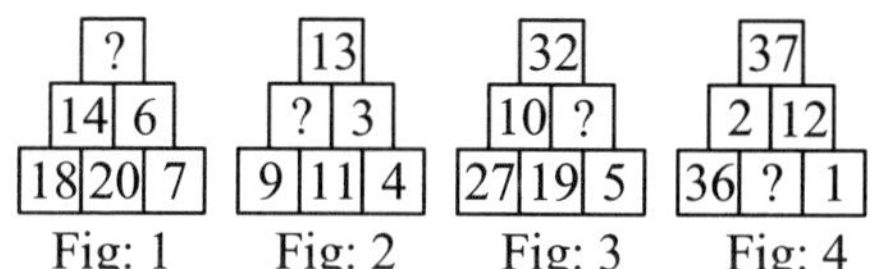


**41.** The missing number in fig. 1 is:
(*a*) 25 (*b*) 20 (*c*) 38 (*d*) 42

**42.** The missing number in fig. 4 is:
(*a*) 12 (*b*) 14 (*c*) 35 (*d*) 34

**43.** The missing number in fig. 2 is:
(*a*) 16 (*b*) 22 (*c*) 7 (*d*) 8

**44.** The missing number in fig. 3 is:
(*a*) 22 (*b*) 37 (*c*) 9 (*d*) 24

**45.** Number in boxes given below follow the same arrangement. Your task is to find out the missiong numbers:

| | 30 | | | | 22 | | | | 57 | |
|---|---|---|---|---|---|---|---|---|---|---|
| 18 | | 12 | | 13 | | 9 | | 30 | | 27 |
| 25 | 36 | 37 | | 19 | 16 | 27 | | ? | ? | ? |

(*a*) 51, 11, 55 (*b*) 15, 9, 32 (*c*) 65, 36, 63 (*d*) 55, 9, 61

## ANSWERS

| 1 | 2 | 3 | 4 | 5 | 6 | 7 | 8 | 9 | 10 |
|---|---|---|---|---|---|---|---|---|---|
| (*c*) | (*b*) | (*d*) | (*b*) | (*b*) | (*d*) | (*a*) | (*d*) | (*a*) | (*b*) |
| **11** | **12** | **13** | **14** | **15** | **16** | **17** | **18** | **19** | **20** |
| (*b*) | (*b*) | (*c*) | (*d*) | (*c*) | (*b*) | (*b*) | (*a*) | (*c*) | (*b*) |
| **21** | **22** | **23** | **24** | **25** | **26** | **27** | **28** | **29** | **30** |
| (*c*) | (*c*) | (*c*) | (*c*) | (*b*) | (*d*) | (*c*) | (*d*) | (*d*) | (*b*) |
| **31** | **32** | **33** | **34** | **35** | **36** | **37** | **38** | **39** | **40** |
| (*b*) | (*a*) | (*d*) | (*d*) | (*d*) | (*b*) | (*b*) | (*b*) | (*d*) | (*b*) |
| **41** | **42** | **43** | **44** | **45** | | | | | |
| (*a*) | (*b*) | (*d*) | (*c*) | (*d*) | | | | | |

## SOME SELECTED EXPLANATORY ANSWERS

**1.** The pattern is as follows:

$5 + 3 = 8$; $8 + 4 = 12$; $12 + 1 = 13$

Therefore, missing number = 12.

**2.** The pattern is as follows:

The numbers 1 to 6 are arranged in three alternate segments.

The smaller number towards the outside.

The numbers 14 to 19 are arranged in the remaining three alternate segments.

The smaller number towards the inside.

Therefore, missing number in the given figure = 14.

**3.** The pattern is as follows:

$7 \times 2 + 1 = 15$; $15 \times 2 + 1 = 31$;

$31 \times 2 + 1 = 63$; $63 \times 2 + 1 = 127$.

Therefore, missing number = $127 \times 2 + 1 = 255$.

**4.** The pattern is as follows:

Keep the middle number intact and square the number on either side i.e.

$213 = (2)^2\ \underline{1}\ (3)^2 = 419$;

$322 = (3)^2\ \underline{2}\ (2)^2 = 924$;

$415 = (4)^2\ \underline{1}\ (5)^2 = 16125$

Therefore, missing number = $215 = (2)^2\ 1\ (5)^2 = 4125$.

**5.** The pattern is as follows:

In the first fig., 2, 3 $\rightarrow$ $23 + 5 = 28$;

In the second fig., 4, 5 $\rightarrow$ 45 + 5 = 50;
In the third fig., 3, 5 $\rightarrow$ 35 + 5 = 40.
Therefore, missing number in the third fig. = 40.

**6.** The pattern is as follows:

In the first figure, $\dfrac{(16+12)}{2} = 14$;

In the socond figure $\dfrac{(21+9)}{2} = 15$

Let the missing number be $x$.

Then, in the third figure, $\dfrac{(10+x)}{2} = 16$

or, $x = 22$

Therefore, Missing Number = 22.

**7.** The pattern is as follows:

Number in the upper part = combination of the numbers obtained by squaring the numbers at the bottom.
In the first triangle, $(3)^2\ (4)^2 = 916$
In the second triangle, $(2)^2\ (3)^2 = 49$
Therefore, Missing Number in the third triangle
$= (1)^2\ (5)^2 = (1)\ (25) = 125.$

**8.** The pattern is as follows: $\dfrac{13+19}{8} = 4$; $\dfrac{71+9}{8} = 10$

Therefore, Missing Number = $\dfrac{128+32}{8} = 20$.

**9.** The pattern is as follows:

Moving anticlockwise, the numbers in alternate segments form the arithmetic series: 36, 33, 30, 27. Moving clockwise, the numbers in remaining segments from the arithmetic series: 25, 23, 21, 19

Therefore, missing number = 19.

**10.** The pattern is as follows:

12, 18, 30 are all multiples of 6;
16, 32, 40 ae all multiples of 8;
And 36, 18, 27 are all multiples of 9
Therefore, Missing Number = 9.

**11.** As, D L

$$\begin{array}{cc} D & L \\ \downarrow & \downarrow \end{array}$$

$$4 + 12 = \frac{16}{2} = 8 + 2 = 10$$

It means, place number of letter will be added and divided by 2, and after division, it is again added by 2.

Similarly,

$$\begin{array}{cc} K & M \\ \downarrow & \downarrow \end{array}$$

$$11 + 13 = \frac{24}{2} = 12 + 2 = \boxed{14}$$

$$\begin{array}{cc} P & V \\ \downarrow & \downarrow \end{array}$$

$$16 + 22 = \frac{38}{2} = 19 + 2 = \boxed{21}$$

**12.** In the first figure → starting from letter A in clockwise direction

$$A \xrightarrow{+3} D \xrightarrow{+3} G \xrightarrow{+3} J$$

and $(7 + 9) \times 2 + \sqrt{4 + 5} = 35$ (middle number)

In the second figure → starting from letter M in clockwise direction

$$M \xrightarrow{+3} P \xrightarrow{+3} S \xrightarrow{+3} V$$

and $(17 + 8) \times 2 + \sqrt{6 + 3} = 53$ (middle number)

In the third figure → starting from letter Y in clockwise direction

$$Y \xrightarrow{+3} B \xrightarrow{+3} \boxed{E} \xrightarrow{+3} H$$

and $(10 + 21) \times 2 + \sqrt{3 + 6} = \boxed{65}$ (middle number)

Hence, ? = E and 65.

**13.** In the first figure → starting from letter A in clockwise direction

$$A \xrightarrow{+2} C \xrightarrow{+2} E \xrightarrow{+2} G$$

and $(7^2 + 5^2) - (4^2 + 3^2) = (49 + 25) - (16 + 9) = 49$ (middle number)

In the second figure → starting from letter I in clockwise direction

$$I \xrightarrow{+2} K \xrightarrow{+2} M \xrightarrow{+2} O$$

and $(8^2 + 4^2) - (6^2 + 2^2) = (64 + 16) - (36 + 4) = 40$

(middle number)

In the third figure → starting from letter Q in clockwise direction

$$Q \xrightarrow{+2} S \xrightarrow{+2} U \xrightarrow{+2} W$$

and $(5^2 + 1^2) - (4^2 + 2^2) = (25 + 1) - (16 + 4) = \boxed{6}$

Hence, ? = S and 6.

**14.** As, $(3 \times 4 \times 5) - 2 = 60 - 2 = 58$

and $(5 \times 6 \times 2) - 2 = 60 - 2 = 58$

and $(8 \times 4 \times 2) - 2 = 64 - 2 = 62$

Similarly, $(7 \times 6 \times 3) - 2 = 126 - 2 = 124$

Hence, number 124 will be come in place of question mark.

**15.** As, $7 \times 9 = 63$

and $5 \times 6 = 30$

Similarly, $4 \times ? = 20$

$$? = \frac{20}{4} = 5.$$

**16.** Starting from letter A in clockwise direction

$$A \xrightarrow{+2} C \xrightarrow{+2} E \xrightarrow{+2} G \xrightarrow{+2} I$$

$$\xrightarrow{+2} K \xrightarrow{+2} M \xrightarrow{+2} \boxed{O}$$

Starting from number 8 in anti-clockwise direction (prime number sequence)

$$8 \xrightarrow{+3} 11 \xrightarrow{+5} 16 \xrightarrow{+7} 23 \xrightarrow{+11} 34$$

$$\xrightarrow{+13} 47 \xrightarrow{+17} 64 \xrightarrow{+19} \boxed{83}$$

Hence, ? = O and 83

**17.** As $1 + 2 + 4 + 3 = 10 \times 5 = 50$

and $3 + 4 + 5 + 2 = 14 \times 5 = 70$

Similarly, $7 + 4 + 9 + 3 = 23 \times 5 = 115.$

**18.** As, $D \xrightarrow{+2} F \xrightarrow{+2} H$

$M \xrightarrow{+3} P \xrightarrow{+3} S$

Similarly, $V \xrightarrow{+4} Z \xrightarrow{+4} \boxed{D}$

**19.** As, $92 + 64 + 52 = 208$

and $70 + 53 + 45 = 168$ ($-40$)

Similarly, $48 + 42 + \boxed{38} = 128$ ($-40$)

**20.** 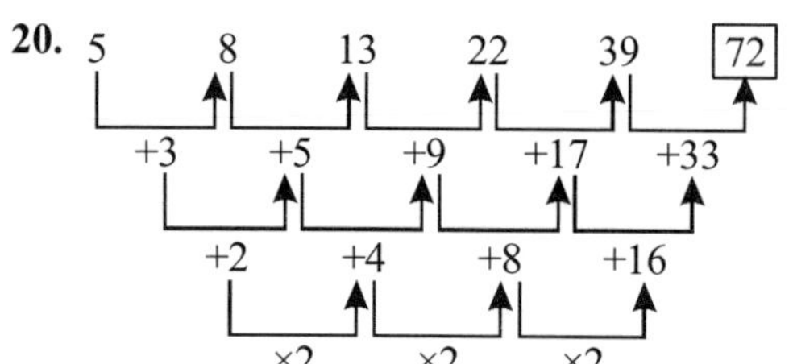


**21.** The sum of the digits of the number in the middle column equals the sum of the numbers in the column to lts left and right. So, in the first row we have $3 + 7 + 0 = 10 = 3 + 7$. In the second row we have $2 + 2 + 4 = 2 + 6$. Thus, in the third row the total of the left and right columns must be equal to $7 + 3 + 0 = 10$. Which means that the number in the right column must be equal to $10 - 1 = 9$.

**22.** 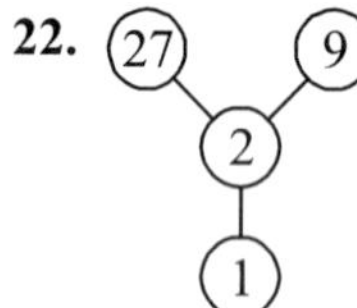


Figure is solved as,

$$27 \div 9 - 2 = 1$$

$$3 - 2 = 1 \quad \Rightarrow \quad 1 = 1$$

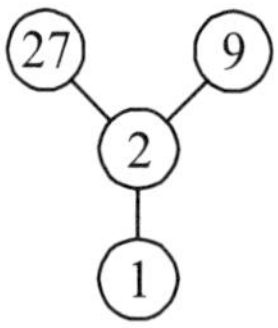

Similarly, second figure

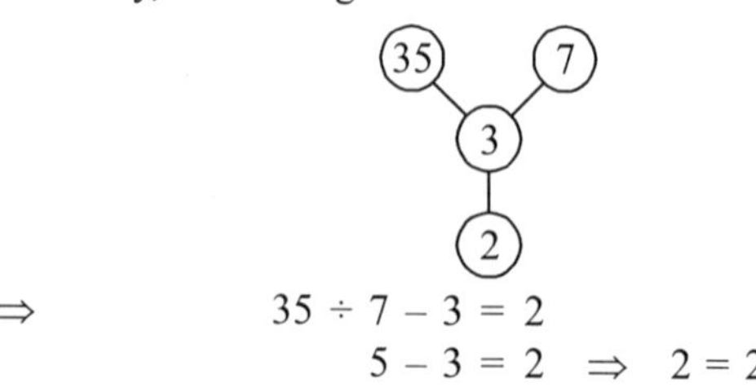


$\Rightarrow$

$$35 \div 7 - 3 = 2$$

$$5 - 3 = 2 \quad \Rightarrow \quad 2 = 2$$

Then,

$\Rightarrow$ $36 \div 4 - 4 = ?$

$9 - 4 = ? \Rightarrow ? = 5$

Hence, the correct option is (*c*).

**23.** Starting from letter A in vowel sequence in clockwise direction

A, E, I, O, U, A, $\boxed{E}$ (outer side)

In inner side, (right half part)

$(7 - 3)^3 = 64$ and $(8 - 2)^3 = 216$

In inner side, (left half part)

$(5 - 4)^3 = 1$ amd $(11 - 8)^3 = \boxed{27}$

Hence, ? = E and 27

**24.** As $5 \rightarrow 126 = 5^3 + 1 = 126$

$6 \rightarrow ? = 6^3 + 1 = \boxed{217}$

**25.** $4 \times 2 \times 3 \times 3 = 72$

$9 \times 4 \times 10 \times 2 = 720$

$6 \times 20 \times 1 \times 6 = \boxed{720}$

**26.** $(3 + 4) \times (3 + 6) = 7 \times 9 = 63$

$(4 + 2) \times (6 + 5) = 6 \times 11 = 66$

$(6 + 3) \times (7 + 5) = 9 \times 12 = \boxed{108}$

**27.** The pattern is as follows:

$5 \times 3 + 4 = 19,$ $6 \times 4 + 5 = 29$

Therefore, Missing Number $= 7 \times 5 + 6 = 41$.

**28.** The pattern is as follows:

Moving clockwise we get,

$$\left(\sqrt{25} + \sqrt{1} + \sqrt{81} + \sqrt{16}\right)^2 = 361;$$

$$\left(\sqrt{4} + \sqrt{16} + \sqrt{9} + \sqrt{64}\right)^2 = 289$$

Therefore, Missing Number $= \left(\sqrt{9} + \sqrt{81} + \sqrt{25} + \sqrt{1}\right)^2 = 324$.

**29.** The pattern is as follows:

Moving clockwise we get,

$$(1^2 + 5^2 + 4^2 + 3^2) \times 10 = 510;$$

$$(3^2 + 4^2 + 6^2 + 2^2) \times 10 = 650$$

Therefore, Missing Number $= (1^2 + 2^2 + 8^2 + 0^2) \times 10 = 690$.

**30.** The pattern is as follows:
In each row, letters follows the sequence +2 *i.e.*,
A, C, E; G, I, K; M, O,Q
Also, in each row, sum of the first two number = The Third number, i.e.
$2 + 4 = 6$; $3 + 5 = 8$; $5 + 9 = 14$
Therefore, in the second row, the missing pair of letters and number K8.

**31.** The pattern is as follows
$1^2 + 1 = 2$; $2^2 + 1 = 5$; $3^2 + 1 = 10$;
$4^2 + 1 = 17$; $5^2 + 1 = 26$; $6^2 + 1 = 37$;
$7^2 + 1 = 50$; $8^2 + 1 = 65$ $9^2 + 1 = 82$
Therefore, the missing number = 26.

**32.** The pattern is as follows:
First row = (second row)$^2$, i.e. $1^2 = 1$; $2^2 = 4$;
$3^2 = 9$; $4^2 = 16$
and third row = 2 × (second row), *i.e.*
$2 \times 1 = 2$; $2 \times 2 = 4$; $3 \times 2 = 6$; $4 \times 2 = 8$
Therefore, missing numbers in the first and the third row are $4^2$, *i.e.* 16 and $4 \times 2$, *i.e.* 8 respectively.

**33.** The pattern is as follows:
Moving clokwise we get,
$3 \times 2 - 1 = 5$; $5 \times 2 - 2 = 8$;
$8 \times 2 - 3 = 13$; $13 \times 2 - 4 = 22$
Therefore, missing number = $22 \times 2 - 5 = 39$.

**34.** Put A = 1, B = 2, C = 3, ...., X = 24, Y = 25, Z = 26
Then the pattern is as follows:
AZ = A + Z = 1 + 26 = 27,
BY = B + Y = 2 + 25 = 27,
CX = C + X = 3 + 24 = 27,
DW = D + W = 4 + 23 = 27,
EV = E + V = 5 + 22 = 27,
FU = F + U = 6 + 21 = 27,
GT = G + T = 7 + 20 = 27,
HS = H + S = 8 + 19 = 27,
and IR = I + R = 9 + 18 = 27
Therefore, the missing pair = EV.

**35.** The pattern is as follows:
Each block comprises two letters and a number. Letters occur in pair with a gap of one letter in the block.

Number in the third column in each row = (Sum of numbers of first and second columns + 2) in the same row
i.e. 4 + 6 + 2 = 12; 18 + 29 + 2 = 49; 36 + 38 + 2 = 76

**36.** The pattern is as follows:
In the first column, $(4 \times 7) - 1 = 27$;
In the second column, $(5 \times 8) - 2 = 38$
Therefore, in the third column,
Missing number = $(6 \times 9) - 3 = 51$.

**37.** The pattern is as follows:

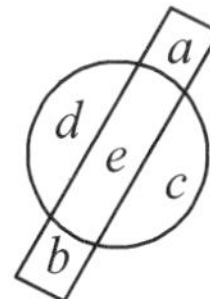


Here,

$$e = (a + b + c + d)^2 - 1$$
$$? = (2 + 3 + 4 + 5)^2 - 1$$
$$= 196 - 1 = 195$$

Therefore, missing number = 195.

**38.** Starting from letter A in anti-clockwise direction:

$$A \xrightarrow{+2} C \xrightarrow{+3} F \xrightarrow{+4} J \xrightarrow{+5} O \xrightarrow{+6} U$$

Starting from number 4 in anti-clockwise direction
$2^2 = 4$, $3^2 = 9$, $4^2 = 16$, $5^2 = 25$, $6^2 = 36$
Hence, ? = U and 36.

**39.** Number of students increase in following order:

1 →(+1) 2 →(+2) 4 →(+3) 7 →(+4) 11 →(+5) 16

∴ Number of students in June = 16.

**40.** In the fist two figures, the number at the top is divided by the number at the right and is then doubled, *e.g.* in the first figure, $\frac{84}{12} = 7$ and $2 \times 7 = 14$. In the second figure $\frac{81}{9} = 9$ and $2 \times 9 = 18$. In the third figure $\frac{88}{11} = 8$. And the missing number will be $2 \times 8 = 16$.

**41.** The pattern is as follows:

The middle number in the third row = Sum of the two numbers in the second row, i.e. 14 + 6 = 20

And sum of the first and the third number in the third row = number in the first row, i.e. 18 + 7 = 25

Therefore, missing number in the first row = 25.

**42.** Same pattern as in the above questions.

Therefore, missing number in the third row = 2 + 12 = 14.

**43.** The pattern is as follows:

sum of the first and the third numbers in the third row = number in the first row, i.e. 9 + 4 = 13,

Let the missing number be $x$.

Then, sum of the two numbers in the second row = The middle number in the third row, i.e.

$$x + 3 = 11 \quad \text{or,} \quad x = 8$$

**44.** Same pattern as in the above questions.
Let the missing number be $x$.
Then, $10 + x = 19$, or, $x = 9$

**45.** The pattern is as follows:
In the first figure,

$18 + 12 = 30$, $(12 \times 2) + 1 = 25$,
$(18 - 12)^2 = 6^2 = 36$, $(18 \times 2) + 1 = 37$.

In the second figure,

$13 + 9 = 22$, $(9 \times 2) + 1 = 19$,
$(13 - 9)^2 = 16$, $(13 \times 2) + 1 = 27$.

So, in the third figure,

$30 + 27 = 57$, $(27 \times 2) + 1 = 55$;
$(30 - 27)^2 = 9$, $(30 \times 2) + 1 = 61$.

So, Missing numbers in the third fig. are 55, 9, 61.

✦✦✦✦

# 12

# Letter and Word formation

## INTRODUCTION

'Word formation' is an advanced level alphabet test. This test is meant to test the ability of the candidate in word building process.

In word formation, a main word is given and we have to choose that word, which can or cannot be formed from the main word. Sometimes a set of English letters are given in a jumbled order and the candidates are asked to arrange them in a meaningful order. In some situations, we are asked to choose particular letters from a word and arrange them to form a meaningful word.

## SOLVED EXAMPLE

**Directions (Qs. 1-2):** *In each of the following questions, a word has been given, followed by four other words, one of which can be formed by using the letters of the given word. Find that word.*

**1.** MEASUREMENT

(*a*) ASSURE (*b*) MASTER (*c*) SUMMIT (*d*) MANTLE

**Sol.** (*b*) MASTER—All the letters of this word are present in the main word.

Hence, 'MASTER' can be formed from the letters of the given word 'MEASUREMENT'.

**2.** COMPENSATION

(*a*) TINY (*b*) COPY (*c*) MENTION (*d*) MOTIVE

**Sol.** (*c*) MENTION—All the letters of this word are present in the main word. Hence, 'MENTION' can be formed from the letters of the given word 'COMPENSATION'.

**3.** If it is possible to make a meaningful word with the 1st, 4th, 7th and 11th letters from the word 'INTERPRETATION', which of the following will be the third letter of that word? If more than one such word can be made, given 'M' as the answer and if no such word can be formed, give 'X' as the answer.

(*a*) T (*b*) R (*c*) M (*d*) X

**Sol.** (*c*) Since, 1st, 4th, 7th and 11th letters are I, E, R and T, respectively. Hence, two meaningful words RITE and TIRE can be formed.

**4.** Which word cannot be formed by using the letters of the word 'NATIONALISATION'

(*a*) NOTATION (*b*) SALINATION
(*c*) INSTALLATION (*d*) SANITATION

**Sol.** (*c*) INSTALLATION—All the letters except second 'L' are present in the main word.

Hence, 'INSTALLATION' cannot be formed from the letters of the given word 'NATIONALISATION'.

## EXERCISE

**Directions (Qs. 1-3):** *In each of the following, questions, a word has been given, followed by four other words, one of which cannot be formed by using the letters from the given word. Find that word:*

**1.** COMMUNICATION
(*a*) ACTION (*b*) UNION (*c*) NATION (*d*) UNISON

**2.** CONCEPTUALISATION
(*a*) STATUS (*b*) POINTS (*c*) NOISE (*d*) TOTAL

**3.** PORTFOLIO
(*a*) RIFT (*b*) ROOF (*c*) FORT (*d*) PORTICO

**Directions (Qs. 4-5):** *In each of the following questions, a word has been given, followed by four other words. One of which can be formed by using the letters from the given word. Find that word.*

**4.** IMMEDIATELY
(*a*) DIALECT (*b*) LIMITED (*c*) DIAMETER (*d*) DICTATE

**5.** COMPANIONSHIP
(*a*) OPEN (*b*) OPIUM (*c*) OPINION (*d*) NATION

**6.** If a meaningful word can be formed beginning with H using the letters SUHRO the fourth letter of that word is your answer. If more than one such word can be formed then 'B' is your answer. If no such word is formed, then 'C' is your answer.
(*a*) B (*b*) C (*c*) U (*d*) R

**7.** If with the third, fourth, fifth, seventh and tenth letters of the word PERSONALITY, a meaningful word is formed, then first letter of the word is the answer. If no word is possible, then 'X' is the answer.
(*a*) O (*b*) T (*c*) R (*d*) X

**8.** Pick the first, second, fourth, fifth and sixth letters of the word REASONING, form yet another word and then write the first and the last letters of the word formed.

(*a*) O & R (*b*) N & E (*c*) S & E (*d*) E & S

**9.** How many meaningful English words can be formed by using any two letters of the word 'NOT'?

(*a*) One (*b*) Two
(*c*) Three (*d*) More than three

**10.** If the letters of the word ARTICULATES can be used as many times as one wants to use, then which one of the following four words cannot be formed?

(*a*) COURTS (*b*) LATER (*c*) ELECTRIC (*d*) ARTICLE

**11.** How many such pairs of letters are there in the word STREAM, each of which has as many letters between them in the word as in the English alphabet?

(*a*) None (*b*) One (*c*) Two (*d*) Three

**12.** How many such pairs of letters are there in the word TEMPORAL each of which has as many letters between them in the word as in the English alphabet?

(*a*) None (*b*) One
(*c*) Two (*d*) More than three

**13.** How many such pairs of letters are there in the word APPREHENSION each of which has as many letters between them in the word as in the English alphabet?

(*a*) Four (*b*) Five (*c*) Six (*d*) Seven

**14.** How many such pairs of letters are there in the word RESIDENTIAL, each of which has as many letters between them in the word as in the English alphabet?

(*a*) Nil (*b*) One (*c*) Two (*d*) Three

**15.** How many such pairs of letters are there in the word DIVERSION each of which has as many letters between them in the word as in the English aphabet?

(*a*) None (*b*) One
(*c*) Two (*d*) More than three

**16.** If the letters of the word VERTICAL are arranged alphabetically, how many letters will remain at the same position ?

(*a*) Four (*b*) Three (*c*) Two (*d*) None of these

**17.** If the order of letters of each of the following words is reversed then which of the following will be a meaningful word thus formed? If more than one such word can be formed mark 'S' as the answer and if no such word can be formed mark 'X' as the answer. NAIL, PAIL, RAIL, MADAM, REST.
(*a*) X (*b*) PAIL (*c*) MADAM (*d*) S

**18.** What will be the rearranged form of the word 'HYDROGEN' if its letters having been arranged in alphabetical order are then substituted by the immediate previous letters in the English alphabet?
(*a*) CDFGMQZ (*b*) EFHIOPSZ (*c*) CDFGMNQX (*d*) CDEGMNQX

**19.** The position of how many letters in the word BRAKES remains unchanged when they are arranged in alphabetical order?
(*a*) One (*b*) Two (*c*) Three (*d*) None of these

**20.** The positions of the first and the sixth letters in the word 'CONTEXTUAL' are interchanged. Similarly, the positions of the second and the seventh letters are interchanged, and so on. Which of the following will be the fourth letter from the right end after the rearrangement?
(*a*) O (*b*) N (*c*) T (*d*) E

**21.** The position of how many letters in the word 'WONDERFUL' will remain unchanged when the letters within the word are arranged alphabetically?
(*a*) None (*b*) One (*c*) Two (*d*) Three

**22.** If in the word 'DISTURBANCE', the first letter is interchanged with the last letter, the second letter is interchanged with the tenth letter and so on, which letter would come after 'T' in the newly formed word?
(*a*) I (*b*) N (*c*) S (*d*) E

**23.** If the first and the second letters in the word 'DEPRESSION' were inter changed, also the third and the fourth letters, the fifth and the sixth letters and so on, which of the following would be the seventh letter from the right?
(*a*) R (*b*) O (*c*) S (*d*) None of these

**24.** If the letters in the word 'COMPARE' are rearranged in such a way that first the vowels within the word are rearranged alphabetically followed by the consonants arranged alphabetically, which of the following will be the fifth letter from the right end after the rearrangement?
(*a*) O (*b*) E (*c*) M (*d*) P

**25.** If the positions of the first and the sixth letters in the word 'CONTAGIOUS' are interchanged, similarly the positions of the second and the seventh letters are interchanged, and so on, which letter will be the second to the right of the fifth letter from the right?

(*a*) O (*b*) N (*c*) I (*d*) T

**Directions (Qs. 26-30):** *If all the letters from A to Z were written as A_C_E_G_ upto Y, i.e., dropping each alternative letter, leaving blank spaces and then all the blanks were filled in with remaining letters in reverse order, i.e. AZCXE V... ending with B, answer the following questions:*

**26.** Which letter is to the right of sixteenth letter from the left end?
(*a*) M (*b*) N (*c*) Q (*d*) R

**27.** Which letters are exactly in the middle of the eighteenth letter from the left and fourteenth letter from the right end?
(*a*) MN (*b*) NO (*c*) OL (*d*) PM

**28.** Which letter would be placed between Q and S?
(*a*) H (*b*) J (*c*) L (*d*) R

**29.** How many pairs of letters in the series are old neighbours from regular alphabetical order?
(*a*) One (*b*) Two (*c*) Three (*d*) None

**30.** Which letters would be to the right and left of G?
(*a*) P and N (*b*) R and T (*c*) F and H (*d*) T and V

**31.** Each letter of the alphabet from Z to A has been given a value from 1 to 26 serially. What is the total value of the word CONSEQUENCE?
(*a*) 137 (*b*) 154 (*c*) 176 (*d*) 196

**32.** In the English alphabet, if all the letters in the even position are substituted by 3, all the letters in odd position are substituted by 5, then what will be the total of the numeric values of the letters of the word 'BEAD'?
(*a*) 16 (*b*) 29 (*c*) 18 (*d*) 20

**33.** If each letter in the English alphabet is attached a value equal to its serial number in the alphabet, which among the following will have the highest sum of the values of all its letters?
(*a*) WIND (*b*) TONE (*c*) BUDY (*d*) MORE

**34.** If each of the twelve digits on a watch is replaced by English vowels *a, e, i, o, u* in sequence (1 by *a*, 2 by *e*, and so on and so forth), the hour hand will be between which pair of vowels at 9 : 30 a.m.?
(*a*) ae (*b*) ei (*c*) io (*d*) ou

**35.** The English alphabet series comprises of 26 alphabets. If in this series, a number of letters in between any 2 adjacent letters are skipped and this skipping gap increases by one, then which of the following series observes the given rule?
(*a*) ACFJO (*b*) AEIMQ (*c*) DINSX (*d*) EHKNQ

**36.** The letters skipped between adjacent letters are the order of 1, 2, 3, 4, .... . Which alternative follows this rule.
(*a*) DFIMS (*b*) DEIMR (*c*) DFINR (*d*) DFIMR

**Directions (Qs. 37-40):** *These questions are based on the following arrangement of symbols, letters and numbers:*

∂ = β F 2 T K S 7 5 # $ P L V 8 @ M 6 ↑ Q G © 9 3 & T Y £

**37.** What will come in place of question mark (?) in the following ?
If ' = → 2', 'K → #', 'P → M', then ' ↑ → ?'
(*a*) 3 (*b*) T (*c*) 9 (*d*) None of these

**38.** How many such letters are there in the arrangement, each of which is either immediately preceded by a symbol or immediately followed by a number?
(*a*) 3 (*b*) 4 (*c*) 5 (*d*) None of these

**39.** How many such numbers are there in the arrangement each of which is either immediately followed by a symbol or immediately preceded by a letter?
(*a*) Nil (*b*) 2 (*c*) 3 (*d*) None of these

**40.** Based on the positions in the above arrangement, if β F ∂ : T & £, the K T 7 : ?
(*a*) © 9 Q (*b*) © G Q (*c*) © 9 ↑ (*d*) 9 © Q

## ANSWERS

| 1 | 2 | 3 | 4 | 5 | 6 | 7 | 8 | 9 | 10 |
|---|---|---|---|---|---|---|---|---|---|
| (*d*) | (*a*) | (*d*) | (*b*) | (*c*) | (*d*) | (*c*) | (*c*) | (*c*) | (*a*) |
| **11** | **12** | **13** | **14** | **15** | **16** | **17** | **18** | **19** | **20** |
| (*b*) | (*d*) | (*b*) | (*c*) | (*d*) | (*d*) | (*d*) | (*c*) | (*b*) | (*a*) |
| **21** | **22** | **23** | **24** | **25** | **26** | **27** | **28** | **29** | **30** |
| (*b*) | (*c*) | (*d*) | (*a*) | (*b*) | (*c*) | (*c*) | (*b*) | (*b*) | (*d*) |
| **31** | **32** | **33** | **34** | **35** | **36** | **37** | **38** | **39** | **40** |
| (*c*) | (*a*) | (*b*) | (*d*) | (*a*) | (*d*) | (*d*) | (*d*) | (*d*) | (*a*) |

## SOME SELECTED EXPLANATORY ANSWERS

**1.** UNISON cannot be formed letter 'S' is not in the given word.

**2.** From the word 'CONCEPTUALISATION' the word which cannot be formed is STATUS as it contains only one 'S'.

**3.** 'PORTICO' word cannot be formed from 'PORTFOLIO' due to the absence of letter 'C'.

**4.** 'LIMITED' is the only word which can be formed by usning the letters of given word.

**5.** 'OPINION' can be formed form 'COMPANIONSHIP'.

**6.** The meaningful word obtained from the given letters beginning with

H = H O U R S
1 2 3 4 5

So, fourth letter or the word 'H O U R S' = R
1 2 3 4 5

**7.** The third, fourth, fifth, seventh and tenth letters of the word

P E [R] [S] [O] N [A] L I [T] Y
1 2 [3] [4] [5] 6 [7] 8 9 [10] 11

are R, S, O, R and T respectively.
The only meaningful word obtained from these letters
= 'R O A S T'
1 2 3 4 5

Therefore, first letter of the word 'R O A S T' = R
1 2 3 4 5

**8.** The first, second, fourth, fifth and sixth letters of the word

[R] [E] A [S] [O] [N] I N G
[1] [2] 3 [4] [5] [6] 7 8 9

are R, E, S, O and N respectively.
The only meaningful word obtained from these letters
= 'S N O R E'
1 2 3 4 5

So, the first and the last letters of the word

[S] N O R [E] = S & E
[1] 2 3 4 [5]

**9.** Words formed using any two letters of the word 'NOT' are as follows:
(*i*) NO (*ii*) ON (*iii*) TO
So, required no. of words = Three.

**10.** The words 'ARTICULATES' does not contain the letter 'O'.
So, the word cannot be formed from the letters of the word 'ARTICULATES'
= C[O]URTS.

**11.** From the given word

19 20 18 5 1 13
S T R E A M

We find that S ( ) T is the only pair having no letter between them as in the alphabetical order. Therefore, there is only one such pair Viz. ST.

**12.** From the given word T E M P O R A L

We find that M (P) O, P ( ) O, P (O) R, P (O R A) L and O (R A) L are the pairs having one letter, no letter, one letter, three letters and two letters respectively between them as in the alphabetical order.

Therefore, there are five such pairs Viz.

MO, PO, PR, PL and OL.

**13.** From the given word A P P R E H E N S I O N.

We find that A (P P R) E, P (P) R, R (E H E) N, H (E N S I O) N and O ( ) N are the pairs having three letters, one letter, three letters, five letters and no letter respectively between them as in the alphabetical order.

Therefore, there are five such pairs Viz.

AE, PR, RN, HN and ON.

**14.** From the given word

18 5 19 9 4 5 14 20 9 1 12
R E S I D E N T I A L

We find that D ( ) E and E (N T I) A are the pairs having no letter and three letters respectively between them as in he alphabetical order. Therefore, there are two such pairs Viz. DE and EA.

**15.** From the given word D I V E R S I O N

We find that I (V E R S I) O, V (E R) S, R ( ) S, R (S I) O, R (S I O) N, and O ( ) N are the pairs having five letters, two letters, no letter, two letters, three letters and no letter respectively between them as in the alphabetical order.

**16.** The new position of letters after the rearrangement or the letters according to English alphabet is as follows:

| Position of letters in the given word | 1 2 3 4 5 6 7 8<br>V E R T I C A L |
|---|---|
| New position of letters according to alphabetical order | A C E I L R T V<br>1 2 3 4 5 6 7 8 |

Therefore, none of the letters will remain at the same position.

**17.** On reversing the order of the given words, we get

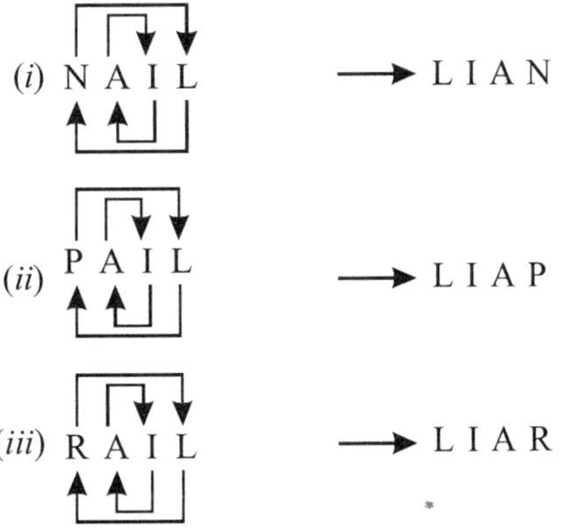

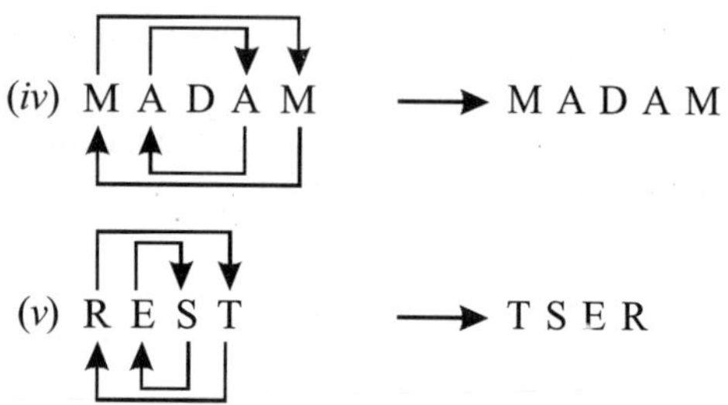


So, among the above five, LIAR and MADAM are meaningful words. Since the number of meaningful words is more than one.

Therefore, our answer is 'S'.

**18.** The given word is

| 8 | 25 | 4 | 18 | 15 | 7 | 5 | 14 |
|---|---|---|---|---|---|---|---|
| H | Y | D | R | O | G | E | N. |

After the rearrangement of the letters of the given word according to English alphabet or in alphabetical order.

We get

| D | E | G | H | N | O | R | Y. |
|---|---|---|---|---|---|---|---|
| 4 | 5 | 7 | 8 | 14 | 15 | 18 | 25 |

Then, the new arrangement of letters are substituted by the immediate previous letters, *i.e.*

| 4 | 5 | 7 | 8 | 14 | 15 | 18 | 25 |
|---|---|---|---|---|---|---|---|
| D | E | G | H | N | O | R | Y |
| −1 | −1 | −1 | −1 | −1 | −1 | −1 | −1 |
| ↓ | ↓ | ↓ | ↓ | ↓ | ↓ | ↓ | ↓ |
| C | D | F | G | M | N | Q | X |
| 3 | 4 | 6 | 7 | 13 | 14 | 17 | 24 |

Therefore, the rearranged form of the word 'HYDROGEN' = CDFGMNQX.

**19.** The new position of letters after the rearrangement of the letters according to English alphabet is as follows:

| | 1 | 2 | 3 | 4 | 5 | 6 |
|---|---|---|---|---|---|---|
| Position of letters in the given word | B | R | A | K | E | S |
| | ↕ | ↕ | ↕ | ↕ | ↕ | ↕ |
| New position of letters according to English alphabet | A | B | E | K | R | S |
| | 1 | 2 | 3 | 4 | 5 | 6 |

Therefore, the positions of letter K and letter S remain unchanged.

**20.** The new arrangement of letters is as given below:

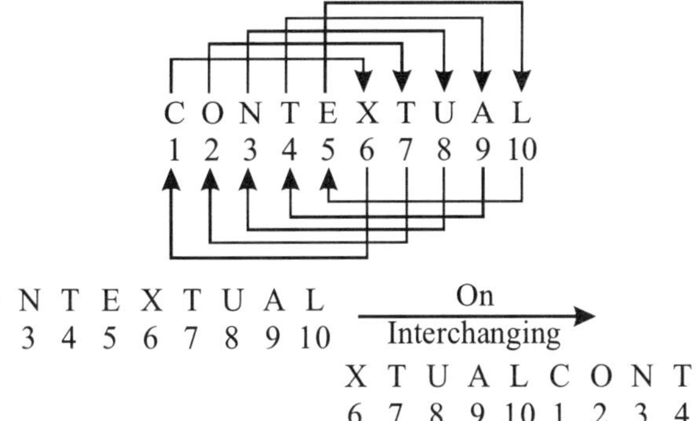


Therefore, the fourth letter from the right end in the new arrangement 'XTUALCONTE' = 'O'.

**21.** The new position of letters after the rearrangement of the letters according to English alphabet is as follows:

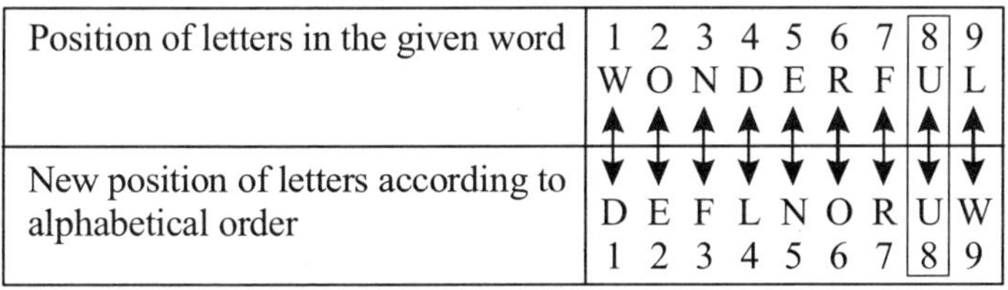

| Position of letters in the given word | 1 2 3 4 5 6 7 8 9<br>W O N D E R F U L |
|---|---|
| New position of letters according to alphabetical order | D E F L N O R U W<br>1 2 3 4 5 6 7 8 9 |

Therefore, the position of letter 'U' only remains unchanged.

**22.** The new arrangement of letters is as given below:

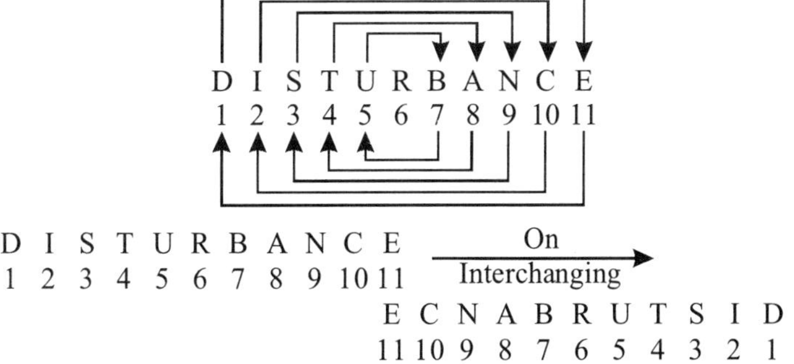


Therefore, the letter comes after letter 'T' in the new arrangement 'ECNABRU<u>TS</u>ID' = 'S'.

**23.** The new arrangement of letters is as given below:

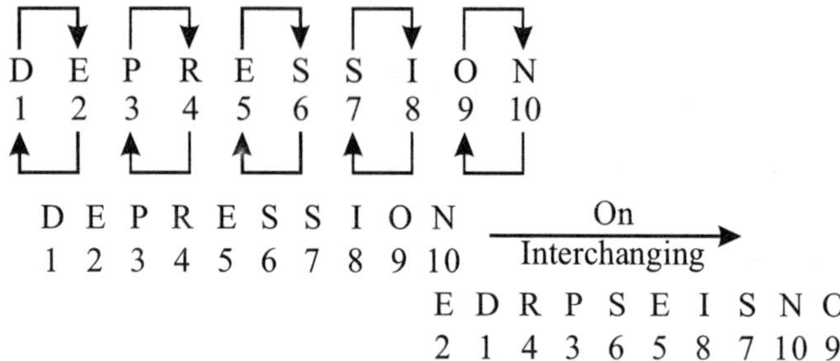

Therefore, the seventh letter from the right in the new arrangement 'EDRPSEISNO' = 'P'

**24.** The vowels in the word 'COMPARE' are O, A and E. Arrangement of vowels in alphabetical order:

A, E, O.

Arrangement of consonants in alphabetical order:

C, M, P, R.

So, the new arrangement:

A E [O] C M P R.

Therefore, the fifth letter from the right end in the new arrangement = 'O'.

**25.** The new arrangement of letters is as given below:

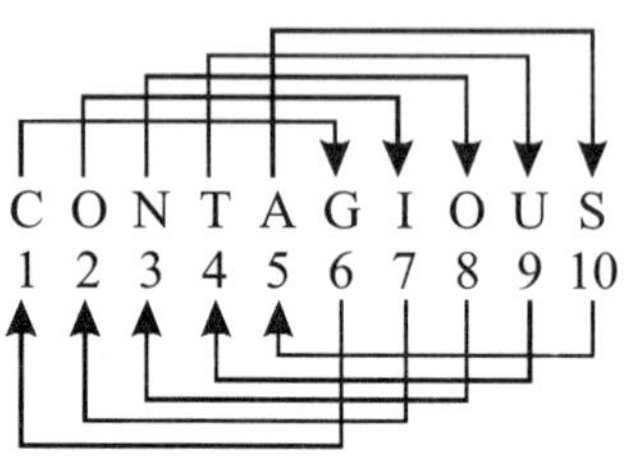

C O N T A G I O U S
1 2 3 4 5 6 7 8 9 10 —On Interchanging→
G I O U S C O N T A
6 7 8 9 10 1 2 3 4 5

So, new arrangement: GIOUSCONTA. Therefore, the second letter to the right of the fifth letter from the right end = (5 – 2) = 3rd letter from the right end = 'N'.

**26-30.**

A Z C X E V G T I R K P M N O L Q J S H U F W D Y B

**26.** The sixteenth letter from the left, i.e. from A = L.

So, the letter to the right of L = Q.

**27.** The eighteenth letter from the, i.e. from A = J.

The fourteenth letter from the right, i.e. from B = M.

MN OL QJ

So, middle letters between MN and QJ is OL.

**28.** Letter J is between Q and S.

**29.** There are two such pairs in the given series containing letters in alphabetical order –MN and NO.

**30.** Letters T and V are to the right and left respectively of letter G in the given series.

**31.** According to the question:

| Letter | Z | Y | X | W | V | U | T | S | R | Q | P | O | N | M | L | K | J | I | H | G | F | E | D | C | B | A |
|---|---|---|---|---|---|---|---|---|---|---|---|---|---|---|---|---|---|---|---|---|---|---|---|---|---|---|
| Numerical Value | 1 | 2 | 3 | 4 | 5 | 6 | 7 | 8 | 9 | 10 | 11 | 12 | 13 | 14 | 15 | 16 | 17 | 18 | 19 | 20 | 21 | 22 | 23 | 24 | 25 | 26 |

So, the total value of the word 'CONSEQUENCE'

= C + O + N + S + E + Q + U + E + N + C + E

= 24 + 12 + 13 + 8 + 22 + 10 + 6 + 22 + 13 + 24 + 22 = 176.

**32.** According to the question:

| Letter | A | B | C | D | E | F | G | H | I | J | K | L | M | N | O | P | Q | R | S | T | U | V | W | X | Y | Z |
|---|---|---|---|---|---|---|---|---|---|---|---|---|---|---|---|---|---|---|---|---|---|---|---|---|---|---|
| Numerical Value | 5 | 3 | 4 | 3 | 5 | 3 | 4 | 3 | 5 | 3 | 4 | 3 | 4 | 3 | 5 | 3 | 4 | 3 | 4 | 3 | 5 | 3 | 4 | 3 | 4 | 3 |

So, the total of the numeric values of the letters of the word 'BEAD'

= B + E + A + D

= 3 + 5 + 5 + 3 = 16.

**33.** Put A = 1, B = 2, C = 3, D = 4, ... X = 24, Y = 25, Z = 26.

WIND → W + I + N + D = 23 + 9 + 14 + 4 = 50.

TONE → T + O + N + E = 20 + 15 + 14 + 5 = 54.

BUDY → B + U + D + Y = 2 + 21 + 4 + 25 = 52.

MORY → M + O + R + E = 13 + 15 + 18 + 5 = 51.

NOSE → N + O + S + E = 14 + 15 + 19 + 5 = 53.

So, the highest sum of the values of all its letters = TONE.

**34.** According to the question, the clock is as shown in the adjoining figure.

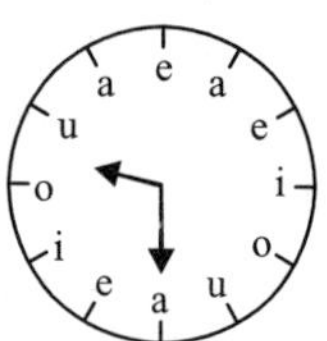


Therefore, the hour hand at 9 : 30 a.m will be between o and u.

**35.** The required pattern is as follows:

A B C D E F G H I J K L M N O
1 (A–C) 2 (C–F) 3 (F–J) 4 (J–O)

**36.** The required pattern is as follows:

D E F G H I J K L M N O P Q R
1 (D–F) 2 (F–I) 3 (I–M) 4 (M–R)

**37.** The pattern is as follows: +3, +4, +5, +6

'= → 2' (+3) ; 'K → #' (+4) ; 'P → M' (+5)

So, '↑ → &' (+6)

**38.** In the given arrangement, there are eight such letters, i.e., F, K, S, P, V, M, Q and T.

**39.** In the given arrangement, there are six such numbers, i.e. 2, 7, 5, 8, 6 and 3.

**40.** The pattern is an follows:

β F ∂ (+1, −3) ; T & £ (−1, +3)

So, K T 7 (−1, +3) ; © 9 Q (+1, −3)

[∵ Second and third; First and fourth have the same pattern respectively].

✦✦✦✦

13

# Place Arrangement

## INTRODUCTION

The process of arranging a group of people or objects as per a prefixed manner is called Place Arrangement. In these questions, some conditions are given, on the basis of which students are required to arrange objects, either in a row or in a circular order.

These types of the questions are asked in various examinations. These types of questions generally involve five to eight individuals arranged in a certain fashion. They may have to be arranged in a row or in a circle.

## TYPE I: LINEAR ARRANGEMENT

In this type of arrangement, we arrange people or objects in a line or row. The arrangement is done only on one 'axis' and hence, the position of people or objects assumes importance in terms of order like first position, second position ... last position. In this type of arrangement, we take directions according to our left and right.

There are few words which must be paid adequate attention, *i.e.* 'between' means sandwiched, 'immediate left' is different from 'to the left'. To understand it let us see some representation.

### One Row Sequence

**(i)** When direction of face is not clear, then we take ourself as base and then the diagram will be as follows:

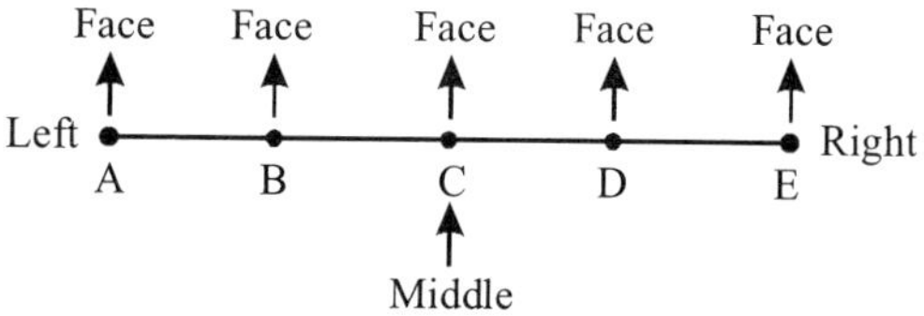

From the above diagram, it is clear that

(*i*) B, C, D, E are right of A but only B is the immediate right of A.

(*ii*) D, C, B, A are left of E but only D is the immediate left of E.

(*iii*) C, D, E are right of B only C is the immediate right of B.

(*iv*) C, B, A are left of D but only C is the immediate left of D.

(*v*) D and E are right of C but only D is the immediate right of C.

(*vi*) B and A are left of C but only B is the immediate left of C.

(*vii*) A is the immediate left of B while E is the immediate right of D.

**(ii)** When direction of face is towards you, then the diagram will be as follows:

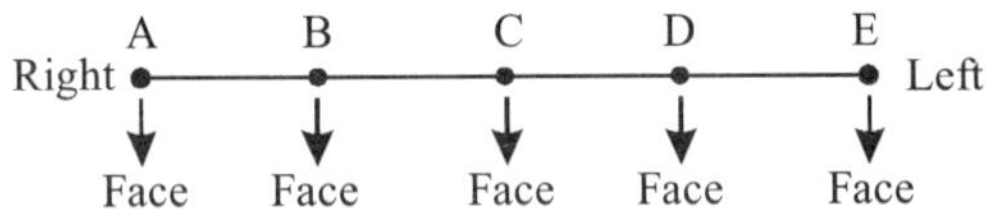


From the above diagram, it is clear that

(*i*) Left of A = B, C, D and E

(*ii*) Right of E = D, C, Band A

(*iii*) B is immediate left of A; C is immediate left of B; D is immediate left of C and E is immediate left of D.

(*iv*) D is immediate right of E; C is immediate right of D; B is immediate right of C; and A is immediate right of B.

## Two Rows Sequence

Let us see 6 persons seating in two rows,

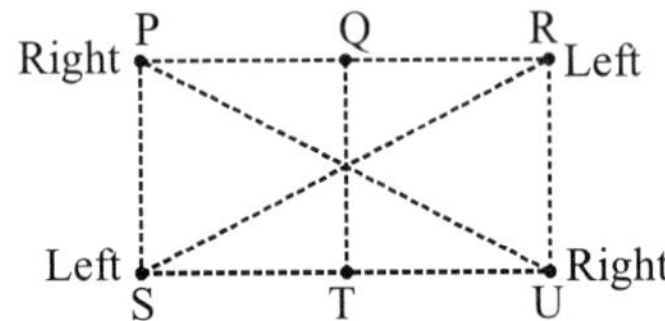


From the above diagram, it is clear that

(*i*) P is sitting opposite S

(*ii*) Q is sitting opposite T

(*iii*) R is sitting opposite U

(*iv*) P and U are sitting in diagonally opposite positions.

(*v*) S and R are sitting in diagonally opposite positions.

## TYPE II: CIRCULAR ARRANGEMENT

In this type of arrangement, we arrange people or objects around a circle or a table. In case of people sitting around a table, the table could be of any shape, *i.e.* rectangular, square, circular, etc.

### Circular Sequence

In this arrangement, some persons are sitting around a circle and they are facing the centre.

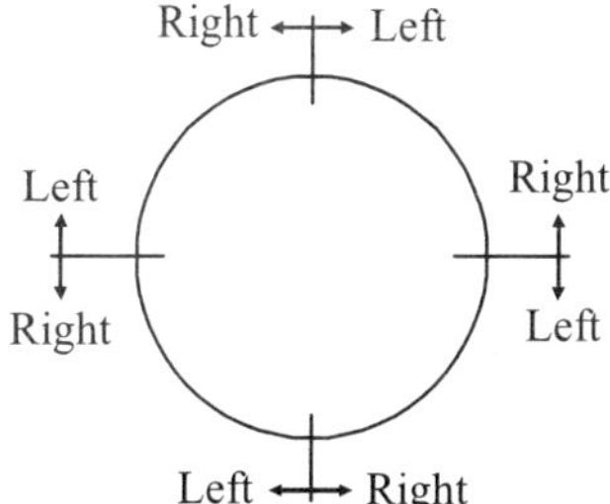


1. Left movement is called clockwise rotation.
2. Right movement is called anti-clockwise rotation.
   (*i*) The above presentation is for 4 persons but the direction is taken in the same manner for any number of persons.
   (*ii*) For rectangular and square arrangement, directions are taken as discussed in the two rows sequence.

The information given in questions specify the position of some or all the persons in the arrangement. The positions are specified through conditions like a particular person is sitting right or left of another person.

After reading the given information, you should draw the shape specified in the question. Following two shapes are of six and eight persons sitting around a circle.

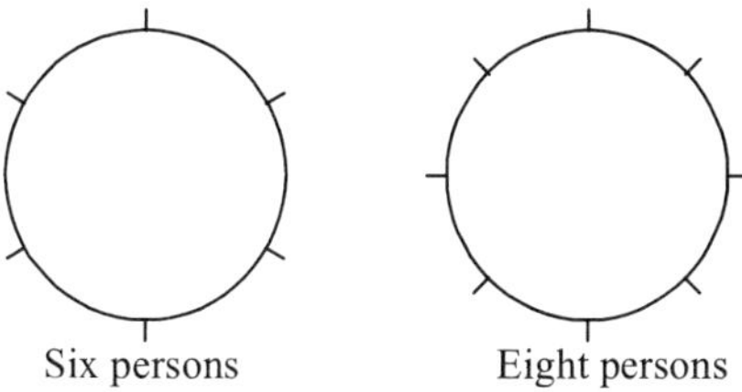

## SOLVED EXAMPLE

**Directions (Qs. 1-5):** *Read the following information carefully and answer the questions given below:*

Six people: C, D, E, F, G and H are standing in a straight line facing North not necessarily in the same order. D is standing second to the right of F. C is standing fourth to the left of H and H is not standing on the extreme end of the line. E is standing second to the right of D.

**1.** What is the position of G with respect to E?
(*a*) Immediate left (*b*) Second to the left
(*c*) Third to the left (*d*) Third to the right

**2.** Which of the following pairs represents the people standing at the extreme ends of the line?
(*a*) FH (*b*) CE (*c*) DE (*d*) CH

**3.** Who is standing second to the right of C?
(*a*) F (*b*) D (*c*) G (*d*) E

**4.** If all the people are asked to stand in an alphabetical order from left to right, the positions of how many will remain unchanged?
(*a*) One (*b*) Two (*c*) Three (*d*) Four

**5.** Four of the following five are alike in a certain way based on their positions in the above arrangement and so form a group. Which of the following does not belong to the group?
(*a*) CG (*b*) GE (*c*) GH (*d*) DE

**Sol. 1 to 5:** D is standing second to the right of F, *i.e.* F * D. E is standing second to the right of D, *i.e.* F * D * E. H is not standing on the extreme end of line and C is standing fourth to the left of H.

So, H must be standing between D and E.

Final position will be as following:

C F G D H E ↑ Facing North

**1.** **(*c*)** G is standing third to the left of E.

**2.** **(*b*)** C and E are standing on the extreme ends of the line.

**3.** **(*c*)** G is standing second to the right of C.

**4.** **(*a*)**

| | | | | | | |
|---|---|---|---|---|---|---|
| Present order | C | F | G | D | H | E |
| Alphabetical order | C | D | E | F | G | H |

So, position of C will remain unchanged.

5. **(*b*)** GE does not belong to that group because there are two people between G and E while in others, there is only one person.

**Directions (Qs. 6-8):** *Read the following information and answer the questions based on it.*

Eight friends A, B, C, D, E, F, G and H are sitting in a circle facing the centre. B is sitting between G and D. H is third to the left of B and second to the right of A. C is sitting between A and G and B and E are not sitting opposite to each other.

6. Who is third to the left of D?
   (*a*) C (*b*) F (*c*) H (*d*) A

7. Which of the following statements is not correct?
   (*a*) D and A are sitting opposite to each other
   (*b*) C is third to the right of D
   (*c*) E is sitting between F and D
   (*d*) A is sitting between C and F

8. Who will be sitting left of G?
   (*a*) C (*b*) D (*c*) H (*d*) B

**Sol. 6 to 8:** From the given information, initial arrangement will be as following:

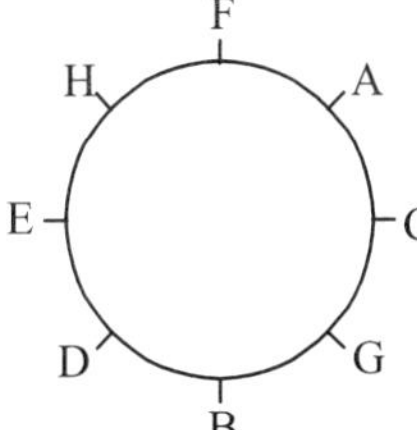


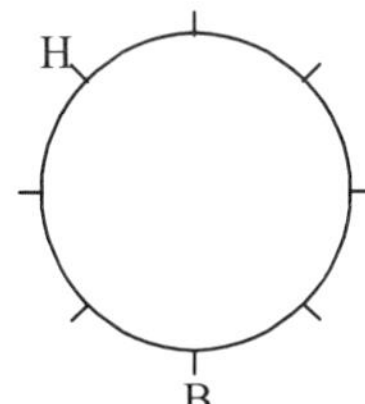


6. **(*b*)** F is third to the left of D.
7. **(*c*)** E is sitting between H and D.
8. **(*d*)** B is left of G.

## EXERCISE

**Directions (Qs. 1 to 5):** *Study the following information to answer the given questions.*

P, Q, R, S, T, V, X and Y are seated in a straight line facing North. P sits fourth to the left of V. V sits either sixth from the left end of the line or third from the right end of the line. S sits second to right of R. R is not an immediate neighbour of V. T and Q are immediate neighbours of each other but neither T nor Q sits at extreme ends of the line. Only one person sits between T and X. X does not sit at the extreme end of the line.

1. What is the position of Q with respect to P?
(*a*) Fifth to the right (*b*) Immediate neighbour
(*c*) Second to right (*d*) Third to left
(*e*) None of these

2. Which of the following represents persons seated at the two extreme ends of the line?
(*a*) P, V (*b*) Y, S (*c*) R, V
(*d*) Y, P (*e*) R, Y

3. How many persons are seated between R and T?
(*a*) One (*b*) Two (*c*) Three
(*d*) Four (*e*) None of these

4. If P is related to Q and S is related to T in a certain way, to which of the following would V be related to following the same pattern?
(*a*) Y (*b*) P (*c*) R
(*d*) S (*e*) X

5. Who amongst the following sits exactly in the middle of the persons who sit second from the left and the person who sits fifth from the right?
(*a*) V (*b*) Q (*c*) T
(*d*) S (*e*) P

**Directions (Qs. 6 to 10):** *Study the following information carefully and answer the given questions following it.*

(*i*) Eleven students A, B, C, D, E, F, G, H, I, J and K are sitting in the first row of a class facing the teacher.
(*ii*) D, who is on the immediate left of F, is second to the right of C.
(*iii*) A is second to the right of E, who is at one of the ends.
(*iv*) J is the immediate neighbour of A and B and third to the left of G.
(*v*) H is on the immediate left of D and third to the right of I.

6. Who is sitting midway between E and H?
(*a*) J (*b*) B (*c*) I
(*d*) G (*e*) None of these

7. Which of the following statements is not true in the context of the above sitting arrangements?
(*a*) There are seven students sitting between K and D
(*b*) G is the immediate neighbour of I and C
(*c*) H is the immediate neighbour of D and F
(*d*) K is between E and A
(*e*) F is third to the right of C

**8.** To obtain the respective seats of all the persons which statement given above is not required?

(*a*) I (*b*) II (*c*) III
(*d*) IV (*e*) None of these

**9.** Besides 'E', who among the following is at the extreme end?

(*a*) K (*b*) F (*c*) B
(*d*) Can't say (*e*) None of these

**10.** Which of the following groups is at the left of I?

(*a*) AJB (*b*) GCH (*c*) HDF
(*d*) GCH (*e*) None of these

**Directions (Qs. 11 to 15):** *Study the following information carefully and answer the questions that follow:*

(*i*) Seven members of a family J, K, L, M, N, O and P are to be seated in a row from left to right. (The one standing at the left end will be called the 1st; the one standing at the right end, the 7th.)

(*ii*) Their professions are lawyer, accountant, social worker, IAS, housewife, commissioner and student, though not necessarily in that order.

(*iii*) The third person is the housewife.

(*iv*) M, who is not the commissioner, will stand after the person who immediately follows N.

(*v*) J is the social worker.

(*vi*) The lawyer stands sixth.

(*vii*) The accountant stands to the immediate left of the commissioner.

(*viii*) P stands to the immediate right of O and to the immediate left of K.

(*ix*) N, the student, stands fifth.

**11.** The person standing first from left is

(*a*) O (*b*) the social worker (*c*) P
(*d*) the commissioner (*e*) L

**12.** The person standing to the immediate left of M is

(*a*) the housewife (*b*) J (*c*) the lawyer
(*d*) K (*e*) the commissioner

**13.** Which of the following correctly matches a person with his/her profession?

(*a*) O-IAS (*b*) K-housewife (*c*) L-commissioner
(*d*) P-lawyer (*e*) M-accountant

**14.** Suppose, P has to go on account of an emergency and the family brings in the family servant Q, who stands to the immediate right of L. The sixth person from the left is now

(*a*) K (*b*) J (*c*) N
(*d*) Q (*e*) M

**15.** If in addition to the changes described in Q. 14 the housewife and her husband, the IAS, agree to interchange places, which of the following will be true?

(*a*) M will stand after O but before J.
(*b*) K will be the only person to the right of L.
(*c*) There will be an equal number of persons to the left and to the right of J.
(*d*) There will be only one person to the right of N and to the left of K.
(*e*) The first and last person will be the same as before.

**16.** In a college party, 5 girls are sitting in a row. P is sitting to the left of M and to the right of O. R is sitting to the right of N but to the left of O. Who is sitting in the Middle?

(*a*) O (*b*) R (*c*) P (*d*) M

**17.** Six persons M, N, O, P, Q, R are sitting in two rows. Each row has three persons Q is not at the ends of any row. P is second to the left of R. O is the neighbour of Q and diagonally opposite to P. N is the neighbour of R. Who is opposite of N?

(*a*) R (*b*) Q (*c*) P (*d*) M

**18.** From A to E, five building are in a row. A is to the right of B; E is to the left of C and to the right of A; B is to the right of D. Which building is exactly in the middle?

(*a*) E (*b*) A (*c*) B (*d*) D

**Directions (Qs. 19 to 23):** *Study the following information carefully to answer these questions.*

Eight members P, Q, R, S, T, V, H and L are sitting in two rows with equal number of members in each row. Members of one row are facing the North and those in the other row are facing the South. Each member in one row is sitting exactly opposite a member in the other row.

P sits in the row facing the North, to the immediate right of H who is exactly opposite of R. L is to the immediate right of R and S is exactly opposite of T who is to the immediate right of P. V does not sit at any of the ends of any row.

**19.** Which of the following members sit at the ends of the same row?

(*a*) TH (*b*) SR (*c*) LQ
(*d*) LT (*e*) None of these

**20.** Who sits opposite of P?

(*a*) L (*b*) Q (*c*) V
(*d*) Cannot be determined (*e*) None of these

**21.** Which of the following members sit exactly opposite each other?
(*a*) VQ (*b*) LV (*c*) VH
(*d*) VP (*e*) None of these

**22.** Who is to the left of V?
(*a*) T (*b*) S (*c*) R
(*d*) L (*e*) None of these

**23.** Who sits to the right of Q?
(*a*) H (*b*) L (*c*) V
(*d*) R (*e*) None of these

**Directions (Qs. 24 to 28):** *Study the following information carefully* to *answer these questions.*

Eight friends A, B, C, D, E, F, G and H are sitting around a circle facing the centre. B is third to the right of A, who is third to the right of C. F is second to the right of E who is not an immediate neighbour of B. D sits second to the left of H, who sits second to the left of G.

**24.** Who sits second of the left of A?
(*a*) G (*b*) D (*c*) H
(*d*) E (*e*) None of these

**25.** Who sits to the immediate left of B?
(*a*) G (*b*) F (*c*) D
(*d*) H (*e*) None of these

**26.** What is the position of H with respect to F?
(*a*) To the immediate right (*b*) Third to the left
(*c*) Second to the left (*d*) Second to the right
(*e*) Third to the right

**27.** Four of the following five are alike in a certain way based on their positions in the given arrangement and so form a group. Which is the one that does not belong to the group?
(*a*) AD (*b*) HG (*c*) EF
(*d*) BF (*e*) CE

**28.** Which of the following pairs has the first person sitting to the immediate right of the second person?
(*a*) BH (*b*) DF (*c*) CF
(*d*) EA (*e*) None of these

**Directions (Qs. 29 to 33):** *Study the following information carefully and answer the given questions.*

A, B, C, D, E, F, G and H are sitting around a square table facing the centre in such a way that four of them sit at four corners of the square while four sit in the middle of each of the four sides.

(*i*) A sits second to right of F. F sits in the middle of one of the sides of the table.

(*ii*) G who does not sit at any of the corners of the table sits second to the right of D.

(*iii*) Only two people sit between D and B (taken from one side).

(*iv*) C is not an immediate neighbour of G.

(*v*) H sits second to left of B.

(*vi*) E is not an immediate neighbour of G or F.

**29.** Who sits exactly between F and A?
(*a*) B (*b*) C (*c*) E
(*d*) H (*e*) None of these

**30.** How many persons sit between A and H when counted in anti-clockwise direction from A?
(*a*) None (*b*) One (*c*) Two
(*d*) Three (*e*) Four

**31.** Four of the following five are alike in a certain way based on their sitting positions in the above arrangement and so form a group. Which is the one that does not belong to that group?
(*a*) D (*b*) F (*c*) A
(*d*) E (*e*) G

**32.** What is the position of F with respect to C?
(*a*) Third to the left (*b*) Immediate to the right
(*c*) Second to the left (*d*) Third to the right
(*e*) Immediate to the left

**33.** What will come in place of the question mark (?) based upon the given sitting arrangement?
AE EH HF ?
(*a*) FE (*b*) HC (*c*) FD
(*d*) DB (*e*) FH

**Directions (Qs. 34 to 38):** *Study the following information carefully and answer the questions given below:*

A, B, C, D, E, F, G, H and K are sitting around a circle facing the centre. F is fourth to the right of A who is third to the right of B. K is fourth to the left of B and third to the right of D. C is third to the right of H. E is second to the left of G.

**34.** Who is to the immediate right of F?
(*a*) B (*b*) G (*c*) E
(*d*) Data inadequate (*e*) None of these

**35.** Who is third to the right of K?
(*a*) F (*b*) E (*c*) G
(*d*) Data inadequate (*e*) None of these

**36.** What is E's position with respect to B?
(*a*) Second to the left (*b*) Third to the right (*c*) Fourth to the right
(*d*) Third to the left (*e*) Fifth to the right

**37.** Who is fourth to the left of G?
(*a*) C (*b*) A (*c*) D
(*d*) K (*e*) Data inadequate

**38.** In which of the following combinations is the third person sitting between the first and the second persons?
(*a*) GFB (*b*) BGH (*c*) ADC
(*d*) KEC (*e*) EGF

**39.** Radha, Sheela, Mahima and Seeta are sitting around a rectangular table. Radha is sitting to the right of Sheela. Mahima is sitting to the left of Seeta. Which of the following pair is sitting opposite each other?
(*a*) Sheela-Seeta (*c*) Radha-Sheela
(*b*) Radha-Seeta (*d*) Mahima-Radha

**40.** Six friends are playing cards sitting around a circte and facing the centre. Kanny is sitting to the left of Danny; Michel is sitting between Boby and Johny Rozer is between Kanny and Boby. Who is sitting to the left of Michel?
(*a*) Danny (*b*) Johny (*c*) Canny (*d*) Boby

**Directions (Qs. 41 to 45):** *Study the following information to answer the given questions.*

(*i*) Eight persons E, F, G, H, I, J, K and L are seated around a square table- two on each side.
(*ii*) There are three lady members and they are not seated next to each other.
(*iii*) J is between L and F.
(*iv*) G is between I and F.
(*v*) H, a lady member is second to the left of J.
(*vi*) F, a male member is seated third to the right of E, a lady member.
(*vii*) There is a lady member between F and I.

**41.** Who among the following are the three lady members?
(*a*) E, H and J (*b*) E, G and J (*c*) G, H and J
(*d*) Cannot be determined (*e*) None of these

**42.** Which of the following is true about J?
(*a*) J is a male member
(*b*) J is a female member
(*c*) Sex of J cannot be determined
(*d*) Position of J cannot be determined
(*e*) None of the above

**43.** Who among the following is seated between E and H?
(*a*) I (*b*) J (*c*) F
(*d*) Cannot be determined (*e*) None of these

**44.** Who among the following is to the immediate left of F?
(*a*) G (*b*) J (*c*) I
(*d*) Cannot be determined (*e*) None of these

**45.** How many persons are seated between K and F?
(*a*) One (*b*) Two (*c*) Three
(*d*) Cannot be determined (*e*) None of these

## ANSWERS

| 1 | 2 | 3 | 4 | 5 | 6 | 7 | 8 | 9 | 10 |
|---|---|---|---|---|---|---|---|---|---|
| (*c*) | (*e*) | (*c*) | (*a*) | (*d*) | (*b*) | (*c*) | (*e*) | (*b*) | (*a*) |
| **11** | **12** | **13** | **14** | **15** | **16** | **17** | **18** | **19** | **20** |
| (*a*) | (*c*) | (*b*) | (*d*) | (*a*) | (*a*) | (*b*) | (*b*) | (*e*) | (*c*) |
| **21** | **22** | **23** | **24** | **25** | **26** | **27** | **28** | **29** | **30** |
| (*d*) | (*b*) | (*a*) | (*a*) | (*c*) | (*e*) | (*d*) | (*b*) | (*b*) | (*c*) |
| **31** | **32** | **33** | **34** | **35** | **36** | **37** | **38** | **39** | **40** |
| (*d*) | (*e*) | (*c*) | (*b*) | (*c*) | (*d*) | (*a*) | (*e*) | (*b*) | (*b*) |
| **41** | **42** | **43** | **44** | **45** | | | | | |
| (*e*) | (*a*) | (*e*) | (*b*) | (*c*) | | | | | |

## SOME SELECTED EXPLANATORY ANSWERS

**6 to 10.**

From (*iii*), A is second to the right of E, who is at one of the ends. So, E is at the left end.

From (*iv*), J is the immediate neighbour of A and B, it implies that J is sitting on the immediate right of A and B is sitting immediate right of J.

E*AJB*G ...(*a*)

From (*ii*) and (*v*), we get the following arrangement

I C H D F ...(*b*)

From the arrangements (*a*) and (*b*), we can get the final arrangement

E K A J B I G C H D F

**6.** There are seven persons which are sitting between E and H. B is in the midway of them.

**7.** H is not the immediate neighbour of D and F

**8.** To get the final arrangement, we require all the statements.

**9.** F is at the extreme end.

**10.** A, J and B are at the left of I.

**11 to 15**

From statements (*iii*), (*iv*) and (*ix*), we can get the following arrangement.

| Position | 1 | 2 | 3 | 4 | 5 | 6 | 7 |
|---|---|---|---|---|---|---|---|
| Name | | | | | N | | |
| Profession | | | House wife | | Student | Lawyer | |

Now, from (*iv*) and (*vii*) statements,

| Position | 1 | 2 | 3 | 4 | 5 | 6 | 7 |
|---|---|---|---|---|---|---|---|
| Name | | | | | N | | M |
| Profession | Ace. | Comm. | House wife | | Student | Lawyer | |

J must be at position 4 and from statement (*viii*), O, P and K are together. So, they are at positions 1, 2 and 3 respectively. The final arrangement will be as following:

| Position | 1 | 2 | 3 | 4 | 5 | 6 | 7 |
|---|---|---|---|---|---|---|---|
| Name | O | P | K | J | N | L | M |
| Profession | Ace. | Comm. | House wife | Social worker | Student | Lawyer | LIAS |

**14.** The new order will be as following

O K J N L Q M

So, sixth person from the left is Q.

**15.** The new order will be as following

O M J N L Q K

So, M will stand after O but before J.

**16.**

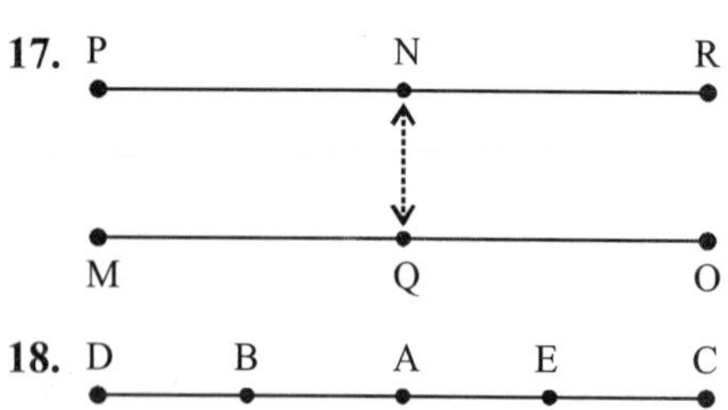


**17.**

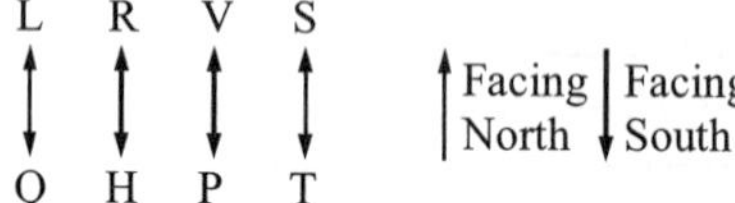


**18.**



**19 to 23.**

According to given information, the final arrangement is as following:



**24 to 28.**

According to the given information, the final arrangement is as following:

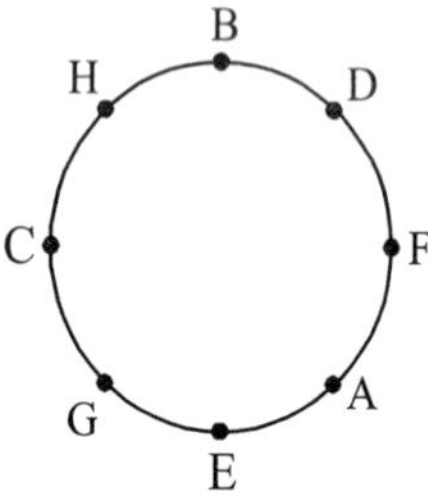


**29 to 33.**

According to given information, the final arrangement is as following:

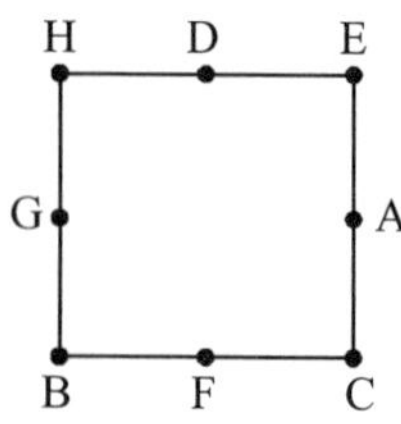

**34 to 38.**

According to the given information, the final arrangement is as following:

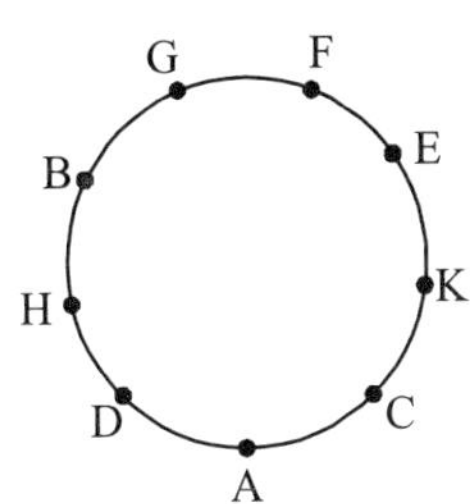


**39.**

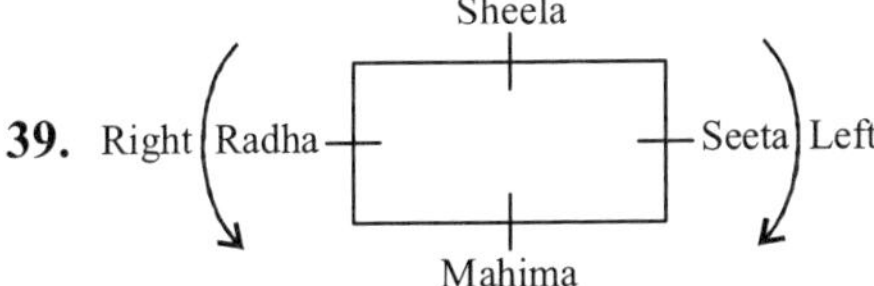


**40.**

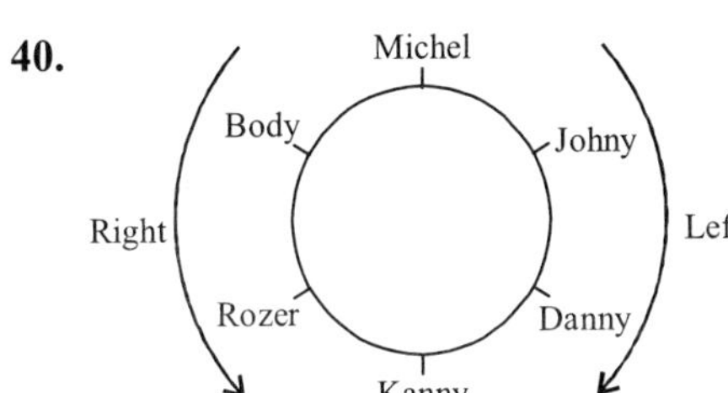


**41 to 45.**

According to the given information, the final arrangement is as following:

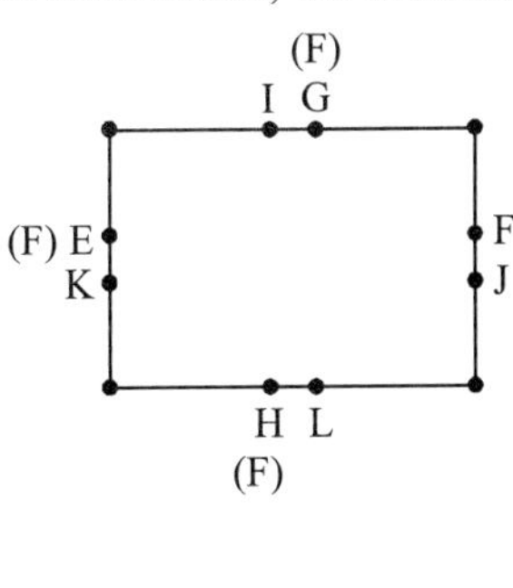


✧✧✧✧

14

# Sequential Input-Output Tracing

In sequential input-output tracing, a specific communication or data or a message consisting/ comprising of haphazard/randomised words or numbers or a combination of both is given as the *input* followed by steps of rearrangement to give sequential *outputs.*

The candidate is required to trace out the pre-fixed pattern/rule in the given reorganization or rearrangement by analysing the steps and subsequently determine the required final output or the last step, etc.

## Three Parts of Input-Output Problems

**1. Arrangement Problems:** In this type of problems, the words or the numbers or the combination of both of the given input arranged in a particular order according to a set of rules/patterns.

**2. Shifting Problems:** In this type of problems, the words or the numbers or the combination of both, of the given input are shifted in a particular order according to a set of rules/patterns.

**3. Arithmetic Problems:** In this type of problems, the given input consists of numbers. By performing different arithmetic operations on the numbers of the given input, we can obtain the subsequent steps or the required final output or the last step or penultimate step.

## Flow-Chart For the Input-Output Problems

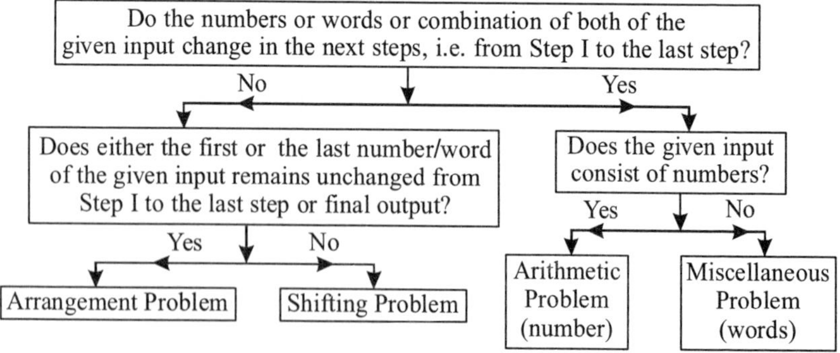

## Part-I: Arrangement Shifting

Either the first or the last word or number of the given input remains unchanged from step I to the last step or final output. Important points:

(*i*) In arrangement problems, *it is not possible to determine the previous steps including input.* We can't proceed or move backward or in reverse direction in a non-cyclical rearrangement.

Therefore, the in these type of problems, earlier steps cannot be determined.

(*ii*) Required number of steps or total steps for *n* words or numbers = at most ($n$ – 1) steps, to arrange the words or numbers finally.

Therefore, the last step or final output = Either ($n$ – 1) steps or less.

(*iii*) Atleast *n* words or numbers must have occupied their due positions or places in *n* step of an arrangement problem.

(*iv*) Last but one or second last or penultimate step = (last step – 1)

### Type–1: Arrangement of Words:

Words are arranged as follows:

(*i*) Original alphabetical order.

(*ii*) Reverse alphabetical order.

### Type-2: Arrangement of Numbers:

Numbers are arranged as follows:

(*i*) Increasing order or ascending order

(*ii*) Decreasing order or descending order

### Type-3 : Arrangement of words and numbers:

Words and numbers are arranged as follows:

(*i*) Numbers are arranged in a descending order while words are arranged in original alphabetical order alternately.

(*ii*) Words are arranged in Reverse alphabetical order while the numbers are arranged in an ascending order alternately.

(*iii*) Numbers are arranged in an ascending order while the words are arranged in reverse alphabetical order alternately.

(*iv*) Words are arranged in the reverse alphabetical order while the numbers are arranged in a descending order alternately.

(*v*) Numbers are arranged as: Largest, smallest, second largest, second smallest and so on.

Words are arranged as : A, Z, B, Y, C, X, ... and so on.

## SOLVED EXAMPLE

**Directions (Qs. 1-4):** *Study the following information carefully and answer the given questions.*

A word and number arrangement machine when given an input line of words and numbers rearranges them following a particular rule in each step. The following is an illustration of input and rearrangement:

**Input :** sale data 18 23 for 95, then 38
**Step I :** data sale 18 23 for 95, then 38
**Step II :** data 95 sale 18 23 for, then 38
**Step III :** data 95 for sale 18 23, then 38
**Step IV :** data 95 for 38 sales 18 23, then
**Step V :** data 95 for 38 sale 23 18, then
**Step VI :** data 95 for 38 sale 23, then 18

Step VI is the last step of the rearrangement of the above input.

As per the rules followed in the above steps, find out in the given questions the appropriate step for the given input.

1. **Input** year 39 stake 47 house full 94 55. How many steps will be required to complete the rearrangement?
   (*a*) Five (*b*) Six (*c*) Four
   (*d*) Seven (*e*) None of these

**Sol. (*b*) Input :** year 39 stake 47 house full 94 55
**Step I :** full year 39 stake 47 house 94 55
**Step II :** full 94 year 39 stake 47 house 55
**Step III :** full 94 house year 39 stake 47 55
**Step IV :** full 94 house 55 year 39 stake 47
**Step V :** full 94 house 55 stake year 39 47
**Step VI :** full 94 house 55 stake 47 year 39
Hence, six steps will be required to complete the arrangement.

2. **Step II of an input is** car 83 lost ever 32 46 74 now.

   How many more steps will be required to complete the rearrangement?
   (*a*) Three (*b*) Four (*c*) Five
   (*d*) Six (*e*) None of these

**Sol. (*b*) Step II :** car 83 lost ever 32 46 74 now
**Step III :** car 83 ever lost 32 46 74 now
**Step IV :** car 83 ever 74 lost 32 46 now

**Step V :** car 83 ever 74 lost 46 32 now
**Step VI :** car 83 ever 74 lost 46 now 32

So, four more steps are required to complete the arrangement.

3. **Step III of an input is** and 79 code 27 18 new goal 34.
   Which of the following steps will definitely be the input?
   (*a*) code and 79 27 18 new goal 34
   (*b*) code 27 18 new goal 34 and 79
   (*c*) code 27 and 18 79 new goal 34
   (*d*) Cannot de determined
   (*e*) None of the above

**Sol. (*d*) Input :** cannot be determined

4. **Input** water full never 35 78 16 height 28
   Which of the following steps wiil be the last?
   (*a*) VI (*b*) VII (*c*) VIII
   (*d*) IX (*e*) None of these

**Sol. (*a*) Input :** water full never 35 78 16 height 28
**Step I :** full water never 35 78 16 height 28
**Step II :** full 78 water never 35 16 height 28
**Step III :** full 78 height water never 35 15 28
**Step IV :** full 78 height 35 water never 16 28
**Step V :** full 78 height 35 never water 16 28
**Step VI :** full 78 height 35 never 28 water 16

Hence, Step VI will be the last step.

**Directions (Qs. 5-9):** *Study the following information carefully and answer the given questions.*

A word and number arrangement machine when given an input line of words and numbers rearranges them following a particular rule in each step. The following is an illustration of input and rearrangement:

**Input :** gone 93 over 46 84 now for 31
**Step I :** 31 gone 93 over 46 84 new for
**Step II :** 31 over gone 93 46 84 new for
**Step III :** 31 over 46 gone 93 84 new for
**Step IV :** 31 over 46 now gone 93 84 for
**Step V :** 31 over 46 now 84 gone 93 for and

Step V is the last step of the rearrangement of the above input.

As per the rules followed in the above steps, find out in each of the following questions the appropriates step for the given input.

5. **Step III of an input is** 15 window 29 93 86 sail tower buy. Which of the following will be step VI?
   (*a*) 15 window 29 tower 86 sail 93 buy
   (*b*) 15 window 29 tower 86 93 sail buy
   (*c*) 15 window 29 towar 93 86 sail buy
   (*d*) There will be no such step
   (*e*) None of the above

**Sol. (*a*) Step III :** 15 window 29 93 86 sail tower buy
**Step IV :** 15 window 29 tower 93 86 sail buy
**Step V :** 15 window 29 tower 86 93 sail buy
**Step VI :** 15 window 29 tower 86 sail 93 buy

6. **Step II of an input is** 19 yr 85 74 near gone 26 store.
   How many more steps will be required to complete the rearrangement?
   (*a*) Three (*b*) Four (*c*) Two
   (*d*) Five (*e*) None of these

**Sol. (*b*) Step II :** 19 yr 85 74 near gone 26 store
**Step III :** 19 yr 26 85 74 near gone store
**Step IV :** 19 yr 26 store 85 74 near gone
**Step V :** 19 yr 26 store 74 85 near gone
**Step VI :** 19 yr 26 store 74 near 85 gone

Hence, four more steps are required to complete the rearrangement.

7. **Step II of an input is** 49 zone car battery 56 87 71 down.
   Which of the following is definitely the input?
   (*a*) car 49 battery zone 86 87 71 down
   (*b*) zone 49 car battery 56 87 71 down
   (*c*) battery car 49 zone 56 87 71 down
   (*d*) Cannot be determined
   (*e*) None of te above

**Sol. (*d*) Input** cannot be determined

8. **Input** news 79 53 glory for 46 29 task.
   Which of the following will be step IV?
   (*a*) 29 task 46 news 53 glory 79 for
   (*b*) 29 task 46 news 53 79 glory for
   (*c*) 29 task 46 news 79 53 glory for
   (*d*) 29 task 79 53 glory for 46 task
   (*e*) None of the above

**Sol. (*b*) Input :** news 79 53 glory for 46 29 task
**Step I :** 29 news 79 53 glory for 46 task
**Step II :** 29 task news 79 53 glory for 46
**Step III :** 29 task 46 news 79 53 glory for
**Step IV :** 29 task 46 news 53 79 glory for

**9. Step III of an input is** 27 tube 34 gas chamber row 74 53.
Which of the following steps will be the last but one?
(*a*) VI (*b*) VII (*c*) VIII
(*d*) V (*e*) None of these

**Sol. (*d*) Step III :** 27 tube 34 gas chamber row 74 53
**Step IV :** 27 tube 34 row gas chamber 74 53
**Step V :** 27 tube 34 row 53 gas chamber 74
**Step IV :** 27 tube 34 row 53 gas 74 chamber So, the step last but one is Step V.

## EXERCISE

**Directions (Qs. 1-7): Study the following information to answer the questions given below:**

A number arranging machine when given an input of numbers, rearranges them following a particular rule in each step. The following is an illustration of input and steps of rearrangement:

| | | | | | | | | |
|---|---|---|---|---|---|---|---|---|
| **Input :** | 48 | 245 | 182 | 26 | 99 | 542 | 378 | 297 |
| **Step I :** | 542 | 48 | 245 | 182 | 26 | 99 | 378 | 297 |
| **Step II :** | 542 | 26 | 48 | 245 | 182 | 99 | 378 | 297 |
| **Step III :** | 542 | 26 | 378 | 48 | 245 | 182 | 99 | 297 |
| **Step IV :** | 542 | 26 | 378 | 48 | 297 | 245 | 182 | 99 |
| **Step V :** | 542 | 26 | 378 | 48 | 297 | 99 | 245 | 182 |

This is the final arrangement and step V is the last step for this input.

**1.** What should be the last step of the following input?
**Input:** 158 279 348 28 326 236
(*a*) 348 28 326 158 279 236 (*b*) 348 28 326 236 158 279
(*c*) 348 28 236 158 279 326 (*d*) 348 28 158 326 236 279
(*e*) None of these

**2.** Below is given the second step of an input. What will be its fourth step?
**Step II:** 298 12 128 36 212 185

(*a*) 298 12 212 128 36 185
(*b*) 298 12 212 36 128 185
(*c*) 298 12 36 212 128 185
(*d*) Cannot be determined
(*e*) None of these

**3.** If the first step of an input is "785 198 32 426 373 96 49", then which of the following steps will be

"785 32 426 49 198 373 96"?

(*a*) Third
(*b*) Fourth
(*c*) Fifth
(*d*) Second
(*e*) None of these

**4.** Below is given the third step of an input. What will be its second step?

**Step III :** 387 42 236 185 92 64

(*a*) 387 42 185 236 92 64
(*b*) 387 42 92 185 236 64
(*c*) 387 42 185 92 236 64
(*d*) Cannot be determined
(*e*) None of these

**5.** What should be the third step of the following input?

**Input :** 239 123 58 361 495 37

(*a*) 495 37 361 123 239 58
(*b*) 495 37 58 361 123 239
(*c*) 495 37 58 123 361 239
(*d*) 495 37 361 239 123 58
(*e*) None of these

**6.** What will be the fourth step for an input whose second step is given below?

**Step:** 765 42 183 289 542 65 110 350

(*a*) 765 42 542 350 183 289 65 110
(*b*) 765 42 542 65 110 183 289 350
(*c*) 765 42 542 65 183 289 110 350
(*d*) Cannot be determined
(*e*) None of these

**7.** How many steps will be required to get the final output from the following input?

**Input:** 39 88 162 450 386 72 29

(*a*) Two
(*b*) Three
(*c*) Four
(*d*) Six
(*e*) None of these

**Directions (Qs. 8-12):** *Study the following information to answer the given questions.*

A word arrangement machine when given an input line of words, rearranges them following a particular rule in each step. The following is an illustration of the input and the steps of rearrangement.

**Input:** going but for crept the light sir

**Step I:** crept going but for the light sir

**Step II:** crept going light but for the sir

**Step III:** crept going light but for sir the

(Step III is the last step for this input)

As per the rules followed in the above steps, find out in the given questions the appropriate step for the given input.

**8.** If the input is 'true se veto be nuke my like', which of the following will be the step IV?

(*a*) like nuke true veto be se my
(*b*) be my like se-true veto nuke
(*c*) be my se like true veto nuke
(*d*) veto true nuke like so be my
(*e*) Cannot be determined

**9.** If the step V of an input is 'more pure soft cat not so sir at', what will be the step II?

(*a*) at so more pure cat not soft sir
(*b*) more pure soft so sir cat at not
(*c*) more pure soft cat so sir at not
(*d*) more so sir soft pure cat at not
(*e*) Cannot be determined

**10.** If the second step of an input is 'clever remand window sales batch tiger never' which of the following will be its sixth step?

(*a*) clever remand window batch sales tiger never
(*b*) window remand clever sales batch tiger never
(*c*) batch never sales tiger clever remand window
(*d*) clever remand window tiger batch sales never
(*e*) It cannot have sixth step.

**11. Input:** the in car as he may me

Which of the following will be the third step for this input?

(*a*) car the in as he may me
(*b*) car may the as in he me
(*c*) car as may he the in me
(*d*) car may the in as he me
(*e*) None of these

**12.** Input: 'more fight cats cough sough acts idea'.

Which of the following steps would be the last step for this input?

(*a*) III
(*b*) IV
(*c*) V
(*d*) VI
(*e*) None of these

**Directions (Qs. 13-17):** *Study the following information carefully to answer the questions given below:*

A number sorting machine .when given an input of numbers, rearranges the numbers in a particular manner step by step as indicated below till all the numbers are arranged in a particular order. Given below is an illustration of this arrangement:

**Input:** 39 121 48 18 76 112 14 45 63 96

**Step I:** 14 39 121 48 18 76 112 45 63 96

**Step II:** 14 39 48 18 76 112 45 63 96 121

**Step III:** 14 18 39 48 76 112 45 63 96 121

**Step IV:** 14 18 39 48 76 45 63 96 112 121

**Step V:** 14 18 39 45 48 76 63 96 112 121

**Step VI:** 14 18 39 45 48 63 76 96 112 121

(This is the final arrangement and Step VI is the last step for this input)

**13.** What will be the step III for the following input?

**Input:** 68 182 39 93 129 46 21 58

(*a*) 21 39 68 93 129 46 58 182 (*b*) 21 39 68 129 93 46 58 182
(*c*) 32 68 39 93 129 46 58 182 (*d*) Can't be determined
(*a*) None of these

**14.** How many steps will be required for last step for the following input?

**Input:** 101 85 66 49 73 39 142 25 115 74

(*a*) 5 (*b*) 6 (*c*) 7
(*d*) 8 (*e*) None of these

**15.** If the second step for an input is as given below, what will be the fifth step for the same input?

**Step II:** 22 49 32 88 69 132 101 185

(*a*) 22 32 49 88 69 101 132 185 (*b*) 22 32 69 49 88 101 132 185
(*c*) 22 32 49 69 101 88 132 185 (*d*) 22 32 49 88 69 132 101 185
(*e*) None of these

**16.** Which of the following will be the third step for the following input?

**Input:** 45 78 97 132 28 16 146 54 99 112

(*a*) 16 28 45 78 97 146 54 99 112 132
(*b*) 16 28 45 97 78 54 99 112 132 146
(*c*) 16 28 45 78 97 132 54 99 112 146
(*d*) 16 28 45 97 78 132 99 54 112 146
(*e*) None of these

**17.** What will be the last step for the following input?

**Input:** 138 63 49 93 89 122 32 71

(*a*) 32 49 71 63 89 93 122 138 (*b*) 32 49 63 71 93 89 122 138
(*c*) 32 49 63 71 89 93 122 138 (*d*) Can't be determined
(*e*) None of these

**Directions (Qs. 18-22):** *Study the following information carefully and answer the questions given below:*

A word arranging machine, when given a particular input, rearranges it following a particular rule. The following is the illustration of the- input and the steps of arrangement:

**Input:** top the name good for is there

**Step I:** is top the name good for there

**Step II:** is for top the name good there

**Step III:** is for the top name good there

**Step IV:** is for the top good name there

(Step IV is the last step of this input.)

**18.** Which of the following is the third step for the following input?

**Input:** lack of a common safe in the

(*a*) a of in the lack common safe (*b*) a of in lack common safe the
(*c*) a in of lack common safe the (*d*) a in of the lack common safe
(*e*) None of these

**19.** If following is the third step of an input, what will be its first step?

**Step III:** no dog was first five forest dense

(*a*) no was dog first five forest dense
(*b*) no first was dog five forest dense
(*c*) no dog first was forest five dense
(*d*) Can't be determined
(*e*) None of these

**20.** If step I of an input is 'If there was no good man', what step would be 'if no man there was good'?

(*a*) Second (*b*) Third (*c*) Fourth
(*d*) Can't be determined (*e*) None of these

**21.** If following is the second step of an input, what will be the fourth step?

**Step II:** is to for while they were going day

(*a*) is to day for they while were going
(*b*) is to day for while they were going
(*c*) is to for day while they were going
(*d*) Can't be determined
(*e*) None of these

**22.** How many steps will be required to get the final output from the following input?

**Input:** Where do you go out of way

(*a*) One (*b*) Three (*c*) Four

(*d*) Eight (*e*) None of these

**Directions (Qs. 23-27):** *Read the following information carefully and answer the questions given below:*

A word-number arranging machine, when given an input as a set of words and numbers, rearranges them following a particular rule and generates stepwise outputs till the rearrangement is completed following that rule.

Following is an illustration of input and steps of rearrangement till the last step.

**Input:** pour ask 57 dear 39 fight 17 28

**Step I:** ask pour 57 dear 39 fight 17 28

**Step II:** ask 57 pour dear 39 fight 17 28

**Step III:** ask 57 dear pour 39 fight 17 28

**Step IV:** ask 57 dear 39 pour fight 17 28

**Step V:** ask 57 dear 39 fight pour 17 28

**Step VI:** ask 57 dear 39 fight 28 pour 17

and Step VI is the last output.

As per the rule followed in the above steps, find out the answer to each of the following questions:

**23.** If the 1st step of an input is "car 17 vas tiger 92 87 like 52", which of the following will be the IVth step?

(*a*) car 92 like 87 tiger 52 17 vas

(*b*) car 92 like 87 17 vas tiger 52

(*c*) car 92 like 87 tiger 17 vas 52

(*d*) car 92 like 17 vas tiger 87 52

(*e*) None of these

**24. Input:** 19 feat 34 28 dog bag take 43

Which of the following steps would be "bag 43 dog 19 feat 34 28 take"?

(*a*) IInd (*b*) IVth (*c*) Ist

(*d*) Cannot be determined (*e*) None of these

**25.** If step II of an input is "cut 97 38 end for 29 46 down", which of the following will be the last step?

(*a*) V (*b*) IV (*c*) VII

(*d*) VII (*e*) None of these

**26. Input:** zeal for 49 31 high 22 track 12

Which of the following will be the IIIrd step?

(*a*) for 49 high 31 track 22 zeal 12

(*b*) for 49 high 31 zeal 22 track 12

(*c*) for 49 high zeal 31 22 track 12

(*d*) for 49 high 31 track zeal 22 12

(*e*) None of these

**27.** If the IVth step of an input is "ago 85 elite 79 exile fat 26 41", which of the following will definitely be the IInd step of the input?

(*a*) ago 85 79 elite fat 41 26 exile

(*b*) ago 85 exile elite4126 fat 79

(*c*) ago 85 26 exile 41 elite 79 fat

(*d*) Cannot be determined

(*e*) None of these

**Directions (Qs. 28-32):** *Read the following information carefully and answer the questions given below:*

A word and number arranging machine when given an input line of words and numbers rearranges them following a particular rule and generates stepwise outputs till the arrangement is completed following that rule.

Following is an illustration of input and steps of rearrangement till the last step.

**Input:** tree cut 92 51 food 17 garden 32

**Step I:** cut tree 92 51 food 17 garden 32

**Step II:** cut food tree 92 51 17 garden 32

**Step III:** cut food 92 tree 51 17 garden 32

**Step IV:** cut food 92 51 tree 17 garden 32

**Step V:** cut food 92 51 garden tree 17 32

**Step VI:** cut food 92 51 garden tree 32 17

And Step VI is the last step of the input.

As per the rules followed in the above steps, find out the answer to each of the questions given below:

**28. Input:** bench 47 63 advance 13 29 again between

Which of the following is the step III of the output?

(*a*) advance again 63 47 bench 13 29 between

(*b*) advance again 63 47 bench between 13 29

(*c*) advance again 63 47 bench between 29 13

(*d*) cannot be determined

(*e*) None of these

**29.** Step III of an input is:

again dark 83 sour 19 21 prey 39

Which of the following steps will be the last but one?

(*a*) V (*b*) VI (*c*) VIII

(*d*) VII (*e*) None of these

**30.** Step IV of an input is:

earn more 82 63 12 31 quite new

Which of the following will definitely be Step II of the output?

(*a*) earn more 12 63 82 31 quite new

(*b*) earn more new 82 63 12 31 quite

(*c*) earn more quite new 82 12 63 31

(*d*) cannot be determined

(*e*) None of these

**31.** Step II of an input is:

desk eagle 12 28 41 69 foreign land

How many more steps will be required to complete the rearrangement?

(*a*) 4 (*b*) 6 (*c*) 5

(*d*) 3 (*e*) None of these

**32.** Input: Bring home 42 73 15 goal 32 type Which of the following steps will be the last one?

(*a*) V (*b*) VI (*c*) IV

(*d*) VII (*e*) None of these

**Directions (Qs. 33-37):** *Study the following information to answer the given questions:*

A word and number arranging machine when given an input line of words and numbers, rearranges them following a particular rule in each step. "The following is an illustration of input and steps of rearrangement:

**Input:** wind packet 19 7 back 12 task 34

**Step I:** 34 wind packet 19 7 back 12 task

**Step II:** 34 back wind packet 19 7 12 task

**Step III:** 34 back 19 wind packet 7 12 task

**Step IV:** 34 back 19 packet wind 7 12 task

**Step V:** 34 back 19 packet 12 wind 7 task

**Step VI:** 34 back 19 packet 12 task wind 7

**Step VII:** 34 back 19 packet 12 task 7 wind

and Step VII is the last step.

As per the rules followed in the above steps, find out in the given questions the appropriate step for the given input.

**33.** If Step I of an input is

59 bead tenure father 38 11 ultimate 24

which of the following will be Step III?

(*a*) 59 bead 38 tenure 11 father ultimate 24
(*b*) 59 bead 38 11 tenure father ultimate 24
(*c*) 59 bead 38 tenure father 11 ultimate 24
(*d*) 59 bead 38 father tenure 11 ultimate 24
(*e*) None of these

**34. Input:** 9 13 about tariff 24 call 29 even.

Which of the following will be step IV?

(*a*) 29 about 24 9 13 tariff call even
(*b*) 29 about 24 call 9 13 tariff even
(*c*) 29 about 24 call 13 9 tariff even
(*d*) 29 about 24 call 13 even 9 tariff
(*e*) cannot be determined

**35.** Which of the following will be the Step III of the following input?

**Input:** 24 12 entry sand butter 51 32 carry

(*a*) 51 butter 32 24 12 entry sand carry
(*b*) 51 butter 32 carry 24 12 entry sand
(*c*) 51 butter 32 carry 24 entry 12 sand
(*d*) 51 24 12 entry sand butter 32 carry
(*e*) None of these

**36.** If Step II of an input is "37 desk 34 garden 5 father victory 17", which of the following steps will be the last step?

(*a*) Step III (*b*) Step V (*c*) Step IV
(*d*) Step VI (*e*) None of these

**37.** If the last step of an input is 41 cost 32 over 28 project 17 violet which of the following must be the input?

(*a*) project 32 cost over 17 41 violet 28
(*b*) project 32 cost over 41 violet 17 28
(*c*) project cost 32 over 41 17 violet 28
(*d*) Cannot be determined
(*e*) None of these

**Directions (Qs. 38-42):** *Study the following information carefully and answer the given questions:*

A word and number arranging machine when given an input line of words and numbers rearranges them following a particular rule in each step. The following is an illustration of input and rearrangement.

**Input:** 93 come home over 32 47 now 26

**Step I:** over 93 come home 32 47 now 26

**Step II:** over 26 93 come home 32 47 now

**Step III:** over 26 now 93 come home 32 47

**Step IV:** over 26 now 32 93 come home 47

**Step V:** over 26 now 32 home 93 come 47

**Step VI:** over 26 how 32 home 47 93 come

**Step VII:** over 26 now 32 home 47 come 93

and Step VII is the last step.

As per the rules followed in the above steps, find out in each of the following questions the appropriate step.

**38.** Step III of an input is:

take 17 mind game 29 73 18 loud

How many more steps are required to complete the sequence?

(*a*) Two (*b*) Three (*c*) Four

(*d*) Five (*e*) None of these

**39.** Step II of an input is:

sky 20 90 37 begin again 11 home

Which of the following is definitely the input?

(*a*) 20 90 37 begin again 11 home sky

(*b*) sky 90 37 20 begin again 11 home

(*c*) 90 20 37 begin sky again 11 home

(*d*) Cannot be determined

(*e*) None of these

**40. Input:** Queen Mary 79 62 17 20 green west

Which of the following steps will be the last but one?

(*a*) VI (*b*) VII (*c*) V

(*d*) VIII (*e*) None of these

**41. Input:** by now 51 32 for 91 20 me

Which of the following steps will be the last?

(*a*) III (*b*) IV (*c*) V

(*d*) VI (*e*) None of these

**42. Input:** fight for all 39 62 25 today 19

Which of the following will be step IV?

(*a*) today 25 for 39 fight all 62 19

(*b*) today 19 for 25 fight all 39 62

(*c*) today 19 for 25 fight 39 all 62
(*d*) Cannot be determined
(*e*) None of these

## ANSWERS

| 1 | 2 | 3 | 4 | 5 | 6 | 7 | 8 | 9 | 10 |
|---|---|---|---|---|---|---|---|---|---|
| (*a*) | (*b*) | (*b*) | (*d*) | (*d*) | (*c*) | (*e*) | (*a*) | (*e*) | (*e*) |
| **11** | **12** | **13** | **14** | **15** | **16** | **17** | **18** | **19** | **20** |
| (*b*) | (*d*) | (*a*) | (*d*) | (*e*) | (*c*) | (*c*) | (*c*) | (*d*) | (*b*) |
| **21** | **22** | **23** | **24** | **25** | **26** | **27** | **28** | **29** | **30** |
| (*a*) | (*e*) | (*b*) | (*e*) | (*a*) | (*c*) | (*d*) | (*e*) | (*a*) | (*d*) |
| **31** | **32** | **33** | **34** | **35** | **36** | **37** | **38** | **39** | **40** |
| (*c*) | (*a*) | (*d*) | (*b*) | (*a*) | (*c*) | (*d*) | (*b*) | (*d*) | (*e*) |
| **41** | **42** | | | | | | | | |
| (*d*) | (*b*) | | | | | | | | |

## SOME SELECTED EXPLANATORY ANSWERS

**(1-7):** From the last step it is clear that there are two alternating series of numbers: One in descending order and the other in ascending order.

When we go through input to step I, we find that the largest no. becomes the first and remaining numbers shift rightward. In the next step, the smallest no. becomes the second and the rest shift rightward. These two steps continue alternately until the two alternate series are formed.

**2. Step II:** 298 12 128 36 212 185
**Step III:** 298 12 212 128 36 185
**Step IV:** 298 12 212 36 128 185

**3. Step I:** 785 198 32 426 373 96 49
**Step II:** 785 32 198 426 373 96 49
**Step III:** 785 32 426 198 373 96 49
**Step IV:** 785 32 426 49 198 373 96

**5. Input:** 239 123 58 361495 37
**Step I:** 495 239123 58 361 37
**Step II:** 495 37 239 123 58 361
**Step III:** 495 37 361 239 123 58

6. **Step II:** 765 42 183 289 542 65 110 350
   **Step III:** 765 42 542183 289 65 110 350
   **Step IV:** 765 42 542 65 183 289 110 350
7. **Input:** 39 88 162 450 386 72 29
   **Step I:** 450 39 88 162 386 72 29
   **Step II:** 450 29 39 88 162 386 72
   **Step III:** 450 29 386 39 88 162 72
   **Step IV:** 450 29 386 39 162 88 72
   **Step V:** 450 29 386 39 162 72 88

**(8-12):** The words are arranged according to the number of letters they have, one at a time. The word with the maximum number of letters is put first. If the two words have the same number of letter, we go for alphabetical arrangement.

8. **Input:** true se veto be nuke my like
   **Step I:** like true se veto be nuke my
   **Step II:** like nuke true se veto be my
   **Step III:** like nuke true veto se be my
   **Step IV:** like nuke true veto be se my
10. **Step II:** clever remand window sales batch tiger never
    **Step III:** clever remand window batch sales tiger never
    **Step IV:** clever remand window batch never sales tiger
    Now, step IV would be the last step.
11. **Input:** the in car as he may me
    **Step I:** car the in as he may me
    **Step II:** car may the in as he me
    **Step III:** car may the as in he me
12. **Input:** more fight cats cough sough acts idea
    **Step I:** cough more fight cats sough acts idea
    **Step II:** cough fight more cats sough acts idea
    **Step III:** cough fight sough more cats acts idea
    **Step IV:** cough fight sought acts more cats idea
    **Step V:** cough fight sough acts cats more idea
    **Step VI:** cough fight sough acts cats idea more

**(13-17):** Here the rule followed is:

**Step I:** The smallest number becomes first and the remaining numbers shift one position rightward. [In case the first number is small then the next number just larger than it will become second and the rest will shift one position rightward and so on.]

**Step II:** The largest number among given numbers be comes last and the remaining numbers shift one position leftward.

[In case the largest number is first from the right end, the second largest number replaces the second number from the right end, and so on.]

These steps are repeated alternately till all the numbers get arranged in ascending order and that will be the last step for that particular input.

**15. Step II:** 22, 49, 32, 88, 69, 132, 101, 185

**Step III:** 22, 32, 49, 88, 69, 132, 101, 185

**Step IV:** 22, 32, 49, 88, 69, 101, 132, 185

**Step V:** 22, 32, 49, 69, 88, 101, 132, 185

Here, Step III will be same as Step I and in Step IV, as the largest-number is already at the end, second largest will come in just one position ahead of the largest.

**16. Input:** 45, 78, 97, 132, 28, 16, 146, 54, 99, 112

**Step I:** 16, 45, 78, 97, 132, 28, 146, 54, 99, 112

**Step II:** 16, 45, 78, 97, 132, 28, 54, 99, 112, 146

**Step III:** 16, 28, 45, 78, 97, 132, 54, 99, 112, 146

**17.** As it is certain that the last step will be strictly in ascending order hence we do not require to go through procedures.

**(18-22):** The words get arranged one by one on the basis of the no. of letters, the word with least no. of words gets arranged first. If the no. of letters is the same, the word that comes first in the dictionary gets arranged first. While one word gets arranged, the others shift rightwards.

**18. Input:** lack of a common safe in the

**Step I:** a lack of common safe in the

**Step II:** a in lack of common safe the

**Step III:** a in of lack common safe the

**20. Step I:** If there was no good man

**Step II:** If no there was good man

**Step III:** If no man there was good

**21. Step II:** is to for while they were going day

**Step III:** is to day for while they were going

**Step IV:** is to day for they while were going

**(23-27):** From the last step, it is clear that the words are arranged in alphabetical order and nos. are arranged in decreasing order alternately. To obtain this output first the word, which comes first in dictionary, comes to the first place and the rest shift one place rightwards. In the next step the largest no. comes to the second place and the rest shift one place rightwards. These two steps occur alternately untill the last step is obtained.

**(28-32):** In the given arrangement, the first and the second places are occupied by words; the third and the fourth by numbers; the fifth and the sixth by words; and the seventh and the eighth by numbers.

Words occupy place in alphabetical order while numbers occupy place in descending order.

Whenever a word or a number gets arranged other elements shift one place rightward.

**28. Input:** bench 47 63 advance 13 29 again between

**Step I:** advance bench 47 63 13 29 again between

**Step II:** advance again bench 47 63 13 29 between

**Step III:** advance again 63 bench 47 13 29 between

**29. Step III:** again dark 83 sour 19 21 prey 39

**Step IV:** again dark 83 39 sour 19 21 prey

**Step V:** again dark 83 39 prey sour 19 21

**Step VI:** again dark 83 39 prey sour 21 19

Since step VI is the last step (because all elements of step III get arranged in step VI), step V is the required step (penultimate step or last but one.)

**30.** Since it is a case of 'Arrangement', previous steps can't be obtained with certainty.

**31. Step II:** desk eagle 12 28 41 69 foreign land

**Step III:** desk eagle 69 12 28 41 foreign land

**Step IV:** desk eagle 69 41 12 28 foreign land

**Step V:** desk eagle 69 41 foreign 12 28 land

**Step VI:** desk eagle 69 41 foreign land 12 28

**Step VII:** desk eagle 69 41 foreign land 28 12

**32. Input:** bring home 42 73 15 goal 32 type
**Step I:** bring goal home 42 73 15 32 type
**Step II:** bring goal 73 home 42 15 32 type
**Step III:** bring goal 73 42 home 15 32 type
**Step IV:** bring goal 73 42 home type 15 32
**Step V:** bring goal 73 42 home type 32 15
Since all the elements of Input get arranged in Step V, it is the last step.

**(33-37):** Here it is the case of arrangement. The logic is: the words get arranged in alphabetical order. Whereas the numbers get arranged in descending order. Numbers occupy odd places in the final steps while words occupy even positions. When any element gets arranged, the previous elements occupying that position shifts one place towards right.

**33. Step I:** 59 bead tenure father 38 11 ultimate 24
**Step II:** 59 bead 38 tenure father 11 ultimate 24
**Step III:** 59 bead 38 father tenure 11 ultimate 24

**34. Input:** 9 13 about tariff 24 call 29 even
**Step I:** 29 9 13 about tariff 24 call even
**Step II:** 29 about 9 13 tariff 24 call even
**Step III:** 29 about 24 9 13 tariff call even
**Step IV:** 29 about 24 call 9 13 tariff even

**35. Input:** 24 12 entry sand butter 51 32 carry
**Step I:** 51 24 12 entry sand butter 32 carry
**Step II:** 51 butter 24 12 entry sand 32 carry
**Step III:** 51 butter 32 24 12 entry sand carry

**36. Step II:** 37 desk 34 garden 5 father victory 17
**Step III:** 37 desk 34 father garden 5 victory 17
**Step IV:** 37desk 34 father 17garden 5 victory
Since all the elements of the input are fully arranged in Step IV, this is the last step of the given input.

**37.** Since it is a case of arrangement, we can't obtain previous steps with certainty.

**(38-42):** An intuitive look at the input and the steps makes it clear that it is a case of arrangement. The input is a combination of words and numbers. Words get arranged according to reverse order of alphabetical arrangement whereas numbers get arranged in ascending order.

In step I, 'over' occupies the first place from the left end and the other elements are pushed one place rightward. Similarly, in step II, '26' occupies the second place from the left end and the other elements are pushed one place rightward.

Thus, alternate arranging of words and numbers finally gives the last step in which the odd places from the left are occupied by words and the even places are occupied by numbers.

**38.** **Step III:** take 17 mind game 29 75 18 loud
**Step IV:** take 17 mind 18 game 29 73 loud
**Step V:** take 17 mind 18 loud game 29 73
**Step VI:** take 17 mind 18 loud 29 game 73
Hence, step VI is the last step. Therefore, three more steps are required to complete the sequence.

**39.** Since it is a case of arrangement, therefore previous steps or input can't be determined with certainty.

**40.** **Input:** queen mary 79 62 17 20 green west
**Step I:** west queen mary 79 62 17 20 green
**Step II:** west 17 queen mary 79 62 20 green
**Step III:** west 17 queen 20 mary 79 62 green
**Step IV:** west 17 queen 20 mary 62 79 green
**Step V:** west 17 queen 20 mary 62 green 79
Hence, step V is the last step. Therefore, the penultimate step (last but one) is step IV.

**41.** **Input:** by now 51 32 for 91 20 me
**Step I:** now by 51 32 for 91 20 me
**Step II:** now 20 by 51 32 for 91 me
**Step III:** now 20 me by 51 32 for 91
**Step IV:** now 20 me 32 by 51 for 91
**Step V:** now 20 me 32 for by 51 91
**Step VI:** now 20 me 32 for 51 by 91
Hence, step VI is the last step for the given input.

**42.** **Input:** fight for all 39 62 25 today 19
**Step I:** today fight for all 39 62 25 19
**Step II:** today 19 fight for all 39 62 25
**Step III:** today 19 for fight all 39 62 25
**Step IV:** today 19 for 25 fight all 39 62

✧✧✧✧

# 15

# Data Sufficiency

## FORMAT OF THE PROBLEM

Data sufficiency measures a candidate's ability to analyse a problem, recognize relevant information and decide whether the information given enough to answer a problem or not.

**Directions:** *The questions below consist of a question followed by two statements labelled as (a) and (b). You have to decide if these statements are sufficient to conclusively answer the question. Give answer:*

(*a*) if statement (I) alone is sufficient to answer the question but statement (II) alone is not sufficient to answer the question.

(*b*) if statement (II) alone is sufficient to answer the question but statement (I) alone is not sufficient to answer the question.

(*c*) if you can get the answer from (I) and (II) together although neither statement by itself suffices.

(*d*) if statement (I) alone is sufficient and statement (II) alone is sufficient.

(*e*) if you cannot get the answer from statements (I) and (II) together but still more data are needed.

## ANALYSIS AND SUGGESTED STEPS

You should note that data sufficiency questions are not new topics in themselves. All you have to do is to analyse the given data and see if you can get the answer to the question using the given data.

When you are attempting a question of data sufficiency you should follow a systematic approach as laid down below. This approach being a systematic one, will save your time. Also, in case you get stuck at any point, it will help your chances of guessing a correct answer because it narrows down the possible answers from five to three or two.

By looking at this format of the question, we would suggest you to try the first statement [labelled (I)] and see if this statement is sufficient. There are two possible outcomes: either the statement will be sufficient or it will not be sufficient. If the former is true, then either 1 or 4 is the correct answer and if the latter be true, then either 2 or 3 or 5 is the correct answer. Thus, we have narrowed down the number of possible answers from five to two or three. Similarly, this procedure can be continued with the second statement. The complete step-by-step approach is explained by the following diagram.

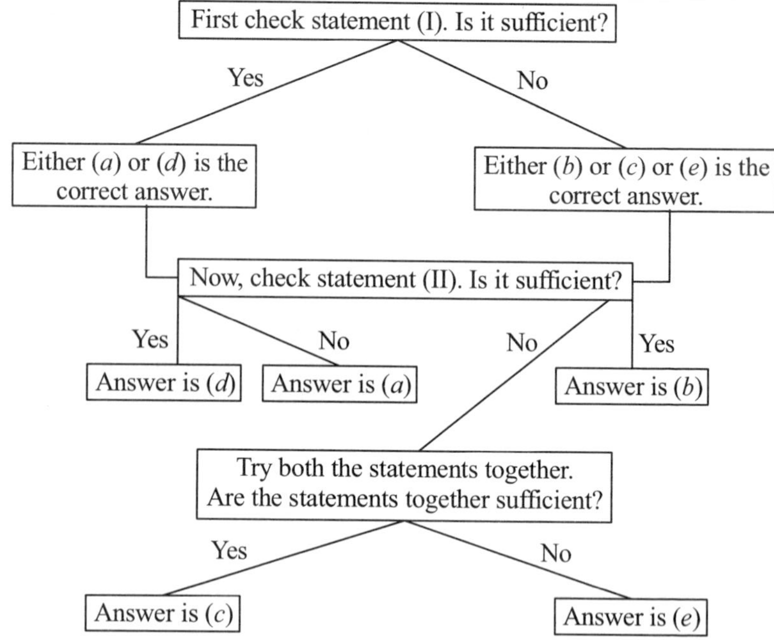


The step-by-step approach outlined here will be sufficient for you to lead to correct answers quickly. However, there are some additional facts which you should keep in mind to have a still quicker approach. These points are discussed below in the following section.

## SOME USEFUL POINTS

### (a) Relationship

In questions that go like "How is Y related to X", the most usual mistake students commit is that they conclude about the relationship without taking the sex into account.

For example, if it is said that X is the son of Y; is it sufficient to conclude that Y is the mother of X? No, because that sex of Y is not known. Y can be either the father or the mother of X.

## (b) Dates

In questions that go like "On which day of the week did the plane reach London" or "What is the birthday of X", You have to find out a "day" or a "date" or an "year". This can be done if (*a*) the day or the date of the same earlier incident (or later incident) is given and (*b*) the exact time-gap between the two incidents is given.

For example, if I am asked to tell "what is Sonu's birth day", a statement that says "Minu's birthday is on 20th March" gives an earlier incident and a statement that says "Sonu was born 5-days after Minu's" gives a clear-cut time-gap between the two incidents. Therefore, the two statements are together sufficient to answer the question although neither itself suffices.

## (c) Comparison

In questions like "Who is the tallest among A, B, C" or "Who is the heaviest among X, Y, Z", we have to make some comparisons. Here, the best way to solve the question by using the mathematical inequalities. For example, if "Sonu is heavier than Manju" you can write it as "S > M". Similarly, Madan is sitting to the left of Ratan and Ratan is sitting to the left of Sudan" can be written as "Madan > Ratan > Sudan". Then the inequalities may be combined to draw the conclusion.

For example, consider the following:

**SOLVED EXAMPLE**

**1.** Among four friends, A, B, C and D; who is the heaviest?

(I) A is heavier than B but lighter than C.

(II) B is not the lightest.

**Sol.** Write statement (I) as: C > A > B.

Now, C and A cannot be lightest as both are heavier than B. So B is not the lightest as per statement II. So D must be the lightest. So, combining; we get

C > A > B > D. ∴ C is the heaviest

Thus, we can answer the question by using both the statements.

## (d) Age

Sometimes the questions go like "What is the age of Shyam?" To help you answer the question, the statements give additional information.

Normally, the informations reduce to mathematical equations and using these mathematical equations, we can solve and find out the age. If one person's age is unknown, we say that there is one unknown. If two persons' ages are not known, we say there are two unknowns. Again, one information gives us one equation. Two different informations give us two equations.

Now, we can easily find out if the given statements are enough to find out a person's age. For this you can follow the following golden rule.

**"If the number of informations is same as the number of unknowns, the data is sufficient; otherwise they are not."**

Let us see some examples in order to understand it.

**2.** Is my son 12 years old?

**Statements:**

**I.** Four years later he will be twenty years younger than me.

**II.** Now, I am twenty years older than him.

**Sol.** This is a deceptive problem. You should notice that there are two unknowns in this case: 'Father' and 'Son'. But how many informations are there? Two? No. There is only one information. Both statements I and II only state that the father is older than the son by 20 years (although the language of I and II are different). So here, we have repetition of data. Since there is one information (one equation) for two unknowns data are insufficient.

**3.** What is the age of Shubham?

**Statements:**

**I.** Twice the age of Shubham, when added to Shyam's age, gives 72 years.

**II.** 10 years later, Shubham will be 38 years old.

**Sol.** Take statement I. Here, no. of unknowns = 2 (Shubham and Shyam) and No. of informations = one. In statement II, however, there is only one unknown (Shubham) and one information. Therefore, statement II alone is sufficient although statement I is not sufficient.

## EXERCISE

**Directions (Qs. 1-35):** *Each of the questions consists of a question and two statements numbered I and II given below it. You have to decide whether the data provided in the statements are sufficient to answer the question. Read both the statements and give answer.*

(*a*) If the data in statement I alone is sufficient to answer the question, while the data in statement II alone is not sufficient to answer the question;

(*b*) If the data in statement II alone is sufficient to answer the question, while the data in statement I alone is not sufficient to answer the question;

(*c*) If the data either in statement I alone or in statement II alone is sufficient to answer the question;

(*d*) If the data even in both statements I and II together are not sufficient to answer the question;

(*e*) If the data in both statements I and II together are necessary to answer the question.

**1.** Among Nitin, Amit, Sudesh, Rekha and Sujata who came last for the programme?

**I.** Nitin came after Amit but not after Sujata.

**II.** Rekha came after Sujata but not after Sudesh.

**2.** Out of the four teams A, B, C and D which team is not likely to win as per the opinion poll?

**I.** As per the opinion poll, chances of team C's winning are more than that of team A but not as much as that of team B, whose chances of winning are more than that of team A.

**II.** As per the opinion poll team C's chances of winning are less than that of team B but not less than that of team D, whose chances of winning are more than that of team A.

**3.** Five friends P, Q, R, S and T are standing in a row facing East. Who is standing at the extreme right end?

**I.** Only P is between S and T; R is to the immediate right of T.

**II.** R is between T and Q.

**4.** What is Sudin's rank in the class of 44 students?

**I.** Ramesh, whose rank is 17th in the class, is ahead of Shyam by 6 ranks, Shyam being 7 ranks ahead of Sudin.

**II.** Suketu is 26 ranks ahead of Sudin and Shyam is 6 ranks behind Sudin while Savita stands exactly in the middle of Shyam and Suketu in ranks, her rank being 17.

**5.** How is P related to N?

**I.** N is sister of M, who is son of Q, whose wife is P.

**II.** M is brother of N and son of Q, whose wife is P.

**6.** What is the distance between villages 'X' and 'Y' by the shortest route?

**I.** Village 'X' is to the North of village 'Z' at a distance of 35 km.

**II.** Village 'Y' is to the west of village 'Z' at a distance of 20 km.

**7.** Among five colleagues, A, B, C, D and E who is the highest salary earner?

**I.** B's salary is less than the sum of the salaries of A and C, but more than the sum of salaries of E and D.

**II.** A's salary is more than that of both E and D but less than that of C who ranks second in the descending order of their salaries.

**8.** Among Q, R, S, T and V who is third from the top when they are arranged in ascending order of their heights?

**I.** T is taller than Q and V but shorter than R.

**II.** R and S are taller than T and Q is shorter than T but taller than V.

**9.** Is Mr 'Y' entitled to get promotion in the month of September, 2002?

**I.** As per his office rules, the only condition for promotion is completion of 12 years of service in a particular grade on 31st December of every year.

**II.** Mr. 'Y' has been working in this office for the last 12 years.

**10.** On which date of a particular year was Aryabhatta commissioned into the Earth's orbit?

**I.** China's secret services claim that it was between 7th and 10th of May.

**II.** The Japan's space research scientists claim that it was between 5th and 10th of May.

**11.** What is the distance (in km) between Achalpur and Durgapur by the shortest route?

**I.** Durgapur is 8 km to the north of Meerapur which is 162 km away from Achalpur.

**II.** Achalpur is 69 km away from Bijnaur which is 28 km away from Durgapur.

**12.** How many employees of bank 'X' opted for VRS?

**I.** 18% of the 950 officer cadre employees and 6% of the 1100 of all other cadre employees opted for VRS.

**II.** 28% of the employees in the age group of 51 to 56 and 17% of the employees in all other age groups opted for VRS.

**13.** Can Rohan retire from office 'X' in January 2000 with full pension benefits?

**I.** Rohan will complete 30 years of service in office 'X' in April, 2000 and desires to retire.

**II.** As per office 'X' rules, an employee has to complete minimum 30 years of service and attain age of 60. Rohan has 3 years to complete the age of 60.

**14.** Who among the three friends A, B and C reached the school first?

**I.** A reached the school at 7.15 am five minutes before the bell rang.

**II.** B reached before C, who reached the school before the bell rang.

**15.** If the first day of a month is Thursday, how many days were there in that month?

**Statements:**

**I.** The fourth Sunday happened to be on 25th.
**II.** The last day of the month was the fifth Saturday of that month.

**16.** Which direction is Shashidhar facing?

**Statements:**

**I.** In the early morning Shashidhar was standing in front of a puppet and the shadow of the puppet was falling to the right of Shashidhar.
**II.** In the early morning Shashidhar was standing on the ground. His shadow was falling behind him when he turned to his left.

**17.** What will be the position of hour hand of a clock at 7.30 PM?

**Statements:**

**I.** There are English letters on the dial of the clock instead of digits.
**II.** The hour hand is at P at 7 o'clock.

**18.** Mahesh's flat is on which floor of the five-floor apartment?

**Statements:**

**I.** His flat is exactly above Ganesh's flat whose flat is exactly above Nitin's first-floor flat.
**II.** Jeevan's flat, which is adjacent to Mahesh's flat, is exactly below Ahmed's flat, who is on fourth floor.

**19.** Who among A, B, C, D and E teaches History?

**Statements:**

**I.** Each one of them teaches only one subject. B teaches Mathematics, while E teaches Science. A or C does not teach Geography. A or D does not teach English.
**II.** C and E are teachers of English and Science respectively and A is the teacher of Mathematics.

**20.** How many books did Dinesh purchase in 'X' bookshop?

**Statements:**

**I.** Dinesh wanted to purchase 65 books, but only 45 books were available in shop 'X'.
**II.** Dinesh selected 37 books but had money to purchase 27 books and asked for some credit to which the shop keeper of 'X' bookstall did not agree.

**21.** On which date in April was Varun born?

**I.** Varun's mother remembers that Varun was born before nineteenth but after fifteenth.

**II.** Varun's sister remembers that Varun was born before seventeenth but after twelfth.

**22.** X is in which direction with respect to Y?

**Statements:**

**I.** Z is to the East of Y, V is to the South of Z, X is to the West of V.

**II.** Z is to the North of X and Y is to the South of Z.

**23.** In a row of 28 girls and boys how many boys are there to the left of Shridhar?

**Statements:**

**I.** If Shridhar is placed after two places to the right then he becomes twelfth from the right.

**II.** Only every third child in the row is girl.

**24.** What is Madhav's birthdate if his sister and mother both are right?

**I.** Madhav's sister remembers that his birthdate is before twentieth but after seventeenth.

**II.** Madhav's mother remembers that his birthdate is after eighteenth but before twenty-third.

**25.** A, B, C and D made their project presentation, one on each day, on four consecutive days but not necessarily in that order. On which day did 'C' make his presentation?

**I.** The first presentation was made on 23rd, Tuesday and was followed by 'D's presentation.

**II.** 'A' did not make his presentation on 25th and one of C and D made his presentation, between A's and B's.

**26.** Which village is to the south-west of village Q?

**I.** Village P is to the west of Village N, which is to the east of village Q.

**II.** Village W is to the south of village N, which is to the west of village Q.

**27.** A, B, C, D and F are seated around a circular table facing at the centre. Who is on the immediate right of B?

**I.** D is between A and F.

**II.** C is between B and F.

**28.** M, J, K, N and D are sitting around a circular table facing the centre, Who among them is sitting on the immediate right of K?

**I.** J is sitting between M and D and D is sitting on the immediate right of N.

**II.** J is second to the left of K and is the second to the right of N.

**29.** Brinda's merit rank is 17th in her class. What is her rank from the last?

**I.** There are 70 students in her class.

**II.** Nisha who ranks 20th in Brinda's class is 51st from the last.

**30.** In a certain code "*al ed nop*" means "We play chess". Which code word means "chess"?

**I.** "*id nim nop*" means "We are honest".

**II.** "*gob ots al*" means "They play cricket".

**31.** How is 'now' written in a code language?

**I.** 'now and then' is written as '*ka da ta*' in that code language.

**II.** 'then you come' is written as '*da ma pa*' in that code language.

**32.** How is Suniti related to the man in the photograph?

**Statements:**

**I.** Man in the photograph is the only son of Suniti's grandfather.

**II.** The man in the photograph has no brothers or sisters and his father is Suniti's grandfather.

**33.** On which day of the week did Sohan visit Chennai?

**I.** Sohan returned to Hyderabad from Chennai on Thursday.

**II.** Sohan left Hyderabad on Monday for Chennai.

**34.** City M is situated in which direction with respect to city D?

**Statements:**

**I.** City K is to the south of city P.

**II.** City M is to the north of city R, which is to the west of city D.

**35.** Who among P, Q, R, S and T is the heaviest?

**I.** Q is heavier than R and T but lighter than only S.

**II.** R is third from the top when they are arranged in descending order of their weight and is heavier than T and P.

**Directions (Qs. 36 to 39):** *Each of the questions below consists of a question and two or three statements given below it. You have to decide whether the data provided in the statements are sufficient to answer the question.*

**36.** Which code represents 'Them' in the given code language?

1. In the code language, 'Se Me Ye' means 'Tell Them Young' and 'Me Yo Na Ye' means 'Wise Young Sharp Tell'.
2. In the code language 'Na Ki Pa Lo' means 'Clever Sharp Come Tomorrow' and 'Ki Po Se Ye' means 'Bring Clever Young Them'.
3. In the code language, 'Pa Na Se Ki Te' means 'Clever Sharp Come Them No' and 'Ki Ni Pa Be Te Na' means 'Yellow Come Sharp Run Clever No'.

(*a*) Only 1 alone is sufficient
(*b*) Either 1 alone or 2 and 3 together are sufficient
(*c*) Only 2 and 3 together are sufficient
(*d*) Only 3 alone is sufficient
(*e*) Either 1 alone or 3 alone is sufficient

**37.** Who is to the North-East of R?

1. S is to the South-East of N, who is to the South-West of P, who is to the North of Q.
2. T is to the North-West of Q, who is to the South of P.
3. R, who is to the North of S, is midway between N and Q, N being to the West of R.

(*a*) All 1, 2, 3 together are required
(*b*) Only 1 and 3 together are sufficient
(*c*) Only 2 and 3 together are sufficient
(*d*) Either 1 and 3 together or 2 and 3 together are sufficient
(*e*) None of these

**38.** What is the rank of Suresh in a class of 17 students?

1. Nitin, having 13th rank from the bottom, is six ranks ahead of Bhupesh, who is two ranks behind Suresh.
2. Bhupesh is .four ranks ahead of Kamlesh.
3. Bhupesh is two ranks behind Suresh and Kamlesh's rank is 15.

(*a*) Only 1 alone is sufficient
(*b*) Either 1 alone or 2 and 3 together are sufficient
(*c*) Only 2 and 3 together are sufficient
(*d*) Only 1 and 3 together are sufficient
(*e*) None of these

**39.** Who is the uncle of L?

1. P, brother of M, is father of L; M is the father of S.
2. R is the father of L's cousin.

(*a*) A alone is sufficient
(*b*) B alone is sufficient
(*c*) Either 1 alone or 2 alone is sufficient
(*d*) Both 1 and 2 together are not sufficient
(*e*) Both 1 and 2 together are necessary

## ANSWERS

| 1 | 2 | 3 | 4 | 5 | 6 | 7 | 8 | 9 | 10 |
|---|---|---|---|---|---|---|---|---|---|
| (*e*) | (*b*) | (*e*) | (*c*) | (*c*) | (*e*) | (*b*) | (*b*) | (*d*) | (*d*) |
| **11** | **12** | **13** | **14** | **15** | **16** | **17** | **18** | **19** | **20** |
| (*d*) | (*a*) | (*d*) | (*d*) | (*b*) | (*c*) | (*d*) | (*c*) | (*a*) | (*b*) |
| **21** | **22** | **23** | **24** | **25** | **26** | **27** | **28** | **29** | **30** |
| (*e*) | (*d*) | (*e*) | (*e*) | (*e*) | (*b*) | (*d*) | (*c*) | (*c*) | (*e*) |
| **31** | **32** | **33** | **34** | **35** | **36** | **37** | **38** | **39** | |
| (*d*) | (*b*) | (*d*) | (*b*) | (*a*) | (*e*) | (*d*) | (*b*) | (*c*) | |

## SOME SELECTED EXPLANATORY ANSWERS

1. **From I:** A > N > S **From II:** S > R > Sud
   From I and II, we get A > N > S > R > Sud
3. **From I:** S P T R **From II:** T R Q East
   Combining I and II, we get, S P T R Q
   Hence Q is at extreme right
4. **From I:** Ramesh = 17th
   ∴ Shyam = (17 + 6 =) 23th
   Sudin = (23 + 7 =) 30th
   **From II:** Savita = 17th

   Suketu ←—25—|→Sudin — 5 — Shyam
   ↑——15→ Savita ←15——↑

   Sudin's rank = 27 th
5. **From I:** P (–) ↔ Q (+)
   |                (P is mother of N)
   (–) N — M(+)
   **From II:** Q ↔ P(–)
   |                (P is mother of N)
   M(+) — N
6. Taking Z as the reference point and using both the equations, we can get the distance between X and Y.
7. **From I:** (A + C) > B > (E + D)
   We can't answer the question on the basis of statement I. We need some more information.

**From II:** C > A > (E + D)

And 'C' has the second position in descending order of their salaries. Hence, B is the highest salary earner.

8. **From I:** R > T > Q, V

   The position of S is not known. Hence I alone is not sufficient.

   **From II:** R, S > T > Q > V

   It is clear that when they are arranged in ascending order, T is third from the top.

9. When were 12 years completed? If Y completed 12 years sometime in 2002, he will be entitled to promotion only after Dec 31, 2002.

10. **From statement I:** Probable dates are: 8th or 9th May

    **From statement II:** Probable dates are : 6th, 7th, 8th or 9th May.

    **From I and II together:** Probable dates are: 8th or 9th May.

12. Statement II gives information in terms of percentage. Hence, this is not sufficient. But I is certainly sufficient.

13. No statements discuss about pension benefits.

14. **From I:** Bell range at 7.15 + 0.05 = 7.20 am

    **From II:** Both B and C reached the school before 7.20

15. (I) gives no additional information; it may be calculated from the statement itself.

    (II) leads us to an answer. Thursday is 1st day (given in the statement). So first Saturday will be the 3rd day. And 5th Saturday = 3 + 4 × 7 = 31st day. Since this is the last day, there were 31 days in the month.

16. **From I:** It means the sun is to the left of Shashidhar and since it is morning, the left of Shashidhar is East. Hence, Shashidhar is facing South.

    **From II:** Sun is to the left of Shashidhar. Hence, he is facing South [Since it is morning].

17. At 7.30 PM, the hour hand of the clock will be between 7 and 8. The alphabet code of 8 cannot known from the given statements.

18. From I, Mahesh's flat is on the 3rd floor.

    From II also, his flat is on the 3rd floor.

19. **From I:** A teaches History among A, B, C, D and E [The names of other four subjects are given in the statement and A teaches none of them.]

    **From II:** Either B or D teaches History.

20. Desire to purchase a thing is not enough; it is the money that matters.

**21. From I:** Varun's birthday may be 16th, 17th or 18th April.

**From II:** Varun's birthday may be 13th, 14th, 15th or 16th April.

Now,

**From I and II:** Varun's birthday is on 16th April.

**23. From I:** The 3rd, 6th, 9th 12th, 15th, 18th, 21st, 24th and 27th positions are occupied by girls.

**From II:** Shridhar is 14th from the right.

Hence, using I & II, we can get the No. of boys required.

**24. From I:** Madhav's birthdate is either on 18th or on 19th.

Hence, statement I alone is not sufficient.

**From II:** Madhav's birthdate is on one of the following dates: 19th, 20th, 21st and 22nd. Hence, statement II alone is not sufficient.

But, from I and II, it is obvious that the birthdate of Madhav is on 19th.

**25. From I:** We get

First presentation: 23rd (Tuesday)

Second presentation : 24th (Wednesday) : D

Third presentation : 25th (Thursday)

Fourth presentation : 26th (Friday)

**From II:** A did not make his presentation on 25th and one of them made his presentation between A and B.

**From I and II:** Both A and B cannot be adjacent and D made the presentation on 2nd day. Therefore, A/B will be 1st and 3rd or 3rd and 1st. Hence, 'C' made the presentation in the end on 26th.

**26. From I:** P ● ● N ● N

Hence, statement I alone is not sufficient.

**From II:** N ● ● Q

● W

Hence, statement II alone is sufficient to answer the question. (village W is the south-west of village Q)

**27. From I:**

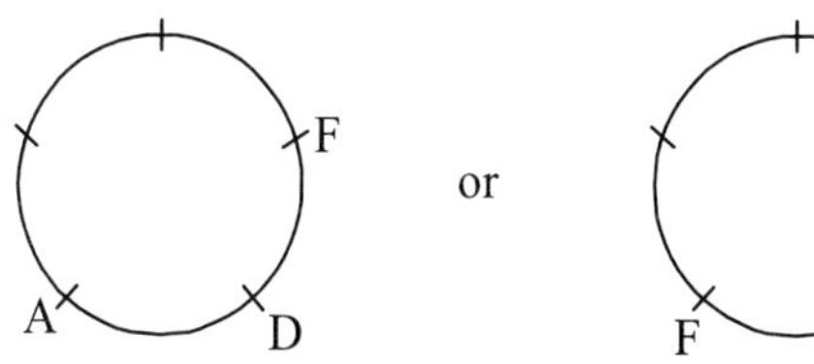

**From II:**

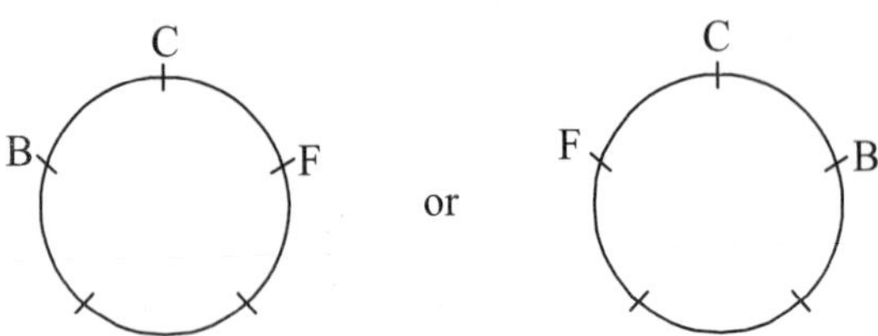


**From I and II:**

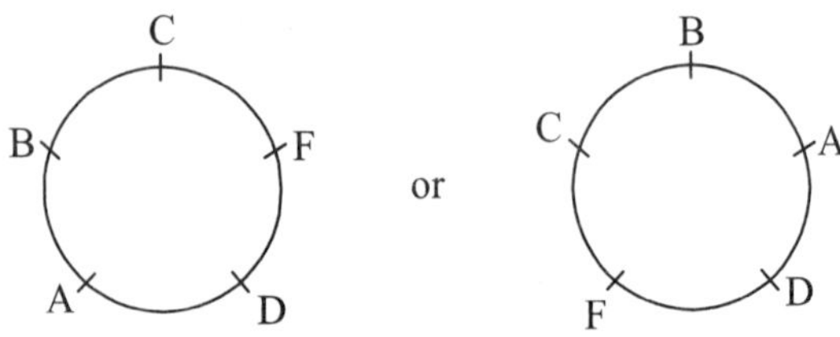


The person who is immediate right of B is either A or C.

**28. From I:**

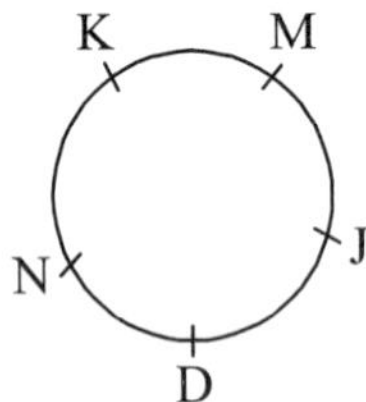


Hence, statement I alone is sufficient to answer the quesion.

**From II:**

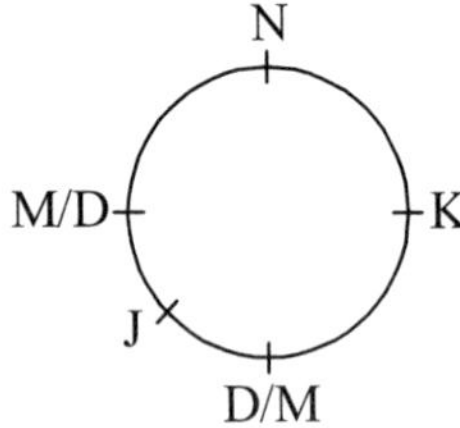


Hence, statement II alone is also sufficient.

**29. From I:** Required rank = 70 – 17 + 1 = 54

**From II:** Total students in Bindra's class = 51 + 20 – 1 = 70

Now, required rank = 70 – 17 + 1 = 54

**30.** **From I:** code for 'We' is '*nop*'.
**From II:** code for 'play' is '*al*'.
Hence, from I and II together code for 'chess' is '*ed*'.

**31.** **From I:** now and then ⇒ *ka da ta* ...(*i*)
**From II:** then you come ⇒ *da ma pa* ...(*ii*)
**From I and II:** Code for *now* is either *ka* or *ta*.
We need some more information.

**33.** Even the information given in both the statement I and II together are not sufficient.

**34.** **From I:** P

K

(No information about city M and D)

**From II:** M

R D

(M is north-west with respect of D.)

**35.** **From I:** S > Q > R and T
Q is lighter than only S. This implies S is the heaviest.
**From II:** ★★ > ★ > R > T and P
Still we need more information to decide who among Q and S is the heaviest.

**39.** (+)P —— M(+)

|    |

L    S

Hence, 'M' is uncle of 'L'.

From (B) it is clear that 'R' is uncle of 'L'.

✧✧✧✧

# 16

# Logical and Venn Diagrams

## INTRODUCTION

In these type of questions, a set of five different figures is given as options. Each figure represents a logical pattern of certain groups of related words wherein each word represents a class. One has to identify the most appropriate logical figure for the set of words given. Some of the relationships represented by these diagrams are given below. Understand the relationship patterns and then attempt the exercise following the explanation.

## EXERCISE

**Directions (1–8) :** *Choose the Venn diagram which best illustrates the three given classes in each question.*

(*a*)

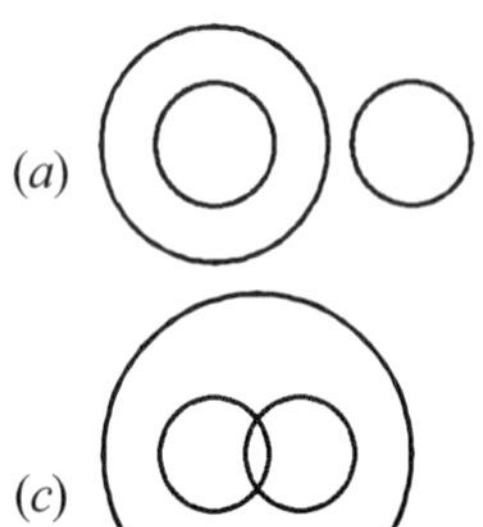

(*b*)

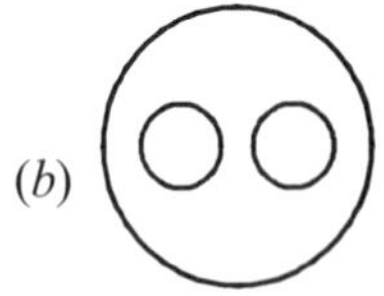

(*c*)

(*d*)

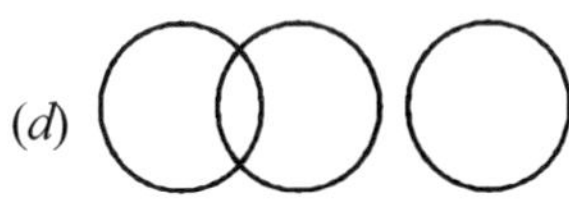

1. Wheat, Grains, Maize
2. Machine, Lathe, Mathematics
3. Biology, Botany, Zoology
4. Atmosphere, Hydrogen, Oxygen
5. Science, Physics, Chemistry
6. Dog, Animal, Pet
7. Sun, Planets, Earth
8. Protons, Electrons, Atoms

**Directions (9–13) :** *Each of the following questions select the diagram out of the five that best represents the relationship among the given words.*

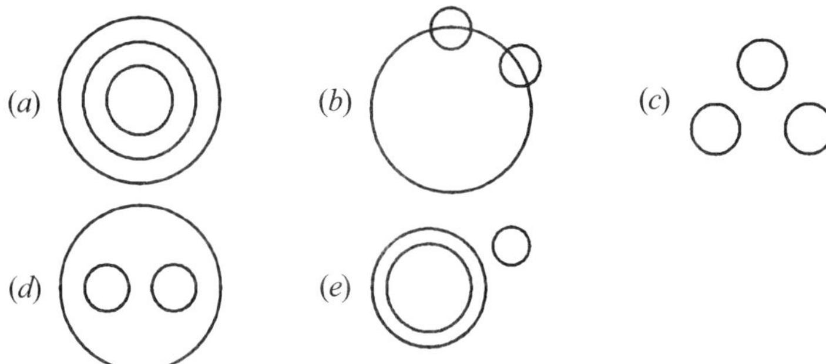


**9.** Cup, Bed, Shoe

**10.** Victoria Memorial, West Bengal, Kolkata

**11.** Society, Children, Young

**12.** Tree, Bark, Pea

**13.** Girls, Beautiful, Flowers

**Directions (14–18) :** *Each of the questions given below contains three elements. These elements may or may not have some intense linkage. Each group of elements may fit into one of the diagrams named (a), (b), (c), (d) or (e). You have to indicate the diagram in which the group of elements fits correctly?*

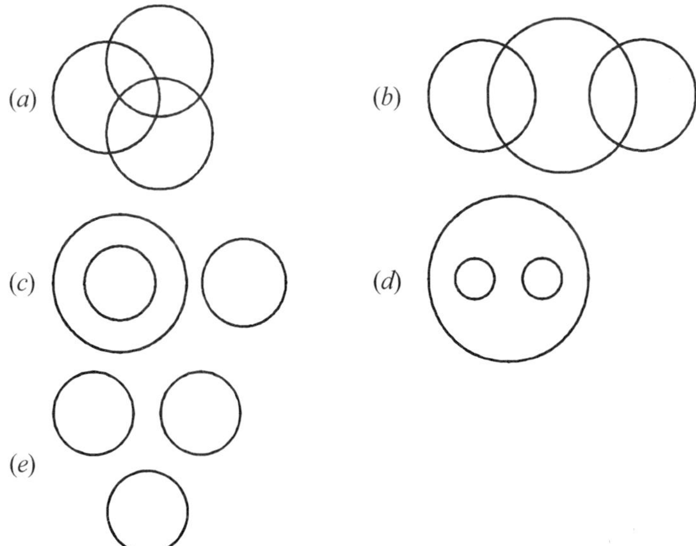

**14.** Person, Philosopher, Writer

**15.** Sweets, Oranges, Fruits

**16.** Clerks, Educated Persons, Government Servants.

**17.** Teachers, Saints, Human beings

**18.** Father, Mother, God

**Directions (19–23) :** *The following questions are based on the diagram given below:*

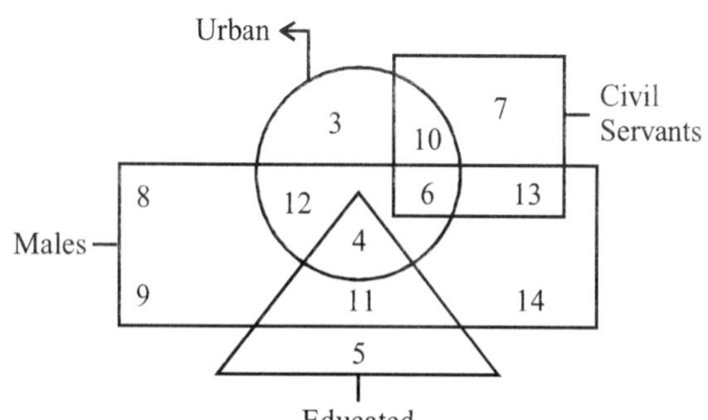


**19.** Who among the following is neither a civil servant nor educated but is urban and not a male?

(*a*) 2 (*b*) 3 (*c*) 6
(*d*) 10 (*e*) 9

**20.** Who among the following is a male, urban oriented and also a civil servant but not educated?

(*a*) 13 (*b*) 12 (*c*) 6
(*d*) 10 (*e*) 4

**21.** Who among the following is a male civil servant, who is neither educated nor belongs to urban area?

(*a*) 7 (*b*) 13 (*c*) 4
(*d*) 1 (*e*) 5

**22.** Who among the following is an educated male who is not an urban resident?

(*a*) 4 (*b*) 5 (*c*) 9
(*d*) 11 (*e*) 12

**23.** Who among the following is a female, urban resident and also a civil servant?

(*a*) 6 (*b*) 7 (*c*) 10
(*d*) 13 (*e*) 11

**Directions (24–28) :** *In the following diagram, there are three figures interlocking each other – a rectangle, a square and a triangle. Each figure represents the class mentioned against it.*

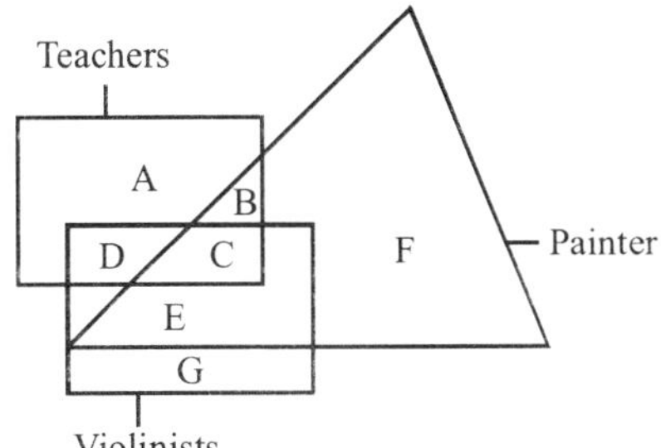


*Study the figure and answer the questions that follows.*

**24.** Painters who are neither teachers nor violinists are represented by
(*a*) A (*b*) B (*c*) C
(*d*) E (*e*) F

**25.** Teachers who are painters but not violinists are represented by
(*a*) B (*b*) C (*c*) D
(*d*) F (*e*) G

**26.** The region which represents painters and violinists but not teachers, is denoted by
(*a*) B (*b*) D (*c*) E
(*d*) F (*e*) G

**27.** Which letter represents teachers who are violinists but not painters?
(*a*) B (*b*) C (*c*) D
(*d*) E (*e*) F

**28.** Which letter represents teachers who are painters as well as violinists?
(*a*) B (*b*) C (*c*) D
(*d*) E (*e*) F

## ANSWERS

| 1 | 2 | 3 | 4 | 5 | 6 | 7 | 8 | 9 | 10 |
|---|---|---|---|---|---|---|---|---|---|
| (*b*) | (*a*) | (*b*) | (*b*) | (*b*) | (*c*) | (*a*) | (*b*) | (*c*) | (*a*) |
| **11** | **12** | **13** | **14** | **15** | **16** | **17** | **18** | **19** | **20** |
| (*d*) | (*e*) | (*b*) | (*b*) | (*c*) | (*a*) | (*d*) | (*e*) | (*b*) | (*c*) |
| **21** | **22** | **23** | **24** | **25** | **26** | **27** | **28** | | |
| (*b*) | (*d*) | (*c*) | (*e*) | (*a*) | (*c*) | (*c*) | (*b*) | | |

## SOME SELECTED EXPLANATORY ANSWERS

**1.** Wheat and Maize are two different items. But both belong to the class of Grains.

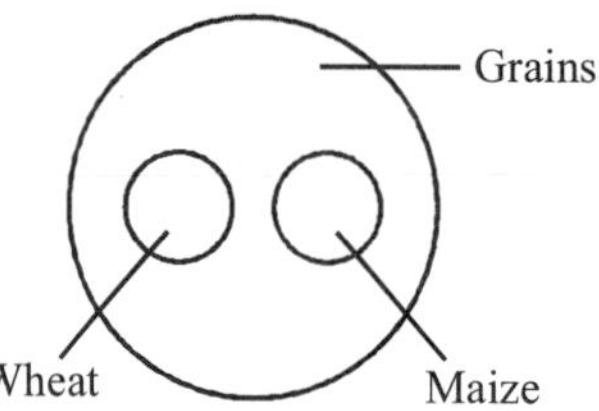


**3.** Botany and Zoology are entirely different from each other. But both are branches of Biology.

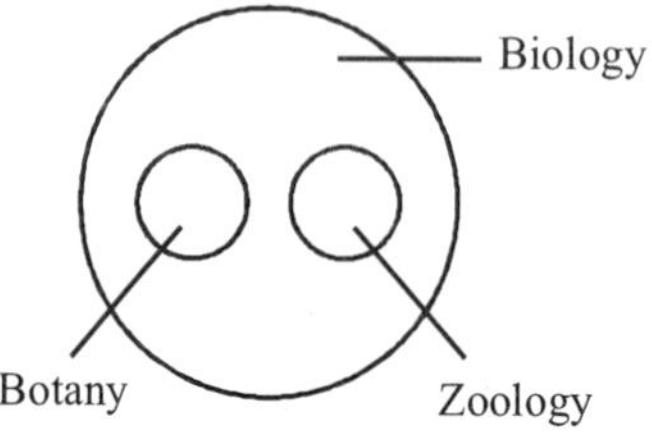


**4.** Hydrogen and oxygen both are component parts of atmosphere

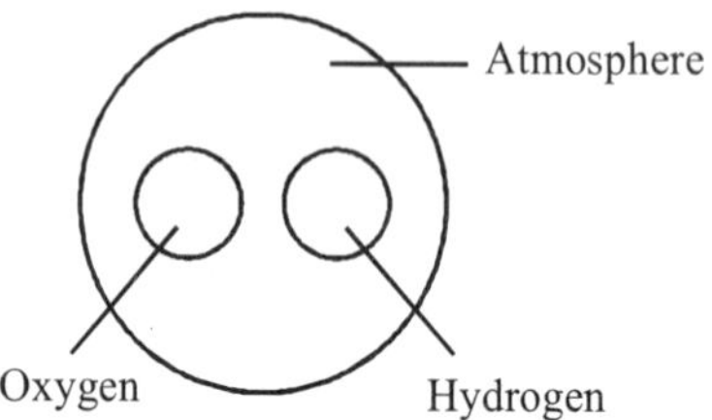


**5.** Physics and Chemistry are entirely different from each other. But both belong to the class of Science.

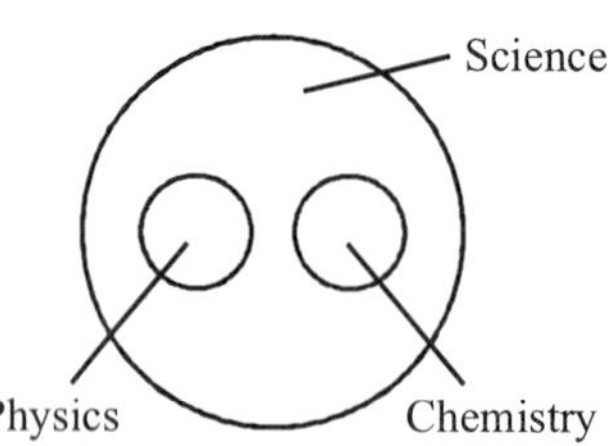

**6.** Some dogs are pets and some pets are dogs. Both dogs and pets are animals.

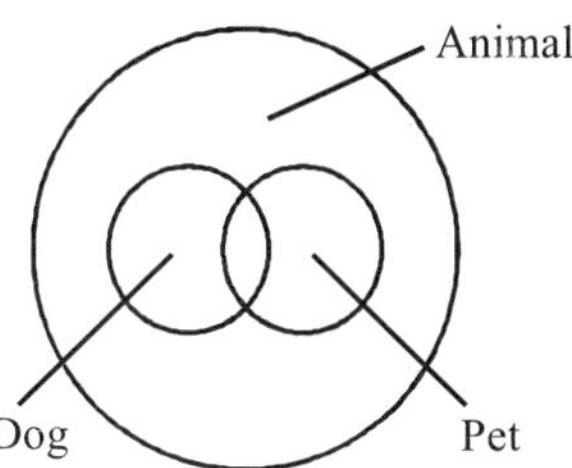


**7.** Earth belongs to the class of Planets. But Sun is entirely different from the two.

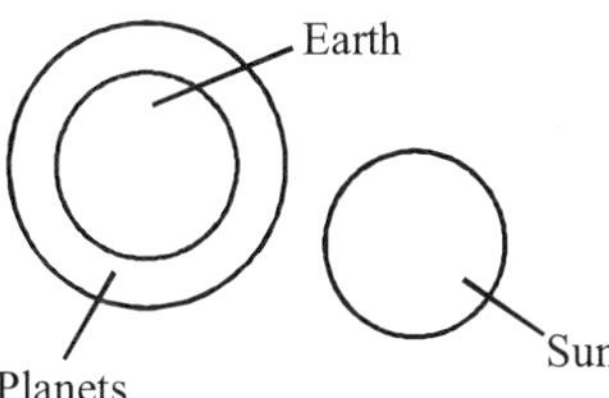


**8.** Protons and Electrons are entirely different from each other. But both are parts of atoms.

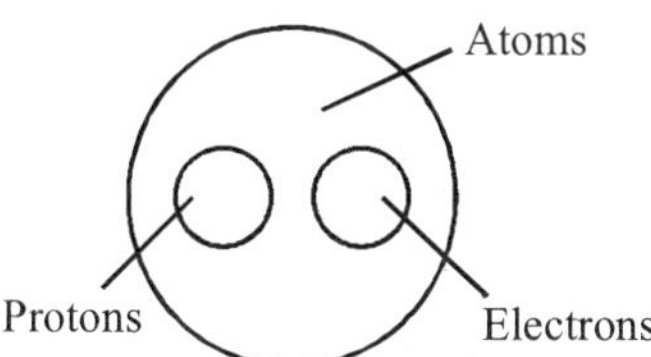


**9.** All the three things are entirely different from one another and bear no relationship among themselves.

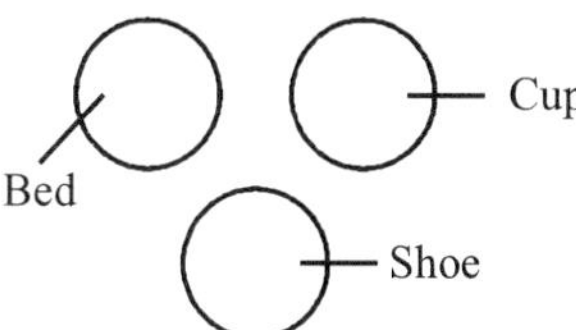

**10.** Victoria Memorial is situated in Kolkata and Kolkata is in West Bengal.

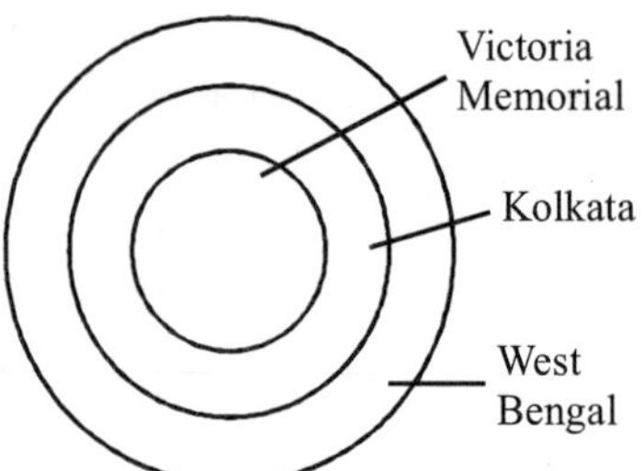


**11.** Society consists of people of different age-groups. Hence, children and young will come under different heads in the society.

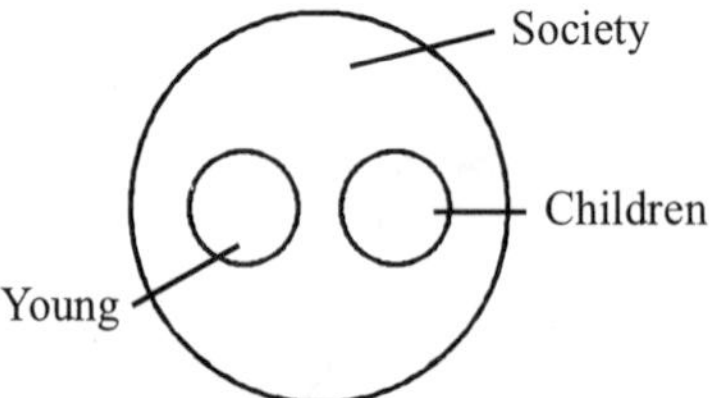


**12.** Every tree has bark but pea grows on plant. So relationship among them is best represented by diagram ***(e)***.

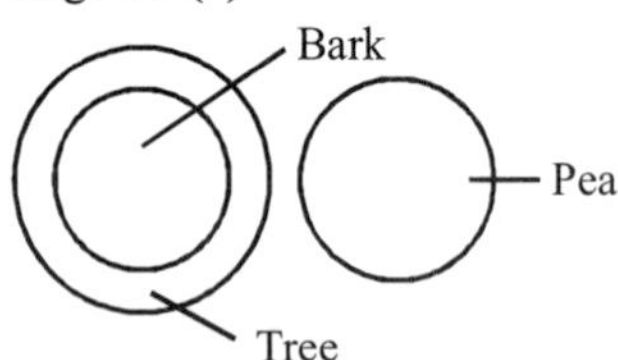


**13.** Some girls and some flowers are beautiful but not all. Some other objects can also be beautiful.

**14.**

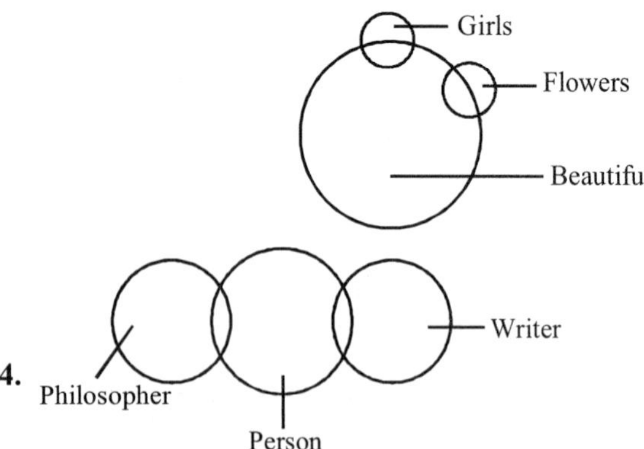

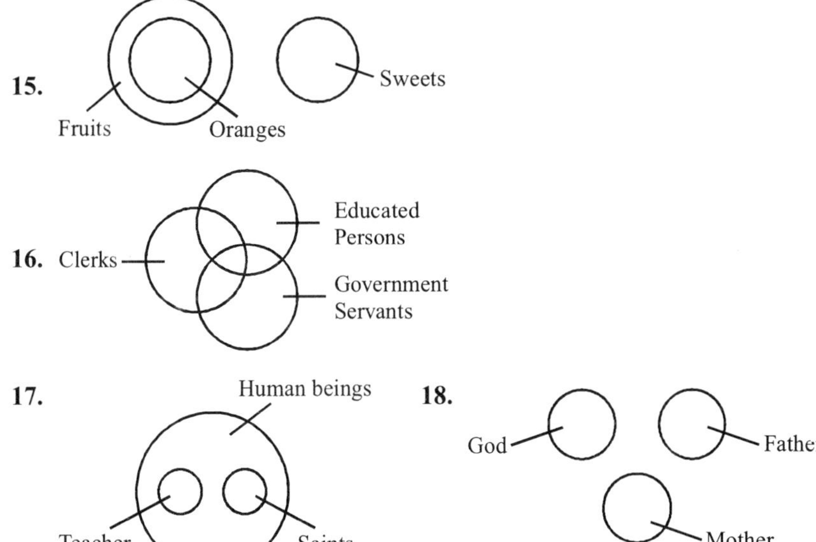


**19.** 3 is satisfying the given condition in the question.

**20.** The person satisfying the given conditions is denoted by the region which is common to the rectangle, circle and the square but lies outside the triangle, i.e. 6.

**21.** The person satisfying the given conditions is represented by the region common to the rectangle and the square but lying outside the triangle and the circle i.e. 13.

**22.** The person satisfying the given conditions is represented by the region which is common to the triangle and the rectangle but lies outside the circle, i.e. 11.

**25.** The persons satisfying the given conditions are represented by the region which is common to the rectangle and the triangle but not the square, i.e. B.

**26.** The persons satisfying the given conditions are represented by the region which is common to the triangle and the square but is not a part of the rectangle, i.e. E.

**27.** The required set of persons is represented by the region which is common to the rectangle and the square but is not a part of the triangle, i.e. D.

**28.** The required set of persons is represented by the letter denoting the region common to the rectangle, triangle and the square, i.e. C.

✧✧✧✧

# 17

# Syllogism

Syllogism is defined as the science of thought expressed in the form of language. It is an important chapter in logical reasoning.

## FORMAT OF THE QUESTIONS

A typical question of syllogism as asked in the competitive examination is being provided below:

**Directions:** *In the following type of questions, two statements are being provided followed by two conclusions A and B. You have to study the two statements and then decide whether, from those two statements,*

(*a*) Only A follows
(*b*) Only B follows
(*c*) Both A and B follow
(*d*) Either A or B follows
(*e*) Neither A nor B follows.

**1. Statements:** 1. All pine trees are coniferous.
2. All coniferous are beautiful.

**Conclusions:** (A) All pine trees are beautiful.
(B) Some beautiful are pine trees.

**2. Statements:** 1. All smart are vociferous.
2. No vociferous is introvert.

**Conclusions:** (A) Some smart are introvert.
(B) Some vociferous are not smart.

## SOME BASIC DEFINITIONS

### Proposition

A proposition is a sentence that makes a statement and gives a relation between two terms. It consists of three parts: (*a*) the subject, (*b*) the predicate and (*c*) the relation between the subject and the predicate.

Some examples of propositions are being given below.

(*i*) All elephants are big.
(*ii*) No schoolboy is disciplined.
(*iii*) Some girls are pretty.
(*iv*) Some wigs are not cute.

## Subject and Predicate

A subject is that part of the proposition about which something is being said. A predicate, on the other hand, is that term of the proposition which is stated about or related to the subject.

Thus, for example, in the four propositions mentioned above, 'elephants', 'schoolboy', 'girl' and 'wigs' are subjects while 'big', 'disciplined', 'pretty' and 'cute' are predicates.

## Categorical Propositions

A categorical proposition makes "a direct assertion. It has no conditions attached with it. For example, "All S are P", "No S are P", "some S are P", etc. are categorical propositions, but "If S, then P" is not a categorical proposition.

**Note:** There is another class of propositions known as 'disjunctive propositions'.

## Types of Categorical Propositions

(*a*) **Universal proposition:** Universal propositions either fully include the subject or fully exclude it. Examples are:

All boys are cute.

No box is square-shaped.

Usually, universal propositions begin with "All", "Every", "Any" etc. or "No", "None of the", "Not a single" etc.

A proposition of the form "All S are F' is called a *universal positive proposition* while a proposition of the form "No S is P" is called a *universal negative proposition.* Further, a universal positive proposition is usually denoted by the letter **'A'** while a universal negative proposition is usually denoted by the letter **'E'**.

(*b*) **Particular proposition:** Particular propositions either only partly include or only partly exclude the subject while making a statement. Examples are:

Some boys are cute.

Some bases are not circular.

Usually, particular propositions have relational clauses like "some", "many", "quite a few" etc. or"some .......... not", "not many", "very little" etc.

A proposition of the form "Some S are P" is called a *particular positive proposition* while a proposition,of the form "Some S are not P" is called a particular negative proposition. Further, a particular positive proposition is denoted by the letter **"I"** while a particular negative proposition is denoted by the letter **'O'**.

*The definition of the **A, E, I, O** propositions are very, very important and the student must have the ability to immediately recognise these types.* With this need in mind we are listing these four types of propositions in the following table:

**Table 1: The four types of propositions**

| Types of Proposition | Universal | Particular, |
|---|---|---|
| Positive | **A** Format: All S are P. | **I** Format: Some S are P |
| Negative | **E** Format: No S are P. | **O** Format: Some S are not P |

## THE EULER'S CIRCLES OR VENN DIAGRAMS

There is a pictorial way of representing the propositions, formulated by Euler, an ancient mathematician. Suppose that the proposition is trying to relate the subject (S) with the predicate (P). Then there are four ways in which the relation could be made according to the four propositions:

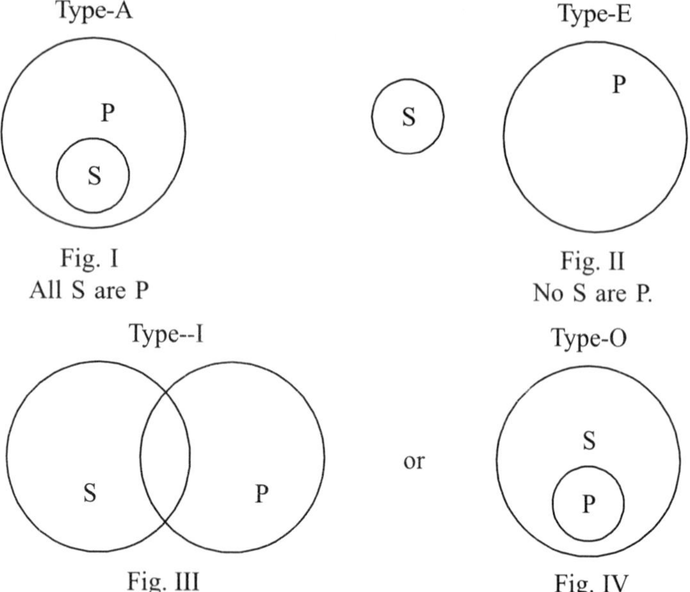


Fig. I
All S are P

Fig. II
No S are P.

Fig. III

Fig. IV

Both figure III and figure IV represent the case— Some S are P.

## IMMEDIATE INFERENCE

Syllogism is a case of immediate inference because in syllogism we draw conclusions from two or more given statements. But, sometimes, we also need to take into account the meaning that follows from a single statement. For example, "Some students are Indians" clearly follows from "Some Indians are students." This is an example of immediate inference.

There are two kinds of immediate inference, we need to know about them. They are:

**I. *Implications* (of a given proposition)**

Suppose we are given a proposition "All birds have feathers". Then this proposition naturally implies that the conclusion "Some birds have feathers" must be true. It is very easy to comprehend because if "all" have feathers, then "some" ("some" is only a part of "all") must have feathers. This example only states that if a given proposition is **A**-type, then it also implies that the **I**-type conclusion must be true. As another example, take the statement "No businessmen are honest". If this statement is true then the conclusion "Some businessmen are not honest" too, must be true. This example illustrates that an **E**-type proposition also implies an **O**-type conclusion.

We are listing various propositions and their implicational relations with the other propositions in the table below.

**Table 2:** Implication from a given proposition

| If the given statement is of type | then the conclusion of the type | | | |
|---|---|---|---|---|
| | **A** is | **E** is | **I** is | **O** is |
| **A** | — | False | True | False |
| **E** | False | — | False | True |
| **I** | Doubtful | False | — | Doubtful |
| **O** | False | Doubtful | Doubtful | — |

*[The reader should not have any difficulty in reading the table given above, For example, the table states that if a statement is of type 'O' then the type 'A' conclusion is definitely false while the type 'E' and type 'I' conclusions are both doubtful, that is, they may or may not be true. Thus, if a statement is*

*Some boys are not meritorious. **(O)***

*Then we have,*

***Conclusions:***

*All boys are meritorious **(A)** = false*

*No boys are meritorious **(E)** = doubtful (may or may not be true).*

*Some boys are meritorious **(I)** = doubtful (may or may not be true)]*

### II. *Conversion*

The second important method of immediate inference is conversion. An example of conversion is given-below:

Let a given statement be "All books are study materials". This is converted to give the conclusion "Some study materials are books."

### How to Convert a Given Proposition?

The following rules are to be employed in order to convert a given proposition:

**Step 1: The** subject becomes the predicate and the predicate becomes the subject.

**Step 2:** The type of the given proposition is changed according to the pattern given in Table 3:

**Table 3: Rules of Conversion**

| A statement of the type | when converted becomes a statement of the type |
|---|---|
| **A** | **I** |
| **E** | **E** |
| **I** | **I** |
| **O** | O-type statement cannot be converted |

[The reader should not have any difficulty in converting a statement. Suppose we have to convert the statement: "No book is readable". Then it is converted according to the two rules stated above. Table 3 says that E-type statement becomes E-type statement after conversion. Also, the subject becomes the predicate while the predicate becomes the subject. Therefore the conclusion will be, "No readable thing is book".]

## THE ANALYTICAL METHOD FOR SOLVING SYLLOGISM

### Step I: Aligning

The first step of the analytical method for solving syllogism consists of aligning of the given sentences.

**Two sentences are said to be aligned if the common term is the predicate of the first and the subject of the second.**

**How to align?**

If the sentences are not already aligned then they can be aligned by

(*i*) changing the order of the sentences and/or (*ii*) converting any one sentence.

For example, consider the following illustrations.

**1. Statements:** **I.** All boys are goodlooking.
**II.** Some boys are Indian.

**Sol.** Here the common term is boys. It is a subject of both the sentences and therefore the sentences are not aligned. Now we can do the aligning in any of the following two ways:

(*i*) **converting the first statement:**

All boys are goodlooking → conversion → Some goodlooking are boys.

Now, the aligned pair is:

Some good looking are boys.

Some boys are Indian.

Or, (*ii*) ***converting the second statement and changing the order of the statements.***

We have,

Some boys are Indian → conversion → Some Indians are boys.

Now, we change the order of the sentences to let the above be the first sentence. Hence, we get an aligned pair.

Some Indians are boys.

All boys are goodlooking

**2. Statements:** **I.** Some girls are cute.
**II.** Some Americans are cute.

We can align the pair by

(*a*) converting the first statement and changing the order of the statements. The aligned pair will be:

[Some Americans are cute.

Some cute are girls (converted form of first statement).]

(*b*) converting the second statement, the aligned pair will be:

[Some girls are cute.

Some cute are Americans (converted form of second statement).]

**An important note:** You may have seen that in order to align a sentence, conversion is necessary when the common term is either a subject in both the sentences or a predicate in both the sentences (see Ex 1 and Ex 2 in previous example). In such cases we have to convert one of the sentences. A question may arise here as "to which of the two statements to choose for conversion. For this, remember the rule of IEA. That is, given a pair of to-be-aligned sentences, the priority should be given, while converting, to I-type statement, to E-type statement and then to A-type statement, in that order. Hence, if in the given pair one sentence is of type I and the other of type A then the sentence of type I should be converted.

**Step II: Use table 4 to draw conclusions**

After step I (which involved aligning the two sentences) has been completed, we are left with the easy and self-explanatory table 4 which can be used to draw conclusions.

**Table 4: To draw conclusions from a pair of aligned statements**

| If the first statement is of the type | and the second statement is of the type | then the conclusion will be |
|---|---|---|
| **A** | **A** | **A** |
| **A** | **E** | **E** |
| A | I | — |
| A | O | — |
| **E** | **A** | **O*** |
| E | E | — |
| **E** | **I** | **O*** |
| E | O | — |
| **I** | **A** | **I** |
| **I** | **E** | **O** |
| I | I | — |
| I | O | — |
| O | A or E or I or O | — |

**Note:** The reader should note that

(*i*) There are only 6 cases where a conclusion can be drawn. These cases are highlighted in the table by bold letters and can be memorised in short form as:

A + A = A

A + E = E

E + A = O* **Short form for table 4**

E + I = O*
I + A = I
I + E = O

(*ii*) The '___' sign in the third column of table 4 means that no definite conclusion can be drawn.

(*iii*) *Table 4 gives correct results if and only if the two sentences have been properly aligned.*

(*iv*) **Format of the conclusion** (very important): The conclusion or the inference is itself a proposition whose subject is the subject of the first statement and whose predicate is the predicate of the second statement. The common term disappears.

(*v*) **The meaning of O*:** In the third column of table 4, we have written O* in place of O at two places. By O* we mean that the conclusion or inference is of type O but its format is exactly opposite the format mentioned in (*iv*). In this case the subject of the inference is the predicate of the second sentence and the predicate of the inference is the subject of the first sentence.

## An Illustrative Example

Draw inferences for the following pairs of statements:

(*i*) All books are hooks.
All hooks are crooks.

(*ii*) All tables are chairs.
All tables are glasses.

(*iii*) Some posters are goodlooking.
All posters are expensive.

(*iv*) Some pencils are torches.
No books are pencils.

**Solution:**

(*i*) **Step I:** The sentences are already aligned.

**Step II:** By table 4 we see that A + A = A. Hence the inference will be of type A. Its subject will be the subject of the first sentence, i.e. *books,* and the predicate will be the predicate of the second sentence, i.e. *crooks.* Hence, inference: All books are crooks.

(*ii*) **Step I:** The common term 'tables' is a subject in both the sentences. Hence, we will have to convert in Order to align: Since both the sentences are of the same type (A), we may convert any of them. We choose to convert the first. Consequently, the aligned pair of sentences is:

Some chairs are tables. (Converted form of All tables are chairs.)

All tables are glasses.

**Step II:** From table 4, I + A = I. Hence, the conclusion will be of type I, its subject being the subject of the first sentence (after aligning has taken place), i.e. *'chairs',* and its predicate being the predicate of the second sentence, i.e. *'glasses'*. Hence, Inference : Some chairs are glasses.

***(iii)*** **Step I:** Again the common term 'posters' is a subject in both the sentences. By the rule of IEA, we convert the I-type statement which is the first statement. Consequently, the aligned pair of sentences is:

Some goodlooking are posters (converted).

All posters are expensive.

**Step II:** I + A = I, hence inference is:

Some goodlooking are expensive.

***(iv)*** **Step I:** The common term 'pencils' is a subject in one sentence and a predicate in the other. Hence, changing the order of the statements is sufficient to align the two sentences. Consequently, the aligned pair will be :

No books are pencils.

Some pencils are torches.

**Step II:** E + I = O*. As we know, O* means that the conclusion is of type O but the subject of the conclusion is the predicate of the second sentence and the predicate of the conclusion is the subject of the first sentence. Hence; inference is:

Some torches are not books.

***Two very important additional steps***

**Step III: Check for any immediate inferences (implication or conversion)**

Consider the following. Here two statements are given, followed by two conclusions.

***(i)*** **Statements:** All books, are chairs.

All chairs are red.

**Conclusions:** (*i*) All books are red.

(*ii*) Some red (objects) are books.

Here, we have (the sentences are already aligned) A + A = A. Hence, the conclusion should be: All books are red. But if we convert this conclusion, we obtain: Some red (objects) are books. Hence, both the conclusions given above should be taken as true.

**Step IV: If no definite conclusions are selected, check for complementary pair:**

Think over the following.

**Conclusions:** (*i*) Some pens are men.
(*ii*) Some pens are not men.

It is easy to understand that one of these conclusions must be true. That is, either some pens will be men or some pens will not be men. This is a typical case where the choice "either (*i*) or (*ii*) follows" is true. Remember that this answer choice follows *even without looking at the statements.* Such pairs of statements are called **complementary pairs**. In a complementary pair, at least one of the two statements is always true.

**Which propositions make a complementary pair?**

Two statements make a complementary pair if

(*a*) both of them have the same subject and the same predicate and

(*b*) they are an I-O type pair or an A-O type pair or an I-E type pair.

Look at the following examples:

**Example:**

**Pair I:** (*i*) All gardens are bulbs.
(*ii*) Some gardens are not bulbs.

**Pair II:** (*i*) Some gardens are bulbs.
(*ii*) Some gardens are not bulbs.

**Pair III:** (*i*) Some gardens are bulbs.
(*ii*) No garden is bulb.

**Pair IV:** (*i*) All gardens are bulbs.
(*ii*) No garden is bulb.

**Pair V:** (*i*) All gardens are bulbs.
(*ii*) Some bulbs are not gardens.

**Comments:** In the above example, pairs I, II and III make a complementary pair each while pairs IV and V don't. In pair I, the first statement is of type A and the second is of type O. An A-O pair makes a complementary pair. In pair II, the first statement is of type I and the second is of type O. An I-O pair makes a complementary pair. In pair III, the first statement is of type I while the second is of type E. An I-E pair makes a complementary pair. In pair IV, the first statement is of type A while the second is of type E. An A-E pair does not make a complementary pair. In pair V, we have an A-O pair and an A-O pair does make a complementary pair, yet this pair will not be a complementary pair because the two sentences do not have the same subject and predicate.

**Note:** Step IV asks you to check for a complementary pair. If you do find a complementary pair you should choose "either of them follows". But remember that step IV is not needed if one of the inferences has already been found to be valid in step II or III. **Step IV is applicable to only those conclusions which do not follow from step II or III.**

## SUMMARY OF THE ANALYTICAL METHOD

Now the discussion of the analytical method is complete. For the reader's benefit, I once again summarise the steps to do a syllogism problem.

**Step I:** Properly align the sentences.

**Step II:** Use table 4 to draw conclusion.

**Step III:** Check for immediate inferences.

**Step IV:** Check for complementary pairs if steps II and III fail.

## THE METHOD OF VENN DIAGRAMS

**Step I:** Draw all possible representations for both the statements separately as given below:

**Note:** *By standard* representation we mean a representation which is the most common and usually sufficient way to denote the statement. For example, "Some X are Y" can be represented as:

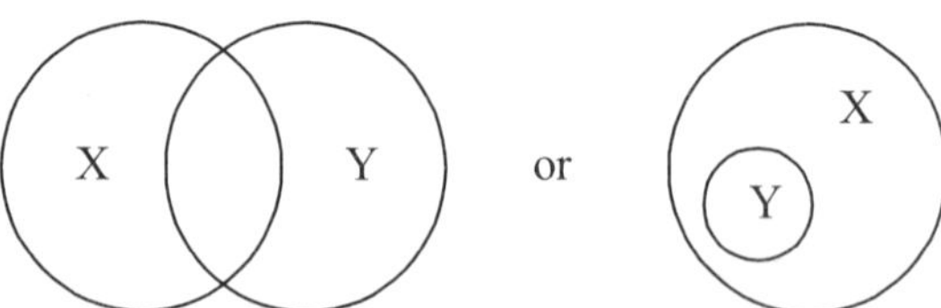


But, for all practical purposes, the first of these representation suffices. And this is the standard representation for an I-type proposition.

Given below is a table of standard representation.

**Tables 5**

| Statement of Type | Standard representation |
|---|---|
| A<br>(All X are Y) | 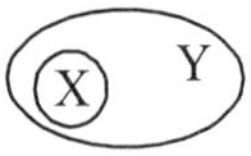 |
| E<br>(No X are Y) | 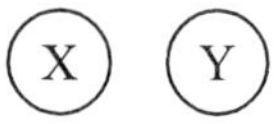 |

| | |
|---|---|
| I<br>(Some X are Y) | X Y |
| O<br>(Some X are not Y) | X Y |

**Step II:** Now try to combine the representations (as drawn in step I) in *as many ways as possible.*

**Note:** When we say as many ways as possible, we mean that you should combine the representations in all possible ways. For example, if statement (1) is "All X are Y" and statement (2) is "Some Y are Z" then the standard representations are:

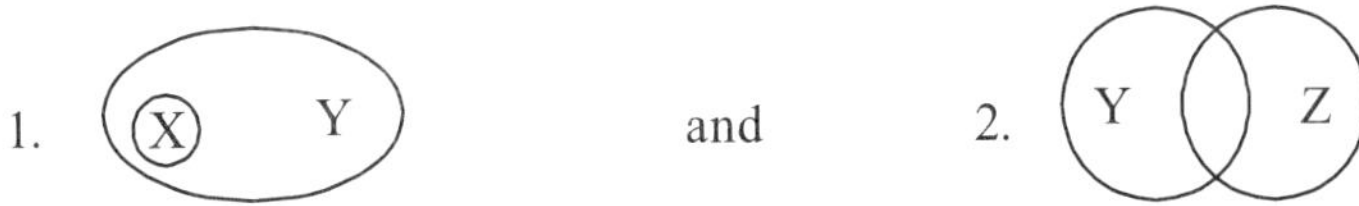


They can be combined in more than one ways. The possible ways are:

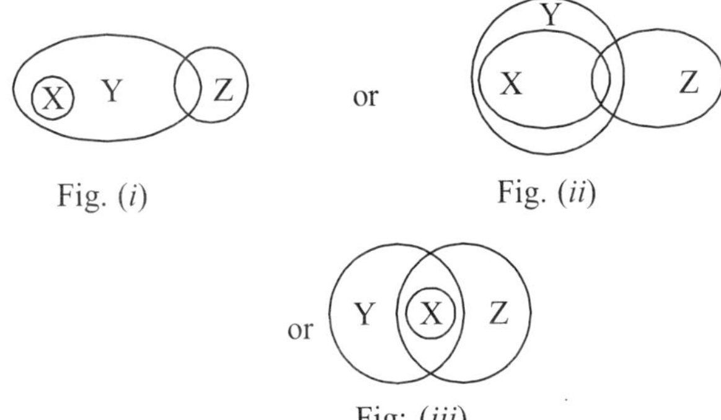


Fig. (*i*) Fig. (*ii*)

or Y X Z

Fig: (*iii*)

Therefore, step II asks you to draw *all* possible combinations.

**Step III:** Finally, make interpretations of the combined figures (obtained from step II). *Any given conclusion will be true* **if and only if** *it is supported by all-the combined figures and no combined figure contradicts it.*

**Example:**

**Statements:** **A.** All cats are bats.

**B.** All bats are tables.

**Conclusions:** **I.** Some tables are bats.

**II.** Some tables are cats.

**Solution:**

**Step I:** Looking at table 5, we draw the standard representations for the two statements:

Let B = bats, C = cats, T - tables.

**Step II:** Now combine fig. (A) and fig. (B) in all possible ways. Fig. (A) and fig. (B) can be combined in only one way. That is:

**Step III:** We see that both conclusions: Some tables are bats and Some tables are cats are supported by the combined figure. Hence, both follow.

## THREE-STATEMENT SYLLOGISM

### Format of the Problem

A typical three-statement syllogism problem reads like this:

**Directions:** *Below are given three statements followed by several conclusions based on them. Examine the conclusions and decide whether they logically follow from the given statements. You have to take the given statements as true even if they appear to be at variance with commonly known facts.*

1. **Statements:** **(A)** All docks are boxes.
   **(B)** Some cars are docks.
   **(C)** No boxes are chocolates.

   **Conclusions:** **I.** Some cars are boxes.
   **II.** No chocolates are docks.
   **III.** Some cars are chocolates.
   **IV.** Some cars are not chocolates.

   (*a*) Only I and IV follow
   (*b*) Only I and II follow
   (*c*) Either III or IV, and I follow
   (*d*) I, IV and II follow
   (*e*) Either III or IV, and I and II follow

### The Method

**Step I:** The first step in solving a three statement syllogism problem involves "carefully choosing the two relevant statements out of the three given statements". You should perform the first step in the following manner.

(*i*) Take a given conclusion.

(*ii*) See the subject and the predicate of this given conclusion.

(*iii*) Now, see which of the two given statements has this subject and predicate.

(*iv*) **A.** If there is one term common between the two statements chosen in the previous part [(*iii*)], these two statements are your relevant statements.

**B.** If there is no term common between the two statements chosen in the previous part [(*iii*)], then all the three statements are your relevant statements. In this case you will have to apply a *chain-like formula.*

## Performing Step I: An illustration

Consider the sample question given above. Here, we take all the four conclusions one by one.

**Conclusion I.** We first take conclusion I. Here, the subject is 'cars' and the predicate is 'boxes'. Now, we see that 'cars' is in statement B and 'boxes' is in statement A. Now look at statements A and B. Do they have a common term? Yes, the common term is 'docks', therefore, A and B are our two relevant statements.

**Conclusion II.** Now, we take conclusion II. Here, the subject is 'chocolates' and the predicate 'docks'. Now, we see that 'chocolates' appears in the statement 'C'. But 'docks' appears in both 'A' and 'B'. So, which of the two should we take? We should take 'A' because *(Note this)* there is a term common between A and C. We would not take B because there is no term common between B and C.

**Conclusion III.** Now, we take conclusion III. Here, the subject is 'cars' and the predicate 'chocolates'. We see that 'cars' appears in 'B' while 'chocolates' appears in 'C'. Now, is there any common term between 'B' and 'C'? We see that there is no term common between 'B' and 'C'. So we will have to use a chain-like formula in this case because all the three statements are, relevant here.

**Conclusion IV.** Same as in conclusion III.

**Note:** It is very important that you understand this first step. If necessary re-read the entire matter once again before going further.

## Step II and III... etc:

Once we have found our relevant statements, the rest of the analysis remains the same as it was discussed earlier. You have to first align the relevant statements; then use the formulae of table 4; then you should also check for any immediate inference and finally, you should check for any complementary pairs.

## A SUMMARY OF THE METHOD

The entire process of solving three-statement syllogism is performed in three simple steps. These three steps have been already described above. To make it clearer, we are giving below the gist of these three steps:

Take a given conclusion.

**Perform step I.** In other words, find out the relevant statements to test this conclusion.

**Perform step II.** In other words, use the formulae to test a given conclusion.

[If more than two statements are relevant for a given conclusion, use the chain-like formulae].

If the given conclusion has been rejected in step II,

**Perform step III: (*i*)** In other words check for immediate inference.

If the given conclusion has still not been accepted,

**Perform step III: (*ii*)** In other words, check for complementary pair.

[**Note:** You do not need to perform Step III (*i*), if a conclusion has already been accepted in step II. Again, you do not need to perform step III (*ii*), if a given conclusion has already been accepted in step III (*i*)].

## COMPLETE STEP-BY-STEP SOLUTION OF EX 1

We hope that the method has become clear to you by now. If there are any doubts, see the detailed solution of Ex 1 that is given below. We have already given the details of step I for Ex 1. So, this solution will start from step II onwards.

**Conclusion I:** We have seen that for this conclusion, statements A and B are relevant. Now we perform step II. For this, we first arrange A and B in such a way that the predicate of the first sentence is the subject of the second. This is done as:

Some cars are docks; (I)

↔

All docks are boxes. (A)

Now we have, I + A = I. So the conclusion will be of type I; it will be "Some cars are boxes." Hence, conclusion I is valid. (Now, we do not need to perform step III because the conclusion has been accepted in step II itself.)

**Conclusion II:** We have seen that statements A and C are relevant for this conclusion (step I). Now we perform step II. For this we write the sentences in such a way that the predicate of the first sentence is the subject of the second. This is done as:

All docks are boxes. (A)

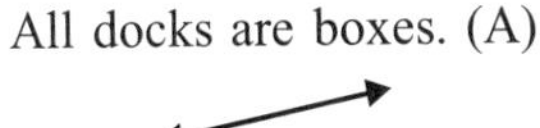

No boxes are chocolates. (E)

Now, we have: A + E = E. Hence, the conclusion will be "No docks are chocolates". Now the given conclusion is: "No chocolates are docks". But "No docks are chocolates" automatically implies "No chocolates are docks". Hence, this conclusion is also valid. [Again we do not need to perform step III because the conclusion has been accepted in step II itself.]

**Conclusion III:** We have seen that all the three statements are relevant to this conclusion (step I). So we should perform step II. For this we should write the three statements in such a way that the predicate of the first sentence is the subject of the second and the predicate of the second sentence is, the subject of the first. This is done as:

Some cars are docks. (I)

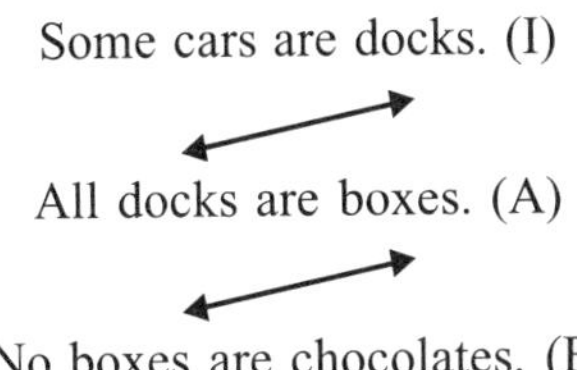

All docks are boxes. (A)

No boxes are chocolates. (E)

Now, we have the chainlike formula:

I + A + E = (I + A) + E = (I) + E = O. Thus, a valid conclusion would be of type O; that is "Some cars are not chocolates". But this is conclusion IV. Hence, conclusion IV is valid. But conclusion III is not accepted in step II. So we perform step III (*i*). We see that "Some cars are not chocolates" does not follow from any of the three given statements alone. So this test fails. Now, we perform step III (*ii*). For this, we will have to first search any other conclusion that has the same subject and predicate. We see that conclusion IV fulfils this condition because the subject and the predicate of conclusions III and IV are the same: 'cars' and 'chocolates' respectively. Again, conclusion III is of type I and conclusion IV is of type O and we know that an I-O pair makes a complementary pair.

Still, we would not choose the choice "either of them follows" unless it is made sure that step II and step III (*i*) fail on conclusion IV too. But we see that conclusion IV is accepted in step II. So, despite the fact that conclusion III and IV make a complementary pair, we do not accept the choice "either of them follows" because conclusion IV is accepted in step II.

**Conclusion IV:** As already explained, it is a valid conclusion.

**Answer: (*d*)** (I, II and IV follow).

## ONE MORE SOLVED ILLUSTRATION

We are presenting a detailed solution of one more example so that you may fully understand the method.

**Example:**

**Statements:** **A.** Some bricks are dogs.
**B.** All kicks are sticks
**C.** No sticks are bricks.

**Conclusions:** **I.** Some dogs are bricks.
**II.** Some dogs are not bricks.
**III.** Some dogs are kicks.
**IV.** Some dogs are not kicks.
**V.** Some kicks are dogs.
**VI.** No kicks are dogs.

(*a*) Either I or II and either III or IV and either V or VI follow
(*b*) Either I or II and IV and either V or VI follow
(*c*) I, IV and either V or VI follow
(*d*) I, IV and VI follow
(*e*) Only IV and VI follow

**Solution**

**Conclusions I and II**

**Step I:** In both these conclusions the subject and the predicate are 'dogs' and 'bricks' respectively. We see that 'bricks' and 'dogs' appear in one statement only in statement A. Hence, only statement (A) is relevant here.

**Step II:** Since only one statement is relevant, step II is not needed.

**Step III:** (*i*) We see that "Some dogs are bricks" follows from "Some bricks are dogs" as immediate inference. Hence, conclusion I is accepted. But conclusion II does not follow from "Some bricks are dogs".

(*ii*) Conclusion I and II make a complementary pair because both have he same subject and the same predicate and they are an I-O pair. But conclusion I has already been accepted; hence "either of them follows" is not a correct choice.

**Conclusions III, IV, V, VI**

**Step I:** In these conclusions 'kicks' and 'dogs' appear as subject and predicate. Now in the given statements, 'dogs' is in statement A while 'kicks' is in statement B. But there is no term common between A and B. This means that all the three statements are relevant to us.

**Step II:** We write the three statements in the following way:

All kicks are sticks. (A)

↔

No sticks are bricks. (E)

↔

Some bricks are dogs. (I)

Now, we have A + E + I = (A + E) + I = (E) + I = O reversed. Hence, a valid conclusion would be "Some dogs are not kicks." Hence, conclusion IV is valid.

**Step III (*i*):** Conclusion IV has been accepted. So we need to perform the remaining steps on conclusions III, V and VI only. We see that none of these three conclusions directly follows from the three given statements alone. Hence, step III (*i*) fails.

**Step III (*ii*):** Conclusions III and IV make a complementary pair because one is of type I and the other of type O, and the subject and the predicate of both are the same. But conclusion IV has already been accepted. Hence, we cannot choose "either of these follows". But conclusions V and VI also make a complementary pair (I-E pair; same subject and predicate) and none of these conclusions has been accepted. Hence "either V or VI follows" would be a correct choice.

**Answer:** (*c*) (I, IV, and either V or VI follow).

## EXERCISE

**Directions (Qs. 1-13):** *In each questions below are two statements followed by two conclusions numbered I and II. You have to take the two given statements to be true even if they seem to be at variance with commonly know facts and then decide which of the given conclusions logically follows from the two statements disregarding commonly known facts.*

Give answer (*a*) if only conclusion I follows.

Give answer (*b*) if only conclusion II follows.

Give answer (*c*) if either conclusion I or conclusion II follows.

Give answer (*d*) if neither conclusion I nor conclusion II follows.

Give answer (*e*) if both conclusion I and II follow.

1. **Statements:** All mangoes are golden in colour. No golden-coloured things are cheap.
   **Conclusions:** **I.** All mangoes are cheap.
   **II.** Golden-coloured mangoes are not cheap.
2. **Statements:** Some engineers are fools. Anand is an engineer.
   **Conclusions:** **I.** Some fools are engineers.
   **II.** Anand is a fool.

**3. Statements:** All cars are cats. All fans are cats.
**Conclusions:** **I.** All cars are fans.
**II.** Some fans are cars.

**4. Statements:** All artists are smokers. Some smokers are drunkards.
**Conclusions:** **I.** All smokers are artists.
**II.** Some drunkards are not smokers.

**5. Statements:** Some dreams are nights. Some nights are days.
**Conclusions:** **I.** All days are either nights or dreams.
**II.** Some days are nights.

**6. Statements:** Some pastries are toffees. All toffees are chocolates.
**Conclusions:** **I.** Some chocolates are toffees.
**II.** Some toffees are not pastries.

**7. Statements:** No gentleman is poor. All gentlemen are rich.
**Conclusions:** **I.** No poor man is rich.
**II.** No rich man is poor.

**8. Statements:** All educated people read newspapers. Rahul does not read newspaper.
**Conclusions:** **I.** Rahul is not educated.
**II.** Reading newspaper is not essential to be educated.

**9. Statements:** Some books are tables. Some tables are mirrors.
**Conclusions:** **I.** Some mirrors are books
**II.** No book is mirror.

**10. Statements:** All hill stations have a sun-set point. X is a hill station.
**Conclusions:** **I.** X has a sun-set point.
**II.** Places other than hill stations do not have sun-set points.

**11. Statements:** All huts are mansions. All mansions are temples.
**Conclusions:** **I.** Some temples are huts.
**II.** Some temples are mansions.

**12. Statements:** Some kings are queens. All queens are beautiful.
**Conclusions:** **I.** All kings are beautiful.
**II.** All queens are kings.

**13. Statements:** All birds are tall. Some tall are hens.
**Conclusions:** **I.** Some birds are hens.
**II.** Some hens are tall.

**Directions (Qs. 14-25) :** *In each questions below are three statements followed by two conclusions numbered I and II. You have to take the three given statements to be true even if they seem to be at variance with commonly known facts and then decide which of the given conclusions logically follows from the three statements disregarding commonly known facts.*

**Give answer (*a*)** If only Conclusion I follows.
**Give answer (*b*)** if only Conclusion II follows.
**Give answer (*c*)** if either Conclusion I or Conclusion II follows.
**Give answer (*d*)** if neither Conclusion I nor Conclusion II follows.
**Give answer (*e*)** if both Conclusion I and II follow.

**14. Statements:** All pots are rings. All bangles are rings. All rings are paints.
**Conclusions:** **I.** Some paints are pots.
**II.** Some bangles are paints.

**15. Statements:** All plastics are wood. No wood is a metal. Some metals are gases.
**Conclusions:** **I.** No plastic is a metal.
**II.** Some gases are plastic.

**16. Statements:** Some forests are huts. Some huts are walls. Some walls are nets.
**Conclusions :** **I.** Some nets are forests.
**II.** Some nets are huts.

**17. Statements:** All chairs are pens. Some pens are knives. All knives are rats.
**Conclusions:** **I.** Some rats are chairs.
**II.** Some rats are pens.

**18. Statements:** All umbrellas are rains. Some rains are clouds. All clouds are storms.
**Conclusions:** **I.** Some storms are umbrellas.
**II.** Some storms are not rains.

**19. Statements:** Some trees are boxes. All boxes are bricks. All bricks are dogs.
**Conclusions:** **I.** Some dogs are trees.
**II.** Some bricks are trees.

**20. Statements:** All stars are moons. All moons are dust. All asteroids are dust.
**Conclusions:** **I.** Some moons are asteroids.
**II.** All stars are dust.

**21. Statements:** All tables are windows. All windows are rooms. All rooms are buses.
**Conclusions:** **I.** Some buses are tables.
**II.** Some rooms are tables.

**22. Statements:** All numbers are digits. All alphabets are numbers. All words are alphabets.
**Conclusions:** **I.** All words are digits.
**II.** Some numbers are not words.

**23. Statements:** All goats are flowers. No flower is branch. Some branches are roots.
**Conclusions:** **I.** Some roots are goats
**II.** No root is goat.

**24. Statements:** Some leaves are roots. Some roots are stems. All flowers are stems.

**Conclusions:** **I.** No flower is a leaf.

**II.** Some leaves are stems.

**25. Statements:** Some desks are tents. Some tents are rivers. All rivers are ponds.

**Conclusions:** **I.** Some ponds are tents.

**II.** Some ponds are desks.

**Directions (Qs. 26-30):** *In each of the questions below are given two statements followed by two conclusions numbered I and II. You have take the two given statements to be true even if they seem to be at variance with commonly known facts. Read the conclusions and then decide which of the given conclusions logically follows from the given statements disregarding commonly known facts. Give answer.*

(*a*) If only conclusion I follows. (*b*) if only conclusion II follows.
(*c*) if either I or II follows. (*d*) if neither I nor II follows.
(*d*) if both I and II follow.

**26. Statements:** All leaders are good team workers.
All good team workers are good orators.

**Conclusions:** **I.** Some good team workers are leaders.

**II.** All good orators are leaders.

**27. Statements:** All terrorists are human.
All humans are bad.

**Conclusions:** **I.** All terrorists are bad.

**II.** No human can be a terrorist.

**28. Statements:** Some teachers are followers.
Some followers are famous.

**Conclusions:** **I.** Some teachers are famous.

**II.** Some followers are teachers.

**29. Statements:** Ship was overturned.
Captain was not traced.

**Conclusions:** **I.** Captain died in the accident.

**II.** Captain is alive.

**30. Statements:** Some dedicated souls are angels.
All social workers are angels.

**Conclusions:** **I.** Some dedicated souls are social workers.

**II.** Some social workers are dedicated souls.

**Directions (Qs. 31-40):** *In each of the questions below are given two statements followed by three conclusions numbered I, II and III. You have to take the given statements to be true even if they seem to be at variance with commonly known facts. Read all the conclusions and then decide which of the given conclusions logically follows from the given statements disregarding commonly known facts.*

**31. Statements:** **1.** All rats are bells.
**2.** All bells are cars.
**Conclusions:** **I.** All bells are rats.
**II.** Some cars are neither bells nor rats.
**III.** No car is rat.
(*a*) Only I (*b*) Only II (*c*) Only III
(*d*) Only II and III (*e*) None follows

**32. Statements:** **1.** All bulbs are tables.
**2.** Some bulbs are pots.
**Conclusions:** **I.** All pots are tables.
**II.** No pot is table.
**III.** Some pots are tables.
(*a*) Only I (*b*) Only II (*c*) Only III
(*d*) Only I and II (*e*) None of these

**33. Statements:** **1.** No room is tiger.
**2.** All tigers are goats.
**Conclusions:** **I.** Some goats are rooms.
**II.** All goats are rooms.
**III.** Some goats are tigers.
(*a*) None follows (*b*) Only either II or III follows
(*c*) Only either I or III follows (*d*) Only II follows
(*e*) None of these

**34. Statements:** **1.** Some books are lamps.
**2.** Some lamps are rods.
**Conclusions:** **I.** Some books are rods.
**II.** No rod is either book or lamp.
**III.** All rods are lamps.
(*a*) Only either I or II follows (*b*) Only I and III follow
(*c*) Only II and III follow (*d*) None follows
(*e*) All follow

**35. Statements:** **1.** All tables are boxes,
**2.** Some boxes are windows.
**Conclusions:** **I.** Some tables are windows.
**II.** All boxes are tables.
**III.** No window is table.

(*a*) None follows (*b*) Only either I or III follows
(*c*) Only either II or III follows (*d*) Only I and II follow
(*e*) None of these

**36. Statements:** **1.** Some men are lions.
**2.** All foxes are lions.
**Conclusions:** **I.** Some foxes are men.
**II.** Some lions are men.
**III.** All lions are foxes.
(*a*) All follow (*b*) Only I and II follow (*c*) Only II follows
(*d*) Only III follows (*e*) None follows

**37. Statements:** **1.** Some cars are roads,
**2.** Some roads are buses.
**Conclusions:** **I.** Some roads are cars.
**II.** Some buses are cars.
**III.** Some buses are roads.
(*a*) All follow (*b*) Only I and II follow
(*c*) Only II and III follow (*d*) Only I and III follow
(*e*) None of these

**38. Statements:** **1.** Some hotels are bricks.
**2.** All bananas are bricks.
**Conclusions:** **I.** Some bananas are hotels.
**II.** Some bricks are hotels.
**III.** No banana is hotel.
(*a*) Only I and II (*b*) Only II and III
(*c*) Only I follows (*d*) Only either I or III and II follow
(*e*) All follow

**39. Statements:** **1.** All birds are flowers.
**2.** All flowers are trees.
**Conclusions:** **I.** Some trees are birds.
**II.** Some flowers are birds.
**III.** All birds are trees.
(*a*) All follow (*b*) Only I and II follow
(*c*) Only I and III follow (*d*) Only II and III follow
(*e*) None follows

**40. Statements:** **1.** All roads are trees.
**2.** No tree is soap.
**Conclusions:** **I.** No soap is road.
**II.** Some trees are roads.
**III.** No road is soap.

(*a*) Only I (*b*) Only II (*c*) Only III
(*d*) None follows (*e*) All follow

**Directions (Qs. 41-45):** *In each question below are given two statements followed by four conclusions numbered I, II, III and IV. You have to take the given statements to be true even if they seem to be at variance with commonly known facts. Read all the conclusions and then decide which of the given conclusions logically follows from the given statements, disregarding commonly known facts.*

**41. Statements:** Some boats are buses.
All trains are buses.

**Conclusions:** **I.** No train is a boat.
**II.** All buses are trains.
**III.** Some buses are boats.
**IV.** Some trains are boats.

(*a*) Either I or IV and III follow (*b*) Only IV follows
(*c*) Only I and III follow (*d*) Only III and IV follow
(*e*) None of these

**42. Statements:** All cups are saucers.
All pots are cups.

**Conclusions:** **I.** All pots are saucers.
**II.** All saucers are cups.
**III.** Some cups are pots.
**IV.** Some saucers are pots.

(*a*) Only I and III follow (*b*) Only II and IV follow
(*c*) Only I, III and IV follow (*d*) All follow
(*e*) None of these

**43. Statements:** All bats are flies.
All rats are bats.

**Conclusions:** **I.** All flies are rats.
**II.** All bats are rats.
**III.** All rats are flies.
**IV.** Some flies are not bats.

(*a*) Only I and III follow (*b*) Only II and IV follow
(*c*) Only III and IV follow (*d*) Only II and III follow
(*e*) None of these

**44. Statements:** Some dogs are cats.
No cat is a cow.

**Conclusions:** **I.** Some cats are dogs.
**II.** Some cows are dogs.
**III.** No dog is a cow.
**IV.** Some cats are not dogs.

(*a*) Only I and II follow (*b*) Only II follows
(*c*) Only III and IV follow (*d*) Only III follows
(*e*) None of these

**45. Statements:** All spoons are bowls.
Some bowls are plates.
**Conclusions:** **I.** Some spoons are plates.
**II.** Some bowls are spoons.
**III.** Some plates are spoons.
**IV.** All bowls are spoons.
(*a*) Only I follows (*b*) Only II follows
(*c*) Only II and III follow (*d*) Only I and II follow
(*e*) None of these

**Directions (Qs. 46-50):** *In each question below are given three statements followed by three conclusions numbered I, II and III. You have to take the given statements to be true even if they seem to be at variance with commonly known facts. Read all the conclusions, and then decide which of the given conclusions logically follows from the given statements, disregarding commonly known facts.*

**46. Statements:** **1.** All papers are books.
**2.** All bags are books.
**3.** Some purses are bags.
**Conclusions:** **I.** Some papers are bags.
**II.** Some books are papers.
**III.** Some books are purses.
(*a*) Only I follows (*b*) Only II and III follow
(*c*) Only I and III follow (*d*) Only I and II follow
(*e*) Only I, II and III follow

**47. Statements:** **1.** Some rats are cats.
**2.** Some cats are dogs.
**3.** No dog is a cow.
**Conclusions:** **I.** No cow is a cat.
**II.** No dog is a rat.
**III.** Some cats are rats.
(*a*) None follows (*b*) Only I and II follow
(*c*) Only II and III follow (*d*) Only III follows
(*e*) I, II and III follow

**48. Statements:** **1.** All locks are keys.
**2.** All keys are bats.
**3.** Some clocks are bats.

**Conclusions:** **I.** Some bats are locks.
**II.** Some clocks are keys
**III.** All keys are locks.

(*a*) Only I and II follow (*b*) Only II and III follow
(*c*) Only I follows (*d*) Only II follows
(*e*) I, II and III follow

**49. Statements:** **1.** Some cars are jeeps.
**2.** All boxes are jeeps.
**3.** All pens are cars.

**Conclusions:** **I.** Some cars are boxes.
**II.** No pen is jeep.
**III.** Some boxes are cars.

(*a*) None follows (*b*) Only I and II follow (*c*) Only II follows
(*d*) Only II and III follow (*e*) Only I follows

**50. Statements:** **1.** Some cups are pots.
**2.** All pots are tubes.
**3.** All cups are bottles.

**Conclusions:** **I.** Some bottles are tubes.
**II.** Some pots are bottles.
**III.** Some tubes are cups.

(*a*) Only I and II follow (*b*) Only II and III follow
(*c*) Only I and III follow (*d*) I, II and III follow
(*e*) None follows

**Directions (Qs. 51-55):** *In each question below, there are three statements followed by three conclusions numbered I, II, and III. You have to take the given statements to be true even if they seem to be at variance with commonly known facts and then decide which of the given conclusions logically follow(s) from the given statements.*

**51. Statements:** Some bottles are bags.
All cards are bottles.
Some pens are bags.

**Conclusions:** **I.** Some pens are cards.
**II.** Some cards are bottles.
**III.** Some pens are bottles.

(*a*) Only I and III follow (*b*) Only II and III follow
(*c*) Only II follows (*d*) Either I or III follows
(*e*) None of these

**52. Statements:** Some doors are windows.
All chairs are tables.
Some chairs are windows.

**Conclusions:** **I.** Some chairs are doors.
**II.** Some tables are windows.
**III.** No table is a window.

(*a*) Only I and III follow
(*b*) Only II and III follow
(*c*) Only II follows
(*d*) Only II and either I or III follow
(*e*) None of these

**53. Statements:** Some stones are bricks.
All plants are stones.
No flower is a plant.

**Conclusions:** **I.** No flower is a stone.
**II.** Some bricks are plants.
**III.** No bricks are plants.

(*a*) Only I follows
(*b*) Only II follows
(*c*) Only III follows
(*d*) Either II or III follows
(*e*) None of these

**54. Statements:** All fishes are bones.
No bone is a dog.
Some cats are dogs.

**Conclusions:** **I.** Some bones are fishes.
**II.** No dog is a fish.
**III.** No cat is a bone.

(*a*) Only I and III follow
(*b*) Only I and II follow
(*c*) Only II and III follow
(*d*) I, II and III follow
(*e*) None of these

**55. Statements:** All glasses are frames.
Some frames are metals.
All blocks are glasses.

**Conclusions:** **I.** All blocks are either metals or glasses.
**II.** Some blocks are metals.
**III.** Some frames are blocks.

(*a*) Only III follows
(*b*) Only II follows
(*c*) Only I follows
(*d*) Only I arid III follow
(*e*) None of these

**56. Statements:** **1.** Some mountains are rivers.
**2.** Some rivers are roads.
**3.** Some roads are windows.

**Conclusions:** **I.** Some windows are roads.
**II.** Some rivers are mountains.
**III.** Some roads are mountains.
**IV.** Some windows are rivers.

(*a*) All follow
(*b*) Only I and II follow
(*c*) Only III and IV follow
(*d*) Only I and IV follow
(*e*) None follows

**57. Statements:** **1.** All benches are trees.
**2.** All trees are flowers.
**3.** All flowers are fruits.
**Conclusions:** **I.** All fruits are benches.
**II.** All trees are fruits.
**III.** Some fruits are flowers.
**IV.** Some flowers are benches.

(*a*) All follow
(*b*) Only II, III and IV follow
(*c*) Only III and IV follow
(*d*) Only II and III follow
(*d*) None of these

**58. Statements:** **1.** Some trains are radios.
**2.** Some radios are waters.
**3.** All tigers are waters.
**Conclusions:** **I.** Some trains are tigers.
**II.** Some trains are waters.
**III.** No water is train.
**IV.** All waters are tigers.

(*a*) None follows
(*b*) Both I and III follow
(*c*) Only either II or III follows
(*d*) Only either I or III follows
(*e*) Only either I or IV follows

**59. Statements:** **1.** Some buses are rivers.
**2.** All rivers are mountains.
**3.** Some roads are mountains.
**Conclusions:** **I.** Some mountains are buses.
**II.** Some roads are buses.
**III.** Some roads are rivers.
**IV.** Some mountains are roads.

(*a*) None follows
(*b*) Only I and II follow
(*c*) Only III and IV follow
(*d*) Only I and IV follow
(*e*) All follow

**60. Statements:** **1.** All lions are jungles.
**2.** Some jungles are rabbits.
**3.** All rabbits are elephants.
**Conclusions:** **I.** Some rabbits are lions.
**II.** Some elephants are jungles.
**III.** Some elephants are lions.
**IV.** Some elephants are rabbits.

(*a*) Only I and III follow
(*b*) Only I and II follow
(*c*) Only II and III follow
(*d*) Only III and IV follow
(*e*) None of these

**61. Statements:** **1.** All books are pens.
**2.** No pens are houses.
**3.** All houses are doors.
**Conclusions:** **I.** No books are houses.
**II.** No books are doors.
**III.** Some doors are pens.
**IV.** Some houses are books.
(*a*) Only I follows
(*b*) Only I and II follow
(*c*) Only II and III follow
(*d*) Only III and IV follow
(*e*) None of these

**62. Statements:** **1.** Some dogs are rats.
**2.** All rats are trees.
**3.** Some trees are not dogs.
**Conclusions:** **I.** Some-trees are dogs.
**II.** All dogs are trees.
**III.** All rats are dogs.
**IV.** All trees are dogs.
(*a*) None follows
(*b*) Only I follows
(*c*) Only I and II follow
(*d*) Only II and follow
(*e*) All follow

**63. Statements:** **1.** Some boys are rains.
**2.** All rains are clouds.
**3.** Some clouds are cars.
**Conclusions:** **I.** Some clouds are boys.
**II.** Some cars are boys.
**III.** Some cars are rains.
**IV.** Some rains are boys.
(*a*) None follows
(*b*) Only IV follows
(*c*) Only I follows
(*d*) Both I and IV follow
(*e*) All follow

**64. Statements:** **1.** All bricks are flowers.
**2.** Some houses are flowers.
**3.** All pens are houses.
**Conclusions:** **I.** Some houses are bricks.
**II.** Some pens are flowers.
**III.** Some flowers are bricks.
**IV.** No pen is flower.
(*a*) Only either II or IV and III follow

(*b*) Only either II or IV and I follow
(*c*) Only either I or II and IV follow
(*d*) None follows
(*e*) All follow

**65. Statements:** **1.** All lions are ducks.
**2.** No duck is a horse.
**3.** All horses are fruits.
**Conclusions:** **I.** No lion is a horse.
**II.** Some fruits are horses.
**III.** Some ducks are lions.
**IV.** Some lions are horses.
(*a*) All follow
(*b*) Only either I or II and both III and IV follow
(*c*) Only either I or IV and both II and III follow
(*d*) Only either I or IV and II follow
(*e*) None of these

## ANSWERS

| 1 | 2 | 3 | 4 | 5 | 6 | 7 | 8 | 9 | 10 |
|---|---|---|---|---|---|---|---|---|---|
| (*b*) | (*a*) | (*d*) | (*d*) | (*b*) | (*a*) | (*d*) | (*a*) | (*c*) | (*a*) |
| **11** | **12** | **13** | **14** | **15** | **16** | **17** | **18** | **19** | **20** |
| (*e*) | (*d*) | (*b*) | (*e*) | (*a*) | (*d*) | (*b*) | (*d*) | (*e*) | (*b*) |
| **21** | **22** | **23** | **24** | **25** | **26** | **27** | **28** | **29** | **30** |
| (*e*) | (*e*) | (*c*) | (*d*) | (*a*) | (*a*) | (*a*) | (*b*) | (*c*) | (*d*) |
| **31** | **32** | **33** | **34** | **35** | **36** | **37** | **38** | **39** | **40** |
| (*e*) | (*c*) | (*e*) | (*d*) | (*b*) | (*c*) | (*d*) | (*d*) | (*a*) | (*e*) |
| **41** | **42** | **43** | **44** | **45** | **46** | **47** | **48** | **49** | **50** |
| (*a*) | (*c*) | (*c*) | (*e*) | (*b*) | (*b*) | (*d*) | (*c*) | (*a*) | (*d*) |
| **51** | **52** | **53** | **54** | **55** | **56** | **57** | **58** | **59** | **60** |
| (*c*) | (*c*) | (*d*) | (*b*) | (*a*) | (*b*) | (*b*) | (*c*) | (*d*) | (*e*) |
| **61** | **62** | **63** | **64** | **65** | | | | | |
| (*a*) | (*b*) | (*d*) | (*a*) | (*e*) | | | | | |

## SOME SELECTED EXPLANATORY ANSWERS

**1. Conclusion I:** 'All mangoes are *golden in colour* + 'No *golden-coloured things* are cheap' i.e. A + E ⇒ E i.e. 'No mangoes are cheap'.
Therefore, conclusion I does not follow.

**Conclusion II:** ∵ 'All mangoes are golden in colour'.
So, substitute 'mangoes' with 'golden-coloured mangoes'
So, 'Golden-coloured mangoes are not cheap'.
[∵ 'No mangoes are cheap"]

Therefore, conclusion II follows.

2. No conclusion follows because the middle term 'engineer' is not distributed even once in the premises.
But conclusion I is the converse of the first premise.
Therefore only conclusion I follows.

3. **Conclusion I & II:** 'All cars are *cats*' + 'All fans are *cats*', i.e. A $\xrightarrow{\text{Conversion}}$ 'Some cats are fans' i.e. I ⇒ A + I ⇒ No conclusion.
Therefore, conclusions I & II do not follow.

4. **Conclusions I & II:** 'All artists are *smokers*' + 'Some *smokers* are drunkards' i.e. A + I ⇒ No conclusion.
Also, none of the conclusions is converse of the given statements.
Therefore, conclusion I and II do not follow.

5. **Conclusion I:** 'Some dreams are *nights*' + 'Some *nights* are days', i.e. I + I = ⇒ No conclusion. [∵ I-type statements cannot be combined]
Therefore, conclusion I does not follow.
**Conclusion II:** 'Some nights are days', i.e. I-type
$\xrightarrow{\text{Conversion}}$ 'Some days are nights, i.e. I- type
Therefore, conclusion II follows.

6. **Conclusion I:** 'All toffees are chocolates', i.e. A-type
$\xrightarrow{\text{Conversion}}$ 'Some chocolates are toffees, i.e. I-type.
Therefore, conclusion I follows.
**Conclusion II:** Some pastries are toffees, i.e. I-type
$\xrightarrow{\text{Conversion}}$ Some toffees are pastries, i.e. I-type
Therefore, conclusion II does not follow.

**Another way:**

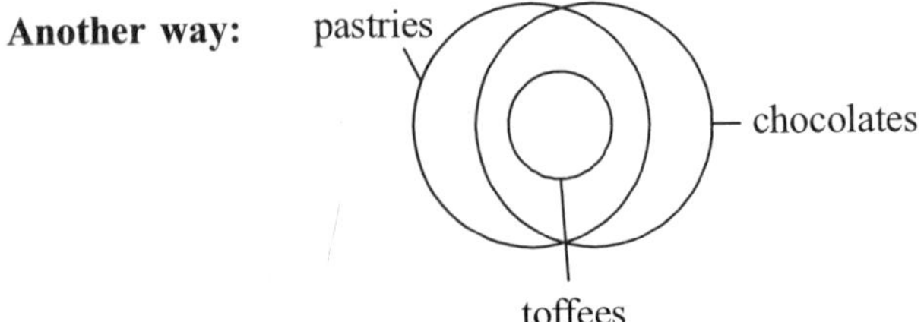

**7. Conclusions I & II :** 'No gentleman is poor', i.e.

E $\xrightarrow{\text{Conversion}}$ 'No poor is *gentleman*' + 'All *gentleman* are rich', i.e. E + A ⇒ $O^+$, i.e. 'Some rich men are not poor'. Therefore, conclusions I and II do not follow.

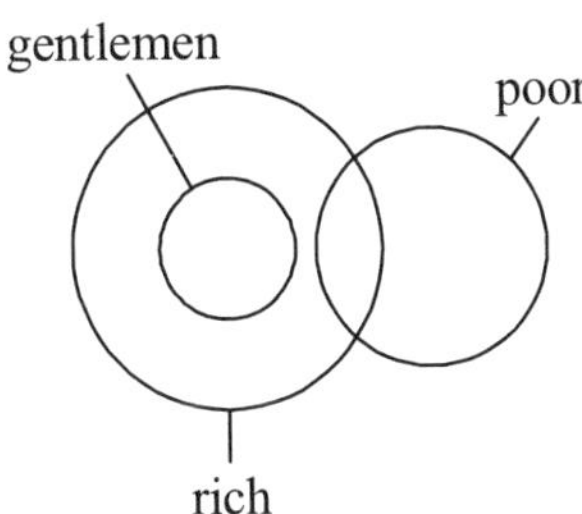


**8.** The conclusion must be universal negative because both the premises are universal and one premise is negative.

Also, the conclusion should not contain the middle term.

Therefore, conclusion I follows but conclusion II does not follow.

**9. Conclusions I & II:** 'Some books are *tables*' + 'Some *tables ate* mirrors, i.e. I + I ⇒ No conclusion.

[∵ I-type statement cannot be combined.]

So, conclusions I and II do not follow.

But they form a complementary I-E type pair.

Therefore, either conclusion I or II follows.

**Another way:**

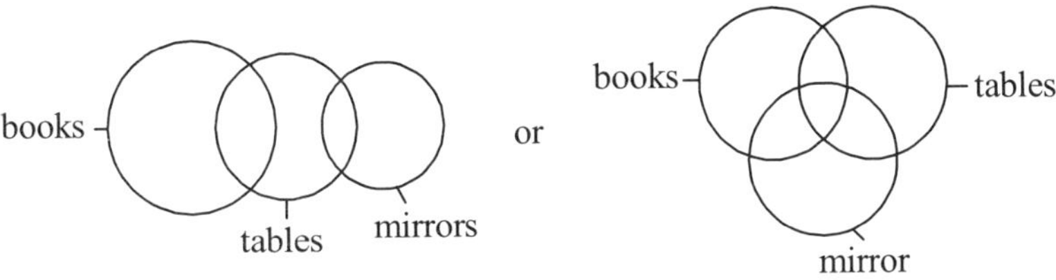


**10.** The conclusion must be universal affirmative because both the premises are universal and affirmative.

Also, the conclusion should not contain the middle term.

Therefore, conclusion I follows but conclusion II does not follow.

**11. Conclusion I:** 'All huts are *mansions*' + 'All *mansions* are temples', i.e.

A + A ⇒ A, i.e. 'All huts are temples' $\xrightarrow{\text{Conversion}}$ 'Some temples are huts.

Therefore, conclusion I follows.

**Conclusion II:** 'All mansions are temples', i.e. A-type $\xrightarrow{\text{Conversion}}$ 'Some temples are mansions', i.e. I-type

Therefore, conclusion II follows.

12. **Conclusion I:** 'Some kings are *queens*' + All *queens* are beautiful', i.e. I + A ⇒ I, i.e. 'Some kings are beautiful'. Therefore, conclusion I does not follow.

**Conclusion II:** 'Some kings are queens', i.e. I-type.

$\xrightarrow{\text{Conversion}}$ 'Some queens are kings', i.e. I-type.

Therefore, conclusion II does not follow.

**Another way:**

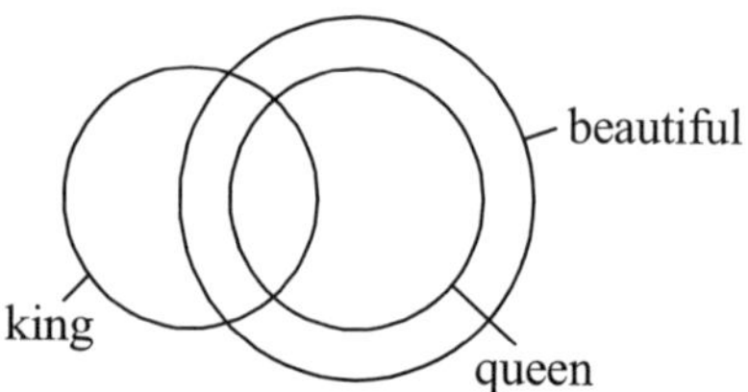


13. **Conclusion I:** 'All birds are *tall*' + 'Some *tall* are hens' i.e. A + 1 ⇒ No conclusion.

Therefore, conclusion I does not follow.

**Conclusion II:** 'Some tall are hens', i.e. I-type

$\xrightarrow{\text{Conversion}}$ 'Some hens are tall', i.e. I-type

Therefore, conclusion n follows.

**Another way:**

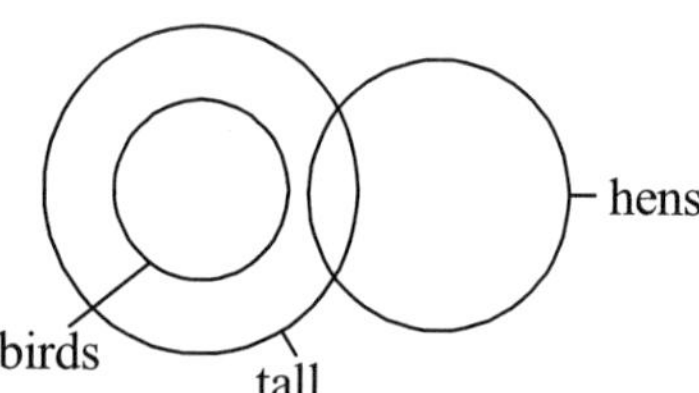


14. **Conclusion I:** 'All pots are *rings*' + 'All *rings* are paints' i.e. A + A ⇒ A, i.e. 'All pots are paints'

$\xrightarrow{\text{Conversion}}$ 'Some paints are pots', i.e. I-type.

Therefore, conclusion I follows.

**Conclusion II:** 'All bangles are rings' + 'All rings are paints', i.e. A + A ⇒ A, i.e. 'All bangles are paints' $\xrightarrow{\text{Implication}}$ 'Some bangles are paints', i.e. I-type.

Therefore, conclusion II follows.

**15. Conclusion I:** According to the given statements, 'All plastics are *wood*' + 'No *wood* is a metal', i.e. A + E ⇒ E, i.e. 'No plastic is a metal'.

Therefore, conclusion I follows.

**Conclusion II:** 'No plastic is a *metal* + 'Some *metals* are gases', i.e. E + I ⇒ $O^+$, i.e. 'Some gases are not plastic'.

Therefore, conclusion II does not follow.

**16.** ∵ I-type statements cannot be combined.

Therefore, neither conclusion I nor II follows.

**17. Conclusion I**: 'All chairs *are pens*' + 'Some *pens* are rats', i.e. A + I ⇒ No conclusion'.

Therefore, conclusion I does not follow.

**Conclusion II:** 'Some pens are *knives*' + 'All *knives* are rats', i.e. I + A ⇒ I i.e. 'Some pens are rats'

$\xrightarrow{\text{Conversion}}$ 'Some rats are pens', i.e. I-type.

Therefore, conclusion II follows.

**18. Conclusion I:** 'All umbrellas are rains' + 'Some rains are storms', i.e. A + I ⇒ No conclusion.

Therefore, conclusion I also does not follow.

**Conclusion II:** According to the given statement, 'Some rains are *clouds*' + 'All *clouds* are storms i.e. I + A ⇒ I, i.e. 'Some rains are storms' $\xrightarrow{\text{Conversion}}$ 'Some storms are rains'. Therefore, conclusion II does not follow.

**19.**

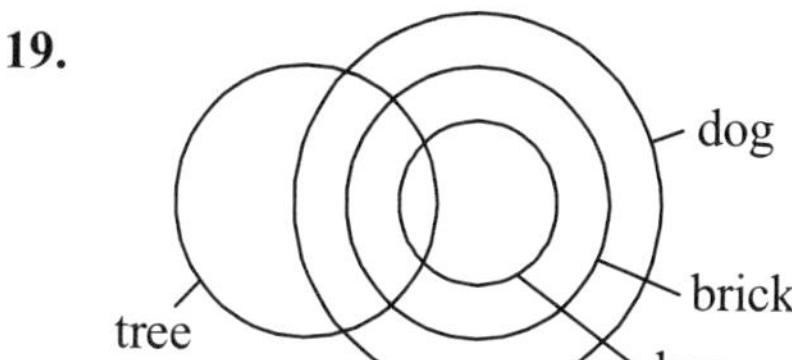


**20. Conclusion I:** According to the given statements, 'All asteroids are dust', i.e.

A $\xrightarrow{\text{Conversion}}$ 'Some dusts are asteroids', i.e. I-type.

So, 'All moons are dust' + 'Some dusts are asteroids i.e. A + I ⇒ No conclusion.

Therefore, conclusion I does not follow.

**Conclusion II:**

'All stars *are moons*' + 'All *moons* are dust'

i.e. A + A ⇒ A i.e. 'All stars are dust'.

Therefore, conclusion II follows.

**21. Conclusion I:** 'All tables are *rooms*' + 'All *rooms* are buses' i.e. A + A ⇒ A i.e. 'All tables are buses' $\xrightarrow{\text{Conversion}}$ 'Some buses are tables'. Therefore, conclusion I follows.

**Conclusion II:** 'All tables are *windows*' + 'All *windows* are rooms' i.e. A + A ⇒ A i.e. 'All tables are rooms' $\xrightarrow{\text{Conversion}}$ 'Some rooms are tables' i.e. I-type.

Therefore, conclusion II follows.

**22.**

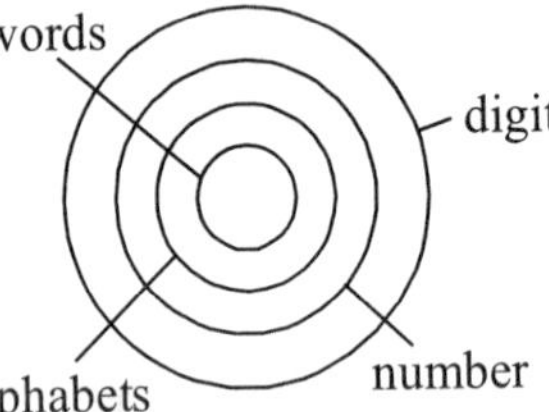


Therefore, both conclusions follow.

**23. Conclusions I & II :** 'All goats are *flowers*' + 'No *flower* is branches' i.e. A + E ⇒ E i.e. 'No goat is branch'.

Now, 'No goat is *branch*' + 'Some *branches* are roots' i.e. E + I ⇒ $O^+$ i.e. 'Some roots are not goats'.

So, Conclusions I and II do not follow. But they form a complementary I-E type pair.

Therefore, either conclusion I or II follows.

**24.** According to the given statements, 'Some leaves are roots' + 'Some roots are stems' i.e. I + I ⇒ No conclusion.

Therefore, neither conclusion I nor conclusion II follows.

**25. Conclusion I :** 'Some tents are *rivers*' + 'All *rivers* are ponds' i.e. I + A ⇒ I i.e. 'Some tents are ponds

$\xrightarrow{\text{Conversion}}$ 'Some ponds are tents' i.e. I-type.

Therefore, conclusion I follows.

**Conclusion II:** 'Some desks are *tents*' + 'Some *tents* are ponds' i.e. I + I ⇒ No conclusion.

Therefore, conclusion II does not follow.

**26.** Conclusion I is the conversion of first statement, hence I follows. But II does not follow because A + A = A i.e. All leaders are good orators but not vice versa.

**31.** Statement (1) + Statement (2) gives the conclusion "All rats are cars" [∵ A + A = A] ⇒ "Some cars are rats". Hence neither conclusion II nor conclusion III follows. Conclusion I does not follow from statement I since conversion of statement (1) will give thc conclusion "Some bells are rats".

**32.** Conversion of statement (1) + Statement (2) gives conclusion III [∵ I + A = I]. Hence, III follows but conclusions I and II do not follow.

**33.** Statement (1) + Statement (2) gives the conclusion "Some goats are not rooms" [∵ E + A = O*]. Thus, conclusions I and II do not follow. Conclusion III follows from statement (2).

**34.** Statement (1) + Statement (2) gives no conclusion [∵ I + I = no conclusion]. Therefore, conclusion I does not follow. Again conversion of statement (2) gives, the conclusion "Some rods are lamps". Hence, conclusions II arid III do not follow.

**35.** Statement (1) + Statement (2) gives no conclusion. [∵ A + I = No conclusion]. Hence, conclusion I and conclusion III do not follow independently. But, conclusion I and conclusion III make a complementary pair (IE type). Hence, either I or III follows. Conclusion II does not follow because "All tables are boxes" gives only the following conclusions:

1. Some tables are boxes.
2. Some boxes are tables.

**36.** Conversion of Statement (1) gives the conclusion "Some lions are men". Hence, conclusion II follows [say statement (3)]. Now, Statement (2) + Statement (3) gives no conclusion [∵ A + I = No conclusion]. Therefore, conclusion I does not follow. Conclusion III does not follow because an A-type statement gives I-type conclusions.

**37.** Statement (1) + Statement (2) gives no conclusion [∵ I + 1 = No conclusion]. Hence, conclusion II does not follow. Conclusion I follows from conversion of statement (1). On a similar basis, conclusion III also follows.

**38.** Conclusion II follows from conversion of statement (1). Now, statement (2) + conversion of statement (1) gives no conclusion [∵ A + I = no conclusion].

Hence, conclusions I and III do not follow. But conclusion I and conclusion III make an IE-type complementary pain. Hence, either conclusion I or conclusion III follows.

**39.** Conclusion III follows because Statement (1) + Statement (2) gives the conclusion "All birds are trees" [∵ A + A = A]. "All birds are trees" implies "Some trees are birds". Hence, conclusion I follows. Conclusion II follows from statement (1).

**40.** Conversion of statement (1) gives conclusion II. Hence, conclusion II follows. Again statement (1) + statement (2) gives conclusion III [∵ A + E = E]. Hence, conclusion III follows. Conclusion I follows from conversion of conclusion III. Hence, All follow.

**45.** All spoons are bowls → conversion → Some bowls are spoons. Hence, II follows. No other conclusion follows.

**51.** II follows as an implication of 2nd statement. 3rd statement + conversion of 1st Statement = I + I = No conclusion. Hence III does not follow. Nor can I be established.

**52.** Some chairs are windows + Some windows are doors (conversion of 1st statement)gives no conclusions [I + I]. Hence I does not follow. Some windows are chairs + Alt chairs are tables = Some windows are tables [I + A = I] → conversion → Some tables are windows. Hence II follows. III is not possible to conclude from the above given statements.

**53.** No flower is a plant + All plants are stones = Some stones are not flowers [E + A = O*]. Hence, I does not follow, 2nd statement + 1st statement gives no conclusion. Hence, II and III do not follow. But II and III make a complementary pair [I - E pair].

**54.** 1st statement + 2nd statement gives: No fish is a dog → conversion → No dog is a fish. Hence II follows. On conversion, the 1st statement gives conclusion I. Some cats are dogs + No dog is a bone [conversion of 2nd statement] gives: Some cats are not bones

[I + E = O]. Hence III does not follow.

**55.** All blocks are glasses + All glasses are frames = All blocks are frames [A + A = A]. On conversion, we get conclusion III.

**56.** Conversion of statement (3) gives conclusion I. Similarly, conversion of statement (1) gives conclusion II. Statement (1) + Statement (2) gives no conclusion [∵ I + I = No conclusion]. Hence conclusion III does not follow. Similarly, statement (2) + statement (3) gives no conclusion [∵ I + I = No conclusion]. Therefore, conclusion IV does not follow.

**57.** Statement (1) + Statement (2) gives conclusion “All benches are flowers” [∵ A + A = A] — on conversion → “Some flowers are benches”. Hence, conclusion IV follows. Again, “All benches are flowers” + “All flowers are fruits” gives conclusion “All benches are fruits”. Hence, I does not follow. Statement (2) + Statement (3) gives conclusion II [∵ A + A = A]. Conclusion III follows from Statement (3) [on conversion].

**58.** Statement (1) + Statement (2) gives no conclusion [∵ I + I = no conclusion]. Therefore, conclusions II and III do not follow. But these two conclusions make complementary pair of IE-type. Therefore, either conclusion II or conclusion III follows. Since Statement (1) + Statement (2) gives no conclusion therefore “train” and “tiger” can’t be related. Hence, conclusion I does not follow. “All tigers are waters” → “on conversion → “Some waters are tigers”. Hence, conclusion IV does riot follow.

**59.** Statement (1) + Statement (2) gives conclusion “Some buses are mountains” [∵ I + A = I] → on conversion → “Some mountains are buses”. Hence, conclusion I follows. Again, Some buses are mountains + Some mountains are roads gives no conclusion [∵ I + I = no conclusion]. Hence, conclusion II does not follow. Again, Statement (2) + “Some mountains are roads” gives no conclusion [∵ A + I = no conclusion]. Hence, conclusion III does not follow. Conclusion IV follows from conversion of Statement (3).

**60.** Only II and IV follow. Statement (1) + Statement (2) gives no conclusion [∵ A + I = no conclusion]. Therefore, conclusion I does not fellow. Again, Statement (2) + Statement (3) gives the conclusion “Some jungles are elephants” [∵ I + A = I] → on conversion → “Some elephants are jungles”. Hence, conclusion II follows. Conclusion III does not follow because Statement (1) + Statement (2) gives no conclusion. Again, All rabbits are elephants gives conclusion IV [on conversion].

**61.** Statement (1) + Statement (2) gives the conclusion “No books are houses” [∵ A + E = E}. Hence, conclusion I follows but conclusion IV does not follow. Again, “No Books are houses” + Statement (3) gives the conclusion “Some doors are not books” [E + A = O*]. Hence, conclusion II does not follow.

Again, Statement (2) + Statement (3) gives the conclusion “Some doors are not pens” [∵ E + A = O*]. Hence, Conclusion III does not follow.

**62.** Statement (1) + Statement (2) gives the conclusion “Some dogs are trees” [∵ I + A = I], Now conversion of “Some dogs are trees” gives conclusion I. Hence, I follows. But conclusions II and IV do not follow. Conversion of statement (1) gives the conclusion “Some rats are dogs”. Hence, conclusion III does not follow.

**63.** Statement (1) + Statement (2) gives the conclusion "Some boys are clouds [$\because$ I + A = I] $\rightarrow$ on conversion $\rightarrow$ "Some clouds are boys". Hence, conclusion I follows. Now, "Some boys are clouds" + Statement (3) gives no conclusion [$\because$ I + I = no conclusion]. Hence, conclusion II does not follow. Statement (2) + statement (3) gives no conclusion [$\because$ A + I = no conclusion]. Hence, conclusion III does not follow. But conclusion IV follows from statement (1).

**64.** Statement (1) + conversion of statement (2) ("Some flowers are houses") gives no conclusion [$\because$ A + I = no conclusion]. Hence, conclusion I does not follow. Statement (3) + Statement (2) gives no conclusion ($\because$ A + I = no conclusion). Hence, conclusions II and IV do not follow. But these two conclusions make a complementary pair (IE-type). Hence, either II or IV follows. Conclusion III follows from conversion of statement (1).

**65.** Only I, II and III follow. Statement (1) +, Statement (2) gives conclusion I [$\because$ A + E = E]. Hence, conclusion I follows but conclusion IV does not follow. Conclusion II follows from conversion of statement (3). Similarly, conclusion III follows from conversion of statement (1).

18

# Clocks and Calendars

## CALENDER

A calendar is a system of organising days for social, administrative, religious or commercial purposes.

A calendar is used to measure the time. This is done by giving names to periods of time, like Days, Weeks, Dates, Months and Years.

1. **Day:** The smallest unit of a calendar is a day.

   ***Example:*** Sunday, Monday, Tuesday, Wednesday, Thursday, Friday, Saturday.

2. **Odd days:** The remainder obtained by dividing the total no. of days by 7 is called the odd days.

   ***Example:*** 124 days ÷ 7 = 5 odd days.

**Counting of day in respect of an odd day:**

| Day | Sun | Mon | Tues | Wed | Thu | Fri | Sat |
|---|---|---|---|---|---|---|---|
| **Odd day** | 0 | 1 | 2 | 3 | 4 | 5 | 6 |

3. **Week:** A week is the grouping of days or a division of a larger grouping such as a lunar month, year, etc. 1 week = 7 days.

   **Week day:** Any day of the week except Sunday.

4. **Date:** The name given to each day is called as a date.

   ***Example:*** 28.08.1983.

5. **Month:** The month is a unit of time used with calendars.

   12 months = 1 year.

   ***Example:*** January, February, March, April, May, June, July, August, September, October, November and December.

| Months | Days |
|---|---|
| January, March, May, July, August, October and December | 31 days |
| April, June, September and November. | 30 days |
| February | 28 or 29 days |

6. **Year:** A year is the amount of time it takes the Earth to make one revolution around the sun.

   **Two types of year:**

   (i) An ordinary year : 365 days

   (ii) A leap year : 366 days

## Points to Remember

1. An ordinary year = 365 days

   (365 days = 52 weeks + 1 day)
2. An ordinary year = 1 odd day
3. In an ordinary year: The first day of a year = last day of the year.

   *Example:* 1st January = Monday and 31st December = Monday.
4. Leap year = 366 days.

   (366 days = 52 weeks + 2 days)
5. Leap year = 2 odd days. [∵ 366 ÷ 7 = 2 (remainder)]
6. In a leap year, the first day and the last day of the leap year are unequal. Last day of the leap year = First day of the leap year + 1 day.

## Important Concepts

(*i*) **Century leap year:** Century leap years always starts *on a Saturday*. Also, February, 29 of such years is always a *Tuesday*.

(*ii*) **Century leap year:** 400, 800,1200,1600, 2000,

(*iii*) **Century ordinary year:** 300, 500, 600, 700, 900,1000,

(*iv*) **Century leap years contain no odd day**

*Example:* 400,800,1200,1600,2000 years each contain no odd day.

(*v*) **Same calendar:** The sum of odd days between the years/months should be zero.

*Example:* 2009 will have the same calendar as that of 2003.

∴ Total no. of odd days between 2003 and 2009 = 7 = 7/7 = 0 odd days.

**(*vi*) The first and the last day of a century year:**

∵ Number of odd days in 100 years = 5.

So, 31st December 100 A. D = Friday

[∵ Monday = 1, Tuesday =. 2, Wednesday = 3, Thursday = 4, Friday = 5, Saturday = 6, Sunday = 7, *i.e.* 0 odd days.]

Therefore, 1st January 100 A.D = Friday

Number of odd days in 200 years = 3.

So, 31st December 200 A.D = Wednesday

Therefore, 1st January 200 A.D = Wednesday.

Number of odd days in 300 years = 1.

So, 31st December 300 A. D = Monday.

## CLOCK

**Clock:** A clock is an instrument used to display and maintain time.

**Minute:** The minute is a unit of time equal to $\frac{1}{60}$th of an hour or 60 seconds.

$$1 \text{ minute} = 60 \text{ seconds.}$$

**Hour:** An hour is a unit of measurement of time of the duration of 60 minutes or 3600 seconds.

$$1 \text{ hour} = 60 \text{ minutes}$$

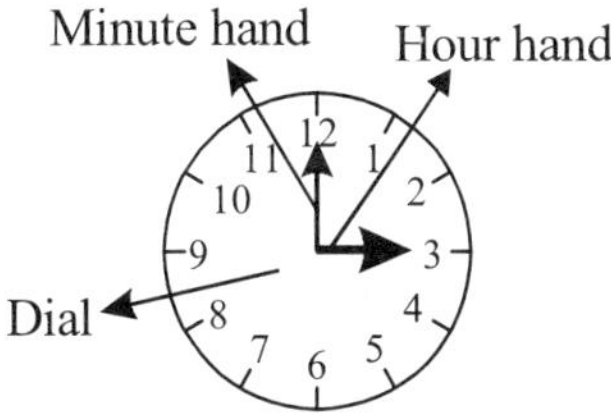


**Fig.** *Clock*

### Important Points

- The face (or dial) of a clock is divided along its circumference into 60 equal spaces called **minutes** spaces. The clock has two hands. The larger one is called **minute hand** which gives minutes and smaller one is called **hour hand** which gives hour.
- The distance between two consecutive numbers = 5 minutes.

- The minute hand moves around the whole circumference of the clock once in one hour.
- The hour hand moves around the whole circumference of the clock once in 12 hours.

  So, the minute hand is 12 times faster than the hour hand.
- The minute hand passes over the 60 minutes spaces while the hour hand goes over the 5 minute spaces.

  So, in 60 minutes, the minute hand gains 55 minutes on the hour hand or $\frac{55}{60}$ minute spaces in 1 minute.
- **Minute Hand:** 1 minute space $= \frac{360°}{60} = 6°$.

  ($\because$ 360° of the circle is divided into 60 minutes)

  So, the minute hand moves 6° in 1 minute or each minute.
- **Hour Hand:** The hour hand moves $\frac{360°}{(12 \times 60)}$

$$= \frac{360°}{720°} = \left(\frac{1}{2}\right)^{\circ} = 0.5° \text{ in 1 minute.}$$

So, the hour hand moves through $\left(\frac{1}{2}\right)^{\circ}$ in each minute or 1 minute.

Angle between hands, $x° = |(30\text{ H} + 0.5\text{ M}) - 6\text{ M}|$

where H and M represent values of hour hand and minute hand.

## Important Concepts

(*i*) The hands of a clock are at right angle, *i.e.* 90° twice in every hour. But two positions of the hands of clock, *i.e.* at 3 o'clock and 9 o'clock are common.

So, in a period of 12 hours, they are at right angles 22 times.

So, in a period of 24 hours or in a day, they are at right angles 44 times.

(*ii*) The hands of a clock point towards each other 11 times in every 12 hour.

[$\therefore$ Between 5 and 7, they point towards each other once at 6 o'clock]

So, in a period of 24 hours or in a day, they are point toward each other 22 times.

(*iii*) When the two hands coincide with each other, then the angle between them is 0°.

In a period of 12 hours, there are 11 coincidences of the two hands.

(*iv*) When the two hands of the clock are perpendicular to each other, then the angle between them is 90°.

In a period of 12 hours, there are 22 coincidences of the two hands.

(*v*) When the two hands are on the same straight line but facing opposite directions, then the angle between them is 180°.

In a period of 12 hours, there are 11 coincidences of the two hands.

(*vi*) The angle between the hands of a clock is always refer as acute/obtuse angle (upto 180°) and not as reflex angle (*i.e.* > 180°).

(*vii*) For every hour the gap is $\frac{60}{13}$.

(*viii*) If two watches move at different speeds, then they show the same time when the gap is 12 hrs or 720 minutes.

## TIME

**A.M.** (L. Ante Meridian): Before Noon

**P.M.** (L. Post Meridian) : After Noon

[**Note:** *Each day begin at midnight (12.00 A.M.)*]

### Important Concepts Regarding Days

(*i*) Yesterday = Today - 1 day.

(*ii*) Tomorrow = Today + 1 day

(*iii*) Day after yesterday = Today

(*iv*) Day before yesterday = Today – 2 days

(*v*) Day after tomorrow = Today + 2 days

(*vi*) Day before tomorrow = Today

(*vii*) Day after the day before yesterday = (Yesterday – 1 day) + 1 day
= Yesterday = Today – 1 day

(*viii*) Day before the day after tomorrow = (tomorrow + 1 day) – 1 day
= tomorrow = Today + 1 day

(*ix*) Day before the day after yesterday = (yesterday + 1 day) – 1 day
= Yesterday = Today – 1 day

(*x*) Pay after the day before tomorrow = (tomorrow – 1 day) + 1 day
= tomorrow = Today + 1 day.

### Important Tips

(*i*) When you get answer in decimals, then remember base is 60.

(*ii*) In the angle calculated does not exists in the given options, then subtract your answer from 360°.

(*iii*) If the angle between the hands is known, then we can easily calculate the time shown by the clock.

(*iv*) At any given point of time the hour hand and the minute hand of a clock make an angle between 0° and 180° with each other.

(*v*) If the time shown by the clock is known, then we can easily calculate the angle between the hands.

(*vi*) Whenever you need to imagine; then imagine the position of hand at exact hour because you know the gap between the hour hand and minute hand and minute hand is behind.

## SOLVED EXAMPLE

**1.** If 18th February, 2005 falls on Friday then what will be the day on 18th February, 2007?

(*a*) Sunday (*b*) Wednesday (*c*) Tuesday
(*d*) Monday (*e*) None of these

**Sol. (*a*)** From the question

18th February, 2005 = Friday.

So, 18th February, 2006 = Friday + 1 day = Saturday.

So, 18th February, 2007 = Saturday + 1 day = Sunday.

[∵ 2005, 2006 and 2007 are ordinary years]

**2.** Imagine that in a calendar year, there were 998 days and 12 days in a week, then no. of odd days in that year will be

(*a*) 5 (*b*) 6 (*c*) 3
(*d*) 2 (*e*) None of these

**Sol. (*d*)** From the question

Number of days in a calendar year = 998.

Number of days in a week of that calendar year = 12.

Therefore, number of odd days in that year = $\frac{998}{12}$

= 83 weeks + 2 odd days = 2 odd days.

**3.** If Thursday was the day after the day before yesterday five days ago, what is the least number of days ago when Sunday was three days before the day after tomorrow?

(*a*) Two (*b*) Three (*c*) Four
(*d*) Five (*e*) Six

**Sol. (*a*)** ∵ Day after the day before yesterday

= (yesterday – 1 day) + 1 day = Yesterday.

Then, five days ago, yesterday = Thursday. (Given)

So, five days ago = Thursday + 1 day = Friday

So, today = Friday + 5 days = Wednesday and tomorrow

= today + 1 day = Wednesday + 1 day = Thursday.

Day after tomorrow = today + 2 days = Wednesday + 2 days = Friday.

So, three days before the day after tomorrow

= (today + 2 days) – 3 days = today – 1 day = Yesterday.

So, it is on Monday that we say 'Yesterday was Sunday'. Therefore, the least number of days ago

= Wednesday – Monday = Two.

**4.** Which two months in a year have the same calendar?

(*a*) April, December (*b*) September, December (*c*) May, August
(*d*) August, December (*e*) None of these

**Sol. (*b*)** Let us discuss each options one by one:

For April, December:

| Months | April | May | June | July | August | September | October | November |
|---|---|---|---|---|---|---|---|---|
| No. of days | 30 | 31 | 30 | 31 | 31 | 30 | 31 | 30 |

Total no. of odd days = 244 = $\frac{244}{7}$ = 6 odd days.

For September, December:

| Months | September | October | November |
|---|---|---|---|
| No. of days | 30 | 31 | 30 |

Total no. of odd days = 91 = $\frac{91}{7}$ = 0 odd days.

For May, August:

| Months | May | June | July |
|---|---|---|---|
| No. of days | 31 | 30 | 31 |

Total no. of odd days = 92 = $\frac{92}{7}$ = 1 odd days.

For August, December :

| Months | August | September | October | November |
|---|---|---|---|---|
| No. of days | 31 | 30 | 31 | 30 |

Total no. of odd days = 122 = $\frac{122}{7}$ = 3 odd days.

Since, there are 0 odd days between September and December.

Therefore, September and December have the same calendar in a year.

**5.** How many degrees does the minute hand covers in the same time in which the hour hand covers 20°?

(*a*) 150° (*b*) 200° (*c*) 180°
(*d*) 240° (*e*) None of these

**Sol. (*d*)** As we know that the hour hand moves through $\frac{1^\circ}{2}$ in each minute, *i.e.*

$\frac{1^\circ}{2}$ = 1 minutes.

So, $20^\circ = \frac{1}{\frac{1^\circ}{2}} \times 20^\circ = 40$ minutes

So, angle covered by minute hand in 40 minute = 6° × 40 = 240°.

**6.** How many times do the hands of a clock coincide in a day?

(*a*) 11 (*b*) 12 (*c*) 24
(*d*) 22 (*e*) None of these

**Sol. (*d*)** As we know that the hands of a clock coincide once in every hour.

So, in a period of 12 hours, the hands of a clock coincide with each other = 11 times.

[∵ Between 11 o'clock and 1 o'clock they coincide only once]

So, the hands of a clock are coincide with each other in a day, *i.e.* in 24 hours = (11 × 2) times = 22 times.

**7.** At what time between 8 and 9 o'clock will the minute hand and the hour hand make and angle of 60° with each other?

**Sol.** From the question,

$\theta = 60^\circ$, h = 8

So, $60 = \frac{11}{2}m - 30 \times 8$

or, $m = \frac{120 + 480}{11} = 54\frac{6}{11}$ minutes past 8 o'clock

Also, $\theta = 30\ h - \frac{11}{2}m.$ $\left[\text{when } 30\ h > \frac{11}{2}m\right]$

So, $60 = 30 \times 8 - \frac{11}{2}m$

or, $m = \frac{480 - 120}{11} = \frac{360}{11} = 32\frac{8}{11}$ minutes past 8 o'clock.

So, the angle between the two hands is 60° when the clock shows = 8 hours $54\frac{6}{11}$ minutes and 8 hours $32\frac{8}{11}$ minutes.

## EXERCISE

**1.** In a month of 31 days, the third Wednesday falls on the 15th. What will be the last day of that month?
(*a*) Fourth Sunday (*b*) Fifth Wednesday (*c*) Fifth Thursday
(*d*) Fifth Friday (*e*) None of these

**2.** If 1st October is Sunday, then 1st November will be:
(*a*) Monday (*b*) Tuesday (*c*) Wednesday
(*d*) Thursday (*e*) None of these

**3.** If 30th January, 2003 was Thursday, what was the day on 2nd March, 2003?
(*a*) Tuesday (*b*) Thursday (*c*) Saturday
(*d*) Sunday (*e*) None of these

**4.** If the 25th of August in a year is Thursday, the number of Mondays in that month is:
(*a*) 3 (*b*) 4 (*c*) 5
(*d*) 6 (*e*) None of these

**5.** If every second Saturday and all Sundays are holidays in a 30 days month beginning on Saturday, then how many working days are there in that month?
(*a*) 20 (*b*) 21 (*c*) 22
(*d*) 23 (*e*) None of these

**6.** If February 1, 2008 is Wednesday, what day is March 3, 2008?
(*a*) Sunday (*b*) Saturday (*c*) Friday
(*d*) Monday (*e*) None of these

**7.** If it was Saturday on 17th December, 2009. What will be the day on 22nd December, 2012?
(*a*) Sunday (*b*) Tuesday (*c*) Friday
(*d*) Monday (*e*) None of these

**8.** Saturday was a holiday for Republic day. 14th of the next month is again a holiday for Shivratri. What day was it on the 14th?
(*a*) Monday (*b*) Tuesday (*c*) Thursday
(*d*) Friday (*e*) Saturday

**9.** If December 2, 2008 was Tuesday, the day on the 217th day after December 2, 2008 would be:
(*a*) Wednesday (*b*) Monday (*c*) Thursday
(*d*) Tuesday (*e*) None of these

**10.** If the day before yesterday was Thursday, when will Sunday be?
(*a*) Today (*b*) Two days after today
(*c*) Tomorrow (*d*) Day after tomorrow
(*e*) None of these

**11.** How many days will there be from 26th January, 2004 to 15th May, 2004 (both days included)?
(*a*) 110 (*b*) 111 (*c*) 112
(*d*) 113 (*e*) None of these

**12.** If the second day of a month is a Friday, which of the following would be the last day of the next month which has 31 days?
(*a*) Sunday (*b*) Monday (*c*) Tuesday
(*d*) Data inadequate (*e*) None of these

**13.** If the day after tomorrow is Saturday, what day was three days before yesterday?
(*a*) Sunday (*b*) Monday (*c*) Thursday
(*d*) Saturday (*e*) None of these

**14.** If 15th August, 2009 is on Saturday, then on which day of the week would the Independence day be celebrated in the year 2109?
(*a*) Sunday (*b*) Monday (*c*) Saturday
(*d*) Thursday (*e*) None of these

**15.** Laxmi Puja would be observed the day after tomorrow. Next week on the same day, the festival of Deepawali would be celebrated. If today is Sunday, then what Would be the day four days after Deepawali?
(*a*) Saturday (*b*) Sunday (*c*) Wednesday
(*d*) Tuesday (*e*) None of these

**16.** How many times do the hands of a clock point towards each other in a day?
(*a*) 11 (*b*) 48 (*c*) 24
(*d*) 22 (*e*) None of these

**17.** At what angle the hands of a clock are inclined at 30 minutes past 6?

(*a*) 45° (*b*) 15° (*c*) 30°
(*d*) 20° (*e*) None of these

**18.** How many times are the hands of a clock at right angles in a day?

(*a*) 22 (*b*) 44 (*c*) 11
(*d*) 24 (*e*) None of these

**19.** How much does the clock gain or lose per day if its hands coincide every 63 minutes?

(*a*) Loses $56\frac{8}{77}$ minutes (*b*) Gains $56\frac{8}{77}$ minutes

(*c*) Loses $56\frac{56}{77}$ minutes (*d*) Gains $75\frac{75}{341}$ minutes

(*e*) None of these

**20.** The angle between the two hands of a clock is 30°, when the hour hand is between 5 and 6, What time does the watch show?

(*a*) 5 hours $21\frac{9}{11}$ minutes (*b*) 5 hours $27\frac{3}{11}$ minutes

(*c*) 5 hours $32\frac{8}{11}$ (*d*) Both (*a*) and (*c*)

(*e*) None of these

**21.** The rotation undergone by the minute hand of a clock as it traverses a distance of 255 minutes is:

(*a*) 810 degrees (*b*) 1530 degrees (*c*) 450 degrees
(*d*) 90 degrees (*e*) None of these

**22.** A watch, which gains uniformly, is 3 minutes slow at 12 noon on Sunday and is 5 minutes 36 seconds fast at 4 pm on the next Sunday. At what time it was correct?

(*a*) 12 am on same day (*b*) 12 pm on Monday
(*c*) 12 am on Tuesday (*d*) 12 am on Wednesday
(*e*) None of these

**23.** A clock, which loses uniformly is 15 minutes fast at 9 am on 3rd of the December and is 25 minutes less than the correct time at 3 pm on 6th of the same month. At what time it was correct?

(*a*) 2.15 am on 3rd (*b*) 2.15pm on 4th (*c*) 2.15pm on 3rd
(*d*) 2.15 am on 4th (*e*) None of these

## ANSWERS

| 1 | 2 | 3 | 4 | 5 | 6 | 7 | 8 | 9 | 10 |
|---|---|---|---|---|---|---|---|---|---|
| (*d*) | (*c*) | (*d*) | (*c*) | (*d*) | (*b*) | (*d*) | (*c*) | (*d*) | (*c*) |
| **11** | **12** | **13** | **14** | **15** | **16** | **17** | **18** | **19** | **20** |
| (*b*) | (*d*) | (*a*) | (*d*) | (*b*) | (*d*) | (*b*) | (*b*) | (*b*) | (*d*) |
| **21** | **22** | **23** | | | | | | | |
| (*b*) | (*d*) | (*b*) | | | | | | | |

## SOME SELECTED EXPLANATORY ANSWERS

**1.** From the question, we have

15th of the month = 3rd Wednesday.

So, 15 + 7 = 22nd of the month = 4th Wednesday.

22 + 7 = 29th of the month = 5th Wednesday.

Therefore, last day of the month i.e. 31st

= 29th of the month + 2 days

= 5th Wednesday + 2 days = 5th Friday.

**2.** From the question, we have

1st October = Sunday

Then, 8th October = Sunday.

We know that every 7th day will be the same day countwise.

15th October = Sunday.

22nd October = Sunday.

29th October = Sunday.

So, 31st October = Sunday + 2 days = Tuesday

So, 1st November = Tuesday + 1 day = Wednesday.

**3.** From the question, we have

30th January, 2003 = Thursday.

So, 6th February, 2003 = Thursday.

13th February, 2003 = Thursday.

20th February, 2003 = Thursday.

27th February, 2003 = Thursday.

We know that every 7th day will be the same day countwise

So, 2nd March, 2003 = Thursday + 3 days = Sunday.

[∵ In an ordinary year, February = 28 days]

**Second Method:**

∵ 30th January, 2003 = Thursday.

So, number of odd days in January, 2003 = 1.

Number of odd days in February 2003 = 28 = 28/7 = 0 odd days.

Number of odd days in March, 2003 = 2 odd days.

So, total number of odd days = 1+ 0 + 2 = 3 odd days.

So, 2nd March, 2003 = Thursday + 3 = Sunday.

**4.** From the question, we have

25th August = Thursday.

So, 22nd August = Thursday – 3 days = Monday.

So, the number of Mondays in August = 5

i.e. on 1st, 8th, 15th, 22nd and 29th.

**5.** From the question, we have

1st of the month = Saturday

So, 8th of the month = Second Saturday = Holiday.

22nd of the month = Second Saturday = Holiday.

Also, 2nd of the month = Sunday = Holiday.

So, 9th of the month = Sunday = Holiday.

16th of the month = Sunday = Holiday.

23rd of the month = Sunday = Holiday.

30th of the month = Sunday = Holiday.

So, total number of Holidays = 2 (Second Saturdays) + 5 (Sundays) = 7.

Since, given month = 30 days.

So, number of working days = (30 - 7) days = 23 days

**6.** From the question, we have

1st February, 2008 = Wednesday,

So, 8th February, 2008 = Wednesday,

15th February, 2008 = Wednesday,

22nd February, 2008 = Wednesday,

29th February, 2008 = Wednesday.

[∵ 2008 is a leap year. So, February = 29 days]

Therefore, 3rd March, 2008 = Wednesday + 3 days = Saturday.

**7.** From the question, we have,

17th December, 2009 = Saturday

So, 17th December, 2012 = Saturday + 4 days = Wednesday.

[∵ 2010 and 2011 are ordinary years. So, number of odd days = 1 + 1 = 2]
[∵ 2012 is a leap year, So, number of odd days = 2]
[∵ 2009 – 2010 = 1 odd day, 2010 – 2011 = 1 odd day,
2011 – 2012 = 2 odd day]

So, 22nd December, 2012 = 17th December, 2012 + 5 days
= Wednesday + 5 days = Monday.

**8.** From the question, we have
26th January = Saturday.
So, 2nd February = Saturday [∵ Republic day = 26th January]
9th February = Saturday
16th February = Saturday.
Therefore, 14th February = 16th February – 2 days
= Saturday – days = Thursday.

**Second method:**
∵ 26th January = Saturday
So, number of odd days from 27th January to 14th February

$$= 19 = \frac{19}{7} = 5 \text{ odd days.}$$

Therefore, 14th February = Saturday + 5 days = Thursday.

**9.** Number of odd days in 217 $= \frac{217}{7} =$ Remainder 0 = 0

Therefore, required day = Tuesday.

**10.** According to the question,
Day before yesterday = Thursday
So, today = Thursday + 2 days = Saturday
Therefore, Tomorrow = Saturday + 1 day = Sunday.

**11.** The total no. of days from 26th January, 2004 to 15th May, 2004 including both days

$$= \left(\frac{6}{\text{Jan}} + \frac{29}{\text{Feb}} + \frac{31}{\text{Mar}} + \frac{30}{\text{Apr}} + \frac{15}{\text{May}}\right) \text{ days}$$

Since 2004 is a leap year. So, number of days in February = 29 days.
= 111 days.

**12.** Since, the number of days in the current month is not mentioned. Therefore, the answer cannot be determined.

**13.** From the question, we have
Day after tomorrow = Saturday
So, today = Saturday – 2 days = Thursday
Also, yesterday = Thursday – 1 day = Wednesday.
Therefore, three days before yesterday = Wednesday – 3 days = Sunday.

**14.** From the question, we have
15th August, 2009 = Saturday
∵ 15th August, 2109 – 15th August, 2009 = 100 years.
So, number of odd days = 5
[∵ We know that 100 years = 5 odd days]
So, 15th August, 2109 = 15th August, 2009 + 5 days
= Saturday + 5 days = Thursday.

**15.** From the question, we have
Today = Sunday
So, the day after tomorrow = Today + 2 days
= Sunday + 2 days = Tuesday = Laxmi Puja
So, next week = Tuesday = Deepawali
As we know that every 7th day will be the same day countwise
Therefore, the day four days after Deepawali = Tuesday + 5 days = Sunday.

**16.** As we know that the hands of a clock point towards each other in every 12 hour = 11 times.
Since, the hands of a clock point towards each other once at 6 o'clock between 5 and 7.
Therefore, the hands of a clock point towards each other in a day, i.e. in 24 hours = 11 × 2 times = 22 times.

**17.** From the formula $\theta = 30h - \frac{11}{2}m$. $\left[\because 30h > \frac{11}{2}m\right]$
According to the question
Here, $h = 6$, $m = 30$.
So, $\theta = 30 \times 6 - \frac{11}{2} \times 30 = 180 - 165 = 15$
Therefore, the hands of a clock are inclined at 30 minutes past 6 at 15°.

**18.** As we know that the hands of a clock are at right angle twice in every hour. So, in a period of 12 hours, the hands of a clock are at right angles = 22 times.

[∵ Two positions of the hands of a clock i.e. at 3 o'clock and 9 o'clock are same.]

Therefore, the hands of a clock are at right angles with each other in a day i.e. in 24 hours = (22 × 2) times = 44 times.

**19.** As we know that in a correct clock, the hands of a clock coincide every $65\frac{5}{11}$ minutes but in case of incorrect clocks, if the hands of a clock coincide is less than $65\frac{5}{11}$ minutes, then the clock gains time. So, Gain in 63 minutes

$$= \left(65\frac{5}{11} - 63\right) = \left(65 + \frac{5}{11} - 63\right) = \left(2 + \frac{5}{11}\right)$$

$$= \frac{27}{11} \text{ minutes} \qquad \left[\therefore\ 65\frac{5}{11} \text{ can be written as } 65 + \frac{5}{11}\right]$$

So, Gain in a day i.e. 24 hours

$$= 24 \times 60 \times \frac{27}{11} \times \frac{1}{63} = \frac{4320}{77} = 56\frac{8}{77} \text{ minutes.}$$

Therefore, the clock gains in a day, i.e. in 24 hours = $56\frac{8}{77}$ minutes.

**20.** From the formulae, $\theta = \frac{11}{2}m - 30h$ $\left[\text{when } \frac{11}{2}m > 30h\right]$

and from the question, we have

Here $\theta = 30°$, $h = 5$.

So, $30 = \frac{11}{2}m - 30 \times 5$ or, $m = \frac{30 \times 2 + 30 \times 5 \times 2}{11}$

or, $m = \frac{60 + 300}{11} = \frac{360}{11}$ or, $m = 30\frac{30}{11}$ minutes past 5 o'clock.

Also, $\theta = 30h - \frac{11}{2}m$ $\left[\text{when } 30h > \frac{11}{2}m\right]$

So, $30 = 30 \times 5 - \frac{11}{2}m$ or, $m = \frac{30 \times 5 \times 2 - 30 \times 2}{11}$

or, $m = \frac{300 - 60}{11} = \frac{240}{11}$ or, $m = 20\frac{20}{11}$ minutes past 5 o'clock.

Therefore, the angle between the two hands is 30°, when the clock shows

$= 5$ hours $30\frac{30}{11}$ minutes and 5 hours $20\frac{20}{11}$ minutes.

**21.** Minute hand of a clock traverses a distance = 255 minutes

Required rotation by the minute hand $= \frac{360}{60} \times 255 = 1530$ degrees

here, Required rotation by the minute hand $= \frac{360}{60} \times$ total distance traverses by the minute hand.

**22.** From the question, we have

Total time from Sunday noon (12 pm) to 4 pm the next Sunday = 7 days 4 hours = 172 hours.

Also, the watch gains in 172 hours = 3 minutes + 5 minutes 36 seconds

$$= 3 + 5\frac{36}{60} = \left(3 + 5\frac{3}{5}\right) \text{ minutes}$$

$$= \frac{43}{5} \text{ minutes.}$$

So, the watch gains 3 minutes in $= \left(\frac{3}{\frac{43}{5}}\right) \times 172$ hours

$$= \left(\frac{3 \times 5 \times 172}{43}\right) \text{ hours.}$$

$$= 60 \text{ hours} = 2 \text{ days } 12 \text{ hours.}$$

Therefore, the watch is correct after 2 days 12 hours from Sunday 12 noon = 12 am on Wednesday.

[∵ 2 days 12 hours + 12 hours = 2 days 24 hours = 3 days].

**23.** From the question, we have

Total time from 9 am on 3rd of the December to 3 pm on 6th of the December = 3 days 6 hours = 78 hours.

Also, the clock loses in 78 hours = (15 + 25) = 40 minutes.

So, the clock loses 15 minutes in $= \frac{15}{40} \times 78 = 29$ hours 15 minutes.

Therefore, the clock is correct after 29 hours 15 minutes from 9 am on 3rd December = 2.15 pm on 4th December.

✦✦✦✦

# 19

# Statement and Conclusions

*'Conclusion' means 'a fact that can truly be inferred from the contents of a given sentence or passage'. It requires a systematic approach to draw inference from the statement.*

A passage is given which is usually from a part of report or an economic essay or any other similar thought provoking subjects. The conclusions drawn may directly follow from the passage, can be inferred from the passage or can be inferred with the help of some keywords.

If an action is being undertaken and if such an action is always taken with a particular type of motive, then such a motive must exist, the use of word 'only' makes the conclusion weak. We are required to analyse the given statements, understand their direct/indirect implications and then decide which of the given conclusion follows logically.

**SOLVED EXAMPLE**

### Types of Questions

There are two types of questions based on statement and conclusion which are generally asked in various competitive examinations.

### Type 1 One Statement and Two Conclusions

In this type of questions, we have one statement and two conclusions. We have to analyse which of the conclusions support the statement.

**Directions (Qs. 1-5):** *In each of the following questions, a statement is given followed by two conclusions numbered I and II.*

**Select option**

(*a*) if only Conclusion I follows
(*b*) if only Conclusion II follows
(*c*) if either Conclusion I or II follows
(*d*) if neither Conclusion I nor II follows
(*e*) if both Conclusions I and II follow

**1. Statement:** These apples are too expensive to be bad.

**Conclusions:**

I. When apples are in short supply, the prices go up.

II. The higher the selling price, the superior is the quality of the commodity.

**Sol.** (*b*) Clearly, 'Too expensive to be bad' means that it cannot be bad because it is expensive. But Conclusion I- short supply favours rising of price is irrelevant to the statement.

**2. Statement:** Cases of bride burning for dowry are not uncommon.

**Conclusions:**

I. Inspite of anti-dowry laws, the ill practice continues.

II. The punishment inflicted on the party concerned is not sufficient.

**Sol.** (*a*) These cases are not uncommon as inspite of anti-dowry laws, the ill practice continues.

**3. Statement:** This world is neither good nor bad. Every one makes his world in his way.

**Conclusions:**

I. Some people like this world very much.

II. Some people hate this world very much.

**Sol.** (*e*) According to statement, both the conclusions are true as everyone makes his world

**4. Statement:** Only good men die on time.

**Conclusions:**

I. No good people live till being old.

II. Every person who live till being old is bad.

**Sol.** (*d*) Both conclusions have the same meaning. Means bad person live till they are old. But according to statement, only good men die in time viz. they live being old. Hence, neither I nor II follows.

## Type 2 One Statement and Three/Four Conclusions

In this type of questions, we deal with questions, which have one statement and three/four conclusions. We have to analyse which of the conclusions supports the statement.

**5. Statement:** All the students in my class are bright. Manish is not bright.

**Conclusions:**

I. Some students are not bright.

II. Manish must work hard.

III. Non-bright ones are not students.

VI. Manish is not a student of my class.

**Sol.** **(*d*)** As Manish is not bright. So, it is clear that he does not belong to my class. As all bright students belong to my class.

## EXERCISE

**Directions:** *In each question below is given a statement followed by the two conclusions numbered I and II. You have to assume everything in the statement to be true, then consider the two conclusions together and decide which of them logically follows beyond a reasonable doubt from the information given in the statement. Give answer.*

(*a*) if only conclusion I follows
(*b*) if only conclusion II follows
(*c*) if either I or II follows
(*d*) if neither I nor II follows, and
(*e*) if both I and II follow

1. **Statement:** Although we have rating agencies like Crisil, ICRA, there is demand to have a separate rating agency for IT companies to protect investors.

   **Conclusions:**

   I. Assessment of financial worth of IT Companies calls for separate set of skills, insight and competencies.

   II. Now the investors investing in IT companies will get protection of their investment.

2. **Statement:** Company "Y" will improve the manufacturing facilities for the production of shaving kits as a result of which capacity would increase and cost would be reduced. — A spokesperson of the Company "Y".

   **Conclusions:**

   I. The products of Company "Y" will better compete the market norms in the quality and cost factor.

   II. There will be demand of shaving kits of Company "Y".

3. **Statement:** Only those candidates with exceptional talent and strong motivation should apply. — An advertisement.

   **Conclusions:**

   I. Candidates not fulfilling these criteria will not be considered.

   II. It is possible to decide clearly who is talented and motivated.

4. **Statement:** Being from a business family, Chandan was apparently convinced by his parents and other family members to join the family trade.

   **Conclusions:**

   I. People should take up their family profession so that family prospers.

   II. It is necessary to keep family members happy by choosing family's business.

**5. Statement:** The maximum number of vacancies for the clerical cadre is 40, which will be filled through this recruitment round — An advertisement of Company 'A'.

**Conclusions:**

I. The Company 'A' may appoint less than 40 clerks in this round.
II. The Company 'A' may appoint 40 clerks in this round.

**6. Statement:** When I no longer enjoy playing cricket or if I feel I am blocking a youngster's place, then only I will quit. — Statement of the captain of country Z's cricket team.

**Conclusions:**

I. Right now the country 'Z' does not have any promising youngster.
II. One who enjoys the game of cricket, has the right to be captain of the country's cricket team.

**7. Statement:** An advertisement—Interest rate will be fixed on the basis of our bank's rate prevailing on the date of deposit and refixed every quarter thereafter.

**Conclusions:**

I. It is left to the depositors to guard their interest.
II. The bank's interest rates are subject to change on a day-to-day basis depending on market position.

**8. Statement:** People in metropolitan city 'X' have welcomed the recent Supreme Court order banning the registration of private vehicles that do not conform to Euro IV emission norms with immediate effect for metropolitan city 'Y' only.

**Conclusions:**

I. City 'X' has quite lower level of vehicular pollution than city 'Y'.
II. Public vehicles do not contribute to the vehicular pollution.

**9. Statement:** The government of State 'A' has sought a waiver of outstanding Central loans of ₹ 4,000 crores and a moratorium on repayment pending the waiver.

**Conclusions:**

I. Unlike other states, State 'A' has no desire to make repayment of its loans.
II. State 'A''s financial condition does not appear to be satisfactory.

**10. Statement:** The cabinet of State 'X' took certain steps to tackle the milk glut in the state as the cooperatives and Government dairies failed to use the available milk. — A news report

**Conclusions:**

I. The milk production of State 'X' is more than its need.

II. The Government and co-operative dairies in State 'X' are not equipped in terms of resources and technology to handle such excess milk.

**11. Statement:** After collision of two vessels in the sea all the crewmen and passengers are declared as missing. — A news report.

**Conclusions:**

I. No one from the two vessels has survived after the collision.

II. A few persons from the two vessels may have survived and are missing.

**12. Statement:** Good health is a luxury in country 'P' where rate of death is very high compared to other nations of that region.

**Conclusions:**

I. People in country 'P' cannot afford to have many luxuries of life.

II. Good health is a gift of nature.

**13. Statement:** The President of XYZ party indicated that 25 independent Members of Legislative Assembly (MLA) are seriously considering various options of joining some political party. But in any case, all of them collectively will join one party only.

**Conclusions:**

I. The 25 independent MLAs will join XYZ party in a short period of time.

II. The 25 independent MLAs will join some other political party in a short period of time.

**14. Statement:** 'We follow some of the best and most effective teaching learning practices used by leading institutes all over the world.' — A statement of a Professor of MN Institute.

**Conclusions:**

I. The MN Institute is one of the leading institutes of the world.

II. Whatever is being followed by world's leading institutes will definitely be good and useful.

**15. Statement:** My first and foremost task is to beautify this city. If city 'X' and 'Y' can do it why can't we do it? — Statement of Municipal Commissioner of city 'Z' after taking over charge.

**Conclusions:**

I. The people of city 'Z' are not aware about the present state of ugliness of their city.

II. The present Commissioner has worked in city 'X' and 'Y' and has good experience of beautifying cities.

**16. Statement:** On metro section of railways, the motormen are frequently required to do overtime during May and June though all vacancies are completely filled as per requirement of this section.

**Conclusions:**

I. Many motormen take leave of shorter or longer duration during this period.

II. Some motormen desire to earn overtime whenever possible.

**17. Statement:** "The Government will review the present policy of the diesel price in wake of further spurt in the international oil prices". — A spokesman of the Government.

**Conclusions:**

I. The Government will increase the price of the diesel after the imminent spurt in the international oil prices.

II. The Government will not increase the price of the diesel even after the imminent spurt in the international oil prices.

**18. Statement:** There has been growing demand for greater powers to meet the increased responsibilities of the councillors in the All-India Councillors Conference.

**Conclusions:**

I. People are mad after powers; they want both money and power.

II. The post of councillors is not merely ornamental.

**19. Statement:** The oceans are a storehouse of practically every mineral including uranium. But like most other minerals, it is found in extremely low concentration—about three gms per 1000 tonnes of water.

**Conclusions:**

I. The oceans are a cheap source of uranium.

II. The oceans harbour radiation hazards.

**20. Statement:** We do not need in India today, extraordinary specialists but those trained ordinary doctors who are dedicated to their profession.

**Conclusions:**

I. We should promote medical profession with dedicated ordinary doctors rather than promoting high by specialised medical education.

II. Extraordinary specialists are not dedicated to their profession.

## ANSWERS

| 1 | 2 | 3 | 4 | 5 | 6 | 7 | 8 | 9 | 10 |
|---|---|---|---|---|---|---|---|---|---|
| (*a*) | (*a*) | (*e*) | (*d*) | (*c*) | (*d*) | (*b*) | (*d*) | (*b*) | (*e*) |
| **11** | **12** | **13** | **14** | **15** | **16** | **17** | **18** | **19** | **20** |
| (*b*) | (*d*) | (*c*) | (*d*) | (*d*) | (*d*) | (*c*) | (*b*) | (*d*) | (*a*) |

## SOME SELECTED EXPLANATORY ANSWERS

**1.** It may be an assumption of the speaker. But certainly it is not a conclusion.

**2.** Improvement in the manufacturing facilities will automatically enhance the quality of its product and reduce the cost. These two things are important to compete in the market. Hence, I follows. II may be an assumption but it is not a conclusion.

**3.** I follows as the ad itself is a screening procedure. II also follows because only such a decision can help a candidate judge his fitness.

**4.** Both are suggestive steps which depend upon person to person. So, both are not conclusions.

**5.** The maximum no. of vacancies is 40. Mathematically, we may represent this as $\leq 40$, i.e. either less than 40 or 40. Hence, either I or II.

**6.** I is not conclusion. Youngsters are available; that is why he is talking about blocking of youngsters' place. II does not follow; 'enjoy the game' is related with his playing, not with his captaincy.

**7.** I does not follow because the statement is silent about the depositors. II follows from the phrase "bank's rate prevailing on the date of deposit". Which means the rates are subject to day-to-day changes.

**8.** I does not follow. It is probable that city 'X' welcomed the order with the expectation that the order would soon be extended in some manner to city 'Y' as well. II also does not follow. That public vehicles have been left out of the order is probably due to other reasons. For example, causing inconvenience to the commuters.

**9.** I does not follow because it makes a comparison with "other states". Now, in the statement, other states are nowhere in the picture. II follows because seeking such loan waivers indicates poor financial condition.

**10.** From the phrase 'milk glut' conclusion I can be determined. As it is given in the statement that these dairies have failed to use the available milk, hence II can be concluded.

**11.** Missing does not necessarily mean "dead", it is quite possible that the persons are alive.

**12.** I does not follows. People of country P might be able to afford some luxuries. II does not follow. Man may strive towards good health.

**13.** As the independent members will join one party only they may join either XYZ party or any other existing party. Hence, I and II together are exahustive.

**14.** II may be an assumption which the professor is assuming before passing his statement. Hence, II does not follow. I may or may not be possible. Hence, I does not follow.

**15.** The public awareness about city Z can't be extracted from the given statement. Hence, I does not follow. II. also does not follow because the information given in the statement may be obtained even without having work experience.

**16.** I does not follow. It might be possible that the railways work is seasonal with more load in summer months. Because of the term *required to do*, nothing can be concluded about their desire. Hence, II does not follow.

**18.** Nothing can be concluded about "money and power" from the given statement. Hence, I does not follow. II follows from the statement. If councillors are not given powers, they can't fulfil their responsibilities and the post of councillors will become useless.

20

# Statement and Assumptions

Assumption is the hidden part of an argument which a person assumes before stating some fact or statement.

In many examinations, we come across questions where candidate is asked to identify an assumption. An assumption is 'something supposed or taken for granted.' In this type of questions, a statement is followed by two or more assumptions. The candidate is required to assess the given statement and decide, which of the given assumptions is implicit in the statement.

There are mainly two types of questions which are generally asked in various competitive examinations.

## SOLVED EXAMPLE

### Type 1. One Statement and Two Assumptions

In this type of questions, a statement is given, followed by two assumptions. You are required to assess the given statement and then decide which of the given assumptions is implicit in the statement.

**Directions (Qs. 1-3):** *One statement given each question mentioned below, followed by two assumptions numbered I and II. You have to consider the statement and the following assumptions and decide, which of the assumptions is implicit in the statement.*

**Select option**

(*a*) if only Assumption I is implicit
(*b*) if only Assumption II is implicit
(*c*) if either I or II is implicit
(*d*) if neither I nor II is implicit
(*e*) if both I and II are implicit

**1. Statement:** Imprisonment for 27 years made Nelson Mandela the President.

**Assumptions:**

I. Only who will be imprisoned for 27 years will become the President.
II. To become the President, imprisonment is a qualification.

**Sol. (*d*)** Nelson Mandela elected as the President on the appeal of people as he struggled for the freedom of Africa and he was dedicated to the nation. Here, statement does not clarify any of the assumptions.

**2. Statement:** The cotton crop continues to be poor even after the introduction of improved variety of cotton seeds.

**Assumptions:**

I. The yield of cotton was expected to increase after introduction of improved variety of seeds.

II. The yield of cotton was inadequate before the introduction of new variety of seeds.

**Sol. (*a*)** Improved variety of cotton seeds has been used in anticipation of good crop. So, Assumption I is implicit. As, Assumption I is implicit Assumption II cannot be implicit as we cannot say whether the yeild was inadequate previously.

**3. Statement:** All existing inequalities can be reduced, if not completely eradicated, by action of governments or by revolutionary change of governments.

**Assumptions:**

I. Inequality is a man-made phenomenon.

II. No person would voluntarily part with what he possesses.

**Sol. (*a*)** It is clear that inequality can be reduced by man's actions. It must be a man-made phenomenon. But the eradication of inequality does not necessarily mean forcing anybody to part with what he possesses.

## Type 2. One Statement and More than Two Assumptions

This type of question also consists of similar type of questions as in type 1, with the difference that three assumptions are given and the candidate is required to choose that group which is implicit in context of the given statement.

**Direction (Q. 4):** *A statement is given, followed by several assumptions. Read the statement, carefully and decide which of the assumptions are implicit in the statement.*

**4. Statement:** "We do not want you to see our product in newspaper, visit our shop to get a full view."

**Assumptions:**

I. People generally decide to purchase any product after seeing the same in the advertisement.

II. Uncommon appeal may attract customers.

III. People may come to see the product.
(*a*) Both I and III are implicit (*b*) Both I and II are implicit
(*c*) Both II and III are implicit (*d*) All are implicit
(*e*) None is implicit

**Sol. (*c*)** It can be inferred from the statement that people also like to see a product before buying. So, I is not implicit. Also, the statement is just an attempt to arouse the people to come and see the shop. So, both II and III are implicit.

## EXERCISE

**Directions (Qs. 1-35):** *In each question below is given a statement followed by two assumptions numbered I and II. An assumption is something supposed or taken for granted. You have to consider the statement and the following assumptions and decide which of the assumptions is implicit in the statement.*

**Select option:**

(*a*) If only assumption I is implicit
(*b*) If only assumption II is implicit
(*c*) If either I or II is implicit
(*d*) If neither I nor II is implicit, and
(*e*) If both I and II are implicit

1. **Statement:** Helping the poor is the real service to humanity.

   **Assumptions:**
   I. Poor people are in need of help from others.
   II. If we do not help the poor, we will not be called human beings.

2. **Statement:** Please do not use lift while going down - an instruction on the top floor of a five-storeyed building.

   **Assumptions:**
   I. While going down the lift is unable to carry any load.
   II. Provision of lift is a matter of facility and not of right.

3. **Statement:** Take this 'oven' home and you can prepare very tasty dishes which you were unable to prepare earlier. — An advertisement of X brand oven.

   **Assumptions:**
   I. The user knows the procedure of recipe of tasty dishes but does not have the proper oven to cook.
   II. Only 'X' brand oven can cook very tasty dishes.

4. **Statement:** "Please note that the company will provide accommodation to only outside candidates if selected." — A condition in an advertisement.

   **Assumptions:**

   I. The local candidates would be having some or other arrangement for their stay.

   II. The company plans to select only local candidates.

5. **Statement:** 'Country A would explore all channels to diffuse current tensions with country B and bring peace on its borders.' — 'Statement of spokesperson of country A.

   **Assumptions:**

   I. Country A is desirous to diffuse current tension and restore peace with country B.

   II. It is desirable to use more than one channel when complex issues are to be settled amicably.

6. **Statement:** The higher echelons of any organisation are expected to be models of observational learning and should not be considered as merely sources of rewards and punishments.

   **Assumptions:**

   I. Employees are likely to be sensitive enough to learn by observing the behaviour of their bosses.

   II. Normally bosses are considered as sources of reward and punishment.

7. **Statement:** Only candidates having B. Tech., B.E., MBA and MCA with at least one year's exposure to software will be considered for admission to our course' — Admission criterion of a reputed software training institute.

   **Assumptions:**

   I. The candidates having requisite background are likely to complete the course successfully.

   II. The institute is choosy about admitting candidates to its courses.

8. **Statement:** Greater public participation results in good, civic governance— Statement of Municipal Commissioner of city 'A'.

   **Assumptions:**

   I. The municipal office is not competent to effect good civic administration.

   II. Good civic governance is a matter of collective will and effort of the people and administration.

9. **Statement:** The nutritional status of children in India is better compared to that in other developing countries.

**Assumptions:**

I. It is not possible to estimate nutritional requirement of children in other countries.

II. India can become a developed country.

**10. Statement:** India must earn a lot of foreign exchange to achieve her target of economic development.

**Assumptions:**

I. India desires to achieve the target of economic development.

II. It is possible for India to earn more foreign exchange.

**11. Statement:** The Government of India has decided to start a track II dialogue with its neighbour to reduce tension in the area.

**Assumptions:**

I. The neighbouring country may agree to participate in the track II dialogue.

II. The people involved in track II dialogue may be able to persuade their respective Governments.

**12. Statement:** The 'X' group of employees' association have opposed Voluntary Retirement Scheme offered to the employees of some organisations.

**Assumptions:**

I. Only those employees who are not efficient may opt for the scheme.

II. The response of the employees may be lukewarm towards the scheme and it may not benefit the organisation to the desired level.

**13. Statement:** In view of the statement on the ongoing strike of work by the employees, the government has agreed to work out an effective social security programme.

**Assumptions:**

I. The striking employees may not be satisfied with the announcement and continue the agitation.

II. The striking employees may withdraw their agitation with immediate effect and start working.

**14. Statement:** The government has set up a fact-finding mission to look into the possible reasons for the recent violence in the area.

**Assumptions:**

I. The mission may be able to come up with credible information about the incidents.

II. The people in the area may cooperate with the mission and come forward to give detailed information related to the incidents.

**15. Statement:** Every citizen must be committed to the social cause; if he is not, his citizenship should be cancelled.

**Assumptions:**

I. It is possible to find out whether a citizen is committed to the social cause or not.

II. Citizenship of any citizen can be cancelled.

**16. Statement:** The head of the organisation congratulated the entire staff in his speech for their sincere effort to bring down the deficit and urged them to give their best for attaining a more profitable position in future.

**Assumptions:**

I. The employees may get motivated and maintain and if possible enhance their present level of work.

II. The employees may now relax and slow down in their day-to-day work as there is no immediate threat of huge deficit.

**17. Statement:** Railway officials have started ten new trains and increased the frequency of fourteen running trains.

**Assumptions:**

I. The existing trains are not sufficient to provide accommodation to all passengers.

II. The new and additional trains would have sufficient passengers so that they will be economically viable.

**18. Statement:** If you are not able to collect the required amount by oral call you must publish an advertisement in a widely read newspaper.

**Assumptions:**

I. People rarely respond to oral call.

II. Generally people are reluctant to read an advertisement in a newspaper.

**19. Statement:** The head of the organisation has decided to reward those employees who will help reducing expenditure substantially by suggesting innovative techniques.

**Assumptions:**

I. The employees may be able to come out with innovative ideas.

II. The employees may be encouraged to apply their mind to earn the reward.

**20. Statement:** Government should deploy the Army at least this year for the rehabilitation of people affected by cyclone because cyclone visits suddenly.

**Assumptions:**

I. The Army should be deployed for all such sudden incidents.

II. Some precautionary plan is being made to prevent destruction caused by cyclone.

**21. Statement:** The Government has decided to overhaul the structure of school fee by linking the school fee with the incomes of parents.

**Assumptions:**

I. Parents will furnish correct information about their incomes to schools.

II. Parents will agree to pay the fee after the overhauling of the fee structure.

**22. Statement:** The Government should engage the Army for the rapid rehabilitation of people affected by the cyclone.

**Assumptions:**

I. Only the Army can rehabilitate the people affected by the cyclone quickly.

II. The Army can take up works other than war also.

**23. Statement:** The X-Airlines has decided to increase the passenger fare by 15 per cent with immediate effect.

**Assumptions:**

I. The demand for seats of the X-Airlines may remain unchanged even after the hike of fare.

II. Other airline companies may also hike the passenger fares.

**24. Statement:** The 'M' Cooperative Housing Society has put up a notice at its gate that salespersons are not allowed inside the society.

**Assumptions:**

I. All the salespersons will stay away from the 'M' Cooperative Housing Society.

II. The security guard posted at the gate may be able to stop the salespersons entering the society.

**25. Statement:** "It has become a necessity to computerise all the functions of our Institute to maintain the present position." — statement of the Director of XYZ Institute.

**Assumptions:**

I. Unless computerised, the Institute will fall behind in the race.

II. The functions of the Institute are too complex to be handled manually.

**26. Statement:** Provide mid-day meals to the children in primary schools to increase the number of students attending schools.

**Assumptions:**

I. Mid-day meals will attract the children to the schools.
II. Those children who are otherwise deprived of good food will attend the schools.

**27. Statement:** "Everyone desires to buy a personal computer." — statement of a college student.

**Assumptions:**
I. Personal computers are not a need but a luxury.
II. Use of personal computer improves quality of skill.

**28. Statement:** "The city's top-ranker for SSC examination this year will be definitely from our school." — Principal of a School 'X'.

**Assumptions:**
I. The teachers of the school have prepared their students thoroughly.
II. Most of intelligent students in the city are studying in School 'X'.

## ANSWERS

| 1 | 2 | 3 | 4 | 5 | 6 | 7 | 8 | 9 | 10 |
|---|---|---|---|---|---|---|---|---|---|
| (*a*) | (*d*) | (*a*) | (*a*) | (*e*) | (*e*) | (*e*) | (*b*) | (*d*) | (*e*) |
| **11** | **12** | **13** | **14** | **15** | **16** | **17** | **18** | **19** | **20** |
| (*e*) | (*d*) | (*b*) | (*e*) | (*e*) | (*a*) | (*e*) | (*d*) | (*e*) | (*d*) |
| **21** | **22** | **23** | **24** | **25** | **26** | **27** | **28** | | |
| (*e*) | (*b*) | (*a*) | (*e*) | (*e*) | (*e*) | (*d*) | (*a*) | | |

## SOME SELECTED EXPLANATORY ANSWERS

**1.** I is implicit: how else can helping the poor be a service? II is not implicit because not all human beings are in the "service" business.

**3.** The term 'which you were unable to prepare earlier' clearly means even though the user knows the procedure of some special preparation, he does not have a proper oven to cook. Hence, I is implicit. The statement assumes that 'X' can cook tasty dishes but does not rule out *all other* ovens from doing so.

**4.** Accommodation to only outside candidates clearly indicates that local candidates will be having their own arrangement for stay. Hence, I is implicit. It is nowhere mentioned that outside candidates will not be selected. Hence, II is not implicit.

**5.** I is implicit. If the desire were not there, why the statement? II is also implicit; hence, the emphasis on "explore all channels".

**6.** I is implicit; that is why the talk of "observational learning". II is also implicit; note the use of the word *merely.*

**7.** I is implicit. That is why the demand for qualification and experience. II is also implicit. Unless the institute were choosy, it would have welcomed one and all, without imposing any restrictions.

**8.** The statement does not point to the competence of anybody. It merely hints at the power of co-operation.

**9.** Assumption I contradicts the statement. Nothing can be assumed about the scale of becoming developed. Hence, II is not implicit.

**10.** I is implicit. Tools for an objective, are talked about only when the desire for such an objective exists. II is implicit because it makes no sense to talk of something without the existence of its possibility.

**11.** A decision to start any sort of dialogue with one's neighbour assumes that the neighbour will also participate in it. Hence, I is implicit. II is implicit because track II dialogue can be meaningful only when the respective Govts agree to abide by it.

**12.** The employees' association is generally concerned with the welfare of employees and not with the benefit of the organisation. Hence, II is not implicit. I, also, is not an assumption.

**13.** Assuming II only, the government has agreed to work, out an effective social security programme.

**14.** Here both the assumptions are valid. If it were not so, there would be no benefit of setting up such mission.

**15.** I is obviously implicit. II is also implicit; that is why cancellation of citizenship has been talked about.

**16.** To motivate the employees and hence for the enhancement of their work, the head of the organisation congratulated the entire staff in his speech and appreciated their effort.

**18.** The tone of the statement only implies that the speaker assumes that newspapers are more effective than oral call. The given assumption I is not implicit because of the word 'rarely'. II is also not implicit because it contradicts the valid assumption. Note that here the valid assumption is "people will read an advertisement in a newspaper".

**19.** Why a reward for a good suggestion? Obviously, authorities are assuming that the reward will enthuse employees to evolve innovative techniques. Hence, II is implicit. On the other side, seeking help from employees in order to evolve an innovative techniques implies that employees may have the required calibre. Hence, I is also implicit.

**20.** I is not implicit (note the word 'at least this year'). II can't be correlated. Hence, II is also not implicit.

**22.** Engaging the Army for the rehabilitation work by the government implies that the government assumes that the Army possesses the required ability to rehabilitate the affected people rapidly. Hence, II is implicit but I is not implicit because of the word 'only'.

**23.** The step taken by the airlines must have been aimed at to earn more revenue. The desired result can't be obtained without assuming I. Hence, I is implicit. II may or may not be an assumption.

**24.** When a notice is given by an organisation to a group of persons, the former assumes that the latter will follow it. Hence, I is implicit.

**25.** I is implicit from the need "to maintain the present position". But why the question of lag? Must be because computers are much more efficient than manual labourers. And this holds true only for complex tasks. Hence II is implicit.

**26.** The scheme will attract the children, particularly those who have no good food available at home. So both assumptions are implicit.

**28.** As a Principal, he trusts his teacher that they would have prepared the students thouroughly. So that they could appear in the list of toppers. Hence I is implicit. Only intelligence cannot be the basis of the Principal's statement. Hence II is not implicit.

# 21

# Statement and Arguments

*Argument is a fact that is being given by a person to support a statement in its favour or against it.*

In this types of questions, a statement concerned with a issue is given, followed by certain arguments in favour or against that statement. These issues may be political, social or economical. You have to find out how some premises help to reach a certain conclusion, some of these make strong arguments while some make weak arguments. Generally, both the arguments are contrary to each other and refer to the positive and negative results of the action as mentioned in the statement issue.

***Arguments can be of two types***

- **Strong Argument** touches the practical and real aspect of the situation as described in the statement.
- **Weak Argument** is very simple, superfluous, ambiguous and long drawn one. These are of minor importance and also may not be directly related to the question.

## Important Points

Following points should be taken into consideration while choosing a strong argument

- A strong argument should give the realistic diagonosis of the situation described in the statement.
- A strong argument should give deep analysis of the topic dealing with the statement.
- A strong argument should relate with the statement and be supported up by facts or established nations.
- A strong argument should not be more reiteration of the situation given in the statement.

## SOLVED EXAMPLE

**Directions (Qs. 1-3):** *Study the following instructions carefully and then answer the questions that follow.*

In making decisions about-important questions it is desirable that a candidate should be able to distinguish between 'strong' and 'weak' arguments so far as they relate to the questions. 'Weak arguments may not be directly related to the questions and may be of minor importance or may be related to the trivial aspect of the question. Each question given below is followed by two arguments numbered I and II. You have to decide which of the arguments is a 'strong' argument and which one is a 'weak' argument.

**Give answer**

(*a*) if only Argument I is strong
(*b*) if only Argument II is strong
(*c*) if either I or II is strong
(*d*) if neither I nor II is strong
(*e*) if both I and II are strong

**1. Statement:** Should small states be formed out of bigger states in India?

**Arguments:**

I. Yes, there will be greater administrative convenience.
II. No, it will jeopardise the national integration.

**Sol. (*e*)** Clearly, if we form smaller states out of bigger ones in India, there will be of greater administrative convenience. Hence, Argument I is strong. Also, it may hamper the national integration. So, Argument II is also strong. Hence, both arguments are strong.

**2. Statement:** Should there be only one entrance test for all the medical colleges— both government and private in India?

**Arguments:**

I. No, each college has unique requirements and decisions on admissions should be left to the concerned colleges.
II. Yes, this will bring in uniformity in the standard of students at the time of admission and will reduce multiplicity.

**Sol. (*b*)** Only Argument II is strong because a common entrance test will bring a uniformity in the standard of students, which is necessary.

**3. Statement:** Should computers be used in all possible sectors in India?

**Arguments:**

I. Yes, it will bring efficiency and accuracy in the work.
II. No, it will be an injustice to the monumental human resources which are at present underutilised.

**Sol. (*e*)** Use of computers does have the positive impact, as mentioned in Argument I but the negative impact as mentioned in Argument II is also worth considering. So, both arguments are strong.

## EXERCISE

**Directions:** *In making decisions about important questions, it is desirable to be able to distinguish between "Strong" arguments and "Weak" arguments in sofar as they relate to the question. "Strong" arguments are those which are both important and directly related to the question. "Weak" arguments are those which are of minor importance and also may not be directly related to the question or may be related to a trivial aspect of the question.*

**Instructions:** Each question below is followed by two arguments numbered I and II. You have to decide which of the arguments is a strong argument and which is a weak argument. Give answer:

(*a*) if only argument I is strong.
(*b*) if only argument II is strong.
(*c*) if either I or II is strong.
(*d*) if neither I nor II is strong and
(*e*) if both I and II are strong.

1. **Statement:** Should government-established higher level Institutes of Technology (IITs) be privatised?

   **Arguments:**

   I. Yes, privatisation will make these institutes financially healthy, competitive and quality-conscious.
   II. Yes, privatisation is the key of the new era - can we survive without it?

2. **Statement:** Should vacations of court judges be reduced?

   **Arguments:**

   I. Yes, it will speed up judicial process and many people are likely to get justice in reasonable time.
   II. Yes, it is a sign of British legacy, why should we carry it further?

3. **Statement:** Should the practice of transfers of clerical cadre employees from one city to another government office be stopped?

   **Arguments:**

   I. No, transfer of employees is a routine administrative matter and we must continue it.
   II. Yes, it involves a lot of governmental expenditure and inconvenience to many compared to the benefits it yields.

**4. Statement:** Should higher qualification be the only criteria for internal promotions in any organisation?

**Arguments:**

I. Yes, why not? In fact only higher qualification is more important than other factors.

II. No, quality of performance and other factors are more important than mere higher qualification in case of internal promotion.

**5. Statement:** Should Indian scientists working abroad be called back to India?

**Arguments:**

I. Yes, they must serve the motherland first and forget about discoveries, honours, facilities and all.

II. No, we have enough talent, let them stay where they want.

**6. Statement:** Should getting primary education be incorporated as a fundamental right in India?

**Arguments:**

I. No, what is the use? Have we fulfilled our duties regarding other fundamental rights?

II. Yes, this is what all the developed countries have done.

**7. Statement:** Should scheme of lotteries be completely stopped in India?

**Arguments:**

I. No, many state governments will have to stop some of their developmental activities which they fund from surplus generated by their lottery scheme.

II. No, many unemployed youths who sell lottery tickets to earn their livelihood will face hardship.

**8. Statement:** With the opening of the economy in India, should all workers unions be banned?

**Arguments:**

I. No, workers unions are not banned in the other economically advanced countries.

II. No, a level-headed worker's union can really do wonders both for workers and economy.

**9. Statement:** Should we grant permission to reputed private companies to construct civil airports for general use in India?

**Arguments:**

I. Yes, why not? It would be both economical and effective.

II. No, it may pose danger to the security and safety of India.

**10. Statement:** Should Government standardize rent for rented houses in big cities in India?

**Arguments:**

I. No, it is an interference in the relationship between landlord and tenant.
II. Yes, Government can do it, provided it has political will to do it.

**11. Statement:** Should old and poorly maintained petrol/diesel vehicles like autorickshaws and taxis which generate heavy pollution be banned for public services in big cities?

**Arguments:**

I. Yes, it will reduce pollution level in these cities which will enhance health of citizen.
II. No, what will the poor autorickshaw/taxi drivers do for their survival?

**12. Statement:** Should Government-dependent loss-making academic institutes like universities/colleges be closed down in India?

**Arguments:**

I. Yes, they are only creating the batches of unemployable young graduates.
II. Yes, none of the developed countries support universities by such massive financing.

**13. Statement:** Should India switch over to a capitalist economy from the present mixed one?

**Arguments:**

I. No, for this to happen there will be a need of constitutional amendments or our prestige will lower.
II. Yes, this is the only way adopted by developing countries.

**14. Statement:** Should admission in schools be controlled by the state government concerned?

**Arguments:**

I. Yes, it will reduce the importance of the members of the school management.
II. No, this will result in delays, compromise with the quality of schools, and give rise to corruption.

**15. Statement:** Should more smaller states be formed from the remaining bigger ones?

**Arguments:**

I. No, a lot of public money will be wasted in the whole process.
II. Yes, this will help in better governance and maximising production in both industrial and agricultural sectors.

**16. Statement:** Should the subsidy on petroleum products be further reduced?

**Arguments:**

I. Yes, the present subsidy is a drain on national resources; let the consumer share the burden.

II. No, this will have a cascading effect and the prices of all the commodities will sharply increase, creating higher rate of inflation.

**17. Statement:** Should the term of the elected members of parliament be reduced to two years in India?

**Arguments:**

I. Yes, even otherwise, the elections are generally held every alternate year in India.

II. No, every round of parliament election needs huge amount of money and it's a national waste.

**18. Statement:** Should India engage into a dialogue with neighbouring countries to stop cross-border terrorism?

**Arguments:**

I. Yes, this is the only way to reduce cross-border terrorism and stop loss of innocent lives.

II. No, neighbouring countries cannot be relied upon in such matters; they may still engage in subversive activities.

**19. Statement:** Should all the utility services be immediately brought under essential services to avoid frequent agitation and strikes by the employees?

**Arguments:**

I. No, otherwise how will the employees voice their grievances and demands?

II. Yes, the employees are becoming more and more greedy and they take the general public for ride by striking work.

**20. Statement:** Should India carry out fresh tests of nuclear weapons?

**Arguments:**

I. Yes, this will send a stern message to the whole world that India is serious about defending herself by any means from aggression,

II. No, the international community will isolate India and this will bring a setback to Indian economy.

**21. Statement:** Should there be more than one High Court in each state in India?

**Arguments:**

I. No, this will be a sheer wastage of taxpayers' money.

II. Yes, this will help reduce the backlog of cases pending for a very long time.

**22. Statement:** Should all the rivers of India be brought under Central Water Commission?

**Arguments:**

I. Yes, it will ensure equal distribution of water to the states.

II. No, because it will be contrary to the geographical conditions in the States.

**23. Statement:** Should all the profit-making public sector units be sold to private companies?

**Arguments:**

I. Yes, this will help the government to augment its resources for implementing the developmental programmes.

II. No, the private companies will not be able to run these units effectively.

**24. Statement:** Should the existing labour laws be changed in the favour of owners?

**Arguments:**

I. Yes, the existing labour laws give much more protection to employees than required and thus production is reduced.

II. No, because owners would exploit employees as before when there were no labour laws.

**25. Statement:** Should the prestigious people be met with special treatment by law if they have committed crime unknowingly?

**Arguments:**

I. Yes, because the prestigious people do not commit crime intentionally.

II. No, it is our policy that everybody is equal before the law.

**26. Statement:** Should India allow the foreign media companies to buy stakes in the print media in India?

**Arguments:**

I. Yes, this will improve the quality of reporting in Indian newspapers by way of expertise and technological upgradation.

II. No, they will divert people's mind from important national issues to trivial issues important to their interests.

**27. Statement:** Should India develop a national water grid by connecting all the rivers in the country?

**Arguments:**

I. No, this is just not possible as we do not have the technical know-how.

II. Yes, this will greatly help the entire country by effectively channelling the excess water to the areas having shortage.

**28. Statement:** Should all students passing out from the government-run colleges and desirous of settling abroad be asked to pay back the cost of their education to the government?

**Arguments:**

I. Yes, such students who study on the resources of the exchequer should be discouraged from leaving the country.

II. No, every citizen has the right to select their place of further study or work and therefore such a condition is unjustified.

**29. Statement:** Should India support all the international policies of United States of America?

**Arguments:**

I. No, many other powerful countries do not support the same.

II. Yes, this is the only way to gain access to USA developmental funds.

**30. Statement:** Should labour reforms be immediately introduced in India?

**Arguments:**

I. Yes, this will help increase the productivity in all the sectors in general and in the public sector in particular.

II. No, many other countries have not implemented this so far.

**31. Statement:** Should all the professional colleges in India be encouraged to run their own courses without affiliation to any university?

**Arguments:**

I. Yes, this is only way to create more opportunities for those who seek professional training.

II. No, this will dilute the quality of professional training as all such colleges may not be equipped to conduct such courses.

**32. Statement:** Should trade unions be banned completely?

**Arguments:**

I. No, this is the only way through which employees can put their demands before management.

II. Yes, employees get their illegal demands fulfilled through these unions.

**33. Statement:** Should the habit of late-coming in educational institutions be checked?

**Arguments:**

I. No, until it affects the work.

II. Yes, discipline must be maintained.

## ANSWERS

| 1 | 2 | 3 | 4 | 5 | 6 | 7 | 8 | 9 | 10 |
|---|---|---|---|---|---|---|---|---|---|
| (*a*) | (*a*) | (*b*) | (*b*) | (*d*) | (*d*) | (*e*) | (*d*) | (*b*) | (*d*) |
| **11** | **12** | **13** | **14** | **15** | **16** | **17** | **18** | **19** | **20** |
| (*a*) | (*d*) | (*d*) | (*b*) | (*e*) | (*e*) | (*b*) | (*b*) | (*d*) | (*b*) |
| **21** | **22** | **23** | **24** | **25** | **26** | **27** | **28** | **29** | **30** |
| (*a*) | (*d*) | (*a*) | (*e*) | (*b*) | (*a*) | (*b*) | (*e*) | (*d*) | (*a*) |
| **31** | **32** | **33** | | | | | | | |
| (*b*) | (*a*) | (*b*) | | | | | | | |

## SOME SELECTED EXPLANATORY ANSWERS

**1.** Argument I is advantageous. Argument II has lack of any theme.

**2.** I is a strong argument. If we have more working days, it is natural that more work can be done. Good qualities or system of even our enemy can be adopted. Hence, II is weak.

**3.** It is not necessary that any practice which has been continued for a long time be right. Hence I is a weak argument. Argument II is strong.

**4.** Neither the reason nor other factors are given in Argument I. Hence, it is weak. On the same grounds II is strong.

**5.** I is not strong. The individual's demands are as important as the motherland's. II is weak because of its complacent attitude.

**6.** I is distorting the argument. II is based on an example which may not apply to India.

**7.** Both are strong because from the economic point of view, we can't ignore either unemployment or revenue loss.

**8.** I is based on example. Hence, it does not follow. II is a vague argument.

**9.** II is strong because national security is a priority area. I is poor since government airports are also effective.

**10.** I is hardly an argument. It merely states the obvious. It says nothing about why the Govt. should not interfere. II deviates from the question. The questions is *why* the Govt. should do it, not *whether* it can do it.

**11.** I is strong because health can't be neglected. II is weak because it is a cry of desperation. Note that it is not strong enough to aver that survival is not possible.

**12.** Unemployment and loss are not related.

**13.** Whenever it has been required, we have amended our constitution. It is illogical and foolish to relate it to our prestige. Hence, I is a weak argument. Every developing country is the product of its own circumstances. Hence, it is not necessary that India should also go on the path of other developing countries.

**14.** The main purpose of decentralisation of power is to run the functions of all units properly. You can't concentrate on all units if you have so many departments to watch over. Hence, II is strong. I is weak because it sort of merely rephrases the statement.

**15.** Here both arguments are strong.

**16.** I is strong because it does not make sense to penalise the rest of the country for something I use. II is strong because if it leads to inflation, even the poor will get trapped.

**17.** Reducing the term is no alternative. Suppose the parliament gets dissolved every six months. Will you then say the term be reduced to six months? Clearly, I is bad logic. II is strong in a country where fiscal deficit is of paramount concern.

**18.** Argument I does not go into the reason while argument II does.

**19.** The reason to club any and all essential utilities under one head is to bring about effeciency in the delivery process.

**20.** Why a fresh test of nuclear weapons? Fresh tests of nuclear weapons will be termed as an exhibition of nuclear weapons. Having nuclear capacity is enough to show a strong defending capacity. In a nutshell, argument I carries a wrong notion. Argument II divulges the bad effects if India carries out fresh tests of nuclear weapons.

**21.** Why more than one High Court? A single efficient High Court is enough to do the job of more than one High Court. Hence, I is strong because it is true that there will be a wastage of money in that case. II is weak because increase in number of High Courts will not necessarily result in quick disposal of pending cases.

**23.** I is strong because it is beneficial for the country. II is weak because it is based on a wrong notion.

**24.** I is strong because we are not in a position to afford less production. II is strong because exploitation of employees is not desirable either.

**25.** Argument I advocates that prestigious people do not commit crime intentionally. Is it true? Answer is 'No'. Hence, I is a weak argument. Argument II is a strong argument.

**26.** I is strong because it says not only about the positive impact of foreign media on our reporting of newspaper but also how this change will come about. II is a weak argument because allowing foreign media companies to buy stakes does not implies that these companies will be given entirely free hand to operate print media in India. Besides, this argument assumes the reader to be stupid.

**27.** I is weak because it does not focuss on the core issue and supports it with a wrong assumption. Note that a need can be fulfilled with the help of other countries if India lacks the required technology. II is a strong argument because optimum and even use of water is desirable.

**28.** Both the arguments I and II are strong. Argument I is strong because optimum use of the resources of the exchequer is desirable. Discouraging such people will lessen the problem of brain-drain. Argument II is strong on the basis of the powers equipped by the Constitution to the citizens.

**29.** Argument I is not strong because India should take its stand according to its need. Argument II is not correct because of the word 'only'. Hence, argument II is not strong.

**30.** Argument I is strong. No doubt, labour reforms will encourage the labour to work more efficiently, which will be helpful in increasing the productivity. Argument II is not strong because it is not a right way of arguing. Basic needs of India may be different from those of other countries.

**31.** Argument 1 is not strong because of two reasons: (i) it is not the only way to create more opportunities for those who seek professional training; (ii) opportunity to get professional training is not enough, quality of the training is equally important. Argument II is strong because charters of degrading of the standard of training can't be ruled out.

**32.** I is the very rationale behind the establishment of trade unions. Hence, I is strong. Illegal demand cannot be fulfilled unless the management is fully convinced of the reasonability of their demands. Hence, II is weak.

**33.** I is not strong because instead of giving a reason, it adds a further clause. II is strong because discipline plays a major role in an educational institution.

✧✧✧✧

22

# Statement and Course of Action

*Course of action is the feasible step taken after an event has happened or is about to happen.*

This test is a framed to test candidate's decision making ability. A person is required to 'Decide' a course of action at every step of his life. In this type of questions, a situation is presented and some courses of action are suggested in the context of that situation. Correct course of action should either reduce the problem or improve the situation which is created by that problem. Course of action should be feasible and should relate with the practical aspect of life.

## Basic Point for a Correct Course of Action

*To solve these questions, the candidates are advised to keep in mind the following important points.*

- Correct course of action should either lessen the problem or improve the situation created by the problem.
- Simple problem must have simple course of action and not a complete are which may create more problems than to solve or reduce it.
- Course of action should be feasible and should relate with the practical aspect of life.
- If any course of action is followed with word 'only' it makes action weak.

## SOLVED EXAMPLE

**Directions (Qs. 1-2):** *Illustrations given below has a statement followed by two courses of action Numbered I and II. You have to assume everything in the statement to be true and on the basis of the information given in the statement, decide which of the suggested courses of action logically follows for pursuing.*

**Give answer**

(*a*) if only I follows

(*b*) if only II follows

(*c*) if either I or II follows

(*d*) if neither I nor II follows

(*e*) if both I and II follow

1. **Statement:** If the retired professors of some institutes are also invited to deliberate on restructuring of the organisation, their contribution may be beneficial to the institute.

   **Courses of Action:**

   I. Management may seek opinion of the employees before calling retired professors.

   II. Management should involve experienced people for the systematic restructuring of the organisation.

**Sol.** **(*b*)** We know it very clearly that retired professors have lots of experience and can give valuable suggestions. Hence, management should involve such experienced people. Seeking permission from the employees is not the right course of action.

2. **Statement:** Incessant rain for the past several days has posed the problem of overflowing and flood as the river bed is full of silt and mud.

   **Courses of Action:**

   I. The people should be made aware about the eminent danger over radio/ television.

   II. The silt and mud from the river bed should be cleared immediately after receding of the water level.

**Sol.** **(*e*)** Each of the courses will provide relief to the victims. Hence, both the given courses of action will favour the solution.

## EXERCISE

**Directions (Qs. 1-25):** *In each question below is given a statement followed by two courses of action numbered I and II. A course of action is a step or administrative decision to be taken for improvement, follow-up or further action in regard to the problem, policy, etc. on the basis of the information given in the statement. You have to assume everything in the statement to be true, then decide which of the two given suggested courses of action logically follows for pursuing.*

**Give answer**

(*a*) if only I follows; (*b*) if only II follows;
(*c*) if either I or II follows; (*d*) if neither I nor II follows; and
(*e*) if both I and II follow

1. **Statement:** The 'X' state government has chalked out a plan for the underdeveloped 'Y' district where 80% of the funds will be placed in the hands of a committee of local representatives.

**Courses of action:**

I. The 'X' state government should decide guidelines and norms for the functioning of the committee.

II. Other state governments may follow similar plan if directed by the Central government.

2. **Statement:** The district administration has agreed to provide necessary infrastructural facilities to the proposed NRI-funded Trust's project of supply of clean water to city 'Z'.

**Courses of action:**

I. The district administration should provide necessary land to the trust by completing due formalities.

II. The district administration should facilitate obtaining electricity and other permissions to the trust.

3. **Statements:** In response to the published tender notice, the company 'Z' has received 57 sealed tenders.

**Courses of action:**

I. The department concerned has to open the tenders and scrutinise them as per the procedure.

II. The purchase committee will have to meet and recommend to the management as the parties have been identified for allotting tenders.

4. **Statement:** The company 'X' has decided to give 10% increase in salary to its employees from next month.

**Courses of action:**

I. The accounts department will have to prepare new salary statement for all employees before due date.

II. Employees' association should ask for more rise in the salary considering the market condition.

5. **Statement:** According to the public health department of State 'X', the supply of contaminated water by the municipality is the main reason of the spread of the disease 'A' in the state.

**Courses of action:**

I. State government should replace the head of the water supply department immediately.

II. State government should provide free water filter to its residents.

6. **Statement:** The proposed strike by the transporters would paralyse day-to-day life of the people.

**Courses of action:**

I. City administrators should engage the transporters successfully in negotiations on their demands in order to pre-empt their strike.

II. City administrators should arrange for alternative public transportation system during the strike.

**7. Statement:** The government of state 'Y' has decided to remove hutments and buildings that have come up beside roads to broaden them in the city 'A'.

**Courses of action:**

I. The government of state 'Y' should rehabilitate the affected residents of hutments/buildings.

II. The government should compensate with reasonable amounts for the targeted houses.

**8. Statement:** The Kharif crops have been affected by the insects for three consecutive years in the district and the farmers harvested less than fifty per cent of produce during these years.

**Courses of action:**

I. The farmers should seek measure to control the attack of insects to protect their crops next year.

II. The Government should increase, the support price of Kharif crops considerably to protect the economic interests of farmers.

**9. Statement:** There was water-logging in the major part of the city due to heavy rain during past few days and the people residing in those areas were forced to shift to other areas.

**Courses of action:**

I. The Government should arrange food and shelter for the displaced people.

II. The fire brigade should be put on high alert to cope with the situation.

**10. Statement:** The cinema halls are incurring heavy loss these days as people prefer to watch movies in home on TV than to visit cinema halls.

**Courses of action:**

I. The cinema halls should be demolished and residential multistoryed buildings should be constructed there.

II. The cinema halls should be converted into shopping malls.

**11. Statement:** It is necessary to adopt suitable measures to prevent repetition of bad debts by learning from the past experiences of mounting non-performing assets of banks.

**Courses of action:**

I. Before granting loan to customers their eligibility for loan should be evaluated strictly.

II. To ensure the payment of instalments of loan, the work, for which loan was granted, should be supervised minutely on a regular basis.

**12. Statement:** Many private sector banks have reduced interest rate on housing loans in comparison to public sector banks.

**Courses of action:**

I. The case should be raised before the regulatory authority for investigation by the public sector banks as they cannot follow such reduction.

II. Public sector banks must adopt such policy to remain in competition.

**13. Statement:** The meteorological department has issued a notification forecasting less rainfall during next year's monsoon.

**Courses of action:**

I. The farmers should be advised to be ready for the eventuality.

II. The government should make arrangement to provide water to the affected areas.

**14. Statement:** There is an unprecedented increase in migration of villagers to urban areas as repeated crop failure has put them into precarious financial situation.

**Courses of action:**

I. The villagers should be provided with alternate source of income in their villages which will make them stay there.

II. The migrated villagers should be provided with jobs in the urban areas to help them survive.

**15. Statement:** Due to inadequate rainfall this monsoon there is a sharp decline in foodgrain production.

**Courses of action:**

I. The government should increase the procurement price of foodgrains to support farmers.

II. The government should subsidise further the prices of seeds and fertilizers for the next season.

**16. Statement:** While laying pipes for one of the utility companies a huge fire broke out due to damage done to the pipeline.

**Courses of action:**

I. All the licences of the utility company should immediately be suspended pending enquiry into the incidence.

II. People residing in the area should be advised to, stay indoors to avoid burn injuries.

**17. Statement:** There have been a large number of cases of Internet hacking in the recent months, creating panic among the Internet users.

**Courses of action:**

I. The government machinery should make an all-out effort to nab those who are responsible and put them behind bars.

II. The Internet users should be advised to stay away from using Internet till the culprits are caught.

**18. Statement:** There is an unprecedented increase in the number of successful students in this year's School Leaving Certificate Examination.

**Courses of action:**

I. The government should make arrangement to increase the number of seats of intermediate courses in existing colleges if feasible.

II. The government should take active steps to open new colleges to accommodate all these successful students.

**19. Statement:** There has been a significant drop in the water level of all the lakes supplying water to the city.

**Courses of action:**

I. The water supply authority should impose a partial cut in supply to tackle the situation.

II. The government should appeal to all the residents through mass media for minimal use of water.

**20. Statement:** The prices of foodgrains and vegetables have substantially increased due to a prolonged strike call given by the truck owners' association.

**Courses of action:**

I. The government should immediately make alternative arrangement to ensure adequate supply of foodgrains and vegetables in the market.

II. The government should take steps to cancel the licenses of all the vehicles belonging to the association.

**21. Statement:** A large number of people visiting India from country 'X' have been tested positive for carrying viruses of a killer disease.

**Courses of action:**

I. The government of India should immediately put a complete ban on people coming to India from country 'X' including those Indians who are settled in country 'X'.

II. The government of India should immediately set up detection centres at all its airports and seaports to identify and quarantine those who are tested positive.

**22. Statement:** It is reported that though Vitamin E present in fresh fruits and fresh vegetables is beneficial for human body, capsuled Vitamin E does not have the same effect on human body.

**Courses of action:**

I. The sale of capsuled Vitamin E should be banned.

II. People should be encouraged to take fresh fruits and fresh vegetables to meet the body requirement of Vitamin E.

**23. Statement:** India has been continuously experiencing military threats from its neighbouring countries.

**Courses of action:**

I. India should engage in an all-out war to stop the nagging threats.

II. India should get the neighbours into a serious dialogue to reduce the tension at its borders.

**24. Statement:** India has now been recognised by the Western world as a vast resource of knowledge and the latter is eager to use the same.

**Courses of action:**

I. India should exploit this opportunity to hasten its economic growth.

II. India should bargain effectively with the Western world and become a superpower in South Asia.

**25. Statement:** It is estimated that about twenty lakh people will visit the city during the ensuing festival.

**Courses of action:**

I. The civic authority should make adequate arrangements to tackle the situation.

II. All the hospitals in the city should be put on high alert in case of any eventuality.

## ANSWERS

| **1** | **2** | **3** | **4** | **5** | **6** | **7** | **8** | **9** | **10** |
|---|---|---|---|---|---|---|---|---|---|
| (*a*) | (*e*) | (*a*) | (*a*) | (*e*) | (*d*) | (*c*) | (*e*) | (*a*) | (*d*) |
| **11** | **12** | **13** | **14** | **15** | **16** | **17** | **18** | **19** | **20** |
| (*e*) | (*b*) | (*e*) | (*a*) | (*e*) | (*d*) | (*a*) | (*a*) | (*e*) | (*a*) |
| **21** | **22** | **23** | **24** | **25** | | | | | |
| (*b*) | (*b*) | (*b*) | (*e*) | (*a*) | | | | | |

## SOME SELECTED EXPLANATORY ANSWERS

**1.** Once it is decided to place funds in the hands of the committee of local representatives, it is necessary to decide guidelines and norms for the functioning of the committee. Hence I follows. II is not related to the statement.

**2.** If district administration has passed any project, it should provide all the required facilities.

**3.** I is the next suitable step, hence follows. The tender is related with which department, is not known. Hence II does not follow.

**4.** I is a reasonable course of action. Hence follows. Nothing about the market condition is known from the statement. Hence II does not follow.

**5.** II is an impractical solution. Hence does not follow. I does not address the problem. The action has to be issue-based, not person-based.

**6.** The first course should be to try their best that transporters don't go on strike. But it necessary that one is prepared with an alternative as well, in case the first course fails.

**7.** The affected residents can be compensated in either ways.

**8.** Both I and II follow. Course of action I will be a precautionary measure, while II will give the farmers a compensation.

**9.** I follows because it will lessen the miseries of affected people. II does not follow. What role can the fire brigade play in a problem caused by heavy rain?

**10.** I is not a proper way to tackle the problem. Because this action will not help reduce the problem. Hence, I is not advisable. On a similar basis II is also not advisable.

**11.** Both I and II are advisable because it will reduce the number of defaulters.

**13.** I is advisable because it will prepare the farmer to face the situation well in advance. II is also advisable because it will be helpful to cope with the problem related to water.

**14.** Only I is advisable because here the core problem is "migration of villagers for survival". I will make environment conducive to villagers to survive and restrict their migration. II is not advisable because it will compound the problem of migration.

**15.** I is advisable because it will bolster the financial condition of the farmers. II is advisable because susidising further the price of seeds and fertilizers will act as a compensation.

**16.** I is not advisable because it is an extreme action. Why should all the licences of the utility company be immediately suspended? II is not advisable because to avoid burn injuries people should be away from the place of incident but not necessarily indoors.

**17.** I is advisable because fear of punishment restricts people from doing offence. Hence, the number of cases of Internet hacking is likely to reduce. II is not advisable because it will hamper the work of Internet users.

**18.** I is advisable because it will lessen the students' problem regarding admission in intermediate courses. II is not advisable because it envisages accommodating all students instead of merely surplus students. Besides, II is an impractical course of action because it will cause delay also.

**19.** I is advisable because partial cut in supply will be useful when water crisis occurs. II is also advisable because minimal use of water by people will help conserve water and ensure smooth supply in future.

**20.** I is advisable because it will reduce the inconvenience of the people. II is not advisable because it is an extreme action.

**21.** I is not advisable because it is a harsh action. II is advisable because it is a proper and rational way.

**22.** I is illogical because Vitamin E capsule is also useful even if it is less effective. Action II is more useful and effective.

**23.** War cannot be an answer to such problems, but dialogue can.

**24.** By exploiting the recognition of the West, India can certainly hasten its economic growth. Hence, I follows. The opportunity to emerge as a super power should not be missed. Hence, II follows.

**25.** I is desirable but II is going too far. A readiness is desirable but "high alert" is alarmist.

# 23

# Assertion and Reason

## INTRODUCTION

The Assertion-Reason Questions are asked to check clarity of the candidate's concepts. In these questions, a statement is given under the heading 'Assertion' and another statement is given under the heading 'Reason'.

Assertion can be defined as

(*i*) A declaration that is made emphatically (as if no supporting evidence is necessary).

(*ii*) Stating or claiming something forcefully.

Reason can be defined as

(*i*) An underlying fact or cause that provides logical sense for a premise or occurrence.

(*ii*) A declaration made to explain or justify action, decision or conviction.

In this test, the combination of Assertion and Reason is given. Candidates are required to relate each other in order to find their correct co-ordination.

## EXERCISE

**Directions** : *In each of the following question, there are two statements labelled as Assertion (A) and Reason (R). Mark your answer as :*

(*a*) if both A and R are true and R is the correct explanation of A;
(*b*) if both A and R are true but R is not the correct explanation of A;
(*c*) if A is true but R is false;
(*d*) if A is false but R is true,
(*e*) if both A and R are false.

1. **Assertion (A):** Light travels in an optical fibre without loss in intensity.
   **Reason (R):** Light undergoes multiple reflections as it passes through the optical fibre.

2. **Assertion (A) :** There are disparities in regional Development on a global scale and within each country too.

   **Reason (R):** Such disparities are mainly due to the lack of adequate skilled labour.

3. **Assertion (A):** There is no vaccine for AIDS.
   **Reason (R):** The AIDS virus changes its genetic code.
4. **Assertion (A):** The length of the day at the equator always remains 12 hours.
   **Reason (R):** The angle of incidence of the Sun's rays at the equator is constant.
5. **Assertion (A):** Middle latitude westerly winds are stronger in the Southern Hemisphere than in the Northern Hemisphere.
   **Reason (R):** Oceans are comparatively cooler in the Southern Hemisphere than in the Northern Hemisphere.
6. **Assertion (A):** China is the most populous country of the world.
   **Reason (R):** Its density of population is much lower than that of India.
7. **Assertion (A):** The amount of dust particles is less in subtropical and temperate areas than in equatorial area.
   **Reason (R):** The atmosphere is dry and windy in the subtropical and temperate areas.
8. **Assertion (A):** The central secretariat is a think tank and treasure house of vital information.
   **Reason (R):** The secretariat carries out a comprehensive and detailed scrutiny of every issue.
9. **Assertion (A):** Subhas Chandra Bose resigned from the Presidentship of the Indian National Congress in his second term.
   **Reason (R):** He became opposed to the Gandhian movement based on non-violence.
10. **Assertion (A):** There has been a growing demand for review of centre-state relationship.
    **Reason (R):** The states have no adequate resources to take up developmental projects.
11. **Assertion (A):** Plaster of paris is used by doctors for setting fractured bones.
    **Reason (R):** When plaster of paris is mixed with water and applied around the fractured limbs, it sets into a hard mass.
12. **Assertion (A):** India enjoys tropical monsoon climate.
    **Reason (R):** India is located within the tropics.
13. **Assertion (A):** The mean is probably the most useful of all statistical measures.
    **Reason (R):** It is the base from which many other important measures are computed.

**14. Assertion (A):** Large deserts are located at low latitudes.

**Reason (R):** Continental drift has moved them to lower latitudes from higher latitudes.

**15. Assertion (A):** We prefer to wear white clothes in winter.

**Reason (R):** White clothes are good reflectors of heat.

**16. Assertion (A):** Ashoka pillars have retained their gloss on their surface.

**Reason (R):** Moisture laden winds do not blow in the areas where it is located.

**17. Assertion (A):** Winds are deflected to their right in Northern Hemisphere and to the left in the southern Hemisphere.

**Reason (R):** Rotation of earth causes the changes in wind direction.

**18. Assertion (A):** Laterite soils are not very productive for crop plants.

**Reason (R):** Laterite soils contain high concentrations of silica and calcium carbonate

**19. Assertion (A):** The ozone layer protects the earth from becoming very hot.

**Reason (R):** The ozone layer filters the solar radiation.

**20. Assertion (A):** The tail of comet is always away from the Sun.

**Reason (R):** The tail of comet is made up of gases and small ice particles.

**21. Assertion (A):** For the production of aluminium, cheap electricity is essential.

**Reason (R):** Extraction of aluminium from its ore requires abundant supply of electricity.

**22. Assertion (A):** Most -of the Himalayan rivers are perennial.

**Reason (R):** They are fed by melting snow.

**23. Assertion (A):** Mercury is the farthest planet from the Sun.

**Reason (R):** Mercury is the smallest planet in the entire solar system.

## ANSWERS

| **1** | **2** | **3** | **4** | **5** | **6** | **7** | **8** | **9** | **10** |
|---|---|---|---|---|---|---|---|---|---|
| (*a*) | (*c*) | (*a*) | (*a*) | (*a*) | (*b*) | (*a*) | (*a*) | (*a*) | (*a*) |
| **11** | **12** | **13** | **14** | **15** | **16** | **17** | **18** | **19** | **20** |
| (*a*) | (*c*) | (*a*) | (*c*) | (*d*) | (*c*) | (*a*) | (*c*) | (*a*) | (*c*) |
| **21** | **22** | **23** | | | | | | | |
| (*a*) | (*a*) | (*d*) | | | | | | | |

## SOME SELECTED EXPLANATORY ANSWERS

1. Light travels in an optical fibre without loss in intensity as it undergoes multiple reflections when it passes through the optical fibre.
2. Main cause of disparities in regional development is due to resources rather than of adequate skilled labour.
3. There is no vaccine for AIDS because the AIDS virus changes its genetic code. [$\because$ a vaccine contains the inactivated germs of the disease.]
4. At the equator, the angle of incidence of the Sun's rays is constant. So, the length of the day always remains for 12 hours at the equator.
5. Oceans are comparatively cooler in the Southern Hemisphere than in the Northern Hemisphere, so middle latitude westerly winds are stronger in the Southern Hemisphere than in the Northern Hemisphere.
6. China with a population of 1317.9 million is the most populous country in the world. Its density of population is 137.7 persons per square km while at present India's density of population is 356.8 persons per $km^2$.
7. In subtropical and temperate areas, the amount of dust particles is less because of dry and windy atmosphere.
8. The central secretariat carries out a comprehensive and detailed scrutiny of every issue and thus is considered as a think tank and treasure house of vital information.
9. Subhas Chandra Bose opposed the Gandhian movement based on non-violence by resigning from the Presidentship of the Indian National Congress in his second term.
10. The states have no adequate resources to take up developmental projects. So, there has been a growing demand for review of centre-state relationship.
11. Plaster of paris is used by doctors for setting fractured bones because when it is mixed with water and applied around the fractured limbs, it sets into a hard mass and keeps the bone joints in a fixed position.
12. India enjoys tropical type of climate, but some part (Northern India is located above $23\frac{1}{2}°$ N that forms tropic belt) is located in temperate zone.

    Therefore, Assertion (A) is true but Reason (R) is false.
13. The mean is probably the most useful of all statistical measures because it is the base from which many other important measures are computed and is also called as measures of central tendency.

An average value generally lies in the central part of the distribution are called the measures of central tendency.

Therefore, Reason (R) is correct explanation of Assertion (A).

**14.** The location of large deserts in lower latitudes is due to descending airs, not due to movement of continental drift. Therefore, Assertion (A) is true but Reason (R) is false.

**15.** Assertion is false because we prefer dark clothes in winter as they absorb heat and keep us warm.

But Reason is correct as white clothes are good reflectors of heat and are worn in Summer.

**16.** Ashoka pillars have retained their gloss on their surface because of the superior quality of the materials used.

**17.** Winds are deflected to their right in Northern Hemisphere and to the left in the Southern Hemisphere due to the rotation of earth.

**18.** In laterite soil, the amount of calcium carbonate is less. So, laterite soils are not very productive for crop plants.

Therefore, Assertion (A) is true but Reason (R) is false.

**19.** The layer of ozone gas found in stratosphere protects the earth from becoming very hot as it absorbs the harmful ultraviolet rays from the sun and thus filters the solar radiation.

Therefore, both Assertion (A) and Reason (R) are true and Reason (R) is the correct explanation of Assertion (A).

**20.** Solar radiations exert pressure on the tiny dust particles and gases, which makes up the tail of the comet. Due to this pressure, the tail of a comet is pushed away from the sun.

**21.** The production of aluminium is done by extracting it from its ore and this process requires an abundant supply of electricity.

**22.** Assertion and Reason both are true. Most Himalayan rivers originating from the Himalayan peaks are perennial because they are fed by the melting snow.

**23.** Assertion is false because Pluto is the farthest planet in the solar system. But Reason is true as Mercury is the smallest planet.

# Cause and Effect

In such type of questions, the candidates are asked to determine whether a given event is the cause or the effect of some other event.

Naturally the cause will always occur before the effect, i.e. cause is always antecedent to an effect. Cause is an event which leads to a said effect and this fact is either scientifically proven or logically expected.

In such questions you are given two statements (I) and (II). These statements may be either independent causes or may be effects of independent causes. One of these statements may be the effect of the other statement. You are required to analyse both the statements and decide which of the following answer choice correctly depicts the relationship between these two statements.

## EXERCISE

**Directions:** *Given below are the pairs of events 'A' and 'B'. You have to read both the events 'A' and 'B' and decide their nature of relationship. You have to assume that the information given in 'A' and 'B' is true and you will not assume anything beyond the given information in deciding the answer. Mark answer:*

(*a*) If 'A' is the effect and 'B' is its immediate and principal cause.
(*b*) If 'A' is the immediate and principal cause and 'B' is its effect.
(*c*) If 'A' is an effect but 'B' is not its immediate and principal cause.
(*d*) If 'B' is an effect but 'A' is not its immediate and principal cause.
(*e*) None of these.

1. **Event (A):** Prices of gold have gone up in the local market.

   **Event (B):** India has won several prizes in design of gold ornaments.

2. **Event (A):** Today, the Prime Ministers of country 'P' and 'Q' have decided to take steps to improve the bilateral relations.

   **Event (B):** Next week a Committee of Foreign Ministers and Senior Officers of country 'P' and 'Q' will workout further steps to improve the relationship.

**3. Event (A):** The sales of cars has dropped in the state 'X' since last Monday.

**Event (B):** The state 'X' has suspended registration of cars which do not confirm to the emission norms stipulated recently.

**4. Event (A):** The revised entry fee for internationally known Taj Mahal monument has been increased to ₹ 50 and ₹ 500 for Indians and foreigners respectively.

**Event (B):** There has been adequate increase in the number of foreign tourists visiting India in view of the improved infrastructure facilities.

**5. Event (A):** The financial position of the Electricity Division of state XYZ has weakened and it has made demand to the government for more subsidies.

**Event (B):** While the Electricity Division of state XYZ has revised the pay and perks of its employees, several subscribers and farmers have refused to pay long pending dues.

**6. Event (A):** We can get anything with money.

**Event (B):** Money is the most important thing today.

**7. Event (A):** Due to mechanisation, the life of human beings is becoming more comfortable in urban areas.

**Event (B):** Life is becoming insecure in urban areas.

**8. Event (A):** The government has decided recently to provide additional dearness allowance to its employees.

**Event (B):** Consumer Price Index is increasing for the last five months.

**9. Event (A):** The children of younger generation do better in their studies.

**Event (B):** The parents of children now realise the importance of education very well.

**10. Event (A):** There is a considerable increase in the number of people having computers.

**Event (B):** Computer education is being made compulsory in schools.

**11. Event (A):** Rickshaw, taxi, tempo and other means of general transportation of city X are on an indefinite strike since the last week.

**Event (B):** The prices of vegetables and other food articles in the city X have increased.

**12. Event (A):** The state government ABC has proposed to start a project "alert citizen" to curb possible crimes and nab the criminals.

**Event (B):** Public cooperation is imperative in controlling crime.

**13. Event (A):** The public transport company of city M has recently changed the routes of some roads to facilitate travellers.

**Event (B):** the public transport company of city M has recently cancelled some routes because there were few commuters.

**14. Event (A):** The sensex crossed 4000-point mark in the stock exchange, the highest mark in last 12 weeks.

**Event (B):** The government announced its credit policy for agriculture.

**15. Event (A):** Recently the traffic jams on MG Road of city 'Z' have not only reduced but the traffic has also become manageable.

**Event (B):** The flyover on MG Road of city 'Z' has recently been made operational and the number of traffic police personnel has been increased.

## ANSWERS

| 1 | 2 | 3 | 4 | 5 | 6 | 7 | 8 | 9 | 10 |
|---|---|---|---|---|---|---|---|---|---|
| (*e*) | (*b*) | (*a*) | (*c*) | (*a*) | (*b*) | (*d*) | (*a*) | (*a*) | (*c*) |
| **11** | **12** | **13** | **14** | **15** | | | | | |
| (*b*) | (*a*) | (*e*) | (*c*) | (*a*) | | | | | |

## SOME SELECTED EXPLANATORY ANSWERS

**4.** There may be several causes for the increment in entry fee in the Taj Mahal. Event (B) may be just one of the causes. It is also possible that the hike in maintenance cost is the other cause of this increment.

**7.** Increase in comfort due to mechanisation gradually leads to decrease in social interactions. This decrease sometimes causes insecurity.

**8.** Dearness allowance of the employee depends on the consumers' price index.

**10.** One of the reasons for increase in number of home computers in their being made compulsory in schools. Other reasons are a general interest in computers for various purposes.

**11.** The prices of vegetables has increased because of the strike of rickshaw, taxi and other general means of transportation. Hence, B is the effect and A is the immediate cause.

**12.** Because of (B), government has started the project "alert citizen" to curb crimes. Hence 'A' is the effect and (B) is the cause.

✦✦✦✦

25

# Analytical Decision-making

## FORMAT OF THE PROBLEM

**Directions:** *Study the following information carefully and answer the questions based on it:*

The following are the conditions for the recruitment of persons as faculty members in a computer education centre. The candidate must:

(*a*) be in the range of 23 years to 28 years as on 1 Nov, 1993.

(*b*) have work experience—teaching experience or programming experience — of not less than two years.

(*c*) have a postgraduate degree in computer application, i.e. MCA, M.Tech. or M.Sc. (Computer Science), with at least 60% marks.

(*d*) obtain at least 25 marks in the interview out of a total of 50 marks.

**In the case of a candidate who:**

(*e*) fulfils the above criteria, he or she shall be appointed as a senior faculty member.

(*f*) has a postgraduate degree in computer application with less than 60% marks but more than 50% marks, he or she shall be appointed as a junior faculty member.

(*g*) is of age more than 28 years but less than 32 years as on 1 Nov, 1993, the case may be referred to the director of the centre.

**On the basis of the above conditions and the information provided about each of the candidates in the question below, you have to decide which of the following courses of action should be taken against each candidate. Please note that you do not assume anything regarding any candidate. The decision should be based only on the information provided. Mark answer:**

(*a*) if the candidate is to be selected as a junior faculty member.

(*b*) if the candidate is to be selected as a senior faculty member.

(*c*) if the case is to be referred to the director of the centre.

(*d*) if the data are inadequate.

(*e*) if the candidate is not to be selected.

**Questions:**

1. Manisha Punjabi is an M.Sc. in Computer Science with 65% marks. Her date of birth is 31st July, 1965. She has been working in an institution as a programmer for the last 4 years.
2. Kishore Garg is an MCA with 61 % marks. His date of birth is 14 August, 1970. He has worked as a computer teacher for 3 years. He has obtained 60% marks in the interview.
3. Babli Sarkar is an M.Tech. with 58% marks. Her date of birth is 31 Dec, 1971. She has been working as a programmer for the last two-and-a-half years. She has obtained 40 marks in the interview.
4. Manish Kumar is an M. Sc.(Comp. Science) with 52% marks. His date of birth is 10 July, 1968. He has been working as a computer teacher for 4 years. He has obtained 40% marks in the interview.
5. Sudha Ranjan is an MCA with 56% marks. She has been working as a programmer for 3 years. Her date of birth is 12 February, 1969. She has obtained 55% marks in the interview.

## Basic Conditions and Additional Conditions

In the problem above, there are four conditions - (*a*), (*b*), (*c*) and (*d*), which are the 'original' conditions. We shall call them, let us say, **"basic conditions".**

Similarly, in the above problem, there are two more' conditions - (*f*) and (*g*), which are to be looked into in cases of exceptions. We shall call them **"additional conditions".** (Please note that (*e*) is not an additional condition as it does not talk of exceptions. It is only a totality of the four basic conditions, given earlier.)

## Suggested Method

The question, as you have seen, has hardly any reasoning to do. It requires very little logic, all you have to do is to see which of some given candidates fulfill some of the given conditions to decide the correct choice.

Therefore, a good method can only save your sometime by being orderly and heat. The following method would be for you.

**Step I:** First of all, write the symbols (*a, b, c, d*) of the basic conditions to the top-left of where the actual questions start (see the arrangement below). Now, write the symbols of the additional conditions (*f* and *g*) below the symbol of that basic condition with which these might be related. For example, (*f*) is a condition about educational qualification and so it is an exception of (*c*). Hence, (*f*) should be written below (*c*). Similarly, (*g*) should be written below (*a*). **To differentiate between the basic conditions and additional conditions,**

**put the basic conditions without brackets and the additional conditions within brackets.**

After performing **step I,** your question-sheet will look like this:

a b c d
(g) (f)
1. Manisha Punjabi is an M. Sc

..............................................

**Step II:** Now look carefully at the answer choices and decide which combination of the conditions leads to which conclusion. For the example given above, the following combinations can be prepared as:

a + b + c + d ⇒ (2) (senior faculty member)

g + b + c + d ⇒ (3) (to be referred to director)

a + b + f + d ⇒ (1) (junior faculty member).

After you have decided the above three combinations, two answer- choices remain — (4) and (5). The answer-choice (5), which states that the candidate is not to be selected, should be chosen when any one or more of the given conditions is violated. The answer-choice (4), which states that the data are inadequate, should be chosen when no information is given about any one or more conditions.

**Step III:** Read each question carefully and compare the facts given in it with the given conditions. Now,

- if a basic condition is fulfilled, put a (✓) mark below it.
- if a basic condition is violated and there are no additional conditions attached to it put a × mark.
- if a basic condition is violated but there exist additional conditions attached to it (like, (a) and (c) in the given example), then if the additional condition is also violated put a (×) mark below it, and if the additional condition is fulfilled put a (✓) mark.
- When no information is given about any condition, put a '?' mark below it.

**Step IV:** Now select your answer choices according to the following rule:

- if there comes an X or (X) anywhere, don't go any further. Choose the choice, not to be selected.
- if there is a '?' below any condition and there are no 'X', then choose "data inadequate."
- if there is neither any 'X' nor any '?', then compare the combination with the three answer-combinations obtained in step II and accordingly select the answer choice.

## EXERCISE

**Directions (Qs. 1-7):** *Study the following information carefully to answer the questions given below:*

The Institute of Technology runs BC college of Engineering. It applies the following criteria for selection of students for admission to the BC College.

The students should:

(*a*) have been born before 1.3.1997 and after 28.2.1994.

(*b*) have obtained minimum 80% marks in aggregate and minimum 90% marks in Maths and Science at HSC.

(*c*) have passed intermediate drawing examination conducted by the State government.

(*d*) be willing to pay a deposit of ₹ 15,000 as laboratory security.

(*e*) be found physically fit in the medical examinations being conducted by the Institute.

However, if a student fulfills all other criteria except

1. criteria (*b*), but has obtained minimum 85% marks in aggregate as well as in Maths and Science his case may be referred to the Vice-President of the Institute.
2. criteria (*c*), but has won award in inter-school drawing competition, his case may be referred to the Principal of the college.
3. criteria (*d*), but is a relative of a member of Board of Trustees of the Institute, his case may be referred to the chairman of the admission committee.

   Based on the above criteria and the information given in each case, you have to take a decision. You are not to assume anything. These cases are given to you as on 28.2.2015.

**Mark Answer If**

A. the student is to be admitted.

B. the student is to be referred to Vice President of the Institute.

C. the student is to be referred to the Principal of college.

D. the student is to be referred to the chairman of the admission committee.

E. the student is not to be admitted.

**1.** Virendra, born on 19th January 1996, has passed the HSC examination with 91% marks in Maths and Science and an aggregate score of 84%. He will manage to pay the amount of ₹ 15,000 as security deposit to the institute. He is medically fit as per the report of the institute's team of doctors. He has passed intermediate drawing examination of the state. However, he could never win a prize in any of the inter-school drawing competitions.

**2.** Narendra, whose date of birth is 21.4.1995 is a student of Electrical Engineering diploma course. He has scored 85% marks in aggregate and 89% marks in Maths and Science at HSC examination. He has done a part-time course in computer operating. He is medically fit as reported by the Institute's medical team. He has passed the state level intermediate drawing examination in 2010, obtaining 'A' grade. He has no problem is paying the amount of deposit.

**3.** Sunita has passed HSC examination with 82% marks in aggregate and 92% marks in Maths and Science. She is found fit in the medical examination and can pay the required amount of deposit. Her date of birth is 1.3.1997. She has passed the state level intermediate drawing examination.

**4.** Asmita is a 19-year-old girl, who has passed her HSC in 2015 with 88% aggregate marks and 93% marks in Maths and Science. She is studying in FY BSc and has secured distinction in the first semester. She had participated in inter-school drawing competitions and has won the awards on two occasions. She is found fit by the medical examiners appointed by the institute. She is the daughter of an industrialist and can pay any amount as deposit.

**5.** Ravi, an 18-year-old boy, is the nephew of an industrialist who is a trustee of the institute. Although he did not appear in the drawing examination of state he has won gold medal in an interschool drawing competition. His aggregate marks in HSC is 81% and the marks in Maths and Science are 91%. He has been found physically fit by the doctors' team appointed by the institute. He is not in a position to pay any amount against deposit.

**6.** Sujit, a 20-year-old boy, has passed his HSC examination securing 87% marks in aggregate and 88% marks in Maths and Science. He is willing to deposit ₹ 15,600 as Lab Security deposit and is found fit by the team of doctors conducting medical examination. He has passed the intermediate drawing examination of the state.

**7.** Ninad, the only son of a Chartered Accountant who is also a trustee of the Institute, has passed the drawing examination of state and has just passed HSC examination securing more than 90% marks in aggregate as well as in Maths and Science. His date of birth is 15.6.1996. He is physically fit as per the medical examination report of the Institute. He cannot pay more than ₹ 10,000 against the security deposit. He has passed the state level intermediate drawing examination with grade B.

**Directions (Qs. 8-14):** *An international bank decided to recruit Management Trainees for its Foreign Exchange department. The following criteria were laid down:*

The candidate must be

1. B. Com., with minimum 65% marks.
2. CA1IB with minimum 50% marks.
3. having working experience of minimum one year in foreign exchange department of any bank.
4. age between 24 years and 30 years as on 1.7.2015.
5. ready to keep a deposit of ₹ 25,000 with the bank.

However, if the candidate fulfils all other criteria except the

(*a*) (*ii*) above, but has completed CAIIB part I with minimum 60% marks his case may be referred to the General Manager.

(*b*) (*iii*) above, but has 4 years experience of working in a bank, his case may be referred to the Chairman.

(*c*) (*i*) above, but has obtained minimum 60% marks at B.Com. as well as CAIIB, his case may be referred to the Managing Director.

Based on the above criteria and the information given in each of the following questions, you have to take the decision in regard of each case. You are not entitled to assume anything. These cases are given to you as on 1st July, 2015.

**8.** Abhijit Kaul is a commerce graduate with 72% marks in graduation and 59% marks at CAIIB examination. He is 28 years old and is working in a bank since 2010 till date. He can keep a deposit of ₹ 25,000 with the Bank.

A. Refer to Managing Director
B. Refer to General Manager
C. Refer to Chairman
D. Candidate is to be selected
E. Candidate is not to be selected

**9.** Manisha is an employee of a private bank in Clerical cadre for past 6 years in its foreign exchange department. She is B.Com. with 70% marks and CAIIB with 60% marks. Her date of birth is 15.6.1988. She is willing to keep a deposit of any amount up to ₹ 50,000 with the bank.

A. Refer to Chairman
B. Refer to General Manager
C. Refer to Managing Director
D. Candidate is to be selected
E. None of these

**10.** Niranjan's father is an industrialist of the city and Niranjan has no problem in keeping any amount as deposit with the Bank. He has completed B.Sc. with 58% marks and CAIIB with 60% marks. He is working in a Public Sector Bank as an officer in the foreign exchange department since the last two years. His date of birth is 24.4.1990.

A. Refer to Managing Director
B. Refer to General Manager
C. Refer to Chairman
D. Candidate is to be selected
E. Candidate is not to be selected

**11.** Mr Subhash Rao has passed his B.Com. examination and CAIIB examination with 62% and 65% marks respectively. He has recently completed 25 years of age in June, 2015. He has joined a foreign bank in 2013 and was placed in its foreign exchange department in January, 2014. He continues to work with the Bank till date. He is ready to keep a deposit of ₹ 25,000.

A. Refer to Managing Director
B. Refer to General Manager
C. Data inadequate
D. Candidate is to be selected
E. Candidate is not to be selected

**12.** Ashutosh, a commerce graduate with 73% marks, has completed CAIIB part I securing 64% marks and will be appearing for CAIIB part II examination. His date of birth is 29.6.1991. He joined a cooperative bank in 2012 and continues to work there. He was posted in the foreign exchange department in 2013 and is working in the same department at present. He can keep the required amount of deposit with the bank.

A. Refer to Chairman
B. Refer to General Manager
C. Data inadequate
D. Candidate is to be selected
E. Candidate is not to be selected

**13.** Rajshekhar, a youth of 26 years age, has completed B.Com. securing 68% marks and is working in a nationalised bank for past two years in its foreign exchange department. He will be appearing for CAIIB part II examination in the next month. He has no problem in depositing ₹ 25,000 with the bank.

A. Refer to General Manager
B. Refer to Managing Director
C. Candidate is to be selected
D. Candidate is not to be selected
E. Data inadequate

**14.** Ranjita, a 25-year-old commerce graduate, is working in a public sector bank since 2012 in its foreign exchange department. She is B.Com. with 75% marks and CAIIB with 58% marks. She has done a diploma course in computer programming. She is willing to keep a deposit of minimum ₹ 25,000 with the Bank.

A. Refer to Chairman
B. Refer to General Manager
C. Data inadequate
D. Candidate is to be selected
E. Candidate is not to be selected

**Directions (Qs. 15-21):** *A reputed Research Institute decided to select research assistant applying the following selection criteria:*

The candidate must

(*a*) be a post-graduate with minimum 60% marks.
(*b*) have at least two research publications.
(*c*) have studied statistics as one of the subjects at graduation.

(*d*) have at least one year's experience in teaching or research.
(*e*) be not less than 25 years and not more than 30 years of age as on 16.7.2015.

However, if a candidate fulfils all other conditions except the:

(*i*) (*b*) above but has done Ph.D., the case may be referred to the Chairman of the institute.
(*ii*) (*a*) above but has secured minimum 50% marks at post-graduation and has also completed M. Phil, the case may be referred to the Director.
(*iii*) (*d*) above but has three years experience of working in industry, the case may be referred to the President.
(*iv*) (*c*) above but has studied Research Methodology at graduate or post-graduate level, the case may be referred to the Executive Director.

Based on the above criteria and the information given in each of the following cases, you have to take a decision. You are not entitled to assume anything. In case you find that the given data is insufficient to make a decision, give 'data inadequate' as you answer. The cases are being given to you as on 16.7.2015.

**15.** Rita has completed 25 years recently, and has a bright academic career all through. She is a B.Sc. in Statistics with distinction. She has done her post-graduation securing 70% marks, and has got her Ph.D. very recently. She is working as a research fellow in a reputed academic institute since 2013.

A. Refer to the Chairman
B. Refer to the President
C. Refer to the Director
D. Not to be selected
E. To be selected

**16.** Divya Bose is a post-graduate having studied Research-Methodology as one of the papers at post-graduation. She secured 75% marks at post-graduation. She is working as a Research Assistant in a private firm since June, 2014 and has got three of her papers published during her tenure in the firm. Her date of birth is 25.4.1988.

A. Refer to the Director
B. Refer to the Executive Director
C. Refer to the Chairman
D. Not to be selected
E. None of these

**17.** Nikita, a 28-year-old lady, is working as an Assistant Teacher in a Junior College since June, 2012. She has completed post-graduation in 2011, securing 68% marks. She regularly writes research papers and has eight to ten publications to her credit. Statistics was one of the papers studied by her at graduation.

A. To be selected
B. Refer to the President
C. Refer to the Director
D. Data inadequate
E. Not to be selected

**18.** Shashidhar, a 27-year-old post-graduate in Statistics with 65% marks, is working as a lecturer in a degree college for past two years. Statistics was his main subject at B.Sc. He is doing M.Phil. and plans to do Ph.D.

A. Refer to the Chairman
B. Refer to the Executive Director
C. Refer to the President
D. Not to be selected
E. To be selected

**19.** Milind, a post-graduate with 55% marks in Commerce, has studied Economics and Statistics in graduation as well as post-graduation. He has also done M.Phil. and has more than five research paper publications. He is teaching in the University since January, 2013. His date of birth is 5.9.1986.

A. Refer to the Chairman
B. Refer to the President
C. Refer to the Director
D. Not to be selected
E. To be selected

**20.** Shirish Kumar has completed graduation with 67% marks having Statistics as a main subject. He has also completed post-graduation with 70% marks. His date of birth is 19.7.1989. He has registered for Ph.D. in 2012 and has four research publications to his credit. He has been working as a lecturer since 2013.

A. Refer to the President
B. Refer to the Chairman
C. Refer to the Director
D. Not to be selected
E. To be selected

**21.** Laxmi has done her graduation and post-graduation in Statistics with 70% and 78% marks respectively. She has registered for Ph.D. and has also got around five research paper publications to her credit. Her date of birth is 17.7.1985. She is working in a private company since 2011.

A. Refer to the Director
B. Refer to the Chairman
C. Refer to the President
D. To be selected
E. Not to be selected

**Directions (Qs. 22-28):** *A company 'XYZ Ltd' has decided to appoint Technical Officers in its Technical Division applying the following eligibility criteria:*

The candidate must be

(*i*) a Science graduate (B. Sc.) with minimum 70% marks.
(*ii*) having postgraduate degree or diploma in Computer Science with minimum 50% marks.
(*iii*) of age not less than 24 years and not more than 28 years as on 1.7.2015.

In addition to the above criteria, he must satisfy at least one or more of the following conditions:

(*a*) The candidate must have work experience of minimum one year.
(*b*) represented school/college team in at least one of the sports at district/state level.
(*c*) participated in drama or music competitions at district/state level.
(*d*) secured distinction in the main subject-of specialisation at B.Sc.
(*e*) secured minimum 60% marks in the post-graduate degree/diploma.

Based on the above conditions and the data given in each of the following cases you have to take decision. You are not supposed to assume anything. All the facts are given as on 1.7.2015.

**22.** Devendra Kumar has done his B.Sc. with specialisation in Chemistry securing 73% marks and has secured distinction in Chemistry. He joined a Chemical company at the age of 23 years and has been working for last two years. He has completed post-graduation in Computer Science with 60% marks.
A. To be appointed - satisfies (*a*) and (*e*) only
B. To be appointed - satisfies (*d*) and (*e*) only
C. To be appointed - satisfies (*a*), (*d*) and (*e*) only
D. Not to be appointed
E. None of these

**23.** Uday is a Science graduate with 75% marks and has done his diploma in Computer Science with 58% marks. His date of birth is 2.7.1991. He has participated in intercollegiate music competitions and has also won the awards.
A. Not to be appointed
B. To be appointed - satisfies (*c*) only
C. To be appointed - satisfies (*e*) only
D. To be appointed - satisfies (*c*) and (*e*) only
E. None of these

**24.** Aniket is a post-graduate in Computer Science with 65% marks and a graduate in Science with 68% marks. He is a dramatist and had always been participating in competitions at state level and has won the state level 'best actor' award. His date of birth is 29.8.1990
A. To be appointed - satisfies (*c*) only
B. To be appointed - satisfies (*e*) only
C. To be appointed - satisfies (*c*) and (*e*) only
D. Not to be appointed
E. None of these

**25.** Nidhi Sharma is an executive in a private company since September, 2014. She has done B.Sc. with Botany as main subject and has secured 72%

marks at B.Sc. with distinction in Botany. She is good at music and has participated in state-level music competitions. She is a postgraduate in Computer Science with 65% marks. Her date of birth is 12.9.1987.

A. To be appointed - satisfies (*a*) and (*c*) only
B. To be appointed - satisfies (*c*) and (*e*) only
C. To be appointed - satisfies (*c*) and (*d*) only
D. Not to be appointed
E. None of these

**26.** Rajiv Kumar, a 25-year-old boy, has completed B.Sc in Computer Science with 76% marks and has also done post-graduation in Computer Science with 68% marks. He is a good dancer and has won prizes in state level dance competitions. He can also sing well.

A. To be appointed - satisfies (*c*) only
B. To be appointed - satisfies (*c*) and (*e*) only
C. To be appointed - satisfies (*e*) only
D. Not to be appointed
E. None of these

**27.** Sushant is a 26-year-old Science graduate with specialisation in Physics. He is working in an electronics company as Sales Officer since August 2013. He has secured 75% marks at graduation. He is a football player and has represented his college team at inter-university level. He has obtained a post-graduate diploma in Computer Science with 54% marks.

A. To be appointed - satisfies (*a*) only
B. To be appointed - satisfies (*a*) and (*b*) only
C. To be appointed - satisfies (*b*) and (*c*) only
D. Not to be appointed
E None of these

**28.** Varsha Khanolkar, a B.Sc with Mathematics as her main subject, secured 79% marks at graduation. She was a kho-kho player and has represented her college team at state level. She has completed her post-graduation in 1998 at the age of 24 years with 56% marks.

A. Not to be appointed
B. To be appointed - satisfies (*c*) only
C. To be appointed - satisfies (*b*) and (*c*) only
D. To be appointed - satisfies (*b*) and (*d*) only
E. None of these

**Directions (Qs. 29-35):** *A public charitable trust desires to select 'Medical Officers' for its rural hospital based on the following criteria:*

The applicant must

(*i*) be holding MBBS degree with minimum 50% marks.
(*ii*) have minimum 4 years of experience of full-time practice in rural areas.
(*iii*) be ready to execute a bond of 3 years of service.
(*iv*) have good knowledge of the local language.

In case of the applicant who satisfies all other criteria except

(*a*) at (*ii*) the above, but has 4 years of full-time experience of either urban or semiurban area and spent at least 5 years in rural area anytime during his life, be referred to Secretary of the Trust.

(*b*) at (*iv*) the above, but has working knowlege of Hindi, be referred to Assistant Secretary of the Trust.

(*c*) at (*i*) the above, but has minimum 45% of marks at MBBS and has done MS or MD with minimum 50%, be referred to the Chief Medical Officer (CMO).

(*d*) at (*iii*) the above, but is ready to give ₹ 25,000 as security money, be referred to the President of the Trust.

Based on these criteria and the information provided below, decide the course of action in each case. You are not entitled to assume anything. If the data provided is not adequate to decide the given course of action, your answer will be 'data inadequate'. All cases given to you fulfil critirion of age and therefore, no details of age are provided. The cases are given to you today.

**29.** Jenifer did her MD after doing her MBBS. She is ready to execute three years bond of service. She has good command over local language as well as Hindi. She has practised for 5½ years in a remote village out of her love for social service. She has obtained 77%, 88%, 47% and 56% at SSC, HSc, MBBS, and MD respectively

A. Refer to Assistant Secretary
B. Data inadequate
C. To be selected
D. Not to be selected
E. None of these

**30.** Durga, after obtaining her MBBS and MS, decided to practise in her native village for five years. She knows the local language very well. Her dispensary and small hospital were very popular in the nearby villages. She plans to go to USA and UK after spending 4 more years in India. She has secured more than 60% marks in all the examinations right from SSC to MS. She is ready to execute a bond of 3 years of service.

A. Refer to CMO
B. Not to be selected
C. Data inadequate
D. To be selected
E. None of these

**31.** Mangesh has secured 47% marks at MBBS and has done his MD with 62% marks. He has 5 years of experience of running a dispensary in a village and can read, write and speak the local language. He is ready to give a bond of only two years of service and is unable to give security money as he wants to start a rural hospital afterwards in Andhra Pradesh.

A. Data inadequate
B. To be selected
C. Not to be selected
D. Refer to the President of the Trust
E. Refer to the CMO

**32.** Siddhant has studied in rural areas while doing his schooling. His father is a farmer. Siddhant completed his MBBS from Mumbai and has six years of experience of practice in a big city. He has good knowledge of the local language and working knowledge of Hindi. He is ready to execute 3 years bond of service. He has done, MS with 53% marks.

A. To be selected
B. Data inadequate
C. Refer to the CMO
D. Not to be selected
E. Refer to the Secretary

**33.** Dr Murthy has stood first at MBBS after having obtained 78% marks. He has also completed MS with distinction. As he is planning to go abroad he is unwilling to give three years bond of service. Dr Murthy is fluent in the local language. He has six years of experience of practice in a rural hospital and he is not in a position to give ₹ 25,000 as a security money.

A. Refer to the President
B. To be selected
C. Not to be selected
D. Data inadequate
E. None of these

**34.** Iquabal Kureshi, the son of a local politician, was born and brought up in a village till attaining SSc. Afterwards he studied in a big city and did his MBBS with 69% of marks followed by MS with 57% marks. He is ready to execute a bond of service for 3 years only. He has very good knowledge of the local language. He has done 4½ years practice in the urban areas. He plans to start a rural hospital after this experience.

A. Refer to the Secretary
B. Refer to the CMO
C. Data inadequate
D. To be selected
E. Not to be selected

**35.** Romila was born and brought up in a big-urban city. Her father is an industrialist. She has secured 87%, 56% and 48% at HSC, MBBS and MD respectively. She is willing to give a bond of 3 years of service. She has worked for 5 years in a rural hospital but can hardly speak the local language. However, she has working knowledge of Hindi. After this experience she plans to settle abroad.

(*a*) Refer to Asst Secretary
(*b*) Refer to President
(*c*) To be selected
(*d*) Not to be selected
(*e*) Data inadequate

**Directions (Qs. 36-42):** *Read the following information carefully and answer the questions given below; Following are the conditions for short-listing candidates for the post of Customer Relations Officers (CRO) for X YZ Ltd.*

The candidate to be called for interview must

(*i*) be a graduate in Science, i.e. B.Sc. with minimum 55% marks.
(*ii*) have at least 3 years experience in selling/marketing.
(*iii*) have participated in debating or drama or sports at the intercollegiate level onwards.
(*iv*) have secured minimum 60% marks in the Written Examination (WE).
(*v*) be ready to deposit Rs 10,000 as security deposit.

However, in case of a candidate who fulfils all these criteria except

(*a*) (iv) the above, but has secured minimum 60% at B.Sc., may be referred to the Chief Manager, Customer Relations (CR).
(*b*) (i) the above, but has passed M.Sc., i.e. Post-Graduation in Science, with minimum 50% marks, may be referred to DGM(CR).

Based on these criteria and information provided below, decide the course of action in each case. You are not entitled to assume anything. If the data provided is not adequate to decide the given course of action, your answer will be 'data inadequate'. All the candidates given below fulfil the criterion for age. Mark answer:

A. Selected for interview
B. Not to be selected
C. Data inadequate
D. Refer to the Chief Manager (CR)
E. Refer to the DGM (CR)

**36.** Krupa is a successful sportsperson having won several prizes in sports and debating at intercollegiate level onwards. At B.Sc., M.Sc. and WE, she has obtained 62%, 55% and 65% marks respectively. She has 5 years experience in sales. Her father is a successful businessman.

**37.** Rohan is the son of a marketing executive. Rohan has obtained many prizes in inter-university debates and drama events. He has worked as marketing executive for 5 years after completing his B.Sc. and M.B.A. with 62% and 70% marks respectively. He is ready to give security deposit of ₹ 10,000. He has obtained 65% marks in WE.

**38.** Chandrakant is a 30-year-old officer who has worked as sales representative for five years. He is a keen sportsman and actor and has won many prizes in college-university level events. He is ready to pay security deposit of

₹ 10,000. He has obtained 67%, 58% arid 55% marks at B.Sc., WE and Diploma in Business Management respectively.

**39.** Kamal Kanchan has 6 years experience in marketing cosmetic products. She has done her B.Sc., M.Sc. and M.B.A. with 65%, 56% and 62% marks respectively. She is ready to pay the security deposit. She is good at debating and has won many prizes in inter-college/university events. She is interested in social work.

**40.** Jadunath is a Science graduate having done postgraduate diploma in Journalism. He is having 4 years experience of marketing consumer products. He is ready to deposit ₹ 10,000 as security deposit. He had been participating in dramas at the intercollegiate level and above and has won many prizes. He has secured 58% and 65% marks respectively at WE and B.Sc. respectively.

**41.** Dinkar has won many prizes in sports at the inter-college/university level. He has seven years experience in direct sales. He has scored 65%, 56%, and 53% marks in WE, B.Sc. and M.Sc. respectively. He is ready to give security deposit and desires to make a career in selling.

**42.** Deepali is a 26-year-old girl having obtained 60% marks at post-graduation, i.e. M.Sc., and 53% and 64% at B.Sc. and WE respectively. Deepali has worked as sales executive for three-and-a-half years. She has obtained. many prizes in inter-collegiate events in debating and is ready to deposit ₹ 10,000 as security deposit.

**Directions (Qs. 43-49):** *Read the following information carefully and answer the questions given below:*

XYZ Institute of Science and Medicine provides scholarships to meritorious students so that they are able to get postgraduate degree in US.

For this, the following criteria have been set:

(*i*) The candidate must be all MBBS graduates with minimum 60% marks.

(*ii*) He/she must have practised at least for 2 yrs in government hospital after completion of his/her MBBS courses.

(*iii*) He/she must have passed Medical Aptitude Test (MAT) with at least 90% marks.

(*iv*) He/she must be between 23 and 26 years of age on 31.01.2015.

However, if the candidate fulfils all the criteria except at

(*a*) (*i*) the above, but has secured at least 54% marks in MBBS along with Diploma in some specialised branches of Medicine, his/her case to be referred to Director, XYZ Institute.

(*b*) (*iii*) the above, but has secured at least 70% marks in MBBS and at least 85% marks in MAT, his/her case to be referred to President; XYZ Institute.

(*c*) (*ii*) the above, but has an MD degree, his/her case to be referred to Vice President, XYZ Institute.

Based on the above criteria and the information given below, you have to take decision in regard to each case. You are not entitled to assume any information.

If the given information is not adequate, then your answer should be 'scholarship not to be given'. All the informations are being given to you on 31.01.2015. Give answer.

A. if the candidate is to be given scholarship
B. if the case is to be referred to Director
C. if the case is to be referred to Vice President
D. if the case is to be referred to President
E. if the scholarship is not to be given

**43.** Dr BK Das has got MBBS and MD degree from Patna. He has also received the award of best medical student. He has completed his MD at the age of 24 yrs. As per the demand he has also got experience of working with the Lucknow government hospital. He has got nearly 95% and 68% marks in MAT and MBBS respectively. He has already enrolled himself in USA.

**44.** Dr Ranjan Kumar is working with 'Herbal Drugs'. He comes from a doctor's family. He received MBBS degree with 73.5% marks at the age of 21 yrs in 2011. He has earned a good name during his 3 yrs' tenure at Jaunpur government hospital. He did MAT but got only 87.5% marks. He has also got published his research paper as a medicine journalist.

**45.** After completing his MBBS degree with 58% marks, Dr Ashok Kumar Verma has worked with the city government hospital for two-and-a-half years. He has got 92% marks in MAT. He was born on Dec 13, 1993. He has successfully got a diploma in paediatrics. He has already enrolled himself in USA.

**46.** Dr Alok Agarwal has had an outstanding career and he has got at least 80 and above percentage of marks from SSC to MBBS. He was born on June 27, 1992. He has got 96% marks in MAT. He has completed his MD with 65% marks while working with a private hospital for nearly two years. After coming back from New York he wants to open 'Rural Hospital' in his. village.

**47.** Dr SN Luthra is not known for his academic excellence but he is a hardworking and enterprising person. He has got 86%, 92%, 65% and 93% marks in ASC, HSC, MBBS and MAT respectively. He has worked with the government hospital for atleast three years. His date of birth is Jan 11, 1990. He wants to settle in USA after his studies.

**48.** Dr Sonia Apte is a dedicated doctor at the age of 25 years and has worked with Thane government hospital for nearly 3 years. She has got 90.40% and 63.5% marks in MAT and MBBS respectively. She wants to reside permanently in USA after her studies.

**49.** Dr Mridula Garg has got 93% marks in MAT. She has passed 3 years in a private hospital after completion of her MBBS with 69% marks. She wants to be a child specialist and has done special diploma in paediatrics. She has attained the age of 25 years in October, 2014. She has got admission for studies in America.

**Directions (Qs. 50-54):** *Study the following information carefully and answer the questions given below:*

Following are the eligibility criteria for becoming member of an exclusive club:

(*i*) The applicant should have annual income of at least ₹ 5 lakhs and should be able to pay one-time membership fee of ₹ 1 lakh.

(*ii*) The annual income and one-time membership fee is relaxed upto 50% for former defence personnel.

(*iii*) For the sons and daughters of the existing members the criterion of annual income is reduced to ₹ 3 lakhs and membership fee to ₹ 70 thousand.

(*iv*) Serving court judges are offered membership free and also the stipulation of annual income is waived.

(*v*) A national level sports personnel is eligible to become a member by paying ₹ 20 thousand as membership fee irrespective of annual income.

Below in each question, data/information about an individual is given. You have to decide, based on the information provided, under which criterion/criteria the individual is eligible to obtain membership. Please note that an individual can be eligible under more than one criteria. You are not to assume anything other than the information provided in each question.

**50.** Ashok Malhotra has been working in a Private Airlines Company as a pilot. His annual income is ₹ 10 lakhs. He is ready to pay ₹ 50 thousand as one-time membership fee. His father is a retired army officer.

A. Not eligible
B. Eligible under (*ii*) and (*iii*) only
C. Eligible under (*ii*) only
D. Eligible under (*iv*) only
E. None of these

**51.** Navin Singh can pay ₹ 70 thousand as membership fee. He has been playing in the national football team and he works in a major public sector bank in the country. His father is a member of the club.

A. Not eligible
B. Eligible under (*v*) only
C. Eligible under (*iii*) and (*v*) only
D. Eligible under (*iv*) only
E. None of these

**52.** Prabhu Sharma's annual income is ₹ 6 lakhs. He is a retired judge of the supreme court. He can pay ₹ 1 lakh as the membership fee. He played cricket for his home state.

A. Not eligible
B. Eligible under (*i*) and (*v*) only
C. Eligible under (*i*) only
D. Eligible under (*i*) and (*iii*) only
E. None of these

**53.** Shobha Patil works in a bank. She represents National Badminton team. Her father is a retired judge of the local high court. Her annual income is ₹ 6 lakhs. She can pay ₹ 1 lakhs as membership fee.

A. Eligible under (*i*) only
B. Eligible under (*v*) only
C. Eligible under (*i*) and (*ii*) only
D. Eligible under (*i*) and (*v*) only
E. None of these

**54.** Meena Jaswani is the daughter of an existing member of the club. Her annual income is ₹ 4 lakh. She can pay ₹ 80 thousand as membership fee. She Works in Indian Navy.

A. Eligible under (*i*) and (*iii*) only
B. Eligible under (*i*) and (*iv*) only
C. Eligible under (*iii*) only
D. Eligible under (*iv*) only
E. Eligible under (*iii*) and (*iv*) only

**Directions (Qs. 55-60):** *Study the following information carefully and answer the questions given below:*

An institute XYZ provides scholarship to its employees for higher studies in the United States of America. Following are conditions for awarding scholarship to the employees. The candidate must:

(*i*) not be more than 30 years of age as on April 1, 2015.
(*ii*) have secured more than 70 per cent marks in post-graduation and 75 per cent marks in graduation.
(*iii*) have at least two years work experience in the XYZ institute.
(*iv*) be ready to sign a bond of two years with the company.
(*v*) have got A or A + rating for his/her works in the last two years.

However, in case of a candidate who fulfils all the criteria EXCEPT.

(*a*) (*ii*) the above, but has secured minimum 60 per cent marks in graduation and postgraduation and he/she has got Ph.D., may be referred to the Director.

(*b*) (*v*) above, but has work experience of three years with ratings B +, A or A+, may be referred to the Chairman.

(*c*) (iv) above, but he/she has to leave the institute and he is ready to pay ₹ 50,000, may be referred to the President.

Based on these criteria and information provided below, decide the course of action in each case. You are not to assume anything. The cases are given to you as on April 1, 2015. If the data provided are not adequate to decide the given course of action, your answer will be "data inadequate".

**55.** Ajit D'Souza is a postgraduate in Physics with 75 per cent marks and passed graduation with 77 per cent marks. He is working in the institute since 2011 and has always got A rating on performance. He was 25 years old at the time of joining the institute. He is keen to seek job in the United States of America.

A. Refer to the Chairman
B. Refer to the President
C. Data inadequate
D. Not to be selected
E. To be selected

**56.** Deepali Mirza is working in XYZ institute for the last two-and-a-half years. Her performance is good and has secured rating A+. She has secured 70 per cent and 75 per cent marks in graduation and postgraduation respectively. She is postgraduate in mathematics. She is ready to sign the bond of two years. Her date of birth is 31.03.1986. She has also done Ph.D.

A. Data inadequate
B. Refer to the Director
C. Refer to the President
D. Refer to the Chairman
E. Not to be selected

**57.** Rajendra Bhave is a postgraduate in Psychology. He had secured 72% marks at postgraduation and 78% marks at graduation. He is working in XYZ institute for more than two years and his performance ratings are A+ and A respectively in the last two years. He is not keen to sign the bond but does not mind paying ₹ 50,000/- if required to leave. His date of birth is 14.8.1985.

A. To be selected
B. Refer to the Chairman
C. Refer to the Director
D. Refer to the President
E. Not to be selected

**58.** 28-years-old Tariqae Anwar is a postgraduate in Chemistry and has registered for Ph.D. He scored 80% and 78% marks at graduation and postgraduation respectively. He is working in the XYZ institute since 2010. His performance ratings in the last three years are B+, A+ and A respectively. He is ready to sign two years' bond with the institute.

A. To be selected
B. Refer to the President
C. Refer to the Chairman
D. Refer to the Director
E. Not to be selected

**59.** Ram Mohan is 28 years old and has done M. Phil, and postgraduation in Economics. His percentage of marks in M. Phil., graduation and post-graduation are 70%, 79% and 76% respectively. He is working in the institute for last four years and his performance ratings are B+, A, B+, A in these years. He is ready to sign a bond for two years.

A. Not to be selected
B. To be selected
C. Refer to the Director
D. Refer to the President
E. Refer to the Chairman

**60.** Harish Chheda has a bright academic career throughout. He has done postgraduation with 65% marks and has submitted Ph.D. thesis. His date of birth is 27.9.1988. He is working for the last three years in the XYZ institute and has always got A ratings for his performance. He is ready to pay ₹ 50,000 in case required to leave.

A. To be selected
B. Refer to the President
C. Refer to the Director
D. Data inadequate
E. Not to be selected

**Directions (Qs. 61-65):** *Read the following information carefully and answer the given questions:*

Following are the criteria for appointing a Personnel Manager for a company. The candidate must

(*a*) not be more than 35 years of age as on 1.6.2015.
(*b*) be a postgraduate in personnel management.
(*c*) have work experience as personnel officer/manager of at least five years.
(*d*) have good command over English.

In the case of a candidate-

(*i*) who satisfies all the criteria except at (A) above but has work experience as personnel manager for at least 10 years, his/her case may be referred to Director (Personnel) for consideration.
(*ii*) who satisfies all the other criteria except at (C) above but has obtained Ph. D. degree in Personnel Management, his/her case may be referred to Managing Director for consideration.

You are given the following cases on 1.6.2015. Deciding upon the information provided in each case in each questions given below and based on the criteria mentioned above, recommend your decision. You are not to assume anything. Mark your answer as per the following:

**Mark answer**

A. if the candidate is to be selected.
B. if the candidate is not to be selected.
C. if the case is to be referred to Director (Personnel).
D. if the case is to be referred to Managing Director.
E. if complete information is not provided.

**61.** Kamini Gadgil is a post-graduate in Personnel Management and was born on 15th August 1982. She has been working in a company for the last 10 years as Personnel Officer.

**62.** Aditi Sahay is a doctorate (Ph.D.) in Personnel Management. She has been working in a company as personnel officer for the last two years. She has good command over English and was born on 2nd November, 1979.

**63.** Vijay Kalkarni is a graduate in Personnel Management. He was 32 years old as on 1st December 2014. He has good command over English and has been working in a company as Personnel Manager for the last 12 years.

**64.** Pradeep Sarkar is post-graduate in Personnel Management and has been working in a company as a Personnel Manager for the last 15 years. He has good command over English and his date of birth is 13th April, 1979.

**65.** Praveen Chopra is post-graduate in Personnel Management and has been working in a company as Personnel Officer for the last 7 years. He has good command over English and his date of birth is 20th March, 1982.

## ANSWERS

| **1** | **2** | **3** | **4** | **5** | **6** | **7** | **8** | **9** | **10** |
|---|---|---|---|---|---|---|---|---|---|
| A | B | E | C | E | B | D | C | D | E |
| **11** | **12** | **13** | **14** | **15** | **16** | **17** | **18** | **19** | **20** |
| A | B | E | D | A | B | A | D | C | E |
| **21** | **22** | **23** | **24** | **25** | **26** | **27** | **28** | **29** | **30** |
| C | C | A | D | E | B | B | E | E | B |
| **31** | **32** | **33** | **34** | **35** | **36** | **37** | **38** | **39** | **40** |
| C | B | C | A | A | C | A | D | C | D |
| **41** | **42** | **43** | **44** | **45** | **46** | **47** | **48** | **49** | **50** |
| A | E | E | D | B | E | A | A | E | A |
| **51** | **52** | **53** | **54** | **55** | **56** | **57** | **58** | **59** | **60** |
| B | B | D | C | C | B | D | A | E | E |
| **61** | **62** | **63** | **64** | **65** | | | | | |
| E | B | B | C | A | | | | | |

## SOME SELECTED EXPLANATORY ANSWERS

**(1-7):**

| Q.No. | 1 | 2(*i*) {a (*i*)} | 2(*ii*) {a (*ii*)} | 3 (*b*) | 4 (*c*) | 5 |
|---|---|---|---|---|---|---|
| **1.** | ✓ | ✓ | ✓ | ✓ | ✓ | ✓ |
| **2.** | ✓ | {✓} | {✓} | ✓ | ✓ | ✓ |
| **3.** | × | ✓ | ✓ | ✓ | ✓ | ✓ |
| **4.** | ✓ | ✓ | ✓ | (✓) | ✓ | ✓ |
| **5.** | ✓ | ✓ | ✓ | (✓) | (✓) | ✓ |
| **6.** | ✓ | (✓) | (✓) | ✓ | ✓ | ✓ |
| **7.** | ✓ | ✓ | ✓ | ✓ | (✓) | ✓ |

$1 + 2(i) + 2(ii) + 3 + 4 + 5 \Rightarrow$ option (*a*)

$1 + a(i) + a(ii) + 3 + 4 + 5 \Rightarrow$ option (*b*)

$1 + 2(i) + 2(ii) + (b) + 4 + 5 \Rightarrow$ option (*c*)

$1 + 2(i) + 2(ii) + 3 + (c) + 5 \Rightarrow$ option (*d*)

**(8-14):**

| Q.No. | 1/(c) | 2/(a) | 3(b) | 4 | 5 |
|---|---|---|---|---|---|
| **8.** | ✓ | ✓ | (✓) | ✓ | ✓ |
| **9.** | ✓ | ✓ | ✓ | ✓ | ✓ |
| **10.** | × | | | | ✓ |
| **11.** | (✓) | ✓ | ✓ | ✓ | ✓ |
| **12.** | ✓ | (✓) | ✓ | ✓ | ✓ |
| **13.** | CAIIB result not out | | | | |
| **14.** | ✓ | ✓ | ✓ | ✓ | ✓ |

$1 + 2 + 3 + 4 + 5 \rightarrow$ selected

$1 + (a) + 3 + 4 + 5 \rightarrow$ General Manager

$1 + 2 + (b) + 4 + 5 \rightarrow$ Chairman

$(c) + 2 + 3 + 4 + 5 \rightarrow$ MD

**10.** In the very step it is known that Niranjan is not satisfying criteria 1 or (*c*) hence, we do not need to go ahead.

**(15-21):**

| Q.No. | a/(*ii*) | b/(*i*) | c/(*iv*) | d/(*iii*) | e |
|---|---|---|---|---|---|
| **15.** | ✓ | (✓) | ✓ | ✓ | ✓ |
| **16.** | ✓ | ✓ | (✓) | ✓ | ✓ |
| **17.** | ✓ | ✓ | ✓ | ✓ | ✓ |
| **18.** | ✓ | | ✓ | ✓ | ✓ |
| **19.** | (✓) | ✓ | ✓ | ✓ | ✓ |
| **20.** | ✓ | ✓ | ✓ | ✓ | ✓ |
| **21.** | ✓ | ✓ | ✓ | (✓) | ✓ |

a + b + c + d + e → to be selected

(*ii*) + b + c + d + e → Director

a + (*i*) + c + d + e → Chairman

a + b + (*iv*) + d + e → Executive Director

a + b + c + (*iii*) + e → President

**(22-28):**

| Q.No. | Candidate | (*i*) | (*ii*) | (*iii*) | (*a*) | (*b*) | (*c*) | (*d*) | (*e*) |
|---|---|---|---|---|---|---|---|---|---|
| **22.** | Devendra | ✓ | ✓ | ✓ | ✓ | × | | ✓ | ✓ |
| **23.** | Uday | ✓ | ✓ | × | | | | | |
| **24.** | Aniket | × | ✓ | ✓ | | | | | |
| **25.** | Nidhi | ✓ | ✓ | ✓ | × | | ✓ | ✓ | ✓ |
| **26.** | Rajiv | ✓ | ✓ | ✓ | | | ✓ | | ✓ |
| **27.** | Sushant | ✓ | ✓ | ✓ | ✓ | ✓ | | | |
| **28.** | Varsha | ✓ | ✓ | ✓ | | ✓ | | | |

**25.** Satisfies (*c*), (*d*) and (*e*).

**(29-35):**

| Q.No. | i/(c) | ii/(a) | iii/(d) | iv/(b) |
|---|---|---|---|---|
| **29.** | (✓) | ✓ | ✓ | ✓ |
| **30.** | ✓ | × | ✓ | ✓ |
| **31.** | (✓) | ✓ | × | ✓ |
| **32.** | – | (✓) | ✓ | ✓ |
| **33.** | ✓ | ✓ | × | ✓ |
| **34.** | ✓ | (✓) | ✓ | ✓ |
| **35.** | ✓ | ✓ | ✓ | (✓) |

i + ii + iii + iv = selected
(c) + ii + iii + iv = referred to CMO
i + (a) + iii + iv = referred to Secretary
i + ii + (d) + iv = refferred to President
i + ii + iii + (b) = referred to Assistant Secretary
Any other combination = not to be selected
Anything missing = Data inadequate

**29.** referred to CMO.

**32.** Marks in his MBBS is not given.

**(36-42):**

| Q.No. | i/(b) | ii | iii | iv/(a) | v |
|---|---|---|---|---|---|
| **36.** | ✓ | ✓ | ✓ | ✓ | – |
| **37.** | ✓ | ✓ | ✓ | ✓ | ✓ |
| **38.** | ✓ | ✓ | ✓ | (✓) | ✓ |
| **39.** | ✓ | ✓ | ✓ | – | ✓ |
| **40.** | ✓ | ✓ | ✓ | (✓) | ✓ |
| **41.** | ✓ | ✓ | ✓ | ✓ | ✓ |
| **42.** | (✓) | ✓ | ✓ | ✓ | ✓ |

(i) + (ii) + (iii) + (iv) + (v) = Option (*a*)
(i) + (ii) + (iii) + (a) + (v) = Option (*d*)
(b) + (ii) + (iii) + (iv) + (v) = Option (*e*)
Anything missing = Option (*c*)

**(43-49):**

| Q.No. | i/(a) | ii/(c) | iii/(b) | iv |
|---|---|---|---|---|
| **43.** | ✓ | ✓ | ✓ | – |
| **44.** | ✓ | ✓ | ✓(b) | ✓ |
| **45.** | ✓ | ✓ | ✓ | ✓ |
| **46.** | ✓ | ✓ | ✓ | × |
| **47.** | ✓ | ✓ | ✓ | ✓ |
| **48.** | ✓ | ✓ | ✓ | ✓ |
| **49.** | ✓ | × | ✓ | ✓ |

(i) + (ii) + (iii) + (iv) = Option (*a*)

(a) + (ii) + (iii) + (iv) = Option (*b*)

(i) + (c) + (iii) + (iv) = Option (*c*)

(i) + (ii) + (b) + (iv) = Option (*d*)

Any other combination or anything missing = Option (*e*)

**43.** When he has completed his MD is not mentioned.

**(50-54):**

| Q.No. | Person | i | ii | iii | iv | v | Answer |
|---|---|---|---|---|---|---|---|
| **50.** | Ashok | × | × | × | × | × | 1 |
| **51.** | Navin | × | × | × | × | ✓ | 2 |
| **52.** | Prabhu | ✓ | × | × | × | ✓ | 2 |
| **53.** | Shobha | ✓ | × | × | × | ✓ | 4 |
| **54.** | Meena | × | × | ✓ | × | × | 3 |

**(55-60):**

| Q.No. | i | ii/(a) | iii | iv/(c) | v/(b) |
|---|---|---|---|---|---|
| **55.** | ✓ | ✓ | ✓ | – | ✓ |
| **56.** | ✓ | (✓) | ✓ | ✓ | ✓ |
| **57.** | ✓ | ✓ | ✓ | (✓) | ✓ |
| **58.** | ✓ | ✓ | ✓ | ✓ | ✓ |
| **59.** | ✓ | ✓ | ✓ | ✓ | (✓) |
| **60.** | ✓ | × | ✓ | (✓) | ✓ |

(i) + (ii) + (iii) + (iv) + (v) = can be selected

(i) + (a) + (iii) + (iv) + (v) = Referred to Director.

(i) + (ii) + (iii) + (c) + (v) = Referred to President.

(i) + (ii) + (iii) + (iv) + (b) = Referred to Chairman.

Anything not given = Data inadequate

Any other combination = Cannot be selected

**58.** Performance rating in the last two years was A + and A.

**60.** Mere submission of Ph.D thesis doesn't mean he has got Ph.D degree.

**(61-65):**

| Q.No. | a/(i) | b | c/(ii) | d |
|---|---|---|---|---|
| **61.** | ✓ | ✓ | ✓ | – |
| **62.** | × | ✓ | (✓) | ✓ |
| **63.** | ✓ | × | ✓ | ✓ |
| **64.** | (✓) | ✓ | ✓ | ✓ |
| **65.** | ✓ | ✓ | ✓ | ✓ |

$a + b + c + d$ = Option A

(i) + $b + c + d$ = Option C

$a + b$ + (ii) + $d$ = Option D

**61.** No information is given about her command over English.

✦✦✦✦

# 26

# Passage and Conclusion

## Degree of Truth and Falsity

In this section of logical reasoning, the question consists of brief passage (which is usually a part of a report or an economic essay or any other similar thought provoking subject), followed by certain inferences based on it.

We can use logic to determine the degree of truth and falsity in an argument.

We can decide whether the opinion or belief is consistent with or follows from other beliefs and opinions expressed in the argument.

The questions that come under this category basically consist of five categories as given below. For a given passage followed by several inferences, you have to examine each inference separately in the context of the passage and decide upon its degree of truth or falsity and then choose the best alternative provided accordingly as:

(*a*) If the inference is 'definitely true', i.e. it directly follows from the facts-given in the passage.

(*b*) If the inference is 'probably true' though not definitely true in the light of the facts given.

(*c*) If you think the data are inadequate, i.e. from the facts given you cannot say whether the inference is likely to be true or false.

(*d*) If you think the inference is 'probably false' though not definitely false in the light of the facts given.

(*e*) If you think the inference is 'definitely false', i.e. it contradicts the given facts.

**Flowchart for evaluation of Inferences**

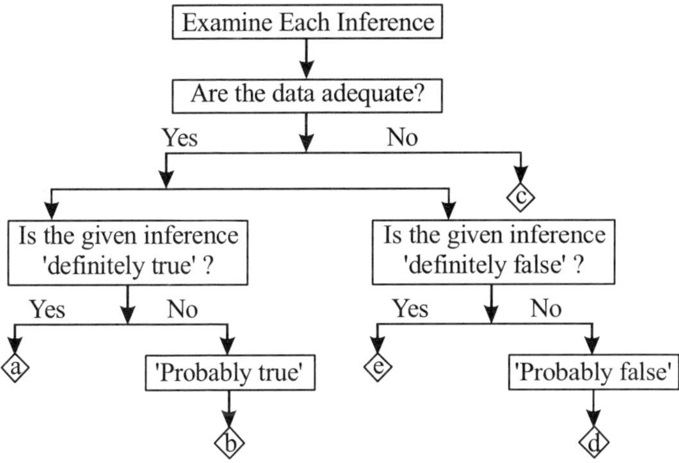


## Important tips to evaluate an inference

(*i*) To evaluate an inference, check whether it can be evaluated with the help of the passage directly.

(*ii*) Check if this inference is directly supported or contradicted by something in the passage.

(*iii*) If an inference cannot be directly related with the passage, check if we can justify or contradict it with the help of an additional assumption.

(*iv*) We should check if the extra assumption we have made to evaluate the inference is universally true to avoid confusion while deriving inferences between the choices "definitely true" and "probably true".

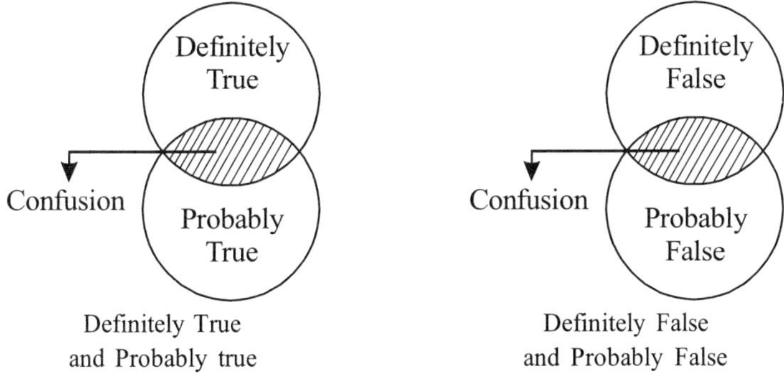


Definitely True and Probably true

Definitely False and Probably False

(*v*) To avoid confusion between the choices "definitely false" and "probably false" we can use the same strategy as given above in (*iv*).

(*vi*) Check if it is possible to make an extra assumption to take the inference as "probably true" to avoid confusion while during inferences between the choices "probably true" and "data inadequate". If we can make a reasonable extra assumption, the answer would be "probably true".

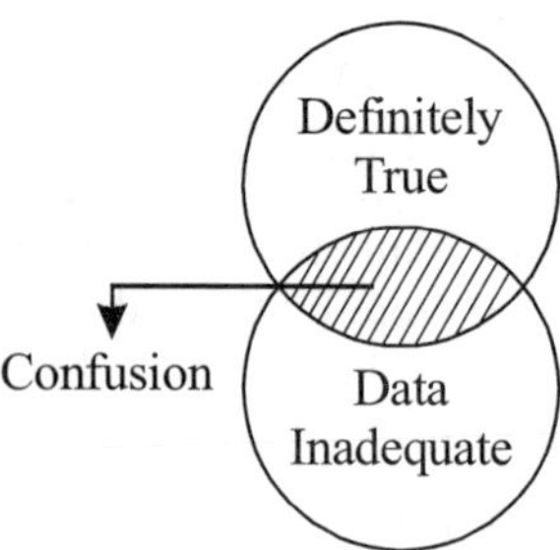


**Fig.:** *Probably True and Data inadequate*

(*vii*) To avoid confusion between the choices "Probably false" and "data inadequate", we can use the same strategy as given above in (*vi*).

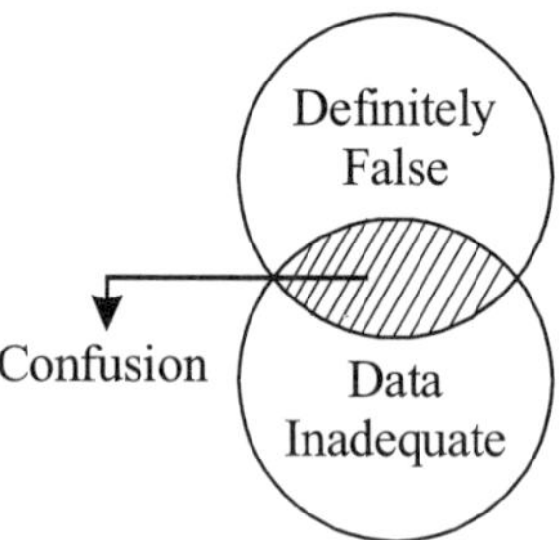


**Fig.:** *Probably False and Data Inadequate*

(*viii*) With the help of some important keywords used in the passage, we can also evaluate an inference.

## EXERCISE

**Directions:** *Below are given passages followed by several possible inferences which can be drawn from the facts stated in the passage. You have to examine each inference separately in the context of the passage and decide upon its degree of truth or falsity. Mark answer:*

(*a*) if the inference is 'definitely true', i.e. it properly follows from the statement of facts given.

(*b*) if the inference is 'probably true' though not 'definitely true' in the light of the facts given.

(*c*) if the 'data are inadequate', i.e. from the facts given you cannot say whether the inference is likely to be true or false.

(*d*) if the inference is 'probably false' though not 'definitely false' in the light of the facts given.

(*e*) if the inference is 'definitely false', i.e. it cannot possibly be drawn from the facts given for it contradicts the given facts.

## PASSAGE - 1

The XYZ Co-operative Milk Marketing Federation of India Limited has targeted a sales turnover of ₹ 10,000 crore by the end of the year 2018. As a part of its projects for the next five years, the federation had envisaged ₹ 100 crore worth of exports per year as against its present exports of ₹ 30 crore per year.

As per the federation's plan, the future network will include 100 offices dealing with about 7500 stockists, who in turn would be covering every taluka headquarters and servicing about 10 lakh odd outlets. Its immediate strategy would be to cater to India's next-door neighbours for exports of milk products.

The main players in this business in the world are India, United States, Europe, New Zealand and Australia, out of which Europe and United States are forced to go for subsidising due to rising labour cost while Australia and New Zealand are far away from India.

**1.** By 2018, more than 90 per cent of product of XYZ will be used for domestic market.

**2.** The federation's emphasis appears to be more on exports than on domestic consumption of its products.

**3.** By 2018, India will be the largest player in the milk industry.

**4.** India does not have an immediate competitor in exporting milk and its products to the neighbouring countries.

**5.** The XYZ Federation may have to train additional man power to enable it to reach all corners of India and its neighbouring countries.

## PASSAGE - 2

There is some controversy about the percentage of population below the poverty line in India. The criteria for the poverty line are based on a person's nutritional requirements in terms of calories. It is assumed that the minimum nutritional requirement per person per day in rural areas is 2400 calories, whereas it is 2200 calories in urban areas. If the household is unable to bear the expenditure for this level of nutrition, it is categorised as below the poverty line. There is also a view that along with calories, the amount of protein intake be treated as a criterion as it is related to the physical energy, mental alertness and resistance to infections.

**6.** Many Indians who are below the poverty line get necessary amount of proteins.

**7.** People who are above the poverty line are less likely to suffer from infections.

**8.** India's poverty alleviation programmes can only succeed after reaching agreement about the poverty line.

**9.** People in urban area do less physical work compared to the people in rural area.

**10.** In other countries, there is no controversy about defining the poverty line.

## PASSAGE - 3

The process of developmental planning in India is greatly dominated by the experts and the technocrats. But it was not always so. Among the initial stalwarts in the Indian planning process, there were only a handful of economists. It was their political conviction and their preconceived political pattern of creating an economy and a society which gave them the specific stability in the path of development. Under the leadership of Indira Gandhi, there was some change in the scenario and the reflection of electoral manifesto of the Congress Party was continually enhanced in the plans.

**11.** In the planning procedure the common man is primary.

**12.** After the independence, our leaders understood the need for framing development-oriented planning and made their desired participation.

**13.** Initially, the Indian planning was free of the influence of ideology of the ruling party.

**14.** Five-year plans in India did not get targeted success because they were not framed by the economists.

**15.** If an economic system is to be enriched then it must be given shape only by the politicians because they understand the thoughts and aspirations of the people.

## PASSAGE - 4

There is a clear link between degraded forests and poverty. It is estimated that one billion of the world's poorest people in about 30 heavily deforested countries would be alleviated from poverty if they are given government support for managing the neighbouring public forest land and sharing benefits within their communities.

The forests face even shakier future with the global population expected to grow by 50 per cent in the next 50 years. To accommodate a growing population's need of more land for food production, we should be making better use of the degraded land through 'Evergreen Revolution'.

**16.** The growth of population is positively linked with growth of forests.

**17.** The developed countries have faster rate of growth of forests compared to the developing countries.

**18.** Evergreen revolution is possible only after controlling rate of growth of population of developing country.

**19.** It is possible to protect and develop forests with the efforts of only the government agencies.

**20.** If a country has a thick forest cover, it is likely to have lower level of poverty.

## PASSAGE - 5

Low vision is a lesser known but widely prevalent eye problem in India. While more than 28 million people in India suffer from low vision in our country, many people do not realize that they have this problem.

Low vision people are neither blind nor do they have full vision. Technically speaking, they score less than 6/18 on visual acuity, and their field of vision is restricted to 10 degrees or less. The people who cannot see very well but whose vision is not helped by the normal glasses are often those suffering from low vision.

**21.** It is possible to detect cases of low vision by using scientific techniques.

**22.** Regular and free check-up of eyes for visual acuity can help reduce cases of low vision among poor people in India.

**23.** The actual number of cases of low vision in India is likely to be more than 28 million.

**24.** The number of cases of low vision in other countries of Asia is quite high compared to India.

**25.** It is possible to produce special glasses in India.

## PASSAGE - 6

There has been a considerable improvement in the economy for the last ten years. Indian economy has witnessed far-reaching changes, e.g. emergence of India as an IT superpower; there has been a wide increase in the global employment for the Indian managers and so have the maximum salaries and so on.

However, there happened a great upheaval in corporations, closure of firms and reduction in the size of institutions. There also occurred infiltration of the "Hire & Fire" culture into the corporations. Employment opportunities have also declined.

**26.** There are certain positive results of reform in economy but there are also some unfavourable effects.

**27.** Before reformation in the economy in our country, there was no "Hire and Fire" culture in the world as a whole.

**28.** India can compete with US as it has emerged as an IT Superpower.

**29.** There are ample employment opportunities for the Indian specialists world over following the closure of some Indian firms.

**30.** The living standard of Indian managers will really improve when they seek jobs in foreign countries.

## PASSAGE - 7

According to the latest numbers, the core sector saw terrific (5.5 per cent) growth recently. This could be a statistical aberration or a flash in the pan. But steel prices are rising and this could be the sign of genuine core sector demand. It will be interesting to see if steel prices continue to maintain an upward trend. That would be a confirmation of sustainability. If steel is indeed in a situation of high demand, it is sure that downstream manufacturing will be doing well. Core sector industries such as heavy construction, mining, steel, etc. are classified as cyclicals. However, the downtrend has lasted so long that one was afraid that these industries were on permanent decline. One doesn't know whether the apparent improvement will translate into rising stock prices over the long term.

**31.** The downstream manufacturing units are expected to have a slowdown in near future.

**32.** For the last few years the core sector has projected a modest growth.

**33.** The growth in core sector in the recent past was much below 4 percent.

**34.** The steel prices will show continuous increase during next few months.

**35.** The price of steel depends on the activities in the core sector.

## PASSAGE - 8

In the initial years, trade policy in our country was primarily aimed at regulating imports regarding the nascent stage of country's development and the need to encourage domestic production through import substitution measures. However, with the onset of liberalisation, the importance of globalisation through trade and making exports the engine of growth of economy has been recognised. Export promotion is now a continuous and sustained effort and specific steps in this direction have been taken and achievements have been made in recent years.

**36.** Achievements made in the economic growth are attributable to maximum possible export and minimum or almost neglible import.

**37.** At present, there are no regulatory clutches on exports as exports is recognised as the main force behind economic growth.

**38.** It is not appropriate to give the credit of economic growth to export.

**39.** Before the implementation of the idea of liberalisation, our trade policy was not much in favour of free import-export.

**40.** Import used to affect domestic production in earlier years.

## ANSWERS

| 1 | 2 | 3 | 4 | 5 | 6 | 7 | 8 | 9 | 10 |
|---|---|---|---|---|---|---|---|---|---|
| (*a*) | (*d*) | (*c*) | (*d*) | (*a*) | (*d*) | (*a*) | (*c*) | (*b*) | (*c*) |
| **11** | **12** | **13** | **14** | **15** | **16** | **17** | **18** | **19** | **20** |
| (*e*) | (*d*) | (*d*) | (*c*) | (*c*) | (*e*) | (*b*) | (*e*) | (*c*) | (*a*) |
| **21** | **22** | **23** | **24** | **25** | **26** | **27** | **28** | **29** | **30** |
| (*a*) | (*c*) | (*a*) | (*c*) | (*c*) | (*a*) | (*d*) | (*c*) | (*c*) | (*b*) |
| **31** | **32** | **33** | **34** | **35** | **36** | **37** | **38** | **39** | **40** |
| (*d*) | (*d*) | (*a*) | (*c*) | (*a*) | (*e*) | (*c*) | (*d*) | (*a*) | (*a*) |

## SOME SELECTED EXPLANATORY ANSWERS

**1.** From the first two sentences it is clear that target sale for domestic market is (10,000 – 100 =) ₹ 9900 crore, which is clearly more than 90 per cent of ₹ 10,000 cr.

**2.** From the data given in the passage, it is clear that domestic consumption is larger than foreign consumption. But as the present data of domestic consumption is not known, hence it is probably false.

**3.** We do not have data about domestic sales and exports of other countries.

**4.** However, a large player does not necessarily mean large exporter.

**5.** Such a possibility exists with expanding network.

**6.** It *appears* to be true because the tone of the passage suggests that calories are the minimum requirement and protein intake additional. So, it is difficult to accept that those who don't get the minimum requirement of calories, i.e. people below the poverty line, would get the necessary amount of proteins.

**7.** People *well above* the poverty line must be those beyond the controversy of the definition. That is, they get sufficient calories as well as proteins. And proteins are related to resistance to infections.

**8.** Poverty alleviation programmes are nowhere in the picture.

**9.** Probably true because of the difference in their nutritional requirements.

**10.** The passage talks only about India.

**12.** The political leaders depended on their preconceived ideas to formulate the policies.

**13.** We are told about the "political conviction" of the "initial stalwarts", who, one presumes, carried the ideology of the ruling party, though one can't be sure.

**14.** The term 'five year plan' is nowhere mentioned in the passage.

**15.** It is not indicated whether our politicians were grassroot politicians who could understand the thoughts and aspirations of the people.

**16.** More population means lesser forest cover.

**17.** Poverty is found in the developing countries.

**21.** The passage clearly says what it means in technical terms. Such measurements can be arrived at only by using scientific techniques.

**22.** Nothing is given about the treatment in the passage.

**23.** From the second line of the passage.

**26.** The first para talks of "positive results" and the second of "unfavourable effects".

**28.** Situation of US economy, especially about IT, is not given.

**30.** Fetching maximum salary by Indian managers is likely to promote living standards. Hence it is probably true.

**31.** See the sentence "If steel is indeed in ........ will be doing well". Since price of steel and its demand are rising therefore, it is likely that downstream manufacturing units will do. well in near future. Hence, inference is false. But we are riot sure about it, hence probably false.

**32.** The core sector was not doing good in the past.

**33.** The word 'terrific' used in the passage makes the inference definitely true.

**34.** Rising steel prices at present does not necessarily mean that the trend will continue during the next few months.

**36.** The second part— minimum or almost negligible import —makes the inference definitely false. Imports are inevitable in an era of globalisation.

**37.** No data is given that says that present regulations have been completely removed or relaxed.

✧✧✧✧

# REASONING

## NONVERBAL

# Non-verbal Reasoning

## NON-VERBAL - REASONING TESTS

The best way to solve reasoning questions easily and quickly is through practice. Practice makes a person perfect and intelligent. One should solve all the previous year's papers of verbal and non-verbal reasoning.

Non-verbal reasoning involves the ability to understand and analyse visual information.

It analyses complex problems using visual reasoning without relying upon language skills.

In this test, all questions are given in the form of diagrams/figures. The purpose of this test is to assess your analytical ability. Generally, a set of four diagrams are given as "Problem Figures". You have to find out the relationship between these figures and apply it to a new situation.

### SERIES

Each question of this type has two sets of figures. The set labelled "Problem Figures" is on the left-hand side consisting of 4 or more figures. The set labelled as "Answer Figures" is on the right-hand side and consists of five figures numbered from A to E. In "Series" type of questions, there is some systematic change occurring in the box from left to right in the 'Problem Figures'. You have to find the nature of this change and decide what will be the next figure, if the same change continues and pick out the one from the "Answer Figures" which can be next or fifth in the row of "Problem Figures".

**Here is an example:**

**PROBLEM FIGURES** **ANSWER FIGURES**

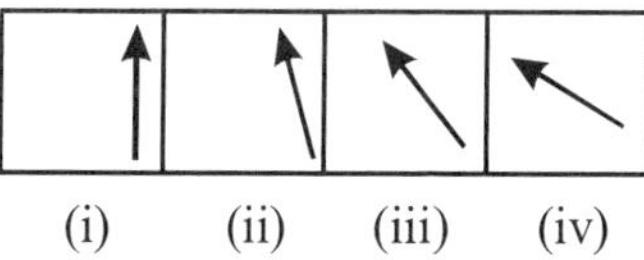

(i) (ii) (iii) (iv)

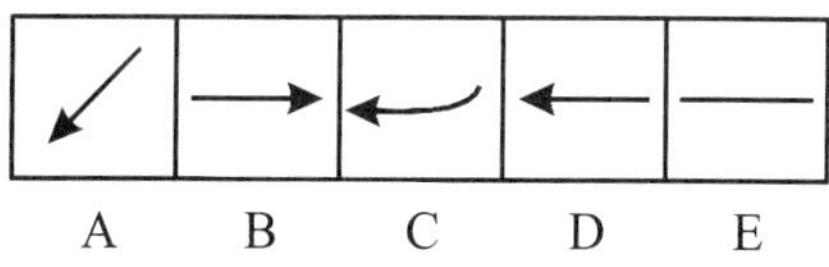

A B C D E

In the above example, you will notice that there are four figures in the "Problem Figures". The arrow in each square (from left to right) is tilting more and more to the left (Anticlockwise) and each time, it tilts to a certain angle. The question is "If the arrow continues to fall at the same angle, what will be its next position, *i.e.* "5th position"? From the extent to which it has tilted to the left in each of the first four squares, it is self evident that it should be lying horizontally. From amongst the five Answer Figures given, the arrow in figure D is horizontal. Hence, the answer is (D). Note that the figures in the 2nd and the 5th square are also lying horizontally. They cannot be the answers because, in the Answer Figure (B), the arrow is pointing towards the reverse direction and in Answer Figure (E) it is a line and not an arrow. The changes which occur in figures in different questions can be of various types. Some of these are:

1. **Rotation:** The elements are rotated clock-wise or anti-clockwise.
2. **Substitution:** A new element replaces an already occuring element there in every successive figure.
3. **Change in element:** The elements in each successive figures are modified or changed.
4. **Combination:** Change involving a combination of two or more of the above.
5. **Rearrangement:** The elements are rearranged in each successive figure.
6. **Addition:** Some elements added in every successive figure.
7. **Subtraction:** Deletion of an element from every succeeding figure.

All elements refer to a line, a dot, a circle or a triangle or any other similar thing which appears in the Problem or Answer Figures.

**Rotation**

**PROBLEM FIGURES** **ANSWER FIGURES**

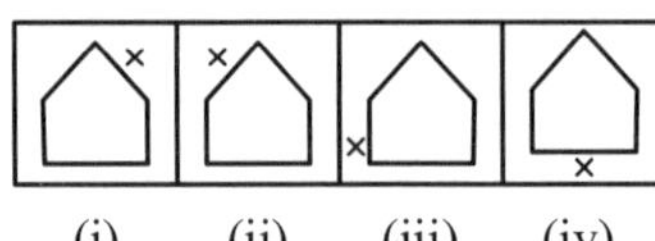

(i) (ii) (iii) (iv)

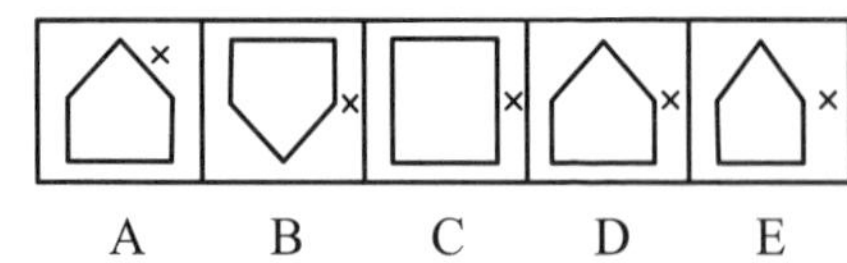

A B C D E

You will observe in the above question that there are two elements in all the Problem Figures– a pentagon and an "×" sign. While the pentagon is stationary, the "×" sign keeps on moving around from side to side in anti - clockwise direction. You can observe that Answer Figure "D" is the correct position of "×". Hence, the answer is D. Note that Answer Figures A, B and E have an element with five sides and an "×" sign. However, they cannot be right answers. In Answer figure "A", the "×" sign has moved one side more than it should have, though the movement is in the right direction, i.e. anti - clockwise. Answer Figure "B" is wrong because the pentagon is upside down. The shape of the pentagon in Answer Figure "E" is different from that in the Problem Figures.

**Substitution**

**PROBLEM FIGURES** **ANSWER FIGURES**

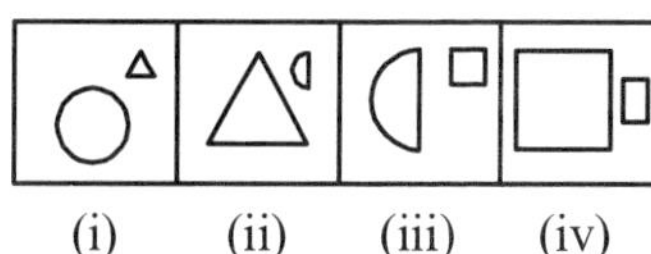

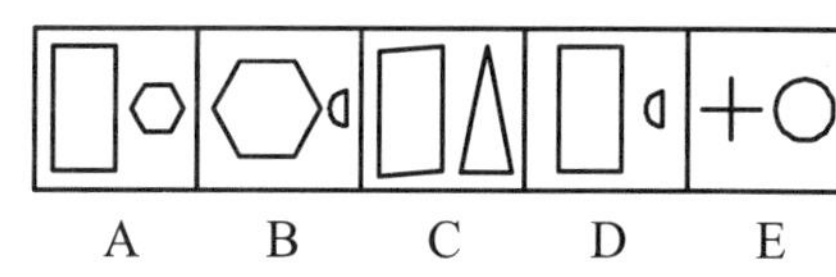

(i) (ii) (iii) (iv) A B C D E

In the above example, you will notice that each figure in the Problem Figures has two elements, a relatively larger element on the left hand side and a smaller element on the right-hand side. Also note that in each successive Problem Figure, the smaller element of the immediately preceding figure moves to the left and becomes larger and an altogether new element (fresh) takes the place of the smaller element. In the last Problem Figure, there is a large square on the left and a rectangle on the right. If the same relationship, as explained above, is extended, the fifth figure should have a larger rectangle on the left and a smaller new figure which so far has not appeared in any of the Problem Figures on the right. You will notice that only Answer Figures A and D have larger rectangles on the left and smaller figures on the right side. Of these, Answer Figure A is the correct answer because the other element in the figure is a small hexagon and has not appeared in any of the Problem Figures. Answer Figure D also cannot be the right answer because from the Problem Figures, it is clear that the element on the right should not have been a half circle which has appeared once. In Answer Figures B & E, the larger element on the left hand side is not a rectangle as it should have been if the sequence is continued. Answer figure C cannot be correct, because both the figures are almost equal.

**Rearrangement**

**PROBLEM FIGURES** **ANSWER FIGURES**

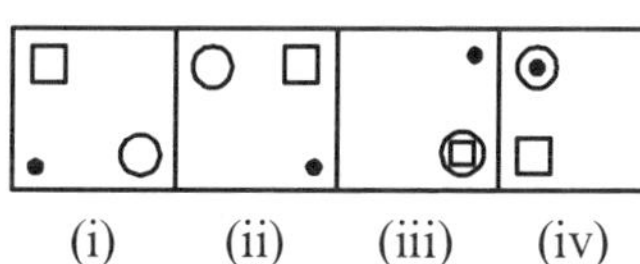

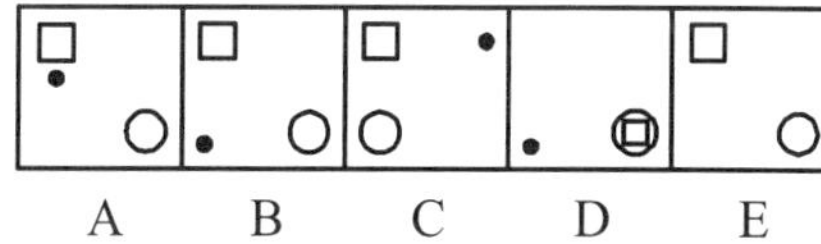

(i) (ii) (iii) (iv) A B C D E

Each of the Problem Figures of the above question has three elements - a dot, a square and a circle. In each successive figure, these three elements change their positions. The circle's position is shifted diagonally from lower right hand corner to top left hand corner. The "dot" is moved from one corner to other corner. The "dot" is moved from one corner to the next in an anti-clockwise direction and the "square" moves from one corner to the other in a clockwise direction. So, in the fifth figure the circle should be at the bottom right corner, the dot in the bottom left hand corner and the square in the top left hand corner. The elements are in the correct positions in Answer Figure B. So "B" is the answer. Note that in Answer Figure "A" the positions of "circle" and the "square" is correct but the position of the "dot" is wrong. It has not moved to the bottom towards left hand corner. In Answer Figure "D", the position of the "dot" and "circle" are correct but the "square" instead of moving in the clockwise direction, has moved in the anticlockwise direction. Answer Figure "E" has only two elements instead of three. The positions of the "circle" and the "dot" in Answer Figure C are wrong.

**Addition**

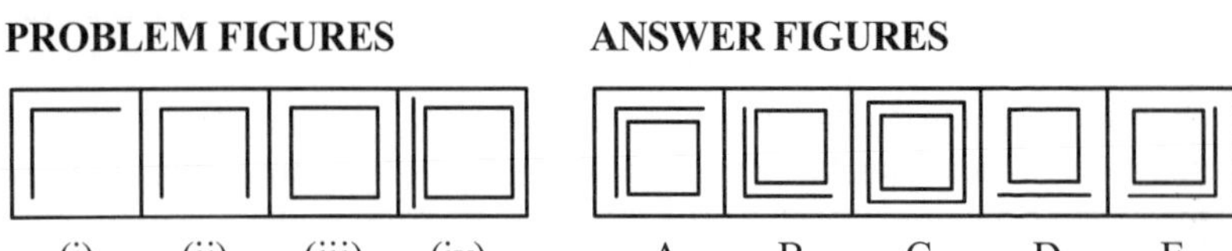


(i) (ii) (iii) (iv) A B C D E

In the above question, you will notice that a line is added in each successive Problem Figure. Also notice that the addition is in the clockwise direction and that none of the lines are joined together. In the 4th Problem Figure, you see that a second line is added, drawn parallel to the line on the left-hand side. So, following the logic of addition of a line in the clock-wise direction, the next line should be drawn parallel to the line on the top. From among the answer figures, it can be seen that "A" is the right answer. Addition takes place in the clock-wise direction.

**Subtraction**

**PROBLEM FIGURES** **ANSWER FIGURES**

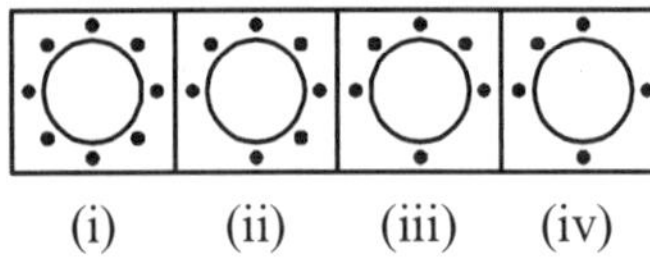

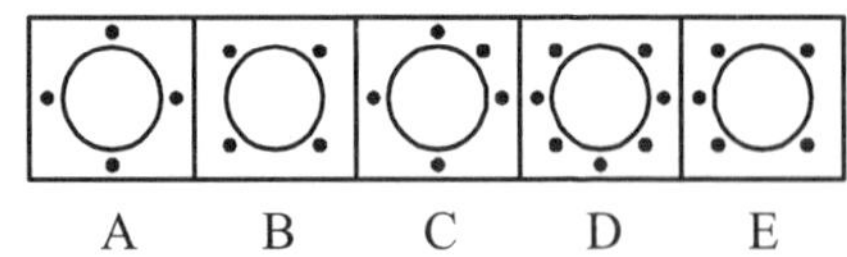

(i) (ii) (iii) (iv) A B C D E

In this type of items, you will find that some element is removed in each successive Problem Figure. In the question given above, the first square has a circle and 8 dots around it. In the next, one dot is missing and in each successive square one additional dot is removed. Now look at the five "Answer Figures". In the correct Answer Figure, there should be four dots. Such figures are only Answer Figures No. A and B. Answer Figures C, D & E cannot be the correct answer because there are more than 4 dots. There are 8 dots in the first Problem Figure of which, one is in the North, one in the East, one in the South, one in the West and one each lies in between the four directions. In the Problem Figures, you will notice that the dots at the North, East, South and West remain intact and only the dots in-between are removed. In the fourth Problem Figure, only one of the dots lies in-between, *i.e.* the dot lies in-between the West and the North. It easily follows that this dot has to be removed. After this dot is removed, the resulting figure will be like the one in Answer Figure "A". So the answer is (A).

**Change in element**

**PROBLEM FIGURES** **ANSWER FIGURES**

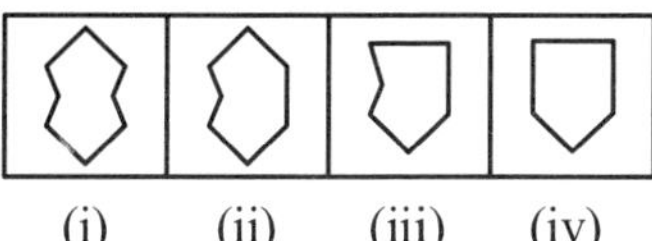

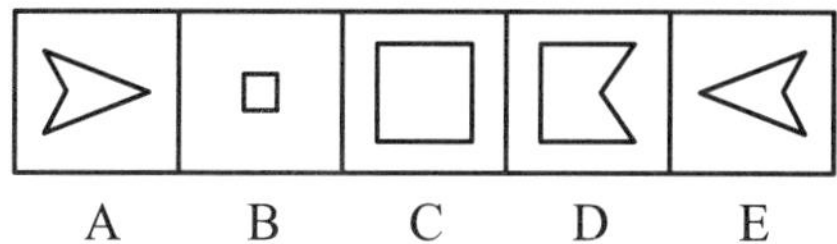

(i) (ii) (iii) (iv) A B C D E

You will notice that in each successive Problem Figures in the question above, two lines straighten up to form a single long straight line. You will also notice that this happens to every two successive short lines in the anti - clockwise direction. When the two remaining short lines in Problem Figure D are straightened, the resulting figure will have an element with four sides. Also note that it should have sides of equal length. Note that Answer Figures A and E have an element with four sides, but the sides are of different lengths. Answer Figure B is not the right choice also, because the square is smaller than the element emerging in each successive Problem Figure. Answer Figure D is wrong because the element has five sides, Hence, Answer Figure "C" is the right answer.

**Combination**

In these questions, figures will be presented in two units. The first unit contains two figures: a black circle and 3 empty circles; and the second unit contains one black square in one figure and a question mark in the other. You have to find out which one of the Answer Figure should be in place of the question mark. You can answer these questions only after you have found out the relation between the two figures in unit one of the Problem Figure. Now look at the example below.

**PROBLEM FIGURES** **ANSWER FIGURES**

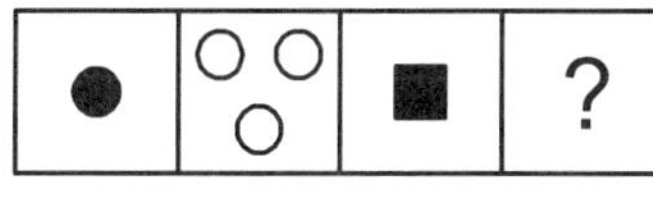


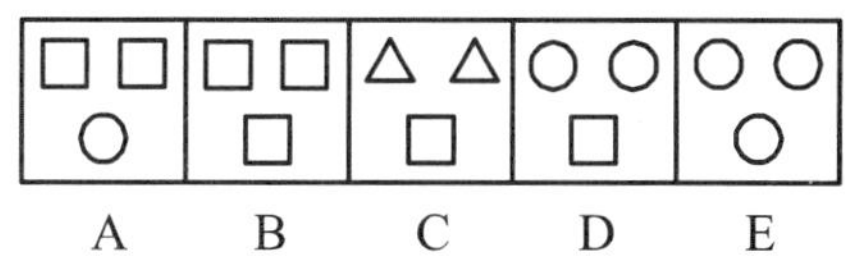

A B C D E

In the first unit, the first square has a darkened circle and the second square has three undarkened circles. The second unit should have a similar combination. So the darkened square should be followed by three undarkened squares, two at the top and one at the bottom. These conditions are satisfied only in Figure B of the Answer Figures. So the answer is B. Note that Answer Figure "A" cannot be the answer because the bottom figure is a circle. Similarly, Figure E has no squares. Answer figure "C" is not a correct answer fig "D" is also wrong because it has circle.

## ANALOGY

Analogy refers to correspondence or similarity in relationship. When a figure exhibits some kind of relationship with another figure on some basis then the two figures are said to be analogous to each other.

Figures are related in some or other ways. Some of them are as follows:

- Based on shape
- Based on orientation of figure
- Based on number of elements
- Based on mirror image
- Based on water image
- Rotation of figure
- Movement of figure
- Replacement of positions of element

In the questions based on analogy, two sets of figures, namely problem figures and answer figures are given. The set of problem figures consists of two parts.

The first part comprises two figures which have some relationship between them on the basis of a certain rule.

The second part comprises of one figure and a sign of '?'. You are asked to select one figure from the set of answer figures to replace '?' but maintaining similar relationship as depicted between the first two figures.

### As for Example

**Directions (Q. No. 1-2):** *The second figure in the first part of the problem figures bears certain relationship to the first figure. Similarly, one of the figures of answer figures bears the same relationship to the first figure of the second part. You have to select a figure from the set of answer figures which would replace the questions mark (?).*

**1.** **Problem Figures** **Answer Figures**

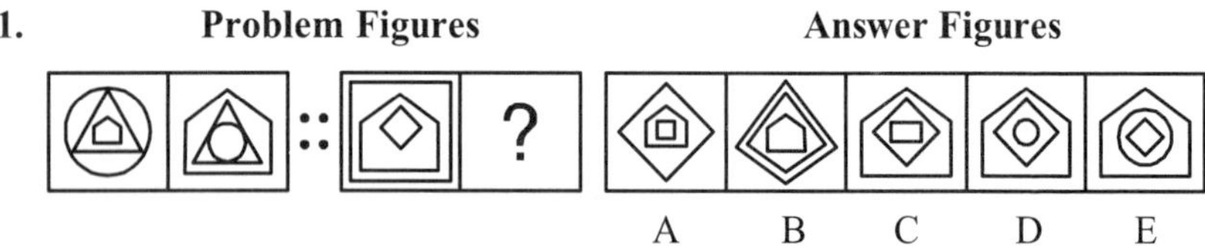


**Answer A.** From problem figure the innermost figure becomes outermost figure and outermost figure becomes the innermost figure, *i.e.*, the first and the third figures are interchanged.

**2.** **Problem Figures** **Answer Figures**

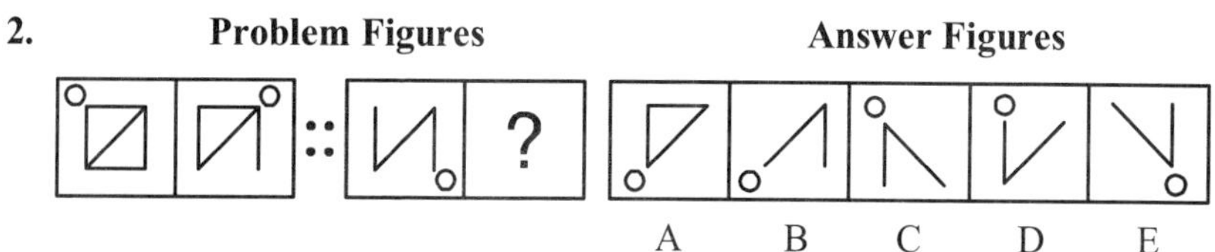

A B C D E

**Answer B.** The symbol 'O' is moving from one corner to another in clockwise direction 90° in each step and one line is removed in each step.

## CLASSIFICATION

Classification is the act or process of putting people or things into a group or a class. In this chapter, we deal with problems of **odd man-out type**.

This test is designed to judge candidates ability to classify or segregate a group of objects, from the given objects, on the basis of their common properties i.e., it is a process of marking out a homogeneous group from a heterogeneous larger group. In this type of questions you will be asked to find out a figure which is different in nature/character from the main group.

In this chapter, we deal with questions which have a set of four/five figures, out of which all except one are alike or have some common nature/characteristics. You will have to select the exclusively different figure from the given set. Here, some examples are given which will illustrate the different types of questions which are generally asked in various competitive examinations.

### As for Example

**Directions (Qs. 1-3):** *Out of these five set of given figures, four are similar in a certain way. One figure is not like the other four/three. Find out the figure which does not belong to the group.*

**1.**

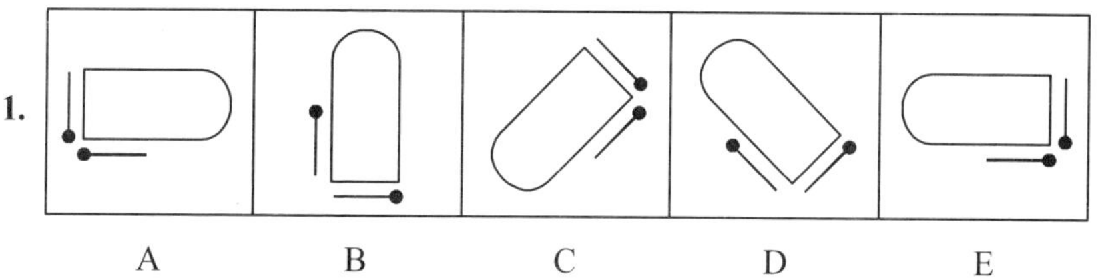

A B C D E

**Answers A:** All the figures are placed straight with base down, then one of the pins lies along base and the other pin lies along left side of the figure. Figure A does not follow this rule and hence, is different from others.

2.

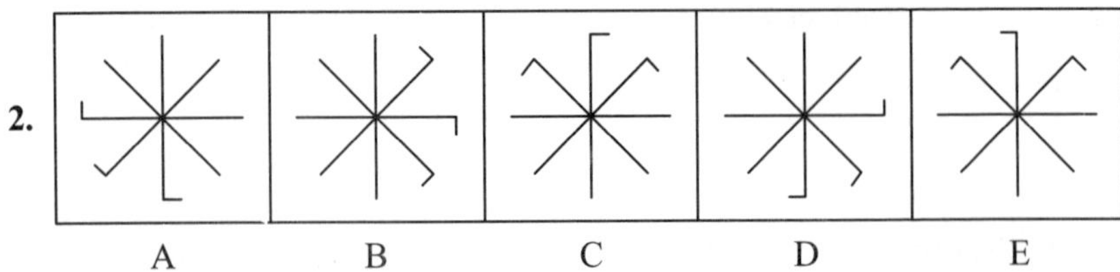


**Answers E:** In all the other figures, the two bent line segments faces clockwise direction and single bent line faces in anti-clockwise direction. In figure E, the case is just the opposite.

3.

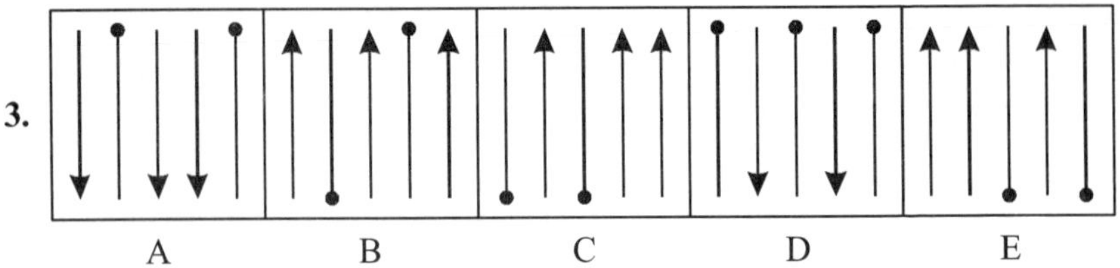


**Answers D:** In all the figures except figure (D), there are two pins and three arrows. In figure (D), there are three pins and two arrows; thus it is different from the others.

## CONSTRUCTION OF BOXES

Formation of figure is using the fragmented part to construct a desired figure. Formation of figure requires a high spatial visualisation skill. As different fragmented parts of a figure are to be combined to form the desired figure.

### As for Example

In this chapter, the two sets of figures are provided, namely **problem figure** and **answer figures**. A candidate is asked to arrange the different components of the problem figure, so as to form one of the answer figure.

Examples given below will give a better idea about the types of questions.

1. Which of the following figures shown below, when folded along the dotted lines, will form a pyramid-shaped box with a rectangular base?

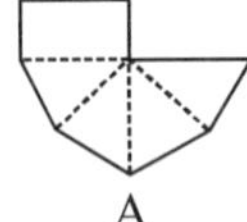
A

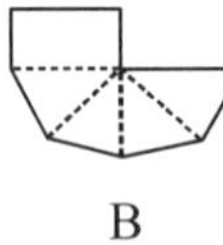
B

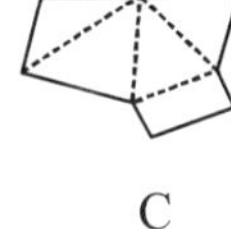
C

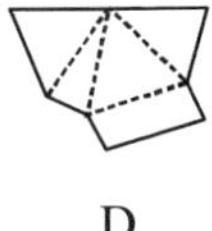
D

**Answers D:** By folding figure D, we get a pyramid-shaped box with a rectangular base as shown below.

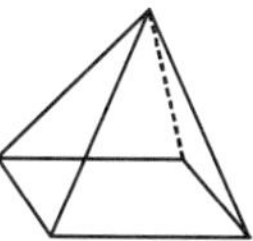

**2.** In the question given below, find out which of the figures can be formed from the pieces given in the problem figure.

**Problem Figure** **Answer Figures**

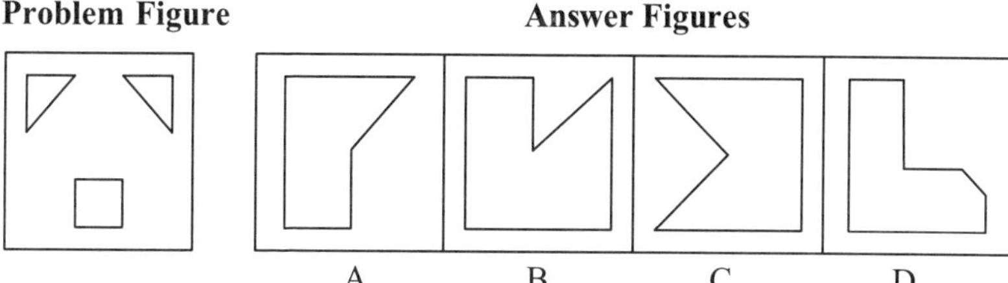


**Answers A:** Using all the components given in the problem figure, we can arrange them as:

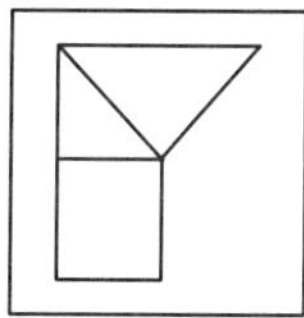

So Option A is the correct answer.

## PAPER FOLDING & CUTTING

### PAPER FOLDING

In these problems, a transparent sheet with designs on either side of a dotted line on it, is provided. The sheet is then folded along the dotted line. You are required to choose a figure which would most closely resemble the pattern when the sheet is folded.

A sample problem is given below:

**Directions:** *In each of the following examples, find from amongst the four response figures the one which resembles the pattern formed when the transparent sheet carrying a design, is folded along the dotted line.*

**1. Transparent sheet** **Response Figures**

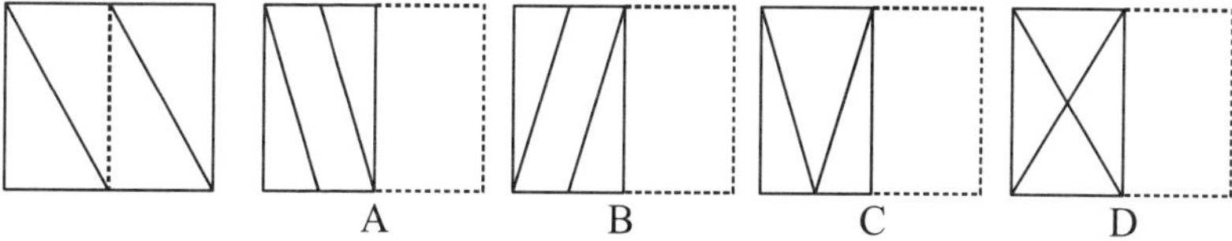

## Suggested Method

Do you remember the method of drawing symmetrical? If the sheet is folded along the dotted line, the symmetrical counterpart of the design in the folded half would emerge on the other half. Therefore, the simple strategy for solving paper-folding problems would be:

(*i*) Draw the reflection of the design in that half which is to be folded, on the other half, assuming a mirror to be kept along the dotted line.

(*ii*) The reflection of the design of the other half and the original design would overlap on the new folded half. This new design, resulting from the overlapping, would be the answer figure.

See the following example to understand the method.

**Answers:** The original design is:

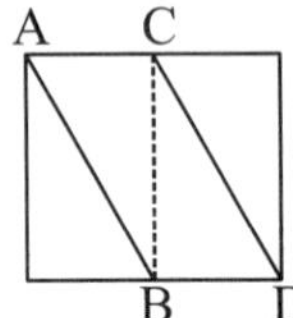


It is folded to the left. Now, what is the image of the design in the folded half, assuming a mirror at the dotted line? In other words, what would be the image in place of the question mark in the figure shown below?

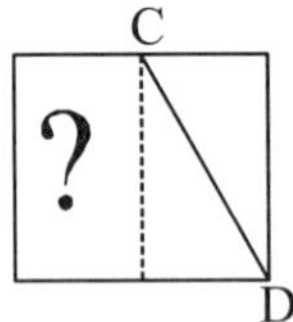


Obviously the image would be along the line CD' as shown:

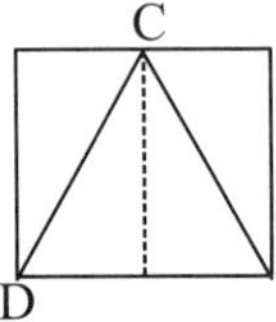


Now, in the answer figure the original design of the unfolded half, i.e. AB, and the reflected design CD' would overlap. Hence, the anwer figure would be:

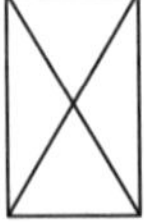

Hence correct answer: (D).

## PAPER CUTTING

In this type of questions, a paper is folded twice (or may be more) and then a cut (or some cuts) is/are made on it. You have to imagine what the paper would look like when it is unfolded back to what it originally was. Usually a set of three figures is given to show the manner in which the paper is folded and the paper is cut. In the first two figures a dotted line together with an arrow on it is given, showing the position and direction of folding. In the third figure, there are marks showing the position and nature of the cut made in the folded sheet. The examinee has to select one of the figures from the set of four answer figures — A, B, C and D that would most closely resemble to the paper when unfolded.

A sample problem is being given below:

Consider the following three figures, marked X, Y, Z, showing one fold in X, another fold in Y and cut in Z. From amongst the answer figures A, B, C and D, select the one showing the unfolded position of Z.

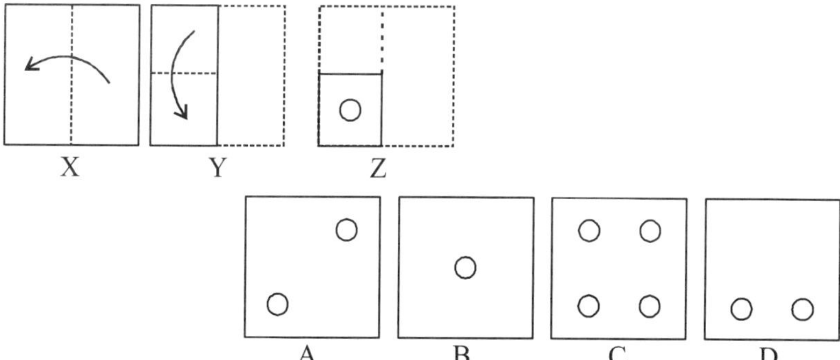


## Explanation

**Backtracking:** The best, easiest and yet the quickest methods to solve the problems would be to use the method of backtracking with the concept of symmetry and reflection. The underlying concept is that when a fold is made on a paper and then a cut is made on the folded half, then the cut would appear on either sides of the half (when the paper is unfolded) and the two cuts would be symmetrically placed about the line of fold. This is explained by the following sequence of diagrams:

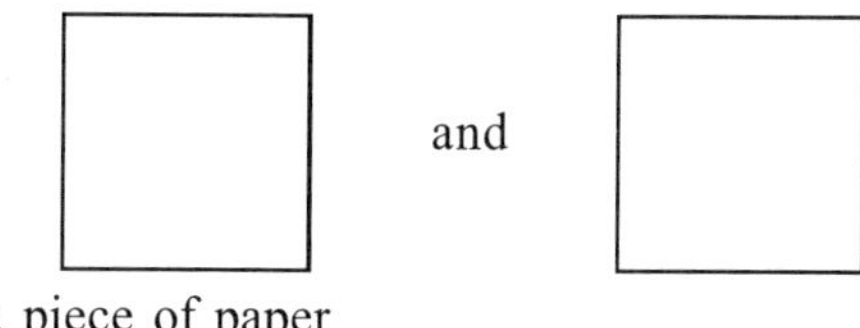


A piece of paper

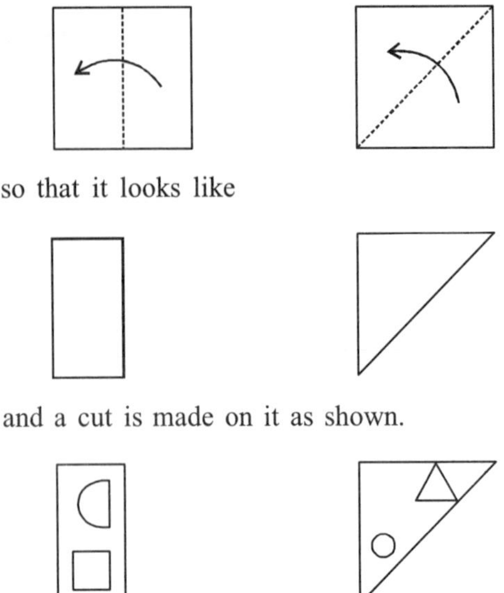

so that it looks like

and a cut is made on it as shown.

then, if the paper is unfolded, a reflection of the two cuts appear on the other half, as if a mirror was placed on the line of fold:

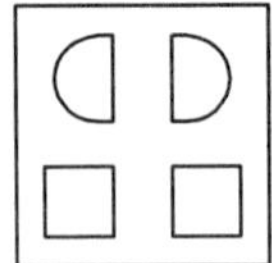

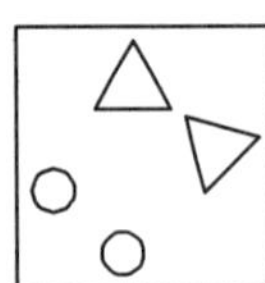

Now, you have understood how the concept of symmetry and reflection works in paper cutting, we are presenting the method of backtracking to solve such problems. Backtracking means going backwards, starting with the last figure and tracing the way back. The steps would be:

I. Start with the last fold. Draw the reflection of the cut on the other side of the line of fold. Hence, draw the diagram of the paper when it is unfolded on the last fold.

II. Now, go to the previous fold. Again draw the reflection of the cuts on the other side of the fold. Repeat this process till the entire paper is unfolded. Since in the usual questions the paper is folded only twice, hence you need to unfold the paper only twice.

We now present some solved examples in order to make you understand the method.

Solution: The cut is = 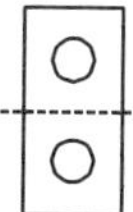

The last fold is =

We draw the reflection of the cut on the other side of the line of fold, we get:

Now, the previous fold is = 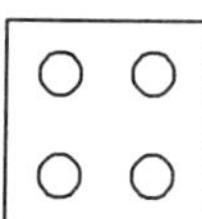

We draw the reflection of the cuts on the other side of the line of fold, we get:

Hence, correct answer (C).

## FIGURES GROUPING & FIGURES MATRIX

Figure matrix is a 2 × 2 as 3 × 3 representation of figures following a certain pattern in the matrix form.

In this chapter, we deal with questions which have either 2 × 2 or 3 × 3 matrix. These matrix are formed by a group of figures. Corresponding rows or corresponding columns follow a certain pattern. You are required to analyse each of the sets to find out the common pattern and on the basis of that, the missing figure is to be identified from a set of alternatives, so as to complete the matrix.

### As for Example

**Directions:** *In the following questions, find out which of the answer figures (A), (B), (C) and (D) completes the figure matrix?*

**Problem Figure** **Answer Figures**

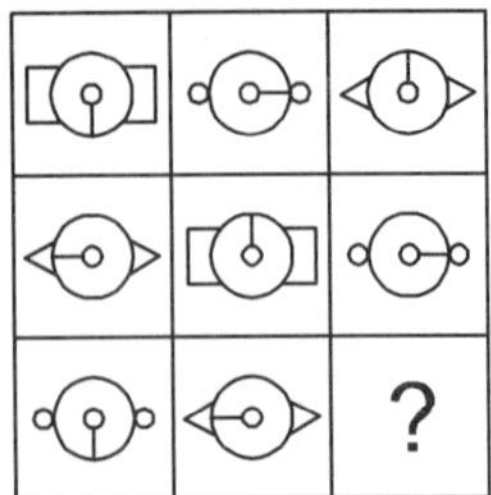

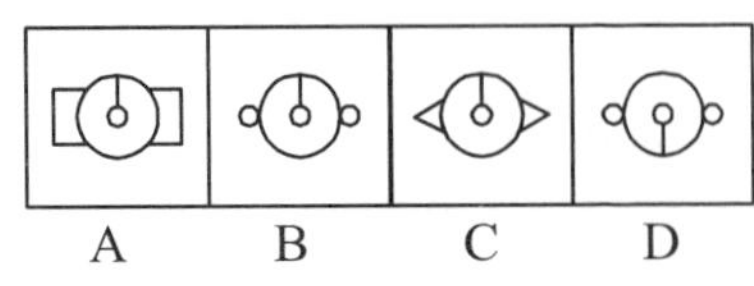

A B C D

**Answers A:** In each row, the central part of the first figure rotates 90° anti-clockwise to form the central part of the second figure and the central part of the first figure rotates 180° to form the central parts of the third figure. Also, in each row, there are three types of geometrical figures: rectangles, circles and triangles.

*When different figures are grouped on the basis of certain pattern, then this is called grouping of identical figures.*

In this chapter, we have a set of few figures which are numbered as 1, 2, 3, 4 and so on. We are required to analyse these figures and classify them into groups consisting of figures having more or less than the same properties. The best answer is to be selected from a given set of fairly close alternatives.

## FIGURE COMPLETION

In this type of questions an incomplete figure is given in which a part, generally a quarter, is left blank. The problem figure is followed by four choice figures. Out of these choice figures, the candidate is required to choose the one which best fits into the blank space so as to complete the original pattern.

A sample question is provided below:

You are given an incomplete figure (X) and four choice figures A, B, C and D. Out of these choice figures, choose the one which best fits into (X) to complete the original pattern.

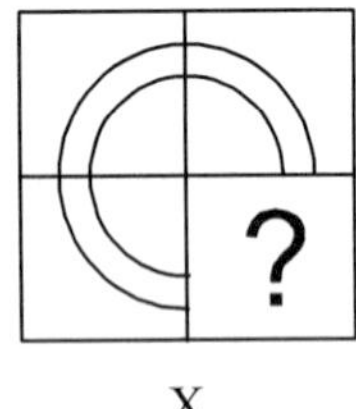

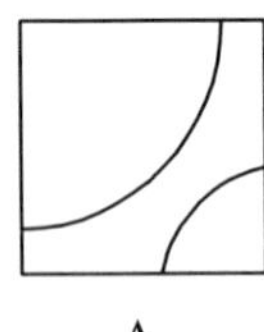

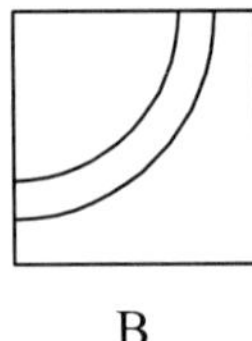

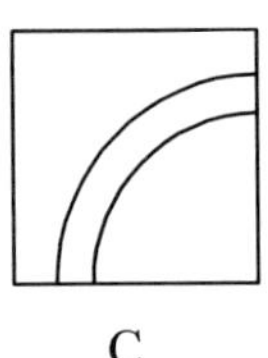

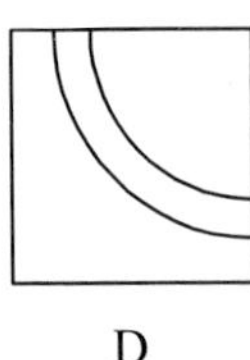

X A B C D

### Suggested Method

What is expected of you in such problems? The expectation is that you complete the pattern in such a way that the figure appears balanced and not haphazard. In other words, the figure should appear symmetrical. Obviously, then you should choose an answer choice that symmetrically fits into the empty box. The first thing that should be done for this is to recognise the axis of symmetry. You should find out the line about which the figure would be symmetrical, if completed. This is not a difficult job and a cursory glance at the figure would be sufficient for you to detect the axis of symmetry. Once you have found out the axis of symmetry, you can draw the image of the figures on one side of the axis by taking this axis as a mirror to find out the pattern of the other side.

However, many problems are so easy that it is totally unnecessary to go in for axis of symmetry and image-reflections. Only a simple inspection could do the job.

The following examples would illustrate the point:

**Answers :** It is obvious by mere inspection that (B) is the correct answer. It is the only choice that completes the two circles, when put in place of the question-mark.

Select a figure from the four alternatives which when placed in the blank space of fig (X) would complete the pattern.

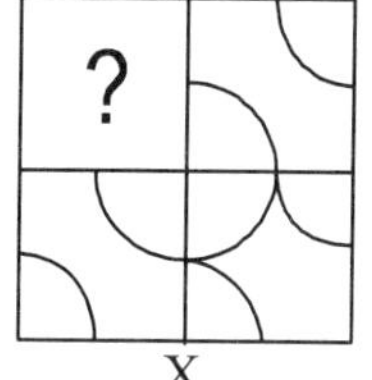


X

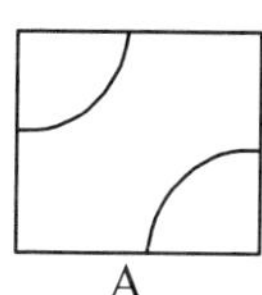

A

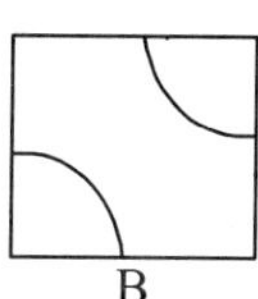

B

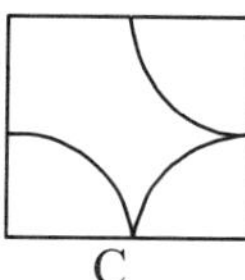

C

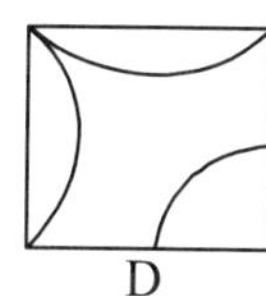

D

**Answers :** Clearly, fig (C) will complete the pattern when placed in the blank space of fig (X), as shown below:

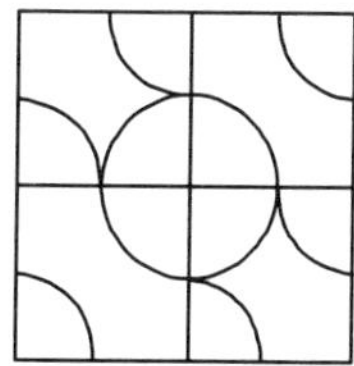

## EMBEDDED (HIDDEN) FIGURE

A figure is said to be an embedded figure when that figure is contained by another figure.

A figure suppose figure (A) is said to be embedded in figure (B), if figure (B) contains a part of figure (A). In this chapter, we deal with questions in which an original figure is followed by four alternative answers. One of the answer figures, is embedded or hidden in the original figure. You are required to select from the alternative that which figure clearly shows the embedded portion of the original figure.

### As for Example

**Directions:** *In the following questions, figure X is embedded in any one of the four alternative figures A, B, C and D. Find he alternative which contains figure X as its part:*

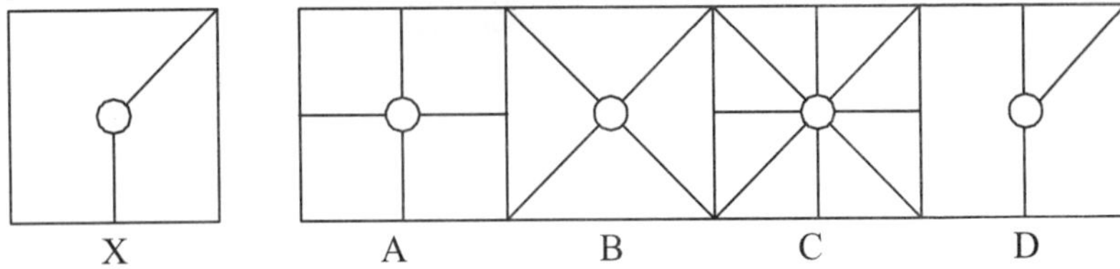


**Answers C:** On close observation, we find figure X is embedded in figure C as shown.

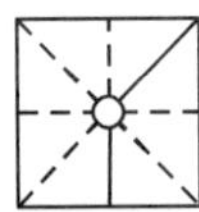

## COUNTING FIGURES

Counting of figure is simply the realisation of different geometrical figure from a complex one.

### As for Example

The questions asked on the counting of figures are designed to test the analytical deposition of candidates and check his ability to count different similar figures in a complex figure. The figures which are asked to count are straight lines, triangles, squares, rectangles etc.

*Examples given below will give a better idea about the type of question asked.*

**1.** How many triangles are there in the given figure?

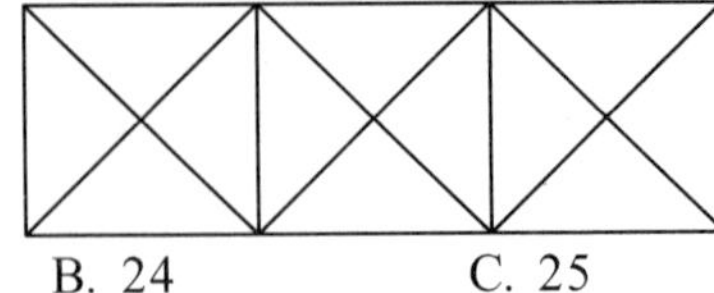

A. 28 B. 24 C. 25 D. 26

**Answers A:** Naming the figure clearly there are 28 triangles in the given figure, they are EOF, AOE, AOB, BOF, ABF, BEF, ABE, AEF, BPF, FPG, CPG, BPC, BFG, BCG, CFG, BCF, GQC, CDQ, DQH, GQH, GDC, GDH, GHC, CDH, AFC, BGD, EBG and FCH:

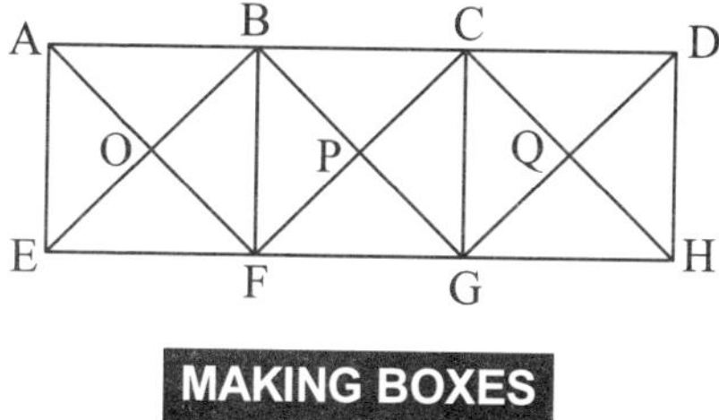


## MAKING BOXES

In this chapter, we deal with a template or a layout of a cube, dice or a box, which can be folded to produce different patterns. To solve these questions, we requires a clear study ot the given loyout and the selection of the figure alternative which can be made from the given layout.

### As for Example

1. Choose from the alternatives, the boxes that will be formed when figure (X) is folded:

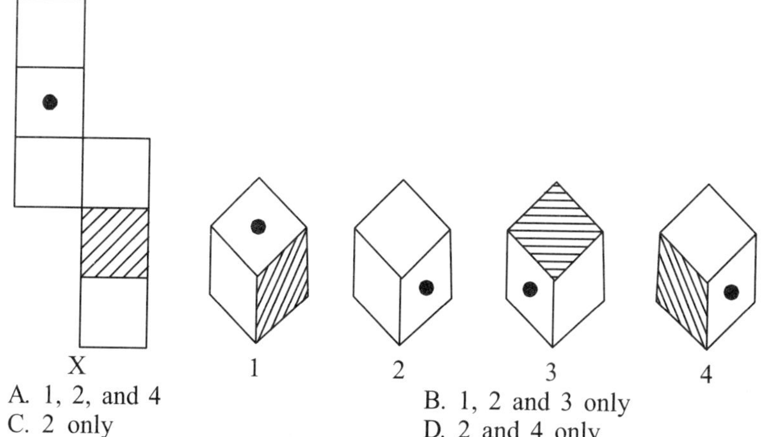


A. 1, 2, and 4
B. 1, 2 and 3 only
C. 2 only
D. 2 and 4 only

**Answers C:** By the rule of third, we infer that the plain square above the dotted square would come opposite the plain square below the dotted square. Similarly, by the rule of third, the other pair of plain squares will also be opposite each other. Hence, the only pair of squares remaining would be opposite each other *i.e.* the dotted square would come opposite the shaded square. Therefore, by the rule of not opposite, an answer choice should not have a dotted square and a shaded square together. But figures 1, 3 and 4 have them together. Therefore, only 2 is correct. Hence, answer choice would be (C).

## MIRROR AND WATER IMAGE

The image of a number or an object my be seen two ways.

(1) By mirror (2) In water by light

1. **Mirror Image:** When an object is placed before the mirror, the left part of the object is seen in the right and vice versa. In other words we may say that its left and right parts get mutually exchanged while its lower and upper parts remain unchanged.

### As for Example

Letter → A → A, B → ᗺ

Digits → 1 → I , 5 → Ƨ

Figure → →

When a mirror is placed at the lower part or the upper part of an object, then in the image position, the object is reversed.

### As for Example

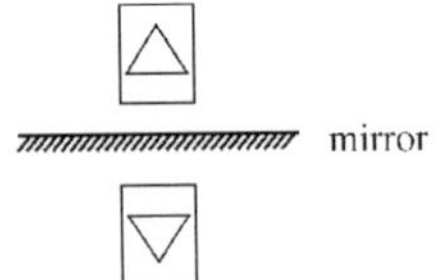


2. **Water Image:** When the image of an object is seen in water in presence of light the upper part and lower part are mutually exchanged while its left and right parts remain unchanged.

### As for Example

| | **Object** | | **Water image** |
|---|---|---|---|
| (1) | SIMULATOR | → | ƧIWՈΓ∀⊥Oᴚ |
| (2) | D6Z7F4 | → | DϱZ⅂Ⅎ4 |
| (3) | SNACK | → | ƧИ∀CK |
| (4) | | → | |

## IDENTICAL COMPONENTS & COMMON PROPERTIES

In this form of reasoning the two given figures share common characteristic features or the problem figure consists of the elements given in one of the answer figures.

This form of reasoning is fairly simple. All one is required to do is to match the components of the key figure or the given figures with the components of the alternative figures. Only one alternative figure will contain the components identical to the given figure. In short, it is a kind of tally work and fairly easy too.

### As for Example

1. Find the figure which has the same common features as the two problem figures:

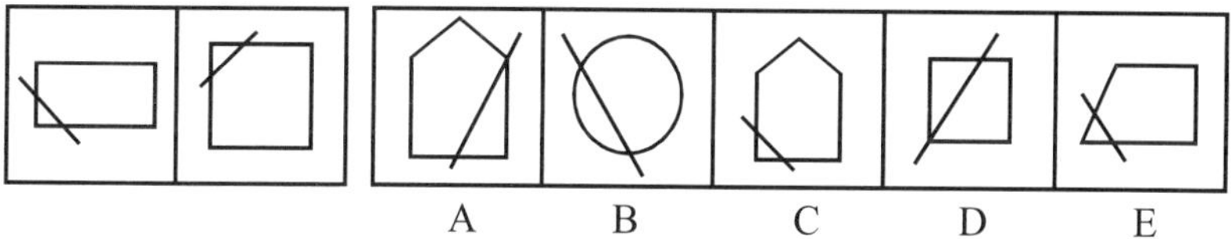


**Answer E :** Each figure is a quadrant and the line segment cuts through its two adjacent sides. Based on this common feature shared by the two problem figures, it is clear that option E is the right answer.

## POINT POSITION

These problems involve the search of similar conditions in the given alternative figures as indicated in the problem figures which contain dots placed in the spaces enclosed between the combinations of geometrical figures. By selecting one of these dots, the region in which this dot is enclosed can be observed, *i.e.* to which of the four figures is this region common. Then one has to look for such a region in the four alternatives. Once this is found, the procedure for other dots, if any, is repeated. The alternative figure which contains all such regions is the right choice for the answer.

### For Example

1. In the given figure there is one diagram marked 'X' with one dot. There are four other figures of which only one satisfies the condition of placement as in 'X'. Find that one.

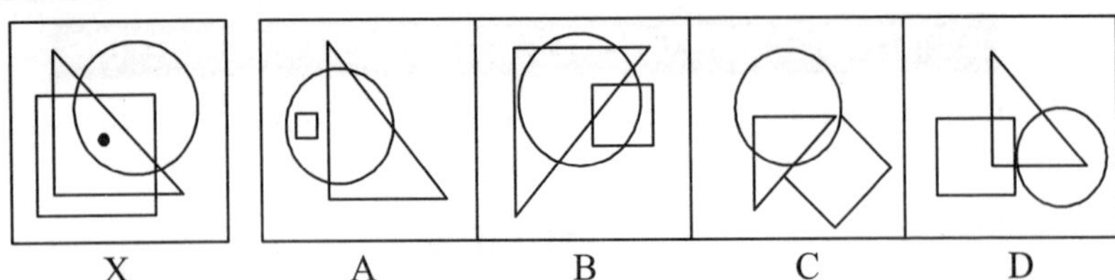


**Answers B:** In figure X, the dot is contained in a region common to all the three figures. Only in figure 'B' such a region is present.

## CUBES AND DICE

These types of questions deal with multi-dimensional figures and problems based on two or three views of the blocks. Such questions are aimed at assessing how well you can analyse the structure of the cubes. In case of questions related to dice, you may be given two or three views of the same dice keeping one face as blank. You are to analyse which number should come in the blank face.

### As for Example

1. Which number is on the face opposite 6?

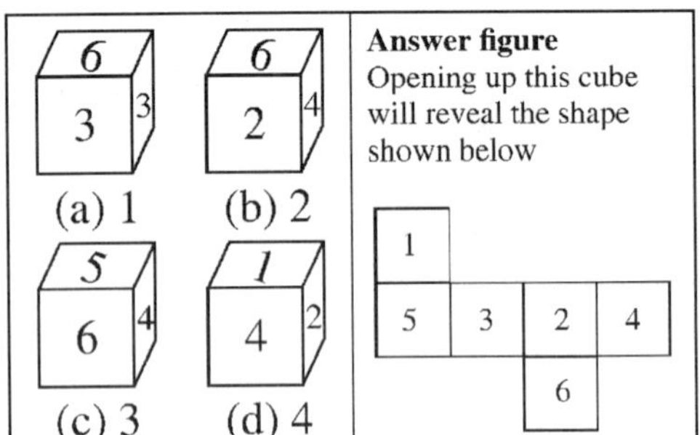


Answer: Fig. (a)

2. How many cubes are stacked in each of the figure below?

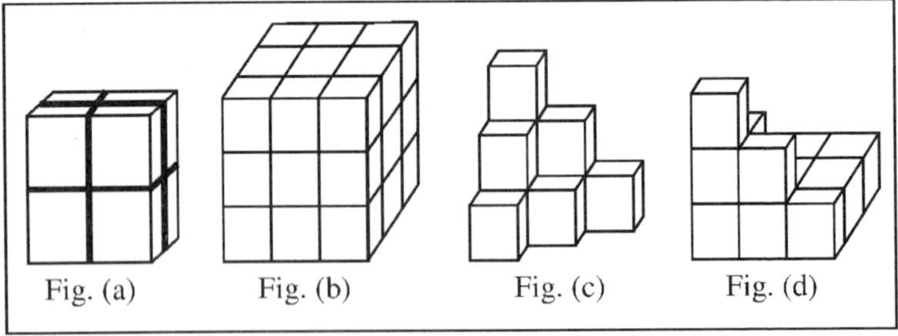


Answer: Fig. (a) 8 cubes; (b) 27 cubes; Fig. (c) 10 cubes; Fig. (d) 13 cubes.

❍ ❍ ❍

# Series

## TYPE I

In this form of non-verbal series, which are the most common, four or five consecutive problem figures form a definite sequence and one is required to select the one figure from the given set of Answer Figures that will continue the same sequence.

One has to try different set of moves, changes, replacements, rotations, repetitions and many more variations to arrive at the logical pattern making the series. Practising alone will sharpen one's skill of solving such sequences.

## EXERCISE

**Problem Figures** **Answer Figures**

1\.

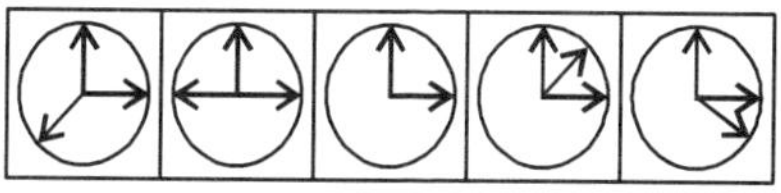

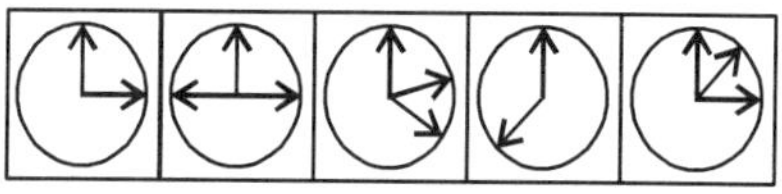

A B C D E

2\.

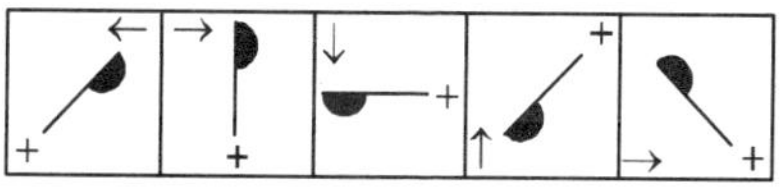

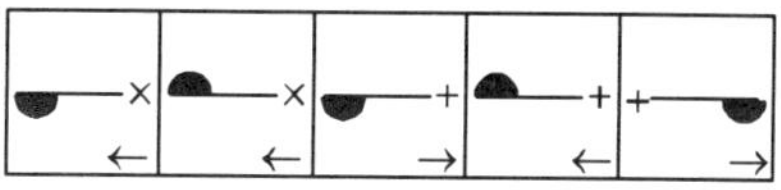

A B C D E

3\.

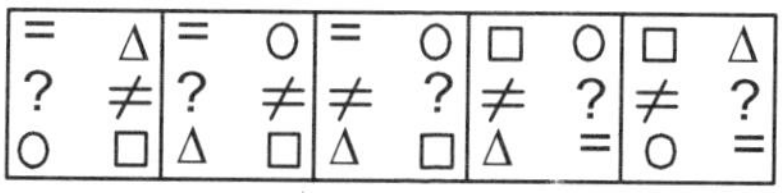

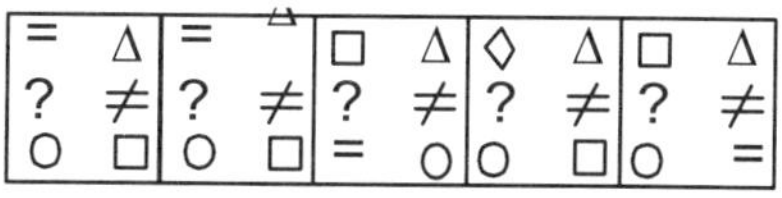

A B C D E

4\.

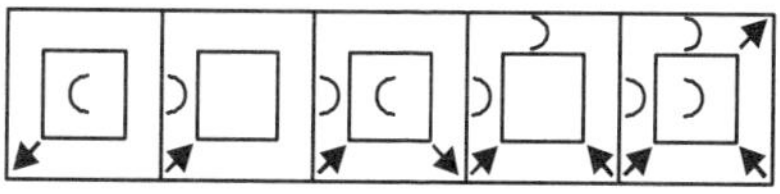

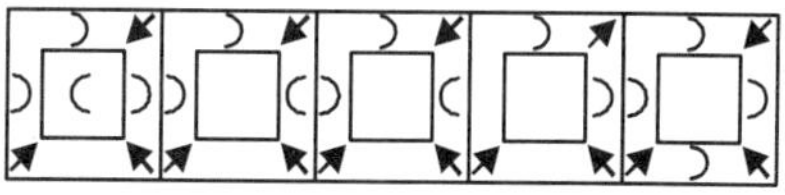

A B C D E

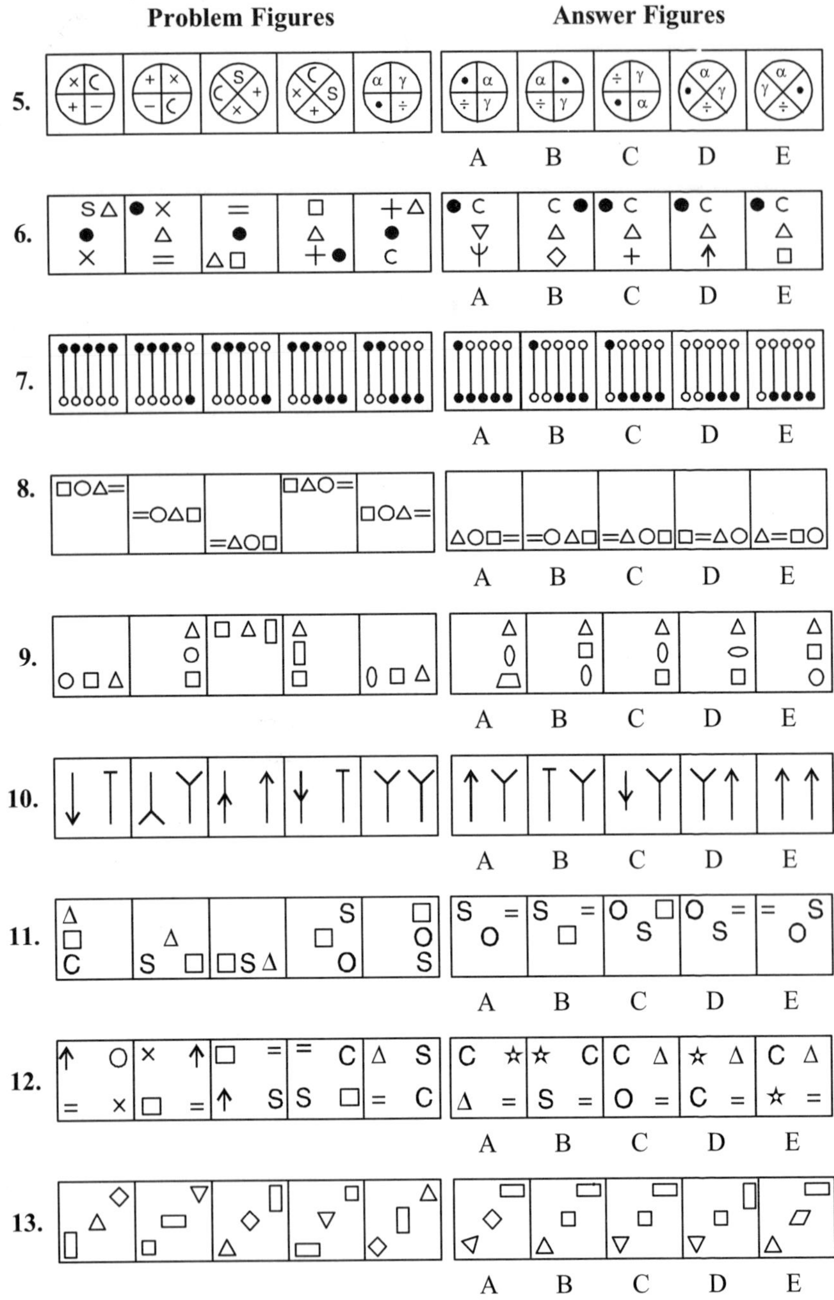
Problem Figures
Answer Figures
5.
6.
7.
8.
9.
10.
11.
12.
13.
A B C D E

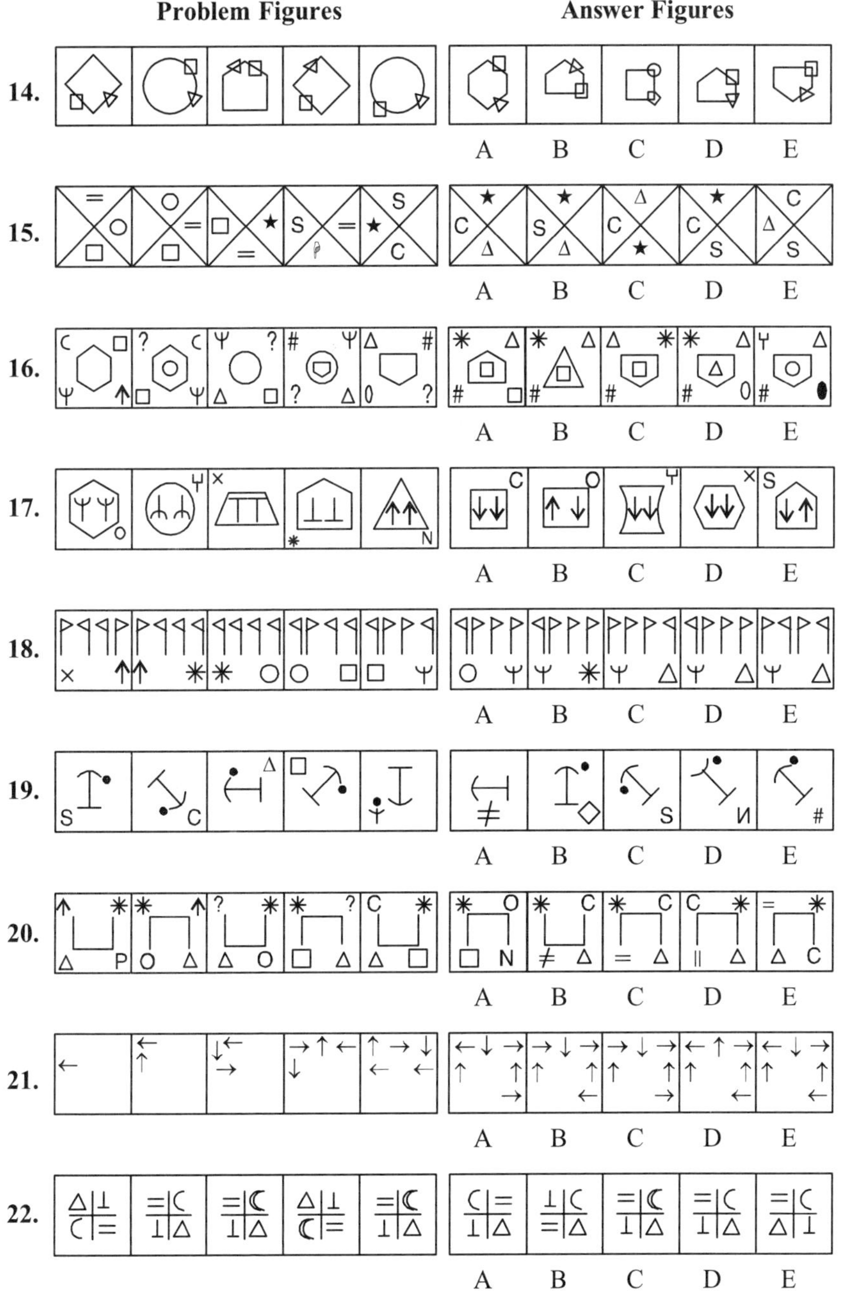
Problem Figures
Answer Figures
14.
15.
16.
17.
18.
19.
20.
21.
22.
A B C D E

**Problem Figures** **Answer Figures**

23. 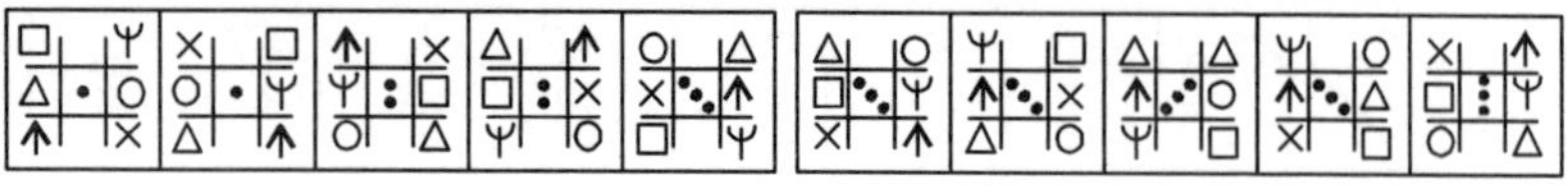 A B C D E

24. 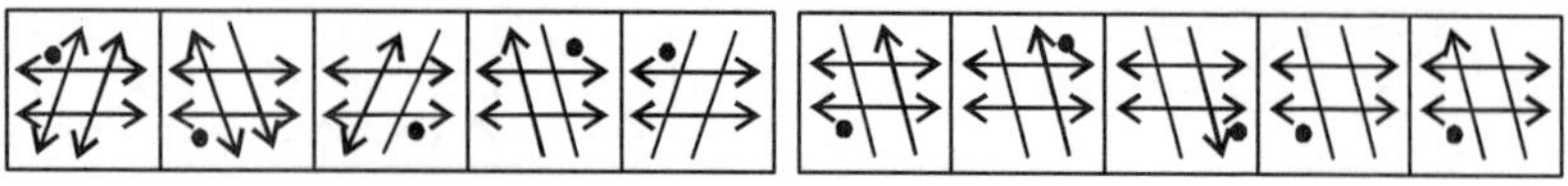 A B C D E

25. 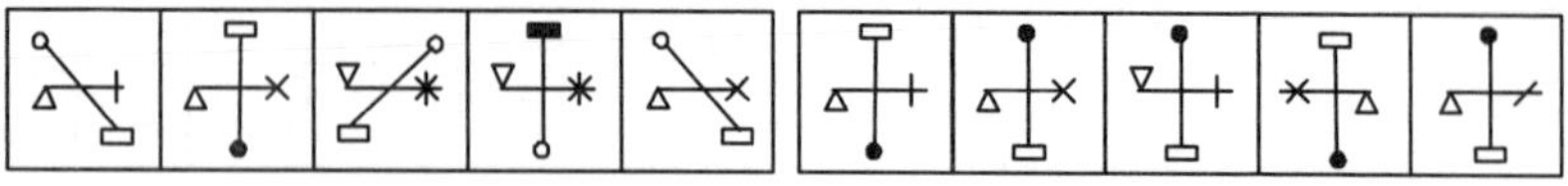 A B C D E

26. 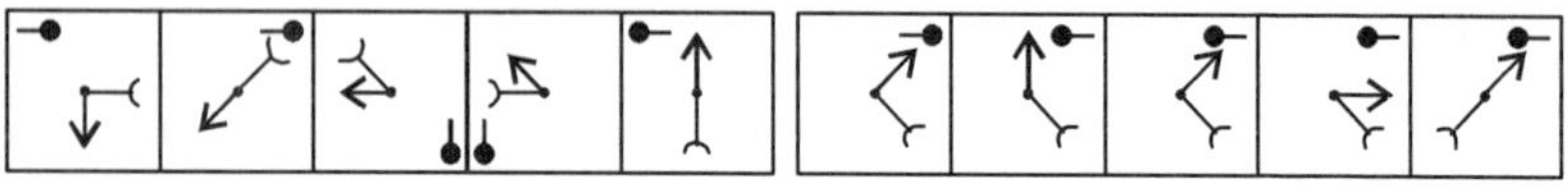 A B C D E

27. 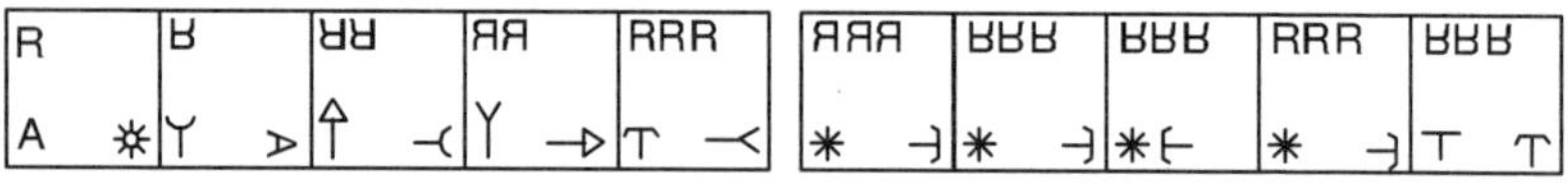 A B C D E

28. 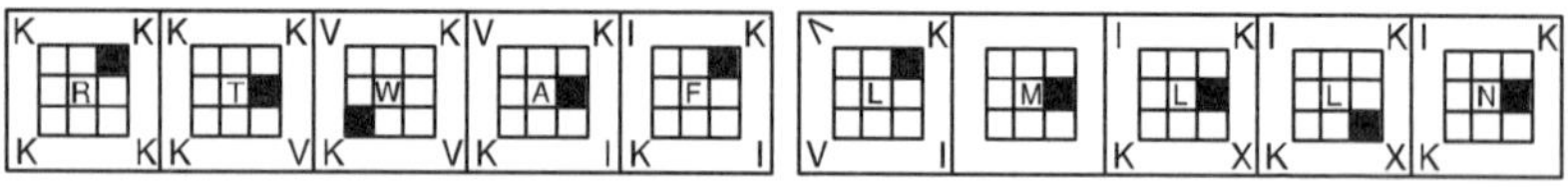 A B C D E

29. 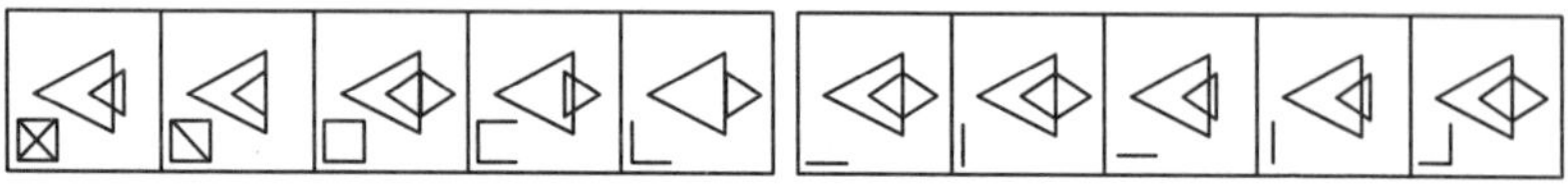 A B C D E

30. 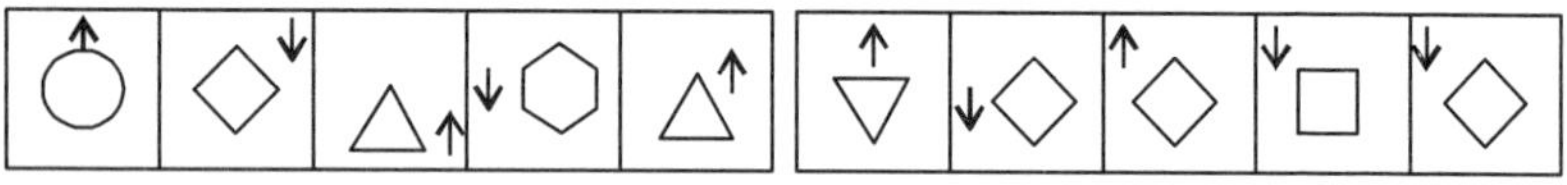 A B C D E

31. 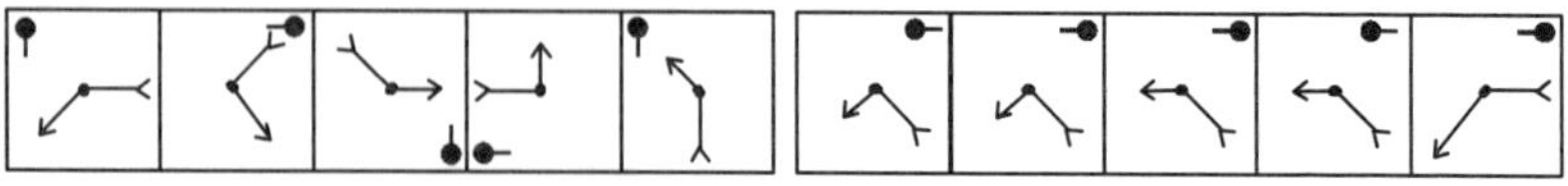 A B C D E

**Problem Figures** **Answer Figures**

32.

A B C D E

33.

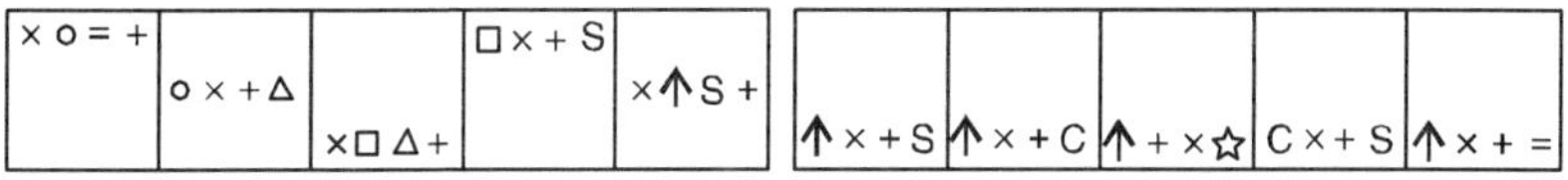

| × o = + | o × + Δ | × □ Δ + | □ × + S | × ↑ S + |
|---|---|---|---|---|

| ↑ × + S | ↑ × + C | ↑ + × ☆ | C × + S | ↑ × + = |
|---|---|---|---|---|
| A | B | C | D | E |

34.

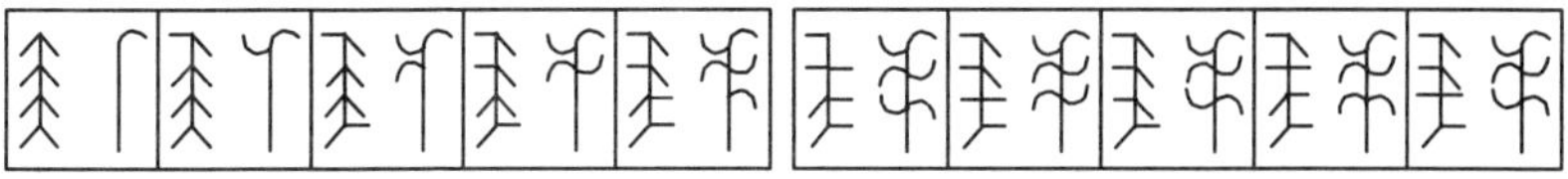

A B C D E

35.

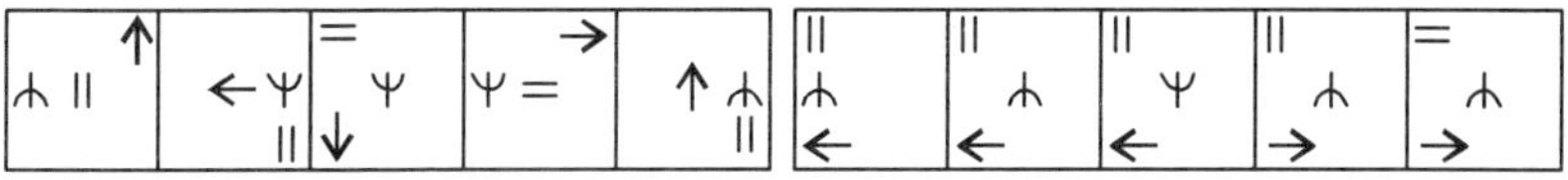

A B C D E

36.

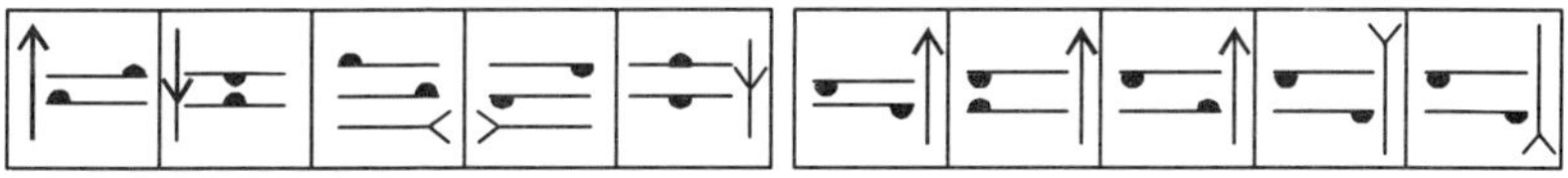

A B C D E

37.

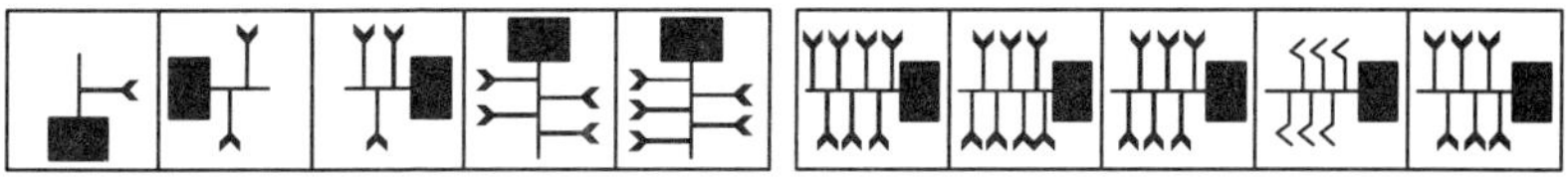

A B C D E

38.

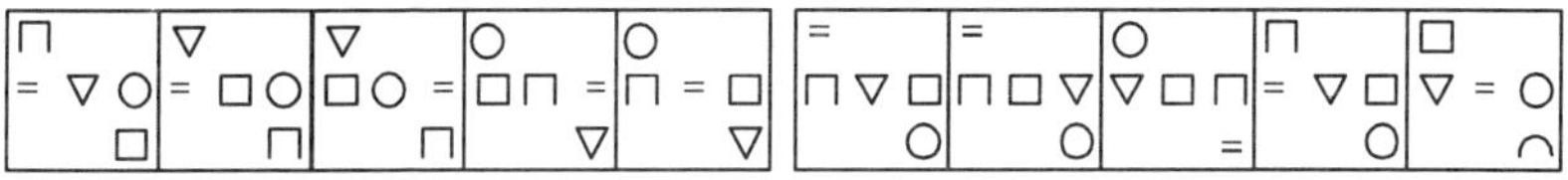

A B C D E

39.

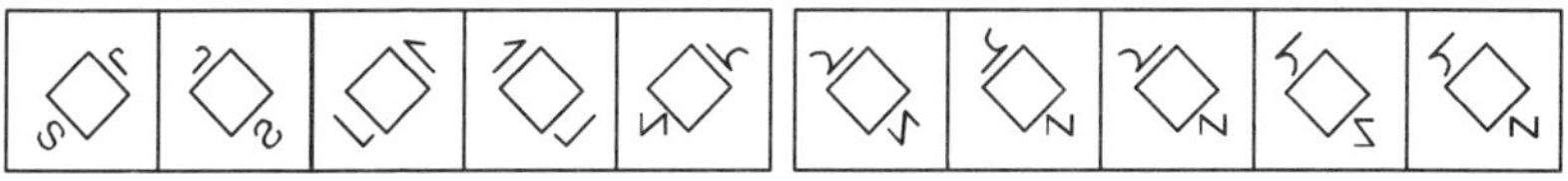

A B C D E

40.

A B C D E

**Problem Figures** **Answer Figures**

41.

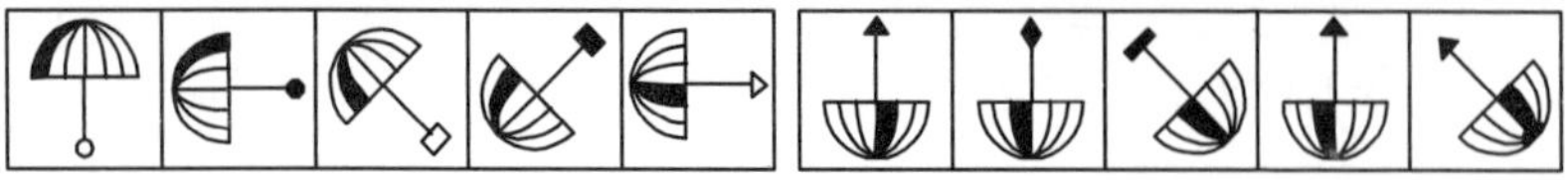

A B C D E

42.

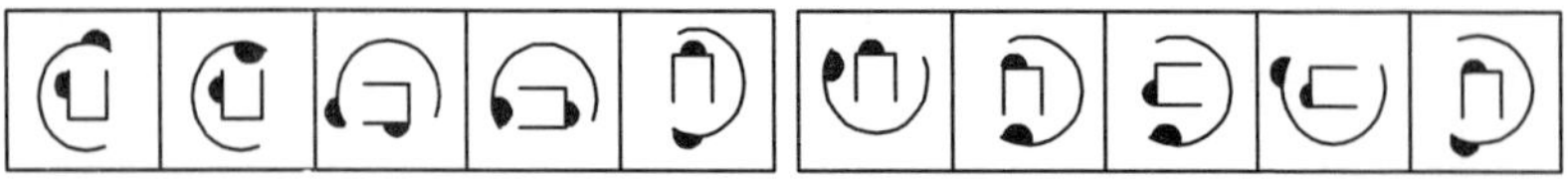

A B C D E

43.

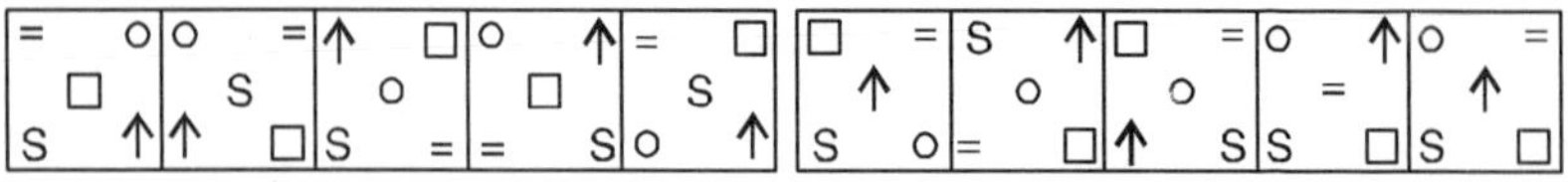

| = O | O = | ↑ □ | O ↑ | = □ |
|---|---|---|---|---|
| □ | S | O | □ | S |
| S ↑ | ↑ □ | S = | = S | O ↑ |

| □ = | S ↑ | □ = | O ↑ | O = |
|---|---|---|---|---|
| ↑ | O | O | = | ↑ |
| S O | = □ | ↑ S | S □ | S □ |

A B C D E

44.

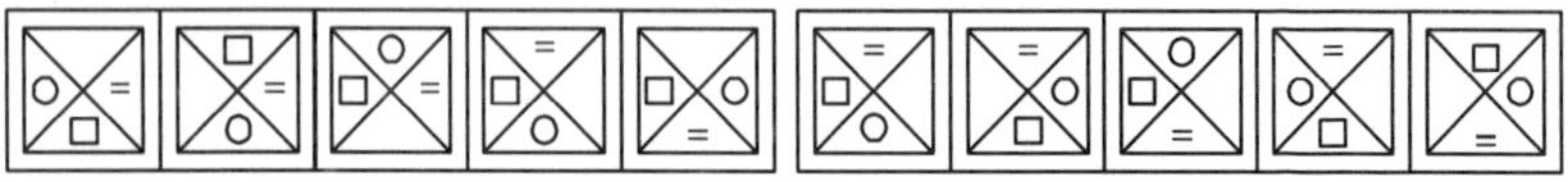

A B C D E

45.

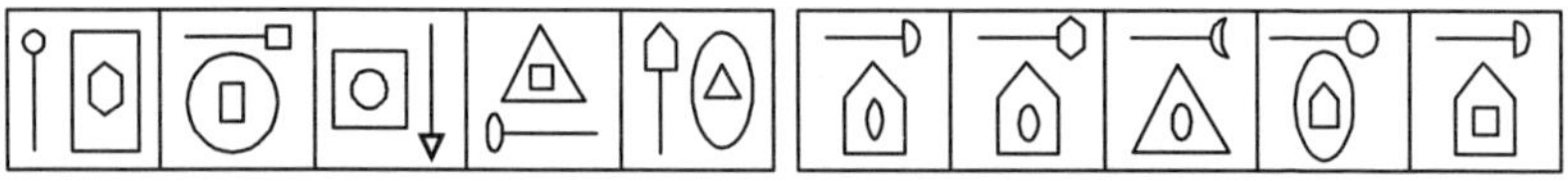

A B C D E

46.

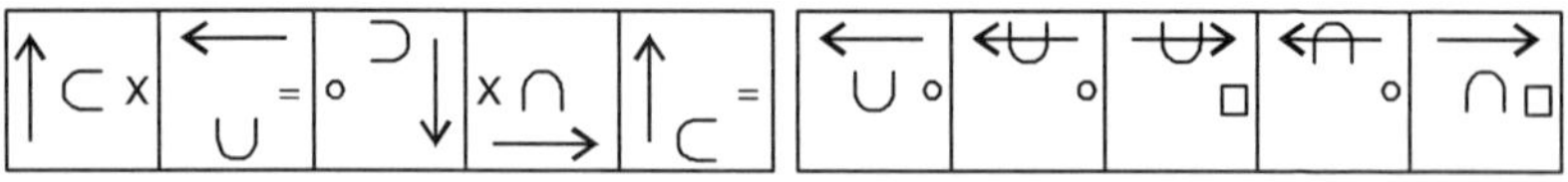

A B C D E

47.

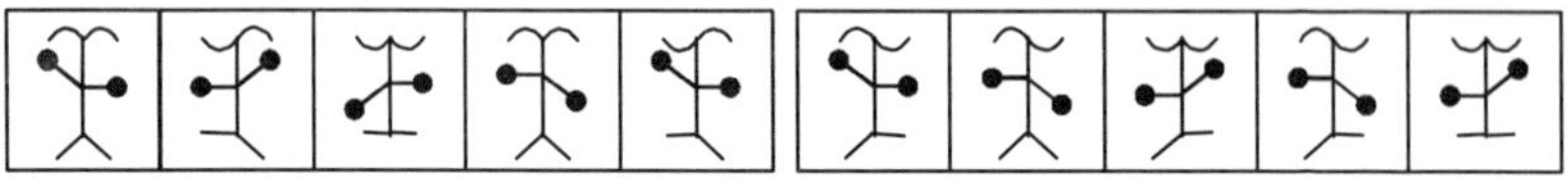

A B C D E

48.

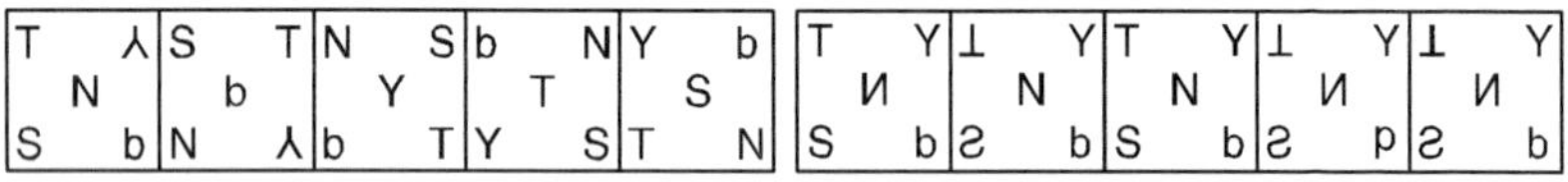

| T ⅄ | S T | N S | b N | Y b |
|---|---|---|---|---|
| N | b | Y | T | S |
| S b | N ⅄ | b T | Y S | T N |

| T Y | ⊥ Y | T Y | ⊥ Y | ⊥ Y |
|---|---|---|---|---|
| И | N | N | И | И |
| S b | Ƨ b | S b | Ƨ p | Ƨ b |

A B C D E

49.

A B C D E

**Problem Figures** **Answer Figures**

50. A B C D E

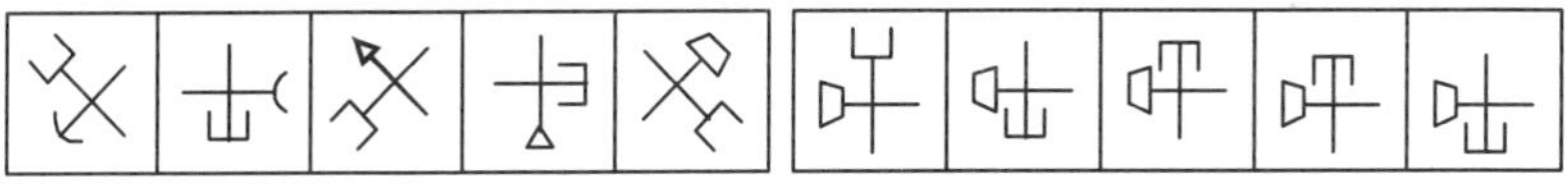

51. A B C D E

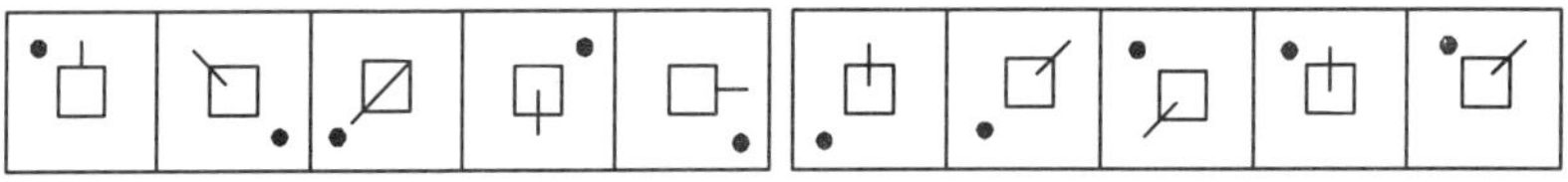

52. A B C D E

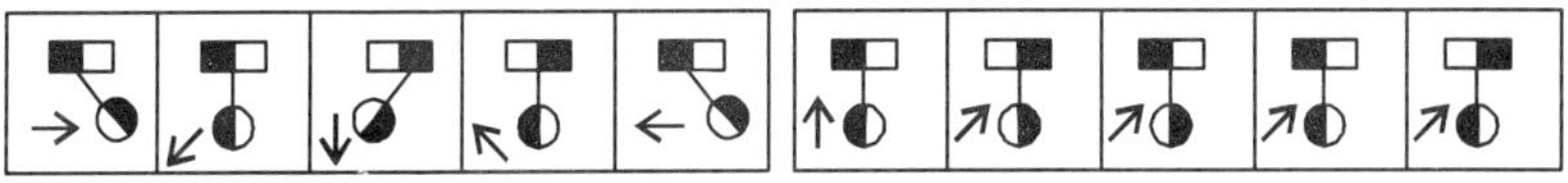

53. A B C D E

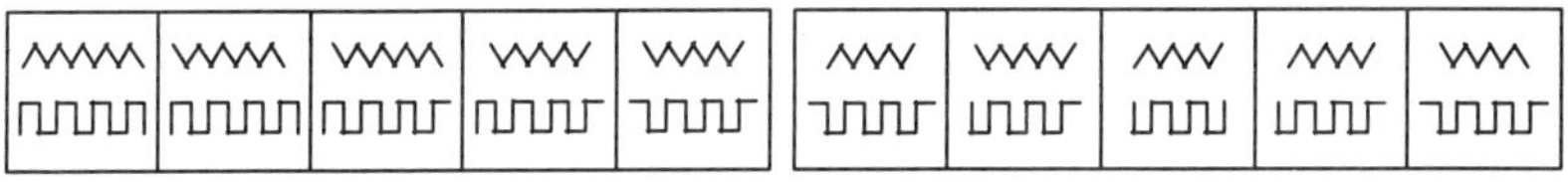

54. A B C D E

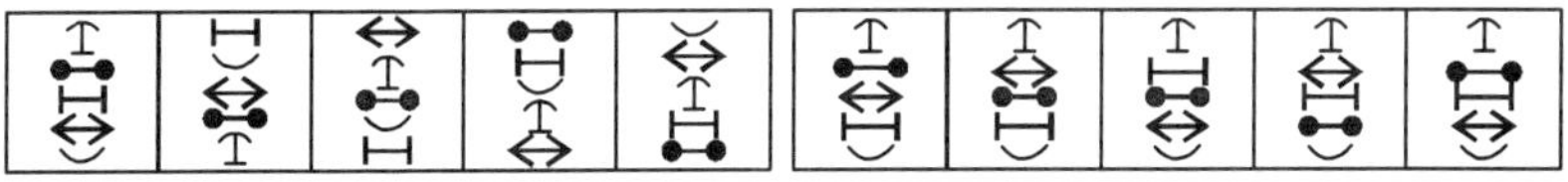

55. A B C D E

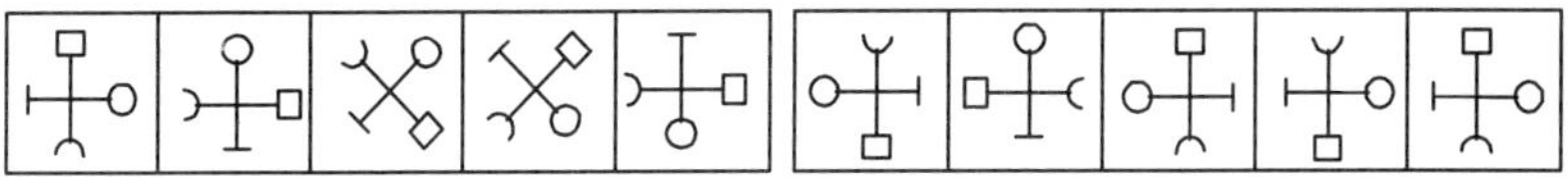

56. A B C D E

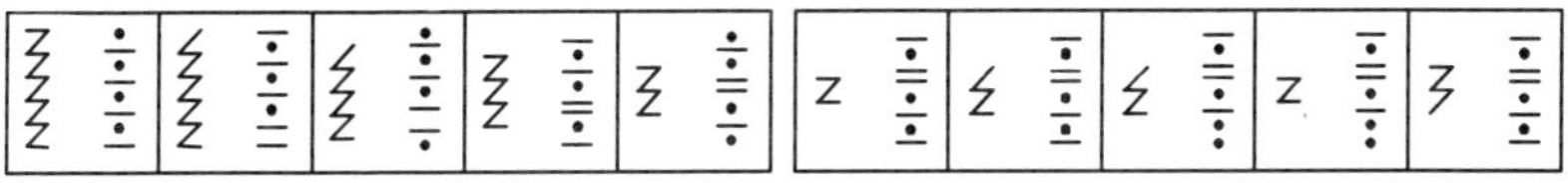

57. A B C D E

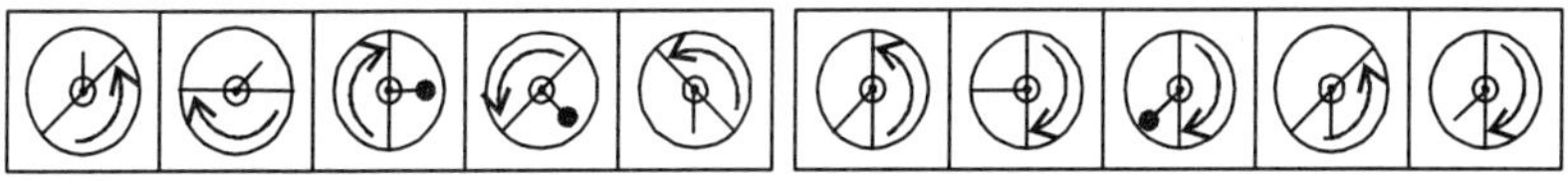

58. A B C D E

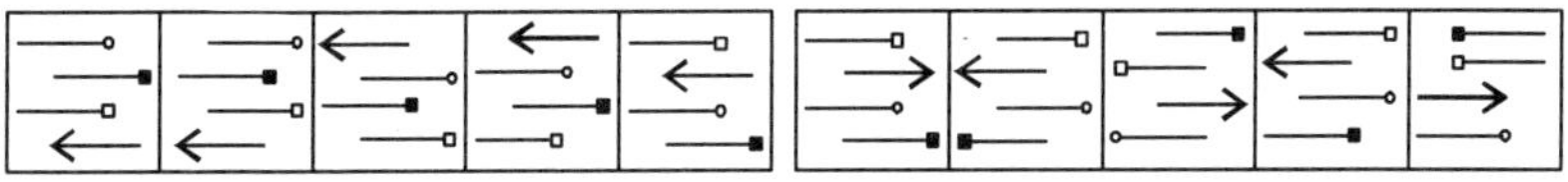

**Problem Figures** **Answer Figures**

59. A B C D E

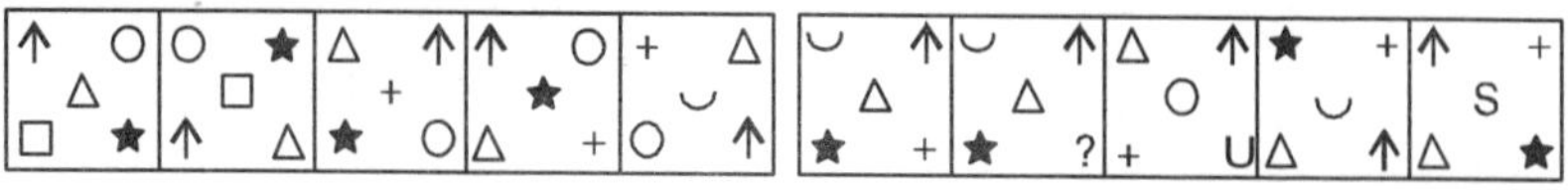

60. A B C D E

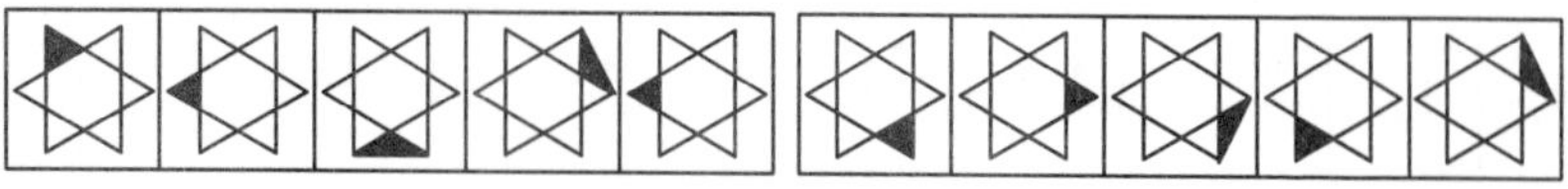

61. A B C D E

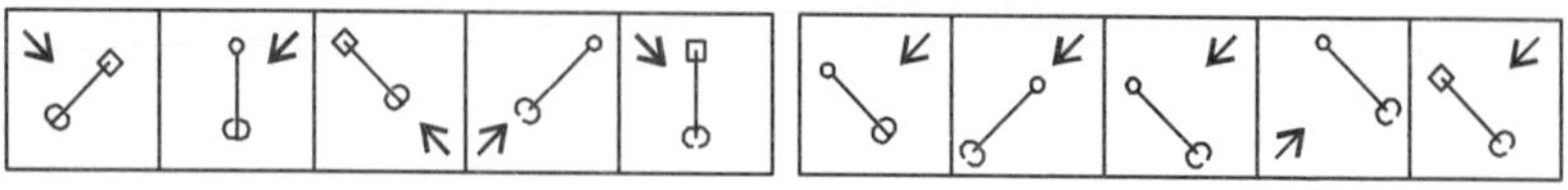

62. A B C D E

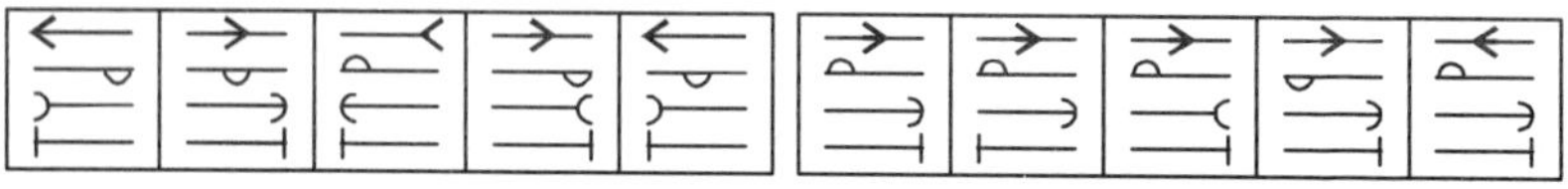

63. A B C D E

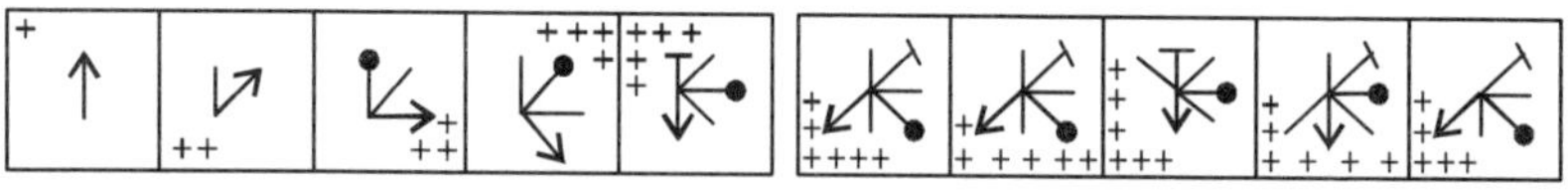

64. A B C D E

65. A B C D E

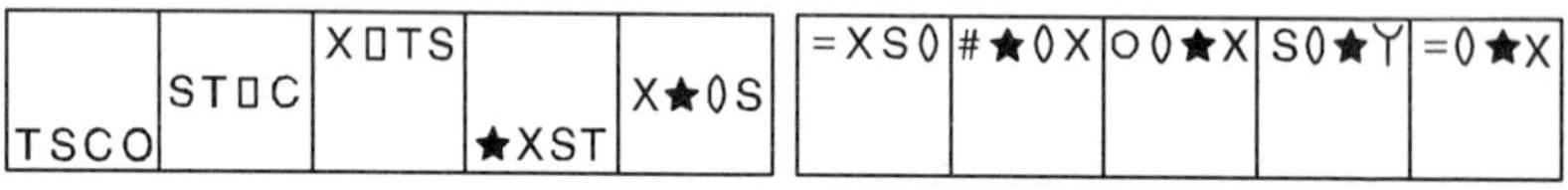

66. A B C D E

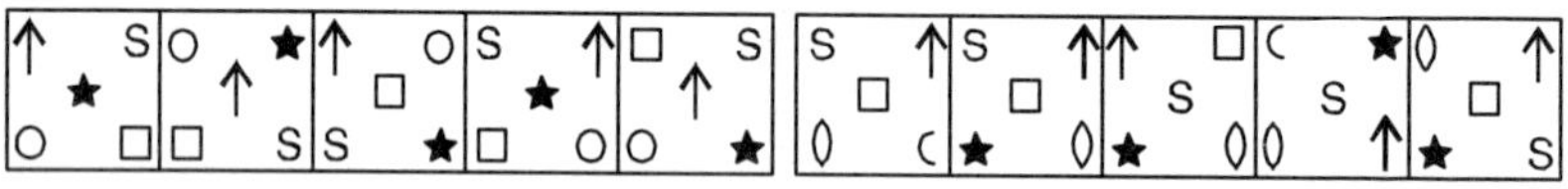

67. A B C D E

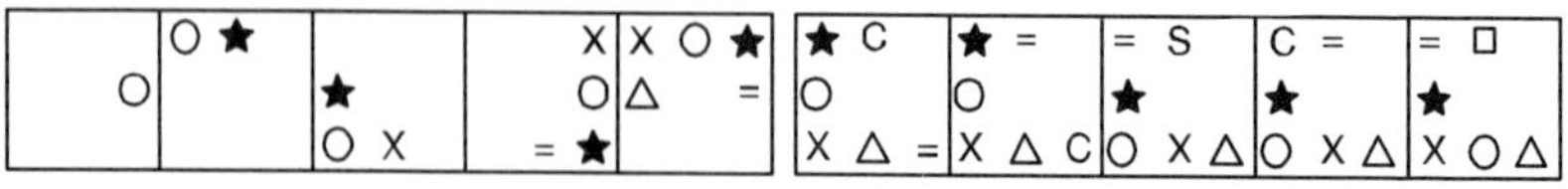

**Problem Figures** **Answer Figures**

68.

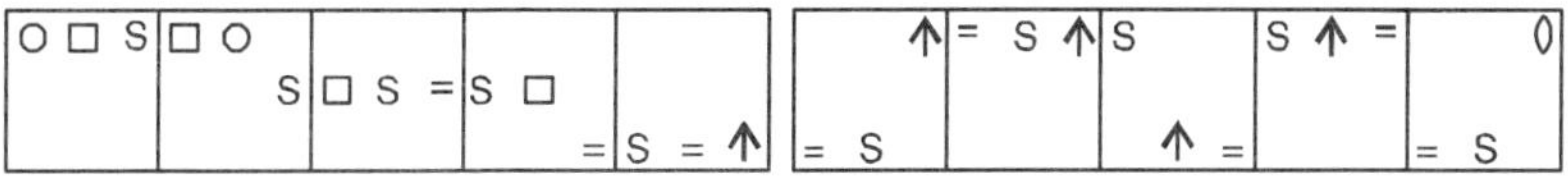

A B C D E

69.

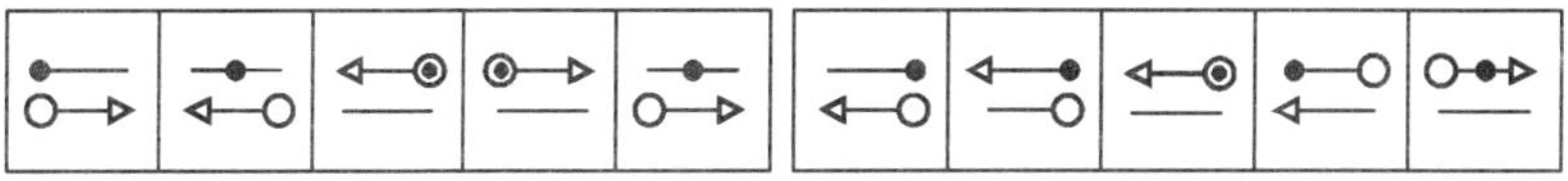

A B C D E

70.

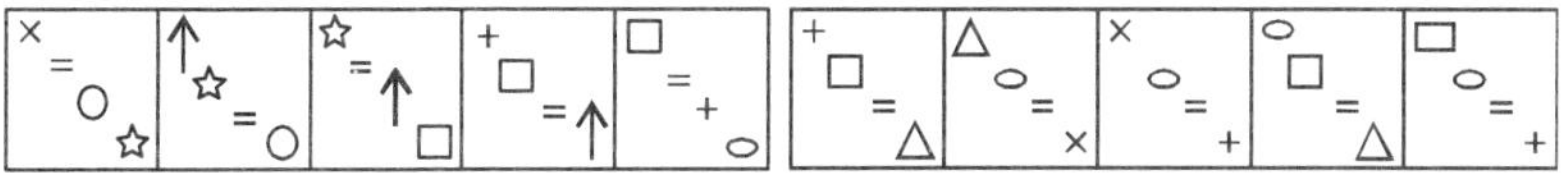

A B C D E

71.

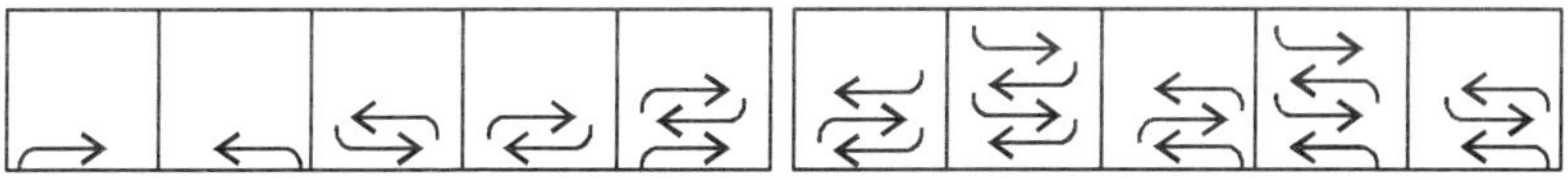

A B C D E

72.

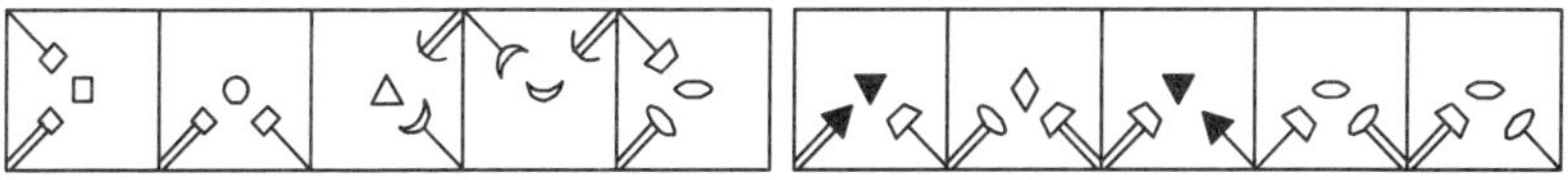

A B C D E

73.

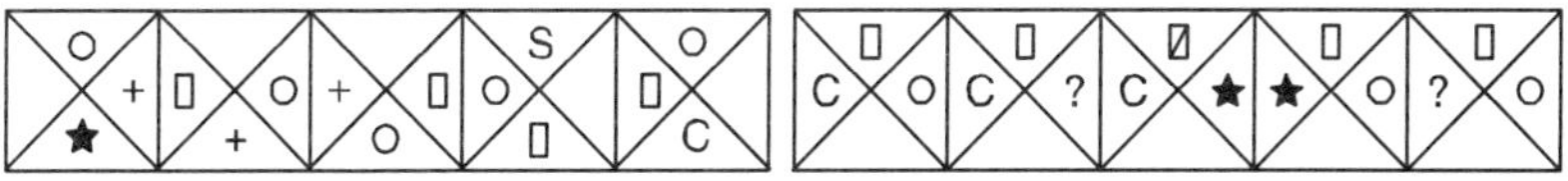

A B C D E

74.

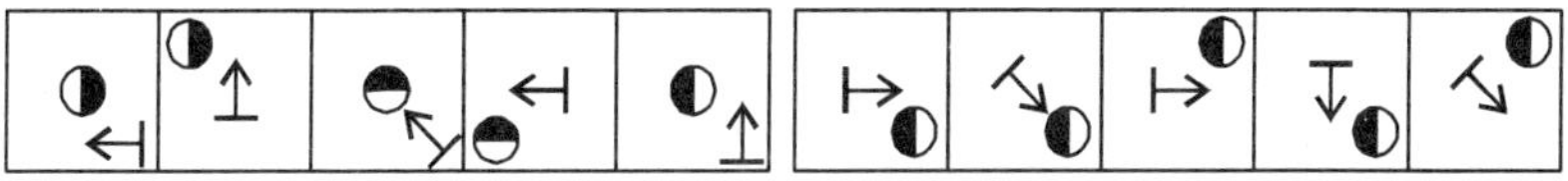

A B C D E

75.

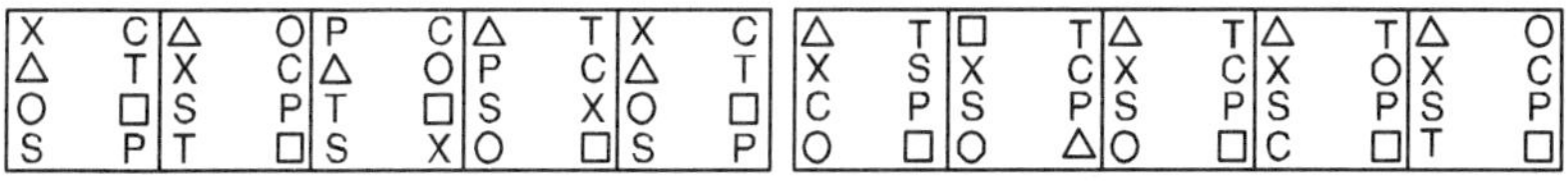

A B C D E

**ANSWERS**

| 1 | 2 | 3 | 4 | 5 | 6 | 7 | 8 | 9 | 10 |
|---|---|---|---|---|---|---|---|---|---|
| C | D | E | C | A | D | B | B | C | E |

| 11 | 12 | 13 | 14 | 15 | 16 | 17 | 18 | 19 | 20 |
|---|---|---|---|---|---|---|---|---|---|
| D | E | C | D | C | D | A | D | E | C |
| **21** | **22** | **23** | **24** | **25** | **26** | **27** | **28** | **29** | **30** |
| E | D | D | A | A | C | B | C | A | E |
| **31** | **32** | **33** | **34** | **35** | **36** | **37** | **38** | **39** | **40** |
| B | B | B | E | B | A | C | A | C | D |
| **41** | **42** | **43** | **44** | **45** | **46** | **47** | **48** | **49** | **50** |
| D | B | C | B | A | B | E | C | A | D |
| **51** | **52** | **53** | **54** | **55** | **56** | **57** | **58** | **59** | **60** |
| E | D | A | E | D | B | E | D | C | B |
| **61** | **62** | **63** | **64** | **65** | **66** | **67** | **68** | **69** | **70** |
| C | A | A | A | E | E | C | A | A | E |
| **71** | **72** | **73** | **74** | **75** | | | | | |
| E | B | B | D | E | | | | | |

## EXPLANATORY ANSWERS

**1.** In figures 1, 3 and 5 moving clockwise, one arrow is turned by 135°, and then the next arrow also by 135°. In figures 2, 4 and answer figure, the above process is applied.

**2.** From figures 1 and 3 to figures 2 and 4 respectively, the element in the centre is turned 45° anticlockwise, the arrow is moved one step anticlockwise and the direction is changed, and the plus sign is moved half step anticlockwise. By the same process answer figure is obtained from figure 5.

**3.** First the places of two elements are interchanged diagonally. Then the places of two elements in the middle row are interchanged. Next, the places of remaining two elements are interchanged diagonally. To continue the sequence the places of two elements in the middle row should be interchanged.

**4.** From figure 1 to figure 2, the direction of the arrow pointing towards the corner is changed and the arc is moved out. From figure 2 to figure 3, one arc is added in the centre and one arrow is added anticlockwise pointing towards the corner. The process is repeated from the beginning. The arcs are moved outside in clockwise manner.

**5.** From figure 1 to figure 2 and from figure 3 to figure 4, the four elements are moved one step clockwise. By the same process answer figure is obtained from figure 5.

**6.** From one figure to the next – the element at the bottom is moved to the top, the element in the centre is moved to the corner in anticlockwise manner at each step, the element in the corner interchanges place with the element in the centre the element on the top is replaced by a new element and is moved to the bottom.

**7.** In the first step the shaded part of the element on the extreme right is shifted down. In the next step the shaded part of the element is made blank. Then two lower blank parts are shaded. Next again one shaded part is made blank. To continue this sequence the shaded part of the next element should be made blank.

**8.** The four elements are moved from top to bottom and the process is repeated. First the places of first and fourth elements are interchanged, then the places of second and third elements are interchanged and the process is repeated.

**9.** From figure 1 to figure 2 and from figure 3 to figure 4, the elements are moved anti-clockwise and the places of last two elements are interchanged. The same process is applied to figure 5 to get the answer figure.

**10.** The direction of two lines making the arrow head of the element on the left is changed, then moved half way up. Again, the direction is changed and then it is moved to the top. The direction of two lines making the arrowhead of the element on the right is turned in three directions from straight to upwards to downwards; and the steps are repeated. For answer figure, the direction of two lines making the arrowhead on the left element should be changed so that the arrowhead of the top is facing upwards and the right element should have the arrow also pointing upwards.

**11.** The arrangement of elements in figures 1, 3 and 5 is in anticlockwise manner. From figure 1 to figure 2 and from figure 3 to figure 4, the first element (anticlockwise) is moved to the centre, the middle element to the almost diagonal corner and the third element is not disturbed but replaced by a new element. By the same process, answer figure is obtained from figure 5.

**12.** From figure 1 to figure 2 and from figure 3 to figure 4 the '=' sign is moved horizontally to the other corner. This corner element is moved to the other corner diagonally, from where the element is moved horizontally to the other corner. The last element to be moved is changed and moved to the position of '=' sign. By the same process answer figure is obtained from figure 5. The changed element is always new.

**13.** The three elements are moved diagonally and the element on the top is placed at the bottom at each step. From one figure to the next, the triangle is turned upside down, the rectangle is turned by 90° and the square by 45°.

**14.** Between figure 1 and figure 4, the hanging triangle is moved to its opposite side. Between figure 2 and figure 5 the hanging square is moved to its opposite side. From figure 3 to answer figure the triangle should be moved to the opposite side. The main figure in the two compared figures is the same.

**15.** From figure 1 to figure 2 and from figure 3 to figure 4, the places of first two elements clockwise are interchanged and the third element is made new.

**16.** From figure 1 to figure 2 and from figure 3 to figure 4, a new design is added inside the central figure, the element of the top left corner is moved to top right corner position, the element on the top right corner is moved diagonally to bottom left position, the element on the bottom left corner is moved horizontally to right corner position, the element on the bottom right corner is moved diagonally to top left corner position and is made new. The changed elements are always new.

**17.** From figure 1 to figure 2 and from figure 3 to figure 4, the two elements inside the figure are turned upside down, the main figure is changed, the element in the corner is moved vertically to the other end and is always new.

**18.** From one figure to the next, the element on the bottom right is moved to the bottom left position and always a new element is placed on the bottom right position. At the top, first the direction of fourth element from the left is changed, then this process of changing direction starts from the first element.

**19.** Figures 1 and 2 are turned 45° clockwise and the element in the corner is always made new to get figures 4 and 5 respectively. The same process is applied to figure 3 to get the answer figure.

**20.** From figure 1 to figure 2 and from figure 3 to figure 4, the places of elements are interchanged horizontally and then only the element on the bottom left is made new, and the element in the centre is turned upside down.

**21.** At each step one horizontal arrow is added clockwise and starting from first arrow the arrows in each figure are turned 90° clockwise and 90° anticlockwise alternately.

**22.** In figures 1, 2 and 3, first the places of elements are interchanged diagonally and then only the style of 'C' is changed. Similarly, in figures 4 and 5 the places of elements are interchanged and in answer figure, only the position of 'C' is changed.

**23.** From figure 1 to figure 2 and from figure 3 to figure 4, the elements are moved in an inverted 'S', *i.e.* 'Z' manner, *i.e.* the bottom right element is moved to top left position, top left element to top right position, top right element to middle right position, middle right element to middle left position, middle left element to bottom left position and bottom left element to bottom right position.

**24.** From one figure to the next the dot is moved two steps anticlockwise and the direction of slant lines is changed. The arrowheads of the slant lines are first removed one by one in clockwise manner and then added one by one in the same manner.

**25.** In figures 1, 3 and 5 the hanging rod is oscillating by 90°. The triangle attached to the horizontal line is moved to the other side of the line and turned upside down. On the right the line is cut by 1, 3 and 2 small lines. In figures 2, 4 and answer figure the elements on the hanging line are shaded alternately. The movement of the triangle is the same as mentioned above and the small lines are in the order of 2, 3 and 1.

**26.** The arrow is turned 45° clockwise at each step. The other arm is turned 45° and 90° anticlockwise alternately. The dot bar is moved one step clockwise each time and rotated 45° clockwise in alternate figures.

**27.** From figure 1 to figure 2 and from figure 3 to figure 4, the element on the top is vertically inverted. The element in the bottom left position is turned 90° clockwise and moved to the bottom right corner and a new element is placed in the bottom left corner position.

**28.** The difference between the letters in the centre is increased by one at each step. The shaded part is the same in figures 1 and 5 and so should be the same in figures 2 and answer figure. Between figures 1, 2 and 3 the two elements, one on bottom right position and the other on top left position, are replaced one by one by other identical elements. Similar process is applied to figures 4 and 5 to get to the answer figure.

**29.** In figures 1, 2 and 3, first the small triangle is moved inside the big triangle and then a small triangle is added on the opposite side. In figures 4, 5 and answer figure, first the small triangle is moved outside the big triangle and then a small triangle is added on the opposite side. At each step one line of the element in the bottom left corner is removed in a set pattern anticlockwise.

**30.** The geometrical figures are in the order of circle—rhombus—triangle—hexagon and from figure 5 the figures are in reverse order, *i.e.*, triangle—rhombus. The arrow is moved ½, 1, 1½, 2 and 2½ steps clockwise and each time its direction is changed.

**31.** In alternate figures, the design in the centre is rotated by 135° anticlockwise. The element in the corner is moved clockwise and turned 90° clockwise at each step.

**32.** From one figure to next, the triangle is turned 45° clockwise, and the line cutting through the triangle is turned 45° anticlockwise. The parts of the small hanging circle are shaded in three different ways – from inside, from outside and in third step it is fully shaded and this style is repeated.

**33.** All the elements are moved half way down two steps and then to the top. The positions of two element on the left are interchanged and the positions of two elements on the right are interchanged, while doing so, first the fourth element is replaced by a new element and then the second. The process is repeated.

**34.** The slanting lines, one on the left side and one on the right side of the vertical line segment are alternately straightened in a set pattern, and one arc is added to the other vertical line segment in a set pattern-two arcs in opposite direction on one side and two arcs in the opposite direction on the other.

**35.** The arrow is rotated 90° anticlockwise at each step and moved on the right diagonal in a set pattern. The two parallel lines are rotated by 90° in alternate figures and moved on the left diagonal in a set pattern. Also observe that the trident is turned upside down after three moves in a set pattern horizontally.

**36.** The shaded semicircle on the top line segment is moved from right to left in a set pattern by changing sides, while the semicircle on the bottom line segment is moved from left to right in a set pattern on the same side. Also, the line segment on the side bears an arrowhead in figure one and two, then changed in figure three and four and changed back to arrowhead in figure five. Figure 'A' continues the series.

**37.** In alternate figures one, three and five, the design is rotated 90° anticlockwise. While in other alternate figures it is rotated 90° clockwise. At each step one line segment with one split end is added on either side of line alternately.

**38.** From figure one to figure two the places of three elements placed diagonally are shifted one place upwards and the top element is placed at the bottom. From figure two to figure three the three elements on the horizontal are shifted one place to the left and the left most element is placed on the extreme right. The above steps are repeated.

**39.** Observe that figure two is the mirror image of figure one. The same is applied to figures three and four. To continue the series, the answer figure should be the mirror image of figure five.

**40.** Observe the series, in every figure the outermost and the innermost shapes are identical while the shape in between is entirely new at each step.

**41.** The umbrella shape is rotated 45° anticlockwise in alternate figures and the shade is moved to the adjacent section in a set order. In two consecutive figures where the base is identical, first base is unshaded while the second is shaded.

**42.** Observe that from figure one to figure two the shade outside the arc is moved inside and the shade on the other element is shifted half way anticlockwise. The same applies to figure three and four. To continue the series, the answer figure should coordinate with figure five.

**43.** At each step the places of equal to sign and the element on its right are inter changed, while the places of other three elements are shifted clockwise.

**44.** All the three elements are moved one section anticlockwise at each step. First the places of the leading two elements are inter changed and then the places of two trailing elements are interchanged. These two steps are repeated.

**45.** The line segment is moved clockwise and bears a new shape each time, which is also the outer shape in the next figure, and this outer shape is enclosed in the next figure.

**46.** The arrow is moved one step clockwise but rotated 90° anticlockwise. The element in the middle is moved on the vertical in a set pattern and rotated 90° anticlockwise. The third element is repeated from figure four and is moved from side to side horizontally in alternate figures.

**47.** Both the dot bars move like a pendulum in a set manner. From figure one to figure two the arc and line segment on the left of the vertical line are moved. From figure two to figure three the arc and line segment on the right of the vertical line are moved. From figure three to figure four both the arcs and the line segments are moved. This process is repeated.

**48.** At each step the bottom left element and two top elements are moved one step clockwise, the bottom right element is moved to the middle, the element in the middle is moved to the bottom left.

**49.** The outer figure is always new; but the first three inner figures are repeated in reverse order from figure four.

**50.** From figure one to figure two, the cross is rotated 135° anticlockwise and the elements attached to its two ends are inverted. The same applies to figure three and figure four. To continue the series the answer figure should coordinate with figure five.

**51.** The dot is moved clockwise two steps and one step alternately. The bar is moved anticlockwise half step and one step alternately. The length of the bar is increased and decreased in a set pattern.

**52.** In figures one, three and five the shade inside the rectangle is moved from side to side, the hanging dot bar is oscillated by 90° left and right, and the arrow is turned 90° clockwise. In figures two, four and answer figure the shade inside the rectangle is moved from side to side, the hanging dot bar is unmoved, and the arrow is turned 90° clockwise.

**53.** From figure one to figure two one line segment on the left of the upper element is removed. From figure two to figure three, one line segment on the right of the lower element is removed. From figure three to figure four, one line segment on the right of the upper element is removed. From figure four to figure five, one line segment on the left of the lower element is removed.

**54.** At each step, beginning from the top, the first, second, third, fourth and fifth (last) elements are moved to the fifth (last), fourth, first, third and second positions respectively.

**55.** The places of circle and square are interchanged and the places of the arc and line segment are interchanged. Then the cross is rotated 45° clockwise. The above two steps are repeated.

**56.** One and two line segments from the top are alternately removed from the zigzag pattern on the left. On the right side when a dot is removed a line segment is added at the base and when a line segment is removed, a dot as added; this process is alternate.

**57.** From figure one to figure two, the diagonal with circle and dot bar are rotated 45° clockwise and the direction of the arrow is reversed. Same applies to the figure three and the figure four. Answer figure E coordinates with figure five.

**58.** Observe that figures one and two are identical and so are figures three and four. Answer figure should be identical to figure five.

**59.** From figure one to figure two the elements on the top and bottom right are shifted one step anticlockwise while the places of remaining two elements are interchanged. From figure two to figure three the places of diagonally opposite elements are interchanged while the element in the centre is replaced by a new element. The above steps are repeated.

**60.** The shade is moved one step anticlockwise in figure two and three after the movement is increased by half step each time.

**61.** Between figure one and figure five, the square is replaced by a circle and vice versa, the direction of the two curves at the base is changed, the arrow is rotated 90° anticlockwise and moved one step anticlockwise. Similarly, answer figure C coordinates with figure three.

**62.** The arrowhead is moved to the right end of the line segment and back in a set pattern and its direction is reversed at each step. The semicircle is moved from right end to the left end of the line segment in a set pattern and is placed on the other side. The arc is moved from end to end of the line segment and its direction is reversed in alternate figures. The bottom element is same in alternate figures.

**63.** In alternate figures the arrow is rotated 90° clockwise, one simple line segment and one line segment with busy end are added in a set pattern and the cross is moved to the diagonally opposite corner and one more sign on either side is added.

**64.** Observe that figure one and figure four coordinate with each other in the manner that the element is rotated 90° clockwise and the straight line at the base is replaced by an arc in the direction of the arrow. Similarly, between figure two and figure five the element is rotated 90° clockwise and the straight line at the base is replaced by an arc in the direction of the curve. Figure A coordinates with figure three.

**65.** All the elements are moved from bottom to top in a set order. From figure one to figure two, the places of two element on the left are interchanged, the places of two elements on the right are interchanged and the element on the left is replaced by a new element. From figure two to figure three the places of two elements on the left are interchanged and they are moved to the right side; the places of two other elements are interchanged and again the element on the left is replaced by a new element. The above process is repeated from figure four onwards.

**66.** From figure one to figure two the element on the top left is moved to the centre, the element in the centre is moved to the top right and all other elements are moved one step clockwise. From figure two to figure three the element on the bottom left is moved to the centre, the element in the centre is moved to the top left and all other elements are moved one step clockwise. To continue, the first element to be moved is picked anticlockwise and the other movements follow clockwise.

**67.** The circle is moved one and a half steps and one step anticlockwise alternately. A new element is added first behind it and then ahead of it in alternate figures.

**68.** From figure one to figure two, the places of two elements on the left are interchanged and the element on the right is moved half step down. From figure two to figure three, the element on the right is moved to the centre, the element of the two together is moved half step down and a new element is placed on the right to complete the row. The above process is repeated.

**69.** The dot is moved on the upper line segment in a set order, the circle is moved anticlockwise at the four ends of the two line segments, and the arrow is moved clockwise at the four ends of the two line segments.

**70.** First the bottom right element is moved to the second position and the two elements shifted down diagonally while the top most element is replaced by a new element. Then, the top left element is moved to the third position and the two elements shifted up diagonally while the bottom right element is replaced by a new element. The above process is repeated.

**71.** From figure one to figure two the arrow is laterally inverted. From figure two to figure three one arrow is added at the bottom in opposite direction to the existing arrow. From figure three to figure four the arrows are laterally inverted, and the process is continued.

**72.** Observe the figures. Figure two corresponds to figure one and figure four to figure three. Of the two corner elements the left element is moved to the diagonally opposite corner and the element in the centre is replaced by a new element. Similarly, Answer Figure 'B' corresponds with figure five.

**73.** From figure one to figure two, the three elements are moved one section clockwise and the leading element is replaced by a new element. The same process follows between figure three and four. Answer figure 'B' corresponds to figure five.

**74.** In this alternate series, in figures one, three and five the circle in the centre is rotated 90° anticlockwise while the arrow is rotated 45° clockwise. In figures two and four the arrow in the centre is rotated 90° anticlockwise while the circle is rotated 90° anticlockwise and moved one step anticlockwise. Answer figure D continues this series from figure four.

**75.** From figure one to figure two, the two top elements and two bottom elements are moved to the second and thirds rows respectively; the elements in the second and the third rows are moved to the top and the bottom rows respectively; and then the places of top right element and bottom left element are interchanged. From figure two to figure three, the movement of elements in the rows is same as above except that in this the places of top left element and bottom right element are interchanged. The above process is repeated.

❍ ❍ ❍

## TYPE II

## EXERCISE

**Directions :** *In each of these questions, there are two sets of figures. The figures placed first are Problem Figures, and those follows are Answer Figures indicated by the letters A, B, C, D and E. A series is established if one of the five Answer Figures is placed at the question-marked space. Figures form a series if they change from left to right according to some specific rule. The letter of the Answer Figure which should be placed in the question-marked space is the answer. All the figures, i.e. three Problem Figures and one Answer Figure placed in the question-marked space should be considered as forming the series.*

Draw figure in one line

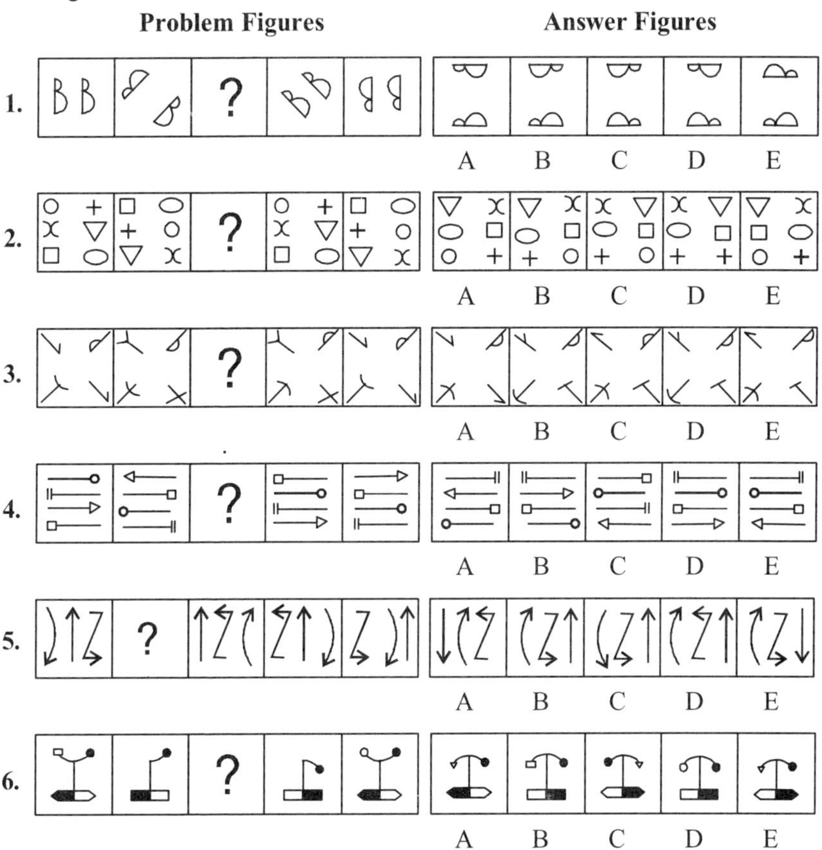

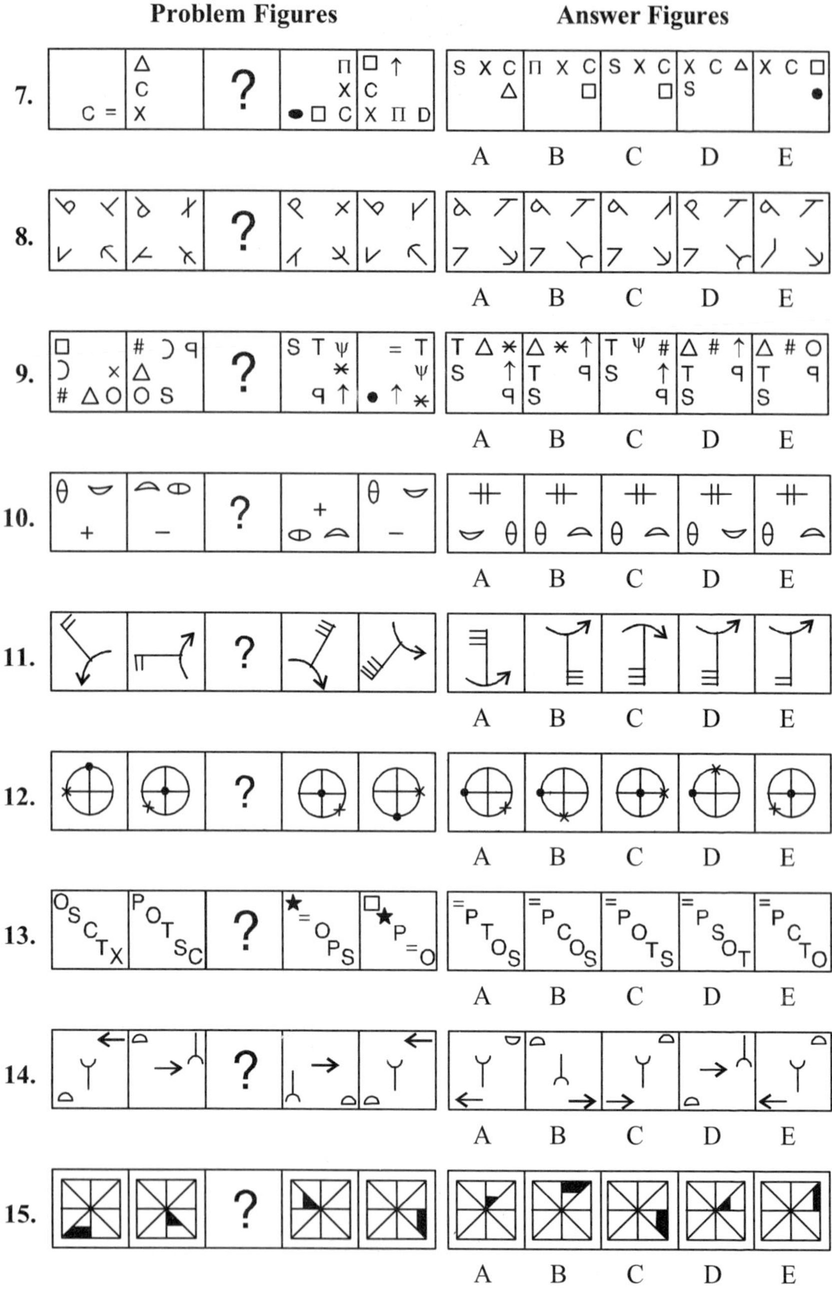

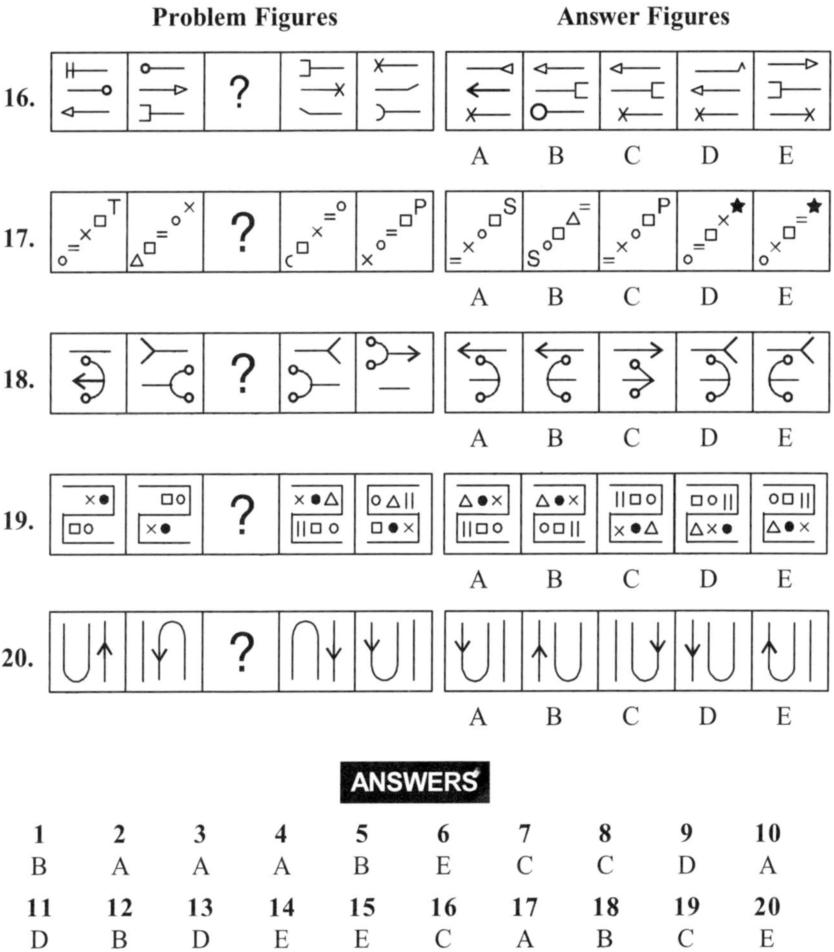


## ANSWERS

| 1 | 2 | 3 | 4 | 5 | 6 | 7 | 8 | 9 | 10 |
|---|---|---|---|---|---|---|---|---|---|
| B | A | A | A | B | E | C | C | D | A |
| **11** | **12** | **13** | **14** | **15** | **16** | **17** | **18** | **19** | **20** |
| D | B | D | E | E | C | A | B | C | E |

## EXPLANATORY ANSWERS

1. In problem figures one, three and five, the element on the left side is moved one step clockwise while the other element is turned 90° anticlockwise and moved one step clockwise. In problem figures two and four, the top left element is moved similar to the left element in problem figure one and the other element is moved similar to the other element in problem figure one. Option 'B' is the right answer.
2. At each step the top left element is moved to the middle right position, the middle right element is moved to the bottom left position, the bottom left

element is moved to the top left position, the top right element is moved to the middle left position, the middle left element is moved to the bottom right position, and the bottom right element is moved to the top right position. Answer figure 'A' completes the series.

3. The arc on the bottom left element is moved half way forward on the line and then the direction is changed and the process is continued. The bottom right and the top left elements are same in alternate figures. The semicircle on the top right element is moved to the other side, shifted half way up on the line, moved to the other side and so on. Option 'A' is the right answer.

4. In alternate figures, the elements are laterally inverted. First the places of first or the top and the third elements are interchanged and the places of second or the bottom or the fourth elements are interchanged. Secondly, the bottom element is moved to the top position. The process is repeated from the beginning. Answer figure 'A' is the right answer.

5. The sequence is : The curved arrow is rotated by 180°, moved to the third place rotated by 180° and moved to the centre. The straight arrow is moved from centre to right to first place, to centre to right. The 'Z' arrow is same in two consecutive figures, it is moved to the other end, moved to the left, its arrowhead moved to the other end, and so on. Answer figure 'B' fits into the question-marked space.

6. The shape of the base is identical in alternate figures, only the shade is moved from one part to the other. The arc holding the elements is also turned to the opposite direction in alternate figures. In odd numbered figures the dot remains on the right side, but the element on the left is new every time. By this process answer figue 'E' fits into the question-marked space to complete the series.

7. The 'C' shape is moved clockwise two steps and three steps alternately. First the element behind it is made new and a new element placed ahead of it, then the element ahead of 'C' is made new and a new element is placed in the end. The above process is repeated in a set order as new elements are added and made new. Option 'C' fits into the question marked space to complete the series.

8. The semicircle of the top left element is first moved to the other side, then it is shifted to the other end and the process is repeated. The line segment of the top right element is shifted half step each time, till it reaches the other end and then it is shifted back. The arc of the bottom right element is also shifted half step to and fro, its direction is same in two subsequent figures. The line segment of the bottom left elements is also moved half

step to and fro, the side is changed at every move and it is always at 45° degrees to the diagonal line. Answer figure 'C' fits into the question-marked space.

**9.** From problem figure one to two, the first and the last (or the sixth) elements are changed; from two to three, the second and the fifth elements are changed; from three to four the third and the fourth elements are changed. The process is again repeated from the beginning. In doing so the elements are moved one step and half step alternately in clockwise manner. Answer figure 'D' is the right choice.

**10.** The oblong shape is moved clockwise and turned by 90°, the half-moon shape moved anticlockwise and rotated by 180°, and the element is the centre is repeated from problem figure four. The above process is repeated. Option 'A' fits into the question-marked space to complete the series.

**11.** The arrowhead is shifted from one end of the arc to the other at each step and the small line segments attached to the straight line are also moved to the opposite side at each step. Also, one line segment is increased in alternate figures. Option 'D' completes the series.

**12.** The cross is moved anticlockwise at angle of 45° on the circumference of the circle while the dot is moved the length of the radius to the centre at a time and then to the circumference a quarter of an arc anticlockwise alternately.

**13.** At each step the topmost element is moved to the second position; the second element to the fourth position, the fourth element to the third position, the third element to the last position and the last element to the topmost position where it is made new. Answer figure 'D' fits into the question-marked space.

**14.** The 'D' shape is moved one step clockwise. The 'Y' shape is turned upside down at each step, moved diagonally half step, first upwards then twice downwards and back. The arrow is inverted and moved diagonally half step, first downwards twice then upwards. Option 'E' is the right choice.

**15.** The shade is moved anticlockwise, the number of sections moved are increased by one at each step and it is moved from side to centre alternately. Option 'E' completes the series.

**16.** Each element is moved half way upwards from bottom to top and then replaced by a new element in a set pattern. With each move the direction of the element is reversed. Answer figure 'C' is the right choice.

**17.** At first step the fifth or the bottom, most element is moved to the second place from top, the second element moved to the fourth place, the fourth element is moved to the third place, the third element is moved to the first or the topmost place and the element on the top which is made new is moved to the last or the fifth place. At second step, i.e. from second problem figure to third problem figure the above process is reversed. The bottom most element is the first and the top most element is the last or fifth. Hereafter, the process is repeated from the beginning. Option 'A' is the right answer.

**18.** The two elements on the sides of the line segment are moved clockwise. The arrowhead is first moved then inverted and the process is repeated. The other element is first inverted then moved and the process is repeated. By this process option 'B' is the right answer.

**19.** From first problem figure to the second the elements on the top are shifted down and vice versa. In fourth problem figure, there are three elements which, as per rule, are also shifted. So, in question marked space only option 'C' can be considered as forming the series.

**20.** Both the elements are turned upside down, their places interchanged and the arrow head moved left from one element to the other. In the question marked space the 'U' shape and the arrowhead should be facing upwards, the line segment should be on the right and the arrowhead should be on the extreme left. To continue the series the next figure has the 'U' shape and the arrowhead facing downwards, the line segment on the right and the arrowhead on the extreme right. Option 'E' fits into the question marked space.

❍ ❍ ❍

# 2

# Analogy

## TYPE I

Analogy refers to correspondence or similarity in relationship. When a figure exhibits some kind of relationship with another figure on some basis, then the two figures are said to be analogous to each other.

Figures are related in some or other ways. Some of them are as follows:

- Based on shape
- Based on orientation of figure
- Based on number of elements
- Based on mirror image
- Based on water image
- Rotation of figure
- Movement of figure
- Replacement of positions of element

In the questions based on analogy, two sets of figures, namely problem figures and answer figures are given. The set of problem figures consists of two parts.

The first part comprises of two figures which have some relationship between them on the basis of a certain rule.

The second part comprises of one figure and a sign of '?'. You are asked to select one figure from the set of answer figures to replace '?' but maintaining similar relationship as depicted between the first two figures.

## SOLVED EXAMPLES

**Directions (Q. No. 1-4):** *The second figure in the first part of the problem figures bears certain relationship to the first figure. Similarly, one of the figures of answer figures bears the same relationship to the first figure of the second part. You have to select a figure from the set of answer figures which would replace the questions mark (?)*

**1.** **Problem Figures** **Answer Figures**

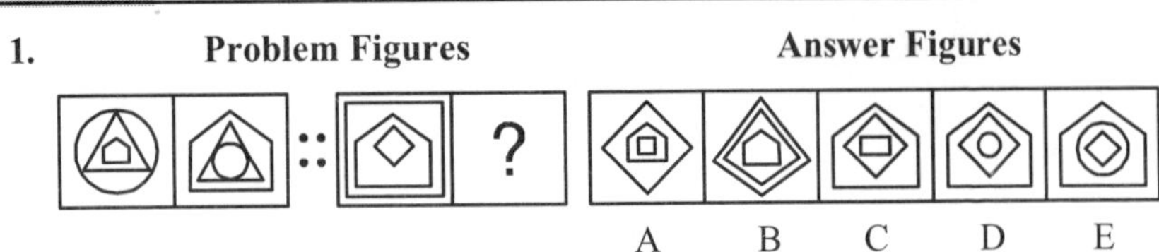

**Answer A.** From problem figure the innermost figure becomes outermost figure and outermost figure becomes the innermost figure, *i.e.* first and third figure interchanged.

**2.** **Problem Figures** **Answer Figures**

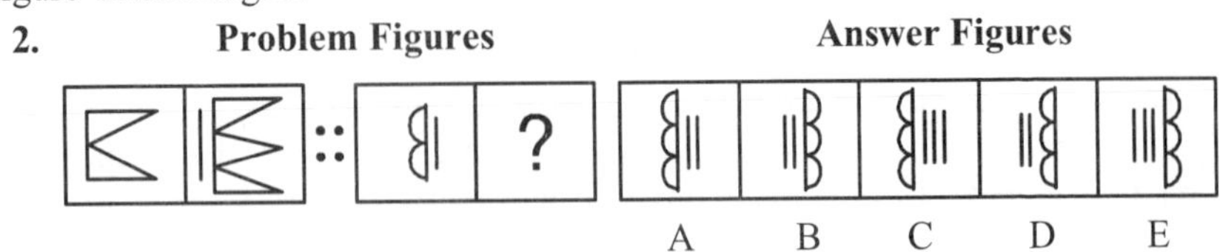

**Answer A.** From problem figure the number of line in inner segment and outer segment increases. So, this happens in first figure.

**3.** **Problem Figures** **Answer Figures**

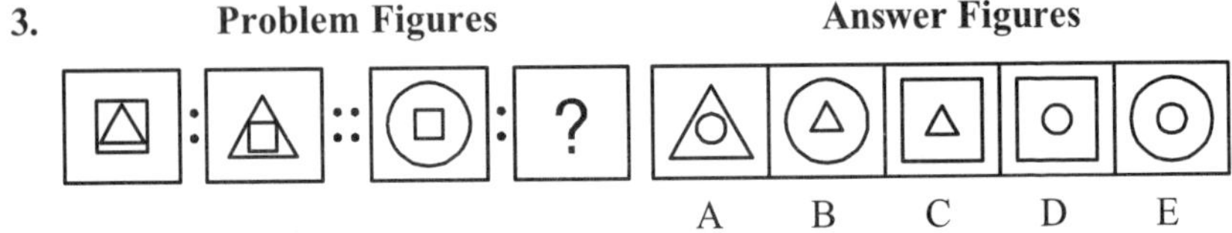

**Answer D.** The outer figure comes inside, the inner figure comes outside.

**4.** **Problem Figures** **Answer Figures**

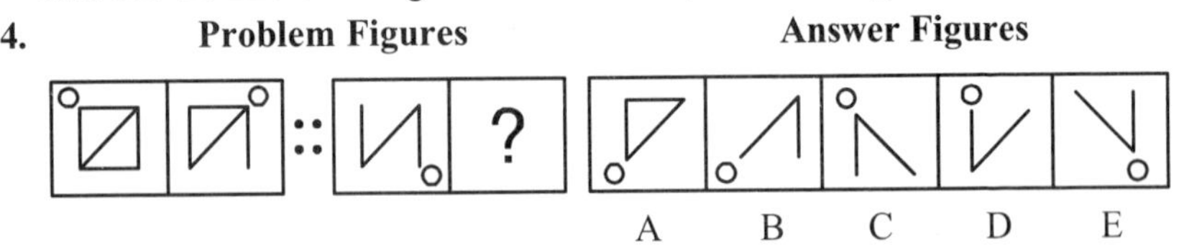

**Answer B.** The symbol 'O' is moving from one corner to another in clockwise direction 90° in each step and one line is removed while second figure is formed.

## EXERCISE

**Problem Figures** **Answer Figures**

1.

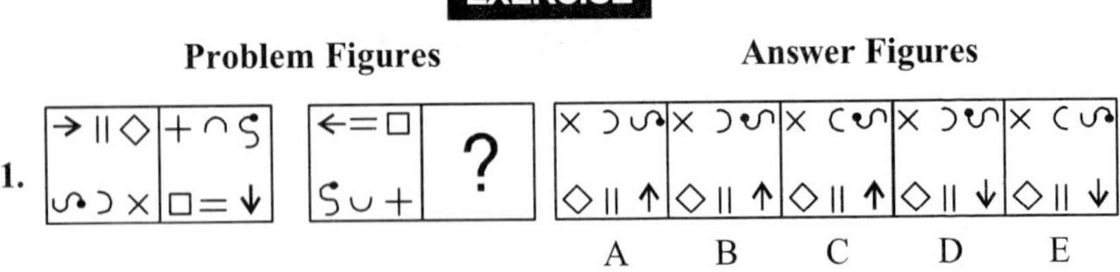

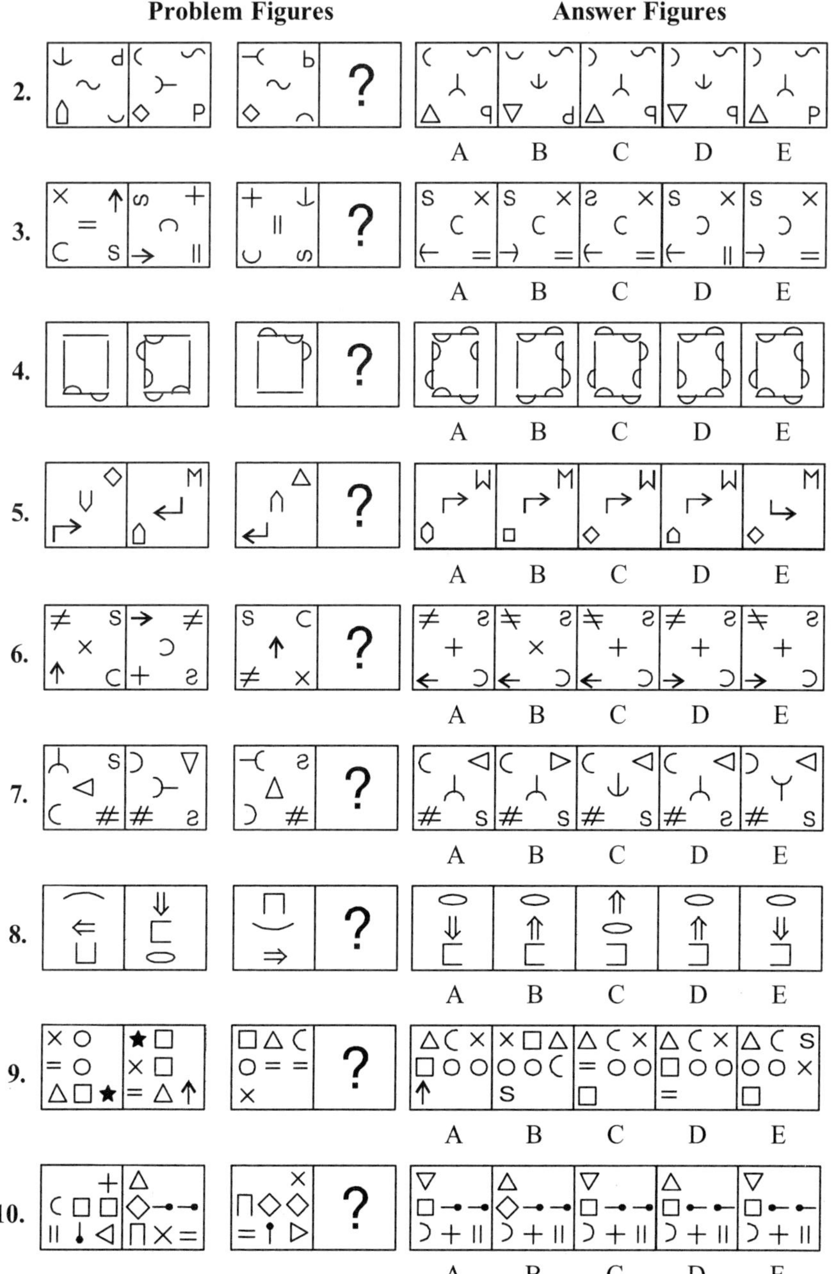
Problem Figures
Answer Figures
2.
3.
4.
5.
6.
7.
8.
9.
10.
A B C D E

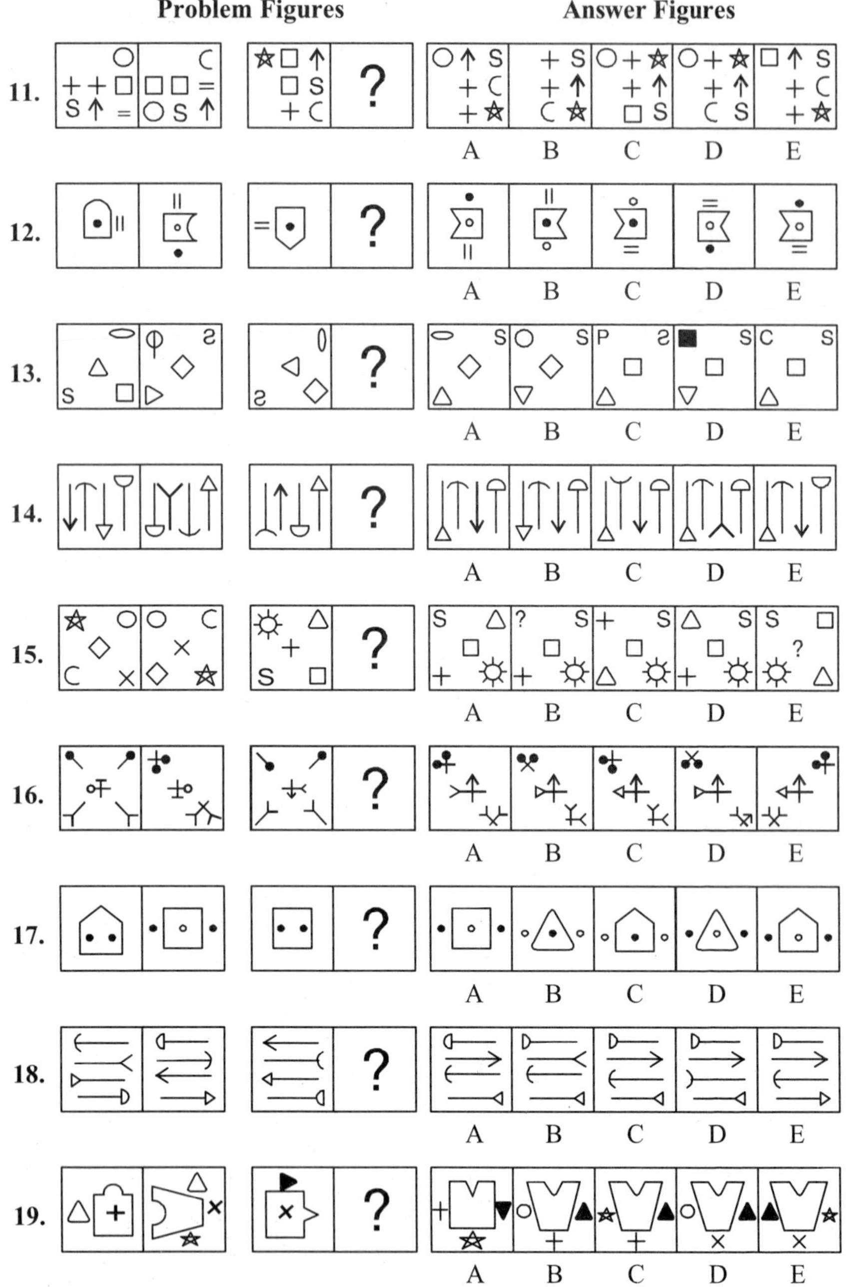
Problem Figures
Answer Figures
11.
12.
13.
14.
15.
16.
17.
18.
19.
A B C D E

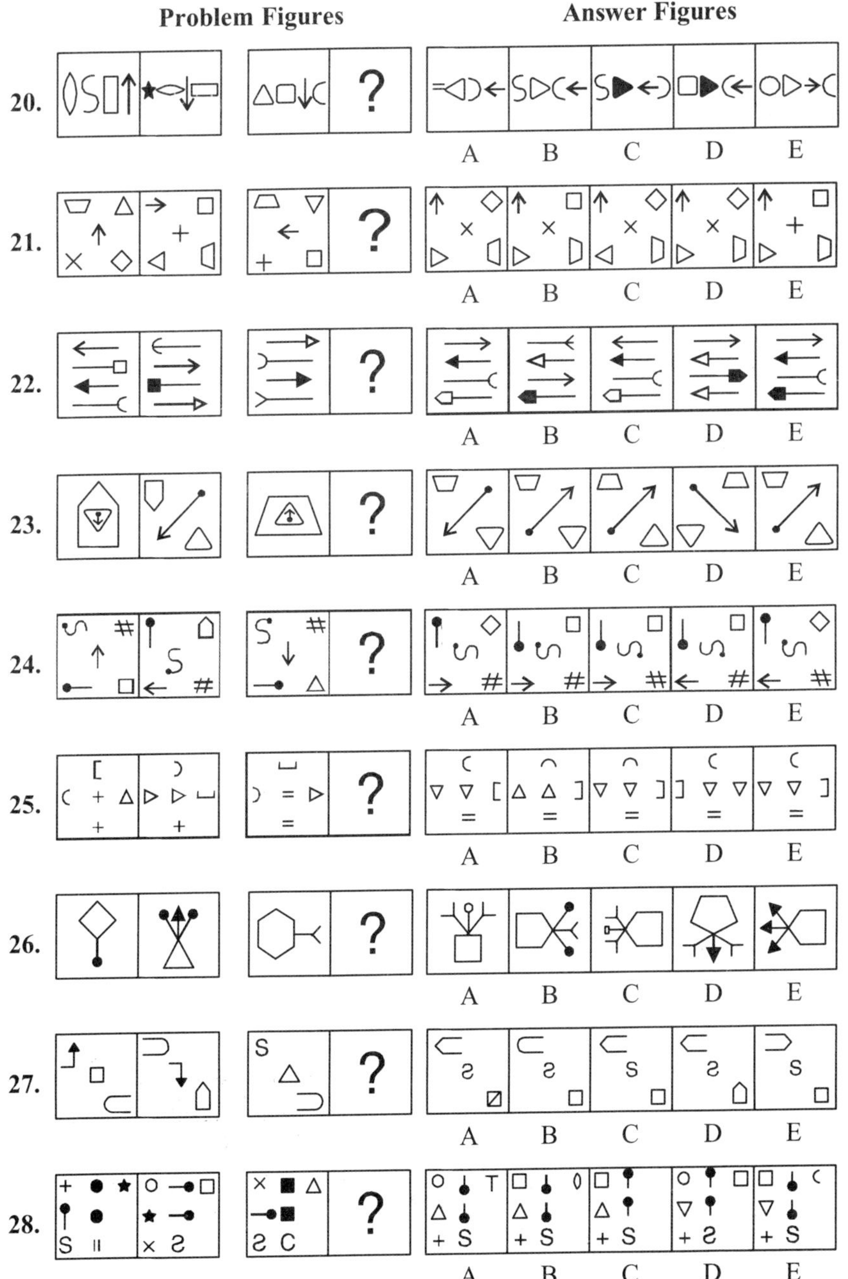
Problem Figures
Answer Figures
20.
21.
22.
23.
24.
25.
26.
27.
28.
?
A B C D E

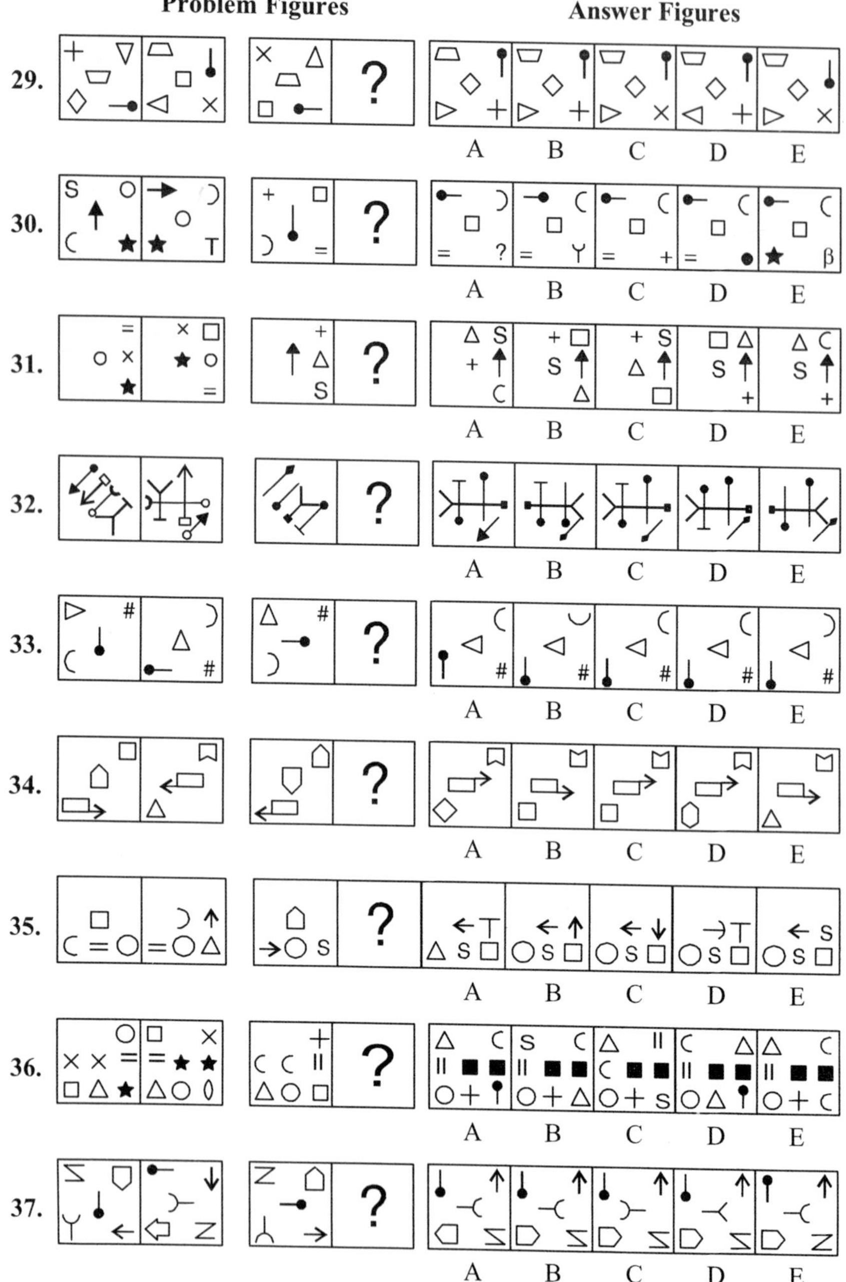
Problem Figures
Answer Figures
29.
30.
31.
32.
33.
34.
35.
36.
37.
A
B
C
D
E

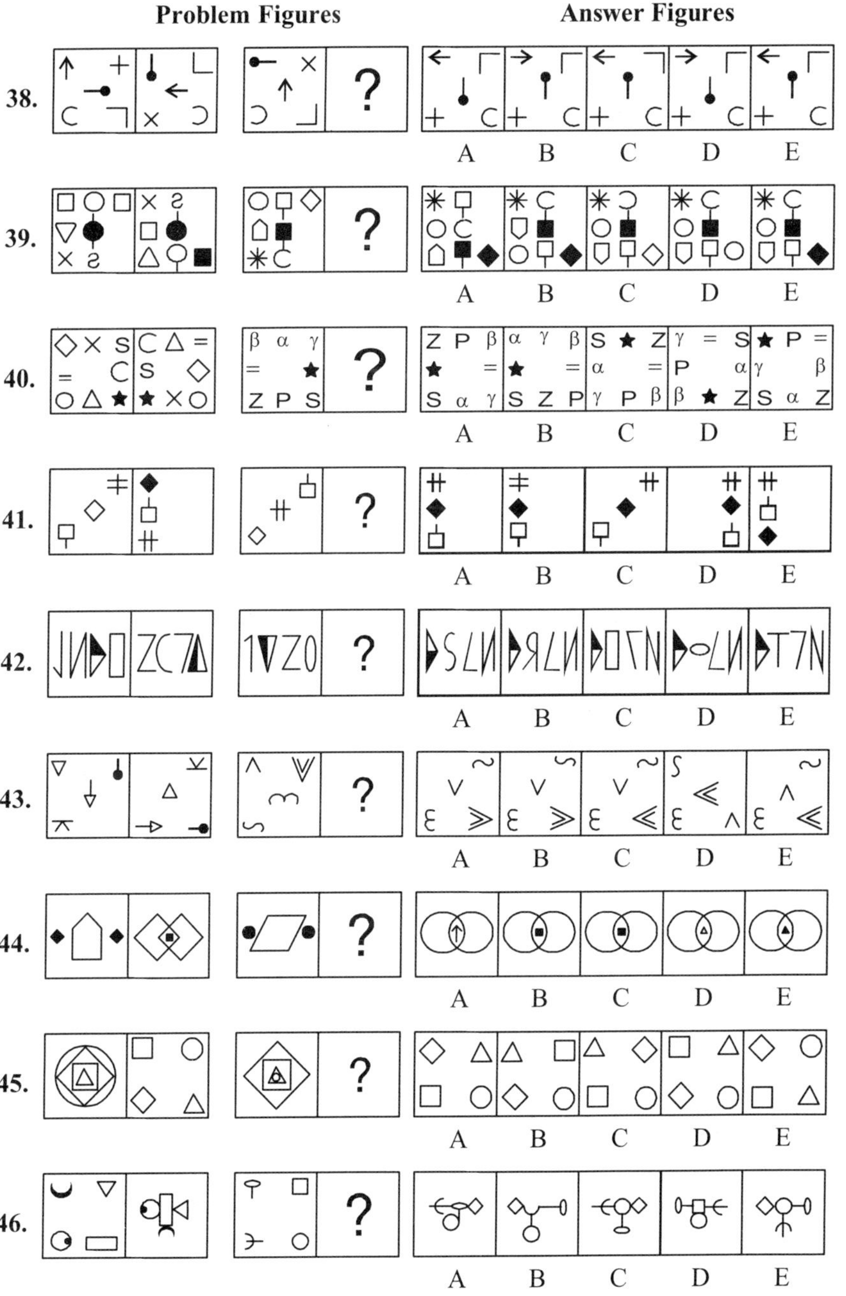
Problem Figures
Answer Figures
38.
39.
40.
41.
42.
43.
44.
45.
46.
A
B
C
D
E

**Problem Figures** **Answer Figures**

**47.** 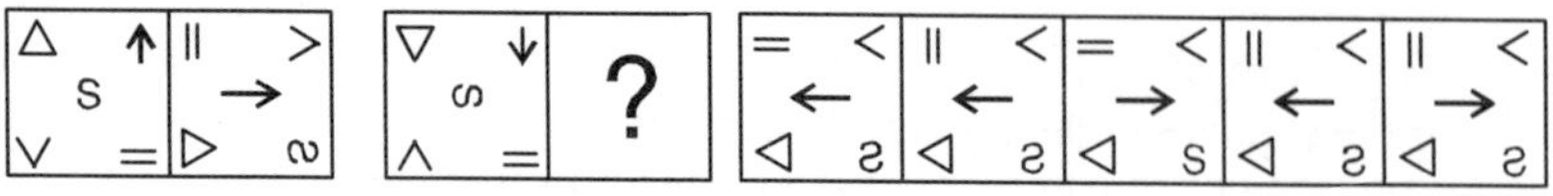 ?

A B C D E

**48.**  ?

A B C D E

**49.** 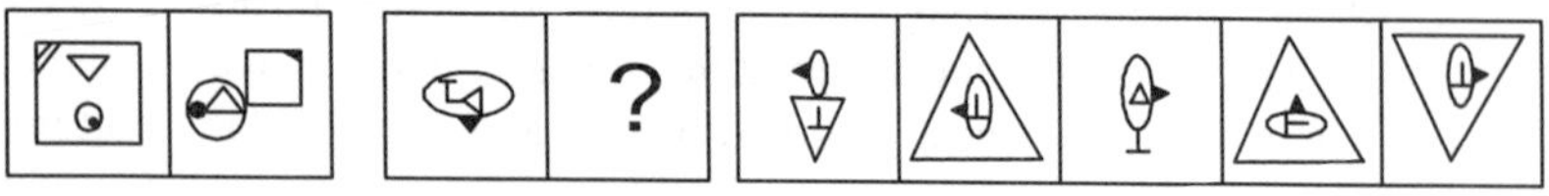 ?

A B C D E

**50.** 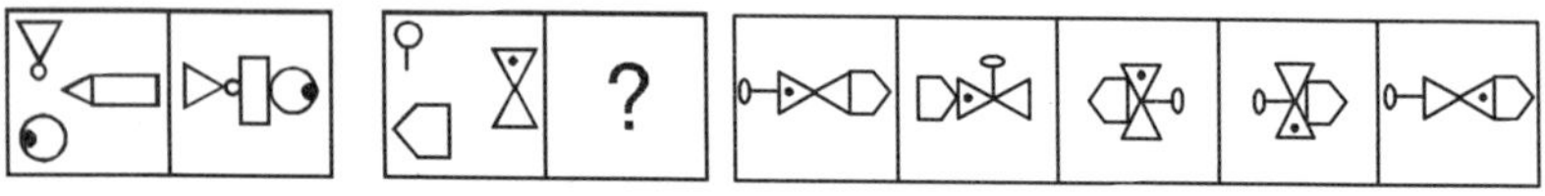 ?

A B C D E

## ANSWERS

| 1 | 2 | 3 | 4 | 5 | 6 | 7 | 8 | 9 | 10 |
|---|---|---|---|---|---|---|---|---|---|
| B | D | A | D | D | E | A | A | A | E |
| **11** | **12** | **13** | **14** | **15** | **16** | **17** | **18** | **19** | **20** |
| A | E | E | A | D | A | D | C | B | B |
| **21** | **22** | **23** | **24** | **25** | **26** | **27** | **28** | **29** | **30** |
| D | D | B | B | E | C | B | B | B | D |
| **31** | **32** | **33** | **34** | **35** | **36** | **37** | **38** | **39** | **40** |
| E | C | C | B | A | A | B | D | E | E |
| **41** | **42** | **43** | **44** | **45** | **46** | **47** | **48** | **49** | **50** |
| B | E | A | E | C | C | D | D | A | A |

## EXPLANATORY ANSWERS

**1.** The places of elements in the four corners are interchanged diagonally and also the places of elements in the top and bottom row are interchanged. The arrow and equal to sign are turned 90° clockwise, the square and the cross are turned by 45° and the S and the C letters are turned 90° anticlockwise.

**2.** The figure in the bottom left corner is replaced by another figure (made of one line less than the first), the element in the bottom right corner is turned 90° clockwise and moved diagonally to the top left corner position, the arc of the element in the top left corner is turned the other side and the element is turned 90° clockwise and then moved to the centre, the element in the centre is laterally inverted and moved to the top right corner position, and the element in the top right corner is turned by 180° and moved to the bottom right corner position.

**3.** The element in the top left corner is turned by 45° and moved horizontally to the top right corner position, the element in the top right is turned 90° clockwise and moved diagonally to bottom left corner position, the element in the bottom left corner is turned 90° clockwise and moved to the centre, the element in the centre is turned by 90° and moved to the bottom right corner position, and the element in the bottom right corner is turned 90° clockwise and moved diagonally to the top left corner position.

**4.** The two loops in the first figure of first set of figures are turned to the opposite side and three loops are added in alternately direction in a set pattern. In the second set of figures there are three loops in first figure; so, four loops should be added in the pattern mentioned above.

**5.** The figure on the top is replaced by a new figure (made of one line more than the first) and moved diagonally to the bottom, the element at the bottom is turned by 180° and moved to the centre, the element in the centre is turned by 180° and the two joined lines are turned the other side and then the element is moved to the top.

**6.** From first figure to the second, cross sign is changed to plus sign, arrow is turned 90° clockwise and the other three elements are horizontally inverted. The movement of elements is — the element in the centre is moved to the bottom left corner position, the element in the bottom left corner is moved up to the top left corner is moved horizontally to the top right corner position, the element in the top right corner is moved down to the bottom right corner position, and the element in the bottom right corner is moved to the centre.

**7.** The element in the top left corner is turned 90° clockwise and moved to the centre, the element in the centre is turned 90° anticlockwise and moved to the top right corner position, the element in the top right corner is laterally inverted and moved down to the bottom right corner position, the element in the bottom right corner is moved horizontally to the bottom left corner position, and the element in the bottom left corner is laterally inverted and moved up to the top left corner position.

8. The changes in elements from the first figure to the second are — the half arc is completed, the arrow like element is turned 90° anticlockwise and the third element is turned 90° clockwise. Also, the element at the top is moved to the bottom and other elements are moved upwards.
9. The element on the left in the first figure is turned 90° anticlockwise and then laterally inverted, and the other element turned by 180° to get the second figure.
10. The single element on the top is turned by 45° and moved to the middle position in the last row, the middle element in the last row is turned 90° anticlockwise and moved to the centre and right positions in the middle row, one of the common elements in middle row is turned by 45° and moved to the left position in the middle row, the element on the left in the middle row is turned 90° clockwise and moved down to the left position in the last row, the element on the left in the last row is turned 90° clockwise and moved horizontally to the bottom right corner position and the element in the bottom right corner is turned 90° clockwise and moved diagonally to the top left corner position.
11. The single element in a row is moved diagonally to its opposite corner, the other elements are shifted in a set pattern. Of the two last elements that are shifted, the second last element is made identical to the third last element and the extreme last element is placed in the corner (from where the sequence started) and made new.
12. The two parallel lines are moved one step anticlockwise and the dot inside the figure is moved out on the side opposite to the parallel lines. The figure in the centre is turned 90° clockwise, the protruding out portion is turned inwards and a blank dot is placed inside.
13. The element in the bottom right corner is turned by 45° and moved to the centre, the element in centre is turned 90° clockwise and moved to the bottom left corner position, the element in the bottom left corner is laterally inverted and moved to the top right corner position and the element in the top right corner is made new and moved to the top left corner position.
14. The elements attached to the fourth and the first vertical lines are shifted to the other end and then the lines are placed at the first and the second positions respectively. The elements attached to the second and the third vertical lines are inverted and then shifted to the other ends, then the lines are placed at third and fourth positions respectively.
15. The element in bottom left corner is moved diagonally to the top right corner position, the element in the top right corner is moved horizontally

to the top left corner position, the element in the top left corner is moved diagonally to bottom right corner position, the element in the bottom right corner is moved to the centre position and the element in the centre is moved to the bottom left corner position.

**16.** The element in the top right corner position is superimposed on the element in the top left corner position and together turned 135° anticlockwise. The element in the centre is turned by 180° and the element in the bottom left corner position is superimposed on the element in the bottom right corner position.

**17.** From first figure to the second, the pentagon (5-line figure) is changed into a square (4-line figure), the shaded dots are moved out one on either side and a blank dot is placed inside the square. Similarly, in the other two figures the square is changed into a triangle (3-line figure), shaded dots moved out and blank dot placed inside the triangle.

**18.** The first element on the top is laterally inverted and moved to the second place. The second element is laterally inverted and the two small line segments are turned inwards to make an arrow, and then the element is moved to the third place. The third element is laterally inverted, the small triangle attached to it is turned by 45°, and then the element is moved to the bottom position. The element at the bottom is laterally inverted and moved to the top as first element.

**19.** The main figure is turned 90° anticlockwise. The figure is changed into a 'V' like shape but the small curved part is turned inwards. The triangle is moved one step clockwise. The plus sign inside the figure is moved out one step ahead of the triangle and turned into a cross. A star sign is added in clockwise manner one step ahead of the cross. In the second set of figures the process is same except that the cross sign is turned into a plus sign.

**20.** The places of first two elements are interchanged and then the first element is made new and the second element is turned 90° clockwise. The places of third and fourth elements are interchanged and then the third element is turned upside down and the fourth element is turned 90° clockwise.

**21.** The element in the top left corner is turned 90° clockwise and moved to the bottom right corner position, the element in the bottom right corner is turned by 45° and moved to the top right corner position, the element in the top right corner is turned 90° anticlockwise and moved to the bottom left corner position, the element in the bottom left corner is turned by 45° and moved to the centre, the element in the centre is turned 90° clockwise and moved to the top left corner position.

**22.** From first figure to the second, the shaded part is unshaded and vice-versa. The three elements from the top are laterally inverted and moved down one step. The attachment to the last element is shifted to the other end of the line and the element is moved to the top position.

**23.** The arrow with a dot inside the two figures is turned 45° clockwise, enlarged and moved out. The outermost and the inner figures are reduced, vertically inverted and moved to top left corner and right corner positions respectively.

**24.** The bottom right corner element is made new and moved to the top right corner position. The top right corner element is moved to the bottom right corner position and the direction of slanting lines is changed. The top left corner element is turned 90° anticlockwise and moved to the centre. The element in the centre is turned 90° anticlockwise and moved to the bottom left corner position. The element in the bottom left corner is turned 90° clockwise and moved to the top left corner position.

**25.** The element on the left is laterally inverted and moved to the top, the element on the top is turned 90° anticlockwise and moved to the right, the element on the right is turned 90° clockwise and moved to the left and this also replaces the element in the centre. The element at the bottom remains unchanged.

**26.** The number of lines making the design in second figure is one less than those making the design in the first figure. The element attached to the design is moved to the other side and duplicated. Also, one new element is placed inbetween the two identical elements.

**27.** The element in the bottom right corner is laterally inverted and moved to the top left corner position, the element in the top left corner is turned upside down and moved to the centre, and the element in the centre is made new by adding one more straight line to its formation and moved to the bottom right corner position.

**28.** The element in the top right corner is moved to the left middle position, the element in the left middle position is turned 90° clockwise and moved to the centre, the element in the centre is replaced by the earlier element and moved to the top middle position, the element in the top middle position is made blank and moved to the top left corner position, the element in the top left corner is turned by 45° and moved to the bottom left corner position, the element in the bottom left corner is laterally inverted and moved to the bottom middle position, and a new element is placed at the top right corner position.

**29.** The element in the top left corner is turned by 45° and moved to the bottom right corner position the element in the bottom right corner is turned 90° clockwise and moved up to top right corner position, the element in top right corner is turned 90° clockwise and moved to bottom left corner position, the element in bottom left corner is turned by 45° and moved to the centre; and the element in the centre is turned upside down and moved to the top left corner position.

**30.** The element in the top left corner is made new and moved to the bottom right corner position, the element in the bottom right corner is moved to the bottom left corner position, the element in the bottom left corner is laterally inverted and moved to the top right corner position, the element in the top right corner is moved to the centre, and the element in the centre is turned 90° clockwise and moved to the top left corner position.

**31.** The element in the top right corner is moved to the bottom right corner position, the element in the bottom right corner is moved to the centre, the element in the centre is moved to the right middle position, the element in the right middle position is moved to the top middle position, and a new element is placed in the top right corner position.

**32.** The element on the top is turned by 180° and moved to the bottom. The second element is turned 135° clockwise and placed in the centre. The third element is turned 135° anticlockwise and placed in the centre, crossing the second element, and the last element in turned 135° clockwise and placed to left of the third element cutting the second element.

**33.** The element in the top left corner is turned 90° anticlockwise and moved to the centre, the element in the centre is turned 90° clockwise and moved to the bottom left corner position, the element in the bottom left corner is laterally inverted and moved to the top right corner position, and the element in the top right corner is laterally inverted and moved to the bottom right corner position.

**34.** The element on the top is changed (made of one line less than the first) and moved diagonally to the bottom, the arrow of the element at the bottom is moved two steps in its direction and then the element is moved to the centre. The element in the centre is turned by 180°, its outward portion is turned inwards and then the element is moved to the top.

**35.** The lines of the figure in the centre are reduced by one, a new figure is made and moved to the bottom right corner position. The element in the bottom right corner and in the centre are shifted to the left. The element in the bottom left corner is laterally inverted and moved to the centre. A new element is added on the right side.

**36.** The element in the top right corner is moved to the centre place in the bottom row, the element in the centre at the bottom row is moved left and the element in the bottom left corner is moved up to the top left corner position, the element in the bottom right corner is shaded and moved up and repeated once on its left, the element in the right of the middle row is moved horizontally to the left, one of the two identical elements is removed and the other one is moved to the top right corner position, and lastly, a new element is placed in the bottom right corner position.

**37.** The element in the top left corner is laterally inverted and moved diagonally to the bottom right corner position, the element in the bottom right corner is turned 90° anticlockwise and moved up to the top right corner position, the element in the top right corner is turned 90° clockwise and moved diagonally to the bottom left corner position, the element in the bottom left corner is turned 90° anticlockwise and moved to the centre, and the element in the centre is turned 90° clockwise and moved to the top left corner position.

**38.** The element in the top left corner is turned 90° anticlockwise and moved to the centre, the element in the centre is turned 90° clockwise and moved to the top left corner position. The element in the top right corner is turned by 45° and moved diagonally to bottom left corner position, the element in the bottom left corner is laterally inverted and moved horizontally to the bottom right corner position, and the element in the bottom right corner is turned by 180° and moved up to the top right corner position.

**39.** The bottom element in the first column is moved to the top, the other elements are shifted down and the last element is vertically inverted. The places of top and bottom elements in the middle column are interchanged and the middle element is vertically inverted. The element in the last column is moved to the bottom and shaded.

**40.** The positions of each of the following two elements are interchanged: *(i)* element in the top left corner and element in the middle on the right side, *(ii)* element in the middle on the top and element in the middle at the bottom, *(iii)* element in the top right corner and element in the middle on the left side, and *(iv)* element in the bottom left corner and element in the bottom right corner.

**41.** The element in the top right corner is moved to the bottom left position, the element in the centre is moved to the top left corner position, and the element in the bottom left corner is moved in the middle of other two elements. It must, however, be noted that in the second figure only the rhombus is shaded, the not equal to sign is turned by 90° and the square with a line segment attached to it is turned upside down.

**42.** The first element is turned 90° anticlockwise and moved to the third place, the second element is laterally inverted and turned 90° anticlockwise and moved to the first place, the third element is laterally inverted and turned 90° clockwise and moved to the fourth and last place, and fourth and last element is made new and moved to the second place.

**43.** The element in the top left corner is turned upside down and moved to the centre, the element in the centre is turned 90° anticlockwise and moved to the bottom left corner position, the element in the bottom left corner is turned upside down and moved diagonally to the opposite corner, and the element in the top right corner is turned 90° anticlockwise and moved to the bottom right corner position.

**44.** The shaded designs on the left and right are unshaded, enlarged and overlapped to form a small section in the middle. The number of lines making the unshaded design in the centre is reduced by one. This new figure is shaded and placed in the middle portion.

**45.** The four designs in figure one are separated in figure two. Starting from the outermost design—the first design is placed at the top right corner position, the second design is placed at the bottom left corner position, the third design is placed at the top left corner position and the fourth (innermost) design is placed at the bottom right corner position.

**46.** The top left element is turned by 180° and moved to the bottom centre position, the top right element is turned 90° clockwise and moved to the right position, the bottom right element is turned by 90° and moved to the centre and the bottom left element is turned by 180° and moved to the left position. All the elements are joined in the second figure.

**47.** The triangle is turned 90° clockwise and moved one step anticlockwise. The 'V' shape is turned 90° anticlockwise and moved diagonally to the other corner. The arrow is turned 90° clockwise and moved to the centre. The 'S' is vertically inverted, turned 90° clockwise and moved to the bottom right corner. The two parallel lines are turned by 90° and moved to the top left corner position.

**48.** The direction of the stand in the middle of the figure is turned to the opposite direction. Of the four hanging elements, the element on the top left is moved to the bottom right side, the element at the bottom right is moved to the top right side, the element at the top right is moved to the bottom left side and the element at the bottom left is moved to the top left position.

**49.** There are two small designs enclosed with in a large design. Of these two, the design on the top is turned upside down. The other design is turned 90° clockwise and enlarged to enclose this small design. The large and outer design in figure one is turned 90° clockwise and placed above the other two designs.

**50.** The element on the right is turned 90° anticlockwise and moved to the centre, the element in the top left corner is turned 90° anticlockwise and attached to the element in the centre on the left, and the element in the bottom left corner is laterally inverted and attached to the element in the centre on the right.

❍ ❍ ❍

## TYPE II

**Directions :** *In each of the following questions, a related pair of figures is followed by five figures. Select the pair that has a relationship similar to that in the original pair.*

**Problem Figures** **Answer Figures**

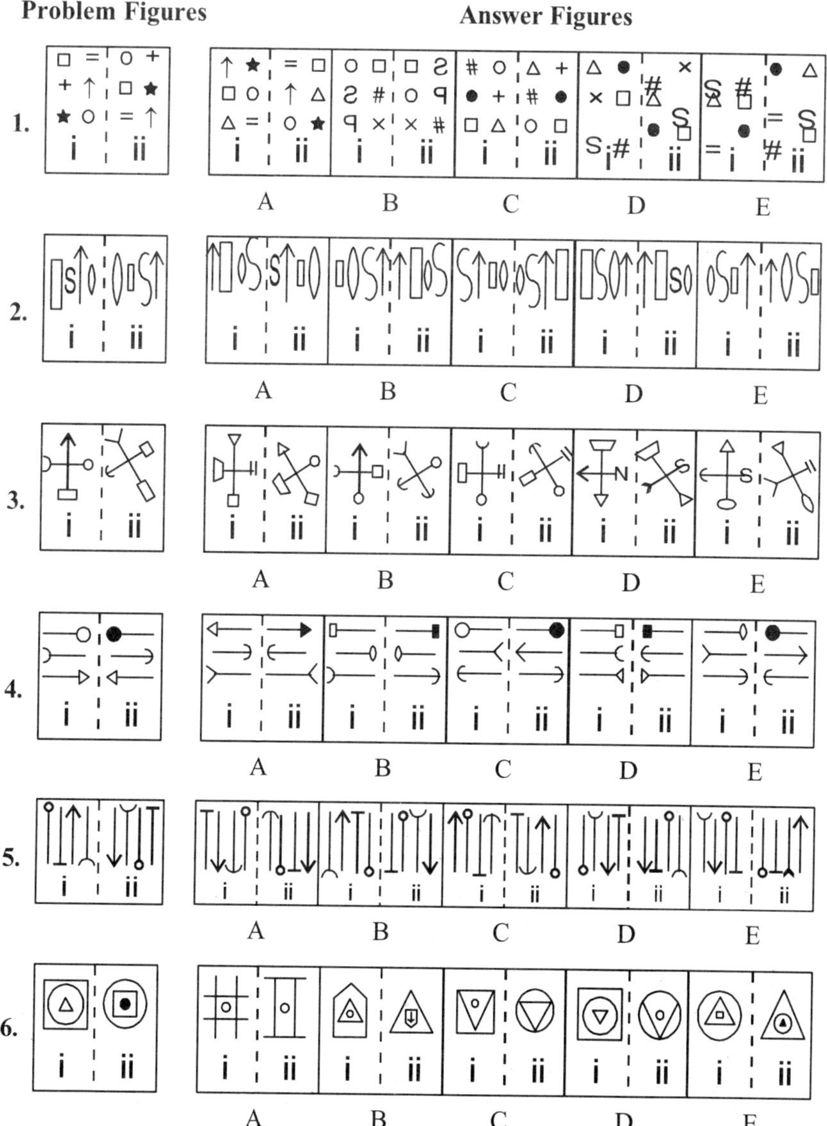

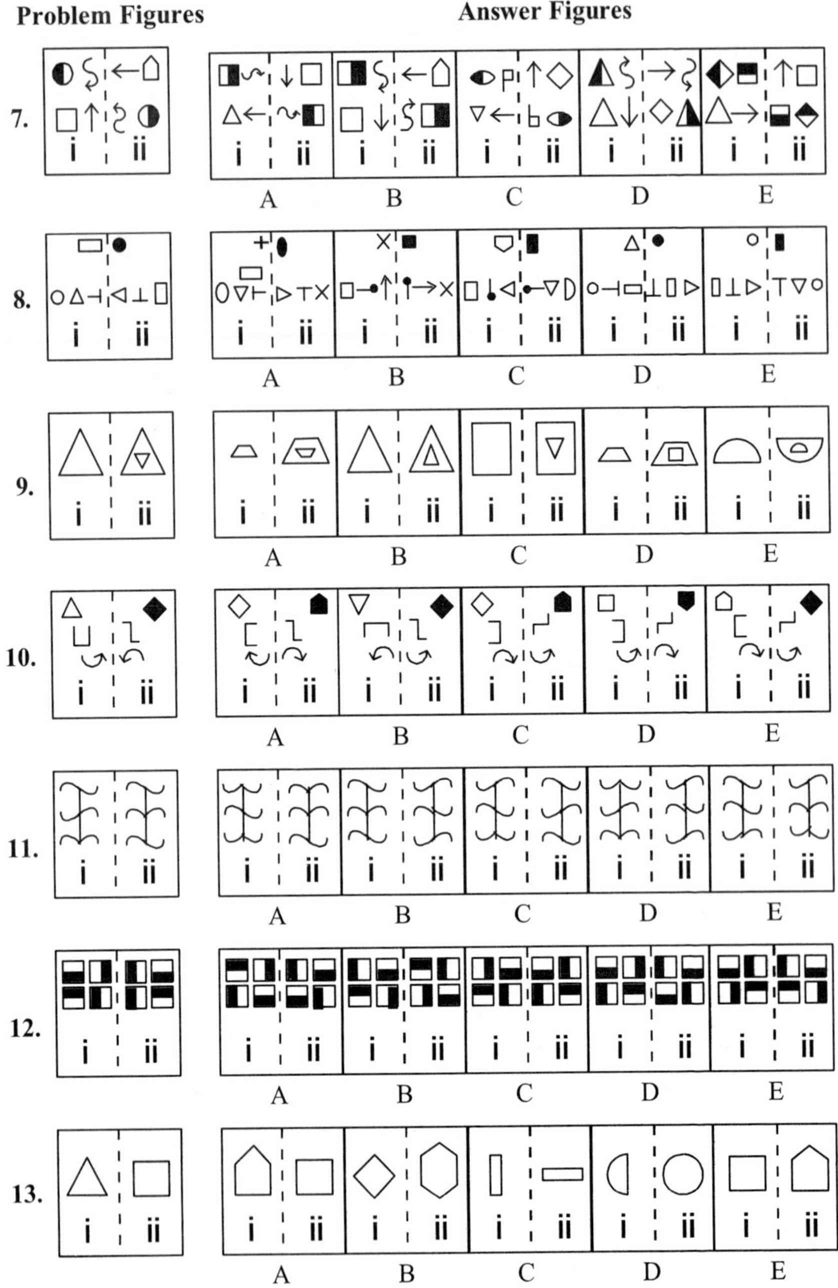
Problem Figures
Answer Figures
7.
8.
9.
10.
11.
12.
13.
i ii
A B C D E

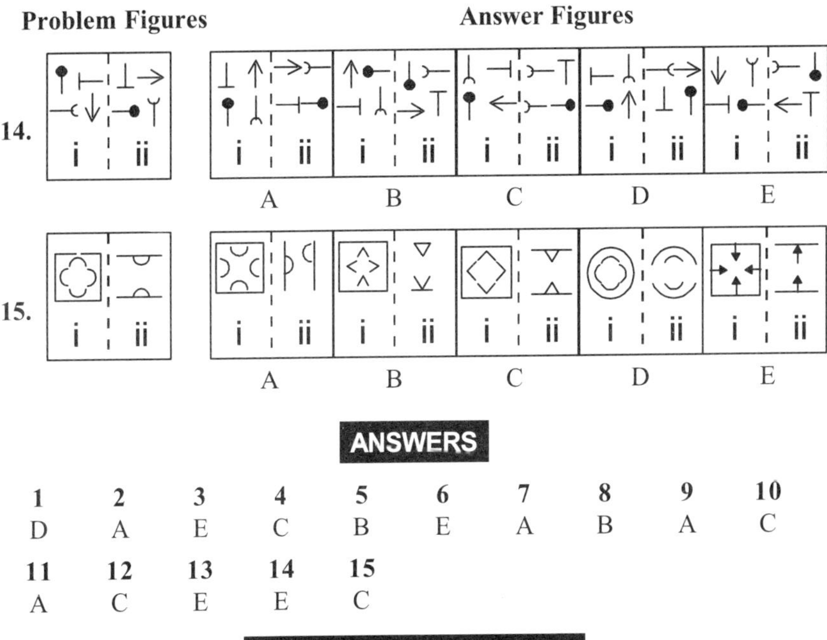


## ANSWERS

| 1 | 2 | 3 | 4 | 5 | 6 | 7 | 8 | 9 | 10 |
|---|---|---|---|---|---|---|---|---|---|
| D | A | E | C | B | E | A | B | A | C |
| **11** | **12** | **13** | **14** | **15** | | | | | |
| A | C | E | E | C | | | | | |

## EXPLANATORY ANSWERS

1. Observe the movement of the units from first part to the second, the top left unit is moved to the middle left position, the middle left unit is moved to the top right position, the top right unit is moved diagonally to the bottom left position, the bottom left unit is moved to the middle right position, the middle right unit is moved to the bottom right position and the bottom right unit is moved diagonally to the top left position.
2. The larger and the smaller elements in first part become smaller and larger respectively in the second. Also, the fourth element on the right becomes the first element on the left in the second part.
3. The cross is turned 90° anticlockwise in the second part. Then the direction of the elements attached to the cross is changed and the element on the top right is replaced by a new element.
4. The units attached to the straight lines in first part are moved to the other side. Then the topmost blank unit is shaded and the the bottom unit is laterally inverted in the second part.
5. All the elements in first part are turned upside down and then 1st, 2nd, 3rd and 4th positioned elements become 3rd, 4th, 1st and 2nd elements in the second part.

6. The innermost figure is removed and the new innermost figure also encloses the other two figures. The innermost and smallest figure is then shaded.
7. All the four elements exchange place diagonally and in doing so the top left element is laterally inverted, the top right element is horizontally inverted, the bottom right element is turned 90° anticlockwise and the number of lines making the element in bottom left is increased by one.
8. From part one to part two, the top right element is turned by 90° and moved down, the lower right and middle elements are turned 90° clockwise and 90° anticlockwise respectively and moved to the left and the lower left element is shaded and moved up.
9. The figure in part one is enlarged as well as reduced and the reduced figure is placed upsidedown inside the enlarged figure in part two.
10. The number of sides making the top left figure is increased by one and a new figure is made, shaded and moved to the top right position. The element in the centre is turned 90° anticlockwise and the small line on the other side is turned by 180°. The element in the bottom right is turned upside down and moved to the bottom left position.
11. The direction of both acs on the top, are on the middle right and arc on the bottom left in first part are turned to the other side in the second part.
12. The bottom left square is turned 90° anticlockwise and the other three turned 90° clockwise in the second part.
13. The number of lines making the figure in first part is one less than the number of lines making the figure in the second part.
14. From part one to part two, the element in the top left is turned 90° clockwise and the other three 90° anticlockwise, also the elements are moved one step anticlockwise.
15. The left and right sides and also the inner elements along the two sides in first part are removed in the second part. The inner elements along the other two sides are inverted.

❍ ❍ ❍

# 3

# Classification

## TYPE I

*Classification is the act or process of putting people or things into a group or a class. In this chapter, we deal with the problems of* ***odd man-out type****.*

This test is designed to judge candidates ability to classify or segregate a group of objects, from the given objects, on the basis of their common properties, i.e. it is a process of marking out a homogeneous group from a heterogeneous larger group. In this type of questions, you will be asked to find out a figure which is different in nature/character from the main group.

In this chapter, we deal with questions which have a set of four/five figures, out of which all except one are alike or have some common nature/characteristics. You will have to select the exclusively different figure from the given set. Here, some examples are given which will illustrate the different types of questions which are generally asked in various competitive examinations.

## SOLVED EXAMPLES

**Directions (Qs. 1-5):** *Out of these five set of given figures, four are similar in a certain way. One figure is not like the other four/three. Find out the figure which does not belong to the group.*

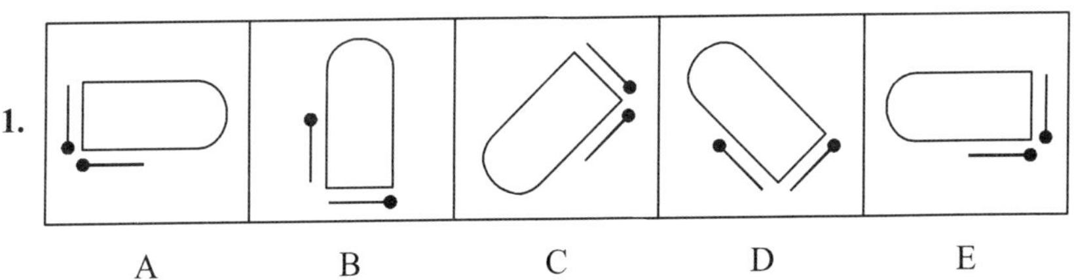


**Answers A:** All the figures are placed straight with base down, then one of the pins lies along base and the other pin lies along left side of the figure. Figure A does not follow this rule and hence, is different from others.

2. 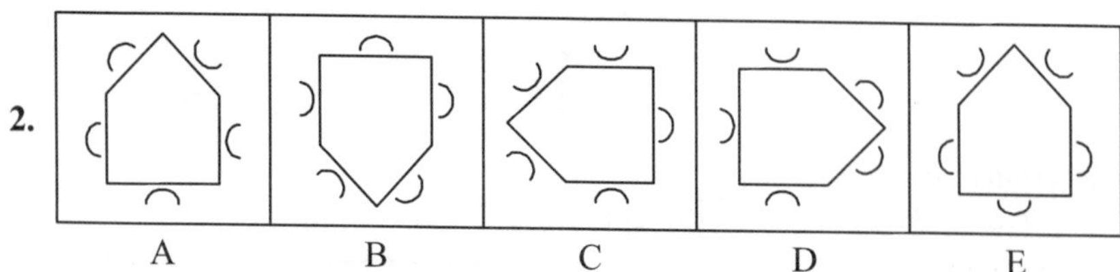

Answers C: All the arcs along the sides of the figure are arranged in such a way that any three arcs adustment are placed in similar fashion, i.e. they face sides of the figure or faces outside. Figure C does not follow this rule and hence, is different from other figures.

3. 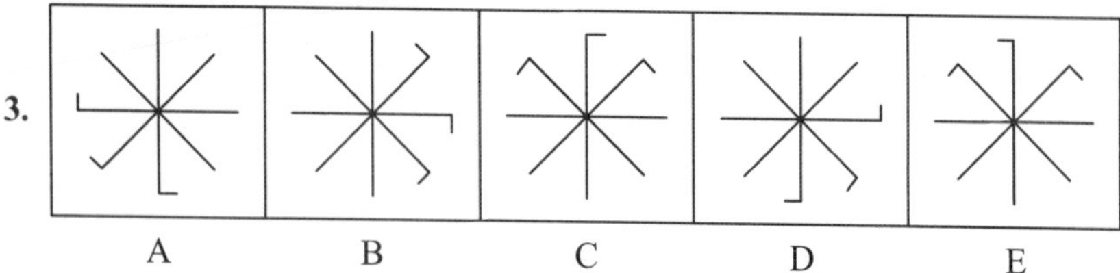

**Answers E:** In all the other figures, two bent lines segments faces clockwise direction and single bent line faces in anti-clockwise direction. In figure E, the case is just the opposite.

4. 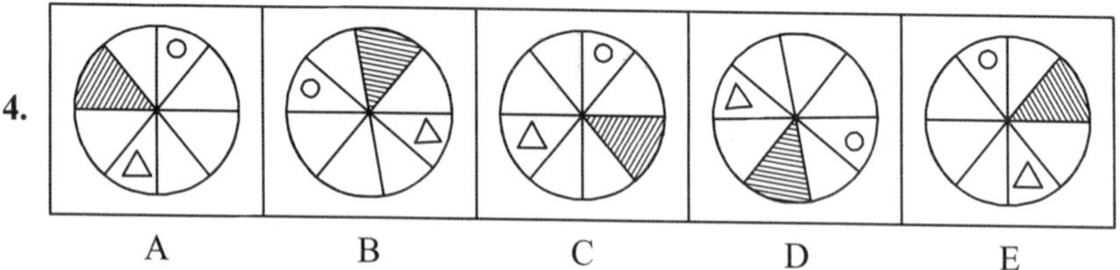

**Answers C:** In all figure, except C the shaded part and the triangle have one empty space similarly the shaded part and the small circle have one empty space in between.

5. 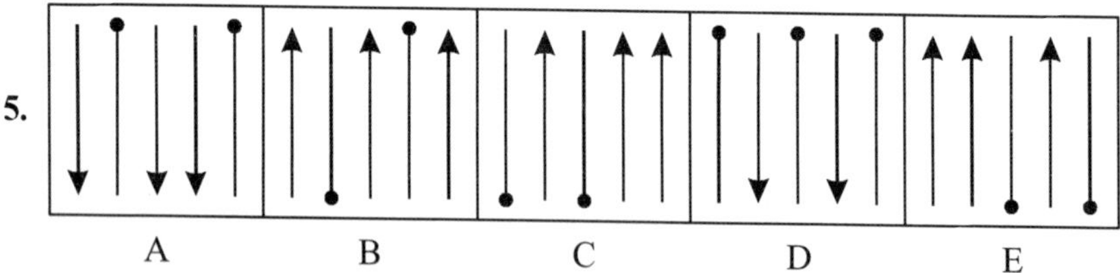

**Answers D:** In all the figures except figure (D), there are two pins and three arrows. In figure (D), there are three pins and two arrows; thus it is different from the others.

**EXERCISE**

**Directions :** *In each of the following questions one of the figures is different from the rest. Spot the figure.*

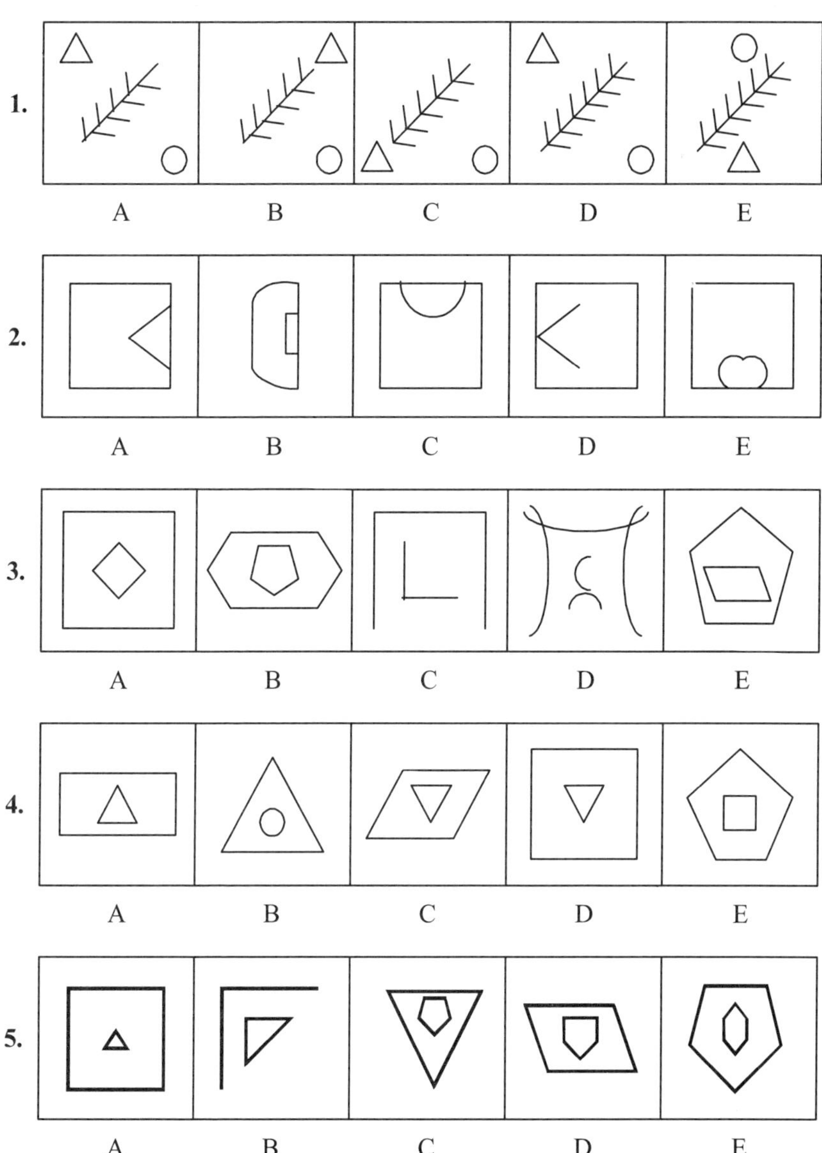

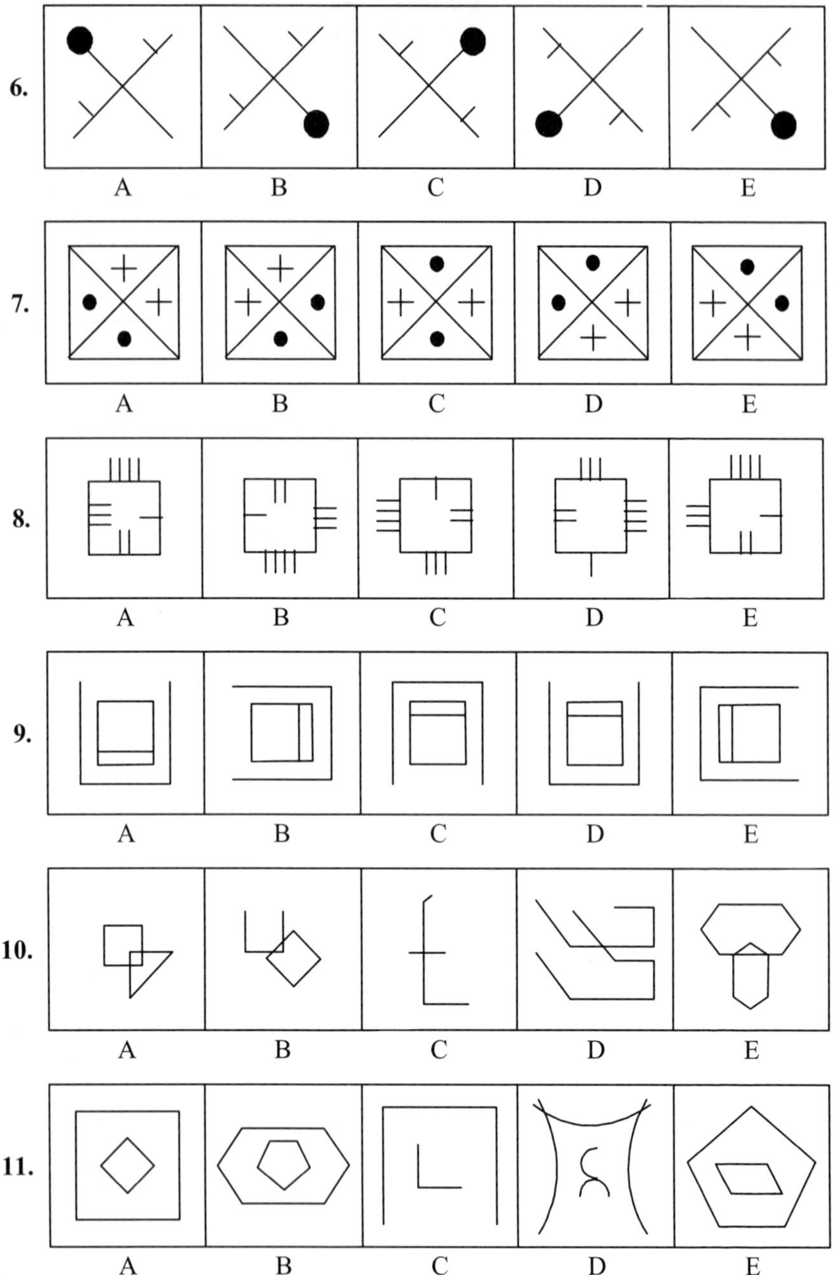
6.
A
B
C
D
E
7.
A
B
C
D
E
8.
A
B
C
D
E
9.
A
B
C
D
E
10.
A
B
C
D
E
11.
A
B
C
D
E

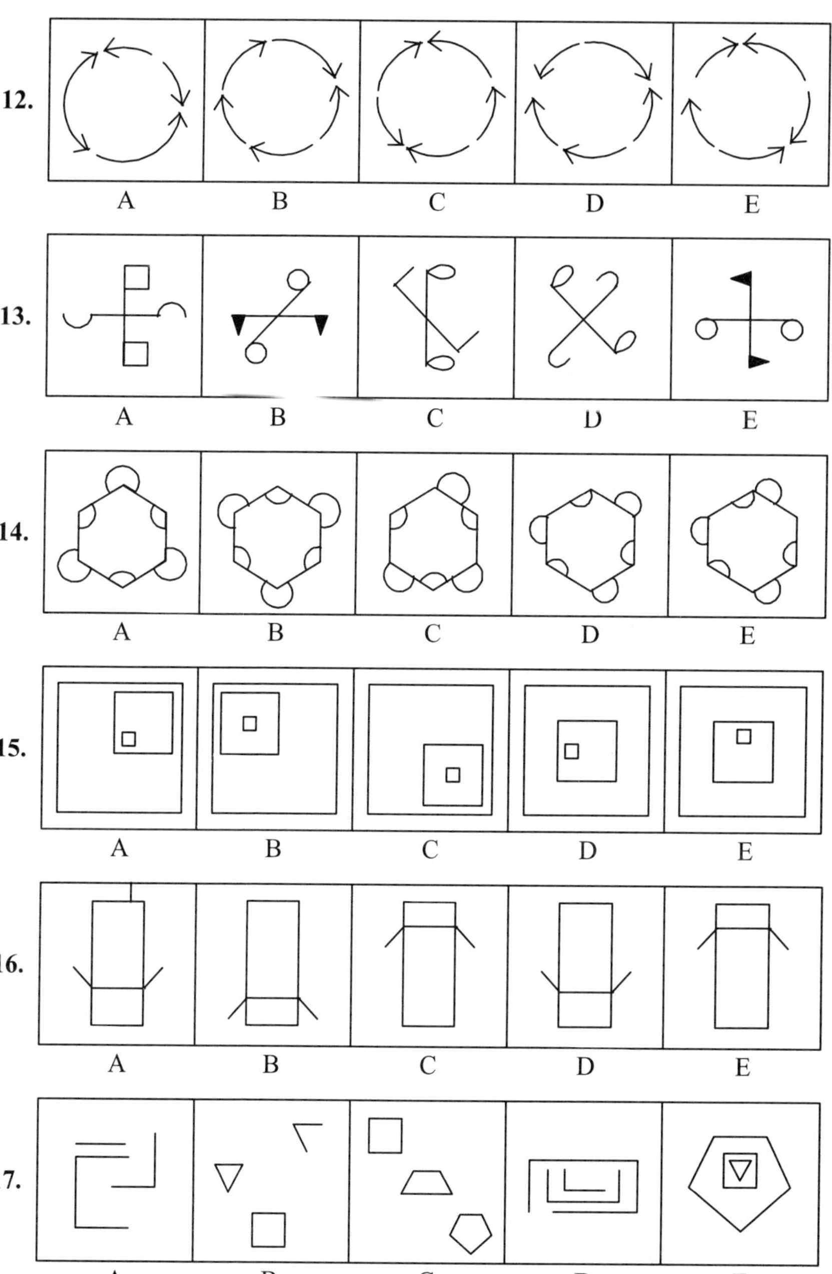
12.
A
B
C
D
E
13.
A
B
C
D
E
14.
A
B
C
D
E
15.
A
B
C
D
E
16.
A
B
C
D
E
17.
A
B
C
D
E

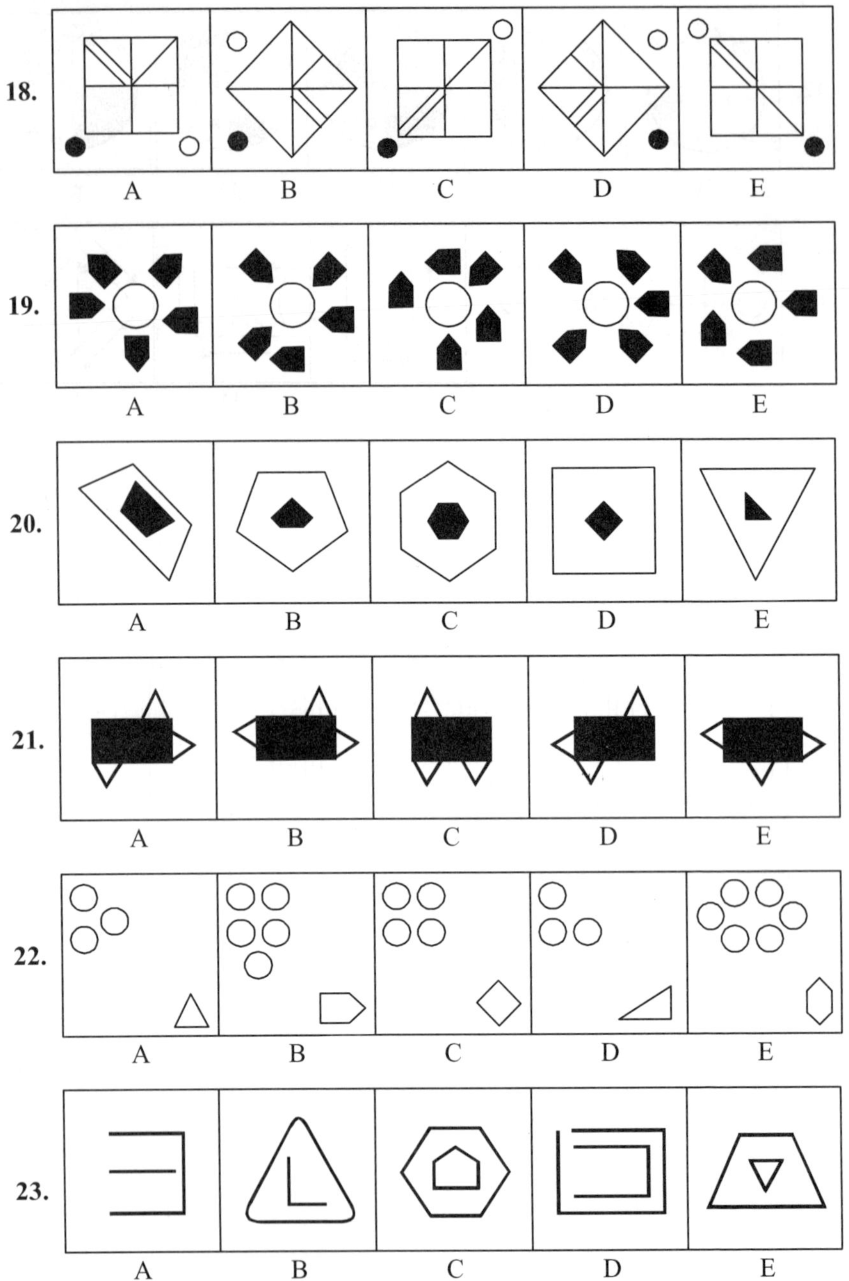
18.
A B C D E
19.
A B C D E
20.
A B C D E
21.
A B C D E
22.
A B C D E
23.
A B C D E

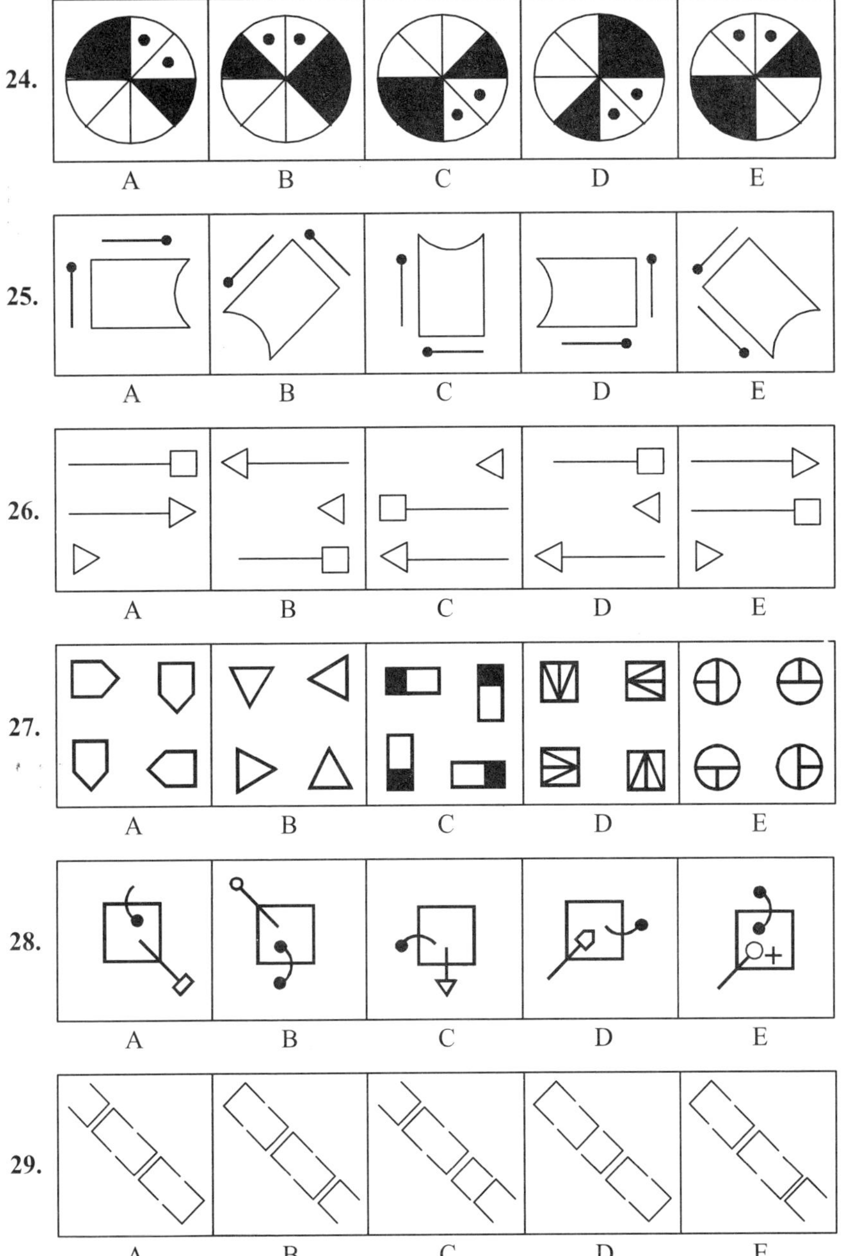
24.
A
B
C
D
E
25.
A
B
C
D
E
26.
A
B
C
D
E
27.
A
B
C
D
E
28.
A
B
C
D
E
29.
A
B
C
D
E

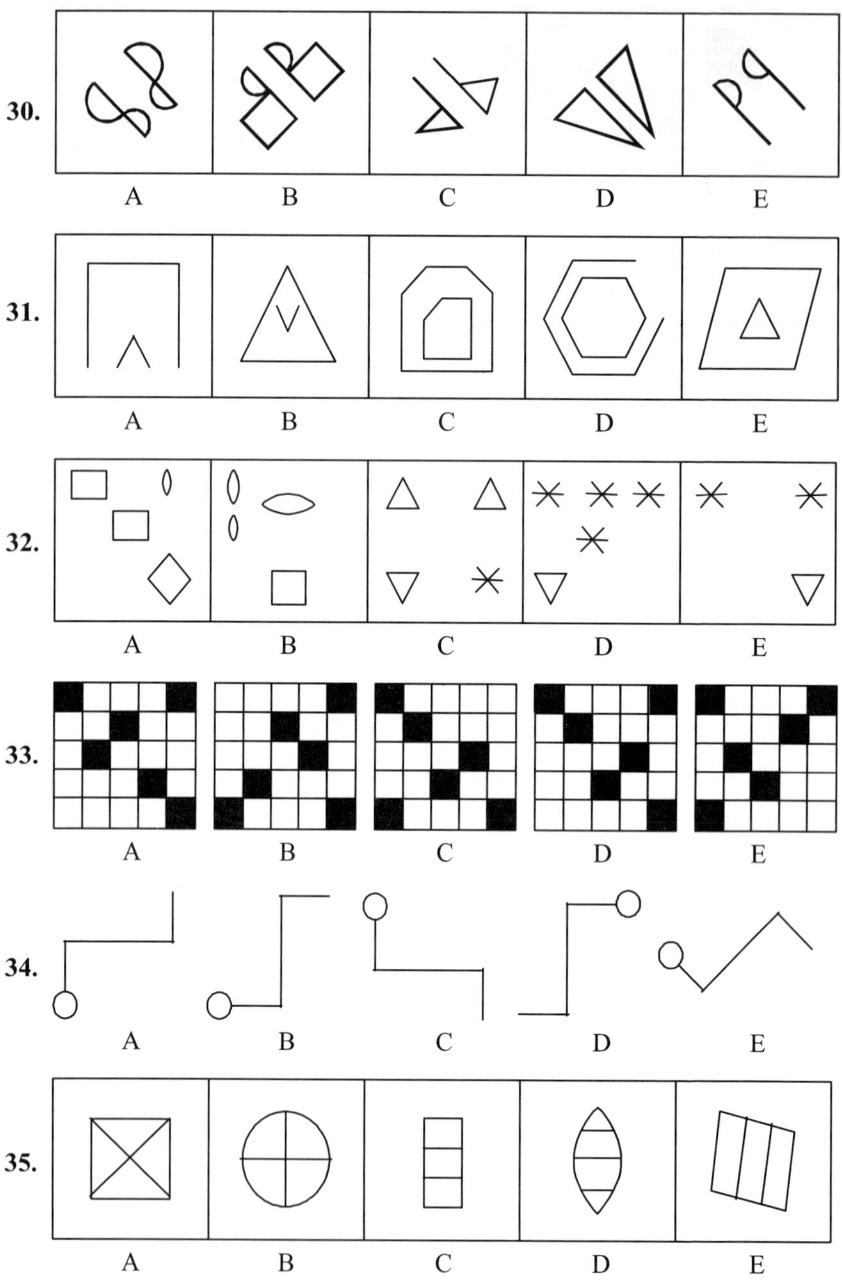
30.
A
B
C
D
E
31.
A
B
C
D
E
32.
A
B
C
D
E
33.
A
B
C
D
E
34.
A
B
C
D
E
35.
A
B
C
D
E

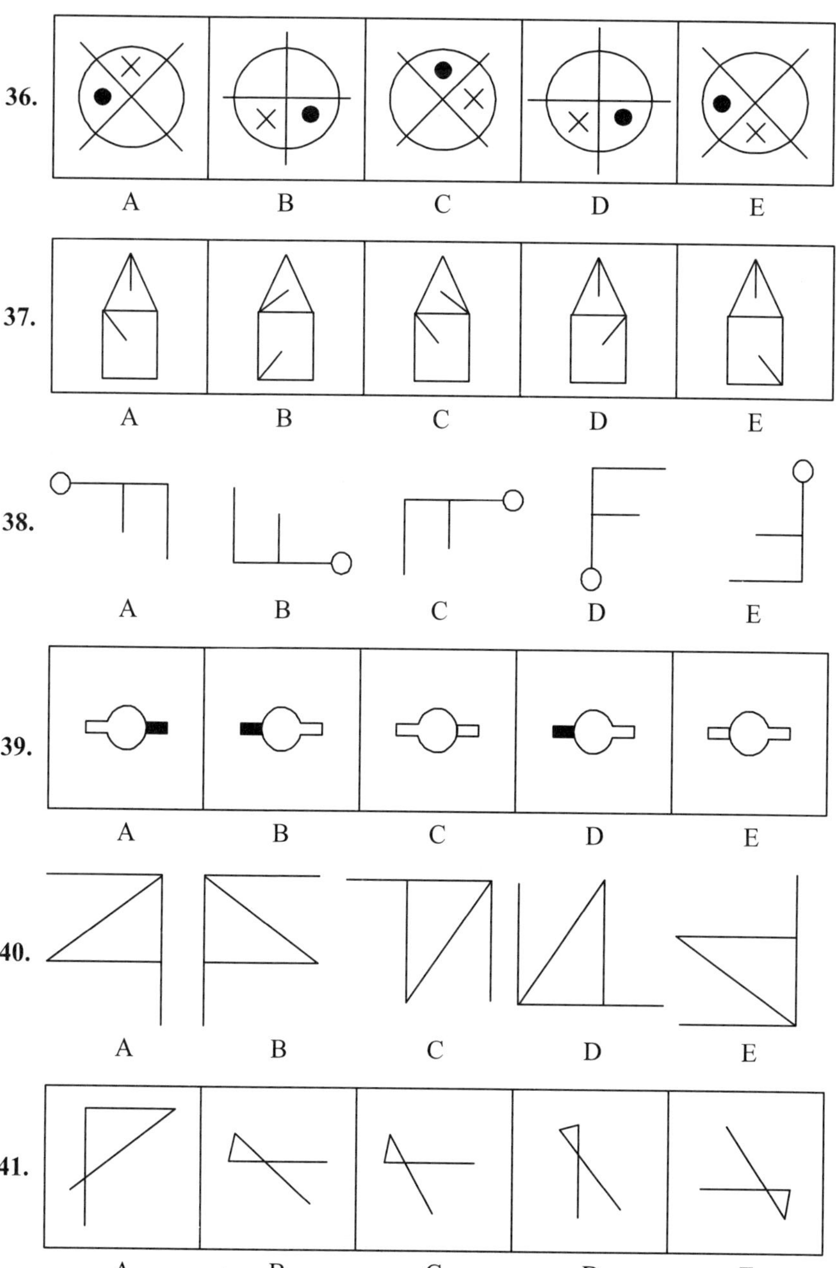
36.
A
B
C
D
E
37.
A
B
C
D
E
38.
A
B
C
D
E
39.
A
B
C
D
E
40.
A
B
C
D
E
41.
A
B
C
D
E

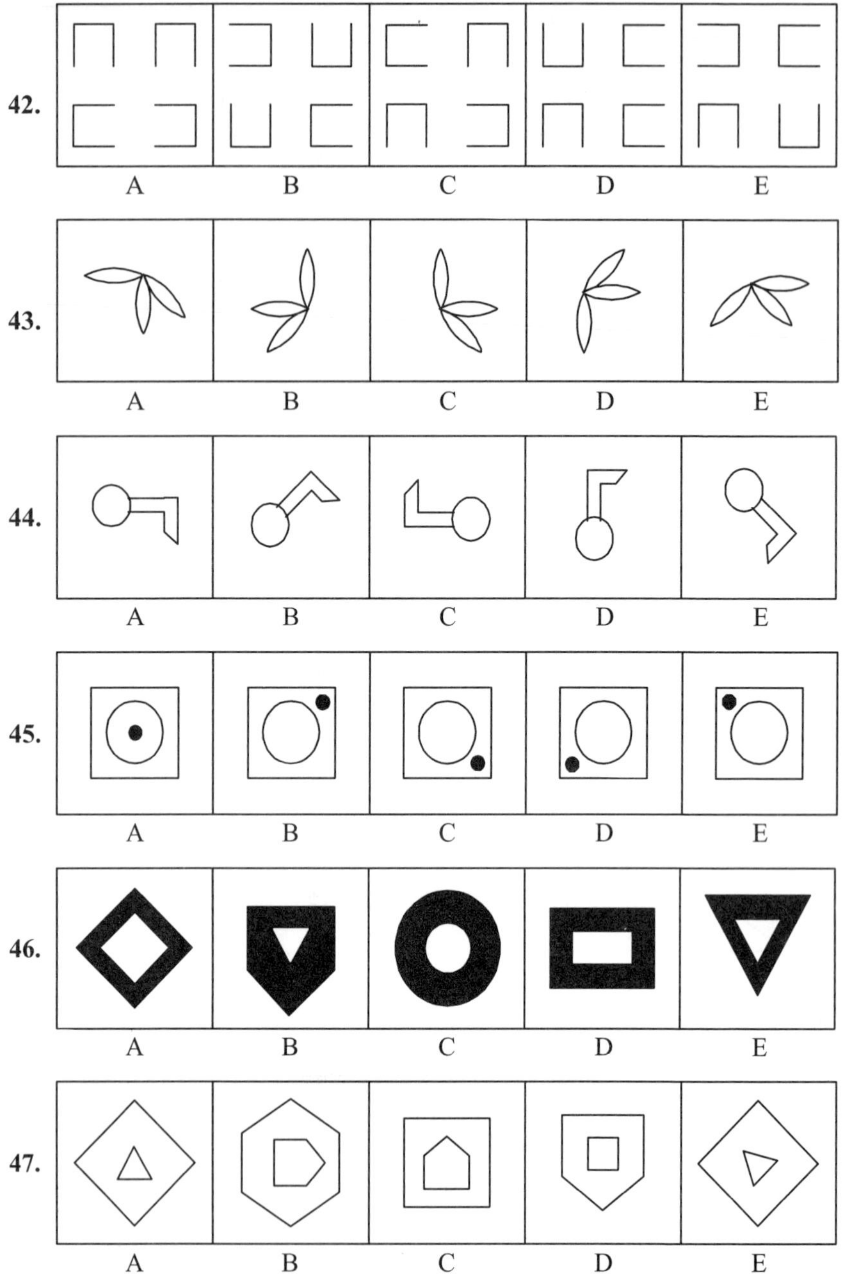
42.
A
B
C
D
E
43.
A
B
C
D
E
44.
A
B
C
D
E
45.
A
B
C
D
E
46.
A
B
C
D
E
47.
A
B
C
D
E

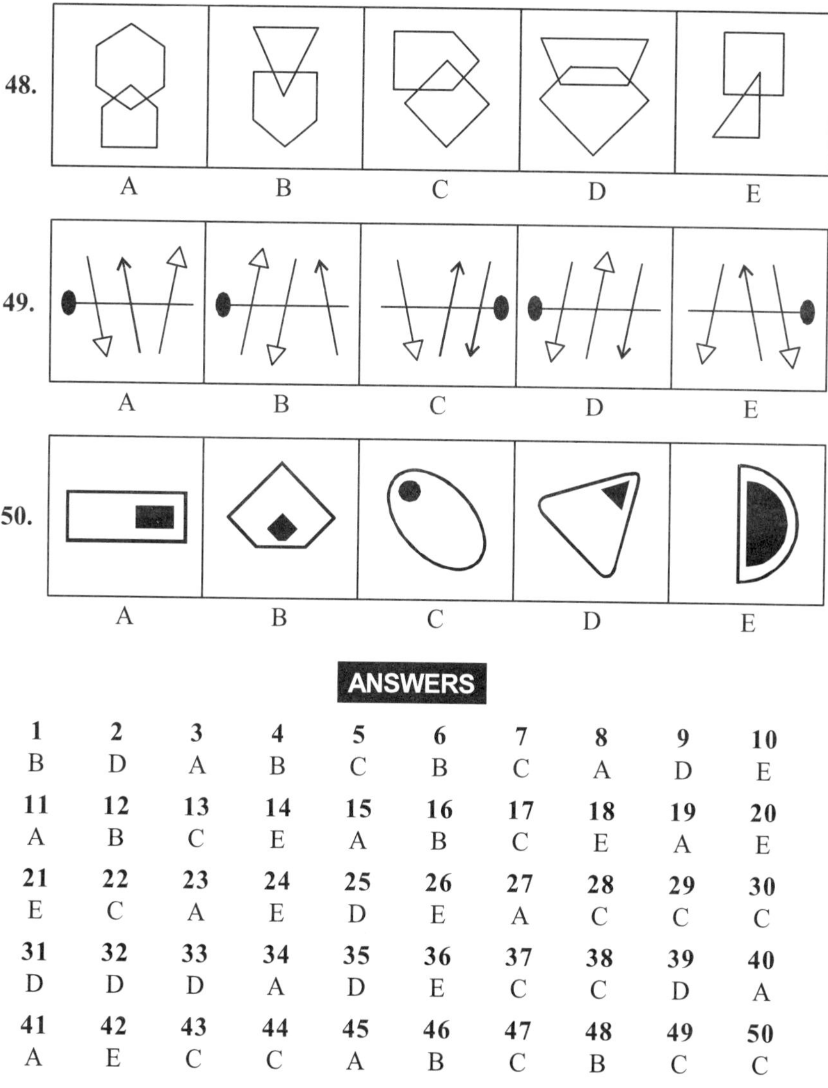


## ANSWERS

| 1 | 2 | 3 | 4 | 5 | 6 | 7 | 8 | 9 | 10 |
|---|---|---|---|---|---|---|---|---|---|
| B | D | A | B | C | B | C | A | D | E |
| **11** | **12** | **13** | **14** | **15** | **16** | **17** | **18** | **19** | **20** |
| A | B | C | E | A | B | C | E | A | E |
| **21** | **22** | **23** | **24** | **25** | **26** | **27** | **28** | **29** | **30** |
| E | C | A | E | D | E | A | C | C | C |
| **31** | **32** | **33** | **34** | **35** | **36** | **37** | **38** | **39** | **40** |
| D | D | D | A | D | E | C | C | D | A |
| **41** | **42** | **43** | **44** | **45** | **46** | **47** | **48** | **49** | **50** |
| A | E | C | C | A | B | C | B | C | C |

## EXPLANATORY ANSWERS

**1.** In all other figures, irrespective of the triangle and circle, the number of small line segments are equal on either side of the line.

**2.** In all other figures the shape inside the square is completed when touching its side. In this figure the inside shape remains open.

3. In all other figures, the number of lines making the larger or outer form is one more than the number of lines making the smaller or inner form.
4. In all other figures, the number of lines making the inner figure is one less than the number of lines making the outer figure.
5. In all other figures, the difference in number of lines making the outer or larger design and the inner smaller design is one.
6. All other figures can be rotated into each other. Only in this figure, the black circle is not on the same side as of the two small line segments.
7. In all other figures, the identical elements are in adjacent sections. In this figure, they are in opposite sections.
8. In all other figures, the three and four small lines protrude outside. In this figure three lines are inside the square.
9. All other figures can be rotated into each other. Only in this figure the smaller part of the contained square is towards the open side of the larger square.
10. In all other figures, the difference between the number of lines making the two designs is one. In this figure, both the designs are made of six lines.
11. Only in this figure, a design made of four lines is enclosed within a design also made of four lines. In all other figures, the outer design is made of one line more than the enclosed design.
12. Only in this figure four arrows are pointing in the same direction, and one arrow in its opposite direction. In other figures, the three arrows are in the same direction and the two are in the opposite direction.
13. In all other figures one line has two elements on the same side and the other line has two elements, one on either side. In this figure both the lines have two elements on the same side.
14. In all other figures, the elements inside as well as outside the hexagon are placed at equal distance. In this figure the outside element at the top is wrongly placed (It should be near the other corner of the same line).
15. In other figures the small square is either in the middle or in the mid of the side of the square containing it. In this figure the small square is in the corner.
16. All other figures can be rotated into each other. In this figure, the small lines are towards the smaller part of the rectangle.
17. There are three designs in each figure, but the number of lines making these designs in all other figures is increased by one. In this figure, there are two designs made of four straight lines.

**18.** In all other figures, the single line inside the square has a black dot on the outside at its opposite side corner, and the two parallel lines have a blank dot on the outside at their opposite side corner.

**19.** In all other figures, at least one or more of the shaded elements are not pointing towards or in just opposite direction of the circle, instead they are on the side of the circle.

**20.** In all other figures, the shaded shape is enclosed within its own shape. In this figure a right angled triangle is enclosed within an equilateral triangle.

**21.** In all other figures, the triangles are drawn at the corners of the sides. In this figure one of the triangles is in the middle of the side line.

**22.** In all other figures, the small circles are joined to form a figure. Except for this figure, all other figures when turned 90° anticlockwise, look like the figure at the base.

**23.** In all other figures, the outer design is made of one line more than the number of lines used to make the inner design.

**24.** In all other figures, the two blank sections in between the shaded sections have the dots. In this figure, the dots are in two of the three unshaded sections.

**25.** In all other figures the line with the dot is drawn in any direction, first at the base and then on the side following the same direction.

**26.** In all other figures, the two triangles are in the same direction. In this figure they are lateral inversions, *i.e.* they are opposite to each other.

**27.** In all other figures, the four elements are placed clockwise and turned by 90°. In this figure, one element does not follow the rule.

**28.** In all other figures, the curve is on the side of the square and the straight line holding an element is cutting the corner.

**29.** In all other figures, the open side of two consecutive identical shapes is facing each other. Only one shape has no shape facing it.

**30.** In all other figures, the two elements are lateral inversions of each other. In this option one triangle is a right angle triangle at the end of the line.

**31.** In all other figures the number of lines making the larger design in one more than the number of lines making the smaller design.

**32.** Only this figure has four identical and one different elements. In all other figures, there are three identical and one different elements.

**33.** All other figures have identical squares shaded. In this option, one shaded square is on the diagonally opposite corner.

**34.** In all other figures, the line segment with the circle is to the right of the straight line. In this option it is on the left side.

**35.** In all other figures, the sub-divided parts are same in size. In this figure, the corne: parts are not the same as the two middle parts.

**36.** In all other figures, the dot and cross are placed clockwise. In this figure they are placed anticlockwise.

**37.** In all other figures, the two line segments are drawn on the same side from the corners of the same line. In this figure, they are drawn on opposite sides.

**38.** All other figures are identical. The two line segments are to the left of the line with a circle in this option.

**39.** In all other figures, one of the sides is the extension of the circle. In this figure both the side parts are seperated.

**40.** All other figures can be rotated into each other. In this figure the triangle is on the left side of the line.

**41.** Only this figure has a large triangle and small extended lines. In all other figures, this feature is reverse.

**42.** In all other figures, two of the four elements are in the same direction and the other two are in the opposite directions.

**43.** Clockwise, in all other figures, the third petal is at 90° to the second. In this figure, the pattern is opposite.

**44.** In all other figures, the slant end of the line is from right to left. In this figure, it is from the left to the right.

**45.** In all other figures, the dot is outside the circle.

**46.** All other figures contain their identical shape within them. In this figure the pentagon contains a triangle.

**47.** In all other figures, the inner design is made of one line less than the number of lines making the outer design.

**48.** In all other figures, the difference between the number of lines making the two intersecting design is one.

**49.** In all other figures, there are two lines with triangle at one end and one line with an arrowhead.

**50.** In all other figures, the inside shaded shape enclosed within the outside shape identical to it.

❍ ❍ ❍

**TYPE II**

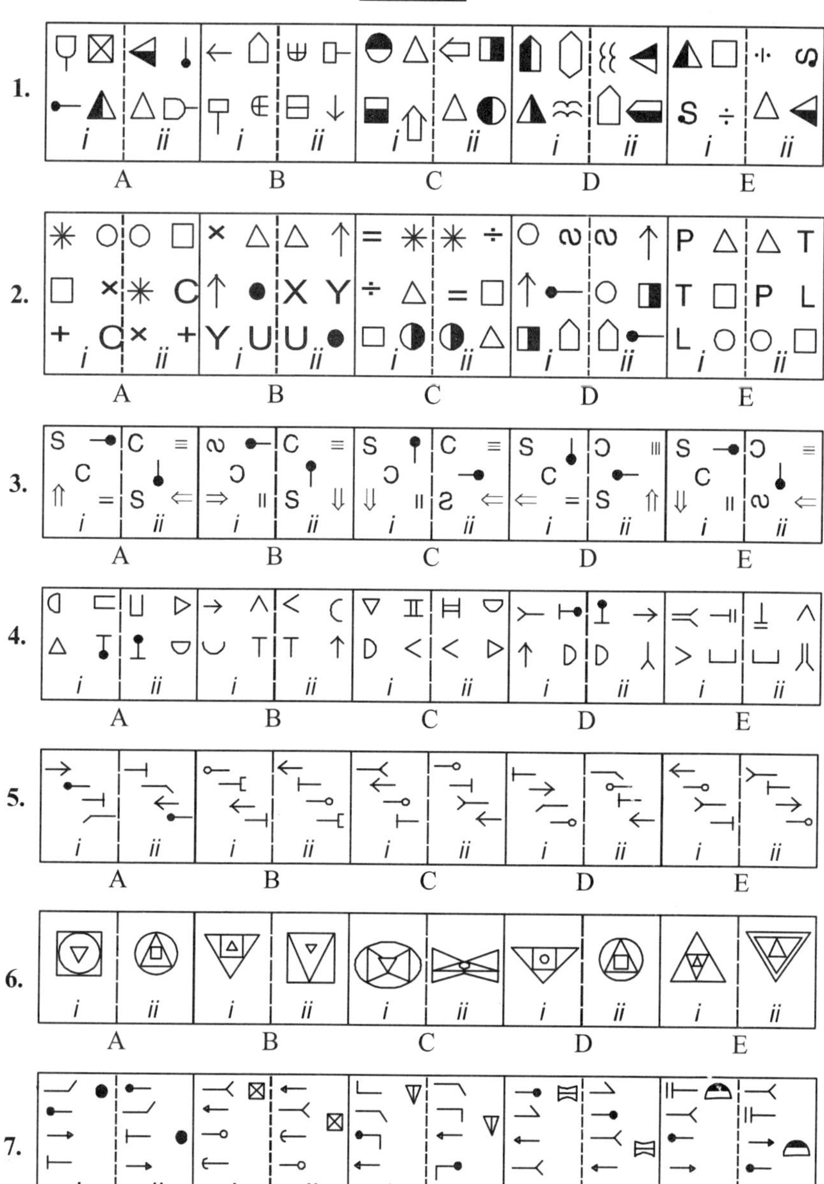

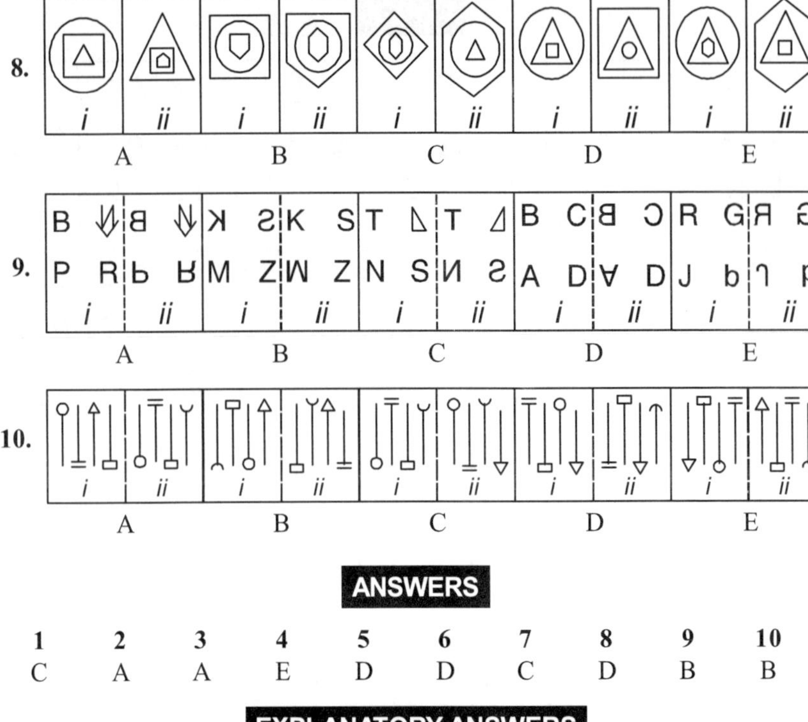

## ANSWERS

| 1 | 2 | 3 | 4 | 5 | 6 | 7 | 8 | 9 | 10 |
|---|---|---|---|---|---|---|---|---|---|
| C | A | A | E | D | D | C | D | B | B |

## EXPLANATORY ANSWERS

1. Three designs are turned 90° anticlockwise while the fourth element on the top right position is changed. Further, the places of the designs are interchanged diagonally in the element II. Here, the fourth design remains unchanged.
2. The two items on the top and the middle left item in element I are moved one step anticlock-wise in element II. Also, the middle right item and the two bottom items in element I are moved one step clockwise in element II. Here, both sets of items are moved anticlockwise.
3. From element I to element II, the 'S' shape is turned 90° clockwise and moved down, the double arrow shape '⇒' is turned 90° clockwise and movd to the right, the two parallel lines one turned by 90°; one parallel line is added and all three lines are moved up, the line with a dot is turned 90° clockwise and moved to the centre and the 'C' shape in the centre is turned by 180° and moved to the top left position. Here, the double arrow is turned anticlockwise.

**4.** From element I to element II, the two designs on the left side are moved diagonally and the two designs on the right are shifted to the left, the top left and the bottom right designs are turned 180° anticlockwise, and the top right design is turned 90° clockwise. In this option, the direction of turn is the opposite.

**5.** The first design is inverted and moved to the third place, the second design is moved to the fourth place, the third design to the first place and the fourth design is inverted and moved to the second place. Option D violates this.

**6.** From element I to element II, the innermost design is turned upside down, the outermost design is reduced and placed inside the innermost design. Here, the innermost design is enlarged and made the outermost design.

**7.** The places of two items on the top are interchanged, the two items at the bottom arc laterally inverted and their places are interchanged and the single item on the right is moved half way down. Here, the four items on the left violate the above rule.

**8.** In all other figures, the innermost design in element I is enlarged as the outermost design in element II and the outermost design in element I is made new and placed as the innermost design in element II. Here, the circle is not changed, but reduced.

**9.** In all other figures, from element I to element II the two items on the top are laterally inverted and the two items at the bottom are turned upside down. Here, the item on the bottom right in element II is not changed.

**10.** From element I to element II the first and the second design are turned upside down, the fourth design is moved to the third place and a new design is placed in the fourth place. Here, the places of first and the second designs is interchanged.

## TYPE III

**Directions :** *In each of the following questions, a related pair of figures (unnumbered) is followed by five numbered pairs of figures. Out of these five, four of them have relationship similar to that in the original pair. Only one pair of figures does not have a similar relationship. Select that pair of figures which does not have a relationship similar to that in the unnumbered pair. The number of that figure is the answer.*

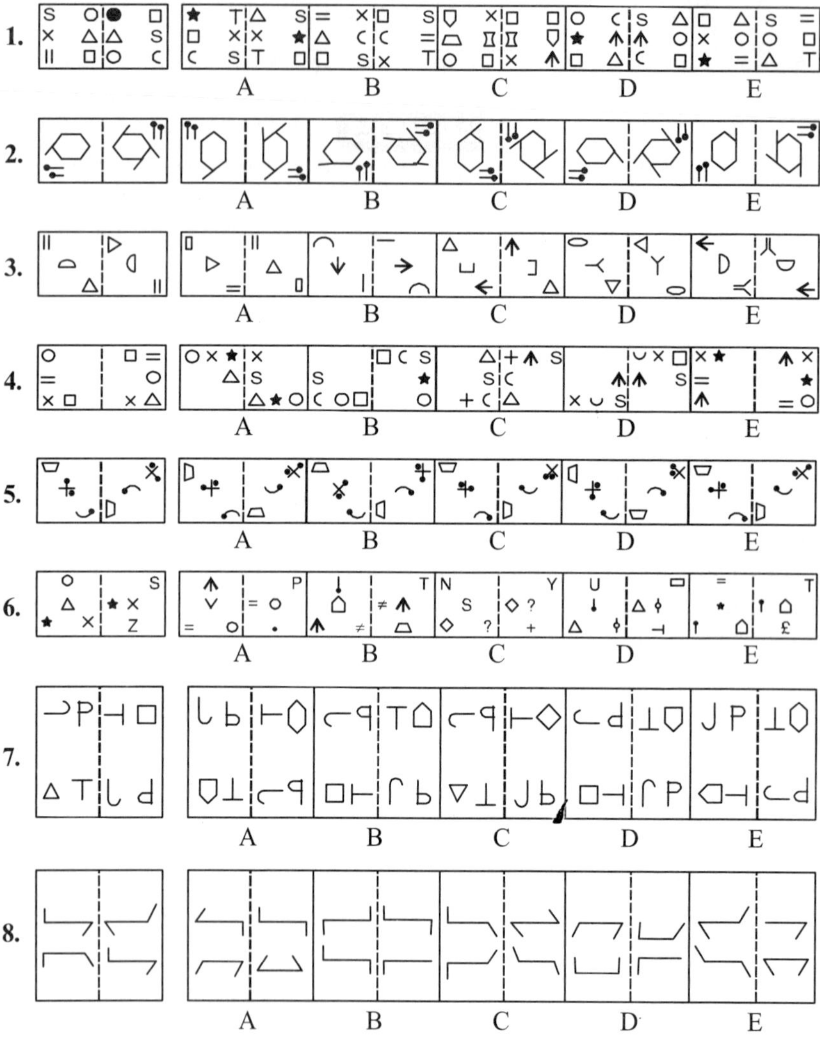

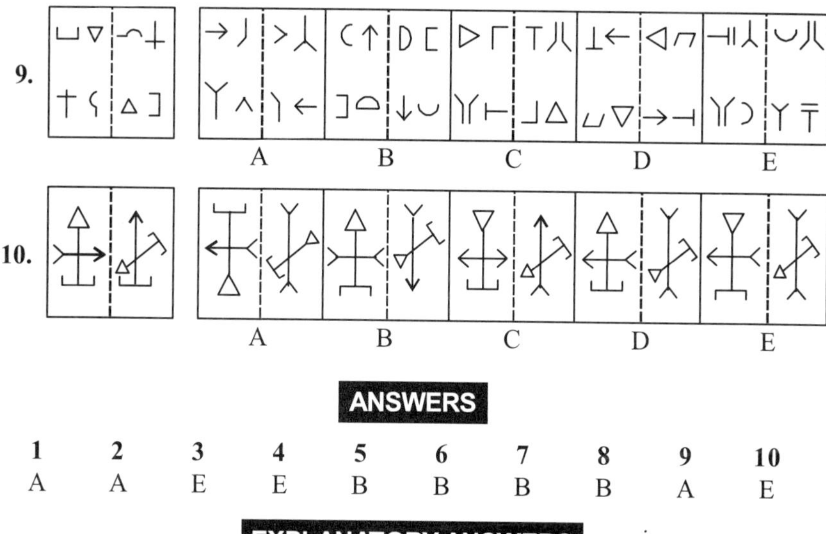

## ANSWERS

| 1 | 2 | 3 | 4 | 5 | 6 | 7 | 8 | 9 | 10 |
|---|---|---|---|---|---|---|---|---|---|
| A | A | E | E | B | B | B | B | A | E |

## EXPLANATORY ANSWERS

**1.** From element I to element II, a new unit is placed in the top left position, the top left unit is moved to the middle right position, the middle right unit is moved to the left position, the middle left unit is replaced by a new unit and placed in the bottom right position, the bottom right unit is moved to the top right position, and the top right unit is moved diagonally to replace the bottom left unit. In option 'A', the middle left unit is not changed when moved to the bottom right position.

**2.** From element I to element II, the places of two units in the corner are interchanged, they are turned 90° clockwise and moved diagonally to the opposite corner. The three extended sides of the figure in element II are in the direction opposite to the direction of one extended side of the figure in element I. In option 'A' all the extended lines are in same direction.

**3.** From element I to element II, of the three units, the bottom unit is rotated 90° clockwise and moved to the top, the middle unit is rotated 90° anticlockwise, and the top unit is moved diagonally to the bottom right position. In option 'E' the middle unit is rotated clockwise.

**4.** From element I to element II starting anticlockwise, the first and the second units are moved 1½ steps clockwise respectively, the third unit ½ step anticlockwise, the fourth unit 2 steps clockwise, and a new unit is placed ahead of the first unit. Option 'E' violates the rules.

**5.** From element I to element II, the unit on the top left is turned 90° anticlockwise and moved to the bottom right corner position, the unit in the centre is turned 135° anticlockwise and moved to the top right position, and the unit in the bottom right is turned by 180° and moved to the centre. In option 'B', the middle unit is turned 135° clockwise.

**6.** From element I to element II the bottom right unit and bottom left unit are moved to the centre and the middle left position respectively. The other two units are removed and the two new elements are placed in the top right and the bottom centre position respectively. In option 'B', the placement of bottom right and the left elements is not right.

**7.** From element I to element II, the top left unit is turned 90° clockwise and moved to the bottom left position, the top right unit is turned by 180° and moved to bottom right position, the bottom left unit is moved to top right position and replaced by a new unit, and the bottom right unit is turned 90° clockwise and moved to the top left position. In option 'B', the top left element violates the rule.

**8.** From element I to element II, the left tip of the top unit is turned 135° clockwise and the right tip rotated by 180°. The left tip of the other unit is rotated by 180° and the right tip is turned 90° clockwise. In option 'B', the left tip of the top unit violates the rule.

**9.** From element I to element II, the units are shifted diagonally opposite. The unit on the right diagonal is inverted, the bottom right unit is rotated 90° clockwise and the top right element is rotated 90° anticlockwise. In option 'A', the top right element violates the rule.

**10.** From element I to element II, the horizontal bar is turned 135° anticlockwise and the unit at the lower end is turned by 180°. The vertical bar is turned 90° anticlockwise and the unit at the lower end is turned by 180°. In option 'E' one more unit at the top is turned by 180°.

❍ ❍ ❍

# 4

# Construction of Boxes

*The formation of figure involves using the fragmented part to construct a desired figure. It requires a high spatial visualisation skill. As different fragmented parts of a figure are to be combined to form the desired figure.*

## SOLVED EXAMPLES

In this chapter, two sets of figures are provided, namely **problem figure** and **answer figures**. A candidate is asked to arrange the different components of the problem figure so as to form one of the answer figure.

Examples given below will give a better idea about the types of questions.

**1.** Which of the following figures shown below, when folded along the dotted lines, will form a pyramid-shaped box with a rectangular base?

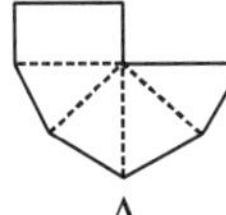
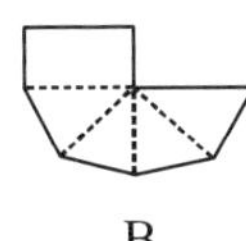
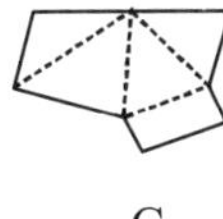
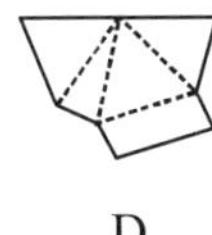

A B C D

**Answers D:** By folding figure D, we get a pyramid-shaped box with a rectangular base as shown below:

**2.** In the question given below, find out which of the figures can be formed from the pieces given in the problem figure.

**Problem Figure** **Answer Figures**

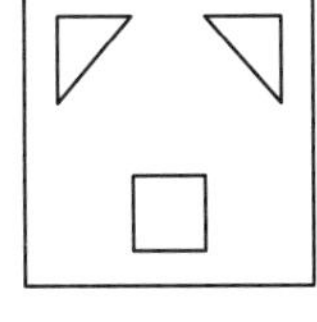
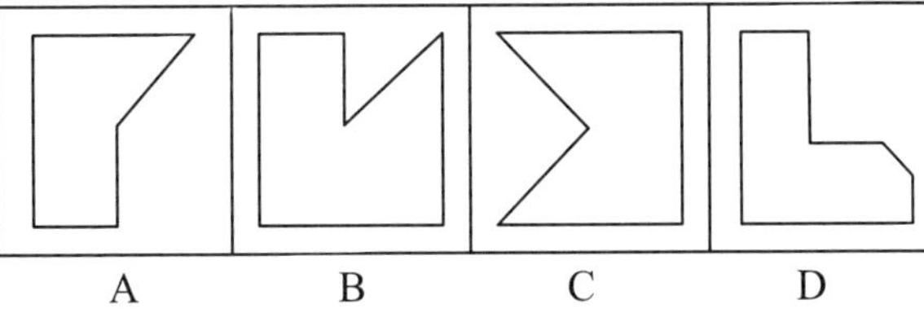

A B C D

**Answers A:** Using all the components given in problem figure we can arrange them as:

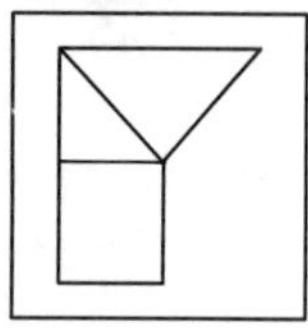

So Option A is the correct answer.

**3.** Select three out of the following five alternative figures which together form one of the four alternatives A, B, C or D and when fitted together will form a complete square.

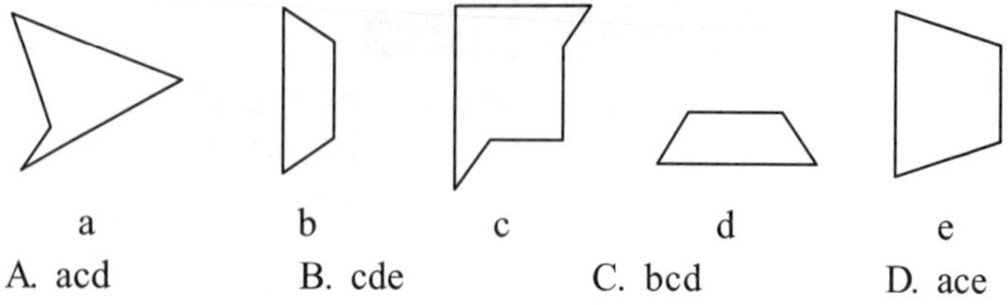

| a | b | c | d | e |
|---|---|---|---|---|

A. acd B. cde C. bcd D. ace

**Answers:** We see the (c) is a part of all the answers. Therefore (c) must be one of the three correct figures. [It must be so because, (c) is the only figure having a right angle.] Now let us check which of the figure fits with C. We see that fig (b) fits with (c) as shown:

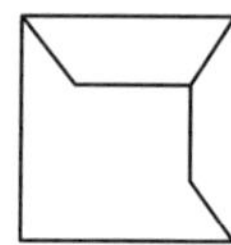

Finally, fig (d) completes the square by fitting into the above combination. The completed square appears as shown below:

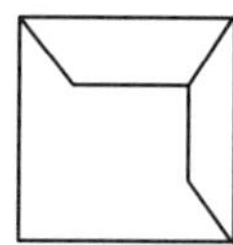

Therefore, (b), (c) and (d) will together form a square.

Hence, alternative C is the answer.

## EXERCISE

**Directions (Qs. 1-9):** *Which one figure can be made out of the given paper cut-outs?*

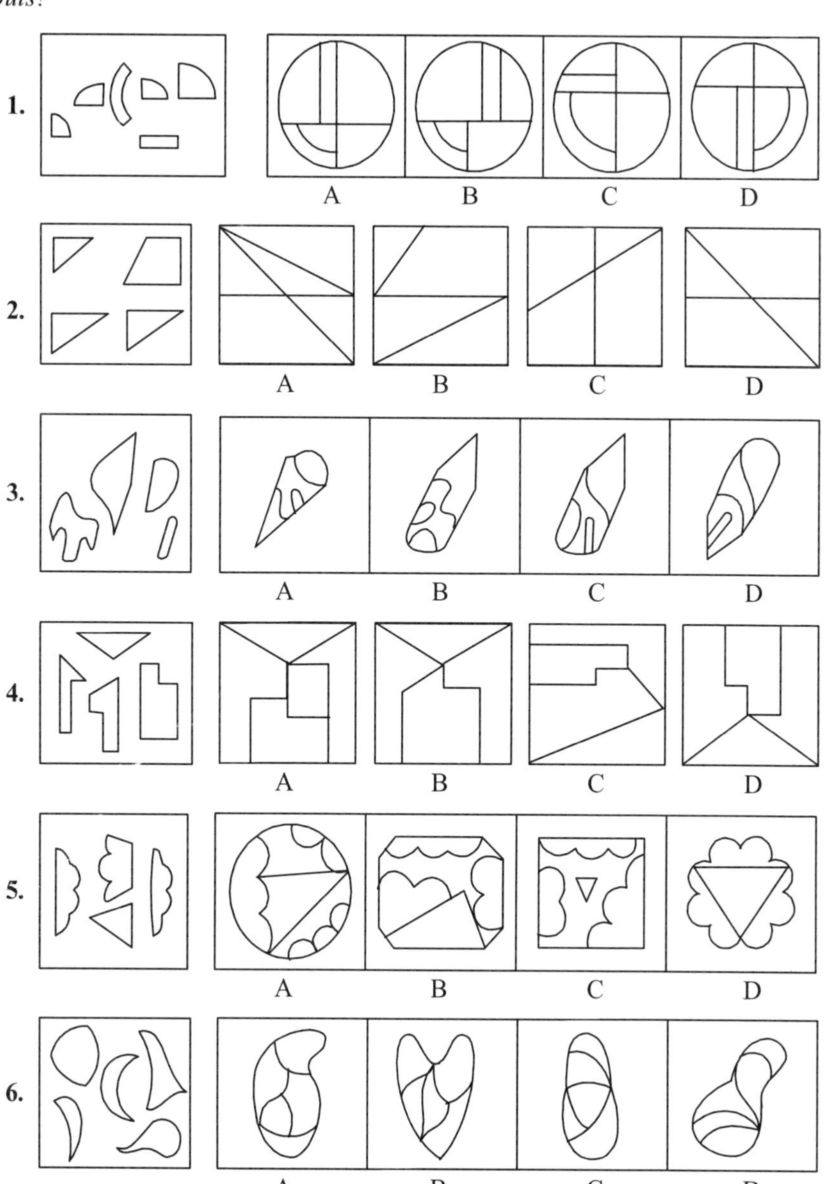

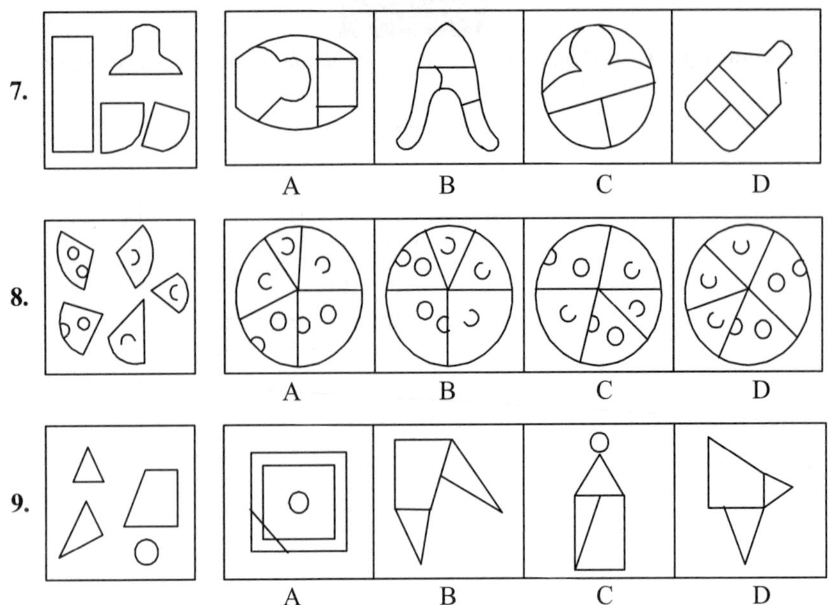


**Directions (Qs. 10-17):** *In each of the following questions, find out the figure from amongst the alternatives A, B, C and D which can be formed from the pieces given in X.*

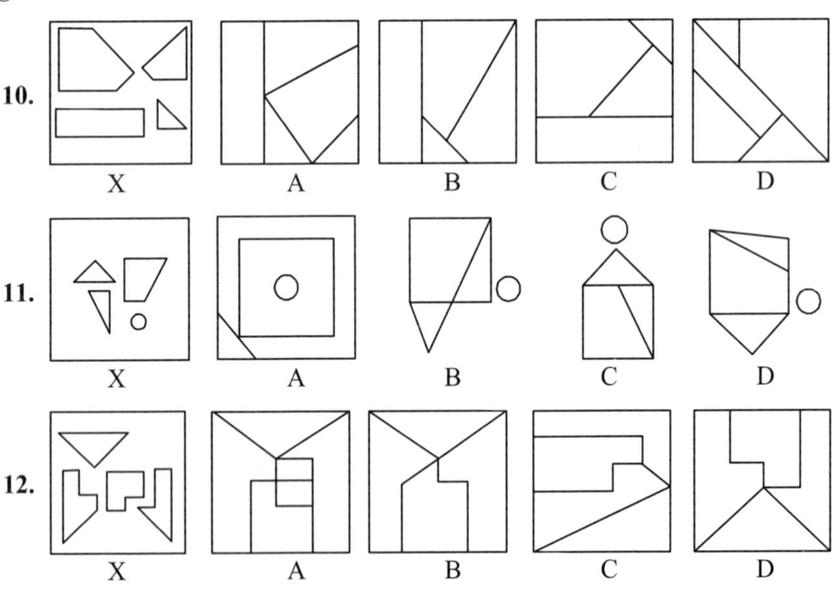

**13.**

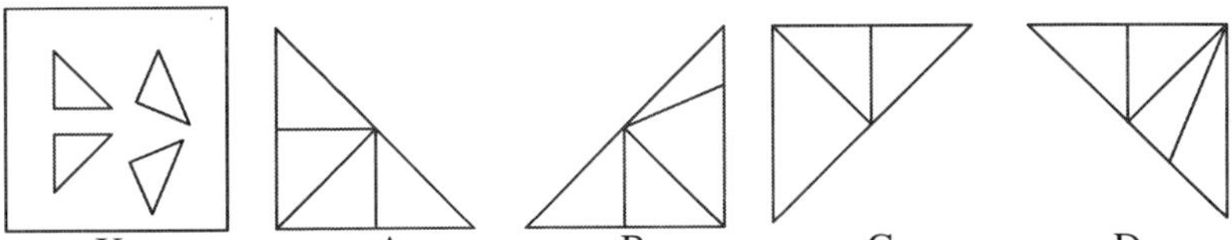

X A B C D

**14.**

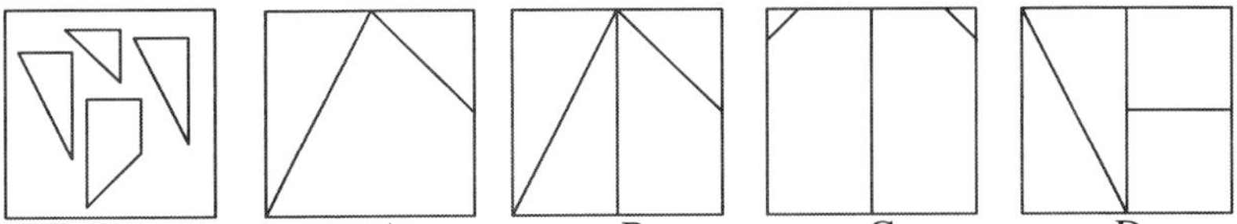

X A B C D

**15.**

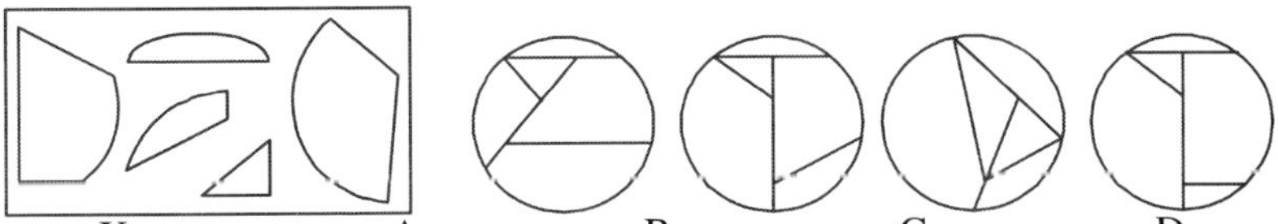

X A B C D

**16.**

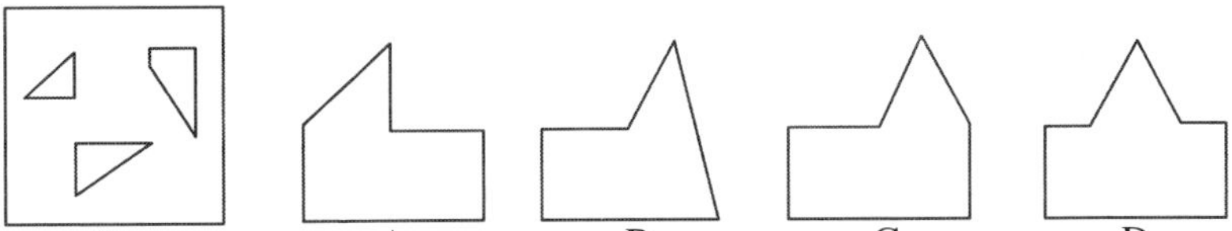

X A B C D

**17.**

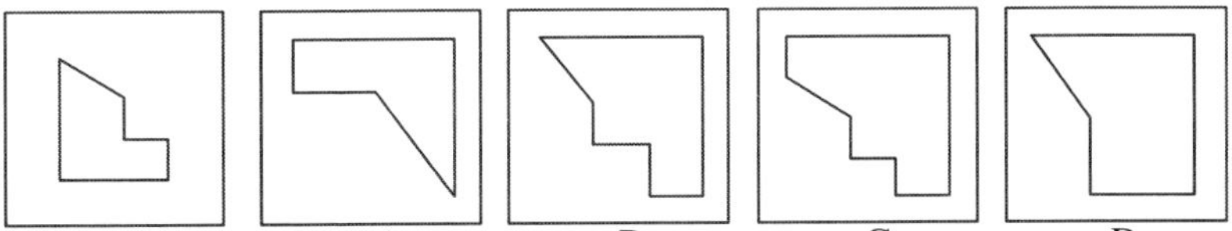

X A B C D

**Directions (Qs. 18-30):** *In each one of the following problems a set of five alternative figures (a), (b), (c), (d) and (e) followed by a set of four alternatives A, B, C and D is provided. You are required to select the alternative which represents three out of the five alternative figures which when fitted into each other would form a complete square.*

**18.**

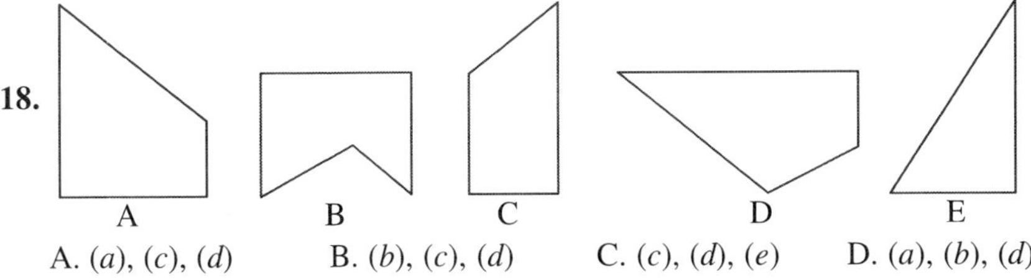


A. (*a*), (*c*), (*d*) B. (*b*), (*c*), (*d*) C. (*c*), (*d*), (*e*) D. (*a*), (*b*), (*d*)

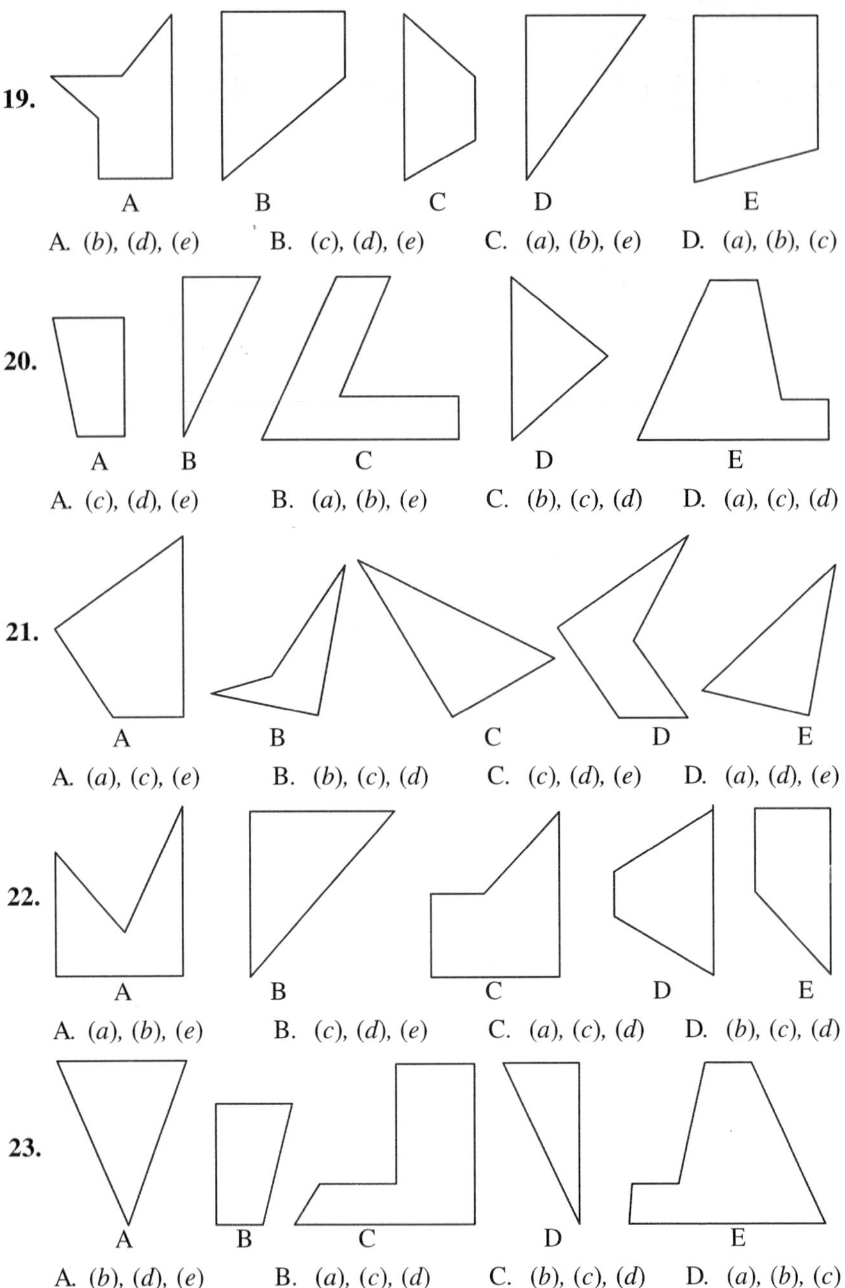


19. A. (*b*), (*d*), (*e*) B. (*c*), (*d*), (*e*) C. (*a*), (*b*), (*e*) D. (*a*), (*b*), (*c*)

20. A. (*c*), (*d*), (*e*) B. (*a*), (*b*), (*e*) C. (*b*), (*c*), (*d*) D. (*a*), (*c*), (*d*)

21. A. (*a*), (*c*), (*e*) B. (*b*), (*c*), (*d*) C. (*c*), (*d*), (*e*) D. (*a*), (*d*), (*e*)

22. A. (*a*), (*b*), (*e*) B. (*c*), (*d*), (*e*) C. (*a*), (*c*), (*d*) D. (*b*), (*c*), (*d*)

23. A. (*b*), (*d*), (*e*) B. (*a*), (*c*), (*d*) C. (*b*), (*c*), (*d*) D. (*a*), (*b*), (*c*)

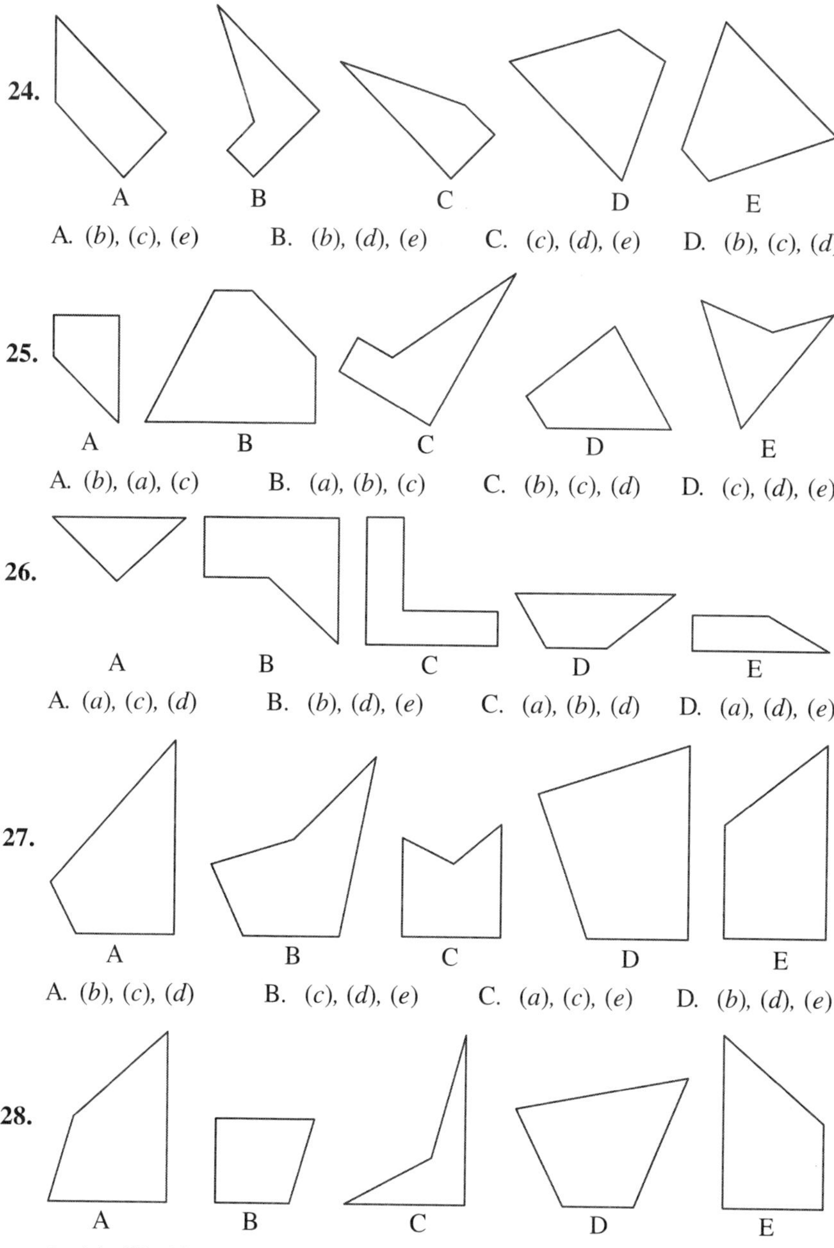

**24.**

A. (*b*), (*c*), (*e*) B. (*b*), (*d*), (*e*) C. (*c*), (*d*), (*e*) D. (*b*), (*c*), (*d*)

**25.**

A. (*b*), (*a*), (*c*) B. (*a*), (*b*), (*c*) C. (*b*), (*c*), (*d*) D. (*c*), (*d*), (*e*)

**26.**

A. (*a*), (*c*), (*d*) B. (*b*), (*d*), (*e*) C. (*a*), (*b*), (*d*) D. (*a*), (*d*), (*e*)

**27.**

A. (*b*), (*c*), (*d*) B. (*c*), (*d*), (*e*) C. (*a*), (*c*), (*e*) D. (*b*), (*d*), (*e*)

**28.**

A. (*a*), (*b*), (*c*) B. (*b*), (*c*), (*d*) C. (*a*), (*d*), (*e*) D. (*a*), (*b*), (*d*)

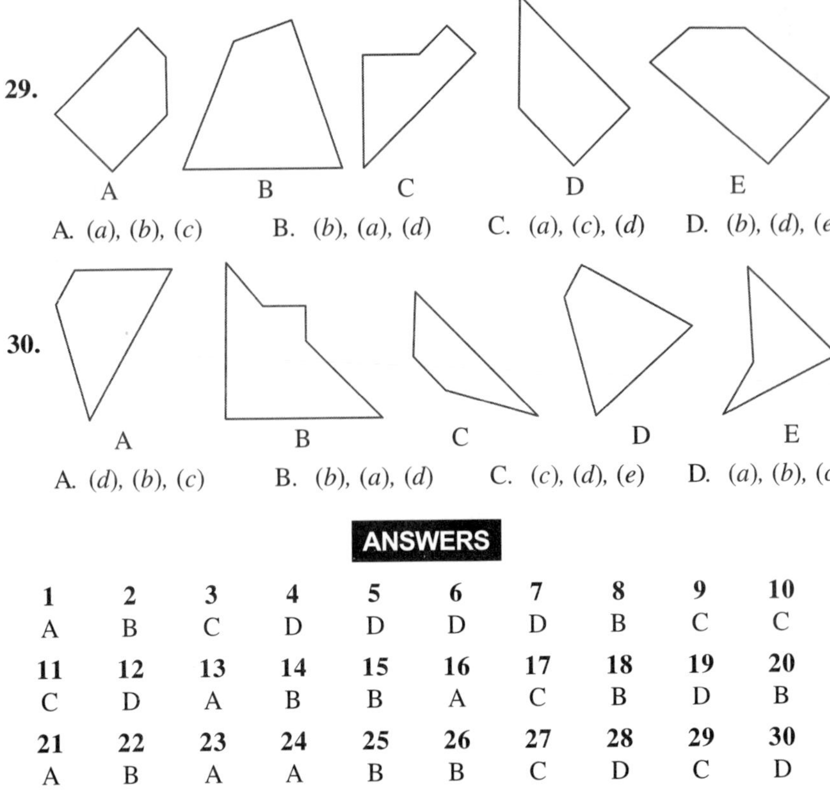


**29.** A. (*a*), (*b*), (*c*)  B. (*b*), (*a*), (*d*)  C. (*a*), (*c*), (*d*)  D. (*b*), (*d*), (*e*)

**30.** A. (*d*), (*b*), (*c*)  B. (*b*), (*a*), (*d*)  C. (*c*), (*d*), (*e*)  D. (*a*), (*b*), (*c*)

## ANSWERS

| **1** | **2** | **3** | **4** | **5** | **6** | **7** | **8** | **9** | **10** |
|---|---|---|---|---|---|---|---|---|---|
| A | B | C | D | D | D | D | B | C | C |
| **11** | **12** | **13** | **14** | **15** | **16** | **17** | **18** | **19** | **20** |
| C | D | A | B | B | A | C | B | D | B |
| **21** | **22** | **23** | **24** | **25** | **26** | **27** | **28** | **29** | **30** |
| A | B | A | A | B | B | C | D | C | D |

❍ ❍ ❍

# Paper Folding & Cutting

## SOLVED EXAMPLES

### PAPER FOLDING

In these problems a transparent sheet, with designs on either side of a dotted line on it, is provided. The sheet is then folded along the dotted line. You are required to choose a figure which would most closely resemble the pattern when the sheet is folded.

A sample problem is given below:

**Directions:** *In each of the following examples, find from amongst the four response figures, the one which resembles the pattern formed when the transparent sheet, carrying a design, is folded along the dotted line.*

**1. Transparent sheet Response Figures**

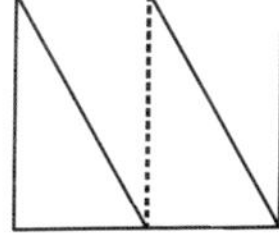

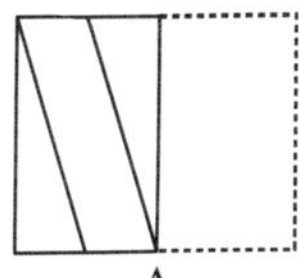

A

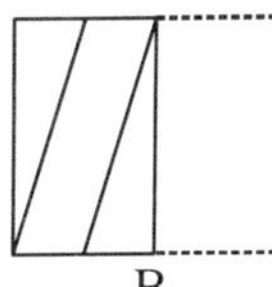

B

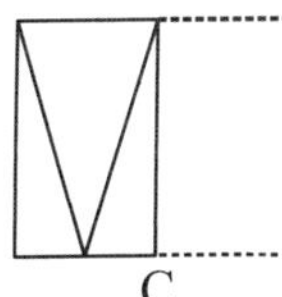

C

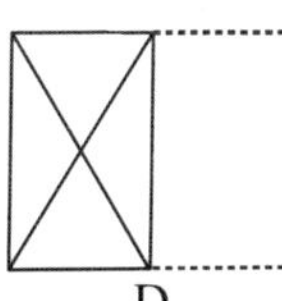

D

### Suggested Method

Do you remember the method of drawing symmetrical figure? If the sheet is folded along the dotted line, the symmetrical counterpart of the design in the folded half would emerge on the other half. Therefore, the simple strategy for solving paper-folding problems would be:

(*i*) Draw the reflection of the design in that half which is to be folded, on the other half, assuming a mirror to be kept along the dotted line.

(*ii*) The reflection of the design of the other half and the original design would overlap on the new folded half. This new design, resulting from the overlapping, would be the answer figure.

See the following example to understand the method:

**Answers:** The original design is:

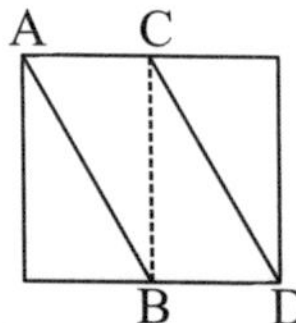


It is folded to the left. Now, what is the image of the design in the folded half, assuming a mirror at the dotted line? In other words, what would be the image in place of the question mark in the figure shown below?

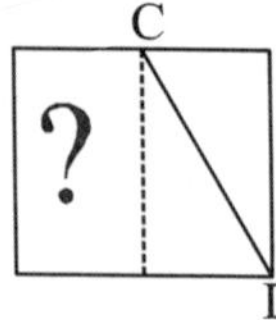


Obviously the image would be along the line CD' as shown:

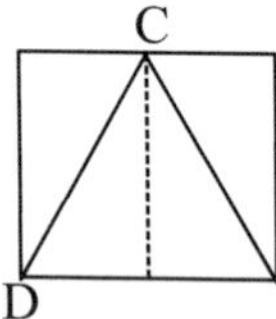


Now, in the answer figure the original design of the unfolded half, i.e. AB, and the reflected design CD' would overlap. Hence, the answer figure would be:

Hence, correct answer: (**D**).

## PAPER CUTTING

In this type of questions, a paper is folded twice (or may be more) and then a cut (or some cuts) is/are made on it. You have to imagine what the paper would look like when it is unfolded back to what it originally was. Usually a set of three figures is given to show the manner in which the paper is folded and the paper is cut. In the first two figures a dotted line together with an arrow on it is given, showing the position and direction of folding. In the third figure there are marks showing the position and nature of the cut made in the folded sheet. The examinee has to select one of the figures from the set of four answer figures A, B, C and D that would most closely resemble the paper when unfolded.

A sample problem is being given below:

Consider the following three figures, marked X, Y, Z showing one fold in X, another fold in Y and cut in Z. From amongst the answer figures A, B, C and D, select the one showing the unfolded position of Z.

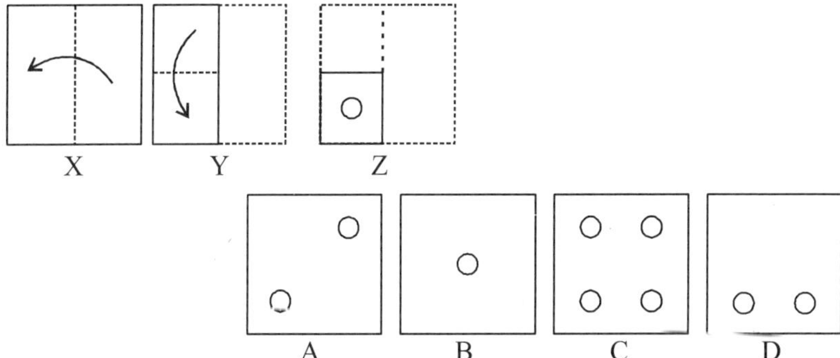


## Explanation

**Backtracking:** The best, easiest and yet the quickest methods to solve the problems would be to use the method of backtracking with the concept of symmetry and reflection. The underlying concept is that when a fold is made on a paper and then a cut is made on the folded half, then the cut would appear on either sides of the half (when the paper is unfolded) and the two cuts would be symmetrically placed about the line of fold. This is explained by the following sequence of diagrams:

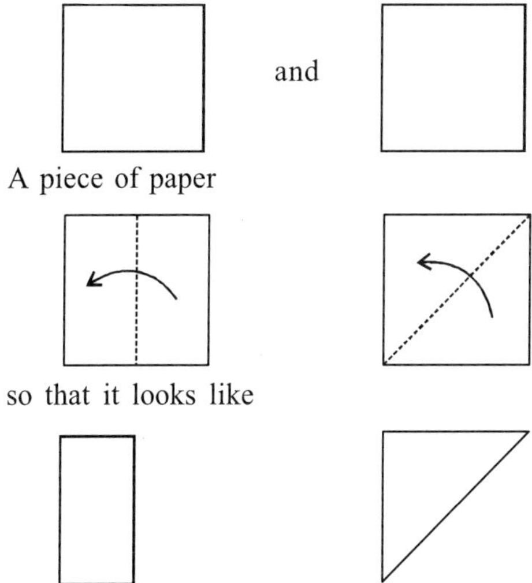

and a cut is made on it as shown

then, if the paper is unfolded, a reflection of the two cuts appear on the other half as if a mirror was placed on the line of fold.

Now, you have understood how the concept of symmetry and reflection works in paper cutting, we are presenting the method of backtracking to solve such problems. Backtracking means going backwards, starting with the last figure and tracing the way back. The steps would be:

I. Start with the last fold. Draw the reflection of the cut on the other side of the line of fold. Hence, draw the diagram of the paper when it is unfolded on the last fold.

II. Now, go to the previous fold. Again, draw the reflection of the cuts on the other side of the fold. Repeat this process till the whole paper is unfolded. Since in the usual questions the paper is folded only twice, hence you need to unfold the paper only twice.

We now present some solved examples in order to make you understand the method.

Solution: The cut is =

The last fold is =

We draw the reflection of the cut on the other side of the line of fold. We get

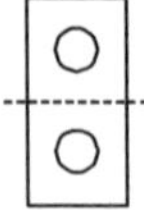

Now, the previous fold is =

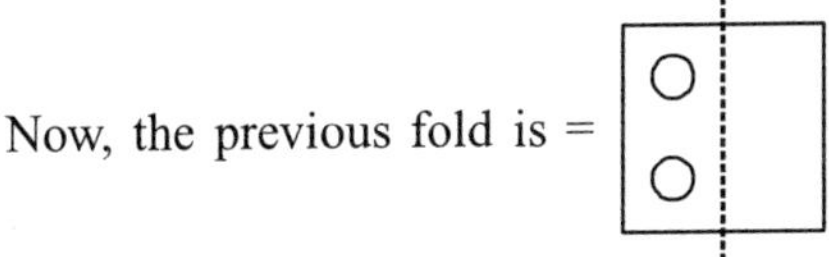

We draw the reflection of the cuts on the other side of the line of fold. We get

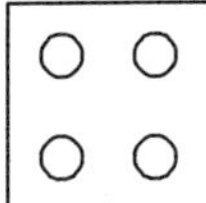

Hence, correct answer (C).

## EXERCISE

**Directions (Qs. 1-20 ):** *In each of the following questions, a piece of paper has been folded and then punched. From the given options figure out the correct responses which shows how it will appear when unfolded.*

**1.**

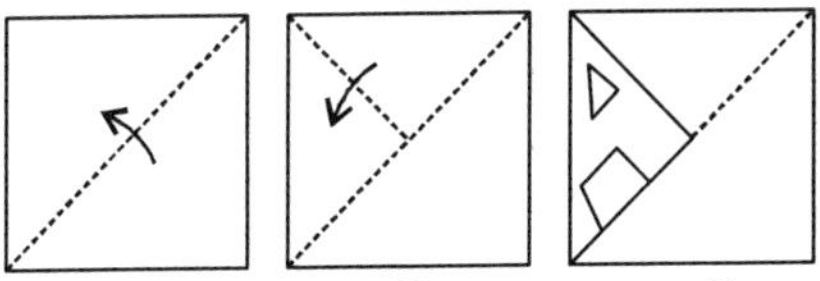

X Y Z

A B C D

**2.**

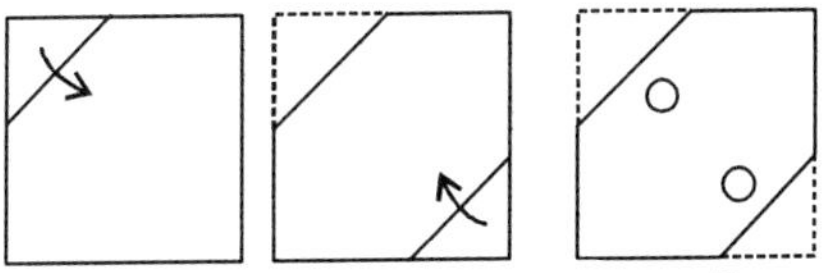

X Y Z

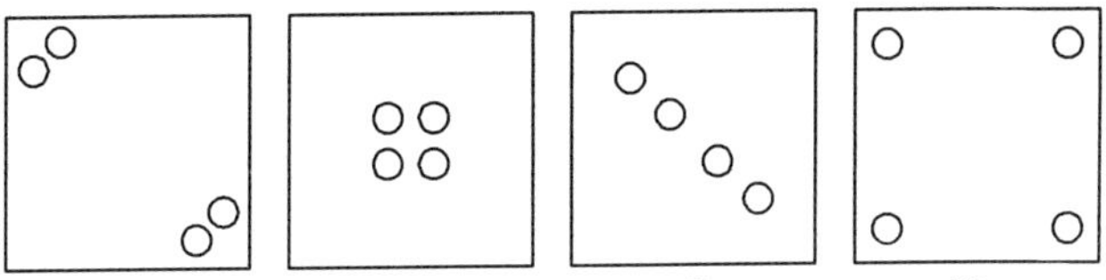

A B C D

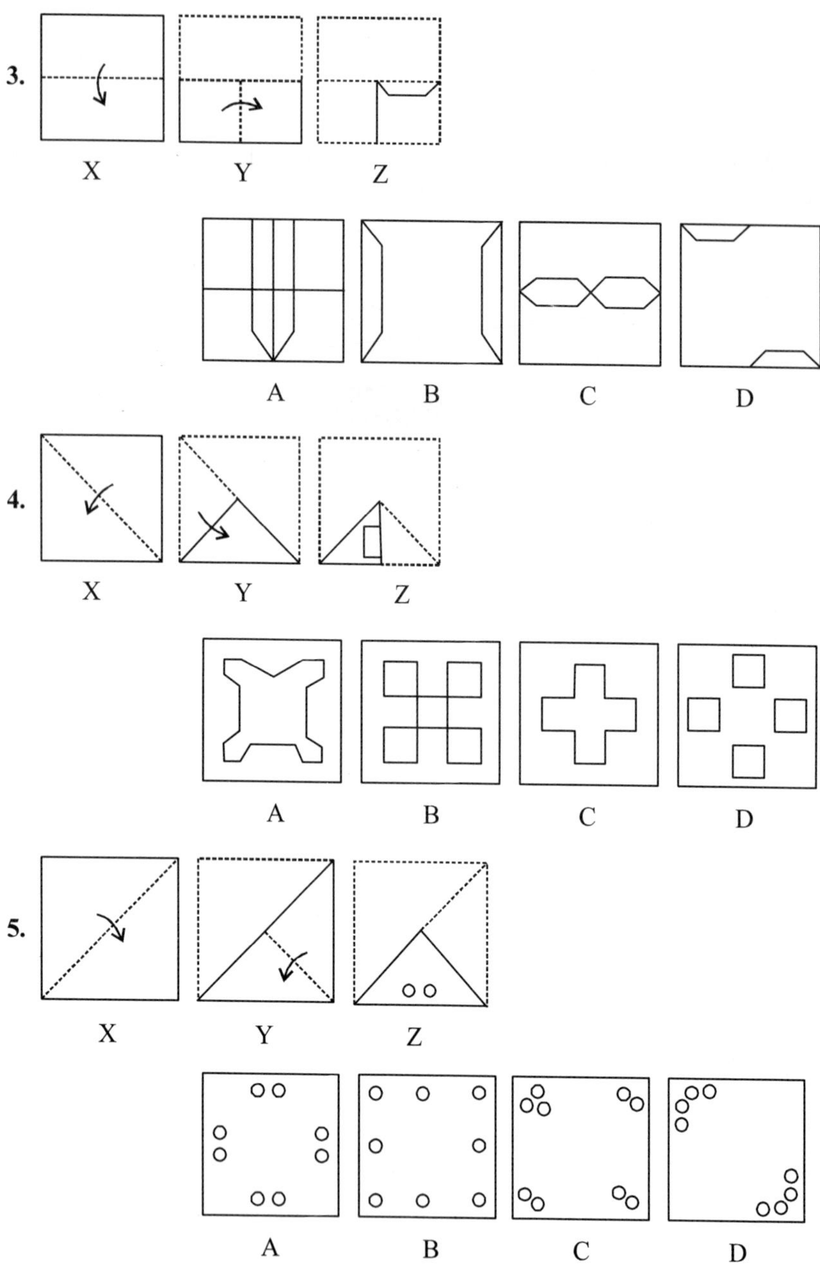
3.
X
Y
Z
A
B
C
D
4.
X
Y
Z
A
B
C
D
5.
X
Y
Z
A
B
C
D

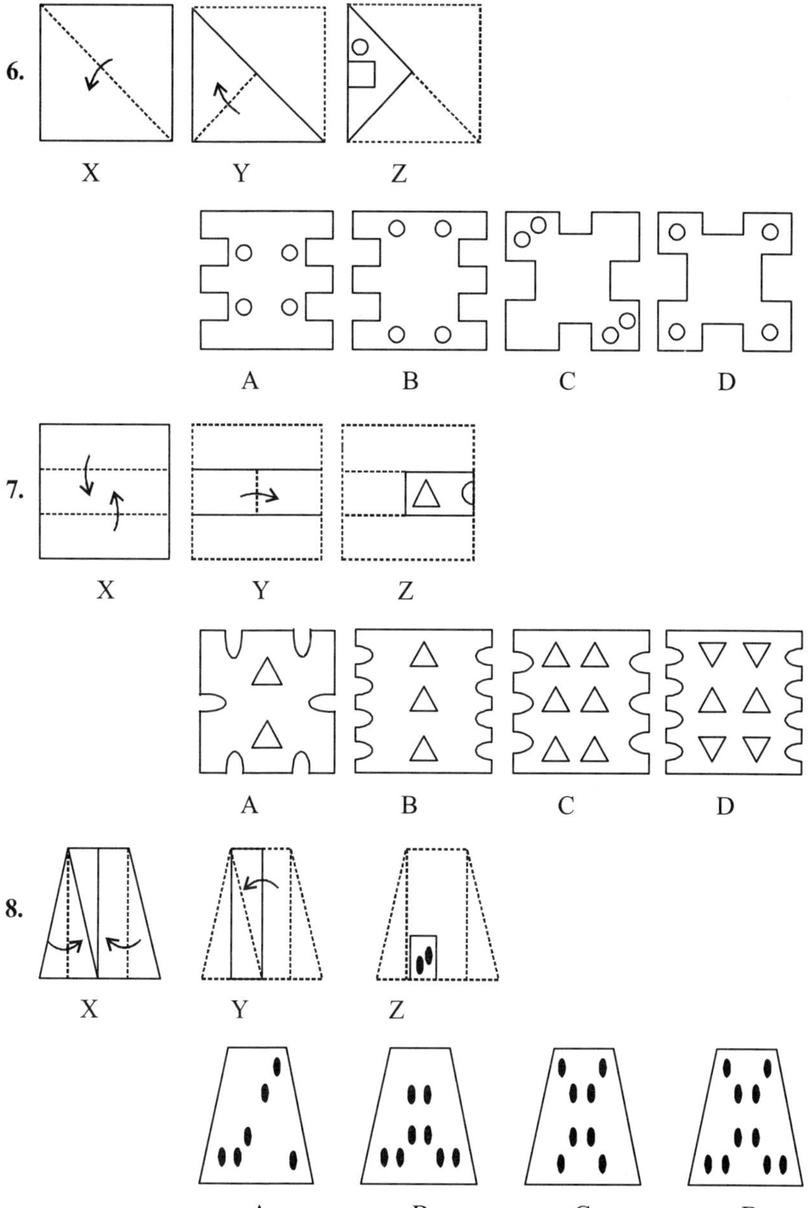
6.
X
Y
Z
A
B
C
D
7.
X
Y
Z
A
B
C
D
8.
X
Y
Z
A
B
C
D

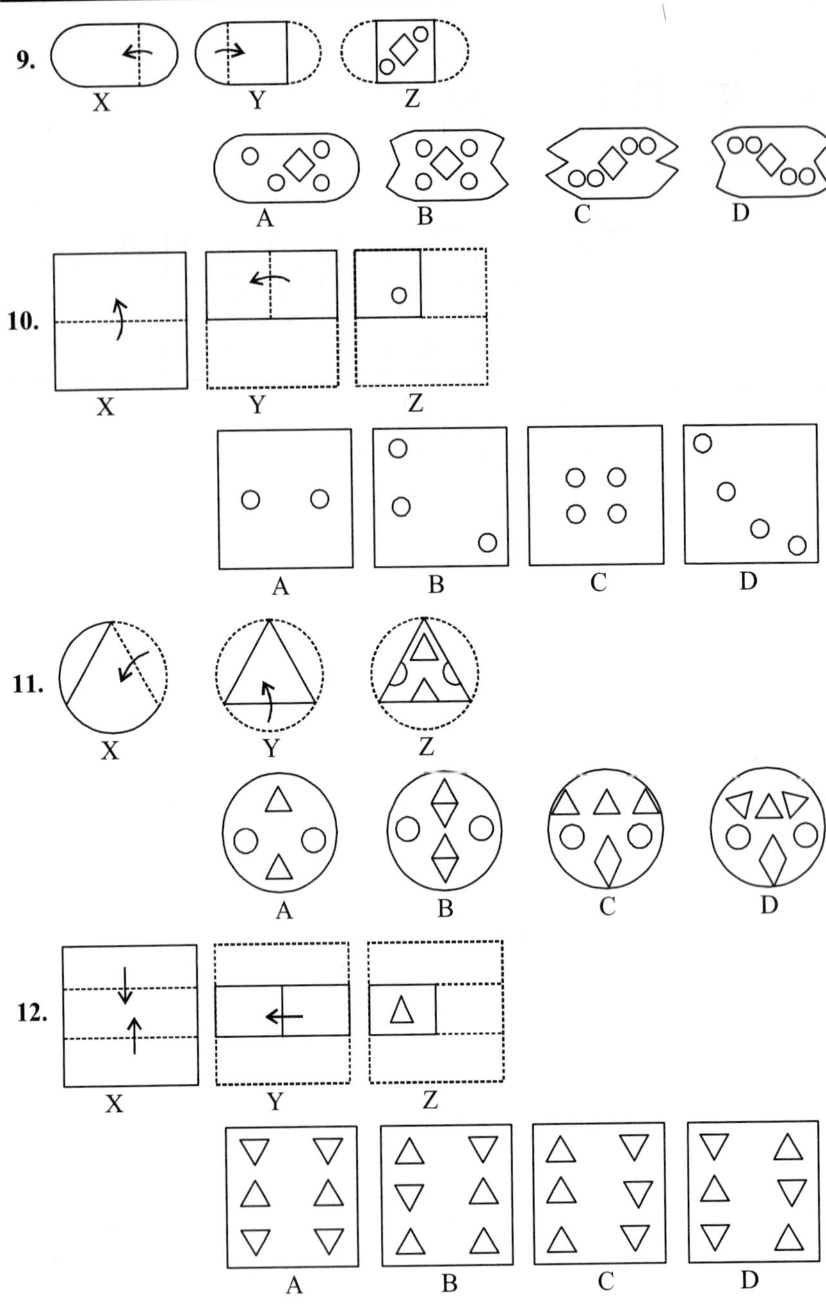
9.
X
Y
Z
A
B
C
D
10.
X
Y
Z
A
B
C
D
11.
X
Y
Z
A
B
C
D
12.
X
Y
Z
A
B
C
D

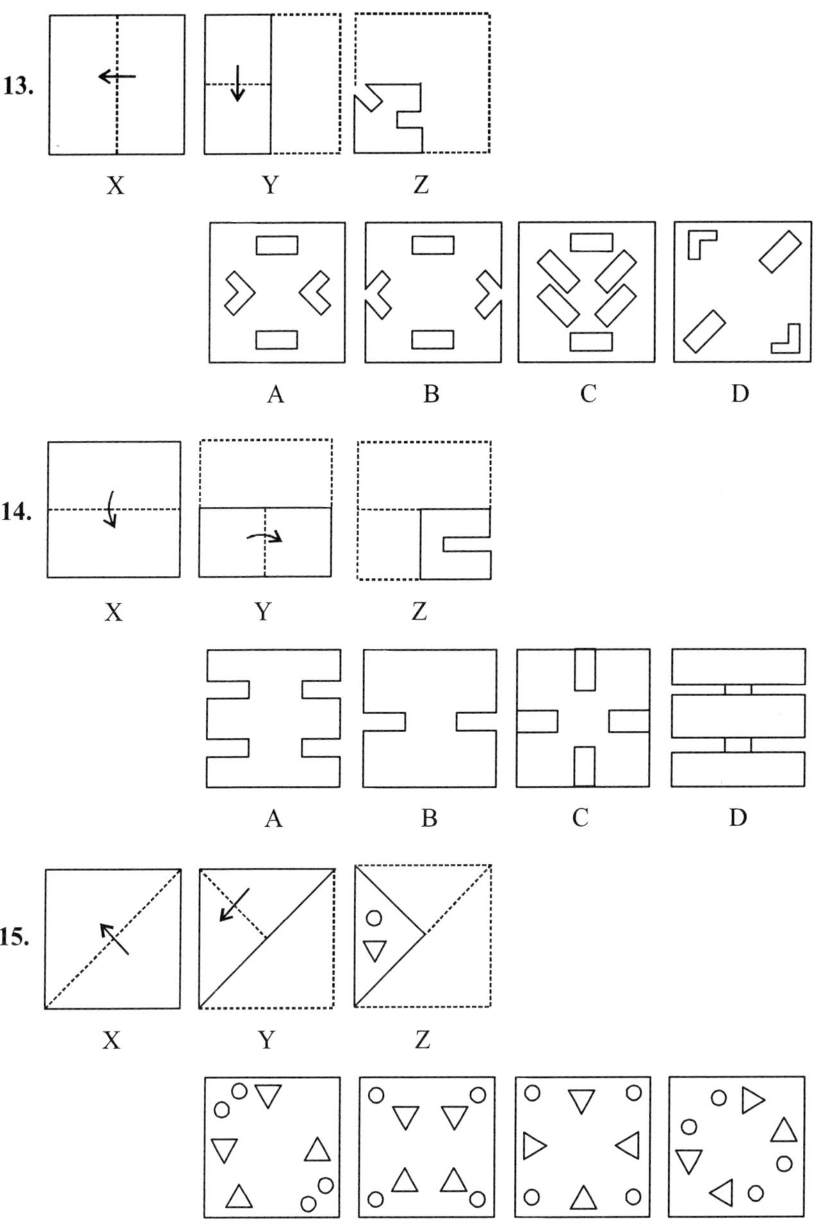
13.
X
Y
Z
A
B
C
D
14.
X
Y
Z
A
B
C
D
15.
X
Y
Z
A
B
C
D

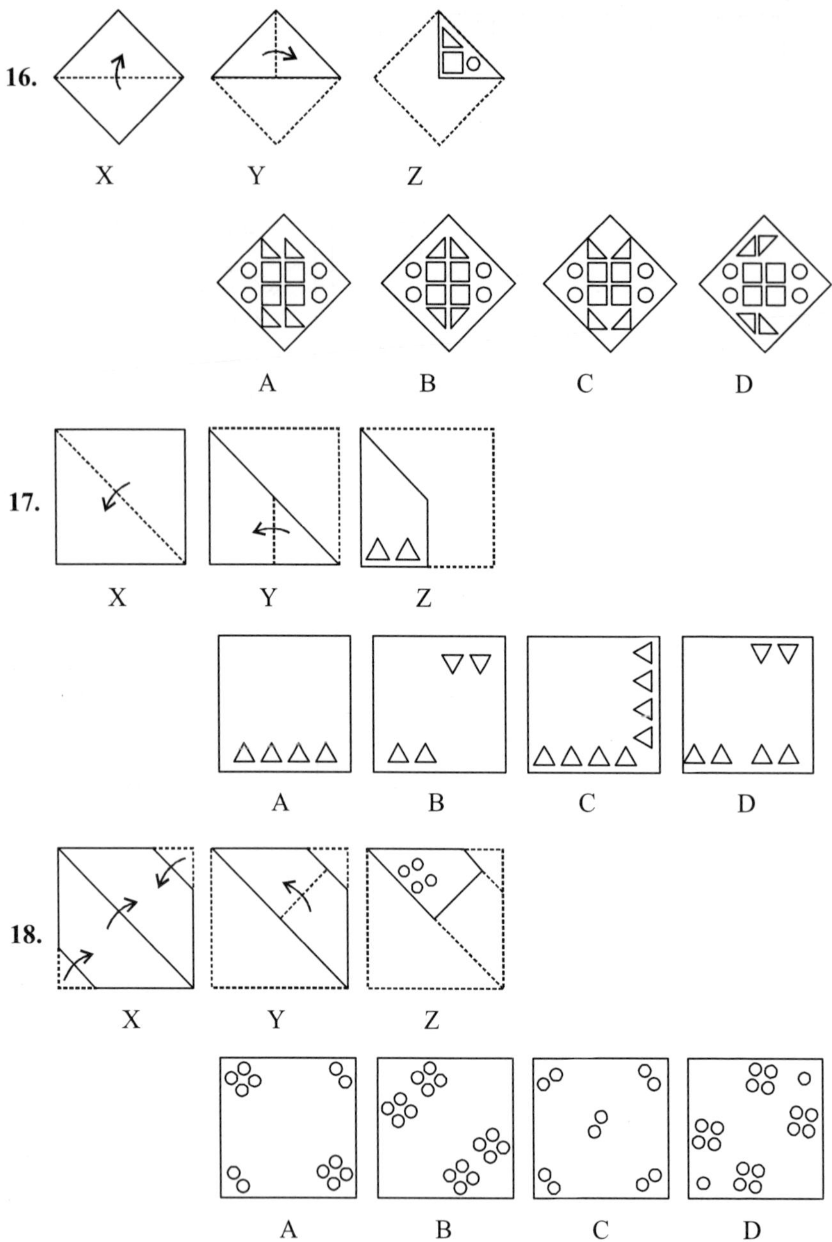
16.
X
Y
Z
A
B
C
D
17.
X
Y
Z
A
B
C
D
18.
X
Y
Z
A
B
C
D

19.

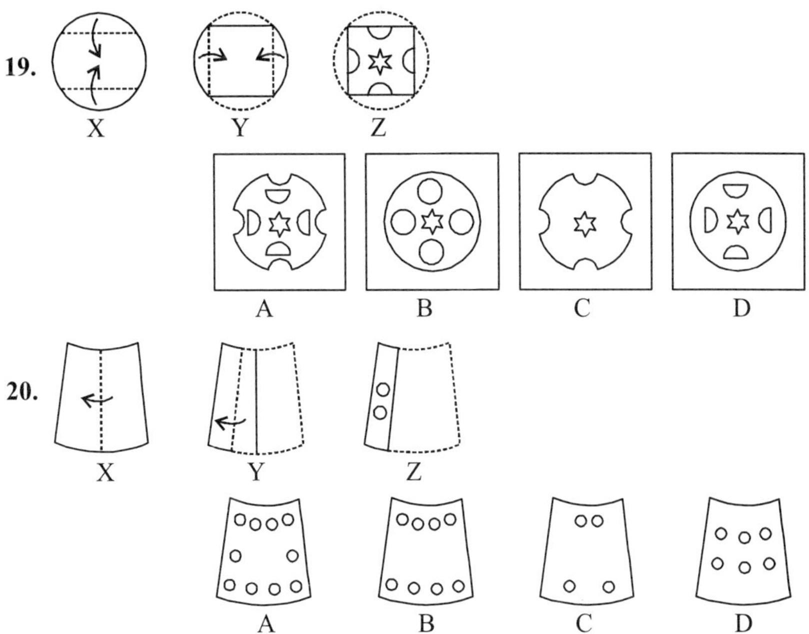


**Directions (Qs. 21-35 ):** *In each of the following problems, a square transparent sheet with a pattern is given. Find out from among four alternative as to how the pattern would appear when the transparent sheet is folded at the dotted line.*

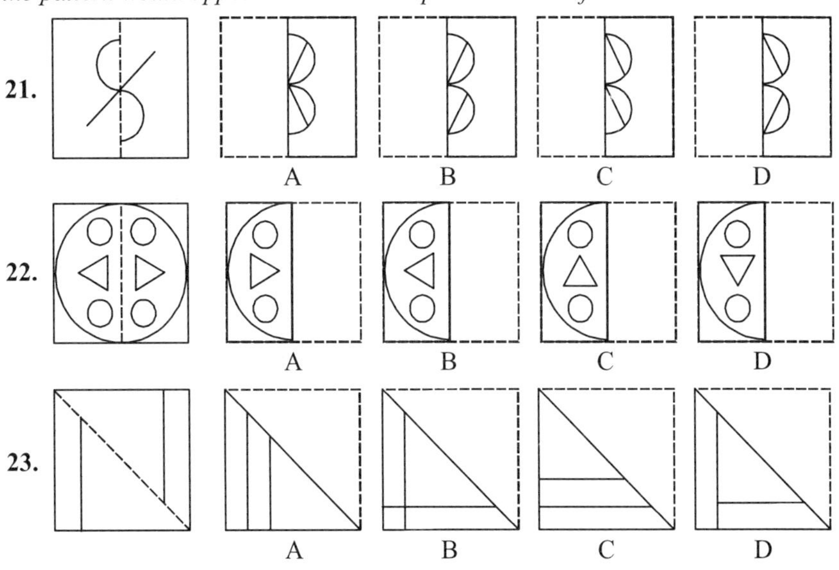

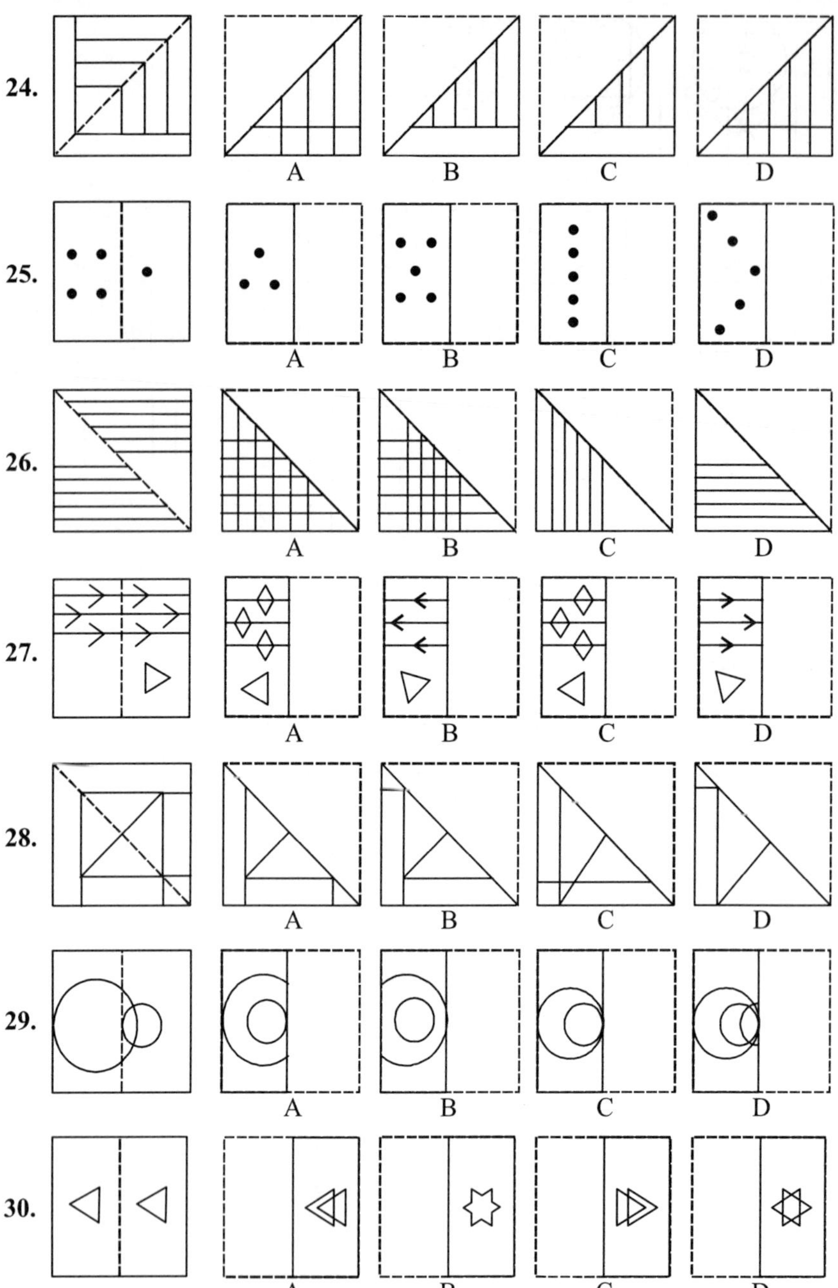
24.
A
B
C
D
25.
A
B
C
D
26.
A
B
C
D
27.
A
B
C
D
28.
A
B
C
D
29.
A
B
C
D
30.
A
B
C
D

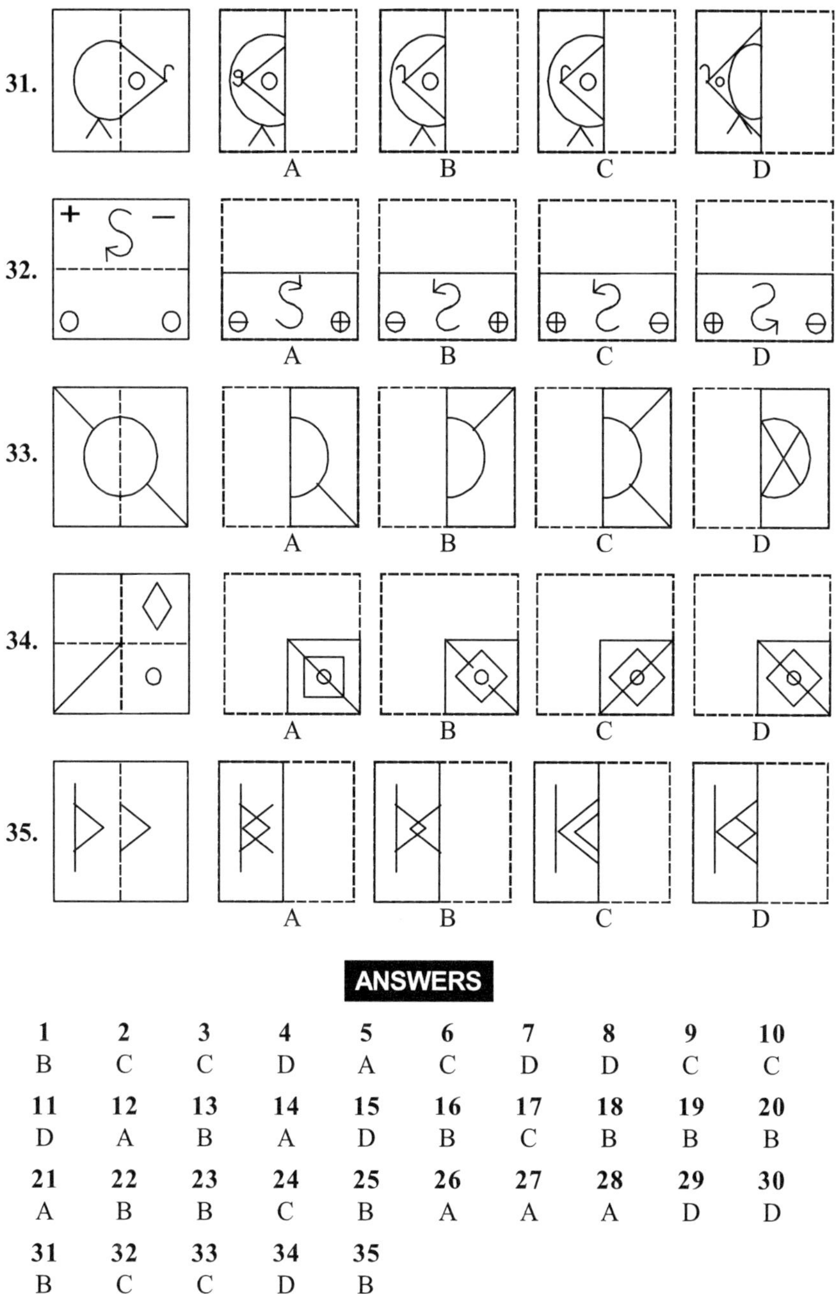


## ANSWERS

| 1 | 2 | 3 | 4 | 5 | 6 | 7 | 8 | 9 | 10 |
|---|---|---|---|---|---|---|---|---|---|
| B | C | C | D | A | C | D | D | C | C |
| **11** | **12** | **13** | **14** | **15** | **16** | **17** | **18** | **19** | **20** |
| D | A | B | A | D | B | C | B | B | B |
| **21** | **22** | **23** | **24** | **25** | **26** | **27** | **28** | **29** | **30** |
| A | B | B | C | B | A | A | A | D | D |
| **31** | **32** | **33** | **34** | **35** | | | | | |
| B | C | C | D | B | | | | | |

❍ ❍ ❍

6

# Figures Grouping & Figures Matrix

*Figure matrix is a 2 × 2 as 3 × 3 representation of figures following a certain pattern in a matrix form.*

In this chapter, we deal with questions which have either 2 × 2 or 3 × 3 matrix. These matrix are formed by a group of figures. Corresponding rows or corresponding columns follows a certain pattern. You are required to analyse each of the sets to find out the common pattern and on basis of that, the missing figure is to be identified from a set of alternatives so as to complete the matrix.

## SOLVED EXAMPLES

**Directions:** *In the following questions, find out which of the answer figures (A), (B), (C) and (D) completes the figure matrix?*

**1. Problem Figure** **Answer Figures**

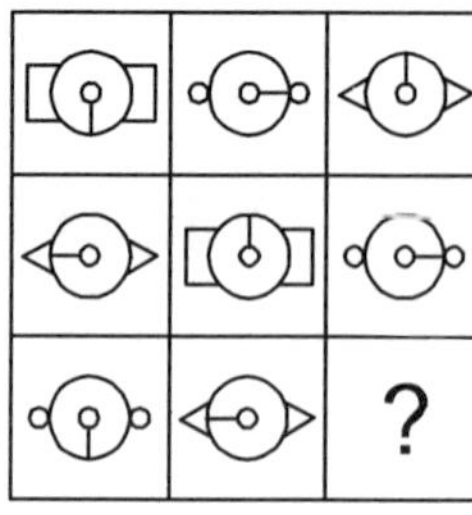


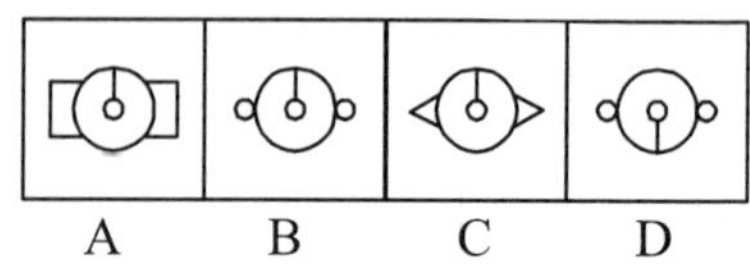


**Answers A:** In each row, the central part of the first figure rotates 90° anti-clockwise to form the central part of the second figure and the central part of the first figure rotates 180° to form the central parts of the third figure. Also, in each row, there are three types of geometrical figures are there rectangles, circles and triangles.

*When different figures are grouped on the basis of certain pattern, then this is called grouping of identical figures.*

In this chapter, we have a set of few figures which are numbered as 1, 2, 3, 4 and so on. We are required to analyse these figures and classify them into groups consisting of figures having more or less than same properties. The best answer is to be selected from a given set of fairly close alternatives.

**Direction:** *In the given question, group the given figures into three classes using each figure only once.*

**2.**

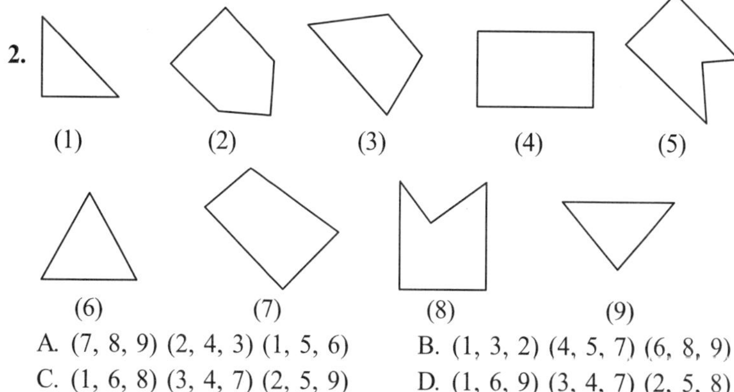

(1) (2) (3) (4) (5)

(6) (7) (8) (9)

A. (7, 8, 9) (2, 4, 3) (1, 5, 6) B. (1, 3, 2) (4, 5, 7) (6, 8, 9)
C. (1, 6, 8) (3, 4, 7) (2, 5, 9) D. (1, 6, 9) (3, 4, 7) (2, 5, 8)

**Answers D :** Figures (1), (6) and (9) are all triangles. Figures (3), (4) and (7) are all quadrilaterals. Figures (2), (5) and (8) are all pentagons.

In this type of questions, you are given a set of usually 6, 7 or 9 figures, which are numbered. The candidate is required to anlyse these figures and classify them into groups consisting of figures having more or less than same properties.

**3.** Group the following figures into three classes on the basis of identical properties.

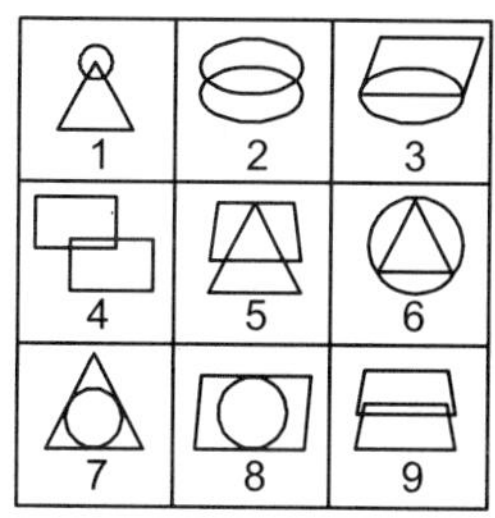


A. 1, 5, 9; 2, 7, 8; 3, 4, 6 B. 1, 5, 6; 4, 7, 8; 2, 3, 9
C. 2, 4, 9; 6, 7, 8; 1, 3, 5 D. 3, 7, 8; 4, 5, 9; 1, 2, 6

**Answers C:** 1, 3, 5 are composed of two dissimilar figures intersecting each other. 2, 4, 9 are composed of two similar figures intersecting each other. 6, 7, 8 contain one figure enclosed inside the other.

Thus, the given nine figures may be divided into three pairs: (1, 3, 5), (2, 4, 9), (6, 7, 8).

## EXERCISE

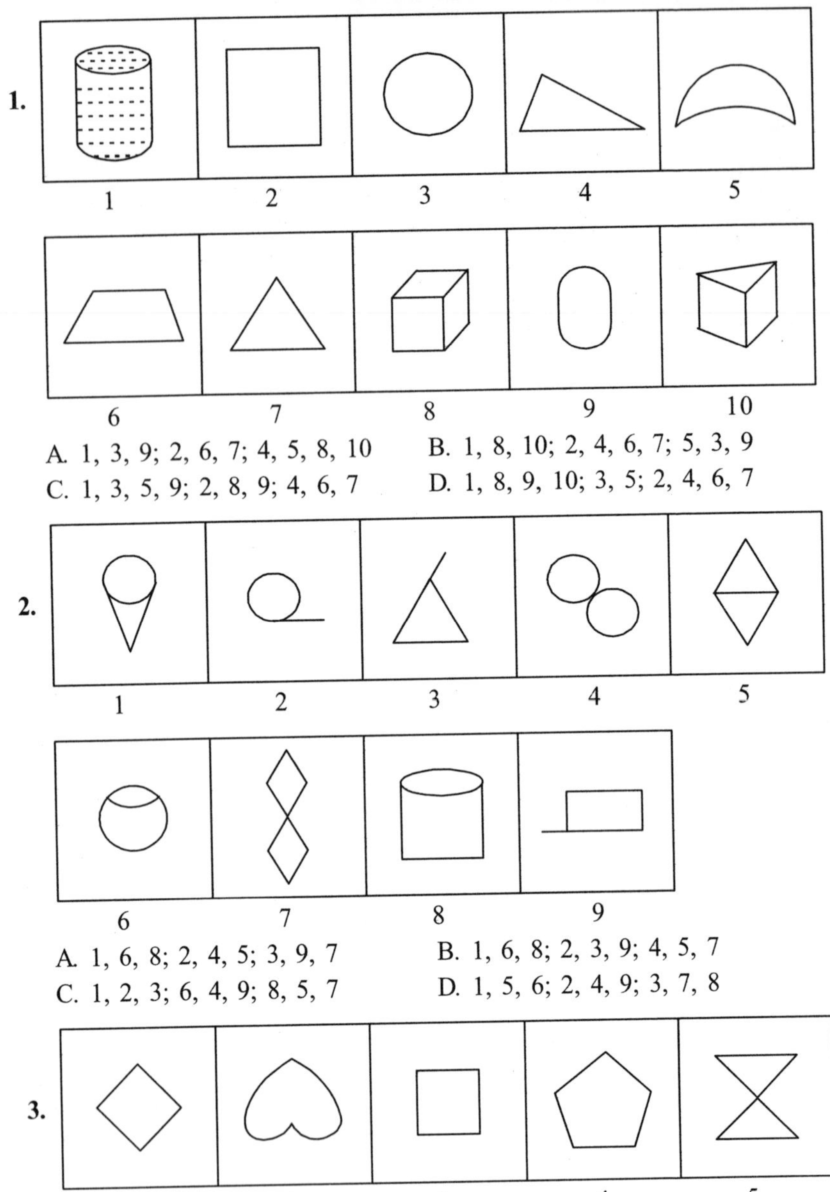

**1.**

A. 1, 3, 9; 2, 6, 7; 4, 5, 8, 10
B. 1, 8, 10; 2, 4, 6, 7; 5, 3, 9
C. 1, 3, 5, 9; 2, 8, 9; 4, 6, 7
D. 1, 8, 9, 10; 3, 5; 2, 4, 6, 7

**2.**

A. 1, 6, 8; 2, 4, 5; 3, 9, 7
B. 1, 6, 8; 2, 3, 9; 4, 5, 7
C. 1, 2, 3; 6, 4, 9; 8, 5, 7
D. 1, 5, 6; 2, 4, 9; 3, 7, 8

**3.**

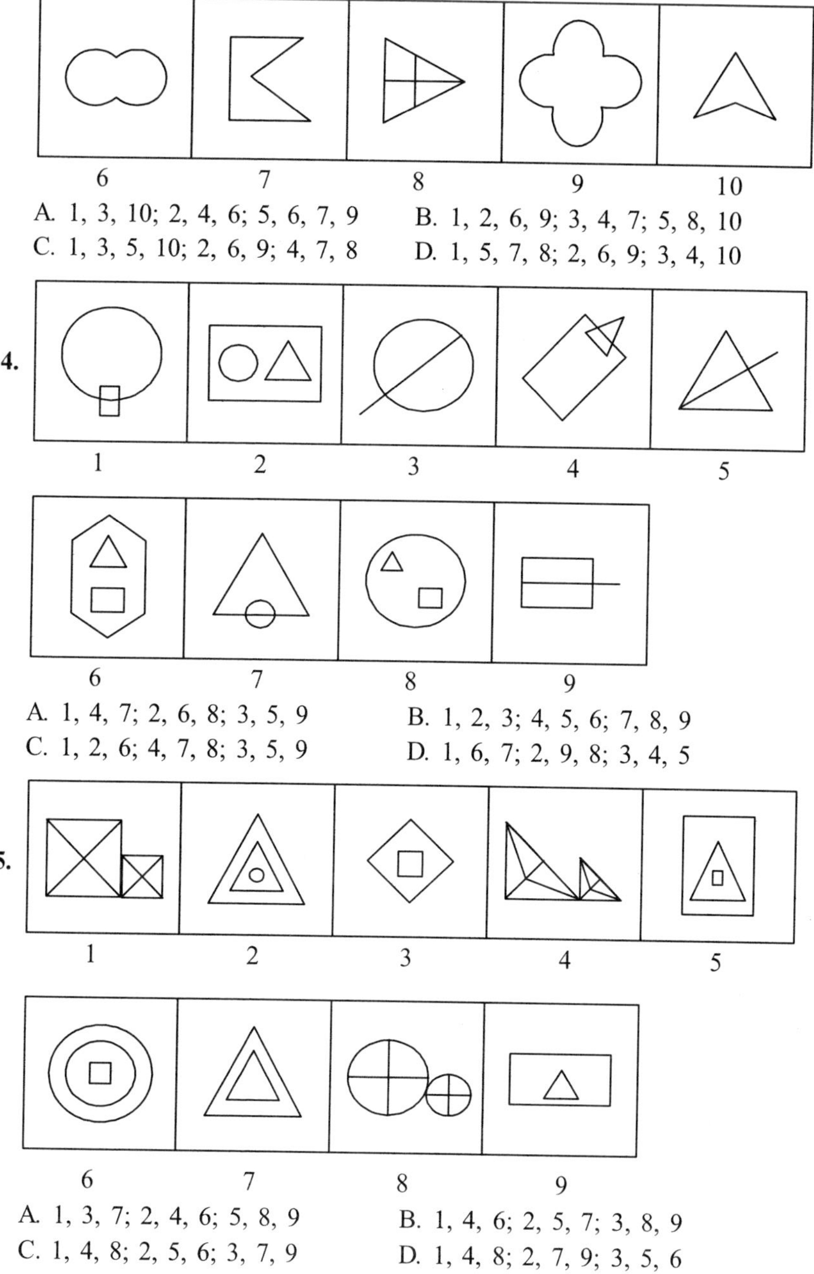


A. 1, 3, 10; 2, 4, 6; 5, 6, 7, 9 B. 1, 2, 6, 9; 3, 4, 7; 5, 8, 10

C. 1, 3, 5, 10; 2, 6, 9; 4, 7, 8 D. 1, 5, 7, 8; 2, 6, 9; 3, 4, 10

**4.**



A. 1, 4, 7; 2, 6, 8; 3, 5, 9 B. 1, 2, 3; 4, 5, 6; 7, 8, 9

C. 1, 2, 6; 4, 7, 8; 3, 5, 9 D. 1, 6, 7; 2, 9, 8; 3, 4, 5

**5.**



A. 1, 3, 7; 2, 4, 6; 5, 8, 9 B. 1, 4, 6; 2, 5, 7; 3, 8, 9

C. 1, 4, 8; 2, 5, 6; 3, 7, 9 D. 1, 4, 8; 2, 7, 9; 3, 5, 6

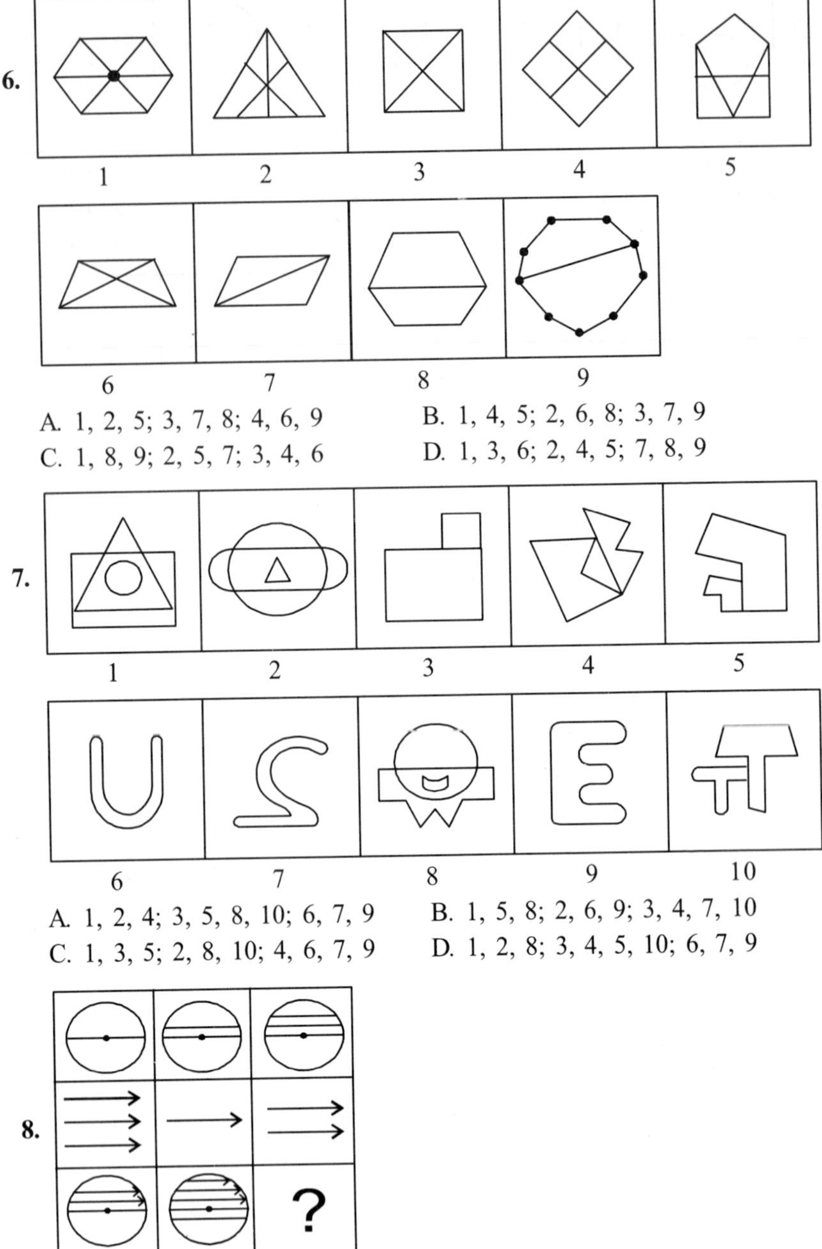


**6.**

A. 1, 2, 5; 3, 7, 8; 4, 6, 9
B. 1, 4, 5; 2, 6, 8; 3, 7, 9
C. 1, 8, 9; 2, 5, 7; 3, 4, 6
D. 1, 3, 6; 2, 4, 5; 7, 8, 9

**7.**

A. 1, 2, 4; 3, 5, 8, 10; 6, 7, 9
B. 1, 5, 8; 2, 6, 9; 3, 4, 7, 10
C. 1, 3, 5; 2, 8, 10; 4, 6, 7, 9
D. 1, 2, 8; 3, 4, 5, 10; 6, 7, 9

**8.**

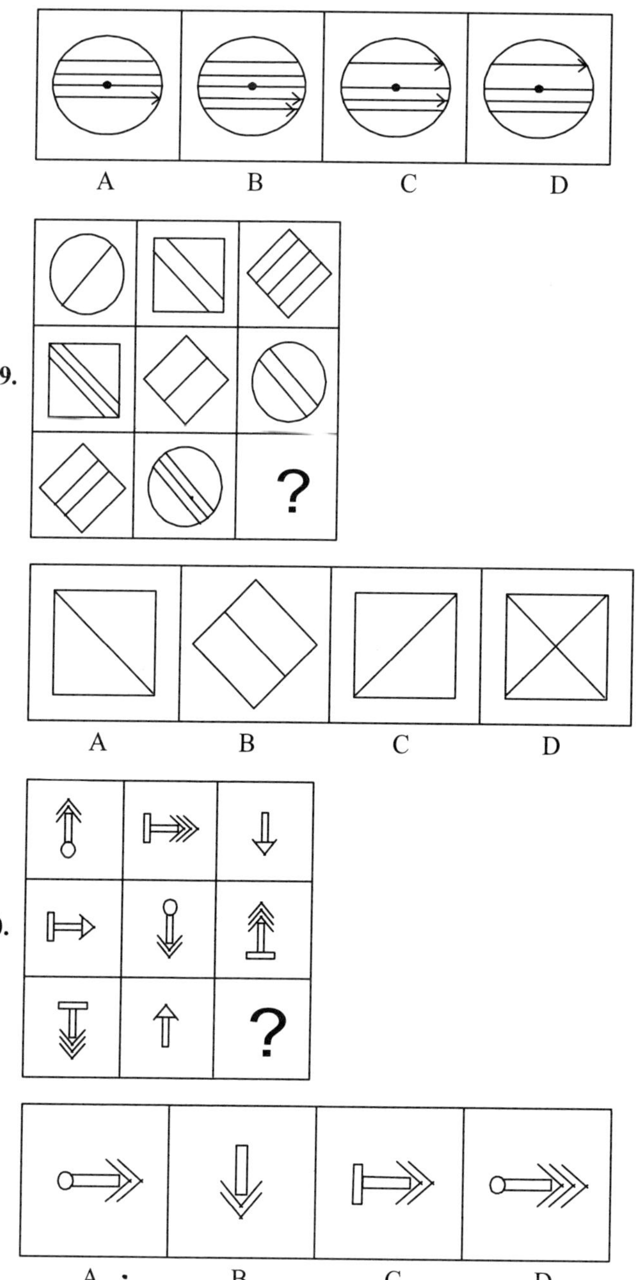
A
B
C
D
9.
?
A
B
C
D
10.
?
A
B
C
D

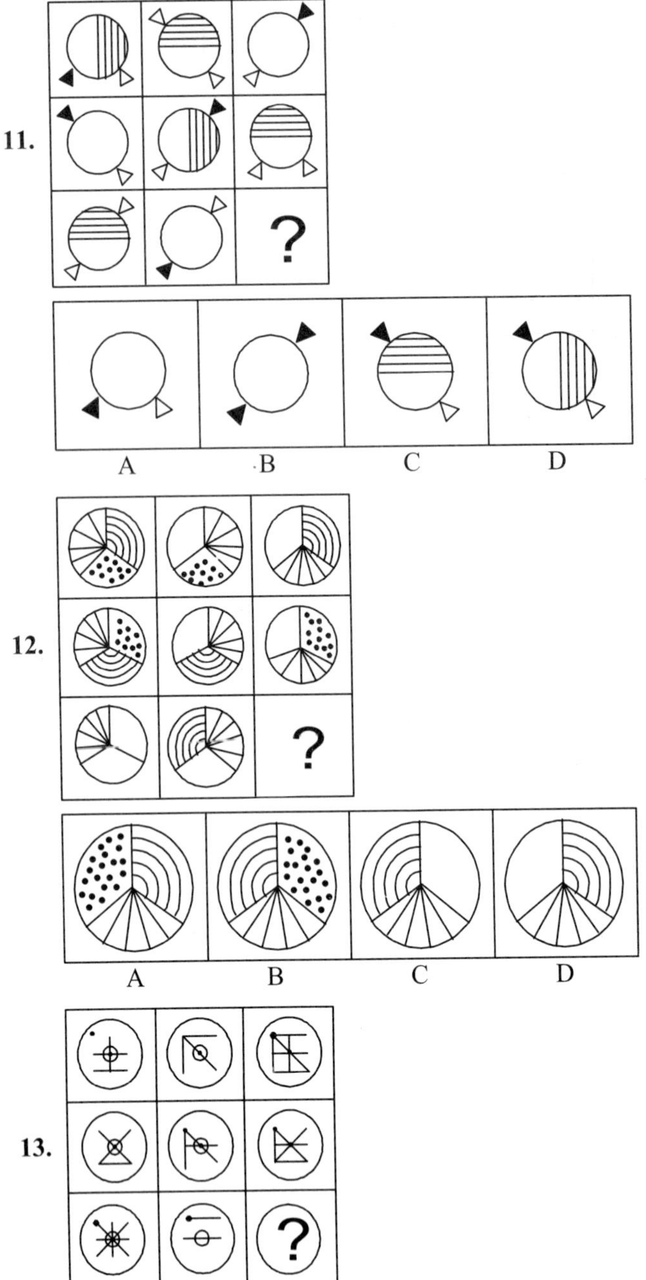
11.
?
A
B
C
D
12.
?
A
B
C
D
13.
?

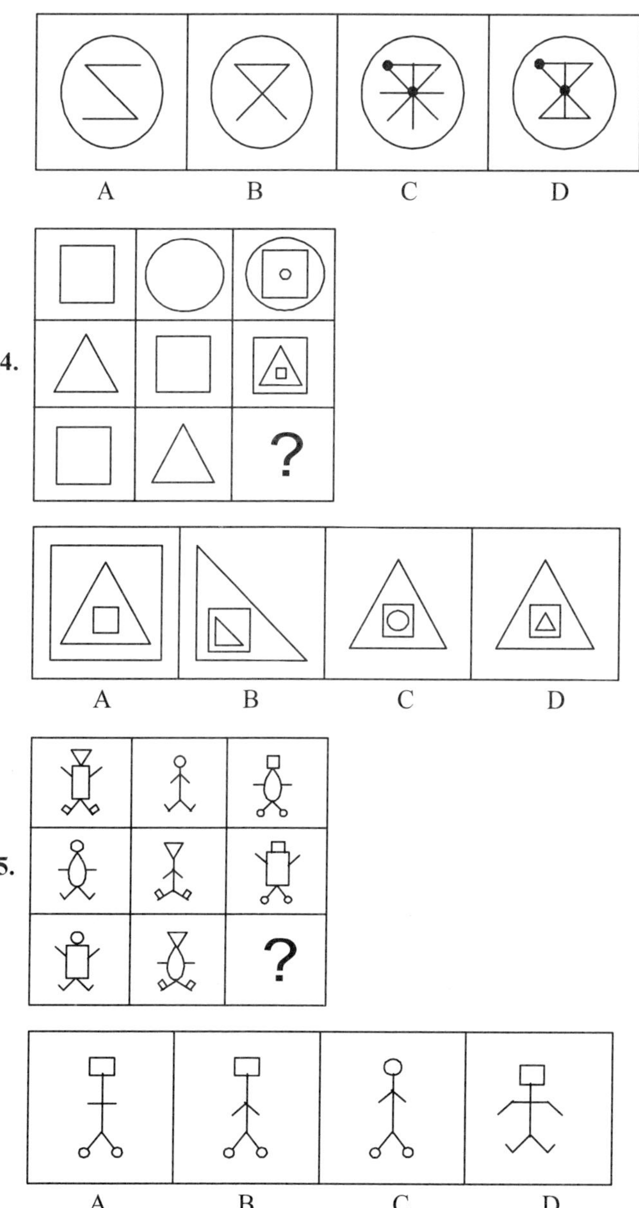


**14.**

**15.**

## ANSWERS

| 1 | 2 | 3 | 4 | 5 | 6 | 7 | 8 | 9 | 10 |
|---|---|---|---|---|---|---|---|---|---|
| B | B | C | A | C | D | D | D | A | A |
| **11** | **12** | **13** | **14** | **15** | | | | | |
| D | C | C | D | B | | | | | |

## EXPLANATORY ANSWERS

1. Figures 1, 8 and 10 are 3-dimensional, figures 2, 4, 6 and 7 are formed by straight lines and figures 5, 3 and 9 are formed by curved lines.
2. Figures 1, 6 and 8 are 3-dimensional, figures 2, 3 and 9 have one straight line joined to the shape and figures 4, 5 and 7 are two identical shapes joined together.
3. Figures 1, 3, 5 and 10 are made of four straight lines; figures 2, 6 and 9 are made of curved lines and figures 4, 7 and 8 are made of five straight lines.
4. Figures 1, 4 and 7 are intersected by a different and smaller shape, figures 2, 6 and 8 contain two enclosed shapes and figures 3, 5 and 9 are divided into two parts and the dividing line is extended.
5. Figures 1, 4 and 8 are two identical forms joined together, figures 2, 5 and 6 contain two identical forms enclosing one different form and figures 3, 7 and 9 contain two forms each.
6. Figures 1, 3 and 6 have diagonals running from corner to corner, figures 2, 4 and 5 have diagonals running from side to side and figures 7, 8 and 9 are bisected by their diagonals.
7. Figures 1, 2 and 8 contain three shapes, figures 3, 4, 5 and 10 are two identical shapes put together and figures 6, 7 and 9 are double-lined alphabet 'U', 'S' and 'E'.
8. In first and second rows, the number of lines and arrows are 1, 2 and 3 each. In the third row the figure contains both lines and arrows of which the latter is on the top side. There are two arrows and one line in first column figure, three arrows and two lines in second column figure, so the figure in the third column should contain one arrow and three straight lines.
9. Each row contains a circle, a square and a rhombus. The figures irrespective of their placement are divided into 2, 3 and 4 parts. In the third row and column, a square will fit the matrix. The dividing diagonal lines are oscillated by 90° at each step. So, the diagonal in the answer square should be running from left corner to the right corner.

**10.** In each row the following features are used once. There are three arrows: one with one line head, one with two line head and one with three line head. Also, their bases are different: one is plain, one has a circle and one has a rectangle. Their directions are upwards, downwards and horizontal to the right.

**11.** In each row one figure is unshaded, one figure contains horizontal lines in top half part and one figure contains vertical lines in right half part. Also, two triangles in each row are shaded.

**12.** In each row the straight lines are moved one section clockwise. The right section in first and third column figures is identical. The bottom section in first and second column figures is identical. And the left section in the second and third column figures is identical. By the rules above, the straight line section should be the bottom section of the option figure, the right section should be blank and the left section should contain the curved lines.

**13.** In each row the figure in the first column superimposed on the figure in the second column is the figure in the third column. Only the circle is missing in the third column figure.

**14.** In each row the figure in the second column forms the outer and the central part, and the figure in the first column forms the middle part of the figure in the third column.

**15.** Each row contains figures containing 3 forms of head and 3 forms of body, 3 forms of hands and 3 forms of legs used only once. In third row the forms left out for the third column figure are: a square head, a straight line body, lowered hands and circled legs. Option B fits the requirement.

❍ ❍ ❍

7

# Figure Completion

## SOLVED EXAMPLES

In this type of questions, an incomplete figure is given in which a part, generally a quarter, is left blank. The problem figure is followed by four choice figures. Out of these choice figures, the candidate is required to choose the one which best fits into the blank space so as to complete the original pattern.

A sample question is provided below:

You are given an incomplete figure (X) and four choice figures A, B, C & D. Out of these choice figures, choose the one which best fits into (X) to complete the original pattern.

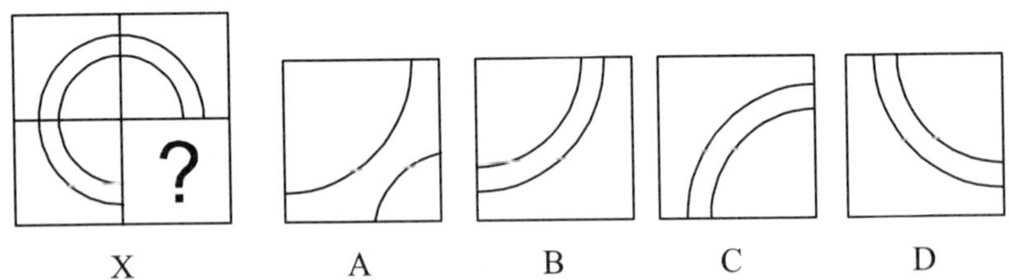


### Suggested Method

What is expected of you in such problems? The expectation is that you complete the pattern in such a way that the figure appears balanced and not haphazard. In other words, the figure should appear symmetrical. Obviously, then you should choose an answer choice that symmetrically fits into the empty box. The first thing that should be done for this is to recognise the axis of symmetry. You should find out the line about which the figure would be symmetrical, if completed. This is not a difficult job and a cursory glance at the figure would be sufficient for you to detect the axis of symmetry. Once you have found out the axis of symmetry you can draw the image of the figures on one side of the axis, taking this axis as a mirror, to find out the pattern of the other side.

However, many problems are so easy that it is totally unnecessary to go in for axis of symmetry and image-reflections. Only a simple inspection could do the job.

The following examples would illustrate the point.

**Answers :** It is obvious by mere inspection that (B) is the correct answer. It is the only choice that completes the two circles, when put in place of the question-mark.

Select a figure from the four alternatives which when placed in the blank space of fig (X) would complete the pattern.

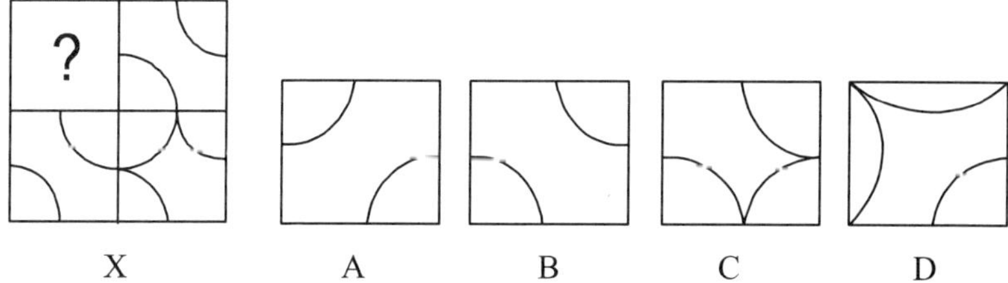


**Answers :** Clearly fig (C) will complete the pattern when placed in the blank space of fig (X), as shown below:

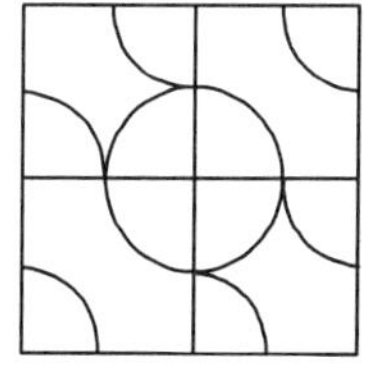

## EXERCISE

**Directions (Qs. 1–29):** *In each of the following questions, complete the missing portion of the given pattern by selecting from the given alternatives A, B, C and D.*

1.

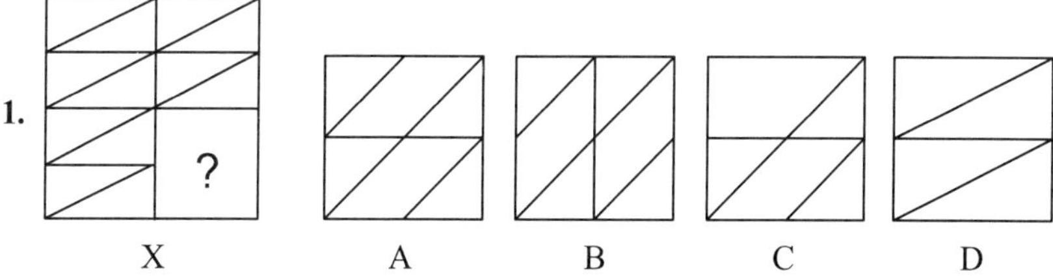

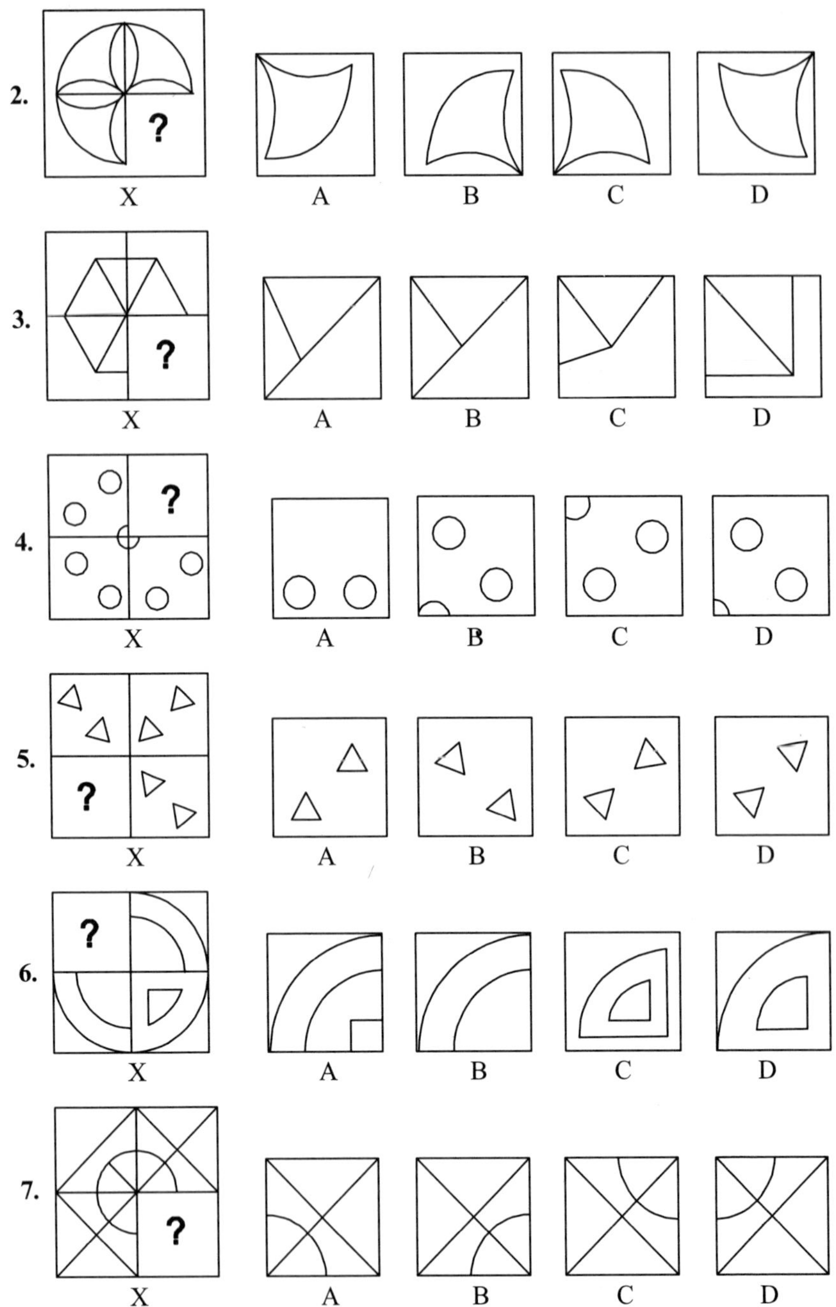
2.
?
X
A
B
C
D
3.
?
X
A
B
C
D
4.
?
X
A
B
C
D
5.
?
X
A
B
C
D
6.
?
X
A
B
C
D
7.
?
X
A
B
C
D

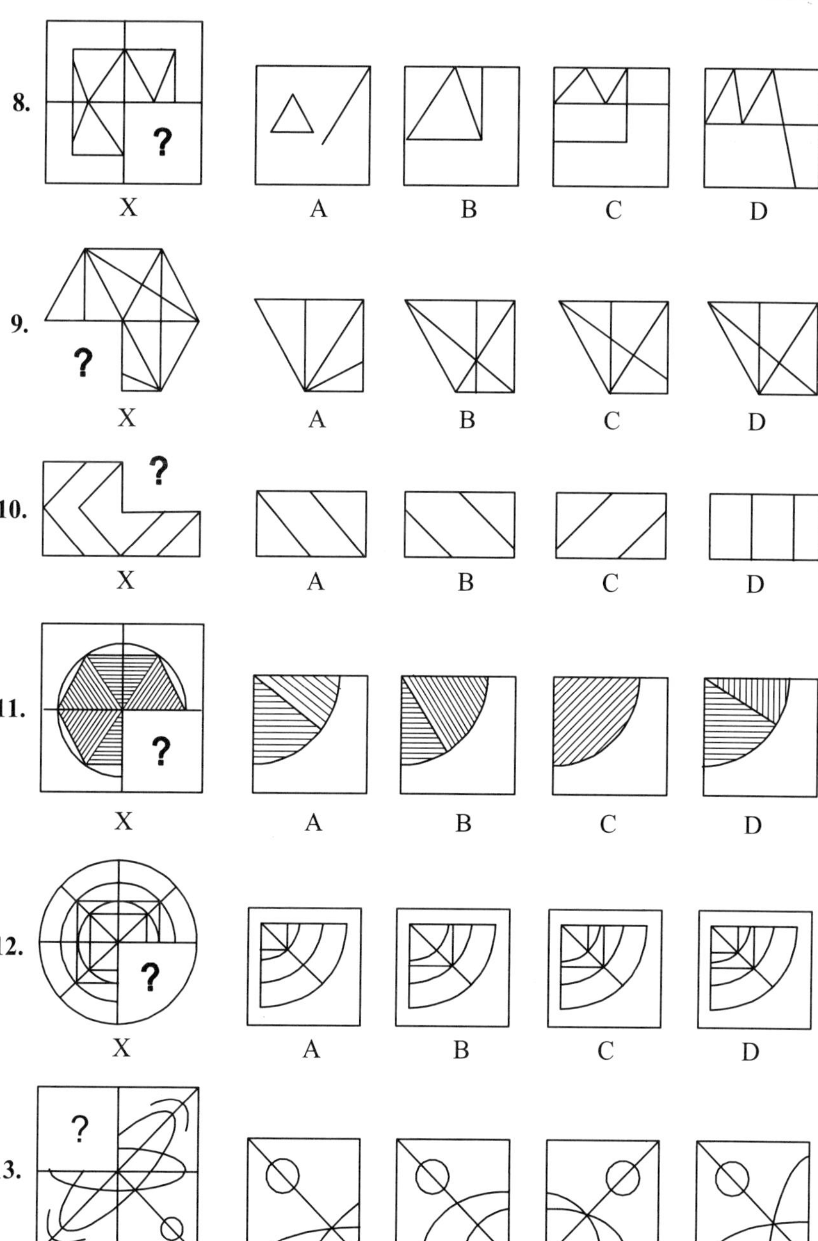
8.
?
X
A
B
C
D
9.
?
X
A
B
C
D
10.
?
X
A
B
C
D
11.
?
X
A
B
C
D
12.
?
X
A
B
C
D
13.
?
X
A
B
C
D

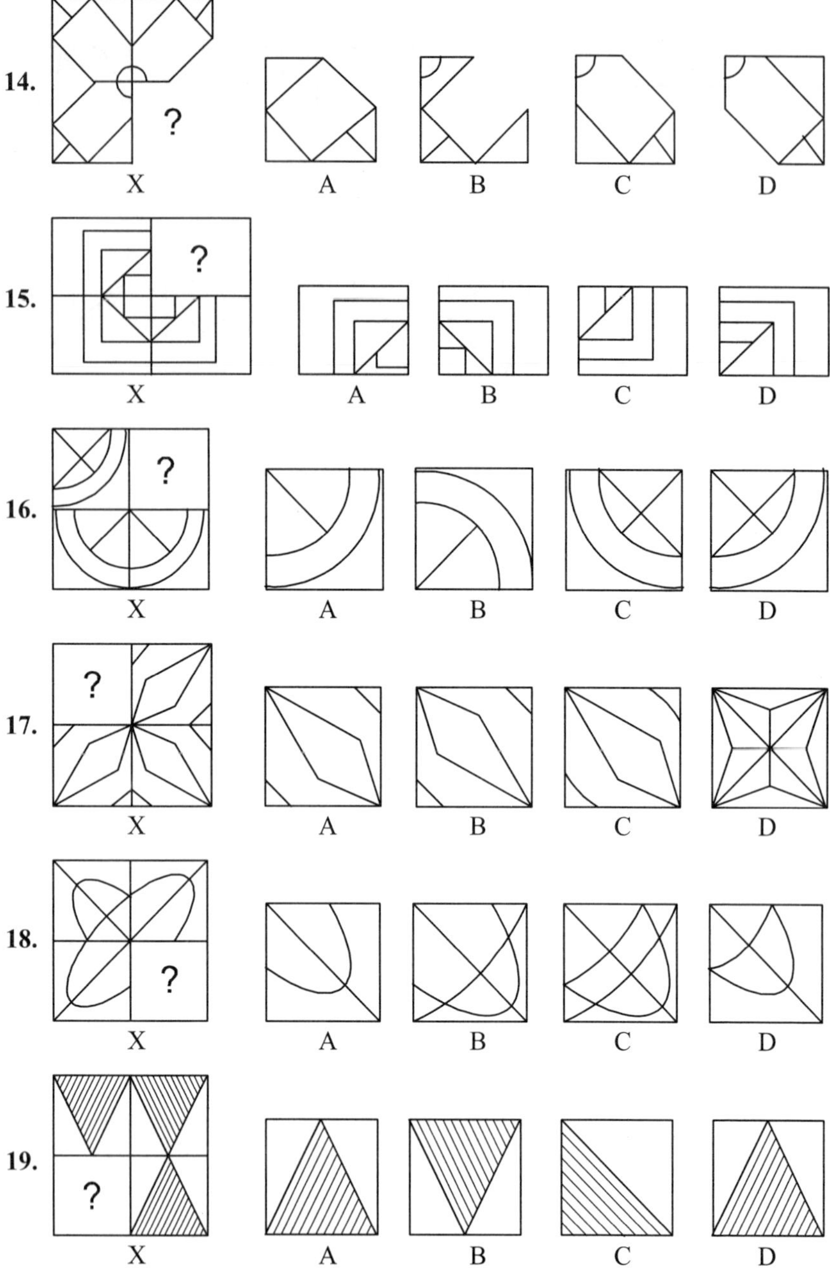
14.
?
X
A
B
C
D
15.
?
X
A
B
C
D
16.
?
X
A
B
C
D
17.
?
X
A
B
C
D
18.
?
X
A
B
C
D
19.
?
X
A
B
C
D

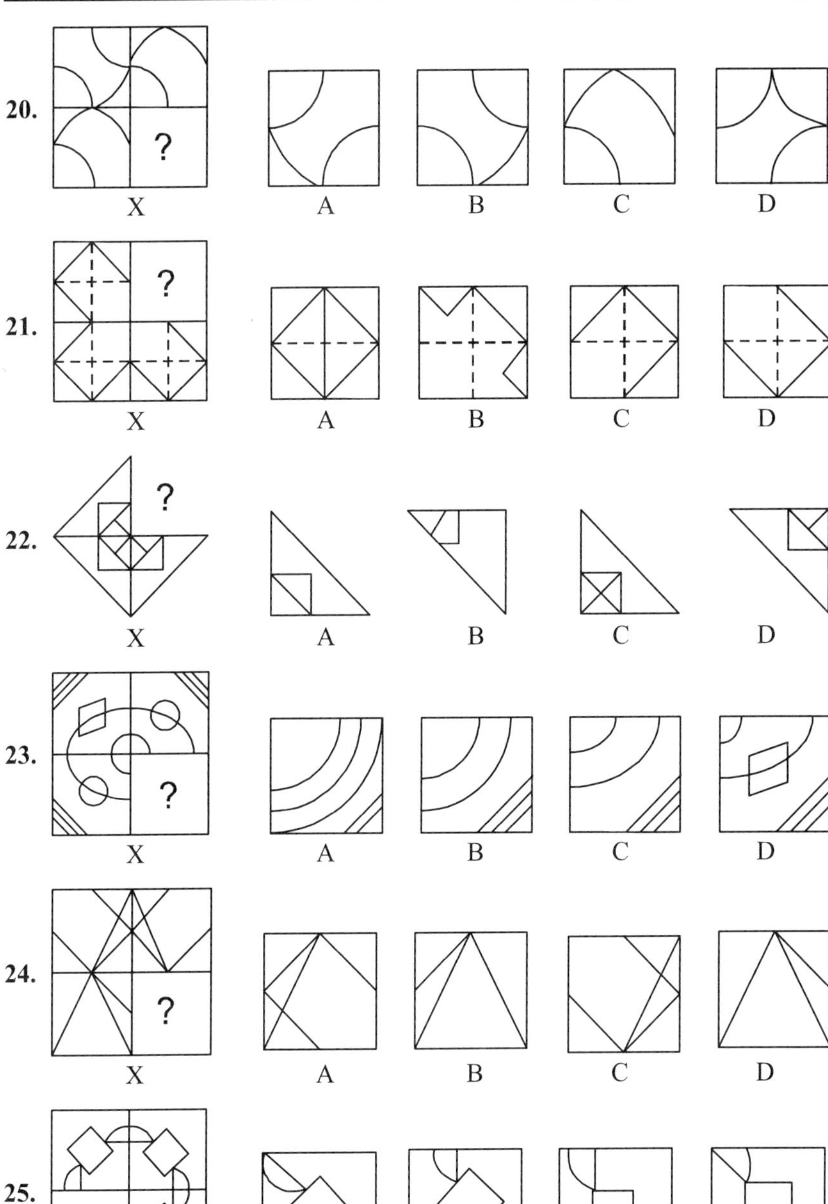
20.
?
X
A
B
C
D
21.
?
X
A
B
C
D
22.
?
X
A
B
C
D
23.
?
X
A
B
C
D
24.
?
X
A
B
C
D
25.
?
X
A
B
C
D

26. X A B C D

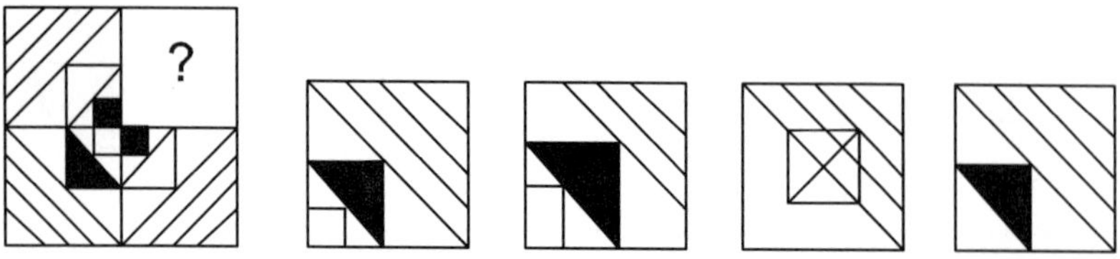

27. X A B C D

28. X A B C D

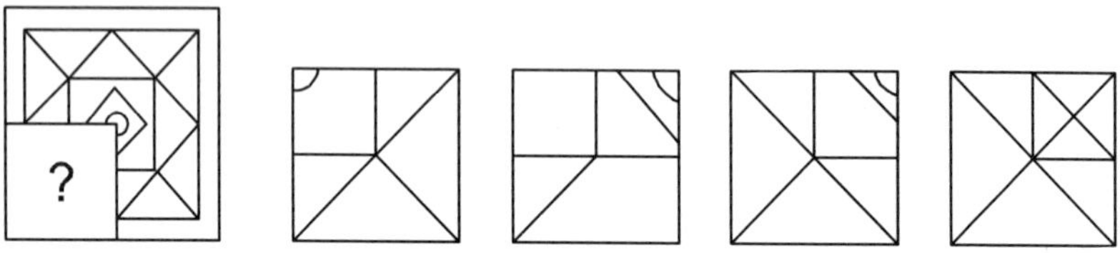

29. X A B C D

**Directions (Qs. 30–32):** *The following problems are based on pattern completion test. A figure is given whose one part / quarter is missing or left blank with some choices, you required to select the best choice which completes the figure.*

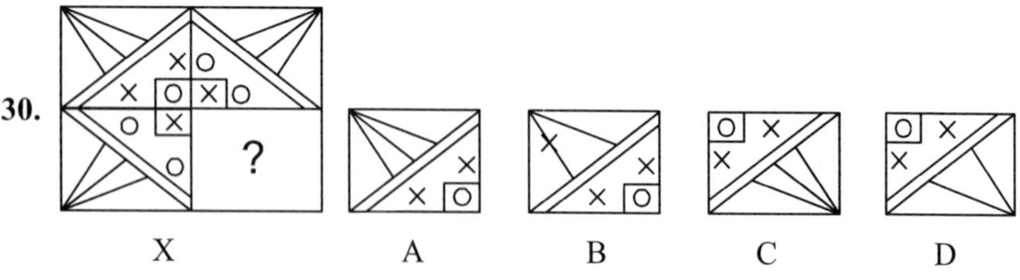
30. X A B C D

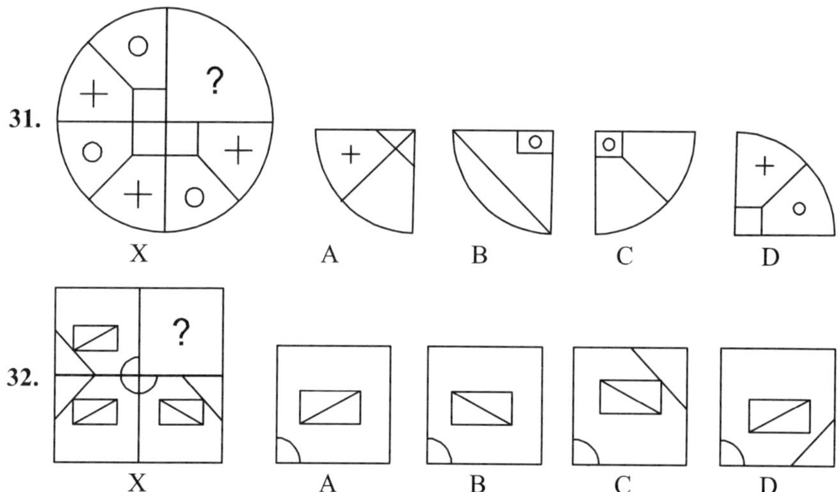


**Directions (Qs. 33–37):** *The following problems are based on pattern completion tets. A problem figure is given whose one part / quarter is missing or left blank with some choices, you are required to select the best choice from answer figures, which completes the figure:*

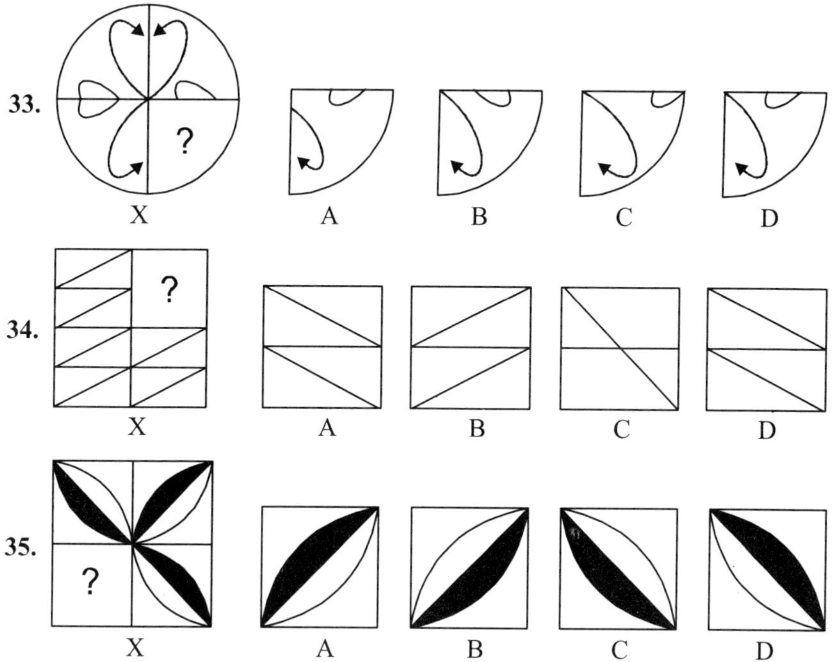

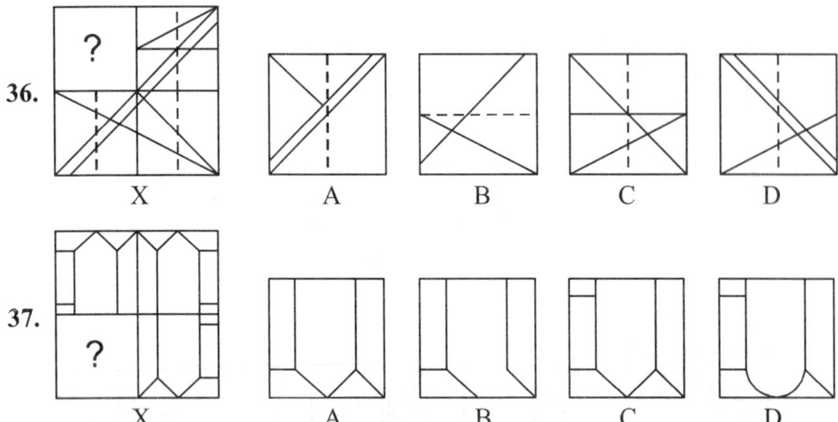


**Directions (Qs. 38–41):** *The following problems are based on the pattern completion test. A figure is given whose one part / quarter is missing or left blank with some choices, you are required to select the best choice from completes the figure:*

38. ?

X A B C D

39. ?

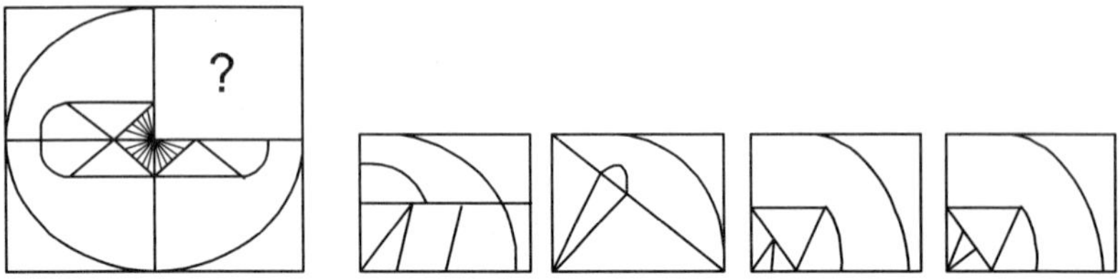

X A B C D

40. ?

X A B C D

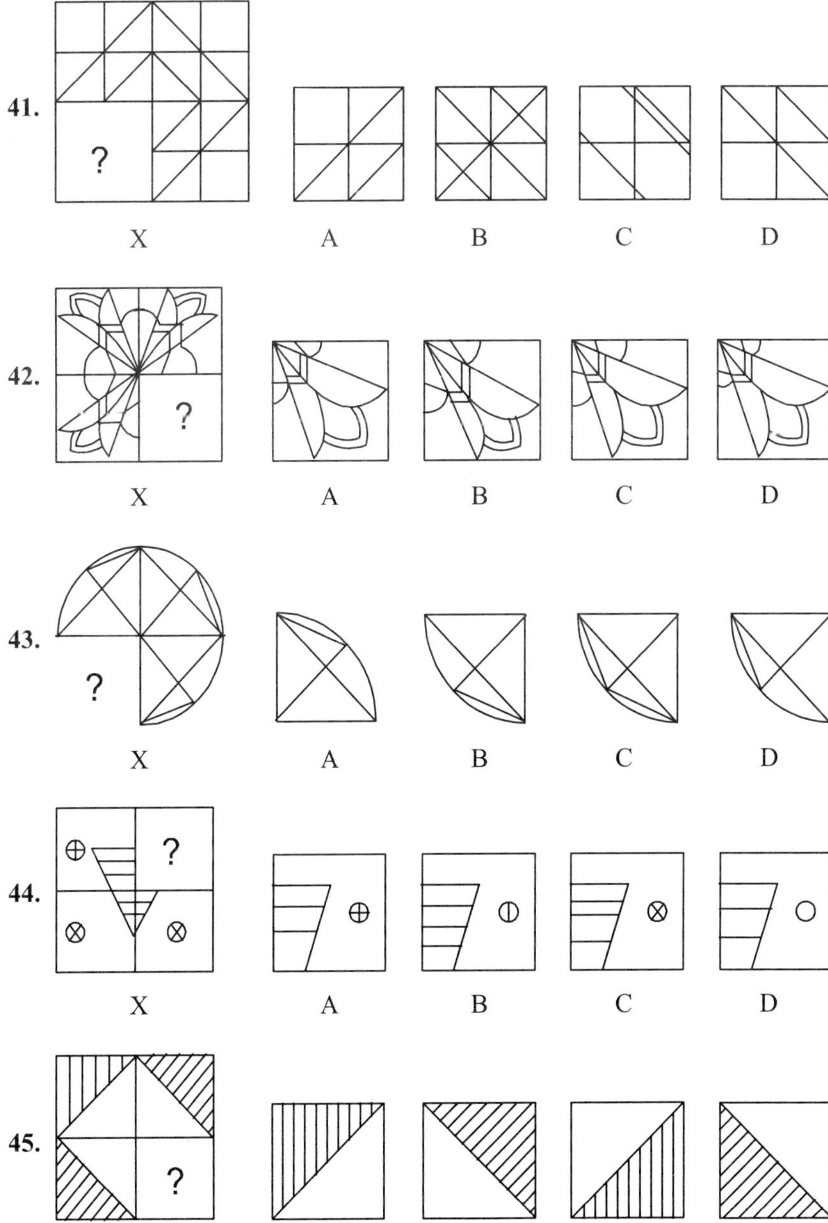
41.
?
X
A
B
C
D
42.
?
X
A
B
C
D
43.
?
X
A
B
C
D
44.
?
X
A
B
C
D
45.
?
X
A
B
C
D

46.

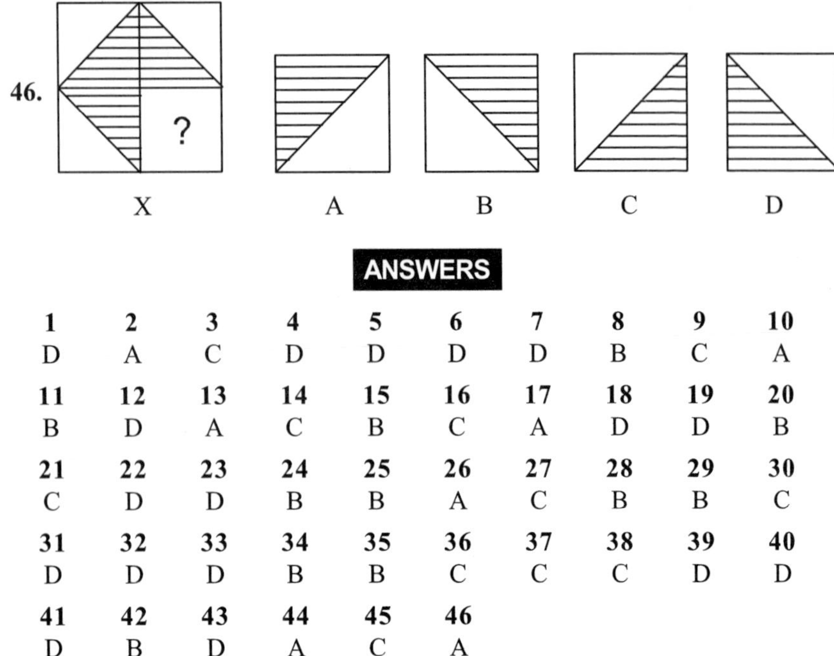


## ANSWERS

| 1 | 2 | 3 | 4 | 5 | 6 | 7 | 8 | 9 | 10 |
|---|---|---|---|---|---|---|---|---|---|
| D | A | C | D | D | D | D | B | C | A |
| **11** | **12** | **13** | **14** | **15** | **16** | **17** | **18** | **19** | **20** |
| B | D | A | C | B | C | A | D | D | B |
| **21** | **22** | **23** | **24** | **25** | **26** | **27** | **28** | **29** | **30** |
| C | D | D | B | B | A | C | B | B | C |
| **31** | **32** | **33** | **34** | **35** | **36** | **37** | **38** | **39** | **40** |
| D | D | D | B | B | C | C | C | D | D |
| **41** | **42** | **43** | **44** | **45** | **46** | | | | |
| D | B | D | A | C | A | | | | |

❍ ❍ ❍

# 8

# Embedded (Hidden) Figure

*A figure is said to be an embedded figure when that figure is contained by another figure.*

A figure suppose figure (A) is said to be embedded in figure (B), if figure (B) contains a part of figure (A). In this chapter, we deal with questions in which an original figure is followed by four alternative answers. One of the answer figures, is embedded or hidden in the original figure. You are required to select from the alternative that which figure clearly shows the embedded portion of the original figure:

## SOLVED EXAMPLES

**Directions:** *In the following questions, figure X is embedded in any one of the four alternative figures A, B, C and D. Find he alternative which contains figure X as its part.*

1.

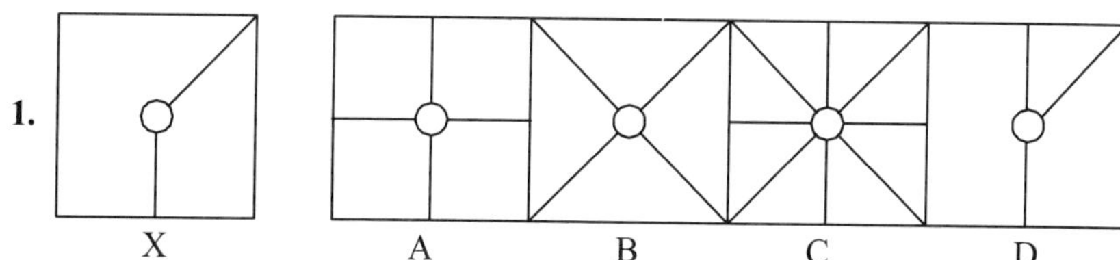


**Answers C:** On close observation, we find figure X is embedded in figure C as shown.

2.

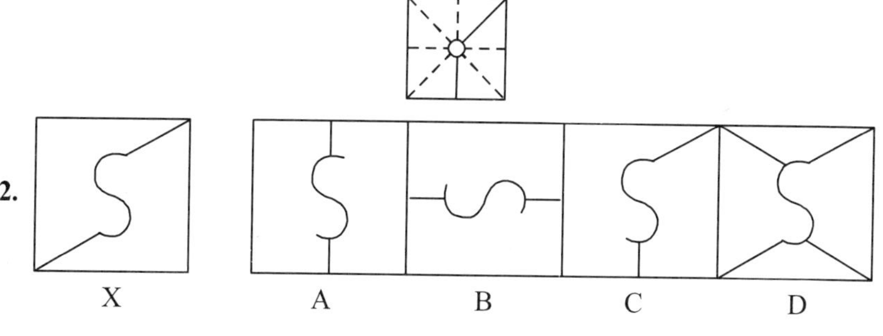

**Answers D:** On close observation figure X is embedded in figure D as shown:

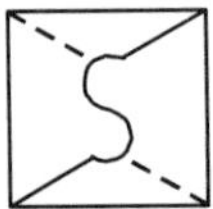

3. Fig. (X) is embedded in any one of the four alternative figures. Find the alternative which contains fig. (X).

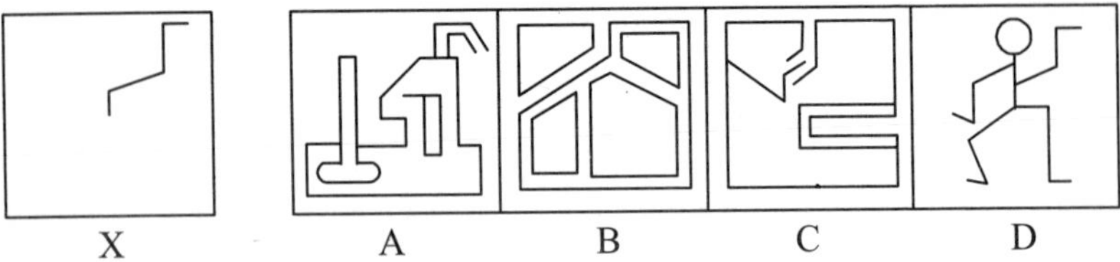


**Answers D:** Fig. (X) is embedded in fig. (D) as shown below:

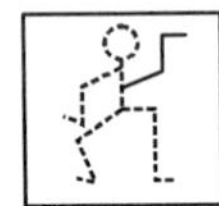

Hence, the answer is (D).

## EXERCISE

**Directions :** *In the questions below (X) embedded in one of the following figures. Find out the correct alternative.*

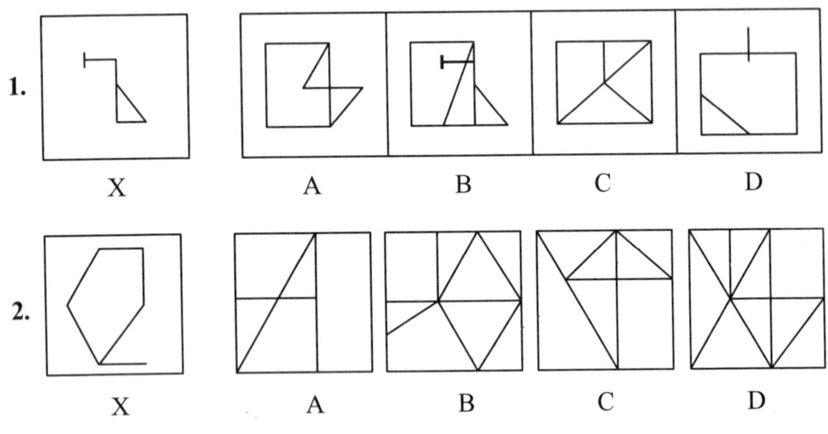

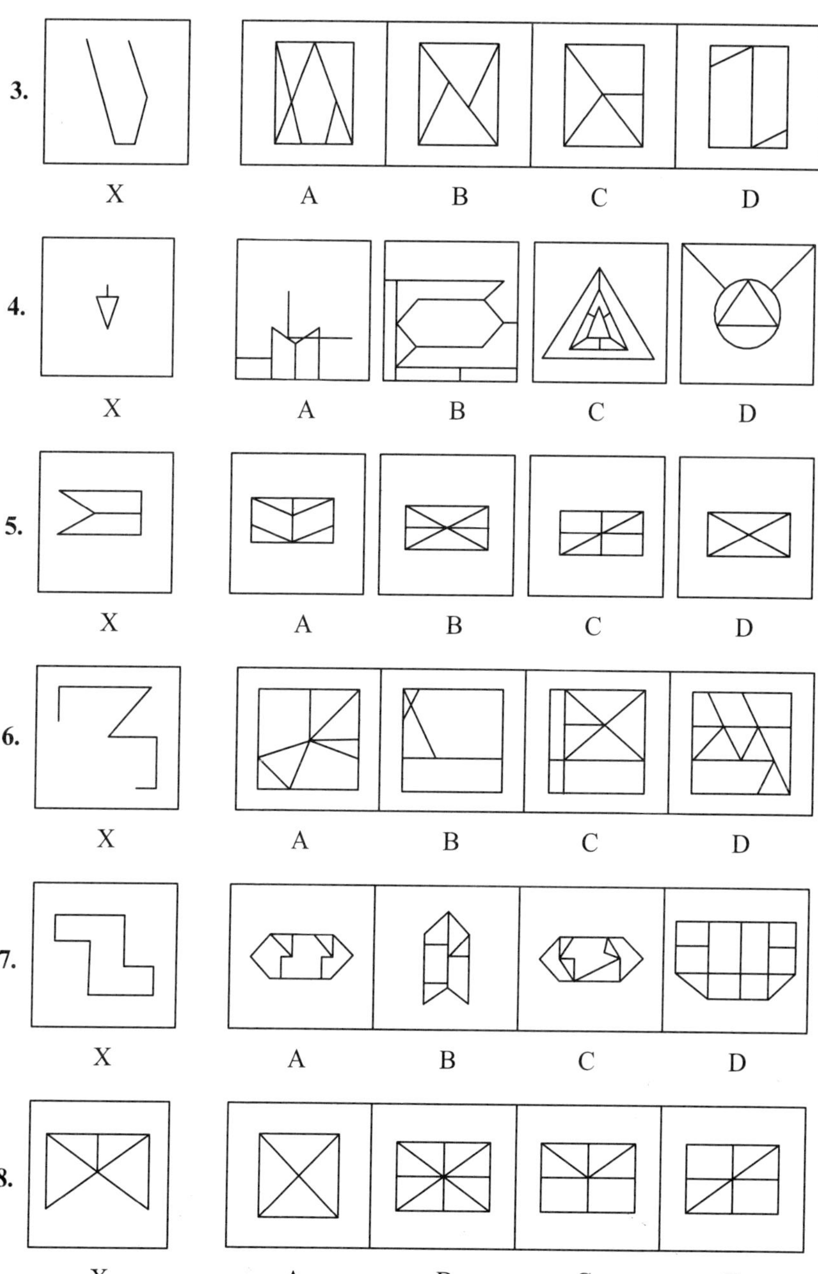
3.
X
A
B
C
D
4.
X
A
B
C
D
5.
X
A
B
C
D
6.
X
A
B
C
D
7.
X
A
B
C
D
8.
X
A
B
C
D

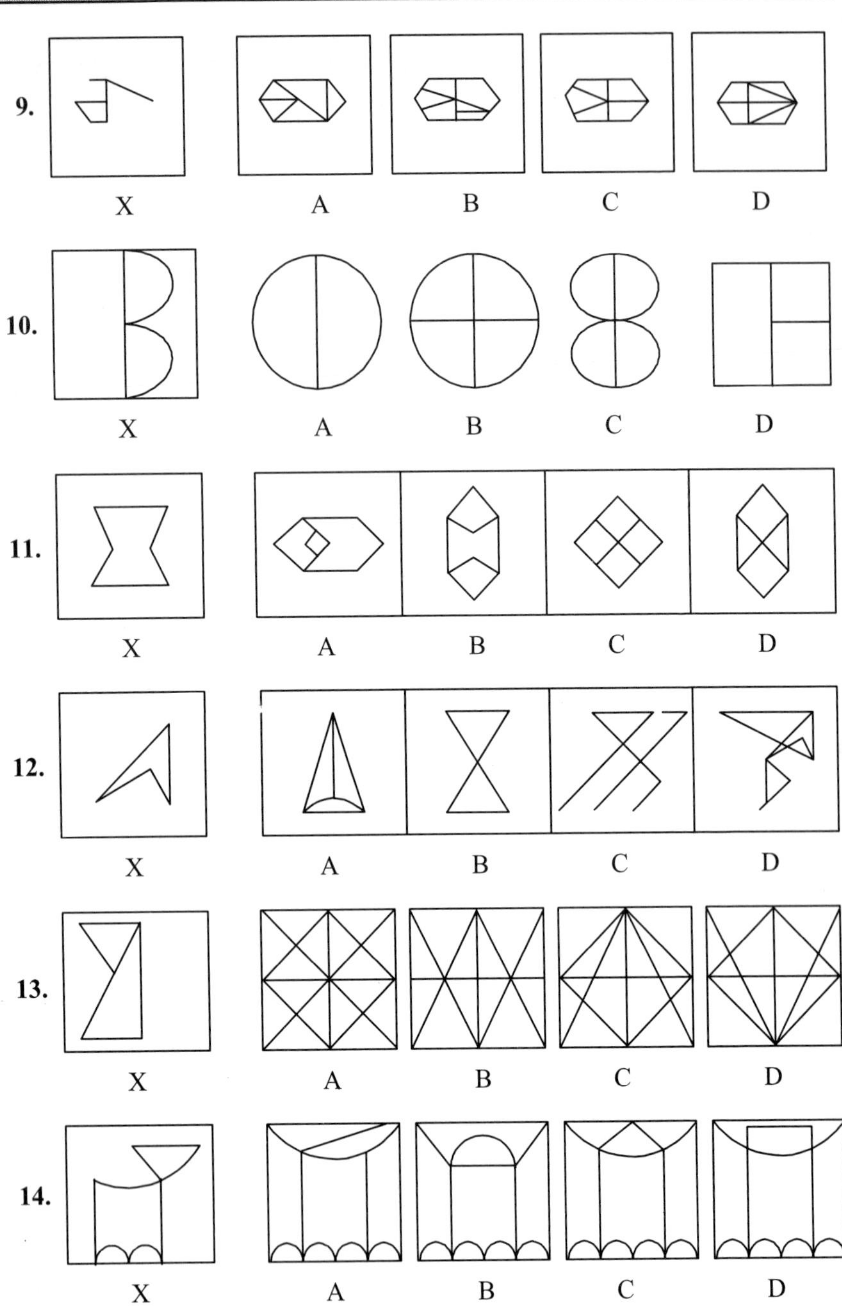
9.
X
A
B
C
D
10.
X
A
B
C
D
11.
X
A
B
C
D
12.
X
A
B
C
D
13.
X
A
B
C
D
14.
X
A
B
C
D

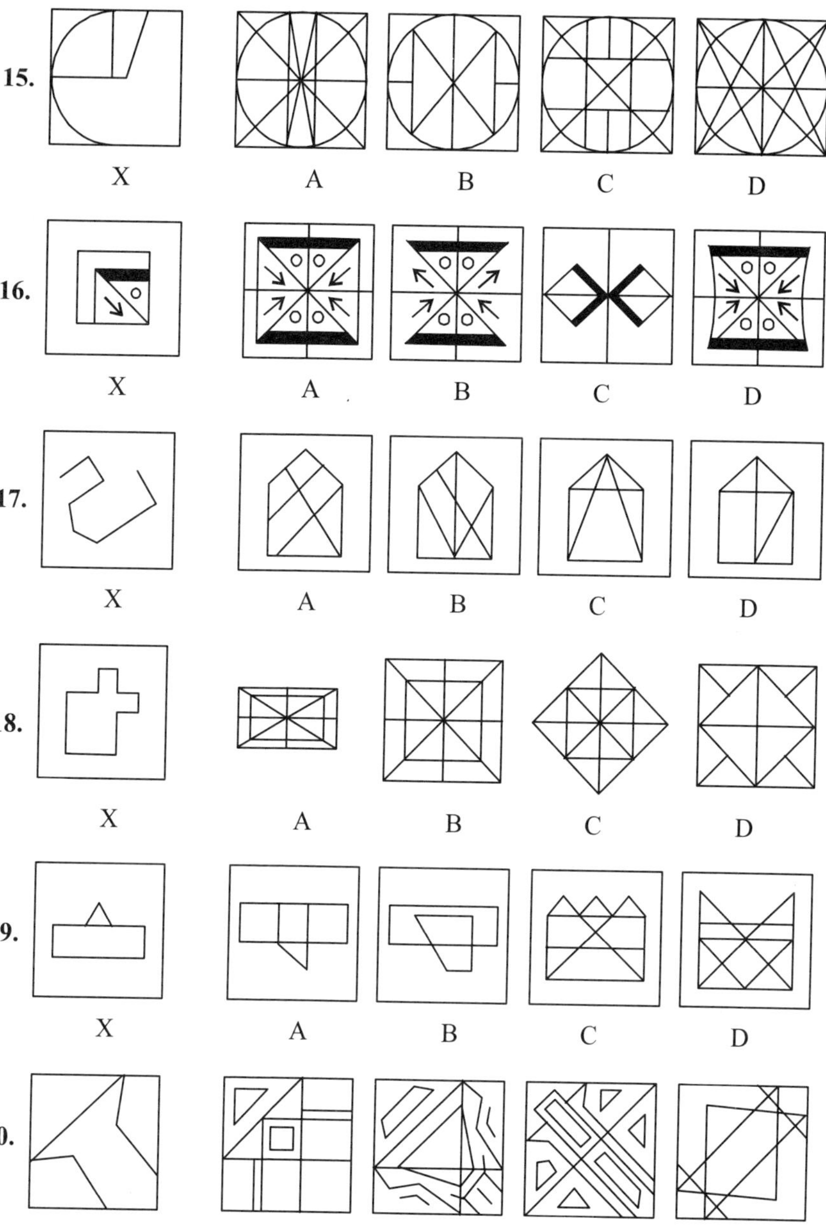
15.
X
A
B
C
D
16.
X
A
B
C
D
17.
X
A
B
C
D
18.
X
A
B
C
D
19.
X
A
B
C
D
20.
X
A
B
C
D

21.

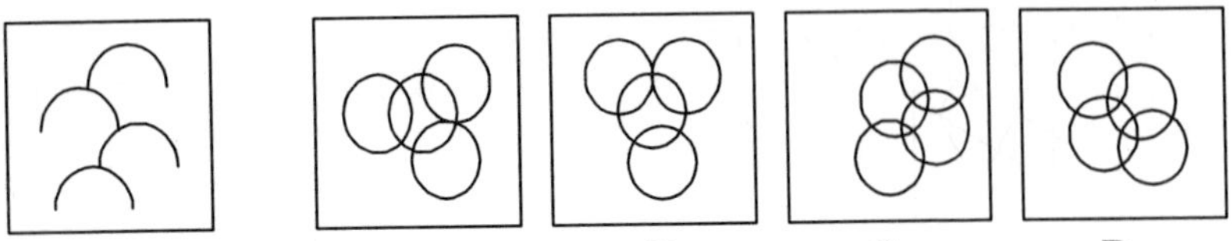

X A B C D

22.

X A B C D

23.

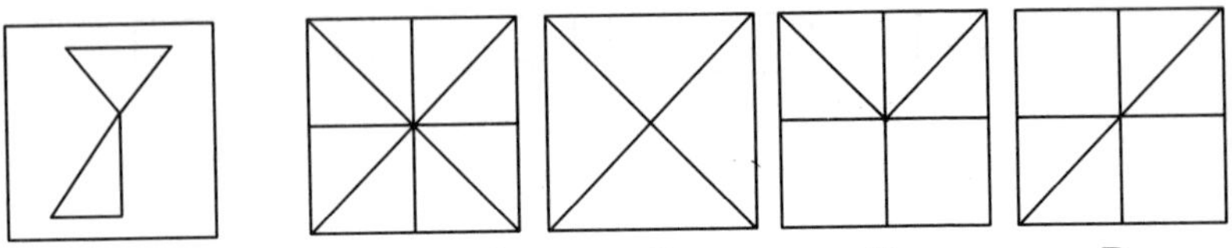

X A B C D

24.

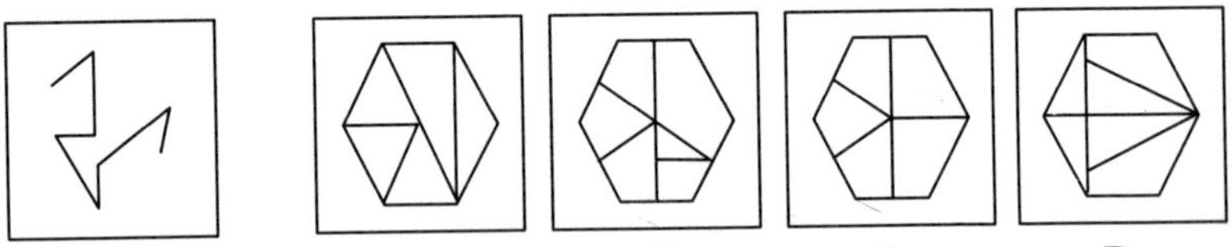

X A B C D

25.

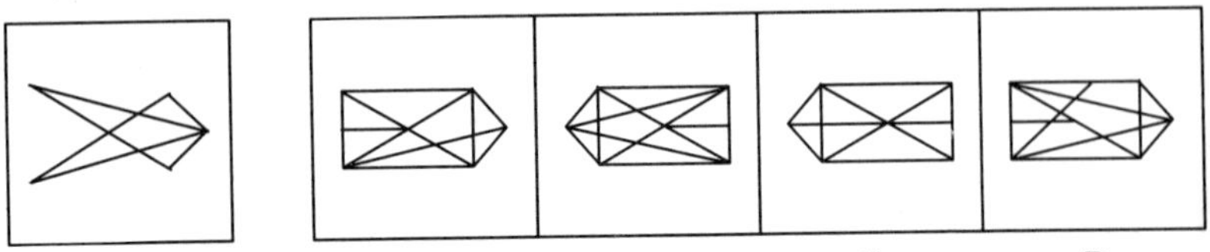

X A B C D

**Directions (Qs. 26-30) :** *In each question given below find the figure form which is embedded in the given pattern.*

26.

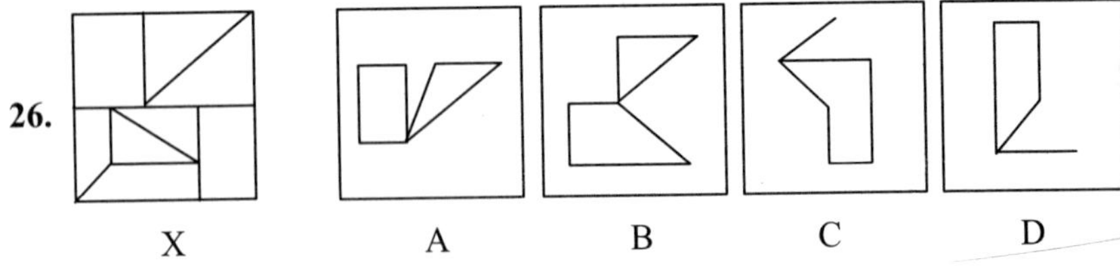

X A B C D

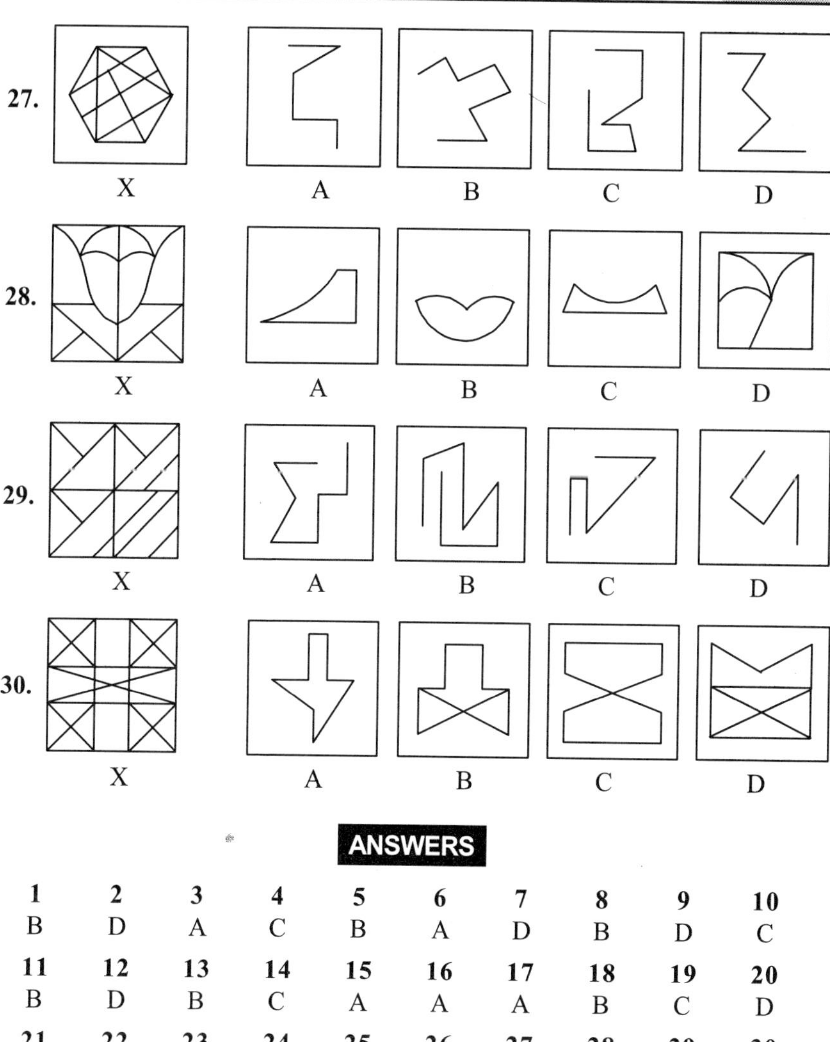


## ANSWERS

| 1 | 2 | 3 | 4 | 5 | 6 | 7 | 8 | 9 | 10 |
|---|---|---|---|---|---|---|---|---|---|
| B | D | A | C | B | A | D | B | D | C |
| **11** | **12** | **13** | **14** | **15** | **16** | **17** | **18** | **19** | **20** |
| B | D | B | C | A | A | A | B | C | D |
| **21** | **22** | **23** | **24** | **25** | **26** | **27** | **28** | **29** | **30** |
| C | B | A | D | B | D | B | D | D | C |

❍ ❍ ❍

# 9

# Counting Figures

*Counting of figures is simply the realisation of different geometrical figures from a complex one.*

## SOLVED EXAMPLES

The questions asked on the counting of figures are designed to test the analytical deposition of candidates and check his ability to count different similar figures in a complex figure. The figures which are asked to count are straight lines, triangles, square, rectangles etc.

*Examples given below will give a better idea about the type of question asked.*

**1.** How many triangles are there in the given figure?

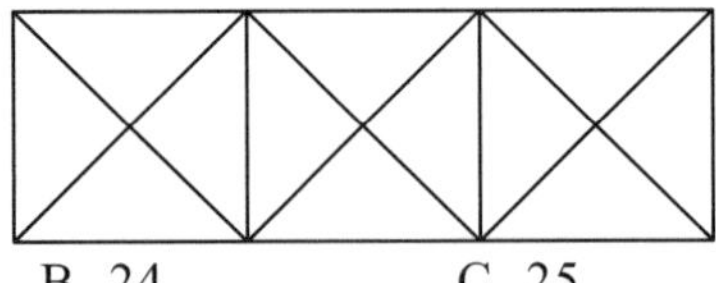

A. 28 B. 24 C. 25 D. 26

**Answers A:** Naming the figure, Clearly, there are 28 triangles in the given figure, they are EOF, AOE, AOB, BOF, ABF, BEF, ABE, AEF, BPF, FPG, CPG, BPC, BFG, BCG, CFG, BCF, GQC, CDQ, DQH, GQH, GDC, GDH, GHC, CDH, AFC, BGD, EBG and FCH.

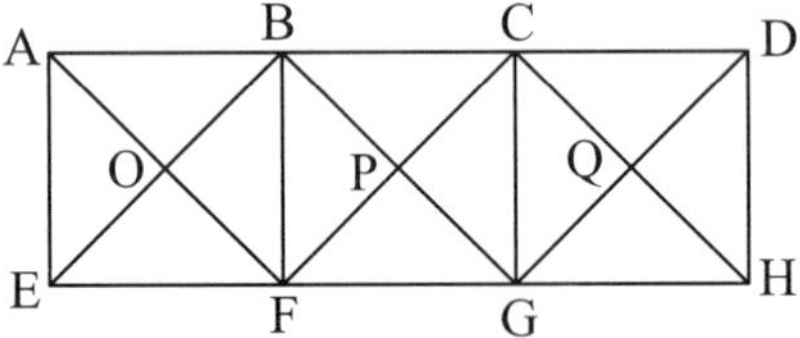


**2.** How many rectangles are there in the figure given below?

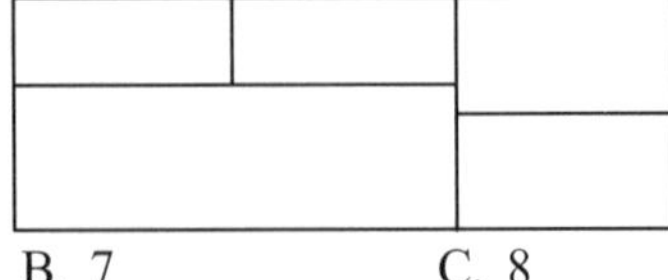

A. 6 B. 7 C. 8 D. 9

**Answers D:** The figure in the question has been labelled as under:

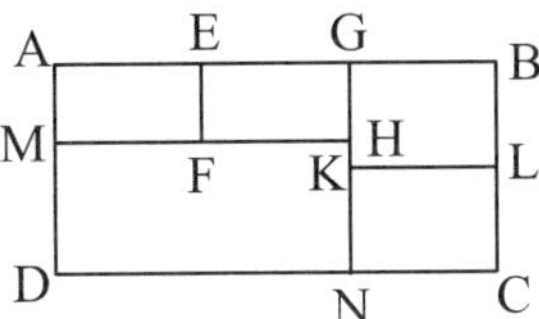


Clearly, there are nine rectangles in the figure given as above, namely AEFM, EGHF, AGHM, GBLK, KLCN, GBCN, MHND, ABCD and AGND.

### Counting pentagons, hexagons, etc.

Counting of pentagons, hexagons, etc. requires a little more visual ability than the previous examples. First of all you should identify the components that make up the pentagon or hexagon. For example, sometimes two triangles and one parallelogram may make up a pentagon, sometime two parallelograms and three triangles may be making a hexagon. So, first you should identify the components making up a pentagon or hexagon and then attempt the counting. See the following example.

**3.** Determine the number of pentagons in the figure that follows:

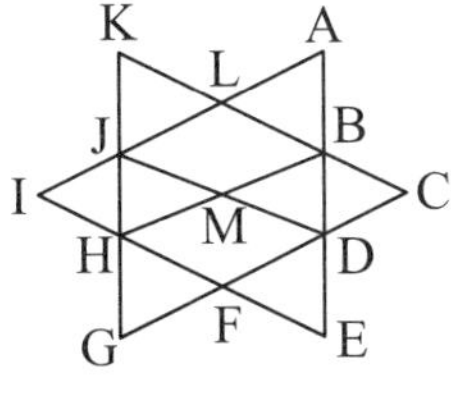


A. 4 B. 5 C. 6 D. 7

**Answers C:** In this case, each pentagon has been formed by the combination of three triangles and two rhombus. Thus, there are six pentagons in the figure, namely ADFHJ, CFHJL,EHJLB, GJLBD,ILBDF and KBDFH.

## EXERCISE

**1.** How many triangles are there in the figure?

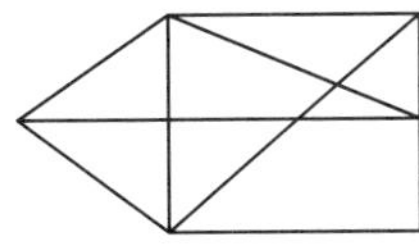

A. 15 B. 14 C. 12 D. 13

**2.** How many triangles are there in the following figure?

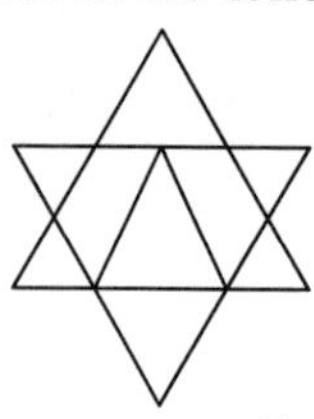

A. 10 B. 11 C. 12 D. 13

**3.** Find the no. of pentagons.

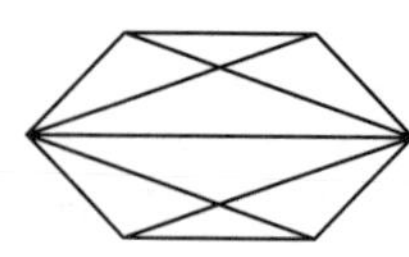

A. 2 B. 3 C. 4 D. 6

**4.** How many pentagons are there in the following figure?

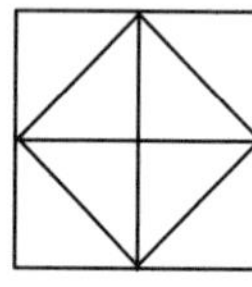

A. 8 B. 6 C. 12 D. 10

**Directions (Qs. 5-6):** *Study the following diagram and answer the questions that follow:*

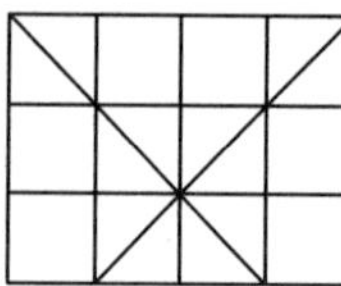

**5.** How many triangles are there in the above figure?
A. 21 B. 23 C. 26 D. 28

**6.** How many squares are there in the above figure?
A. 18 B. 20 C. 22 D. 24

**7.** How many squares and triangles are there in the following figure?

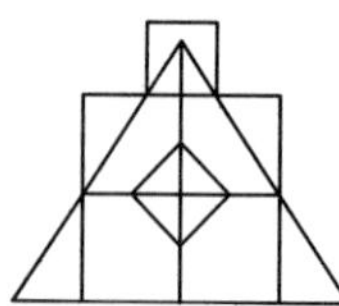

A. 7, 21 B. 8, 18 C. 8, 15 D. 7, 17

**8.** How many triangles are there in the figure?

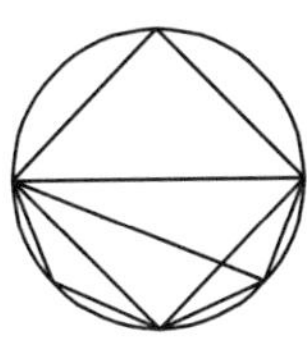

A. 8 B. 10 C. 11 D. 12

**9.** How many rectangles are there in the given figure?

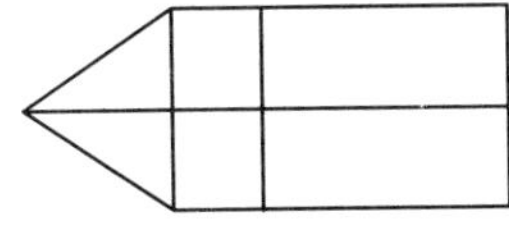

A. 6 B. 7 C. 8 D. 9

**10.** How many triangles and squares are there in the given figure?

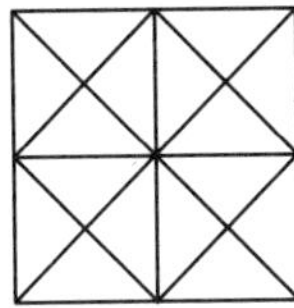

A. 44 triangles, 10 squares
B. 14 triangles, 16 squares
C. 24 triangles, 6 squares
D. 24 triangles, 9 squares

**11.** How many triangles are there in the following figure?

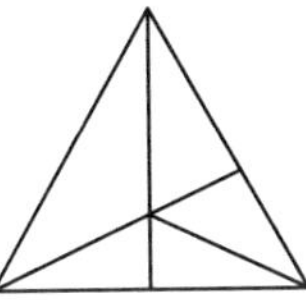

A. 9 B. 10 C. 11 D. 12

**Directions (Qs. 12-13):** *Study the figure below carefully and answer the following questions?*

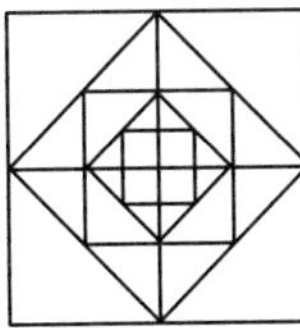

**12.** How many squares are there in the fugure?

A. 15 B. 16 C. 17 D. 18

**13.** How many rectangles are there:
A. 25 B. 26 C. 29 D. 28

**Directoins (Qs. 14-15):** *Study the figure below carefully and answer the following questions?*

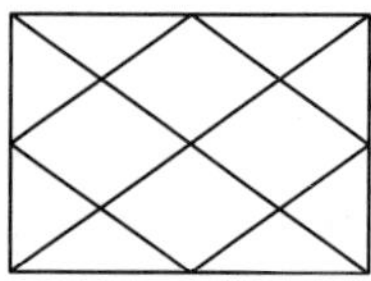

**14.** How many triangles are there?
A. 20 B. 16 C. 18 D. 26

**15.** How many parallelograms are there?
A. 4 B. 7 C. 10 D. 8

**16.** How many quadrilaterals are there in the figure given below?

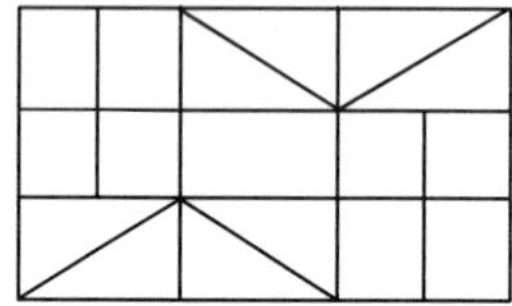

A. 64 B. 60 C. 58 D. 56

**17.** How many squares can you find in this diagram altogether?

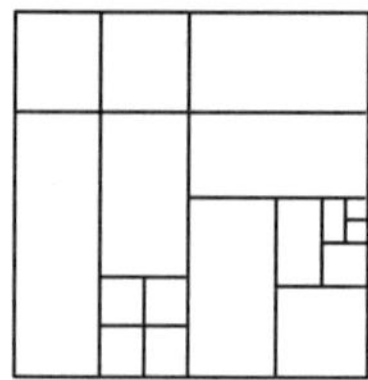

A. 14 B. 15 C. 16 D. 17

**18.** The number of triangles in this figure is:

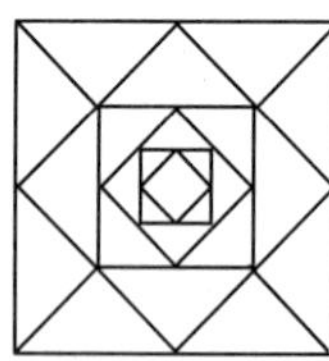

A. 20 B. 22 C. 26 D. 28

**19.** How many triangles are there in this figure?

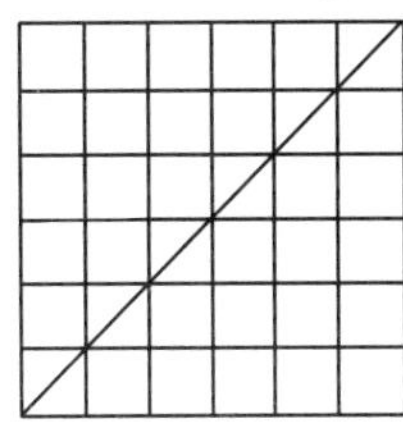

A. 42 B. 41 C. 40 D. 39

**20.** How many triangles are there in this figure?

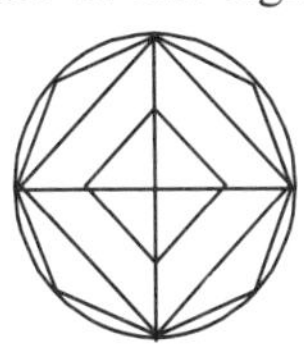

A. 18 B. 16 C. 20 D. 22

**21.** How many parallelograms are there in this figure?

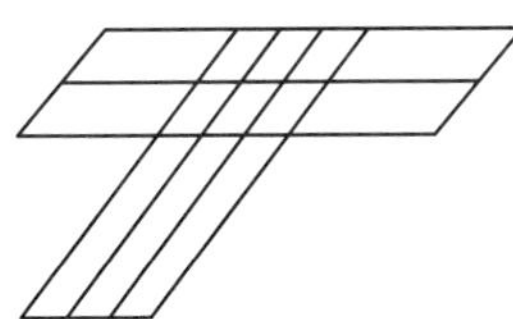

A. 40 B. 43 C. 41 D. 49

**22.** How many triangles are there in the figure given below?

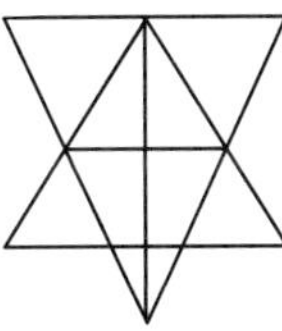

A. 19 B. 21 C. 20 D. 22

**23.** How many squares are there in the figure given below?

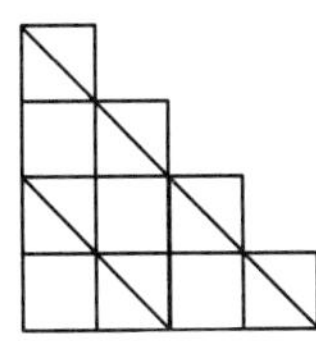

A. 10 B. 11 C. 13 D. 14

**24.** How many squares are hidden in this figure?

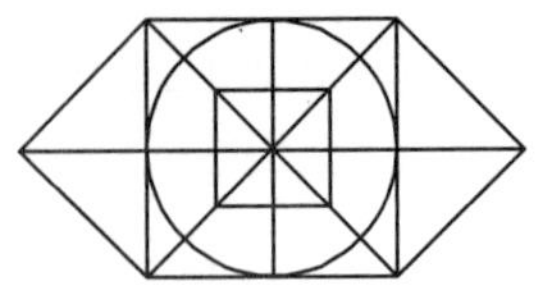

A. 7 B. 8 C. 9 D. 10

**25.** How many triangles are there in the figure given below?

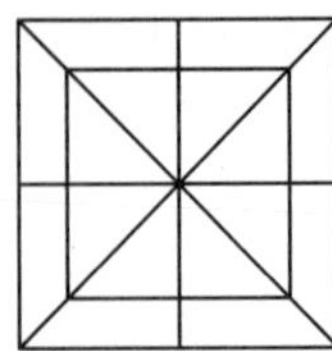

A. 28 B. 36 C. 24 D. 32

**26.** How many straight lines are used to make the figure given below?

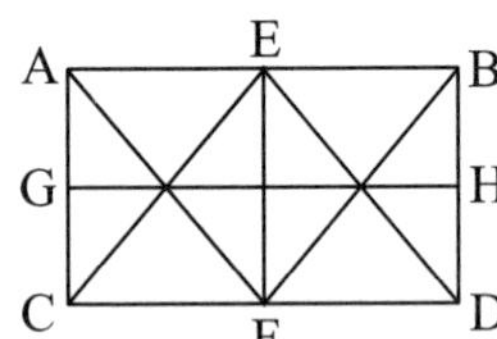


A. 8 B. 6 C. 10 D. 12

**27.** How many squares are there in this figure?

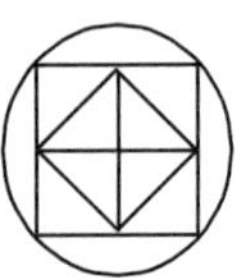

A. 4 B. 6 C. 8 D. 5

**28.** The number of circles in this figure is:

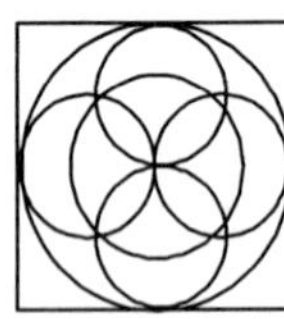

A. 6 B. 5 C. 2 D. 3

**29.** Count the number of parallelograms in the figure given below:

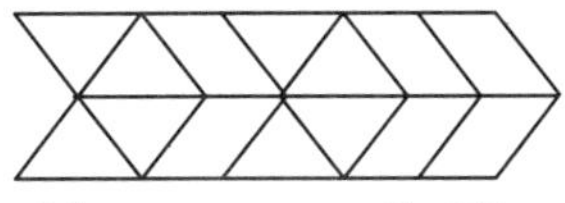

A. 35 B. 36 C. 37 D. 38

**30.** How many squares are there in this figure?

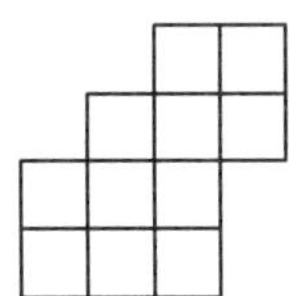

A. 11 B. 14 C. 15 D. 18

## ANSWERS

| 1 | 2 | 3 | 4 | 5 | 6 | 7 | 8 | 9 | 10 |
|---|---|---|---|---|---|---|---|---|---|
| A | B | D | C | C | B | A | B | D | A |
| **11** | **12** | **13** | **14** | **15** | **16** | **17** | **18** | **19** | **20** |
| D | C | C | A | C | B | A | D | A | C |
| **21** | **22** | **23** | **24** | **25** | **26** | **27** | **28** | **29** | **30** |
| D | B | C | D | D | C | B | A | B | C |

## EXPLANATORY ANSWERS

**1.** Label all the vertices of the given figures as shown:

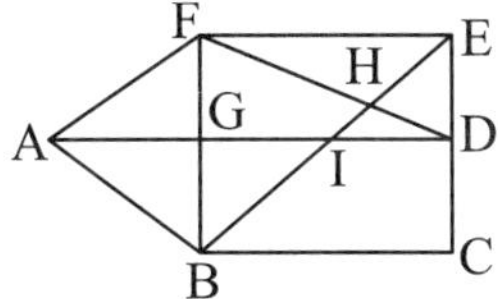


First count the simple triangles. These are AFG, AGB, FGD, FEH, EHD, IHD, GIB, FEB, EEC. Next count triangles composed of two small triangles. These are: AFB, FED, EID, AFD, AIB, FBH.

Thus there are (9 + 6 =) 15 triangles.

**2.** Possible triangles are: ALJ, JFI, IBH, HEK, KCM, MDL, GIH, AGI, GHC, DFE, ACB. So, there are 11 triangles.

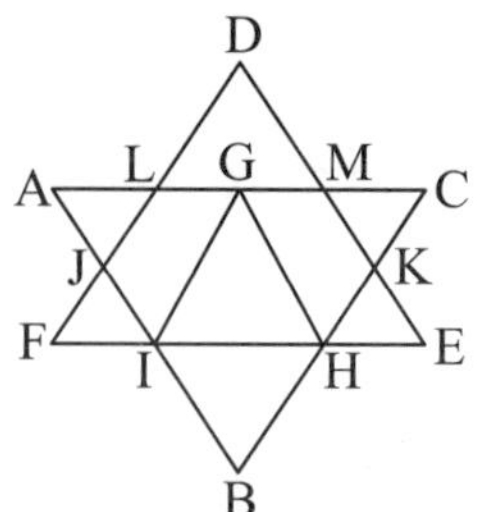


**3.** The possible pentagons in the given figure are: EFACD, FABDE, BAFDC, CBAED, AGDCB, AHDEF.

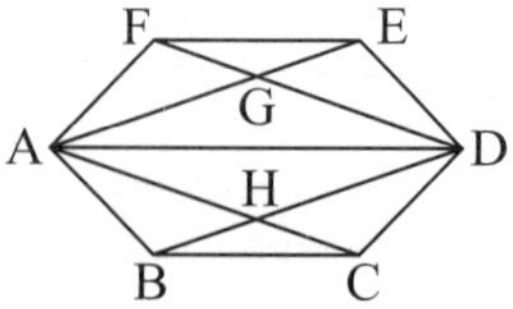


**4.** Possible pentagons are: AEHGF, DHGFE, CHEFG, BGHEF, EFBCD, FGCDA, GHDAB, HEABC, FEHGI, EHIGF, HIEFG, EIFGHE.

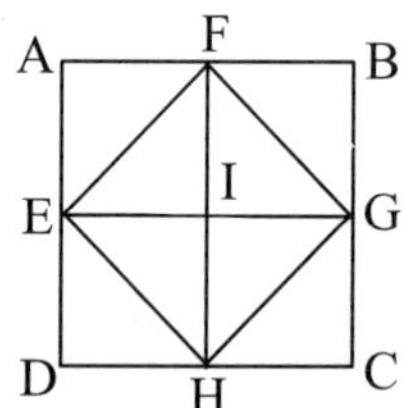


**5-6.** Label all the vertices of the given figure as shown:

**5.** Simple triangles are: AON, AOB, OST, OPT, STK, KTJ, TJI, TRI, PQT, TQR, DQE, QEF.

Triangles composed of two triangles are: OTK, TKI, TIQ, TQO.

Triangles composed of four triangles are: QKJ, QOK, OKI, OIQ.

Other possible triangles are: ALI, AMT, ETG, ACT, CTE, AET.

Thus, there are: 12 + 4 + 4 + 6 = 26 triangles.

**6.** Possible squares are: ABON, NOSM, MSKL, BCPO, OPTS, STJK, CDQP, PQRT, TRIJ, DEFQ, QFGR, RGHI, ACTM, NPJL, BDRS, OQIK, CEGT, PFHJ, ADIL, BEHK.

**7.** The no. of triangles and squares in the following are:

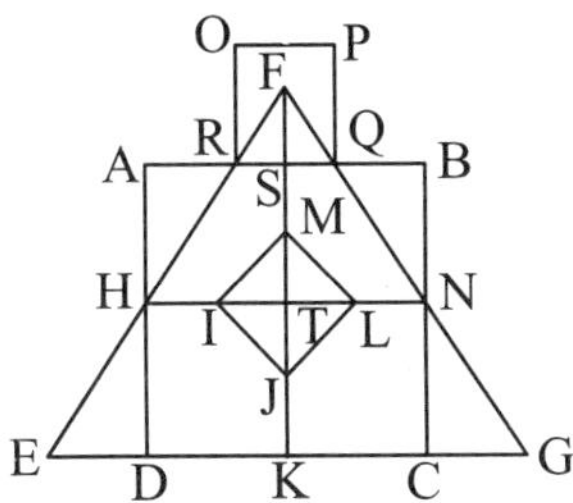


Simple triangles are: FRS, FSQ, MIT, MTL, ITJ, TLJ, ARH, HED, NCG, QBN.

Triangles composed of two triangles are: IML, ILJ, IMJ, MLJ.

Other possible triangles: FHT, FEK, FTN, FKG, FRQ, FHN, FEG.

Thus, there are 10 + 4 + 7 = 21 triangles.

Possible squares are: OPQR, ASTH, HTKD, SENT, TNCK, IMLJ, ABCD (7 squares).

**8.** Simple triangles are: ABC, AFE, FGD, GDC, AGC, AEG.

Triangles composed of two triangles are: ADC, AED, EDC, AEC.

Thus, there are (6 + 4 =) 10 triangles.

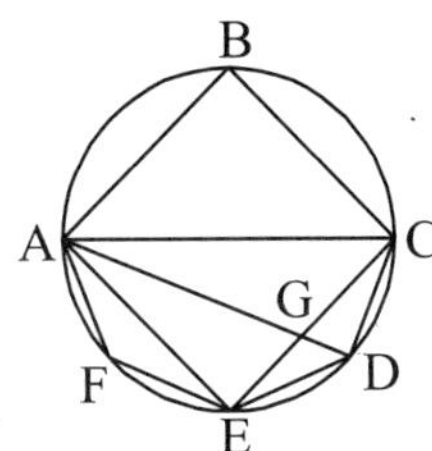


**9.** The possible rectangles in the given figure are:

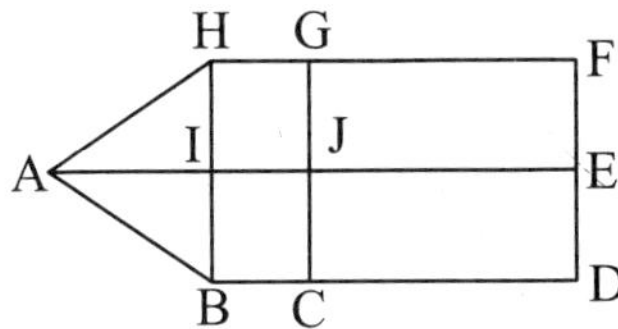


HGJI, IJCB, GFEJ, JEDC, HGCB, GFDC, HFEI, IEDB, HFDB.

**10.** The possible triangles and squares in the given figures are:

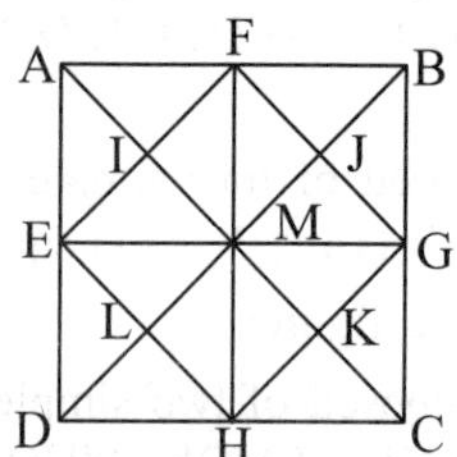


Simple triangles are: AEI, AFI, IBM, IFM, FJM, FJB, JBG, MJG, EML, ELD, LDH, LMH, MGK, KGC, KHC, MKH.

Triangles composed of two triangles are: AEF, AFM, EFM, EMA. FMB, MBG, FMG, FBG, MGC, MHC, MHG, HOC, EDM, EMH, DHM, DME.

Triangles composed of four triangles are: ABM, AMD, MDC, MBC, EFH, GFH, EHG, EFG.

Triangles composed of eight triangles are: ABD, ADC, BDC, ABC.

Thus, there are (16 + 16 + 8 + 4 =) 44 triangles.

Possible squares are: AFME, FBGM, MGCH, EMHD, EIML, IFJM, MJGK, MKHL, EFGH, ABCD.

**11.** The possible triangles in the given figure are: ADE, DEC, DCF, BDF, BDA, DEC, DC A, AFC, AFB, EEC, ABE, ABC.

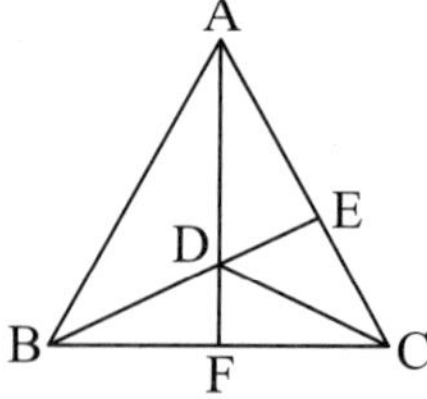


**12.** All the vertices in the figure are labelled as:

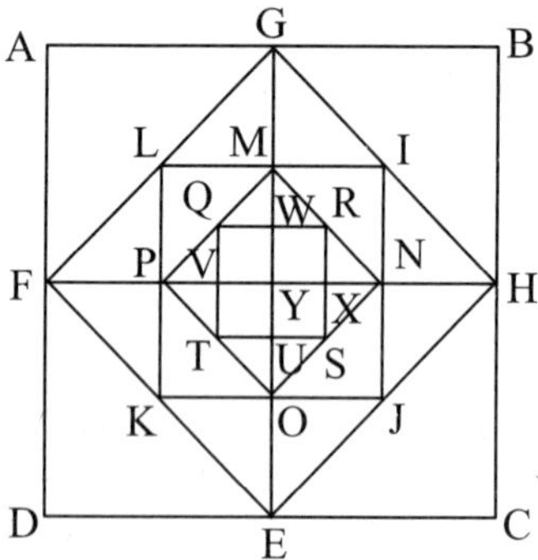

Simplest squares are GFEH, MNOP, QWYV, WRXY, YXSU, VYUT, MINY, LMYP, PYOK, YNJO, GBHY, AGYF, FYED, YHCE, *i.e.* there are 14 such squares.

The squares, each composed of four simple ones, are QRST, LIJK, and ABCD, *i.e.* there are in all (14 + 3 = 17) squares in the figure.

**13.** Use the label of the above figure:

The rectangles, each composed of two simple square, are QRXV, VXST, WRSU, QWUT, LIMP, PNJK, LMOK, MUO, ABHF, FHCD, AGED and GBCE, *i.e.* there are all 12 such rectangles.

Hence, Squares + Rectangles = (17 + 12) = 29.

**14.** Label all the vertices of the given figure as shown:

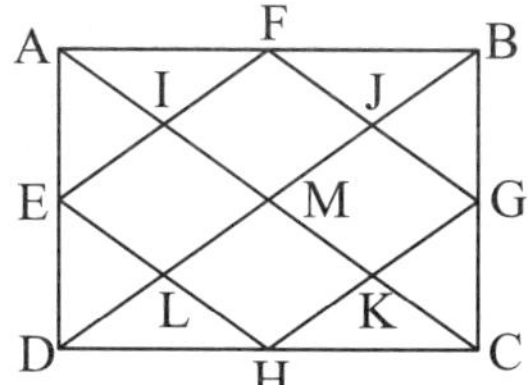


Simple triangles: AIE, ELD, LDH, KHC, KCG, GJB, JBF, FIA.

Triangles composed of two small triangles (enclosed area other than triangles are also included): AEF, DEH, HCG, GFB, ADM, MDC, MCB, AMB.

Triangles composed of four small triangles (enclosed area other than triangles are also included): ADB, DEC, ADC, ABC.

**15.** Simple parallelograms: ABCD, IFJM, MJGK, LMKH, EIML.

Parallelograms composed of two parallelograms: EFJL, LJGH, EIKH, IFGK.

Parallelograms composed of four parallelograms: EFGH.

Thus, there are (5 + 4 + 1 =) 10 parallelograms.

**16.**

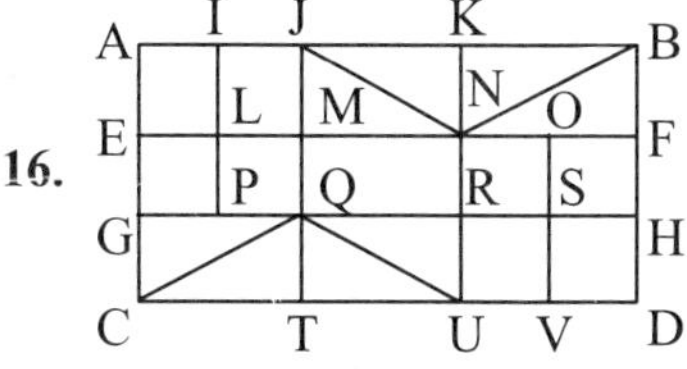


The main four sided figure is ABDC, *i.e.* 1 quadrilateral

The simplest four sided figures are : AILE, IJML, ELPG, LMQP, MNRQ, NOSR, OFHS, RSVU and SHDV, *i.e.* 9 quadrilaterals.

The quadrilaterals divided into two parts are: AJME, AIPG, IJQP, EMQG,

LNRP, JKNM, KBFN, MOSQ, NFHR, NOVU, OFDV, GQTC, QRUT and RHDU, *i.e.* 14 quadrilaterals.

The quadrilaterals divided into three parts are:

IKNL, ENRG, LOSP, MFHQ, JKRQ, JNUQ, MNUT and QSVT, *i.e.* 8 quadrilaterals.

The quadrilaterals divided into four parts are: AKNE, JBFM, EOSG, LFHP, GRUC, QHDT, AJQG, EMTC, KBHR and NFDU, *i.e.* 10 quadrilaterals.

The quadrilaterals divided into five parts are: IBFL, EFHG, GSVC and JKUT, *i.e.* 4 quadrilaterals.

The quadrilaterals divided into six parts are: ABFE, GHDC, AJTC and KBDU, *i.e.* 4 quadrilaterals.

The quadrilaterals divided into seven parts are : AKRG, JBHQ, ENUC and MFDT, *i.e.* 4 quadrilaterals.

Other quadrilaterals are : IBHP, EOVC, ABHG, EFDC, AKUC and JBDT, *i.e.* 6 quadrilaterals.

So, the total number of quadrilateals is:

1 + 9 + 14 + 8 + 10 + 4 + 4 + 4 + 6 = 60.

**17.** 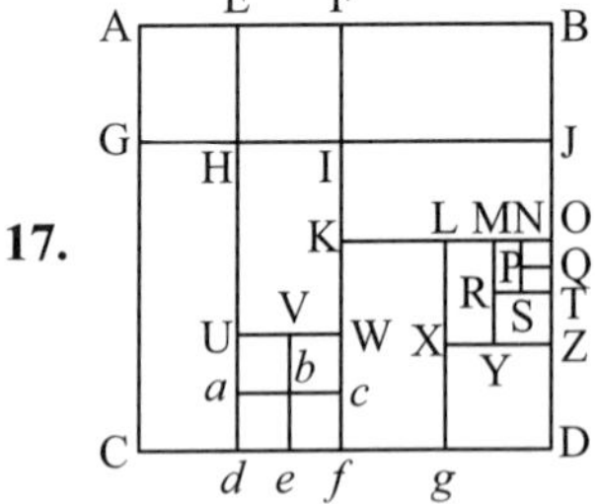


The main square is : ABDC, *i.e.* 1 square

The simplest squares are : AEHG, EFIH, NOQP, PQTS, RTZY, XZDg, uVba, VWcb, abed and bcfe, *i.e.* 10 squares.

Other squares are : MOTR, LOZX and uWfd, *i.e.* 3 squares.

So, the total number of squares are 1 + 10 + 3 = 14.

**18.** 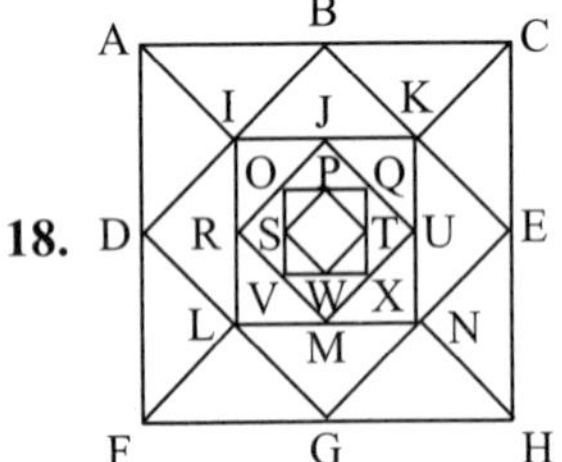

The simple outer triangles are : AID, AIB, BIK, BCK, CKE, KEN, ENH, NGH, NGL LFG, DLF and DLI, *i.e.* 12 triangles.

The simple middle triangles are : IJR ORV, RLM, VXM, UMN, QUX, KJU and JOQ *i.e.*, 8 triangles

The simple innermost triangles are : OSP, PQT, SVW and TWX, *i.e.* 4 triangles. The bisected triangles are : ABD, BCE, DFG and EGH, *i.e.* 4 triangles

So, the total number of triangles is: 12 + 8 + 4 + 4 = 28.

**19.** 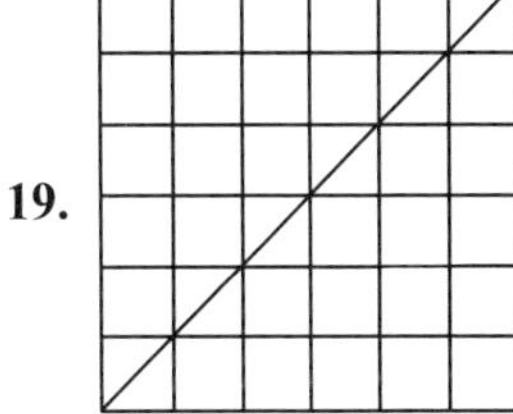

In such figures the manner of calculating the triangles is:

$1 \times 2 = 2$

$2 \times 3 = 6$

$3 \times 4 = 12$

$4 \times 5 = 20$

$5 \times 6 = 30$

$6 \times 7 = 42$

$7 \times 8 = 56$ and so on.

Here, the square grid has 6 rows and columns each. So the calculation will be $6 \times 7$ and the total number of triangles are 42.

**20.** 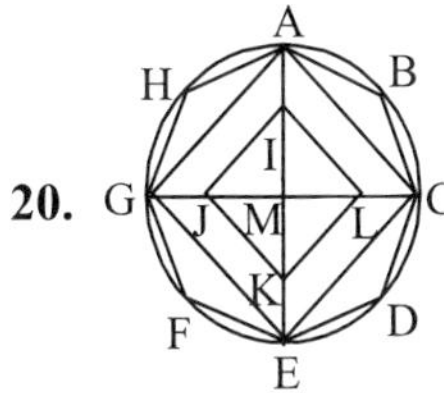


The simplest triangles are ABC, CDE, EFG, GHA, JIM, IML, MLK and JMK, *i.e.* 8 triangles.

The bisected triangles are : JIK, IJL, IKL and JLK, *i.e.* 4 triangles.

Other triangles divided into two parts are : AGM, AMC, GME and MCE, *i.e.* 4 triangles.

Other triangles are : AGC, AGE, ACE and GCE, *i.e.* 4 triangles

So, the total number of triangles is:

8 + 4 + 4 + 4 = 20

**21.** 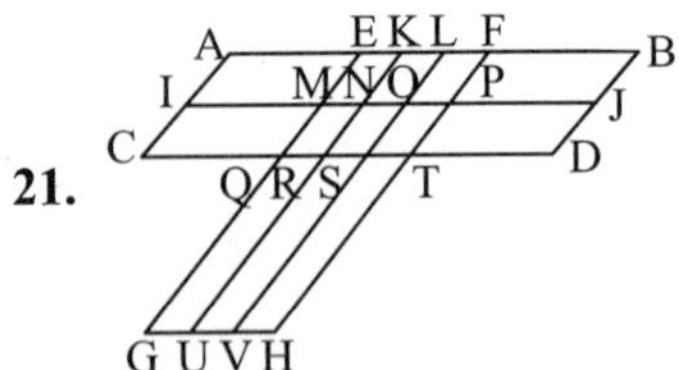


The main parallelograms are : ABDC and EFHG, *i.e.* 2 parallelograms

The simplest parallelograms are : AEMI, EKNM, KLON, LFPO, FBJP, IMQC, MNRQ, NOSR, OPTS, PJDT, QRUG, RSVU and STHV, *i.e.* 13 parallelograms.

The parallelogram divided into two parts are: AKNI, ELOM, KFPN, LBJO, INRC, MOSQ, NPTR, OJDS, QSVG, RTHU, AEQC, EKRQ, MNUG, KLSR, NOVU, LFTS, OPHV and FBDT, *i.e.* 18 parallelograms.

The parallelogram divided into three parts are : ALOI, EFPM, KBJN, IOSC, MPTQ, NJDR, QTHG, EKUG, KLVU and LFHV, *i.e.* 10 parallelograms.

The parallelogram divided into four parts are: AFFI, EBDQ, IPTC and MJDQ, *i.e.* 4 parallelograms.

Other parallelograms are : ABJI and IJDC, *i.e.* 2 parallelograms:

So, the total number of parallelogram are :

2 + 13 + 18 + 10 + 4 + 2 = 49.

**22.** 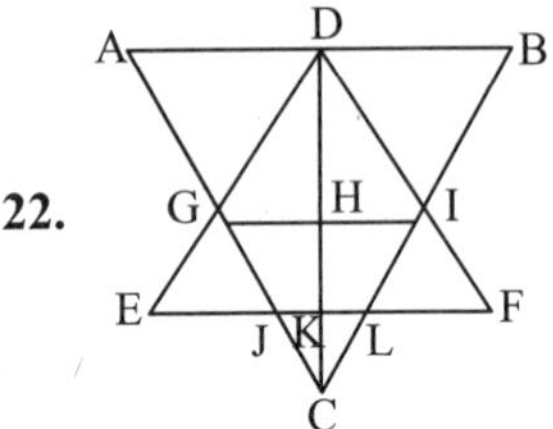


The main triangles are ABC and DEF, *i.e.* 2 triangles

The simplest triangles are : ADG, DGH, DHI, DBI, GEJ, JKC, KLC and ILF *i.e.* 8 triangles

The bisected triangles are : DGI and JLC, *i.e.* 2 triangles.

The triangles divided into three parts are : DGC, DIC, DEK and DKF, *i.e.* 4 triangles.

Other triangles are : ADC, DBC, GIC, GHC and HIC, *i.e.* 5 triangles.

So, the total number of triangles is. 2 + 8 + 2 + 4 + 5 = 21.

23. 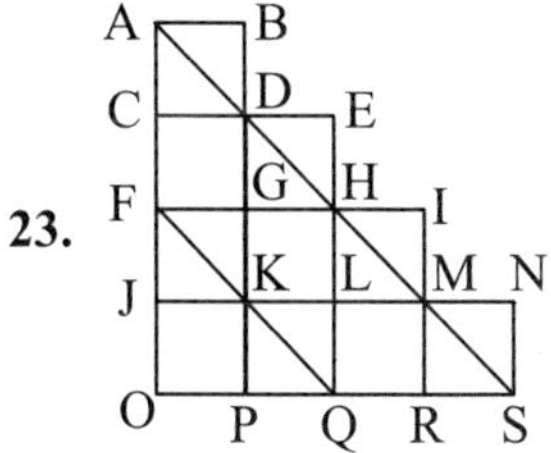


The simplest squares are: ABDC, CDGF, DEHG, FGKJ, GHLK, HIML, JKPO, KLQP, LMRQ and MNSR, *i.e.* 10 squares.

Other squares are : CELJ, FHQO and GIRP, *i.e.* 3 squares.

So, the total number of squares is 10 + 3 = 13.

24. 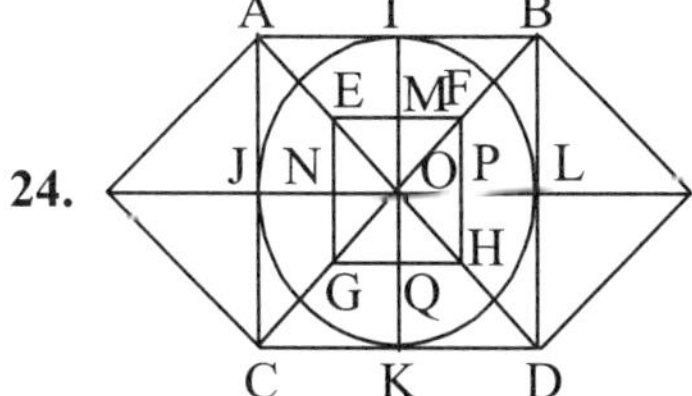


The main squares are ABDC and EFHG, *i.e.* 2 squares.

The simplest outer squares are AIOJ, IBLO, JOKC and OLDK, *i.e.* 4 squares

The simplest inner square are EMON, NOQG, MFPO and OPHQ, *i.e.* 4 squares

There are no other squares formed in the figure.

So, the total number of squares is:

2 + 4 + 4 = 10

25. 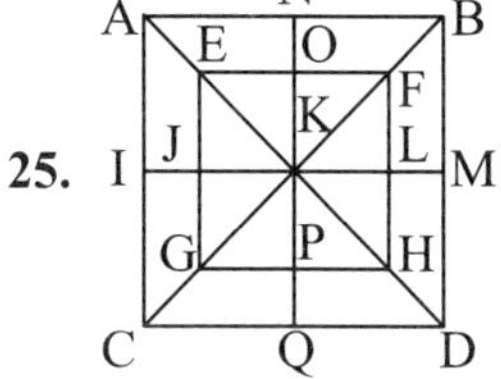


The larger triangles are : ABC, BCD, ABD and ACD, *i.e.* 4 triangles

The smaller triangles are : EFH, EGH, EFG and FGH, *i.e.* 4 triangles.

The simplest triangles are : EJK, EOK, OFK, JKG, FKL, KLH, KGP and KPH *i.e.* 8 triangles.

The bisected triangles are: AKC, ABK, CKD, KBD, EKG, EKF, KHG, KHF, *i.e.* 8 triangle.

Other triangles are : ANK, NKB, KBM, KMD, KQD, KQC, KCI, IKA, *i.e.* 8 triangles.

So, the total number of triangles is:

4 + 4 + 8 + 8 + 8 = 32.

**26.** The method of counting is given below.

The horizontal lines are AB, GH and CD, *i.e.* 3 lines, the vertical lines are AC, EF and BD, *i.e.* 3 lines, the diagonal lines are CE, FB, AF and ED, *i.e.* 4 lines, therefore the total number of straight lines is:

3 + 3 + 4 = 10.

**27.** The squares are counted in this manner:

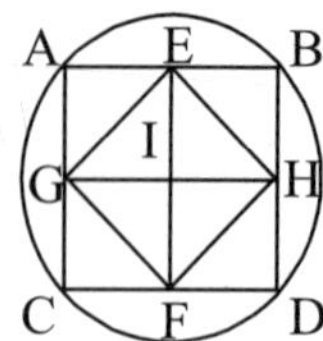


There is one main square ABDC divided into four parts by lines EF and GH. So, all the 5 squares are ABDC, AEIG, GIFC, EBHI and IHDF. The square in the middle is EGFH. The total number of squares are 5 + 1 = 6.

**28.**

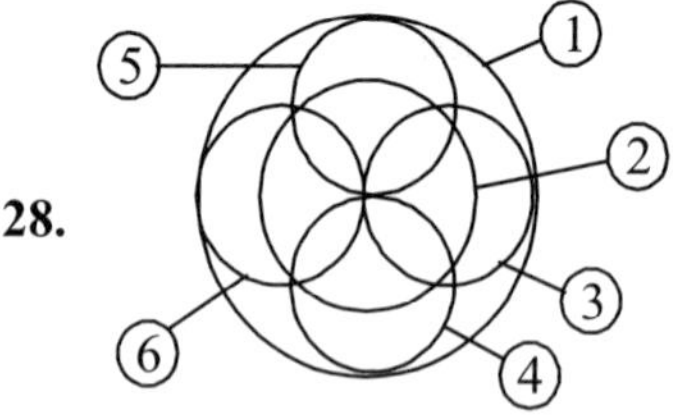


There are two main circles and four smaller circles intersecting each other. So, the total number of circles is 2 + 4 = 6.

**29.**

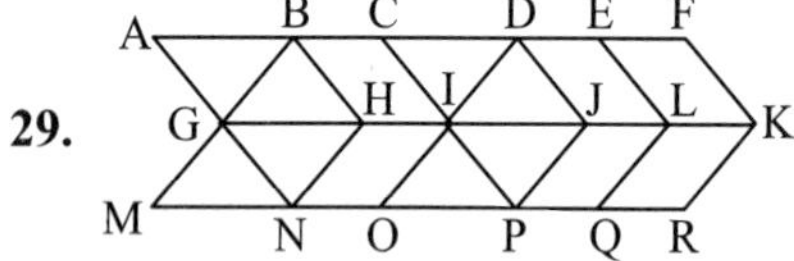


The main parallelograms are AFKG and GKRM, *i.e.* 2 parallelograms.

The simplest parallelograms are: BCIH, DELJ, EFKL, HION, JLQP and LKRQ, *i.e.* 6 parallelogram.

The parallelograms divided into two parts are: ABHG, CDJI, DFKJ, GHNM, IJPO, JKRP, GBHN and IDJP, *i.e.* 8 parallelograms.

The parallelograms divided into three parts are : ACIG, BDIG, BDJH, CELI, GIOM, GIPN, HJPN and ILQO, *i.e.* 8 parallelograms.

The parallelograms divided into four parts are:

BELH, CFKI, HLQN and IKRO, *i.e.* 4 parallelograms.

The parallelogram divided into five parts are: ADJG, BFKH, GJPM and HKRN, *i.e.* 4 parallelograms.

Other parallelograms are : AELG, GLQM, ACPN and BDOM, *i.e.* 4 parallelograms.

So, the total number of parallelograms are :

2 + 6 + 8 + 8 + 4 + 4 + 4 = 36.

**30.** 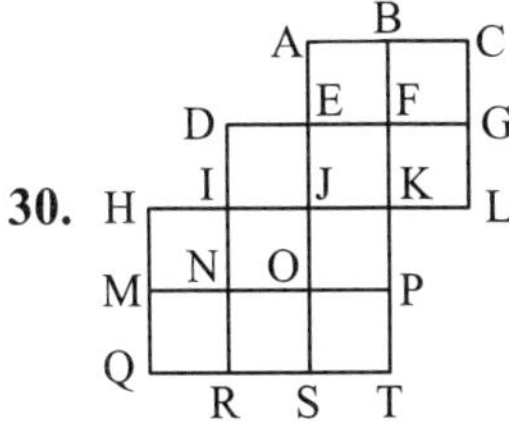


The simplest squares are : ABFE, BCGF, DEJI, EFKJ, FGLK, HINM, IJON, JKPO, MNRQ, NOSR and OPTS, *i.e.* 11 squares.

Other squares are : ACLJ, DFPN, HJSQ and IKTR, *i.e.* 4 squares.

So, the total number of squares is 11 + 4 = 15.

❍ ❍ ❍

# 10

# Making Boxes

In this chapter we deal with a template or a layout of a cube, dice or a box, which can be folded to produce different patterns. To solve these questions we require a clear study of the given layout and the selection of the figure alternative which can be made from given layout.

## SOLVED EXAMPLES

**1.** Choose from the alternatives, the boxes that will be formed when figure (X) is folded.

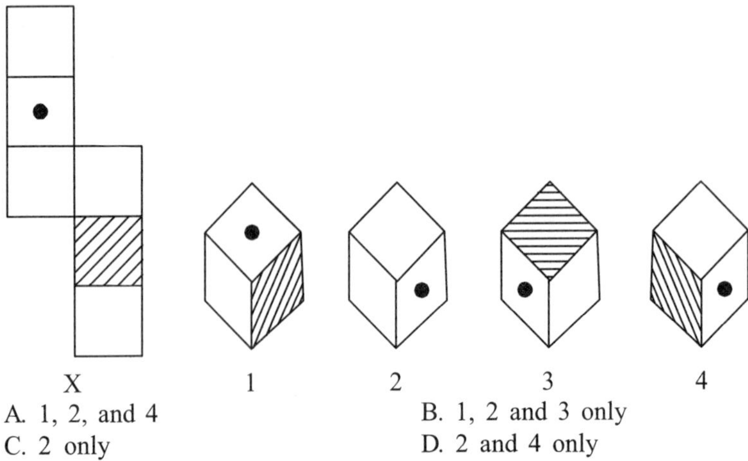


A. 1, 2, and 4 B. 1, 2 and 3 only

C. 2 only D. 2 and 4 only

**Answers C:** By the rule of third, we infer that the plain square above the dotted square would come opposite the plain square below the dotted square. Similarly, by the rule of third, the other pair of plain squares will also be opposite each other. Hence, the only pair of squares remaining would be opposite each other, *i.e.* the dotted square would come opposite the shaded square. Therefore, by the rule of not opposite, an answer choice should not have a dotted square and a shaded square together. But figures 1, 3 and 4 have them together. Therefore, only 2 is correct. Hence, answer choice would be (C).

## EXERCISE

**Directions:** *Choose from the alternatives, the boxes that will be formed when figure (X) is folded.*

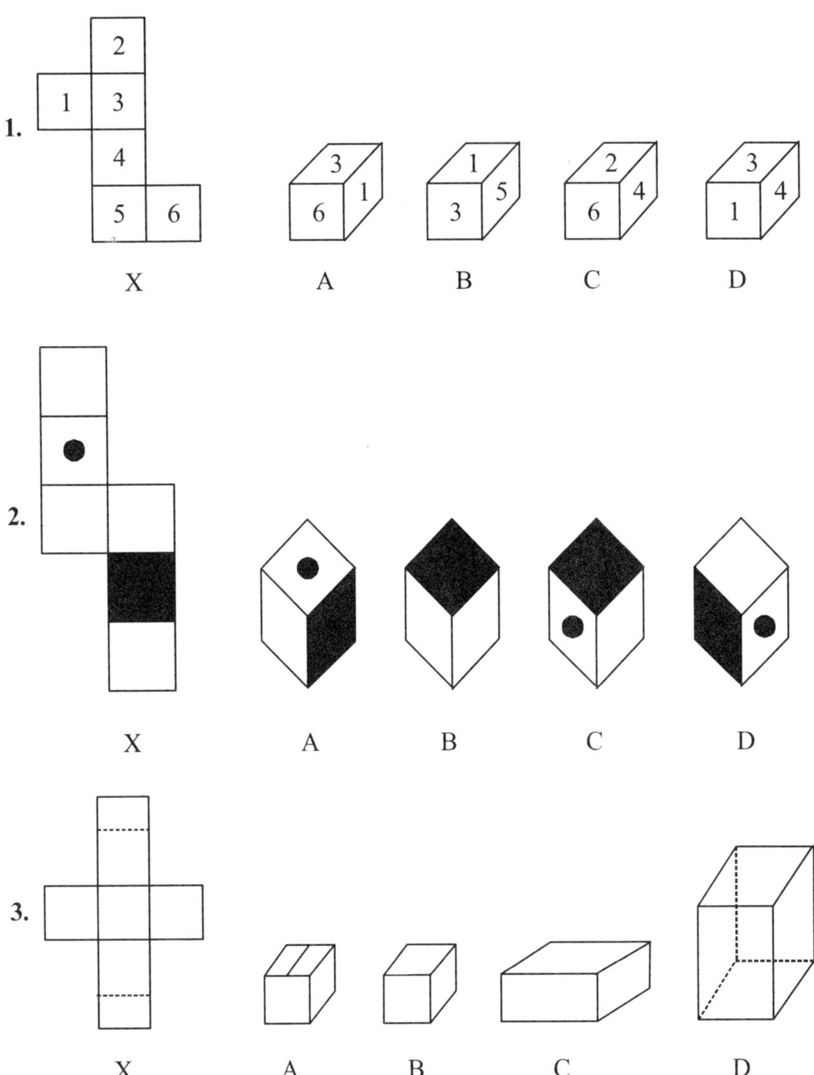

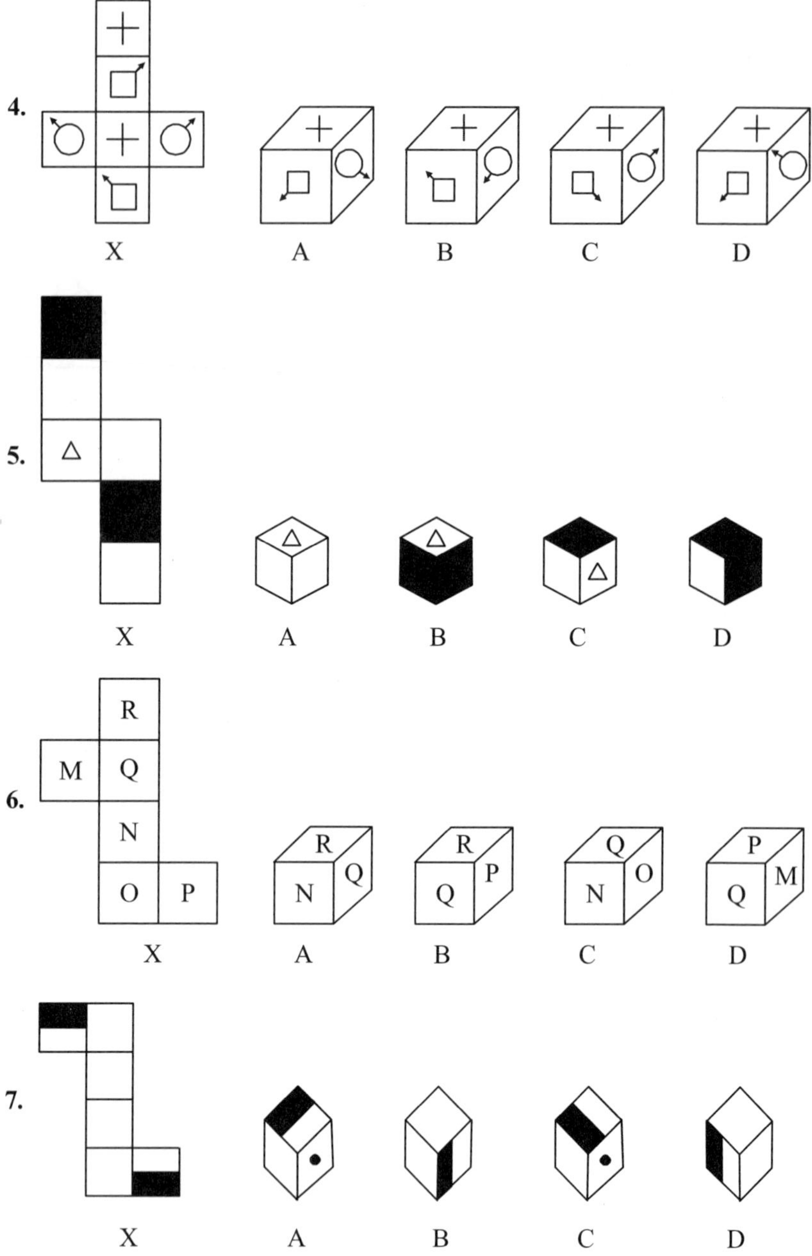
4.
X
A
B
C
D
5.
X
A
B
C
D
6.
R
M
Q
N
O
P
X
A
B
C
D
7.
X
A
B
C
D

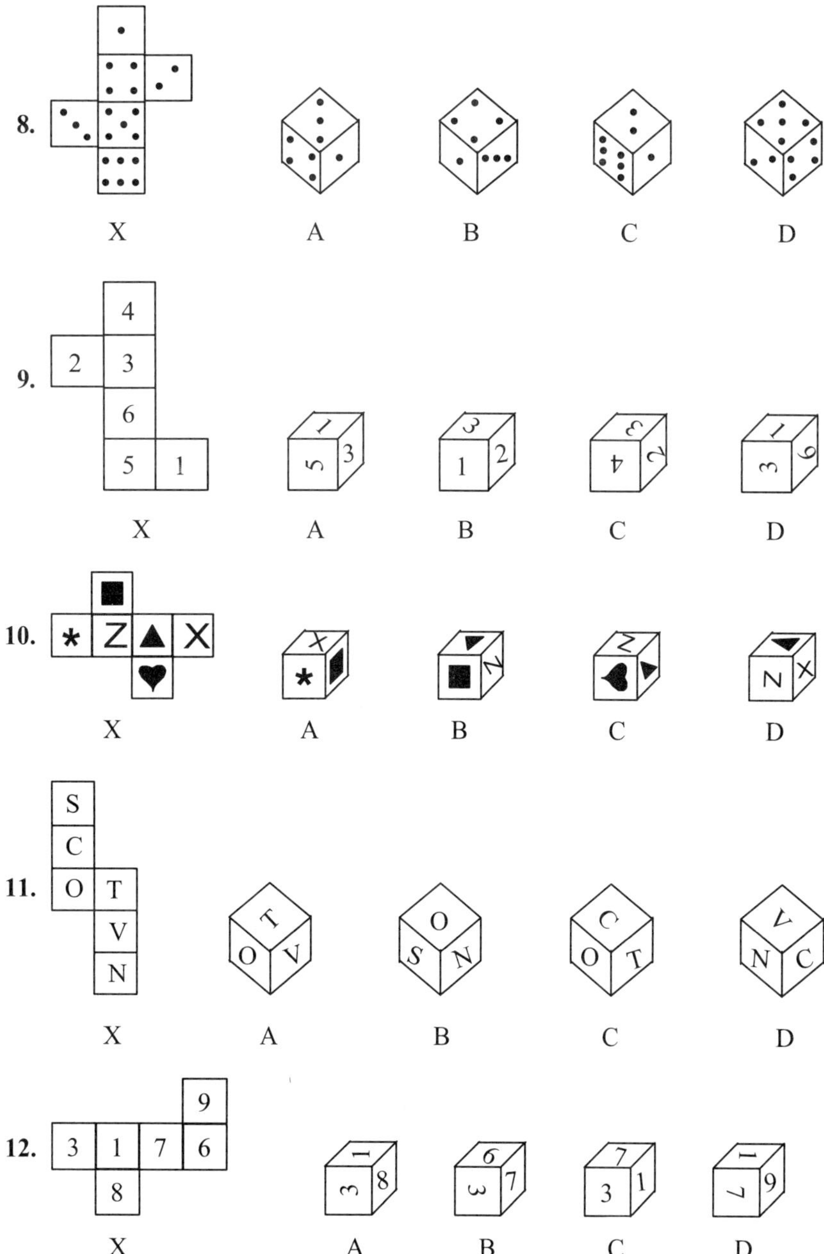
8.
X
A
B
C
D
9.
4
2
3
6
5
1
X
A
B
C
D
10.
Z
X
X
A
B
C
D
11.
S
C
O
T
V
N
X
A
B
C
D
12.
9
3
1
7
6
8
X
A
B
C
D

**13.**

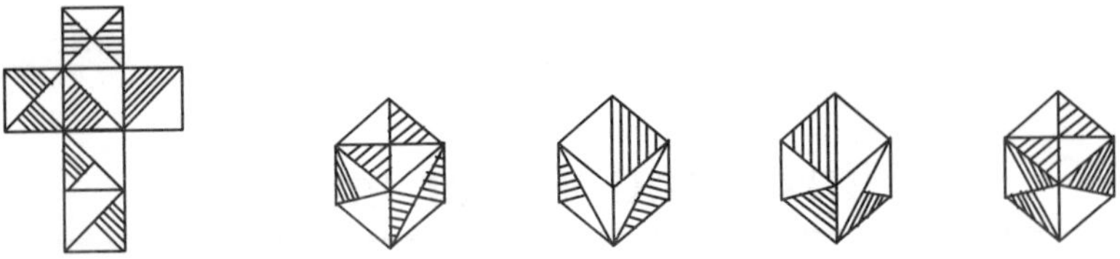

X A B C D

**14.**

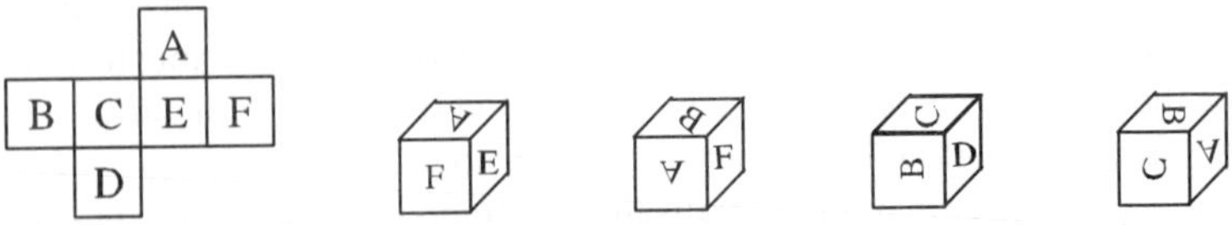

A
B C E F
D

X A B C D

**15.**

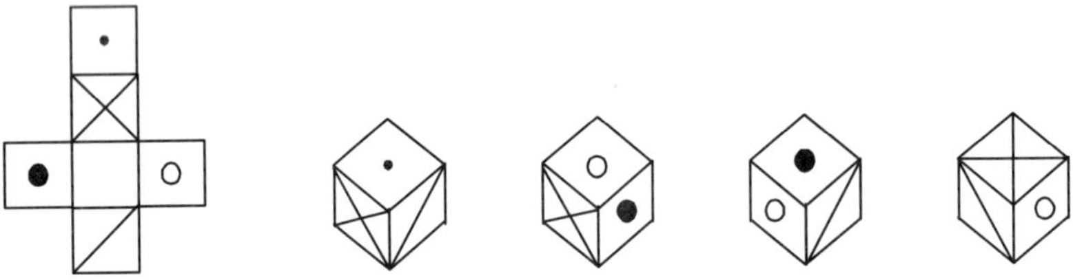

X A B C D

## ANSWERS

| 1 | 2 | 3 | 4 | 5 | 6 | 7 | 8 | 9 | 10 |
|---|---|---|---|---|---|---|---|---|---|
| D | B | A | A | B | B | A | D | B | C |
| **11** | **12** | **13** | **14** | **15** | | | | | |
| C | A | C | C | D | | | | | |

# 11

# Mirror and Water Images

These types of problems are based on the mirror images or reflections of numbers, letters and figures. While attempting such questions one must be able to visualise clearly the questioned reflections, be they on vertical plane or on horizontal plane. Study the chart and information given below. The visualisation of letters and numbers is easier than the visualisation of figures for the simple reason that the figures have many forms and all cannot be summed up.

**Mirror Images (MI) of Numbers**

| *Number* | *MI* | *Number* | *MI* |
|---|---|---|---|
| 0 | 0 | 5 | ट |
| 1 | I | 6 | ∂ |
| 2 | Ƨ | 7 | Γ |
| 3 | Ɛ | 8 | 8 |
| 4 | ᔦ | 9 | ϱ |

**Note :** MI of 0 and 8 remain unchanged

**Water Images (WI) of Numbers**

| Numbers : | 0 | 1 | 2 | 3 | 4 | 5 | 6 | 7 | 8 | 9 |
|---|---|---|---|---|---|---|---|---|---|---|
| WI : | 0 | I | ᘔ | 3 | ᔭ | ᘓ | ϱ | ㄥ | 8 | ∂ |

**Note :** WI of 0, 3 and 8 remain unchanged.

Exceptions in style need caution. For example

3 will be 3, or 8 will be 8.

**Water Images of Capital Letters**

| Letters : | A | B | C | D | E | F | G | H | I | J | K | L | M |
|---|---|---|---|---|---|---|---|---|---|---|---|---|---|
| WI : | ∀ | B | C | D | E | Ⅎ | ⅁ | H | I | ſ | K | Γ | W |
| Letters : | N | O | P | Q | R | S | T | U | V | W | X | Y | Z |
| WI : | И | O | b | Ό | ᴚ | ƨ | ⊥ | ∩ | Λ | M | X | ⅄ | Z |

**Note :** WI of C, D, E, H, I, K, O and X remain unchanged.

### Mirror Images of Capital Letters

| Letter | MI | Letter | MI | letter | MI |
|---|---|---|---|---|---|
| A | A | J | Ⴑ | S | Ƨ |
| B | ᗺ | K | ꓘ | T | T |
| C | Ɔ | L | ⅃ | U | U |
| D | ᗡ | M | M | V | V |
| E | Ǝ | N | И | W | W |
| F | ꟻ | O | O | X | X |
| G | Ꮹ | P | ꟼ | Y | Y |
| H | H | Q | Ϙ | Z | Ƹ |
| I | I | R | Я | | |

**Note :** HMI of A, H, I, M, O, T, U, V, W, X and Y remain unchanged.

Exceptions in style need caution. Example : A will be A, or X will be X.

### Mirror Images of Small Letters

| Letter | MI | Letter | MI | Letter | MI |
|---|---|---|---|---|---|
| a | ɒ | j | ᒑ | s | ƨ |
| b | d | k | ʞ | t | ɟ |
| c | ɔ | l | l | u | u |
| d | b | m | m | v | v |
| e | ɘ | n | n | w | w |
| f | ʇ | o | o | x | x |
| g | ϱ | p | q | y | γ |
| h | ᖹ | q | p | z | ƹ |
| i | i | r | ɿ | | |

**Note :** MI of o, v, w and x remain unchanged.

### Water Images of Small Letters

| Letter : | a | b | c | d | e | f | g | h | i | j | k | l | m |
|---|---|---|---|---|---|---|---|---|---|---|---|---|---|
| WI : | ɐ | p | c | q | ә | ɟ | ƃ | ɥ | ¡ | ɾ | ʞ | l | ɯ |
| Letter : | n | o | p | q | r | s | t | u | v | w | x | y | z |
| WI : | u | o | b | d | ɹ | ƨ | ʇ | n | ʌ | ʍ | x | λ | z |

**Note :** WI of c, o and x remain unchanged. Letter l has exceptions: if it is a straight vertical line – l then it remains unchanged.

## SOLVED EXAMPLES

**1.** Choose the correct mirror reflection of the figures given below from among the given answer choices:

FIXING

A. GNIXIF B. ƎИIXIꟻ C. ƎИIXIF D. ƎNIXIꟻ

**Answers B:** Choice (A) is incorrect because it givens G is it is and not the mirror image. Choice (C) is incorrect because it does not invert F. Choice (D) is not correct as it does not invert N. Hence, (B) is correct.

**2.** Which of the answer choices is the correct water reflection of:

DL2CA34

A. DΓ2CV34 B. ᗡΓ2CV34 C. DΓ2CV34 D. ᗡΓ2CV34

**Answers A:**

## EXERCISE

**Directions (Qs. 1–10):** *In each question below which is the exact mirror image?*

**1.** LATERAL

A. ΓAЯETAΓ B. ⅃AЯƎTA⅃ C. LARETA⅂ D. ⅃AЯETAL

**2.** DOCTOR

A. ROTƆOᗡ B. ᗡOƆTOЯ C. ЯOTƆOᗡ D. ЯOTƆOᗡ

**3.** 7892

A. 2687 B. 2987 C. 2987 D. 2987

**4.** 247593

A. 395742 B. 395742 C. 395742 D. 395742

**5.** CHEAPER

A. ЯƎPAƎHƆ B. ЯƎꟼAƎHC C. ЯƎꟼAƎHƆ D. ЯƎꟼAEHC

**6.** GZ5QRh

A. hЯQ5ZG B. hЯQ5ZG C. hRQ5ZG D. hЯQ5ZG

**7.** 2JKS

A. SKL2 B. SKJ2 C. SKL2 D. SKL2

**8.** plaque

A. ɘupɒlq B. ɘuq blp C. qlapue D. ɘuqɒlp

**9.** 7↑FN8

A. 8Иꟻ↑7 B. 8Nꟻ↑7 C. 8ИF↑7 D. 8NF↑7

**10.** yk19G

A. ᘓ9Ɩʞʎ  B. ᘓϱIꓘʎ  C. ᘓϱɪʞʎ  D. ᘓϱƖʞʎ

**Directions (Qs. 11–15):** *Find the mirror image of figure X from the given alternatives:*

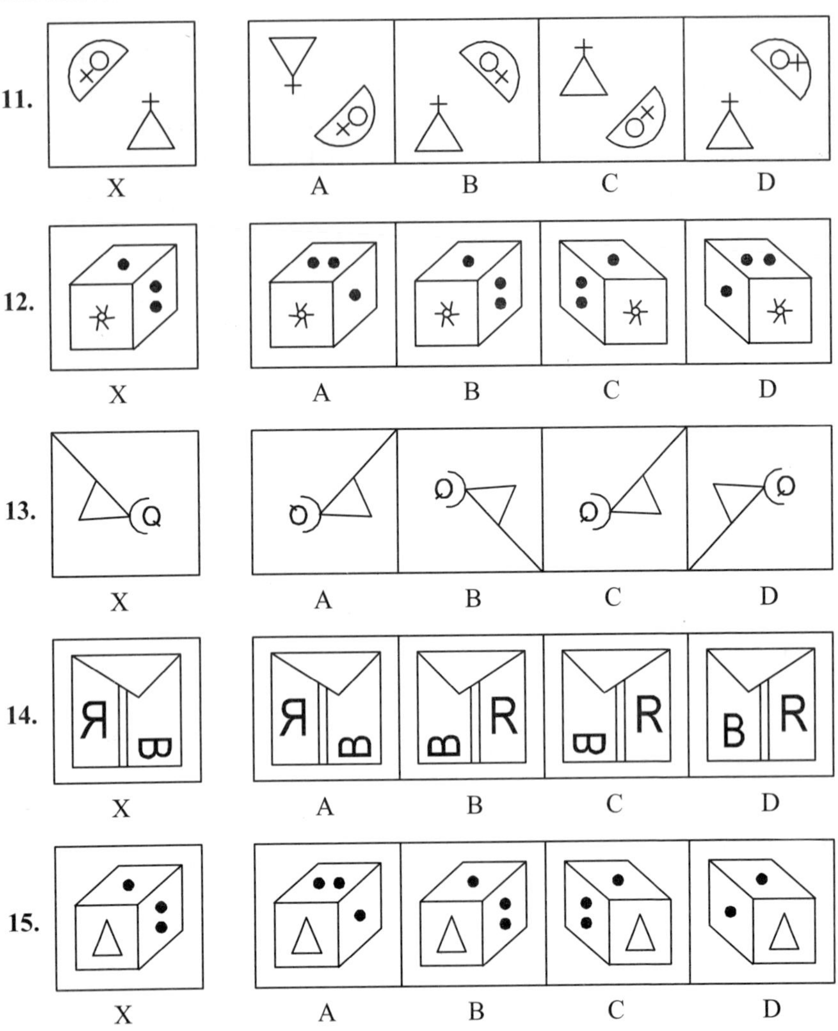

**Directions (Qs. 16–20):** *In each question below which is the exact water image?*

**16.** ↓OF2xq

A. ↑OꟻƧxd  B. ↑OEƧxd  C. ↑OEƧxp  D. ↑OƧExd

**17.** MJ7KL

A. ꟽႱ⅃KΓ B. ꟽႱ⅃KΓ C. ꟽႱ⅃ꓘL D. ꟽႱ⅃ꓘL

**18.** SAVOUR

A. ƧѴΛOՈꓤ B. ƧѴΛOՈꓤ C. ƧAΛOՈꓤ D. ƧѴΛOՈR

**19.** 3*7$OP

A. 3*⅃$Od B. 3*7$Oᑲ C. 3*⅃$Oᑲ D. 3*⅃$Od

**20.** 4320

A. ᔭ320 B. ᔭƐ20 C. ᔭƐ20 D. ᔭ320

**Directions (Qs. 21–25):** *Choose the correct water image of the given words/numbers from the alternatives:*

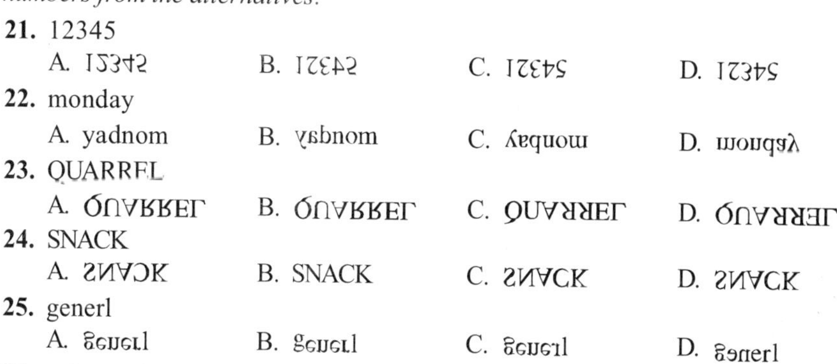

**21.** 12345

**22.** monday

**23.** QUARREL

**24.** SNACK

**25.** generl

**Directions (Qs. 26–30):** *Find the water image of X from amongst the given alternatives.*

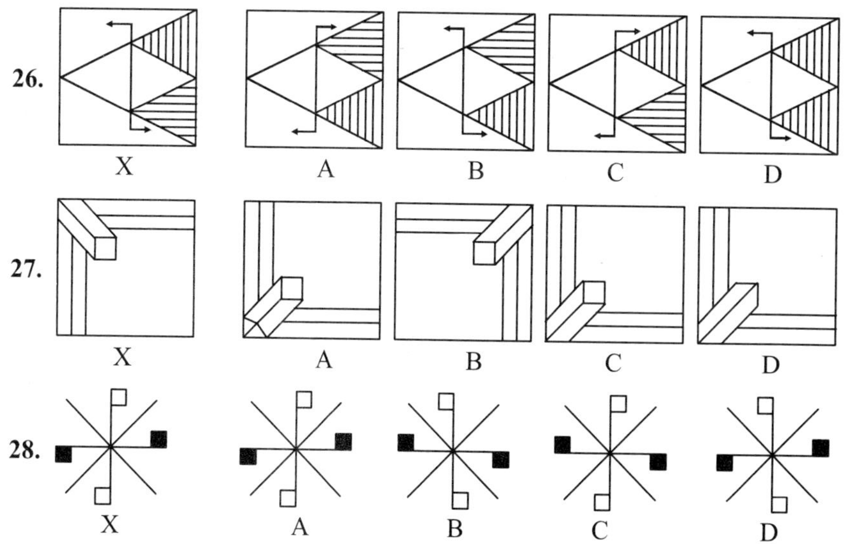

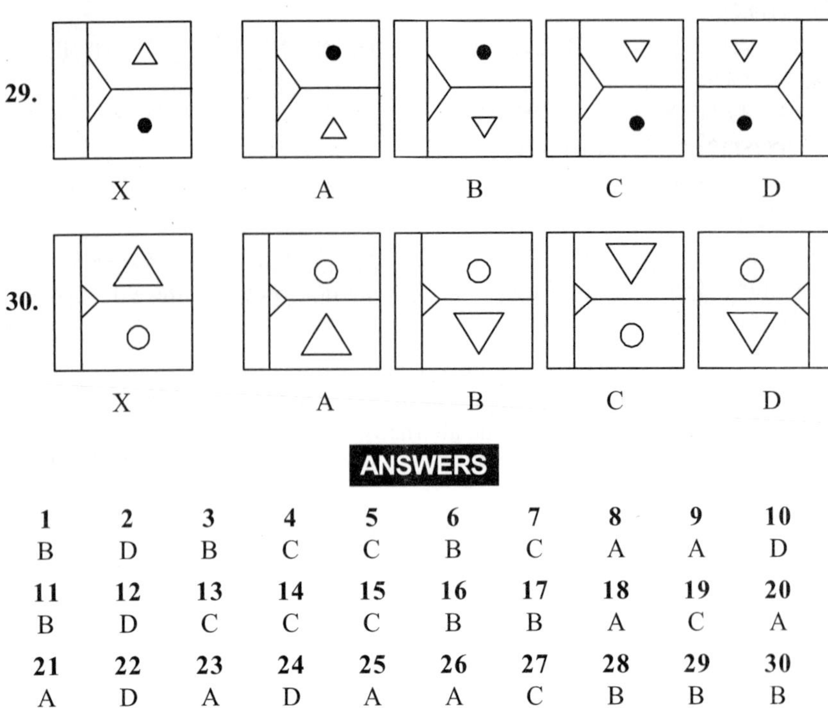


## ANSWERS

| 1 | 2 | 3 | 4 | 5 | 6 | 7 | 8 | 9 | 10 |
|---|---|---|---|---|---|---|---|---|---|
| B | D | B | C | C | B | C | A | A | D |
| **11** | **12** | **13** | **14** | **15** | **16** | **17** | **18** | **19** | **20** |
| B | D | C | C | C | B | B | A | C | A |
| **21** | **22** | **23** | **24** | **25** | **26** | **27** | **28** | **29** | **30** |
| A | D | A | D | A | A | C | B | B | B |

❍ ❍ ❍

12

# Identical Components & Common Properties

In this form of reasoning, the two given figures share common characteristic features or the problem figure consists of the elements given in one of the answer figures.

This form of reasoning is fairly simple. All one is required to do is to match the components of the key figure or the given figures with the components of the alternative figures. Only one alternative figure will contain the components identical to the given figure. In short, it is a kind of tally work and fairly easy too.

## SOLVED EXAMPLES

1. Find the figure which has the same common features as the two problem figures.

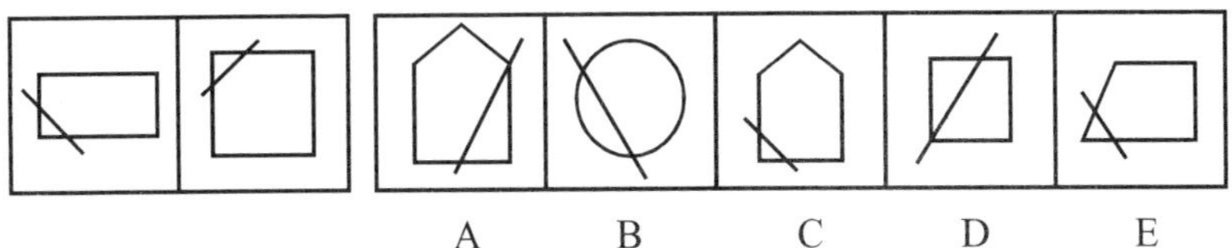

A B C D E

**Answer E :** Each figure is a quadrant and the line segment cuts through its two adjacent sides. Based on this common feature shared by the two problem figures it is clear that option E is the right answer.

2. Here, a figure is given, its components are given in one of the four alternative figures. Find this one.

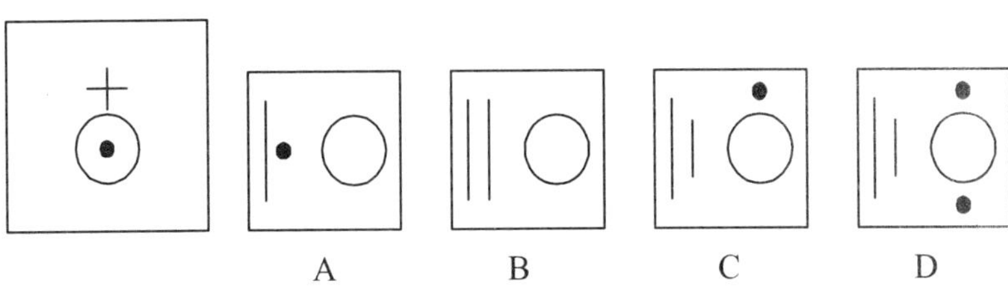

A B C D

**Answer C :** A quick observation reveals that the given figure has a dot, a circle, and two line segments of different length that form a cross. Similarly, in alternative figure 'C' there is a dot, a circle and two line segments of different length.

**2.** In which figure, the specified components of the key figure are found?

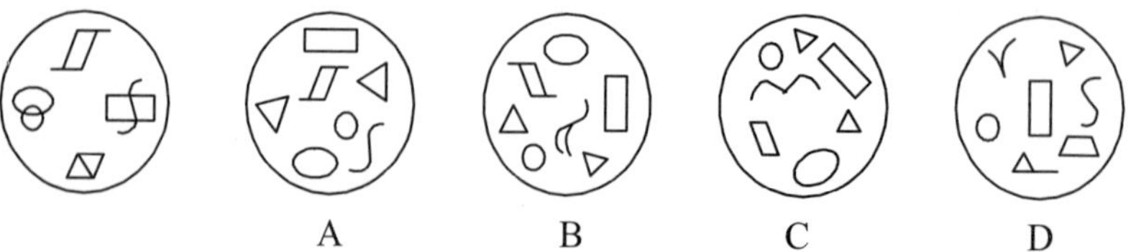

A B C D

**Answer A :** Observe the key figure closely. When each component is to be placed separately, the figure shall contain a rectangle with two extended sides, an oval, a circle, a rectangle, one 'S' shape and two triangles. Answer figure 'A' matches perfectly containing all the components.

## EXERCISE

**Directions (Qs. 1–10):** *In each question below two problem figures are given. These are followed by five answer figures. The two Problem Figures have some common characteristic features. You have to find out the Figure out of the five given Answer Figures which has the same commonlity. The letter of that figure is the answer.*

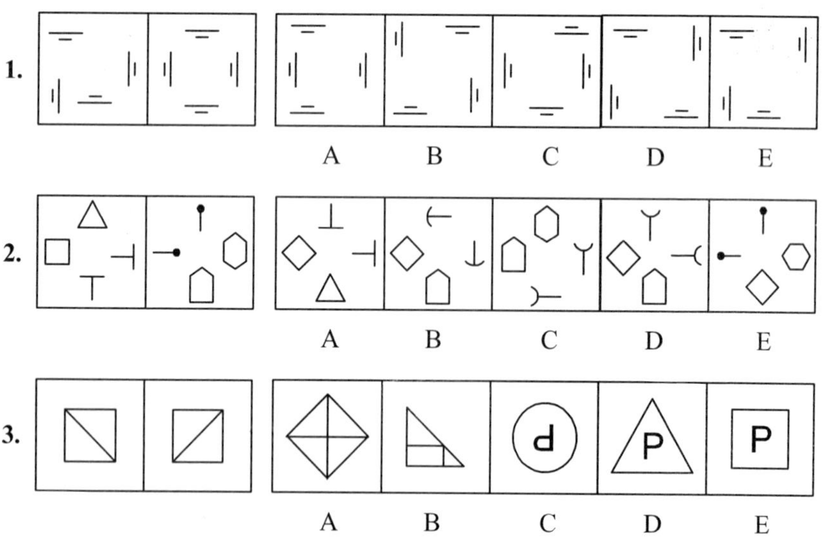

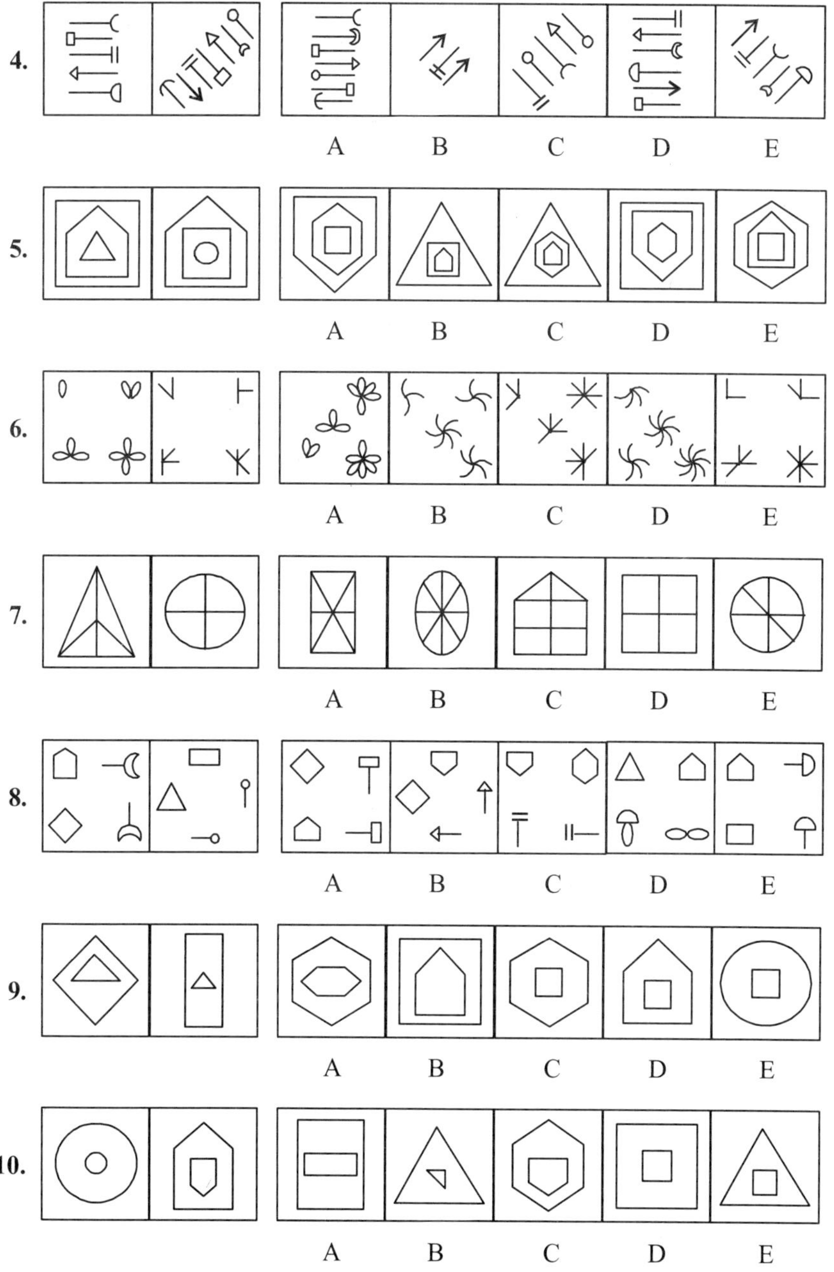
4.
A
B
C
D
E
5.
A
B
C
D
E
6.
A
B
C
D
E
7.
A
B
C
D
E
8.
A
B
C
D
E
9.
A
B
C
D
E
10.
A
B
C
D
E

**Directions (Qs. 11–20):** *In the following questions, a key figure is given. Its components are given in one of the four alternative figures. Find this one:*

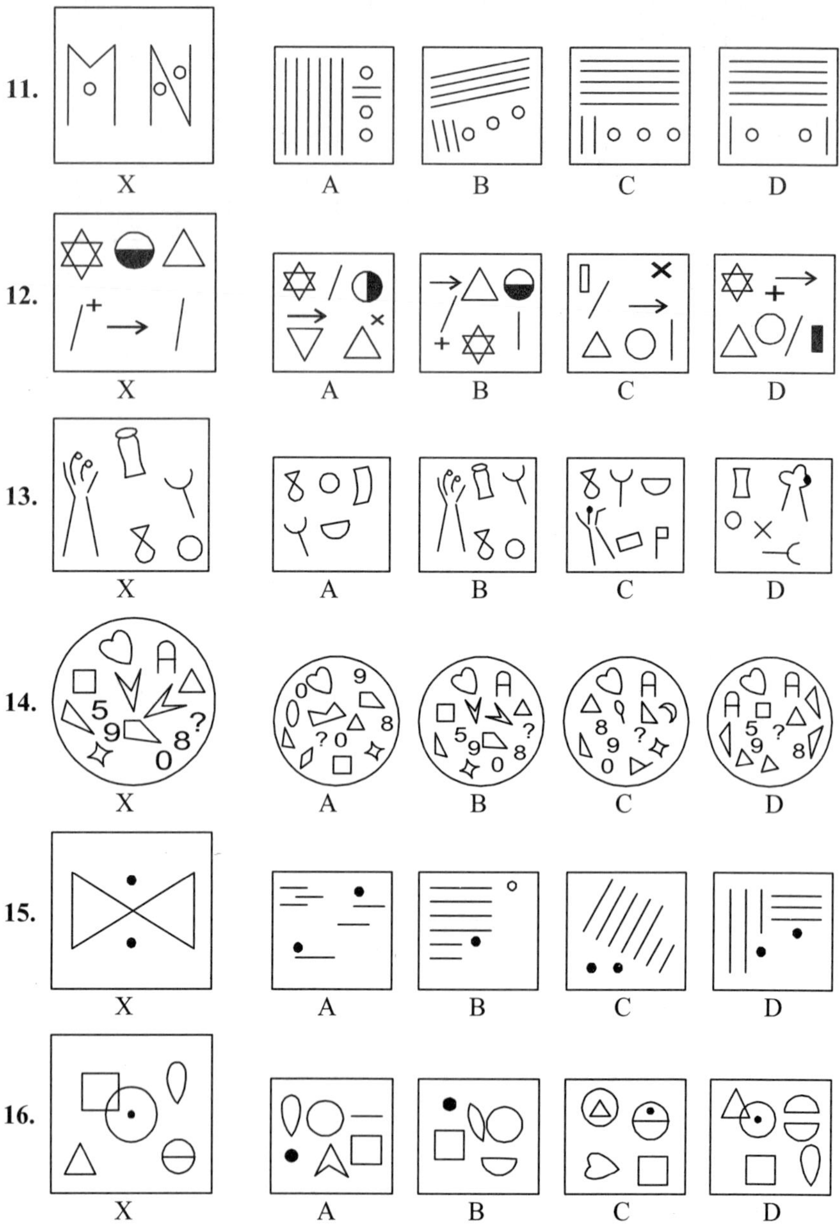

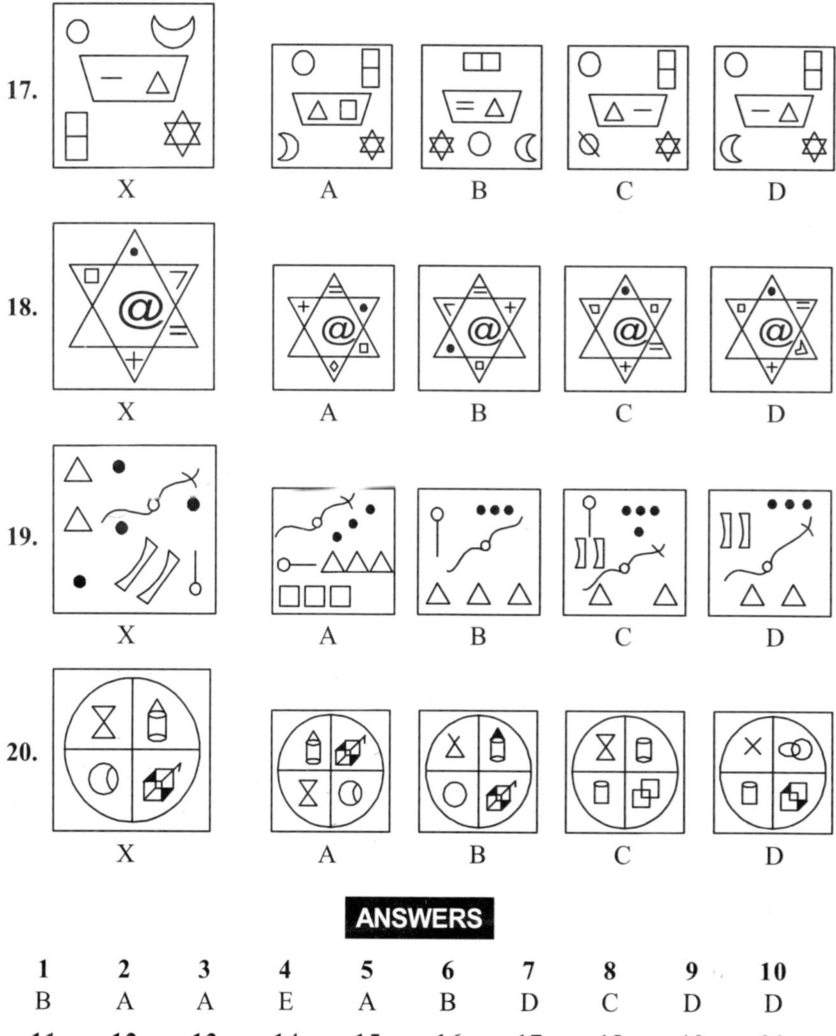


**ANSWERS**

| 1 | 2 | 3 | 4 | 5 | 6 | 7 | 8 | 9 | 10 |
|---|---|---|---|---|---|---|---|---|---|
| B | A | A | E | A | B | D | C | D | D |
| **11** | **12** | **13** | **14** | **15** | **16** | **17** | **18** | **19** | **20** |
| C | B | B | B | A | D | D | B | C | A |

❍ ❍ ❍

13

# Point Position

These problems involve the search of similar conditions in the given alternative figures as indicated in the problem figures which contain dots placed in the spaces enclosed between the combinations of geometrical figures. By selecting one of these dots, the region in which this dot is enclosed can be observed, *i.e.* to which of the four figures is this region common. Then one has to look for such a region in the four alternatives. Once this is found, the procedure for other dots, if any, is repeated. The alternative figure which contains all such regions is the right choice for the answer.

## SOLVED EXAMPLES

**1.** In the given figure, there is one diagram marked 'X' with one dot. There are four other figures of which only one satisfies the condition of placement as in 'X'. Find that one:

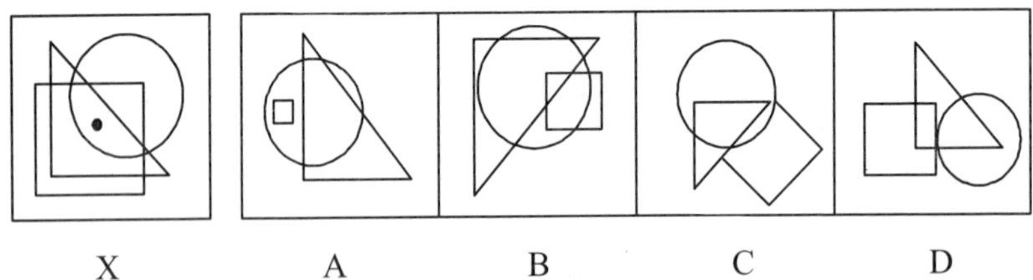

X A B C D

**Answers B:** In figure X, the dot is contained in a region common to all the three figures. Only in figure 'B' such a region is present.

## EXERCISE

**Directions (Qs. 1–20):** *In each of the following questions, there is a diagram marked (X) with one or more dots. There are also four other figures marked (A), (B), (C) and (D); only one figure is the same as the (X) marked figure. Choose the same figure and indicate the right sign on that figure.*

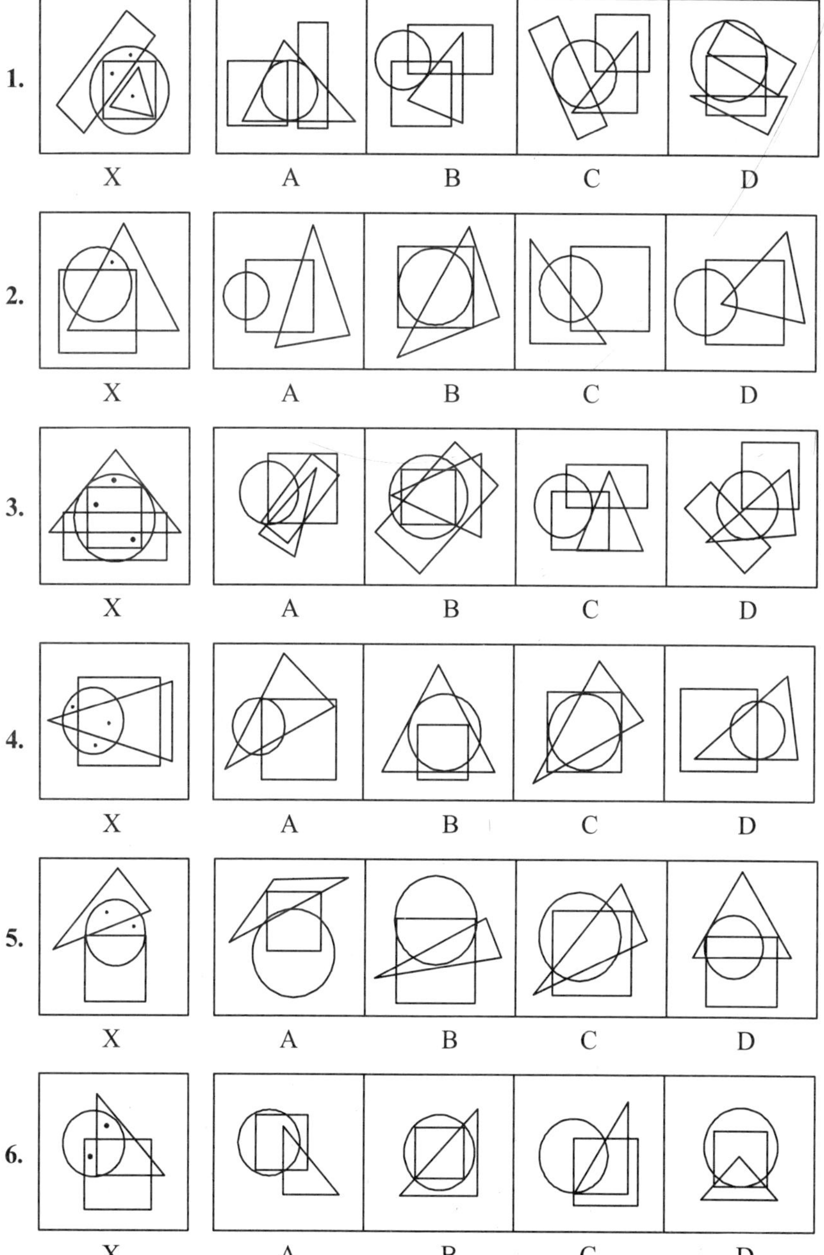
1.
X
A
B
C
D
2.
X
A
B
C
D
3.
X
A
B
C
D
4.
X
A
B
C
D
5.
X
A
B
C
D
6.
X
A
B
C
D

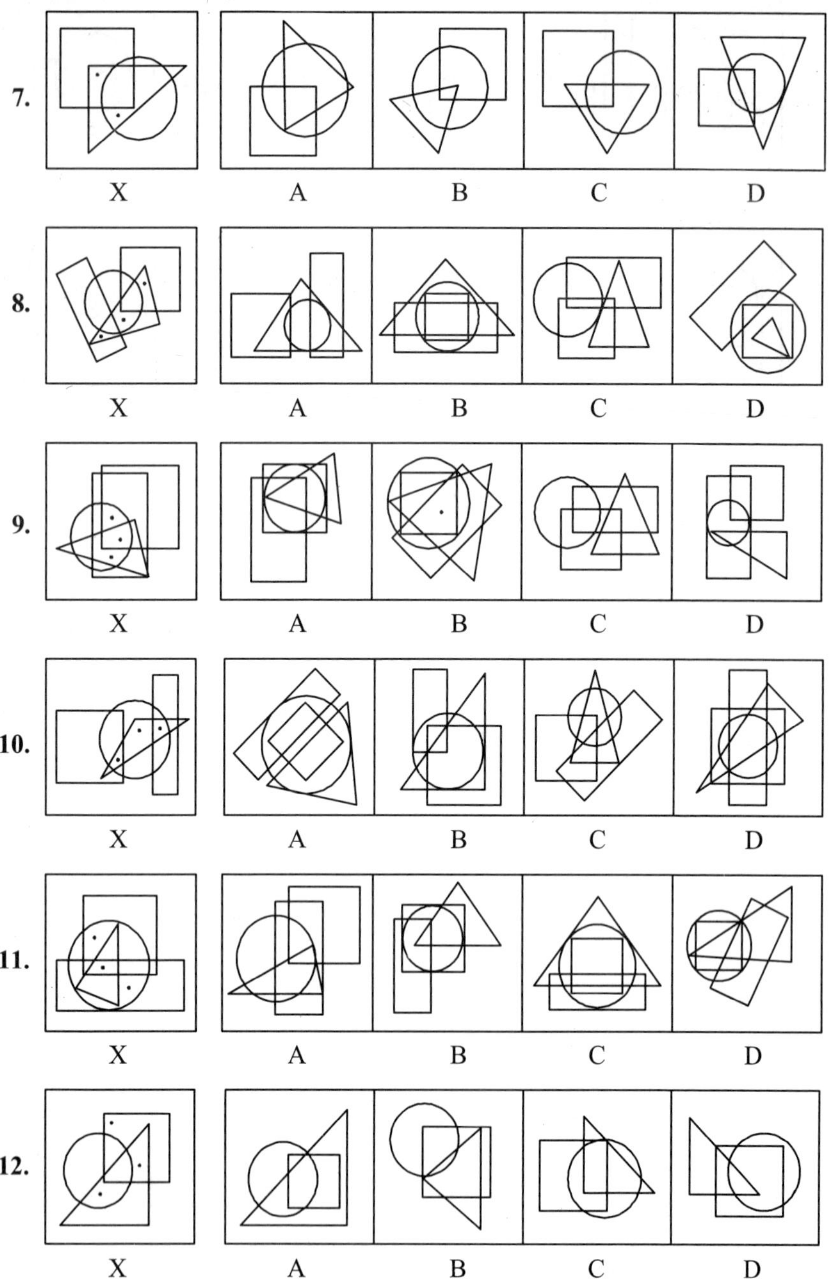
7.
X
A
B
C
D
8.
X
A
B
C
D
9.
X
A
B
C
D
10.
X
A
B
C
D
11.
X
A
B
C
D
12.
X
A
B
C
D

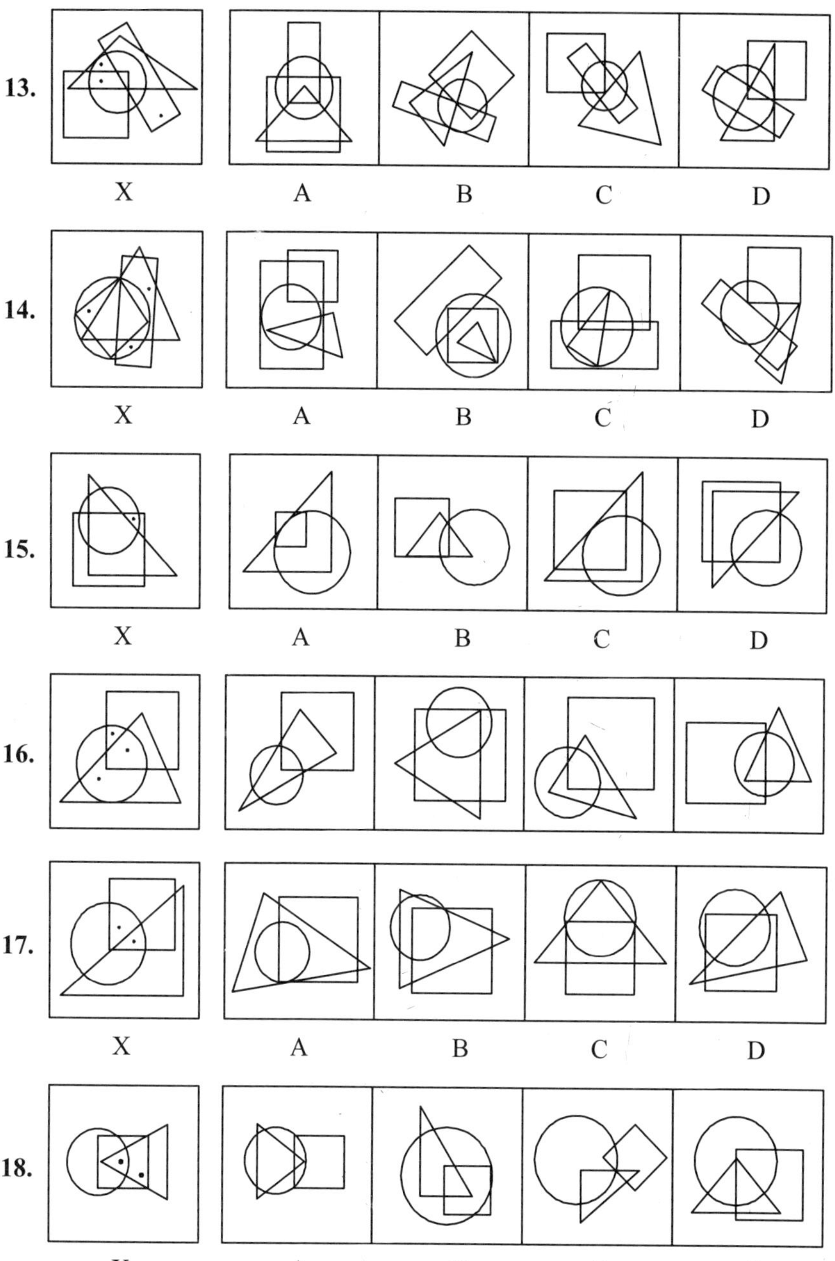
13.
X
A
B
C
D
14.
X
A
B
C
D
15.
X
A
B
C
D
16.
X
A
B
C
D
17.
X
A
B
C
D
18.
X
A
B
C
D

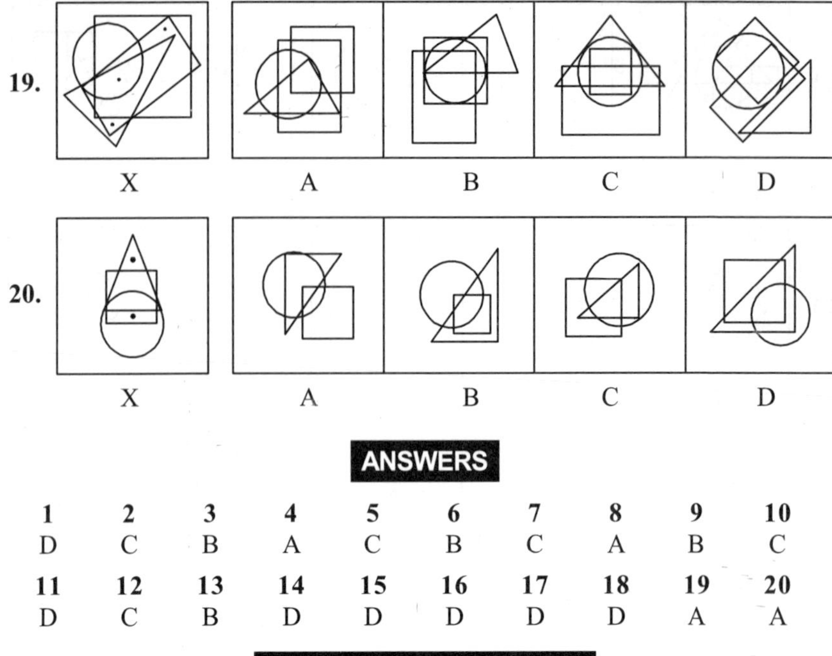


## ANSWERS

| 1 | 2 | 3 | 4 | 5 | 6 | 7 | 8 | 9 | 10 |
|---|---|---|---|---|---|---|---|---|---|
| D | C | B | A | C | B | C | A | B | C |
| **11** | **12** | **13** | **14** | **15** | **16** | **17** | **18** | **19** | **20** |
| D | C | B | D | D | D | D | D | A | A |

## EXPLANATORY ANSWERS

**1.** Figure (X) contains three dots in the region common to the circle and rectangle. The second dot in the region common to circle, square and triangle and the third dot in the region common to circle, square and rectangle. The same region shown in the figure "D".

**2.** In figure (X), the only one dot lies in the region common to the circle and triangle. Such a region is represented in the figure "C".

**3.** Figure (X) contains three dots; one dot in region common to the circle and triangle; one dot in region common to triangle, circle and square and one dot in region common to rectangle, circle and square respectively. Figure "B" contains all the three types of region.

**4.** Figure (X) contains three dots in the region common to the circle, the second dot in the region common to square rectangle and triangle and the third dot in the region common to the circle and square. Only figure ''A'' contains all these three types of regions.

**5.** The figure (X) contains two dots in the region common to circle and circle-triangle. The same region shown only in figure (C).

**6.** Figure (X) contains two dots in the region common to the triangle and circle and the other dot in the region common to the square and circle. Only figure 'B' contains the region common to the circle and triangle, so the answer "B" is right.

7. The figure (X) one of the dots lies in the region common to the circle and triangle and the other dot is common in the region square and triangle. Figure (A), (B) and (D) does not contain any region common to triangle and square.
8. In the figure (X), there are three dots in the region common to the triangle and square. The second dot in the region common to the circle and triangle, and the last dot in the region common to the rectangle and triangle. Such relation is shown only in the figure "A".
9. In figure (X), there are three dots in the region common to square, rectangle and circle. The second dot is common in the region circle, square, triangle and rectangle, and the last dot is in the region common to the circle, triangle and rectangle the same region is represented in the figure B.
10. In figure (X), one dot lies in the region common to the circle, rectangle and triangle. The second dot lies in the region common to circle and triangle, and the third dot common in the region circle, triangle and square. The same relation shows in the figure "C".
11. Figure (X) contains three dots one in the region common to the circle and square. The second in the region common to the circle, triangle, square and rectangle, and the third in the region circle and rectangle. Only figure "D" contains all these regions.
12. The dot position is inside the square, square and triangle and the third dot is common in the region circle and triangle. The same condition holds in figure "C".
13. The dot position is in the region rectangle, circle and rectangle also the circle, triangle and square. The same condition holds in figure "B". So the right Answers is "B".
14. Figure (X) contains three dots in the region common to circle and square. The second dot is common in the region common to triangle and rectangle and the third dot is in the region common to the circle and rectangle. Only figure "D" of contains all the three types of region.
15. In the (X) marked figure, the position of dot is common to circle and square lies in the figure "D".
16. Figure (X) contains three dots one in the region common to circle and square, the second is in the region circle, square and triangle, and the third in the region circle and triangle. Only figure "D" contains all these types of region.

**17.** The figure (X) contains two dots in the region common to circle and square and the second is common to the region circle, square and triangle. The same region shown only in the figure "D".

**18.** The figure (X) contains two dots, one dot is in the region common to the square and triangle, and the other dots is common in the circle, square and triangle, only figure "D" contains both the types of region.

**19.** Figure (X) contains three dots in the region common to rectangle and square the second dot in the region common to circle, triangle, square and rectangle and the third dot is in the region common to rectangle and triangle. Only figure A contains all these types of region.

**20.** Figure (X) contains three dots in the region common to triangle, square and the third dot in the region common to the circle and square. The same region is shown only in the figure A.

❍ ❍ ❍

14

# Cubes and Dice

The questions related to the problems on cubes and dice are aimed to check the imaginative power of the candidate. The candidate must have the ability to visualise three-dimensional (3D) objects. To attempt such questions some basic facts should be kept in mind and the visualisation ability should be combined with fast and accurate calculations.

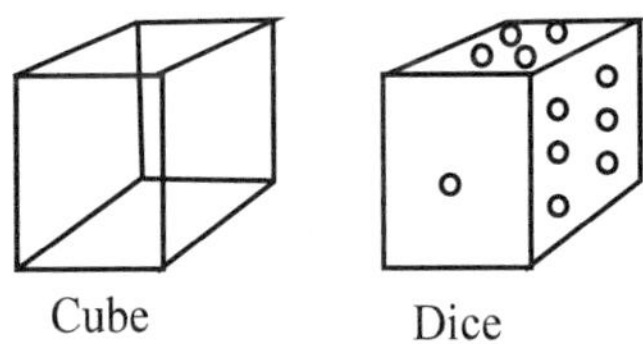

Cube Dice

- Cube has six faces/sides and eight corners.
- Dice has six faces/sides.
- Problems are based on the same or different coloured faces.
- Problems are based only on the value occurring on the six faces.
- Problems are based on cutting the cube into specified number of smaller equal parts.

Diagrammatically, the explanation of a cube can be understood easily by taking one side of the cube.

| | | |
|---|---|---|
| a | b | a |
| b | c | b |
| a | b | a |

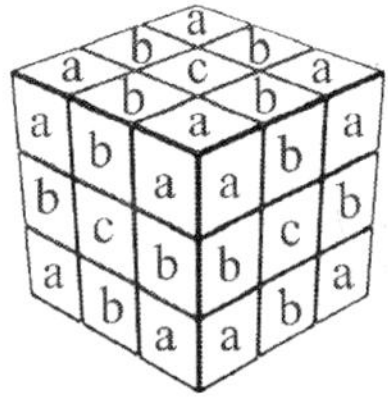

This cube is divided into $3 \times 3 \times 3 = 27$ equal small cubes.

There are four corner cubes 'a', so $4 \times 2$, *i.e.* 8 cubes that have 3 sides/faces exposed.

There are four middle cubes 'b', so $4 \times 3$, *i.e.* 12 cubes that have 2 sides/faces exposed.

There is one middle cube 'c', so 1 × 6, *i.e.* 6 cubes that have 1 side/face exposed. There will be 1 smaller cube right in the centre of this bigger cube none of whose face or side is exposed.

So, this bigger cube has 8 + 12 + 6 + 1, *i.e.* 27 smaller cubes.

To count the number of smaller cubes, the above explanation can be generalised as follows:

- Number of smaller cubes with three surfaces exposed = 8
- Number of smaller cubes with two surfaces exposed = $(n-2) \times 12$
- Number of smaller cubes with one surface exposed = $(n-2)^2 \times 6$
- Number of smaller cubes with no surface exposed = $(n-2)^3$

  Here, $n$ = Number of division on the surface of the bigger cube

$$n = \frac{\text{Length of edge of big cube}}{\text{Length of edge of one smaller cube}}$$

## Counting the Number of Cubes/Blocks in the Given Figures

When the number of cubes (or blocks/cuboids) in a figure needs to be counted, the procedure is described with the help of the following illustrations.

### SOLVED EXAMPLES

**1.** Count the number of blocks in the given figure:

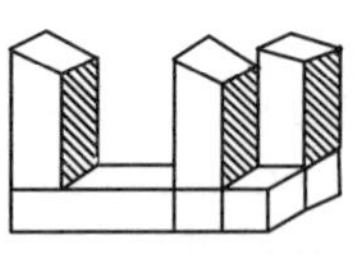

A. 6 B. 7 C. 8 D. 9

**Answers B:** It is clear from the figure that there are four blocks in the lower layer close to the ground. Also, there are 3 blocks standing over the lower layer of blocks.

Thus, there are 4 + 3 = 7 blocks in the given figure.

**Direction:** *Read the following information carefully to answer the questions that follows.*

A cube is colured red on two opposite faces, blue on two adjacent faces and yellow on two remaining faces. It is then cut into two halves along the plane parallel to the red faces. One piece is then cut into four equal cubes and the other one into 32 equal cubes.

**2.** How many cubes will not have any coloured faces?

A. 0 B. 16 C. 4 D. 8

**Answers C:** Only 4 smaller cubes from inside the cube will have none of their faces painted.

**3.** Two positions of a dice are shown below. Identify the number at the bottom when the top is '3'?

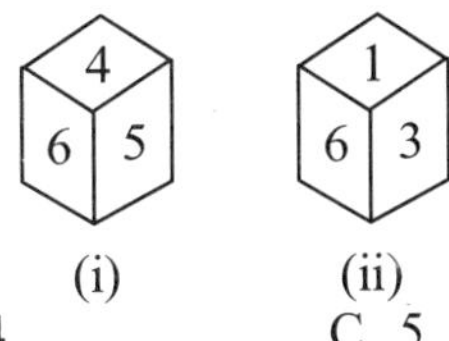


(i) (ii)

A. 2 B. 4 C. 5 D. 16

**Answers C:** Using both dice, we can say 1, 3, 4 and 5 are adjacent sides of 6. So, 2 is opposite to 6. Here, 4 and 6 are adjacent to 5. So, either 1 or 3 is opposite to 5. But 1 and 3 both are adjacent and when 1 is at top, then 3 is its adjacent side. So, 3 lies opposite of 5. Hence, when the top is 3, then the number at the bottom will be 5.

## EXERCISE

**1.** Twenty-seven cubes are arranged in a block as shown below. How many cubes will be surrounded by other cubes on all sides?

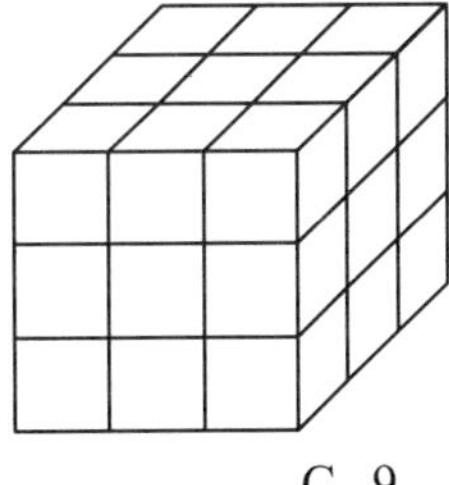

A. 3 B. 1 C. 9 D. 6

**2.** If the cube is turned twice to the right, which will be the hidden numbers?

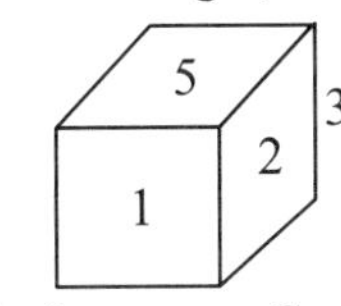


A. 1, 2, 5 B. 3, 4, 6 C. 1, 2, 6 D. 2, 3, 5

**3.** Two positions of a dice are shown below. If 1 is at the bottom which number will be on the top?

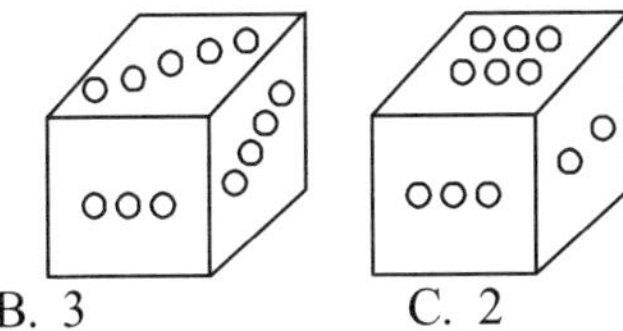

A. 4 B. 3 C. 2 D. 5

**Directions (Qs. 4–8):** *A cube is coloured red on one face, green on the opposite face, yellow on another face and blue on a face adjacent to the yellow face. The other two faces are left uncoloured. It is then cut into 125 smaller cubes of equal size. Answer the following questions based on the above statement.*

**4.** How many cubes are uncoloured on all the faces?
A. 27 B. 36 C. 48 D. 64

**5.** How many cubes have at least one green face ?
A. 4 B. 5 C. 16 D. 25

**6.** How many cubes are coloured red on one face, and have the remaining faces uncoloured?
A. 8 B. 10 C. 12 D. 16

**7.** How many cubes are coloured blue on one face, red or green on another face and have four uncoloured faces?
A. 8 B. 12 C. 16 D. 23

**8.** How many cubes have at least two coloured faces?
A. 23 B. 21 C. 20 D. 19

**Directions (Qs. 9–10):** *A cube painted blue on all the faces is cut into 125 cubes of equal size. Now answer the following questions:*

**9.** How many cubes are not painted on any face?
A. 8 B. 16 C. 27 D. 54

**10.** How many cubes are painted on one face only?
A. 8 B. 16 C. 36 D. 54

**Directions (Qs. 11–15):** *Six dices with their top faces erased have been given. The opposite faces of the dices have dots which add up to thirteen. Work out the number of dots on the top faces, according to the question, spot your answer from amongst the given alternatives:*

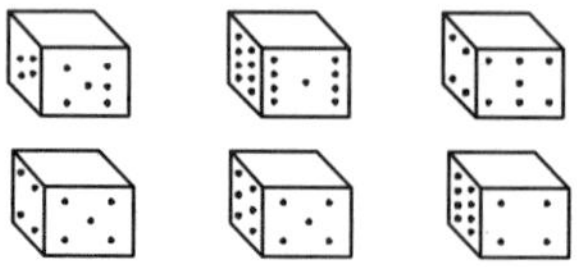

**11.** If even numbered dices have odd number of dots at their top faces, what would be the total number of dots?
A. 19 B. 18 C. 17 D. 16

**12.** The odd numbered dices have even number dots at their bottom faces, what would be the total number of dots?
A. 20 B. 22 C. 24 D. 18

**13.** If dices II, V and VI have even number of dots at their bottom faces, what would be the total number of dots?

A. 18 B. 20 C. 16 D. 24

**14.** If dices I, II and III have odd number of dots on their upper faces and dices IV, V and VI have even number of dots on their bottom faces, then what would be the difference in the total numbers of top face dots between these two sets?

A. 8 B. 4 C. 0 D. 1

**15.** If dices I, III and IV have odd number of dots at their top faces, what would be the total number of dots?

A. 15 B. 18 C. 21 D. 17

**Directions (Qs. 16–17):** *Six sides of a cube are coloured with different colours. Yellow is opposite to white and blue is between red and green. One side is black.*

**16.** Which colour is opposite to blue?

A. red B. black C. green D. yellow

**17.** Which colour does not touch red side?

A. green B. yellow C. white D. blue

**Directions (Qs. 18–22):** *Study the following information and answer the questions given below:*

(*i*) A rectangular wooden block is having length 6 cm, breadth 4 cm and height 1 cm.

(*ii*) Both sides having dimension 4 cm. 1 cm are painted with black colour.

(*iii*) Both sides having dimension 6 cm. 1 cm are painted in red colour.

(*iv*) Both sides with dimension 6 cm. 4 cm are painted in green colour.

(*v*) The block is cut into six equal parts of 1 cm each (from 6 cm side) and into 4 equal parts of 1 cm each (from 4 cm side).

**18.** How many cubes will have all three colours black, green and red each atleast on one side?

A. 6 B. 12 C. 10 D. None of these

**19.** How many cubes will be formed?

A. 6 B. 12 C. 16 D. 24 or these

**20.** If cubes having only "black as well as green" colour are removed then how many cubes will remain?

A. 4 B. 8 C. 12 D. None of these

**21.** How many cubes will have two sides with green colour and remaining 4 sides without any colour?

A. 12 B. 10 C. 8 D. 4

**22.** How many cubes will have 4 coloured sides and 2 sides without colour?
A. 8 B. 4 C. 16 D. 10

**Directions (Qs. 23-25):** *Study the information given below:*

The six faces of a cube are coloured black, brown, green, red, white and blue.

(*i*) Red is opposite of black
(*ii*) Green is between red and black
(*iii*) Blue is adjacent to white
(*iv*) Brown is adjacent to blue
(*v*) Red is at the bottom

**23.** Which colour is opposite of brown?
A. White B. Red C. Green D. Blue

**24.** Which of the following can be deduced from (*i*) and (*v*)?
A. Black is on the top B. Blue is on the top
C. Brown is on the top D. Brown is opposite of black

**25.** The four adjacent colours are:
A. black, blue, brown, red B. black, blue, brown, white
C. black, blue, red, white D. blue, black, red, green

**Directions (Qs. 26-30):** *The following questions are based on dice numbered 1 to 6 in different ways as indicated in each of the questions.*

**26.** If 1 is adjacent to 2, 4 and 6, which one of the following statements is necessarily true?
A. 3 is opposite to 5 B. 3 is adjacent to 5
C. 1 is adjacent to 3 D. 2 is opposite to 6

**27.** If 1 is opposite to 2 and adjacent to 3 and 4, which one of the following statements is necessarily true?
A. 3 is opposite to 5 B. 4 is opposite to 6
C. 3 is opposite to 4 D. 2 is opposite to 6

**28.** If 1 is adjacent to 2, 3 and 5, which one of the following statements is necessarily true?
A. 1 is adjacent to 4 B. 1 is adjacent to 6
C. 2 is adjacent to 5 D. 4 is adjacent to 6

**29.** If 1 is opposite to 5 and 2 is opposite to 3 then:
A. 4 is adjacent to 5 and 6 B. 6 is adjacent to 3 and 4
C. 2 is adjacent to 4 and 6 D. 4 is adjacent to 3 and 6

**30.** If 2 is opposite to 3 and adjacent to 4 and 6, which one of the following statements is necessarily true?

A. 1 is adjacent to 2 and 3 B. 4 is adjacent to 2 and 6
C. 4 is opposite to 6 D. 1 is opposite to 5

**Directions (Qs. 31-33):** *A solid cube with each side 3 cm has been painted red, blue and green on pairs of opposite faces. It is then cut into small cubes with each side 1 cm. Answer the questions that follow:*

**31.** How many cubes have only one face painted?
A. 6 B. 4 C. 12 D. 9

**32.** How many cubes have one face painted red and one face painted green?
A. 12 B. 8 C. 6 D. 14

**33.** How many cubes are painted blue on one face and either red or green on another face?
A. 4 B. 6 C. 8 D. 12

**Directions (Qs. 34- 38):** *A cube is coloured red on two opposite faces, blue on two adjacent faces and yellow on the two remaining faces. It is then cut into two halves along the plane parallel to the red faces. One piece is then cut into four equal cubes and the other one into 32 equal cubes.*

Now answer the following questions based on the above :

**34.** How many cubes do not have any red face?
A. 8 B. 16 C. 20 D. 24

**35.** How many cubes have each a yellow face with other faces blank?
A. 4 B. 14 C. 16 D. 17

**36.** How many cubes have at least two coloured face?
A. 20 B. 24 C. 28 D. 32

**37.** How many cubes do not have any coloured face?
A. 0 B. 2 C. 4 D. 8

**38.** How many cubes have at least one blue face?
A. 4 B. 14 C. 16 D. 17

**Directions (Qs. 39 & 40):** *The questions are based on the following statement :*

A cube is painted red on two adjacent faces, yellow on two opposite faces and green on the remaining faces. It is cut into 64 smaller cubes of equal size.

**39.** How many cubes have three faces painted?
A. 4 B. 8 C. 16 D. 32

**40.** How many cubes are painted on two faces only and that too with the same colour?
A. 0 B. 4 C. 8 D. 16

## ANSWERS

| **1** | **2** | **3** | **4** | **5** | **6** | **7** | **8** | **9** | **10** |
|---|---|---|---|---|---|---|---|---|---|
| B | D | B | C | D | D | A | B | C | D |
| **11** | **12** | **13** | **14** | **15** | **16** | **17** | **18** | **19** | **20** |
| A | A | A | B | D | B | A | D | D | D |
| **21** | **22** | **23** | **24** | **25** | **26** | **27** | **28** | **29** | **30** |
| C | B | A | A | D | B | D | D | C | A |
| **31** | **32** | **33** | **34** | **35** | **36** | **37** | **38** | **39** | **40** |
| A | A | C | B | A | A | C | D | B | B |

❍ ❍ ❍